Data Warehousing

Building the Corporate Knowledge Base

International Thomson Computer Press is
A division of International Thomson Publishing Inc.
The ITP Logo is a trademark under license.

For more information, contact:

International Thomson Computer Press
20 Park Plaza, 13th Floor
Boston, MA 02116
USA

International Thomson Publishing Europe
Berkshire House
168–173 High Holborn
London WCIV 7AA
England

Thomas Nelson Australia
102 Dodds Street
South Melbourne, 3205
Victoria
Australia

Nelson Canada
1120 Birchmount Road
Scarborough, Ontario
Canada M1K 5G4

International Thomson Publishing Southern Africa
Bldg. 19, Constantia Park
239 Old Pretoria Road, P.O. Box 2459
Halfway House, 1685 South Africa

International Thomson Publishing GmbH
Königswinterer Strasse 418
53227 Bonn
Germany

International Thomson Publishing Asia
221 Henderson Road #05-10
Henderson Building
Singapore 0315

International Thomson Publishing Japan
Hirakawacho Kyowa Building, 3F
2-2-1 Hirakawacho
Chiyoda-ku, 102 Tokyo
Japan

International Thomson Editores
Campos Eliseos 385, Piso 7
Col. Polanco
11560 Mexico D.F. Mexico

International Thomson Publishing France
1, rue st. Georges
75 009 Paris France

QEBFF 16 15 14 13 12 11 10 9 8 7 6 5 4 3 2

Library of Congress Cataloging-in-Publication Data

(available upon request)

ISBN: 1-85032-856-0

Publisher/Vice President: Jim DeWolf, ITCP/Boston
Manufacturing Manager: Sandra Sabathy Carr, ITCP/Boston
Technical Editor: Thomas King
Project Manager: Trudy Neuhaus
Project Director: Chris Grisonich/ITCP Boston
Marketing Manager: Kathleen Raftery, ITCP/Boston
Copy Editor: J.W. Olsen

Production: Jo-Ann Campbell • mle design • 562 Milford Point Road • Milford, CT 06460

Data Warehousing

Building the Corporate Knowledge Base

Tom Hammergren

International Thomson Computer Press

I(T)P® An International Thomson Publishing Company

London • Bonn • Boston • Johannesburg • Madrid • Melbourne • Mexico City • New York • Paris
Singapore • Tokyo • Toronto • Albany, NY • Belmont, CA • Cincinnati, OH • Detroit, MI

To Kim, my loving wife.
You listen, you love, you care.
Thanks for the extraordinary support!

Table of Contents

Acknowledgments

Gratitude is the most exquisite form of courtesy.

—Jacques Maritain

Writing a book is much harder than it sounds and involves extended support from a multitude of people. Though my name is on the cover, many people were ultimately involved in the production of this work. As I began to think of all the people to whom I would like to express my sincere gratitude for their support and general assistance in the creation of this book, the list grew enormous.

Probably my most important thank you is to my wife, Kim, and loving children, Brent and Kristen. They created an environment in which I could successfully complete this book—an accomplishment that I share with them and one that forced all of us to sacrifice a lot.

Then there were the combined efforts of the outstanding support crew that comprised Carole McClendon and her wonderful staff at Waterside Productions; Jim DeWolf, Trudy Neuhaus, Jerry Olsen, and their support staff at International Thomson Publishing; Sandy Emerson, Jose Cartagena, and their associates within Sybase Publications; Alan Rottenberg, Lynne Angus, Mickey Gill, Jean Peirre, and those behind the scenes at

Cognos; Cathy Murray at Sybase for her wonderful administrative support and the reviewers, including Thom King, who provided valuable insight and suggestions for changes to make this book meaningful. One very special thank you needs to be extended to Jo-Ann Campbell who almost single handedly brought the final graphics together for this book. This book could have never come into being without the efforts of these individuals, who hung in there with me through the entire process.

It would also be tough not to thank those who have formed my life personally, including my mother and father, Betty and Gordon Hammergren, who sacrificed many times and supported me through the good, the bad, and the ugly times of my life. Without their lifelong commitment of support and teaching, I would never have become who I am. My sisters, Jane and Beth, have also been there throughout my life, to challenge my mind and relieve my stress. To them, I say a million thanks—and I owe you. Also—my wife's family, whose spirited debates and ongoing support have never deviated. When you have so many people who believe in you, it is easy to accomplish what I have.

Then there are the business colleagues and mentors who have taught me all they know and challenged me to push the envelope of technology and knowledge more than once. This list includes Don Leonardo and Eric Schurr, who convinced me early in my career to enter this crazy software industry, then further taught me to never become complacent or quit. This list also includes the customers who taught me what quality and compassion really mean—especially those of you at The Proctor & Gamble Company with whom I worked during the creation of PowerPlay and Impromptu in my days at Cognos. The list also includes those who showed enormous faith in me during those early creative days at Cognos and the birth of the Business Intelligence Division (formerly the Desktop Division), including Jeff Papows, Ron Zambonini, Mike Potter, Alan Rottenberg, Jim Sinclair, Joe Smarkala, Graham MacIntosh, Robin McNeill, Rob Rose, Glen Rassmussen, Colin McAlpin, Rick Soderstrom, Ron Nordine, Mike Green, Mickey Gill, Sue Hardeman, Barb Paradis, and everyone else from the PowerPlay and Impromptu teams.

Finally, I would like to thank you, the reader, for purchasing this book. I hope it will help you to achieve success and continue your education. I look forward to sharing more with you in the future and hope you will share your ideas, compliments, criticisms, and suggestions with me as you experience them. Contact me at *hammergren@objx.com*. Also, monitor our World Wide Web site for valuable support information. The URL is: *http://www.objx.com*.

Prologue

What Will the Future Bring?

The past is of no importance. The present is of no importance. It is with the future that we have to deal. For the past is what man should not have been. The present is what man ought not to be. The future is what artists are.

—*Oscar Wilde*

Somewhere in the year 2000. . . .Tom has risen to chief strategist in his enterprise. The corporate realm looks to him to formulate the company strategy—its vision, its direction, its production plans—all forged within his jurisdiction. Many of his colleagues are awestruck with how this former leader of their corporate Information Systems came to such power. Yet upon further investigation, it is apparent how he achieved this feat and how he came to control so much.

TOM: Computer, we are trying to determine the current demographics associated with those people who are not loyal to our products or our competitors products.

COMPUTER: Tom, the key indicators suggest that your product support base has been growing among those people who earn between $75,000 and $150,000 annually. They tend to own their own home, be married, live in suburbs, and frequently shop at superstores or malls that carry complete products for all facets of life. The competition has gained a strong hold around people with incomes of $50,000 to $75,000. These people tend to be less established, *more mobile in their professions, and single with little family responsibility. They tend to live in major metropolitan areas and show shopping habits that are supplied by specialty shops. The area of the population that is noncommittal is those people who make less than $50,000 and, based on their income, rent an apartment versus own a home and frequently have little discretionary money to purchase the products marketed by you and your competitors.*

TOM: When they buy from us, what causes them to do so?

COMPUTER: Based on research from the Consumer Data Agency, promotional sales that feature sensitive messages, compassionate stars, and aggressive rebates attract this constituency. We have samples from your company and your competitors. Would you like to see the video promotion, print promotion, in-store promotion. . . ?

TOM: Show me the video and in store promotions for my company and the company who sold the most promotional units, if it wasn't us.

TOM (after reviewing the promotions): What would such a promotion cost? When would be the best time to run such a promotion? How many new customers would the promotion attract? Would the promotion net a profit and potentially an increased loyal customer base? Show me how it might look to the consumer over cable TV as well as in the store of the future.

The dialog continues as Tom enters the holodeck demonstrating the virtual reality encapsulation of the future store and how the consumer would be presented with the promotion.

The Future Will Bring the Corporate Knowledge Base

In a stroke of madness, all of us have begun to drive an information system craze called data warehousing. While the technology marketplace is going through a data warehousing boom, many people are asking, "what is a data warehouse?" This technology market focuses on providing users with a uniform source of corporate information, a *corporate knowledge base.*

The problem in data warehousing is that many people can explain what a data warehouse is, but few know how to build a data warehouse. The following are among the many reasons for this problem.

- Many people do not understand the difference between operational and analytical systems
- The techniques and tools used to design database systems do not support the important aspects of data warehouses, including multidimensional data, aggregations, and summary-level data

- The knowledge of how to design, implement, and administer a data warehouse is only available to those who have experience in building data warehouses

Even with these inherent problems, the data warehouse marketplace is growing significantly. The reason for this growth stems from more than 20 years of data in corporate computers for the operational aspects of a business. Executives are now demanding to learn why they have been storing that data for all these years. *Who are my customers? What are the behavior patterns of my customers? What are my customers' buying trends and how are they affected by marketing campaigns? How is product quality related to customer satisfaction? How well does my sales force forecast sales? How quickly do I turn over my inventory? What factors help increase repeat business with my customers? With whom do I do 80 percent of my business?* And so forth.

Information Systems professionals need to harness the data available in their current systems to allow for easy, yet unpredictable business queries and questions. However, the industry currently lacks a uniform methodology for capturing the data that is needed and transforming it into building and delivering a data warehouse.

This book has been written to solve the problems we have just mentioned. From the inception of an executive telling an Information Systems professional to build a data warehouse to the creation of a data warehouse, this book explains the entire process. This book provides you with the techniques in designing, modeling, and delivering a data warehouse. These techniques have been linked together to form a comprehensive methodology, *the information packaging methodology*, that allows Information System professionals to build and deliver their specific company's data warehouse.

Information Packaging Methodology

The information packaging methodology focuses on the entire process, beginning with gathering business requirements from users, analyzing and modeling these requirements, creating a data warehouse, and finally administering and maintaining the data warehouse system. By beginning with and focusing on business requirements—the desires of users—the methods discussed in this book allow Information System professionals to deliver *business intelligence* in a more effective fashion than ever before.

The purpose behind data warehousing was not born yesterday. However, it has evolved from previous user-oriented support systems such as information centers, decision support systems, and executive information systems. Yet, the data warehousing market is still in its infancy.

As the futuristic conversation above suggests, great advances in data warehousing will be made in the coming years. These advances include improvement of the quality of data, enhanced content, usability improvements, and general improvements in the overall process of data warehousing. To achieve these results, we must find a better way to deliver information through a more strategic use of technology. Businesses are beginning to focus how Information Systems can improve the way they do business. Data warehousing is leading these efforts, because a data warehouse provides a competitive asset—information characterized as business intelligence.

Why This Book?

The overall shift in information systems and technologies as described in the above conversation will take time. Most of us cannot afford to wait for this Xanadu to be delivered by software companies and must forge ahead and build it on our own. The ultimate information access system requires most enterprises to build the proper technical vision and a more stable, adaptable architecture. A data warehouse will reside in this new architecture. For some of us, the data warehouse revolution has hit; others are still trying to get to where they need to be. Wherever you are in this process, one thing is clear: Data warehousing has forced us to take another look at the way we manage our corporate data assets.

This is the first in a series of books that focuses on improving your ability to deliver data warehousing solutions based on an adaptable architecture. In this book, we focus on the information packaging methodology that allows you to rapidly deliver data warehousing strategies and solutions. These techniques immediately assist you and your enterprise in better managing information assets as well as in transforming the managed information into business intelligence.

Within the information packaging methodology disclosed in this book, several key concepts will emerge. The following are among these concepts.

- **Architecture**—or how do you build the correct foundation for your company's data warehouse?
- **Process**–or how do you formulate a team and build a repeatable process for data warehousing in your company?
- **Content**—or how do you deliver the proper information to your users while focusing on delivering adaptable and reusable data structures?

- **Access**—or how do you get everyone in your corporation with a need to know online with the information in a data warehouse?

Future books in this series will cover how technology improves the data warehousing process. The areas of focus will include technologies such as the Internet and multimedia (images, audio, video, and the like). Each of these books is derived from our personal experiences as well as many discussions with those building data warehouse solutions. We hope that these books will enlighten you and assist you in creating better information assets in your enterprise and in broadening the ability of users to access this information.

We have written this book with a goal to develop and cultivate the information packaging methodology in you and your organization, allowing you to deliver your own data warehouse in a highly adaptable architecture that will absorb the information requirements of your users for years to come.

Who Should Read This Book?

This book is for Information Systems professionals who need to deliver or understand how to build a data warehouse. This includes, among others, project managers, architects, database administrators, data modelers, analysts, and developers.

Information System professionals actively engaged in or contemplating the development of a data warehouse will benefit the most from this book. The techniques disclosed in the chapters that follow provide the first fully integrated life cycle development process for delivering data warehouses—the information packaging methodology. Those who follow these techniques will find development of data warehouses more effective, more comprehensive, and more accepted by their user community. The goal of these techniques is to deliver an easily maintained set of objects that manage and maintain the proper data for delivering business intelligence. Therefore, the book present topics of interest for a cross section of data warehouse project teams.

The Future Data Warehouse: An Adaptable Data Architecture

With technology advances such as the information superhighway (the Internet and its World Wide Web), information systems are beginning to become as commonplace as telephones. When a company originates, it tend to purchase the necessities—and computing resources are beginning to appear as a necessity. The productivity that these systems offer us is enormous, and businesses are beginning to leverage the concepts of electronic transfers as legal tender for business deals.

Even our children are becoming highly computer literate. Our sons and daughters are more proficient in automated technologies than we were at their age. What does this mean? Are we learning how to better use technology? Are we correcting past ills of information systems?

Great work still must be done to get our information systems in line with an enterprise's overall mission. Most of the innovations of the future will be more nuts-and-bolts oriented, but the most important in our opinion are the concepts and advancement of a data architecture.

The overall data architecture of our future will provide an all-encompassing definition of the real-world data that drives a business. This architecture will bring together the operational systems that are fixated on daily transactions and the ability for a company to stay operational as well as the historical and external data used to analyze important measurements within our purview, allowing us to recreate a business for the future. This shared-data concept is not far from reality for those who have begun the process of warehousing information.

Shared Data

The concept of shared data begins with the premise that an item of data should be collected only once from the person or data source in the best position to produce that data. This data source is called the system of record, or official data source. This system of record has the primary responsibility to maintain the data on a timely basis to ensure that it is accurate and broadly sharable to other systems.

Overall, this approach eliminates the problems caused when data is maintained by more than one system of record. The format of the data will be more consistent to the needs of a total enterprise, not just one specific organization. Perhaps the most important aspect of this is that the value of shared data will be realized when consistent data is available to all people who need the information throughout an enterprise.

The impact to an overall enterprise is that business decisions will truly be *informative* decisions—that is, based on a corporate knowledge base. Currently, in most environments the same data is maintained differently on opposing schedules and is not shared. After input into one system and passed to another, the data takes on a life of its own, never to link back to the original source. The result is that the information that is provided is rejected as inaccurate or incomplete, and business decisions lack the factual information required to make them anything more than a manager's intuition. With shared data, there is only one source. The data will be complete, and the decision making process and subsequent recommendations will be factual—derived from a corporate knowledge base, the sole source of information.

This concept also provides greater control over the quality of the information in a shared data environment. Because only one system of record has the responsibility for maintaining specific data, management can measure quality in performance and enforce standards. In today's environment, it is difficult to determine what the source is and who has the responsibility for maintaining the data.

This concept also provides a major cost benefit to enterprises. Fewer systems are needed to maintain the information, and fewer people are involved in the care and feeding of the data. The net effect is the following.

- More time can be spent analyzing the data
- A greater degree of confidence can be placed in the information produced from the data
- Less time will be wasted trying to find, match, and verify the accuracy of the data

Getting to a Uniform Data Source

Information systems will more than likely never physically support a universal database concept. Though many software companies tout such solutions, the reality is that every corporation use many—sometimes up to 10—different database vendors to manage the corporation's data assets. Therefore, a strategy that supports multiple data sources is required.

It is often easier to discuss this in a dual strategy. A dual database strategy is a concept that sources standard, shareable data from data capture (operational) and data access (decision support) environments. Data capture systems and processes are used to enter business transactions and reference data. This data is subsequently processed, formatted, and sent to a data warehouse. Within this data warehouse, the data is stored according to subject areas from which it can be accessed directly in a fully ad hoc manner or through other preoptimized formats.

Such a dual-database strategy calls for data to be stored in both the data capture and the data access environments. The data capture environment allows for updates to the data, while the data access environment freezes the data and allows only reading. There are clear-cut reasons for such a strategy. Here are two of the main reasons.

- **Data consistency** Most enterprises must have stability and completeness in their decision support data. Based on current systems implementations and design practices, data consistency is not always maintained in a database for reporting and decision support. If reporting or decision support functions were performed against such a database, different results would be obtained at different points in the day. This problem is resolved by providing a separate, consistent database for reporting and decision support. The dual-database strategy provides better data consistency, with one database used for transaction management while the other database is used for decision support.
- **Performance** Current technology doesn't allow for update and read activities to effectively occur simultaneously on one database. Thus, a dual-database strategy provides better performance, with one database for operational update activities and one for decision-support read activities. By creating two separate databases, each database can be individually tuned for optimal performance. The number of indexes on an update-intensive transaction database can be minimized, while the number of indexes on a read-only intensive decision-support database can be maximized. Each of these designs provides its respective constituency with the maximum performance for a given environment.

Because processing demands seem to keep pace with technology performance, you can expect current performance limitations in technology to persist long into the future. If these technology limitations are eventually corrected, performance no longer will be a driving issue for an architecture.

In the center of these multiple data sources, a repository of information can be maintained that serves both data capture and data access functions. *Metadata repository* refers to a dictionary that provides details about data—or as some refer to it, data about data. This information includes an inventory of data sources and their associated standards.

Information Packaging

As we begin a data warehousing process, we clean our data. The data is transformed and placed into information packages. These information packages are surprisingly standard across companies. Every company has customers, products, locations, charts of accounts, and many other common subjects. The core data in each of these subjects finds itself standardizing across similar businesses. However, there is a need for additional data that is secondary to the overall information package. This data is created and maintained as strategic and as a unique interest to its owner.

As technology and its overall implementation in enterprises evolve, common templates can be developed to assist companies in managing their information packages. This standardization of subject areas may be one component that the data warehouse market gives back to the Information Systems community. As we begin to standardize for reporting purposes, we may begin to realize that there are common objects with common methods. A data warehouse makes the selection method robust, while the operational systems extend the capture and maintenance methods.

In Summary

The computer software industry has begun to focus on several key areas that will improve the solutions our users receive in data warehousing. As you will see in solutions that are beginning to be delivered in the data warehouse marketplace, these advances include those that follow.

- **Logical application partitioning** Many vendors are beginning to split front-end query reporting tools into a presentation engine and a computational, expression engine. Though they have done this for some time from an engineering perspective, the user is now beginning to see this physical split in the areas of decision support agents and application servers. These advances allow users' workstations to properly present the data, while a more powerful, potentially parallel processing machine works to obtain and properly filter the requested data.
- **Open connectivity among application partitions** The vendor community is realizing that the one-tool-fits-all mentality does not match users' needs. Therefore, tools that allow multiple best-of-breed applications to better integrate with each other are beginning to appear. The ability to distribute briefing books that provide a standard information base for the management community allows integration of various objects, whether these are Executive Information System reports, Decision Support System reports, spreadsheets, plans, or news feeds. The compound document is growing in importance for the data warehousing community as it has for the office automation community.
- **Object support of data and logic** As you will see in this book, the concept of universally defining entities to be managed in a data warehouse along with their associated load modules and access modules is a growing technique that will revolutionize the speed and productivity for deploying a data warehouse. Though not

entrenched in an object-oriented database or language, the techniques focus heavily on the principles of reuse and productivity. Further, data and code are closely tied to one another.

- **Industry standard objects** These objects currently comprise the weakest area of data warehousing, though in some communities this is either evolving or stable. For instance, the consumer packaged goods industry has a standard set of objects, such as markets and product coding standards. Health care, on the other hand, is only evolving with clear definitions for the data structures behind a uniform patient record. Those industries that rely most on data interchange are the obvious choices for leadership in this area.
- **More advanced and technology-rich application vendor partnerships** Application vendors and the ability to better utilize application vendor data stores have recently evolved to the point that many vendors who focus on transformation of data are selling targeted transformation modules for an application. This trend will continue to evolve with the enormous popularity of applications such as PeopleSoft and SAP.

Genesis of This Book

This book has been written after much prodding from colleagues to disclose the techniques we have used over the years to develop data warehouses and decision support systems for many major corporations, something we refer to as the information packaging methodology. This methodology is based on years of experience working with, designing, and delivering decision support systems and data warehouses to corporations in various market segments.

Probably, our most significant experience came while working at Cognos Corporation while developing PowerPlay and Impromptu in conjunction with a world-class leader in the consumer packaged goods industry, The Proctor and Gamble Company. While working with Cognos and their strategic partner, P&G, we learned some strategy and technique required to deliver a good decision-support database and data warehouse: *focus on what the user needs*. Companies such as P&G are great consumers of data. As they digest and formulate this data, it becomes a marketing weapon and a corporate asset, and it helps them guarantee that they are putting a quality, competitive product on the market that in fact meets the demands of their constituents.

Our experiences at Cognos also exposed us to many other companies, including Dun & Bradstreet and their SmartStream series; Equifax and their demographic information services; and AT&T and their sales management programs. All of these experiences have allowed us to build a strong understanding and methodology focused on delivering successful data warehousing. These experiences, which yielded many successes as well as failures, have been educational and allowed us to fine-tune the techniques described in this book.

During the coming years, we will experience more improvements to this methodology. However, we feel that, after reading this book, you will have a much stronger understanding of how to successfully deliver what your users want from a data warehouse. A corporate knowledge base provides information—or probably better stated, knowledge—of how a business is doing and what can be done to improve it. Whether that knowledge is based on quality, profitability, or other metrics, it should be a strategic weapon in every corporate arsenal that drives productivity and competitiveness. This is why we chose the title *Data Warehousing: Building the Corporate Knowledgebase.* Delivery and maintenance of this knowledge base is what our job is in the data warehousing sector.

When Will the Future Be Here?

Some questions are nearly impossible to answer; when the future goals that we have observed in this prologue will be achieved is one of them. But our hope is that the information in this book will spark your creativity, allowing you to move closer to the future. Time and enormous amounts of money will be required to create the ultimate environment to support the user community. However, with a little fortitude and common sense, you can create a mini-Xanadu for your users, giving them information to better perform their job, while making your company more knowledgeable and competitive.

Meanwhile, you can watch those who wait for the ultimate solution. By the time that solution is available, your company may have acquired those who waited—or they may have disappeared! Either way, our recommendation is to not wait for the technical community to come to you to deliver the future. Create your own future—your own solutions. Don't believe the marketing hype that tends to surround the technology industry. Challenge the technology industry and force it to deliver what you really need. Soon enough, the future will be here—maybe you will be the person in the dialog that began this chapter or the one that follows.

TOM (or insert your name): Computer, please distribute this modified hologram to the focus group members, who will review it through their own holodecks. If everything works out, we can deploy this promotion next week and capture market share from our competitors.

Four weeks later at an executive luncheon:

CEO: Tom here has done it again. He and his computer assistant have developed a promotional strategy that maximized our promotional investment to gain 20 percent market share from the previously uncommitted prospect base that we and our competitors have been targeting. Tom, please share how you and your assistant came to be so productive.

TOM: Well, it all started four years ago when I. . . .

SECTION I

Introduction

1

The Data Warehouse Market Explosion

Knowledge in the form of an informational commodity indispensable to productive power is already, and will continue to be, a major—perhaps the major—stake in the worldwide competition for power. It is conceivable that the nation-states will one day fight for control of information, just as they battled in the past for control over territory, and afterwards for control over access to and exploitation of raw materials and cheap labor.

—Jean François Lyotard

Data warehousing has become the craze of the 1990s. Companies around the world are trying to harness the information that has been stored on their computers for years. Why are these companies spending millions of dollars trying to harness this information? After considering the quotation from Jean François Lyotard, you may have a better understanding of the answer to this question.

The reality of business, and in many ways of our lives in general, is that a data-driven society has arisen. Think for a moment: How do you personally make decisions? You can't do much in a day without utilizing or being presented with tons of information. Consider the following.

- The Dow Jones Industrials Average was up 30.5 points
- The interest rate dropped one percent
- Your superstar basketball player is averaging 27 points and nine rebounds per game
- The temperature is 32 degrees, five degrees above the average for this day of the year
- Quarterly earnings were up 16 percent; however, annual earnings were up only eight percent

The above figures require different data to determine if the metrics are good or bad.

- *The Dow Jones Industrials Average was up 30.5 points.* This is good news to the person who has a portfolio containing industrial stocks. However, if your portfolio is filled with stocks in the high technology sector, this is only a data point to you–not information.
- *The interest rate dropped one percent.* This is good news to the person who is applying for a new mortgage. On a home valued at $150,000 for a 30 year mortgage, this reduction of the interest rate would save $103.63 per month—a total of $37,306.80 over the life of the loan.
- *Your superstar basketball player is averaging 27 points and nine rebounds per game.* If you are this player's coach, this is enough to start the player for the next game. For an opposing coach, this type of information generates a good degree of heartburn and a new defensive strategy.
- *The temperature is 32 degrees, five degrees above the average for this day of the year.* The 32-degree temperature is good information to tell you how to dress yourself and your children. You will no doubt be wearing a winter coat when outside.
- *Quarterly earnings were up 16 percent; however, annual earnings were only up eight percent.* Eight percent may be good. At least this data lets you know that the quarter was better than the year as a whole. This as well may be good information.

Every aspect of everything we do has some way to be measured. Average cost savings, average spending, market share, percent increase—all of these items are important data points that assist in a decision making process. If you think about the aspects of your own life, imagine living without this type of data. How would you determine the following?

- Your pay raise requirements
- How much of a mortgage you can afford
- What kind of clothing to wear
- Where to invest your money
- When to service your car

Some people are better at understanding this type of data and transforming it into information. In our competitive society, these people tend to be the leaders in their prospective fields. And no field is lacking in leaders.

- A brand manager who understands how to increase sales in his or her product while decreasing sales in a competitor's product will provide more value to an employer than a brand manager who does not understand this concept
- A stock broker who understands the industry averages as well as other data points on companies that he or she is buying and selling will better interpret financial information, allowing the stock broker to make better investments and yield higher returns than competitors
- A manufacturer who understands how much scrap is generated within the manufacturing process and if the scrap can be utilized again in the same or another processes, will reduce waste and expense achieving better profitability than other manufacturers
- A project manager who understands what it really takes to build a system in time, resources, and money will rise above others in the areas of estimation, expectation setting, and delivery capabilities
- A politician who understands the polls and the community at large can better service constituents while ignoring negative information that will not affect the politician's performance
- A doctor who statistically understands the treatment options and the desired outcomes for the various ailments he or she sees in a day will have a better treatment record than that of colleagues
- An athlete who understands an opponent's weaknesses will better exploit those weaknesses to overcome and win challenges

Being able to harness this type of data makes people more capable of making decisions—intelligent, fact-based decisions. If you now take these personal data points and compound them, you will see what most business managers and leaders face on a daily basis.

- How do I manage my payroll?
- How do I trim spending?
- How many new employees will we need next year?
- How many outside consultants do we need to cover a short-term need?
- When will we need to replace the equipment on the factory floor?
- Is it better to purchase or to lease?

Decisions are typically made from an information base—*data that has been collected over the years*. For most personal decisions, the data that we draw upon is stored in one of the most complex computing systems—the human brain. However, some decisions utilize data derived from external sources such as reference manuals, personal notes, and diaries. After all, the human brain, like other computer systems, must be archived or purged from time to time, and tends to not store all of the data required to make an informed decision.

The information that we use to formulate decisions typically is based on data gathered from previous experiences—what is right and what is wrong. Data warehouses capture similar data, allowing business leaders to make informed decisions based on previous business data—what is right about the business and what is wrong about the business. Because decision making is improved when one analyzes similar historical situations, many corporations are defining the information produced by querying a data warehouse as *business intelligence*.

What Is a Data Warehouse?

So, what is a data warehouse? Literally, the words that make up this term have definitions as follows.

- **Data** Facts and information about something
- **Warehouse** A location or facility for storing goods and merchandise

A data warehouse system has the following characteristics.

- It provides a centralization of corporate data or information assets
- It is contained in a well-managed environment
- It has consistent and repeatable processes defined for loading operational data
- It is built on an open and scaleable architecture that will handle future expansion of data
- It provides tools that allow its users to effectively process the data into information without a high degree of technical support

As characterized in Figure 1.1, a data warehouse is similar to traditional warehousing of products within the manufacturing industry. Within the information systems world, there is a need to accomplish the following steps, which are keyed to Figure 1.1.

1. Produce or purchase the materials required to build finished inventory; that is, *capture operational data*
2. Take materials and produce finished inventory; that is, *transform the operational transaction data*
3. Store the finished inventory until it is required within the distribution channels; that is, *store the transformed data in a data warehouse*
4. Ship the finished inventory to the distribution channel based on demand; that is, *deliver business intelligence upon receipt of a user data request or query*

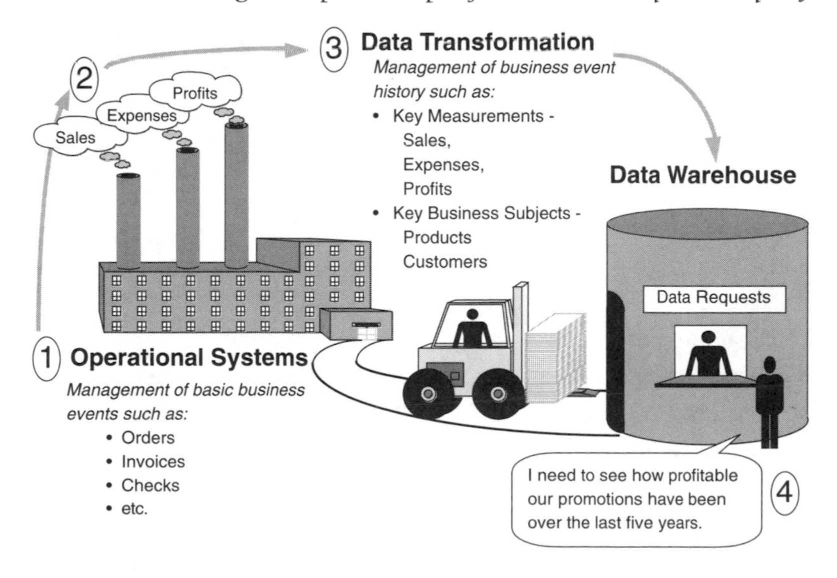

Figure 1.1: *Data warehousing is analogous to a manufacturing process*

Data warehouse systems have become a rapidly expanding requirement for most information system departments. What is causing this astronomical growth? We would respond that no one circumstance has launched us into this new paradigm. The concepts behind the data warehouses of today have been around for years. In the past, there were information centers, executive information systems (EIS), and decision support systems (DSS).

The reasons for growth in this area stem from many places. With regard to data, most companies now have access to more than 20 years of data on managing the operational aspects of their business. With regard to user tools, the technology of user computing has reached a point where corporations can now effectively allow the users to navigate corporate databases without a high need for technical support. With regard to corporate management, executives are realizing that the only way to sustain and gain an advantage in today's economy is to better leverage information.

Operational Systems Versus Data Warehousing Systems

Prior to discussing more details of data warehouse systems, it may be beneficial to note some of the differences between operational and data warehousing systems.

Operational Systems

Operational systems are those that assist a company in its day-to-day business to respond to events or transactions. As a result, operational system applications and their data are highly structured around the events they manage. These systems provide an immediate focus on business functions and are typically run in an on-line transaction processing (OLTP) computing environment. The databases associated with these applications are required to support a large number of transactions on a daily basis. Typically, operational databases are required to work as fast as possible. To gain performance within these operational systems, personnel who support these systems have sacrificed ease of use. Strategies for increasing performance include keeping these operational data stores small, focusing the database on a specific business area or application, and eliminating database overhead in areas such as indexes.

An example of an operational system is documented in the accounting system flow illustrated in Figure 1.2. The sales part of the accounting system will assist in better processing orders. When a customer purchases a product, the system managing this function will register the sale, process shipment information, reduce the available inventory, and and so on. This system, as a whole, allows users to better manage their orders, invoices, receipts, and payroll. But will it help them understand who their customers are or what drives the sales of their products?

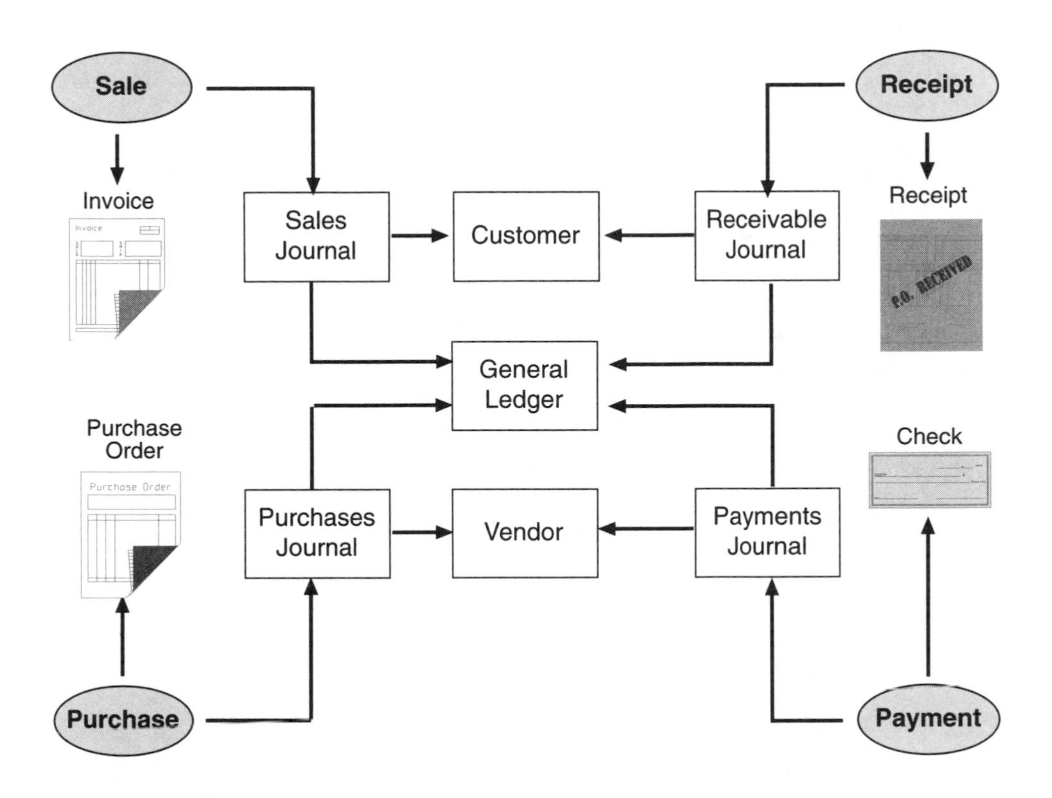

Figure 1.2: *Accounting system flow that illustrates the events and transactions managed by this operational system*

Data Warehouse Systems

Most companies today have a relatively good handle on their operational systems and are now focusing on pulling information contained within these systems to define what they have done right (and therefore should continue to do) as well as what they have done wrong (and should focus on not allowing to happen again). This data is being captured and stored in data warehouses.

Operational system applications and their data are highly structured around the events they manage. Data warehouse systems are organized around the trends or patterns in those events. Operational systems manage events and transactions in a similar fashion to manual systems utilized by clerks within a business. These systems are trained to handle individual transactions according to the established business rules. Data warehouse systems focus on the business needs and requirements that are established by managers, who need to reflect on events and develop ideas for changing the business rules to make these events more effective.

Operational systems and data warehouses provide separate data stores. A data warehouse's data store is designed to support decision support queries and applications. The separation of a data warehouse and operational system serves multiple purposes.

- It minimizes the impact of reporting and complex query processing on operational systems
- It preserves operational data for reuse after that data has been purged from operational systems
- It manages the data based on time, allowing the user to look back and see how the company looked in the past versus the present
- It provides a data store that can be modified to conform to the way the users view the data
- It unifies the data within a common business definition, offering one version of reality

A data warehouse assists a company in analyzing its business over time. Users of data warehouse systems can analyze data to spot trends, determine problems, and compare business techniques in a historical context. The processing that these systems support includes complex queries, ad hoc reporting, and static reporting (such as the standard monthly reports that are distributed to managers). The data that is queried tends to be of historical significance and provides its users with a time-based context of business processes.

Differences Between Operational and Data Warehousing Systems

While a company can better manage its primary business with operational systems through techniques that focus on expense reduction, data warehouse systems allow a company to identify opportunities for increasing revenues, and therefore for growing the business. From a business point of view, this is the primary way to differentiate these two mission critical systems. However, there are many other key differentiations between these two systems, such as the following.

- **Size and content** The goals and objectives of a data warehouse differ greatly from an operational environment. While the goal of an operational database is to stay small, a data warehouse is expected to grow large—to contain a good history of the business. The information required to assist us in better understanding our business can grow quite voluminous over time, and we do not want to lose this data.
- **Performance** In an operational environment, speed is of the essence. Can you imagine requiring hours to enter an order into a system? Would a customer put up with this? The answer typically is no. However, in a data warehouse some requests—"meaning-of-life" queries—can take hours to fulfill. This may be acceptable in a data warehouse environment, because the true goal is to provide better information, or business intelligence. For these types of queries, users are typically given a personalized extract of the requested data so they can further analyze and query the information package provided by the data warehouse.
- **Content focus** Operational systems tend to focus on small work areas, not the entire enterprise; a data warehouse, on the other hand, focuses on cross-functional subject areas. For example, a data warehouse could help a business understand who its top 20 at-risk customers are—those who are about to drop their services—and what type of promotions will assist in not losing these customers. To fulfill this query request, the data warehouse needs data from the customer service application, the sales application, the order management application, the credit application, and the quality system.
- **Tools** Operational systems are typically structured, offering only a few ways to enter or access the data that they manage, and lack a large amount of tools accessibility for users. A data warehouse is the land of user tools. Various tools are available to support the types of data requests discussed earlier. These tools provide many features that transform and present the data from a data warehouse as business intelligence. These features offer a high degree of flexibility over the standard reporting tools that are offered within an operational systems environment. Some of the more interesting features include the ability for people to perform "drill-down" analysis and "slice-and-dice" operations on the dimensions contained within information packages, or business models, as depicted in Figure 1.3.

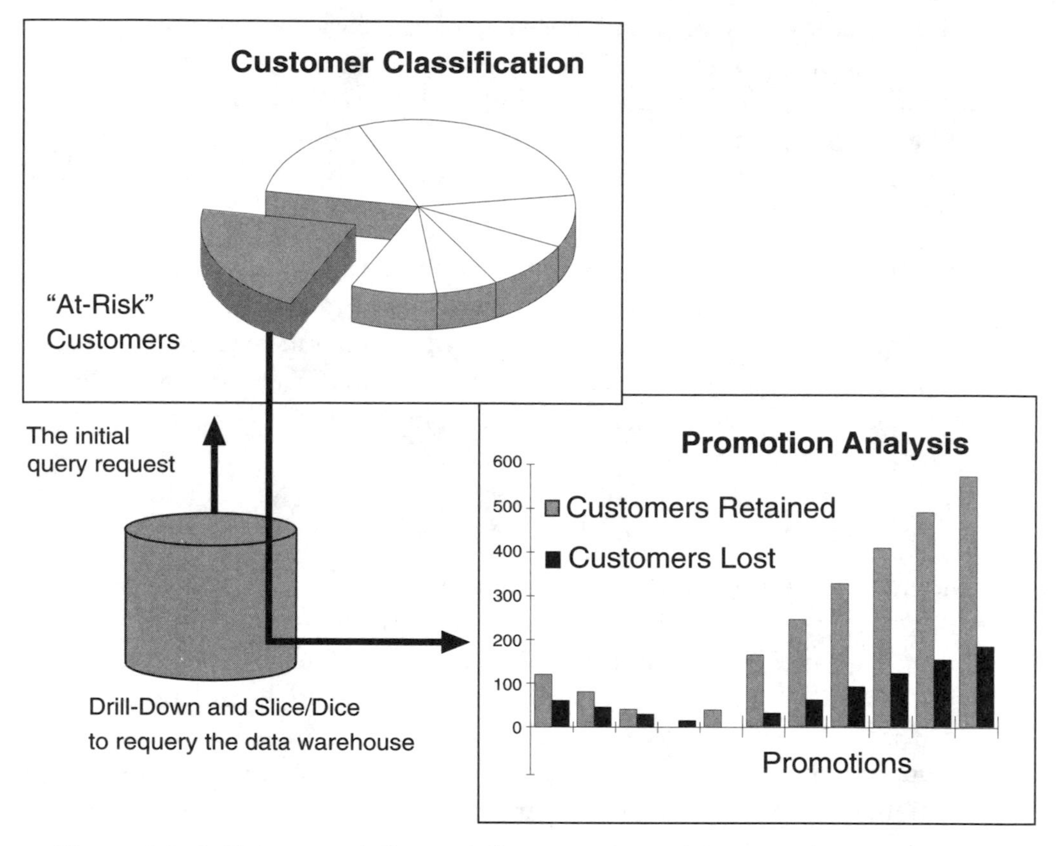

Figure 1.3: *Drill-down and slice-and-dice operations of data warehouse information*

Drill-down analysis allows the user to explore the levels of summarized data within a warehouse. As shown in Figure 1.3, a user may begin with a view of all customer classifications. One such grouping might be at-risk customers. The user could select this slice within the pie chart and drill down on that dimension. From that view of the data, the user could then select another dimension, promotions, and isolate queries specifically to the at-risk customers. Iterative queries could then be launched to investigate other associated data. This is an example of slicing and dicing of data among different subject and measurement areas. (These concepts will be discussed in greater detail in later chapters.)

Why the Need for Data Warehousing Systems?

To answer user questions, information system professionals need to harness the data available within their current systems and allow for easy to complex, unpredictable business queries. The user's questioning process can be characterized as a rapid-fire interviewing process; it is not as simple as one question and the resultant answer. Typically, the answer to one question leads to one or more additional questions. The data warehousing systems of today require support for dynamic iterative analysis—delivering answers in a rapid fashion.

Driven by the need to gain competitive advantage in the marketplace, organizations are now seeking to convert their operational data into useful business intelligence—in essence fulfilling user information requirements. Better access to information results in competitive advantage for business functions such as customer service, customer retention, sales forecasting, budgeting, quality management, and employee retention. However, the information required by these users must cross operational system boundaries and provide better quality data. Therefore, consistency and accuracy are keys to providing a solution to users of a data warehouse system.

In our experience, the need to cross functional business boundaries and provide quality data is often cited as a way to improve the quality of the overall business. And data warehouse systems, often characterized by query processing, can also assist in other areas, as noted below.

- **Consistent, quality data** A hospital system with which we consulted had a severe data quality problem within its operational system that captured information about the people serviced. The hospital needed to log all people who came through its doors regardless of the data that was provided. This meant that someone who checked in with a gun shot wound and told the staff his name was Bob Jones and who subsequently lost consciousness and died would be logged into the system identified as Bob Jones. This posed a huge data quality problem, because Bob Jones could have been Robert Jones, Bobby Jones or James Robert Jones. There was no way of distinguishing who this person was. You may be saying to yourself, big deal! But if you look at what a hospital must do to assist a patient with the best care, this is a problem. What if Bob Jones were allergic to some medication required to treat the gun shot wound? From a business sense, who was going to pay Bob Jones' bills? From a moral sense, who should be contacted regarding Bob Jones' ultimate outcome? All of these directives had driven this institution to a proper conclusion: They needed a data warehouse. This information base, which they called a clinical repository, would contain quality data on the people involved with the institution—that is, a master people database. This data source could then assist the staff in analyzing data as well as improving the data capture, or operational system, in improving the quality of data entry. Now, when Bob Jones checks in, they are prompted with all of the previous Bob Joneses who have been treated at all five of their facilities. The person entering the data is presented with a list of valid Bob Joneses and several questions that allow the staff to better match the person to someone who was previously treated by the hospital.

- **Expense reduction** In another customer situation, we were presented with the best reason for implementing a data warehouse that we have ever seen. This customer had a relatively nice size office, which was approximately 10 feet by 14 feet. Within his office were the traditional desk, credenza, two guest chairs, and a file cabinet. However, there was no room to move in the office. The customer had purposely placed the boxes containing the monthly reports that had been distributed to his various offices around the world against one wall. This was a wonderful visual aidc to characterize the expense created by the operational system reporting—in an area approximately seven feet long by five feet high by four feet wide sat boxes of computer printouts. This project manager's questions were: What does this cost us to produce? To distribute? To develop? And so on. How much of the data content in these reports do we use? He discovered that it was typically very little. Why? Because the data took so long to produce and distribute that it was out of synch with the users' requirements. We also had a customer who solved a similar problem with a data warehouse implementation. The company indexed the paper reports on-line and allowed users to select the pages of importance to them through an ad hoc searching method. At that point, the data was downloaded electronically to the users' personal workstations. The customer saved a bundle of money just by eliminating the distribution of massive paper reports.
- **More timely data access** As noted earlier, reporting systems have become so unwieldy that the data that they present is typically unusable after it is placed in users' hands. What good is a monthly report if you don't get it until the end of the following month? How can you change what you are doing based on data that old? You can, but it is not a timely change. The reporting backlog has never dissipated within information system departments; typically it has grown. Granting users access to data on a more timely basis allows them to better perform their business tasks. It also can assist in reducing the reporting backlog, because users take more responsibility for the reporting process.

- **Improved performance and productivity** Removing Information Systems professionals from the reporting loop and empowering users results in internal efficiency. Imagine for a moment that you had no operational systems and had to hunt down the person who recorded a transaction to better understand how to improve the business process or determine whether a promotion was successful. The truth is that all we have done is automate this nightmare with the current operational systems. Users have no central sources for information and must search all of the operational systems for the data that is required to answer their questions. A data warehouse assists in eliminating information backlogs, reporting backlogs, information system performance problems, and so on by improving the efficiency of the process, eliminating much of the information search missions.

Improved data quality, timely data access, support for organizational change, improved productivity, expense reduction—all of these items seemingly support the business mission and should result in the business gaining significant competitive advantage. This may answer the question: Why are corporations building data warehouse systems? Frequently, the competitor that obtains the best information fastest gains significant competitive advantage over others within its field. However, it should be noted that, even with a data warehouse, companies still require two distinct kinds of reporting: those that provide notification of operational conditions needing response and those that provide general information, often summarized, about business operations. The notification style reports should still be derived from operational systems, because detecting and reporting these conditions is part of the process of responding to business events. The general information reports indicating operational performance typically used in analyzing the business are managed by a data warehouse.

Data warehouse implementations are in their infancy. But as technology and innovation evolve, warehouses will store vast amounts of information to assist us in reliving an experience—shortening the learning cycle involved with understanding the past, and in many ways the future. An interesting twist to all of this is that data warehouses will expand our knowledge into areas in which we are not so comfortable or experienced. Data warehouses will not only derive information from you personally, but also from the business as a whole—or more important to you—from other individuals' information. This data will contain information on successes and failures. And we can tap into this knowledge base. Therefore, as we grow into different business roles, those that proceeded us will help to mentor us through their recordings into the corporate data warehouse. These individuals can mentor us without even being there; their legacy is their business information.

If your carry out the concepts of data warehousing to their fullest potential, you can imagine a real-life Star Trek—reliving scenes in a hologram, querying data banks via voice interfaces, the computer giving you a response full of prioritized options and recommending the best, allowing you to narrow your decision scope.

With this vision of data warehousing, we prefer to define a data warehouse in a future sense as the *business or corporate knowledge base*. The data warehouse will contain information that is pertinent to the key measures of the business and that allows users to extend these measures, assisting them in assimilating enough information to make informed decisions. It will not make decisions for you. Business cycles change too frequently to ever assume that a data warehouse could make business decisions; however, data warehouses can prioritize your options and recommend which might be the best.

The Warehousing Process

Data warehousing provides a means to make information available for decision making. An effective data warehousing strategy must deal with the complexities of the modern enterprise. Data is generated everywhere, and controlled by different operational systems and data storage mechanisms. Users demand access to data, anywhere and anytime, customized to their needs and requirements. Therefore, a data warehouse must fit within the business model—not dictate it. Also, the technology that is utilized to deliver a data warehouse must be flexible enough to evolve with changes in the business and user requirements.

A data warehouse enables executives, managers, analysts, and users to query and analyze enterprise data across many facets of their business. Data warehousing allows users to perform complex analysis on this data that has been extracted, aggregated or summarized to fit particular criteria, manipulated to derive new data, reformatted or filtered to remove unwanted or unnecessary data, and integrated with other data sources.

The job of a data warehouse is to prepare the current transactions from operational systems into data with a historical context required by the users of the data warehouse. This data preparation includes aggregating and time stamping the data for future analysis. This preparation of the data allows users to perform trend analysis in a larger context on the business results that are managed by the data warehouse.

The process outlined to deliver a data warehouse assists the information systems staff in the following areas.

- Assembling data for decision making
- Transforming data into a consistent view that is usable by the business
- Distributing data where it is needed within the business

- Furnishing high-speed access to the user with tools such as popular PC software

Example of the Data Warehousing Process

The following is a high-level example of the data warehousing processing flow within a manufacturing system.

1. Database triggers create capture changes within plant-based operational systems. The captured data are stored in tables that will assist the data warehouse in understanding what incremental data has changed within plant applications.
2. A centralized warehouse process selects the current data from each of the updated plant tables based on the incremental changes in step 1, and inserts it into a staging area of the data warehouse; that is, into temporary tables. These tables will be filled with transactions from all plants and further processed for inclusion into the data warehouse.
3. After the data is successfully inserted into the staging area, the plant update tables are refreshed to reflect the completion of the data movement.
4. Staging area data is converted into the final data warehouse transaction format.
5. The data warehouse is taken off-line.
6. The updated data is inserted into the data warehouse production tables.
7. After all of the data is successfully inserted into the data warehouse production tables, the staging area tables are refreshed.
8. The data warehouse is brought back on-line, making the data available to all users.

Components of a Data Warehouse System

Many components make up a data warehouse system. This system begins with the current operational systems, part of the back-end process required to support the data warehouse, and ends with the users' tool suite from which they access and manipulate the data contained within the data warehouse. In the middle is a distribution process that allows the data warehouse to support its users in a localized rather than a centralized fashion. As with other systems, underlying technologies cover all of these processes, such as security, which controls not only the feeding process for the data warehouse on the back end, but also the user accessibility on the front end of the data warehouse. The components of a data warehouse process are shown in Figure 1.4.

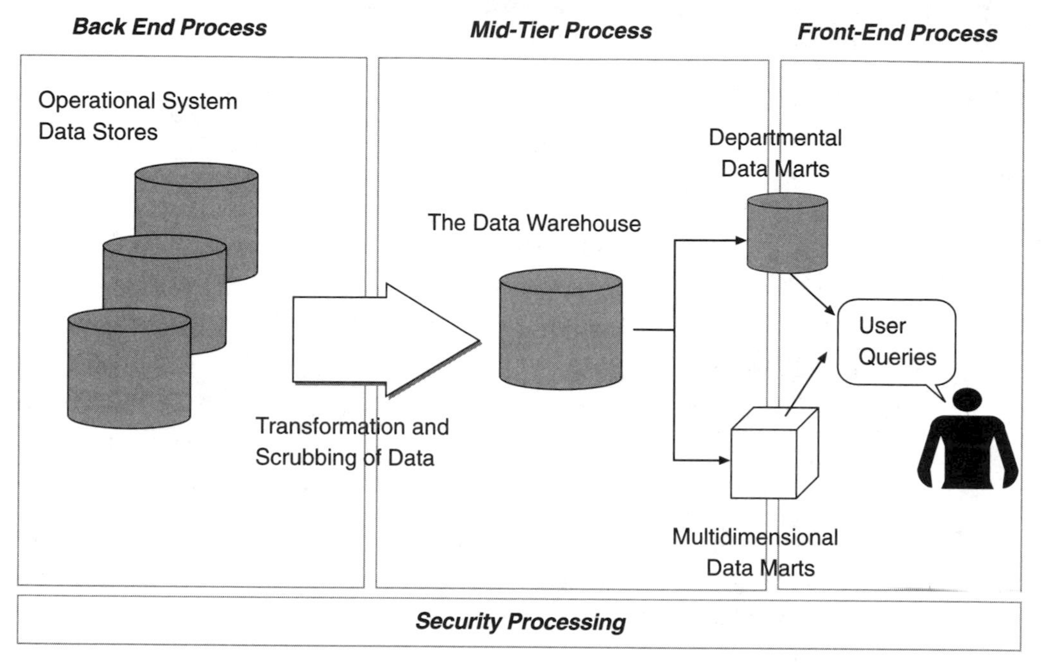

Figure 1.4: *Components of a data warehouse process*

Back-End Process

The back-end process of data warehouse systems utilizes operational systems data stores to populate the staging area within the data warehouse. This process includes the following.

- **Data collection** The data collection process for a data warehouse starts with the current operational systems. This back-end processing for the data warehouse needs to be fragmented into manageable processing chunks. Operational systems generate the transactions that must be processed and entered into the data warehouse. There must be a way within the data warehousing system architecture to intercept and collect data that has changed in the operational system to feed the data warehouse input processing.

- **Data gathering** After we have collected the changes within operational data stores, the back-end processing of the data warehouse must gather all related data to those transactions that have been collected over time. The data collection process typically only captures key information that will drive data gathering processes.

The back-end processing prepares the data into a transaction base that updates and feeds the data warehouse system. This process is by far the most complex within the entire data warehousing system, because we are dealing with multiple legacy data sources, some of which may be easy to manipulate and while most may not.

Mid-Tier Process

The mid-tier process of data warehouse systems utilizes a staging area to finalize the data that will be made available to users within the data warehouse. The staging area is sometimes formally referred to as an operational data store. This process includes the following.

- **Data scrubbing** After we have gathered all related information from operational data stores, the data must be scrubbed to give it a proper, uniform format and definition prior to its placement within the data warehouse.
- **Data placement and distribution** Upon completing the scrubbing, the data must be placed within the data warehouse—in a central location, in a remote location, or in a combination of the two.
- **Standard report compilation and indexing** After the data has been placed in each of the data warehouse data stores, standard reports that are contained within the data warehousing system must be compiled and indexed. After this process is completed, the reports—much like the raw data within the data warehouse—will be made available on-line to the users, avoiding paper distribution.

Mid-tier processing updates the data contained in the staging area of the data warehouse, making it an information base that is more digestible by the ultimate consumer, the users of the data warehouse system. Objectively, this phase should focus on minimizing the down time of the data warehouse while updating its content.

Front-End Process

The front-end process involves granting the proper access to users for the information contained within the data warehouse as well as repopulating any catalog or metadata information required by the users' tool suite. The goal of most data warehouse projects should be to drive this process into the power user's territory and out of the Information Systems space. However, several critical applications need to built for the less sophisticated user of the data warehouse. This process is similar to the traditional application development process. The tasks contained here include updating the applications that access the data warehouse with new content information as well as improving accessibility through proper view or catalog definitions within the users' tools. For example, the front-end application and overall process may present users with metadata that informs them that the financial data provided by the warehouse is accurate through the end of the latest processing time period.

Sample Data Warehouse Reports

It is impossible to show you a complete data warehouse implementation. However, in the many chapters to follow you will be presented with several data warehouse fragments. Typically, these are real-life samples of systems in which we have personally been involved. Because most data warehouse implementations are built to gain competitive advantage, we have presented the information in a modified format so that corporate secrets have not been given away.

The examples that follow in the next sections present the users' window into their data warehouses. These reports are presented utilizing popular tools for business intelligence applications, Cognos' PowerPlay and Impromptu. Each of these applications has had major impact on the company that implemented it. These examples cover only a small fraction of the companies' overall data warehouse. However, they should assist you in better understanding the goals, objectives, and final visualization of a data warehouse through the user interface.

Telecommunications—Sales Analysis

Most companies have objectives that their sales force must attain for the corporation to deliver upon its business plan. The telecommunication provider on which this example is based set specific targets for each of its branches on the three types of sales activities listed below.

- **Installed accounts or base accounts** The business desired to maintain and grow revenues within accounts that already had their products. This included selling more product to them as well as showing their installed customers how to better utilize their current services.
- **New accounts or new business** The business also set a goal not to become stagnant. Each branch had specific targets for generating new business within its territory, thereby expanding the business. These targets were lower than the installed or base account targets, because it is much more difficult to sell to a stranger than to a friend. However, the company wanted its sales personnel to focus on expanding the territories and wanted to compensate those who excelled in this area.

- **Win back accounts** Because the telecommunications business is very competitive, the company set objectives on winning back customers that for one reason or another it had lost over the years. This is a time consuming process. However, after accounts were won back from a competitor, they tended to be much more loyal and it was easier than ever to sell new products to them. If they were not won back, these accounts tended to be negative references for their products and expanded problems in growing a given territory.

It was the job of sales management to monitor the progress that each of the territories was making toward the business goals. The data that fed this system came from various operational and personal data stores, including the order management system, the budgetary system, and the forecasting system. The graphic in Figure 1.5 was utilized to see how current sales were progressing.

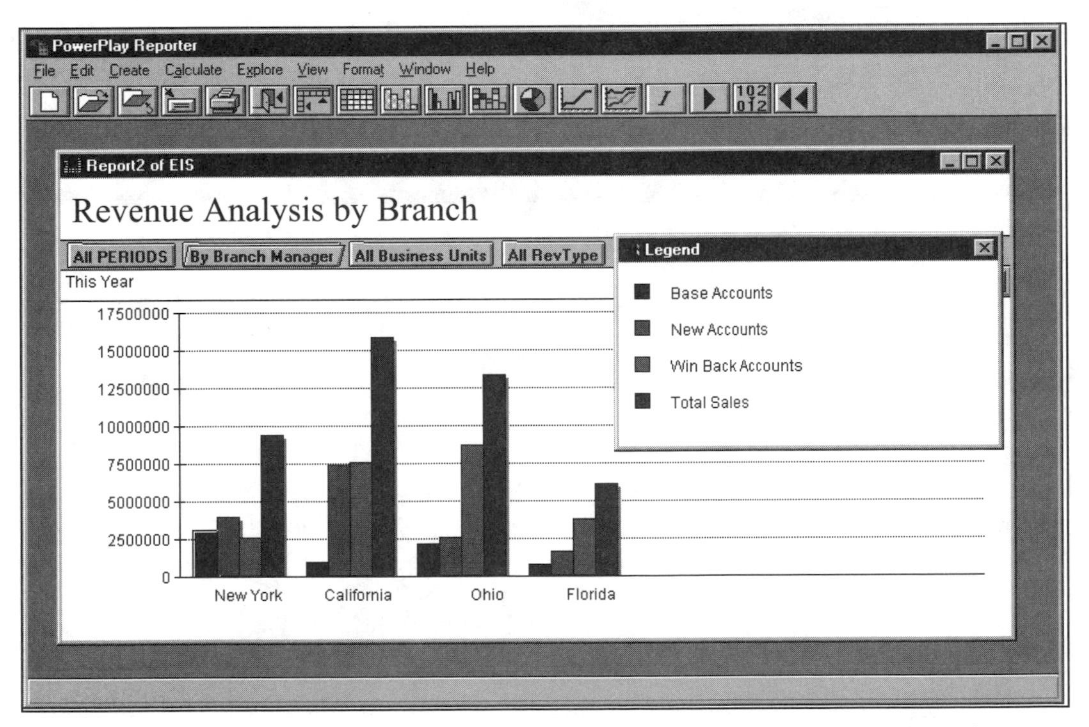

Figure 1.5: *Sample data warehouse report—revenue type analysis by branch*

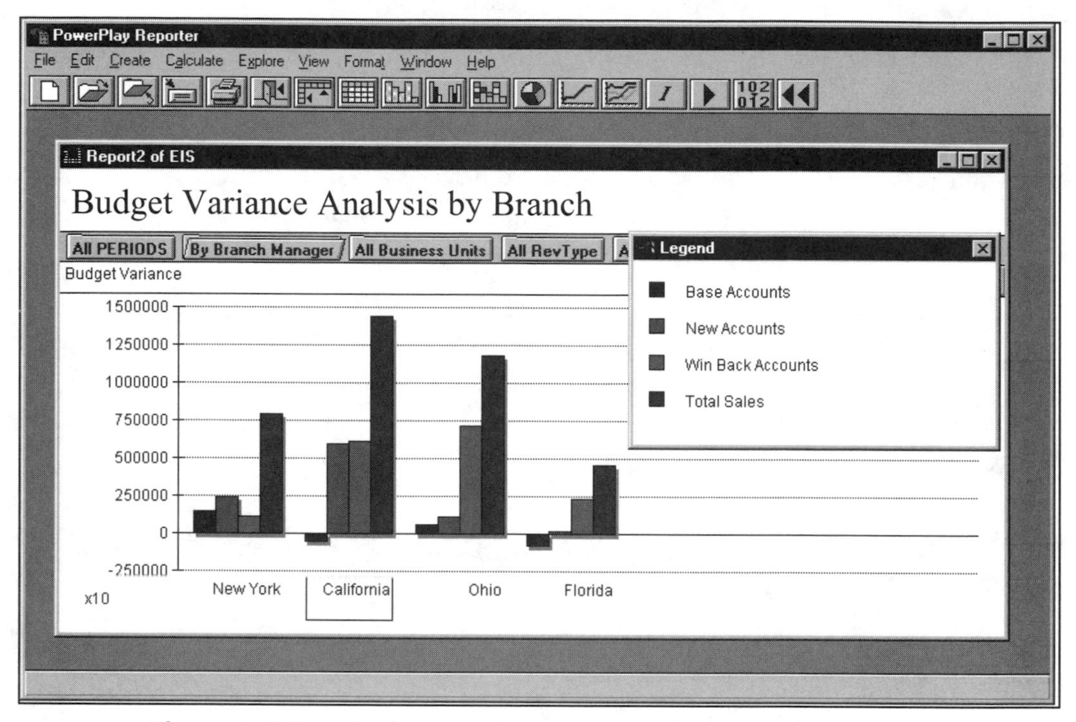

Figure 1.6: *Sample data warehouse report—budget variance report*

The graphic in Figure 1.6 told a more complete story. This graphic shows how each branch was fairing based on the plan that was established at the beginning of the year. As you can see, California and Florida were falling behind their sales numbers for base accounts.

This project resulted in early intervention to guide the business in achieving its overall business goals. Sales managers received data on a timely basis, which allowed them to make adjustments and guide the sales representatives who worked for them in areas that previously were not known until the quarterly reporting system provided the data.

Brand Management—Target Marketing

Brand managers tend to gauge their business' success on their ability to penetrate defined markets. This example was an application produced for a consumer packaged-goods company that desired to better understand who its customer was and what distribution channels were most successful. This data warehouse application focused on demographic analysis and assisted brand managers in understanding market segments that were most receptive to a promotion or marketing campaign.

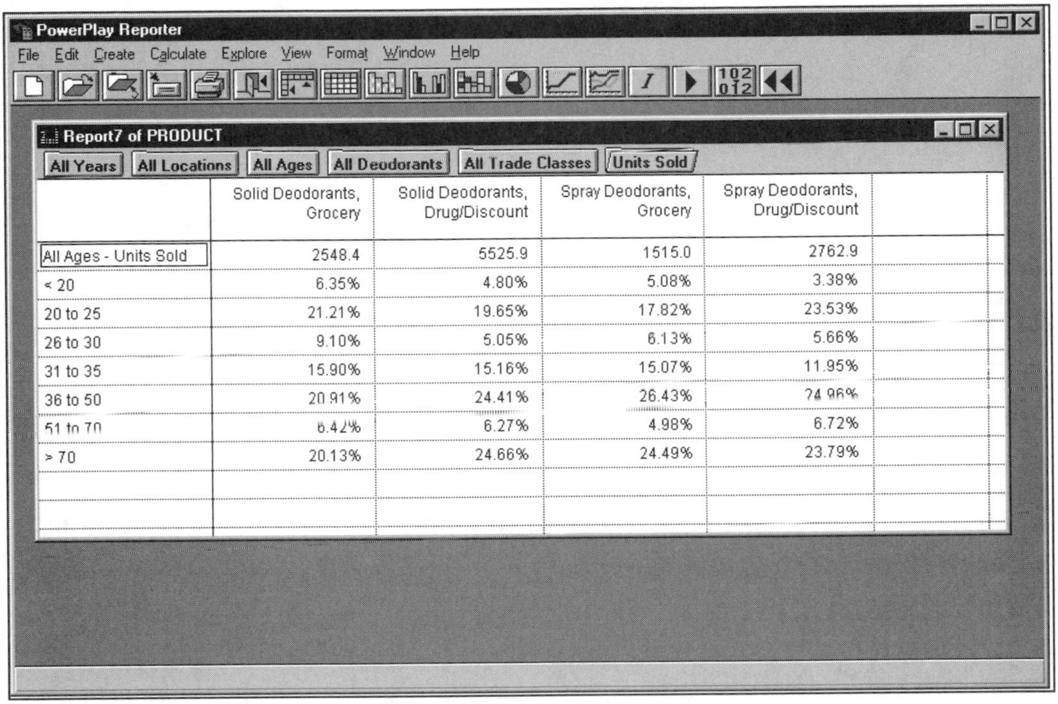

PowerPlay Reporter

File Edit Create Calculate Explore View Format Window Help

Report7 of PRODUCT

All Years | All Locations | All Ages | All Deodorants | All Trade Classes | Units Sold

	Solid Deodorants, Grocery	Solid Deodorants, Drug/Discount	Spray Deodorants, Grocery	Spray Deodorants, Drug/Discount
All Ages - Units Sold	2548.4	5525.9	1515.0	2762.9
< 20	6.35%	4.80%	5.08%	3.38%
20 to 25	21.21%	19.65%	17.82%	23.53%
26 to 30	9.10%	5.05%	6.13%	5.66%
31 to 35	15.90%	15.16%	15.07%	11.95%
36 to 50	20.91%	24.41%	26.43%	24.96%
51 to 70	6.42%	6.27%	4.98%	6.72%
> 70	20.13%	24.66%	24.49%	23.79%

Figure 1.7: *Sample data warehouse report—brand demographic report*

The report in Figure 1.7 shows a demographic breakdown by age. The percentage breakdown explains the units sold by product and distribution channel to these age groups. This type of report is typical of market segmentation reports utilized in many industries by product and brand management to gauge the effectiveness of marketing promotions and campaigns.

This report explains key items to a brand manager, including the following.

- The age groups less than 20, 26 to 30, and 51 to 70 tend not to purchase the products of this business
- Most product is sold via the Drug/Discount sales channel

This is one of many reports utilized by the brand managers of this company to improve promotions based on age category demographics and distribution channels. The brand managers were able to better determine where their consumers were purchasing product and focus their promotional efforts where they would not be wasted. Efforts such as these greatly enhanced the users' capabilities to execute their jobs through informed decisions.

Manufacturing—Labor Hours

Plant managers constantly monitor trends and watch for anomalies within their labor hours. The reports presented in Figures 1.8 and 1.9 are from a data warehouse that assisted plant managers in keeping a closer watch by period and cost center of the labor hours that were logged. Overtime labor is more expensive than regular labor hours. Therefore, overtime should only be utilized when the company really requires it. Up to this point, the process of monitoring these activities occurred on a manual basis. No system captured this data except for the payroll system, which was ill-equipped to produce such a report. Therefore, a system was built to capture this data and other cost information to assist in managing the expense of the manufacturing process. These reports helped plant managers understand when they had stresses in the production systems and when they should budget for more overtime hours. The reports also assisted the managers in controlling costs.

The reports presented here and the data contained within the data warehouse allowed the user to easily navigate the information. Figure 1.8 is a summary report by period of regular and overtime hours.

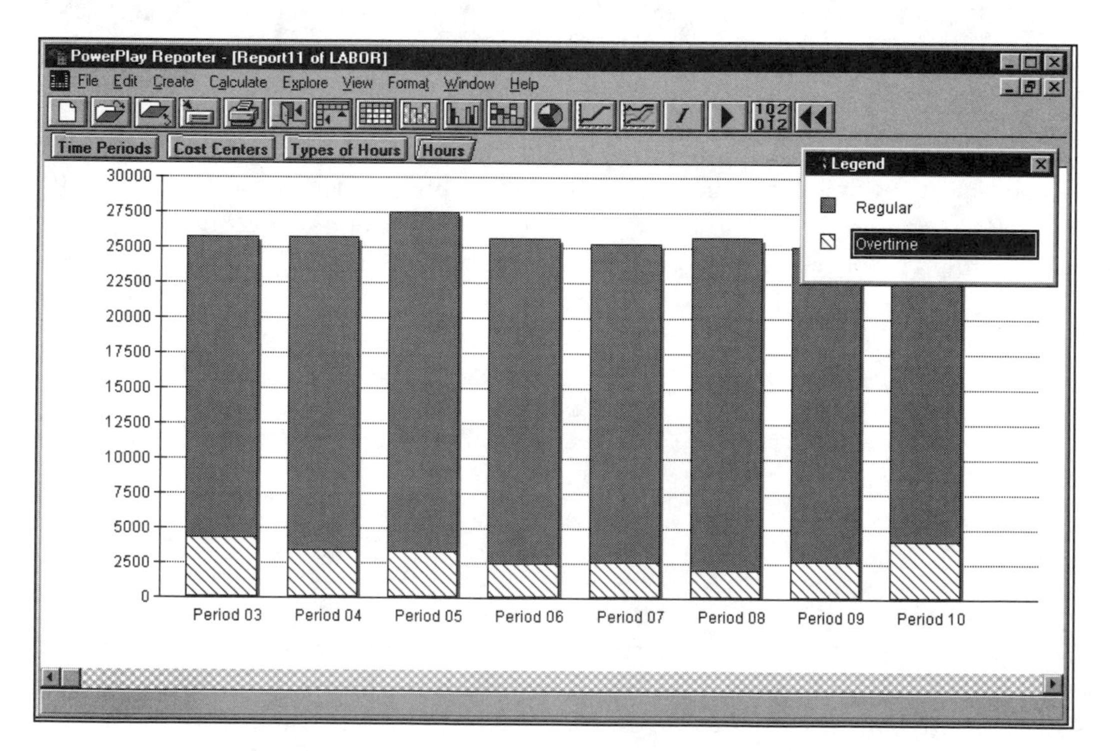

Figure 1.8: *Sample data warehouse report—labor hours*

The report in Figure 1.9 was derived from the one shown in Figure 1.8. The user activity to derive the report in Figure 1.9 included drilling down on the overtime hours, isolating on overtime hours, and swapping the hours coordinate with the cost center dimension. The resultant report allowed plant managers to see by cost center where the overtime hours were being applied. This report also shows that the trend for overtime hours had begun to decrease; however, in periods 9 and 10 the overtime hours were on the rise. Depending on business cycles, this might have raised concern.

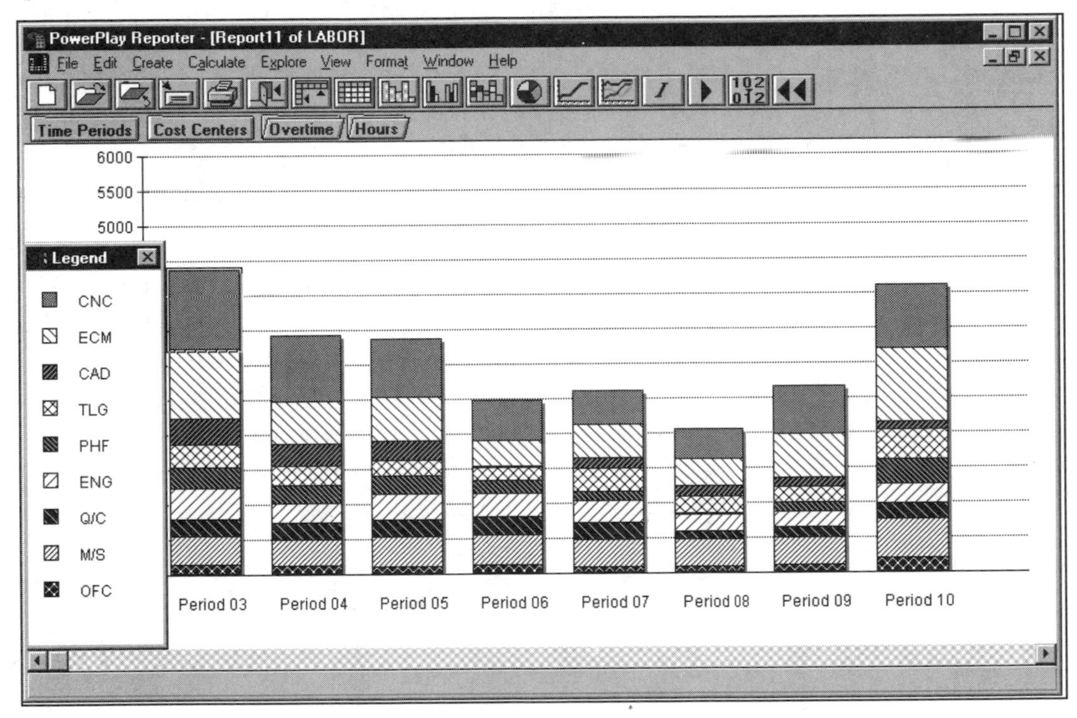

Figure 1.9: *Sample data warehouse report—labor hours by cost center*

Summary

Data warehouse systems have and will be the foundation for dynamic companies. The process of data warehousing has many correlations to the manufacturing industry—hence the term of warehousing. With the goal of placing information into the hands of people who need it, the data warehouse is providing its users with a corporate knowledge base. The business intelligence derived from a data warehouse and given to its users can greatly enhance a company's capabilities in growth and revenue expansion. Individuals who figure out where their markets are going and how their markets have handled product introductions, promotions, and other revenue-growing techniques will be the ones who gain the most competitive advantage.

A data warehouse can assist your company in the following ways.

- Better utilization of information from current operations to run the whole business more effectively
- Better business intelligence
- Enhanced customer service
- Better management of corporate assets and liabilities
- Monetary savings through elimination of reporting expenses
- Increased effectiveness of decision-making personnel; assisting in increasing profits

To achieve these and other types of benefits, a data warehouse must formulate data at different levels of granularity, from detailed data to highly summarized and aggregated data. The historical data that is collected and stored in a data warehouse will enhance your users' capabilities to perform trend analysis and make long-term strategic decisions. The more current the content of the data warehouse, the better you can enhance your business' ability to support the day-to-day decision-making process.

The data that feeds a data warehouse is derived from a variety of data stores, including the following.

- Operational systems residing on a variety of heterogeneous platforms
- Data that is external to operational systems, originating from nonoperational parts of the business
- Data that is external to the company, originating from public databases, such as demographic or financial data

A data warehouse provides your company with a single version of reality that is characterized over time. This gives you a true picture of what has occurred historically—the good, the bad, and the ugly. If the data in a data warehouse can be refreshed at intervals closer to the business decision process, those users requiring information to make decisions become more capable of making informed decisions. This includes the ability to shrink the gap between a business' leading and trailing indicators, creating a process of decision making based on a shorter business cycle. If the duration of a decision-making process can be decreased, corporations gain significant competitive advantage and are able to grow their organizations' revenues at an accelerated pace. This is what your company's data warehouse team should strive for.

Building the corporate knowledge base is no longer a fantasy; and with the proper techniques, it can be done in an organized and highly productive manner. In the next chapter, What Factors Drive a Successful Data Warehouse Project?, we provide you with 10 steps that can help you make your data warehousing project a success.

2

What Factors Drive a Successful Data Warehouse Project?

If you are a genius and unsuccessful, everybody treats you as if you were a genius. But when you come to be successful, when you commence to earn money, when you are really successful, then your family and everybody no longer treats you like a genius, they treat you like a man who has become successful.

—Pablo Picasso

Data warehouse projects differ from those that most development staff have experienced. Many companies plow into the development effort without placing themselves in a position where they can be successful. We find amazing how many data warehouse projects have significant cost overruns or are never delivered. In the information systems world, cost and time are our measures of success, and far too many data warehouse projects result in management grading them as failures. To assist you in avoiding failure, we list some key requirements to make a data warehouse project succeed. These items may seem basic; however, you would be amazed at the basics that are dropped when pressure to deliver is placed on a project team. If you want a successful data warehouse project, make sure to address the following issues. Each of these issues is discussed in the separate sections that follow.

- Obtain management commitment
- Begin with a manageable project
- Clearly communicate realistic expectations
- Assign a user-oriented manager
- Use proven methods
- Design based on queries rather than on transactions
- Only load data that is needed
- Define the proper data source, or system of record
- Clearly define unique subjects
- Force use of, and reference to, the data warehouse

Obtain Management Commitment

The most important quality in a leader is that of being acknowledged as such.

—*André Maurois*

The proper sponsor is critical for the success of a data warehouse. The project sponsor must be a high-level executive within the company. Examples of a proper sponsor include vice president of sales, vice president of marketing, vice president of manufacturing, and vice president of operations. This person will become the driving force required to correctly complete your project and will give the project credibility beyond that of a traditional development project. Support by an executive delivers a strategic vision to a data warehouse and the respect of the entire organization. This support assists you in gaining access to information that otherwise would be difficult to receive. This information may come from interviewing someone who typically would not see you, from documents that are viewed as strategic to the company, or from general insight of what the company views as strategic. Your project's sponsor allows you to apply a sense of urgency with those from whom you will need to obtain information, avoiding unnecessary delays.

Based on the strategic importance of your sponsor to the overall organization, it is also important to realize that you will not have a dedicated sponsor, only someone on whom you can depend in times of need. Typically, your sponsor will establish or assist you in establishing a steering committee that will represent him or her. The steering committee is a high-level, decision-making authority with guidance or direction from the executive sponsor. Some sponsors will actively manage the steering committees, while others manage through delegation. However, both the sponsor and the steering committee will provide the required user backing to make your project successful.

As well, your sponsor or the appointed steering committee will assist you on the business side of the project. Because data warehouse projects often do not show tangible cost savings benefits, the sponsor can assist, even fight for, the financial requirements of the project. After all, the reason sponsors have achieved their positions in the company is that they are good business people. They will be able to assist in building the proper business plan to justify the costs of the data warehouse project, eliminating any problems with attaining the proper resources such as equipment, software, people, location, and training.

If your sponsor lacks enthusiasm and commitment, you may want to immediately confront him or her to understand why. Data warehouses are built for the business to gain significant competitive advantage. Most development organizations are more in tune with technologies than they are with the goals of individual business organizations. The sponsorship chain from the user community, including the executive sponsor and steering committee, will help the development staff stay focused and deliver what is needed by the business. Without that focus, projects drift. Make sure to communicate this with your sponsor, who can guarantee that the organization views your project as a strategic investment, not just another tactical system.

It is our experience that the lack of an executive sponsor or a high level user steering committee is the number one reason for failure of data warehouse projects. Data warehouses that are driven solely by the information systems department tend to run over budget and seldom deliver what the user desires. Therefore, if you have started a project and have yet to formulate such a sponsor—stop and get one.

Begin with a Manageable Project: A Subject-Oriented Data Warehouse

Method goes far to prevent trouble in business, for it makes the task easy, hinders confusion, saves abundance of time, and instructs those that have business pending both what to do and what to hope.

—*William Penn*

You should not set out to create an enterprise data warehouse; this scope is far too large for any development team and will more than likely never be completed. Data warehouses are complex—probably the largest integration effort ever undertaken by those who do so. These projects require the coordination of multiple vendors' components as well as internal organizations within a company. Based on these complexities, you should start with a small and manageable aspect of the business, a subject-oriented data warehouse.

A subject-oriented data warehouse is a smaller scale data warehouse that focuses on a given part of the business in need of the most assistance. However, the development team must build an architecture that supports the concept of the enterprise data warehouse, a plug-and-play or building-block approach to data warehouse development as shown in Figure 2.1. A subject-oriented data warehouse focuses on laying the groundwork for an enterprise data warehouse by slowly automating the areas required by the business in a more manageable fashion—by building a decision support database and infrastructure.

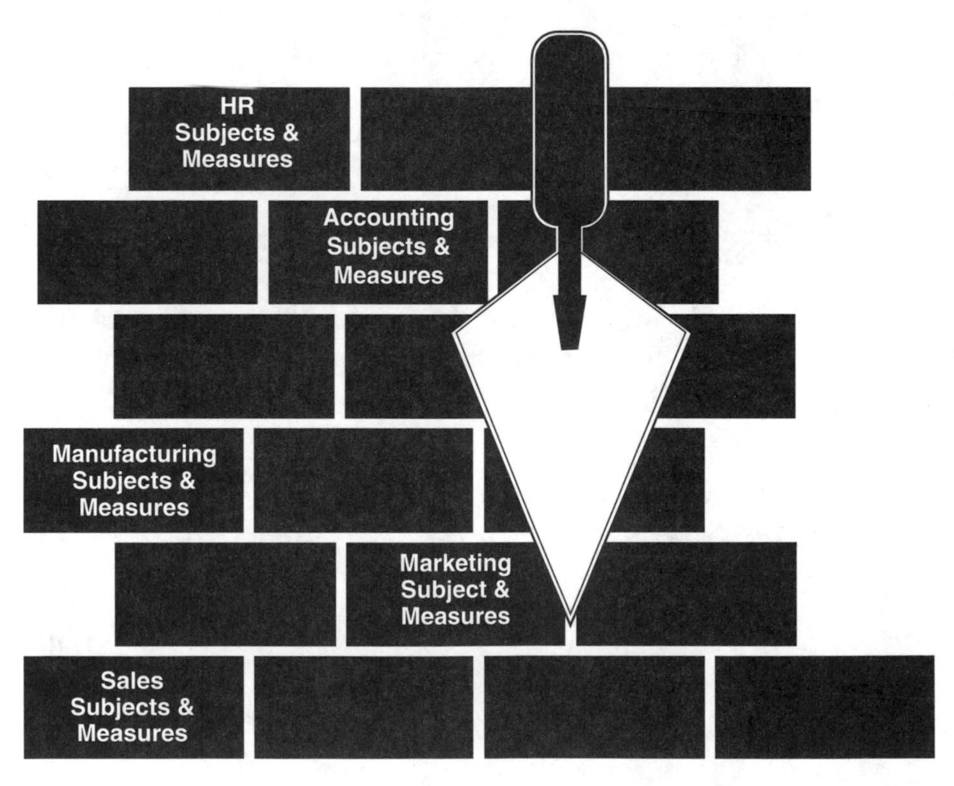

Figure 2.1: *Building-block approach to data warehousing*

When selecting candidate applications for subject-oriented data warehouse implementations, you should focus on areas that will provide the highest value to the organization if the project succeeds, while at the same time reducing the risk to the organization should the project fail.

As you can see in Figure 2.2, attempting to deliver an enterprise data warehouse that supports all of the labeled systems would be a daunting task. The benefits of starting with smaller, more manageable projects have proven their worth over time, especially in the area of client/server systems, of which data warehousing typically is one. Our experience with small projects like those described here also has shown that the costs of a data warehouse infrastructure declines for each subject-oriented data warehouse implementation. This is primarily due to the reuse of the contents of the subject areas managed within subject-oriented data warehouses.

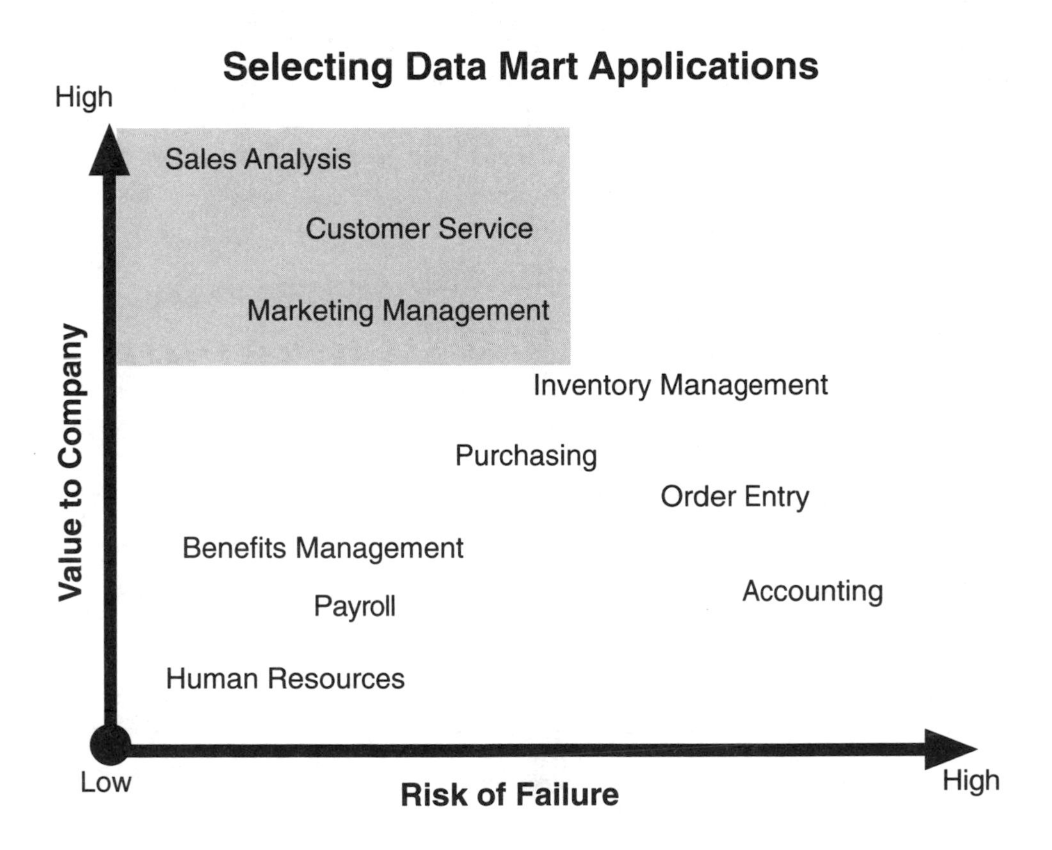

Figure 2.2: *Business area selection for a subject-oriented data warehouse*

The first implementation of a subject-oriented data warehouse will have a relatively high entry cost that is directly associated with the lack of an architecture, a data model, and the tools to properly implement the system. During the initial subject-oriented data warehouse project, the development team faces numerous challenges in these technical areas as well as the large task associated in discovering what the user's perception and expectations are for the data warehouse. The architectural work will begin to define how the systems will interconnect. The tool selection work will define how the data will be accessed. And most important, data modeling exercises will allow the project to begin to define the subject areas that will be contained in the enterprise data warehouse.

Over time, subject areas will be reused within different subject-oriented data warehouses, allowing the development team to allocate less time and cost for data modeling and analysis. For example, an initial subject-oriented data warehouse may develop subject areas such as customer, product, and location. Each of these subject areas will be reused within sales management, marketing management, product management, and operation planning subject-oriented data warehouses. Therefore, if the subject areas are developed within a sales management subject-oriented data warehouse, the costs associated with analysis and development of these subject areas will not reoccur in the other subject-oriented data warehouse projects. The effects of reuse on costs associated with analysis and development are depicted in Figure 2.3.

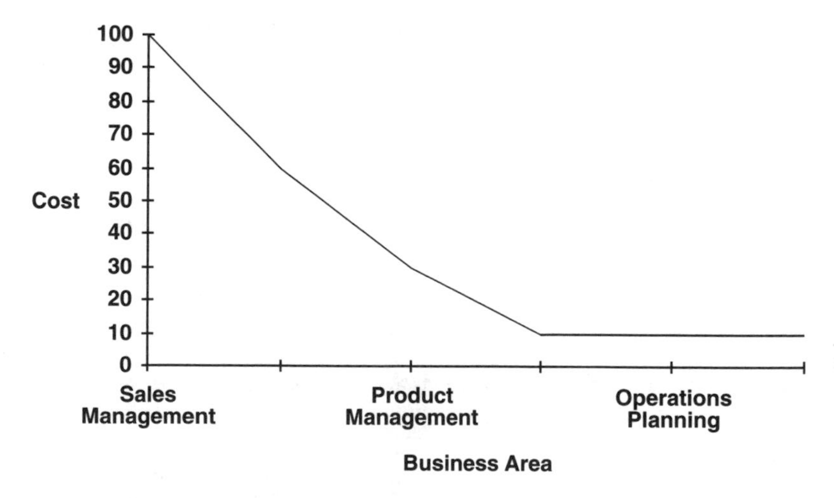

Figure 2.3: *Cost of data warehouse development based on reuse*

However, the generalization that subject areas will fit the need of future subject-oriented data warehouses is not always true. At times during the development of additional subject-oriented data warehouses, it becomes apparent that one of the subject areas within the data warehouse does not match the needs of the new business area. This forces the development effort to incorporate further analysis and development of the affected subject areas. Each business area utilizing the affected subject area must be reanalyzed to verify that the change will not severely impact the production subject-oriented data warehouses. The effects of this reanalysis upon costs is illustrated in Figure 2.4.

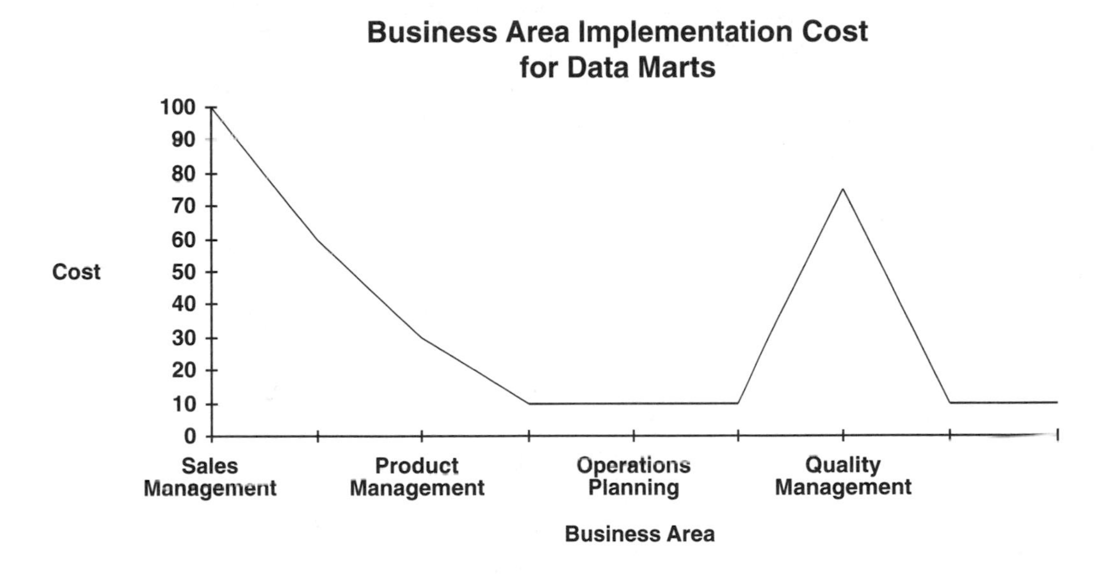

Figure 2.4: *Cost of data warehouse when reanalysis must occur*

The recommended strategy for building your data warehouse involves a methodology that focuses on smaller development cycles and rapid deliverables, such as subject-oriented data warehouses, and a methodology that focuses on the reuse of data entities. This approach gives users deliverables at a greater frequency and allows the project team to grow its expertise based on more rapid review cycles.

Undertaking a significantly larger project is another source for failure of data warehousing projects. Again, you should analyze your own situation. Are you starting a project whose first deliverable is more than a subject-oriented data warehouse? If so, consider resizing into a more manageable project before commencement.

Clearly Communicate Realistic Expectations

I know not anything more pleasant, or more instructive, than to compare experience with expectation, or to register from time to time the difference between idea and reality. It is by this kind of observation that we grow daily less liable to be disappointed.

—Samuel Johnson

Project management encompasses many things, including estimation, resource management, and budget management. However, the most important aspect of managing a project is communication. Nobody appreciates surprises when those surprises involve project or budgetary overruns, but surprises in lack of functionality are an even ruder awakening for those paying. Effective communication with proper project management will ensure that you do not commit to unrealistic time lines or system capabilities.

The job of communication is a job of expectation setting. This type of communication is one of the most important things you can do in any project, and a data warehouse project is no exception. The importance within a data warehouse project lies in the fact that your users probably are of a different kind than that to which you are accustomed. Time lines, functionality, and budget must be managed and effectively communicated to customers. Your sponsor or steering committee should focus heavily on the communication and expectation aspects of the project.

Make sure not to overstate the capabilities of a data warehouse. Much like the old adage of *garbage in, garbage out,* computers are dumb and only do what you tell them. Data warehousing requires some level of business intelligence in the user of the system. We hope that a data warehouse will help managers make better decisions, but there is no guarantee of that. A data warehouse gives its users better information from which they must make the decisions.

As a project manager or team member, verify that you are establishing realistic scope, goals, objectives, functionality, and time lines. These items should then be effectively communicated to the users with frequent, consistent updates to the plan. An effective communication strategy will assist you in avoiding surprises and give the project a success rating by users and management.

Assign a User-Oriented Manager for the Project

You see things and you say, "Why?" But I dream things that never were and I say, "Why not?"

—George Bernard Shaw

Selecting a project manager for your data warehouse project should be done carefully. It is not wise to assume that just any project manager will do. To properly guide and develop a data warehouse, the project manager and other key development personnel require a user-oriented mindset. The project manager should be able to work from the outside in on the project.

What does this mean? The project manager must be able to place himself or herself in the user's role, understanding what the deliverable will look and feel like. From that position, the project manager gains significant insight into leading his or her team to the delivery of the data warehouse. This top-down management style allows the project manager to drive from a position where the end is in mind and no deviation from that end will occur unless it enhances the end product and makes the users of the data warehouse more successful. A user-oriented project manager has a much easier time envisioning cross-functional boundary systems.

To deliver a successful data warehouse, the project manager must be understand and deliver what the user wants. It is not advisable to put your best technical project manager in this role. You need someone who is a good project manager and clearly understands the business for which the company is striving to be the best. This manager must think and act like users—not like technologists.

Technology-oriented project managers tend to loose focus of the end. As new technologies become available in the marketplace, they lose focus of the deliverable and have a strong desire to establish a new plan based on the new technology. Within a data warehouse environment, it is critical to stay on course and make modifications based on the established development cycles of subject-oriented data warehouses.

The project manager is required to interact frequently with users. As all of us know, communication is key to ensuring that a project succeeds. Assigning someone who cannot communicate or who quickly becomes frustrated with users is a death shot to a data warehousing project.

Use Proven Methods

The effectiveness of our memory banks is determined not by the total number of facts we take in, but the number we wish to reject.

—*Jon Wynne-Tyson*

Though a data warehouse may be a new type of system, the tasks at hand are no different than in the past—and we cannot forget the past. Client/server development was the first time we saw information systems professionals incurring significant memory loss regarding what the past had taught them. When you ask individuals with a mainframe background to show you their policies, procedures, and standards for system development processes, they will take you to a room filled with books much like a library. Ask the same question in the client/server world and you may get a 20-page document.

Why are we forgetting the past? The answer still alludes us. We firmly believe that what was done in the past with regard to system development life cycles, project management, and policies governing these tasks was, to some degree, overkill. It took us far too long to deliver systems. However, many valuable lessons have been learned and should be the foundation on which we build our future systems. Data warehousing is just another system. Albeit complicated in different areas than traditional systems, it still is just a system. It intersects our corporate, departmental, and personal systems, and offers a melding of these systems. Over several decades, we've learned some effective methods for developing software and managing information systems projects. Using these methods improves the probability that a data warehouse project will succeed. We need to take the techniques that were most successful in all of these platforms and merge them into a standard methodology for delivery of high-quality systems to our user community.

As part of defining a data warehouse development process, you need to adopt policies, procedures, and standards to provide a basis for comparison to assess the size, content, value, and quality of an activity. Items that should have documented policies, procedures, and standards include the following.

- Project management
- Development plans
- Design documentation
- Modeling techniques
- Prototyping techniques

- Test plans
- Quality assurance plans
- Review and audit processes
- Usability testing
- Change management
- Problem reporting and tracking
- Configuration management

These policies, procedures, and standards are required, especially in situations in which many people, products, and tools must coexist. These items are essential for a data warehouse project, because they establish common support environments. The ability to support data warehouse development will become much easier when everyone knows and understands a common way of doing the same task. Some of the benefits of this include: resources may be moved between projects; over time, training needs will be reduced; and a uniform method for reviewing work and the status of projects will be developed.

Defining the best common practices for data warehouse development also promotes consistent use of tools and methods. This approach facilitates your team through the development life cycle and greatly enhances the maintainability of the final deliverables. It is hard to envision a well-established and efficient development shop allowing every manager, designer, developer, and tester to use their personal conventions. In such an environment, quality debates have no basis for mutual agreement and are prone to non-resolution. Approved practices for development within a data warehouse provide a framework to support the development decision-making process.

Design Must Be Focused on Queries, Not on Transactions

An audience is never wrong. An individual member of it may be an imbecile, but a thousand imbeciles together in the dark—that is critical genius.

—Billy Wilder

The design of a data warehouse is far different from an operational database design. The process modeling techniques, which often form the basis of an operational system's design, offer little assistance to those designing and developing a data warehouse.

A data warehouse is a data-driven and query-driven system in which the focus must be more oriented to data modeling. Your data modeling efforts should focus on delivering a database that is easy and fast to navigate. You will find that a user's query process is rapid fire and reiterative. Therefore, the associated database design must understand that queries may not be well defined. You will also find that you cannot afford the time and dedicated effort to tune every query a user sends to a data warehouse. Instead, you need to define a system that allows users to continue their current query behaviors and that supports and promotes this type of behavior. The system is nothing more than the data source for a lot of users to query; therefore, you should place emphasis on data organization and layout, including indexes, physical data placement, memory utilization, and query access patterns. This means that we will build a system that breaks many of the rules that we have previously learned in our data modeling history. That is, the demon of denormalization will become our angel of mercy!

The focus of operational systems is the on-line transaction processing needs or the meeting of response time requirements of volatile transactions. With this focus, data structures have become highly normalized to eliminate data redundancy. Denormalization is viewed negatively by most database or data administrators. This negative view often stems from the rich on-line transaction processing (OLTP) background developed by these critical information system professionals.

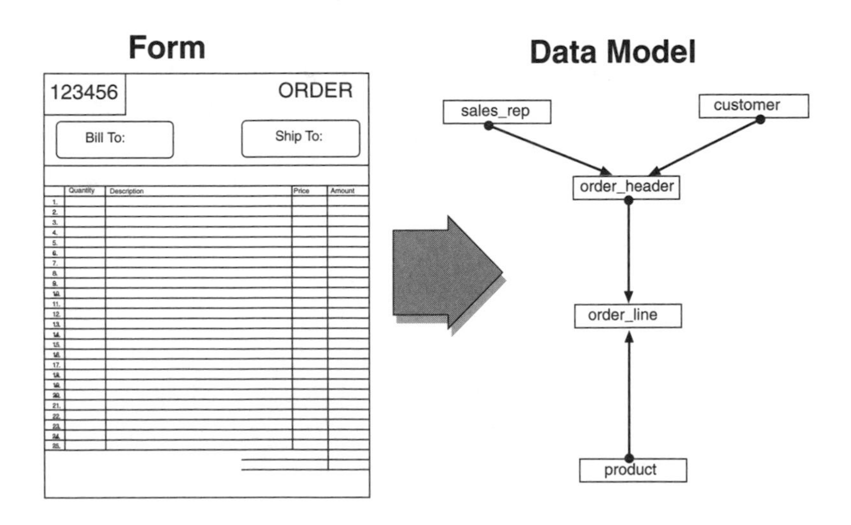

Figure 2.5: *The normalization of an order form*

Normalization and denormalization can best be characterized by the paper based systems utilized prior to computers. A form, such as an order, was utilized to record business transactions. These forms were stored in a filing cabinet, typically in alphabetic order. The retrieval of information was easy and standard. Any time that users of this system wanted to look up a customer's orders, they just took the first letter of the name and opened that drawer. The normalized database structures of an order form are depicted in Figure 2.5.

When computerized information systems arrived, professionals realized that it would be more efficient to build data structures that in essence tore up the form and placed different sections in different files—customer, order header, order lines, parts, and so forth. However, this posed a problem to the user of the system as it became difficult to piece all of the information—the order forms—back together. The relationship between traditional and computerized record retrieval is illustrated in Figure 2.6.

Old way of retrieving customer order information

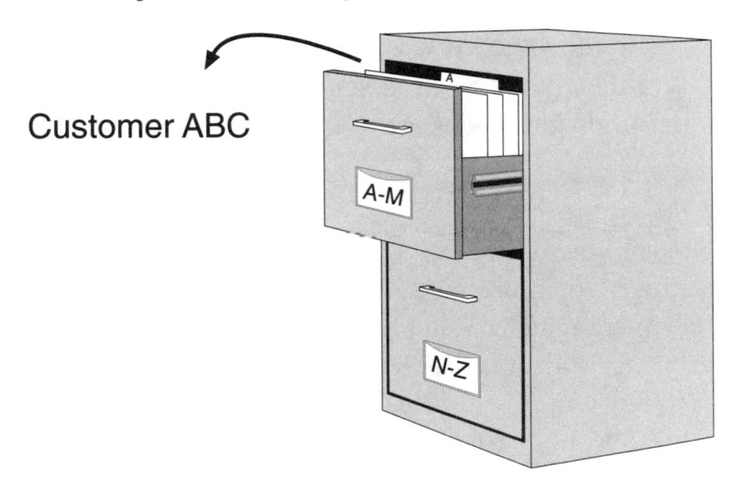

New way of retrieving customer order information

```
select
  ordhd.id, prod.desc, ordln.qty, prod.up, (ordln.qty*prod.up) as "Amount"
from
  ordln, ordhd, prod, cust, sale_rep
where
  (ordln.id = ordhd.id and ordln.pid = prod.pid and ordhd.cid = cust.cid
  and ordhd.srid = sale_rep.srid) and cust.name = 'ABC'
```

Figure 2.6: *Retrieval of customer order information*

Tearing apart the data used by a form is called normalization, in which we compartmentalize data that belongs together in its own file and avoid storing it redundantly. The art of putting the form back together in one location can be viewed as denormalizing. This denormalizing has typically only happened on paper through standardized reports.

Data warehousing has increasingly added denormalization to its modeling techniques and physical implementations. These techniques improve the user's ability to navigate the historical, business data without information system professional intervention. Remember, a data warehouse strives to provide users with direct access. For this reason, most data warehouses are not as concerned with transactions as they are with the overall business impact of a given event. Also, a data warehouse contains data that is typically read-only, or static. Therefore, data redundancy or denormalization is a technique utilized to support ease of use and efficiency of query processing within a data warehouse.

Only Load Data That Is Needed

The word that gives the key to the national vice is waste. And people who are wasteful are not wise, neither can they remain young and vigorous. In order to transmute energy to higher and more subtle levels, one must first conserve it.

—*Henry Miller*

If you ask users what data they need in a data warehouse, they will respond, "Everything!" The current user community sentiment is that the Information Systems department has been totally inept in delivering the information users require to get their job done. So they will take all of the data and get someone from outside the company who knows how to deliver what they want in a timely fashion.

Many data warehouses begin with this data dumping technique when the Information Systems department establishes a philosophy of: *We will give them everything, then see what they use.* We must remember why they are users and we are Information Systems professionals. We need to control what actually goes into a data warehouse. At the same time, we need to begin rebuilding rapport with the user community.

Data should not be placed into a data warehouse without justification or cause. There is a fine line between want and need, and your data warehouse project team must manage this line. Just because data is used operationally, or just because data is in a database, is not just cause for inclusion in a data warehouse. We do not want to create a data junkyard.

The size of the data that will be loaded into a data warehouse is a critical bottleneck that impacts your ability to succeed in the final delivery of a data warehouse. As noted earlier, data warehouses can grow quite large. Therefore, you should scrutinize the usefulness of data that is placed in a data warehouse. Verify data requirements with the user community during the design phase of your project through the interview and review process.

User interviews will present you with the requirements, potentially for the first time. Take your notes and formulate a design. Then, return to the users and validate your design and assumptions, describing what capabilities you feel the users will have with the data content. Give the users a chance to provide feedback on the design. When they do, have them rank the information with which they have been presented as *required*, *important*, *nice to have*, or *not needed*. You can take this information and enhance your design one more time. Upon completion of this design, present and validate your design again with the user community. The users will probably resist these frequent meetings. However, over time they will begin to appreciate the meetings, realizing that you are looking out for their best interest by formulating a solid design. If you encounter any resistance in this process, remember your sponsorship chain and leverage it; let the sponsor or steering committee manage the conflict. After you begin to successfully deliver your subject-oriented data warehouses, the user community will realize that you don't live your life to make their lives miserable.

Improper design with lots of extraneous data makes a data warehouse unwieldy and fat, containing meaningless data that must be maintained and that slows the process. Extraneous data buries important data and adversely affects ease of use. The user community will be impacted and irritated as they wade through data that has little value to them. You should not take an "I told you so" attitude after the fact. Remember, users have been starved for information and will want a quick solution. But like other information systems, no silver bullet will immediately solve their information requirements.

You must manage data placement from the onset. Failure to do so yields a data warehouse that we characterize as a data junkyard. If the data that is placed in a data warehouse is extraneous to the business process or its key performance measures, it will just sit there and rust. And when users must wade through this unneeded data, they quickly become disenchanted with you and your data warehouse. The lesson here is, do not create a data junkyard.

Define Proper Data Sources: Metadata Mapping

Our treasure lies in the beehive of our knowledge. We are perpetually on the way thither, being by nature winged insects and honey gatherers of the mind.

—*Friedrich Nietzsche*

Data is everywhere, and most of it we don't currently control. Historically, the data associated with operational systems has been locked in mainframe computer systems. These glass-house systems have driven users to build their own personal databases, which allow them to better understand the cross-functional data and the data that most impacts their specific job. These systems and data sources have grown with companies.

When scouring the land for data, you will begin to see a distributed organization that is supported by various systems and system architectures. Often, you find five payroll systems, three accounting systems, 10 budgetary systems, and numerous more human resource applications. Figure 2.7 illustrates the evolution of a business' computer system needs as a business grows.

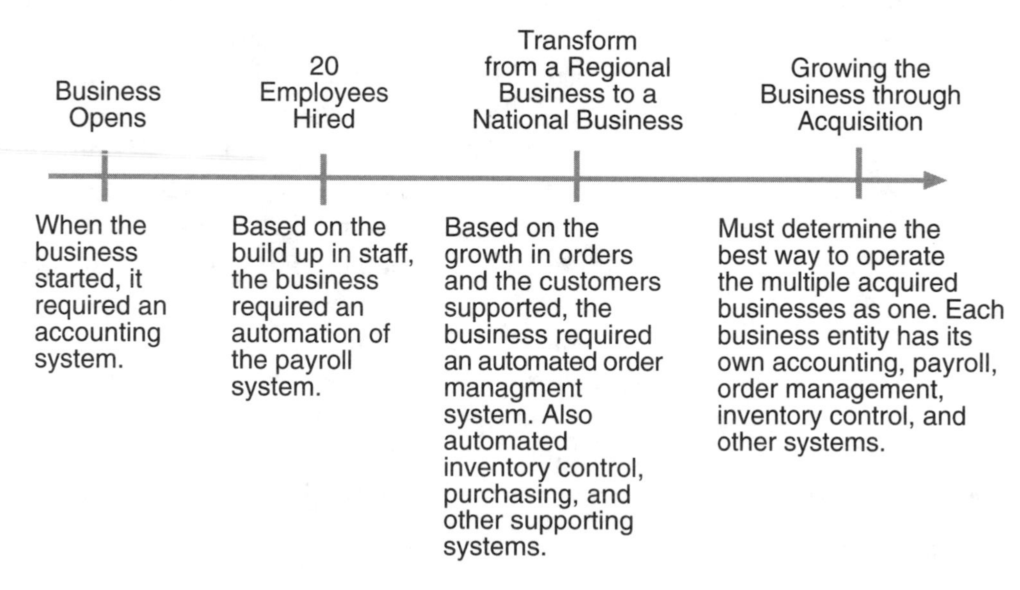

Figure 2.7: *Business systems grow as a business evolves*

The complications of multiple operational systems managing the same business events and transactions are typically prevalent in organizations that have grown through acquisitions. These companies may have allowed the separate entities to proceed with their own information systems strategies. And now you have the wonderful job of trying to centralize all of that data. Figure 2.8 depicts incompatible infrastructures that result through corporate acquisitions.

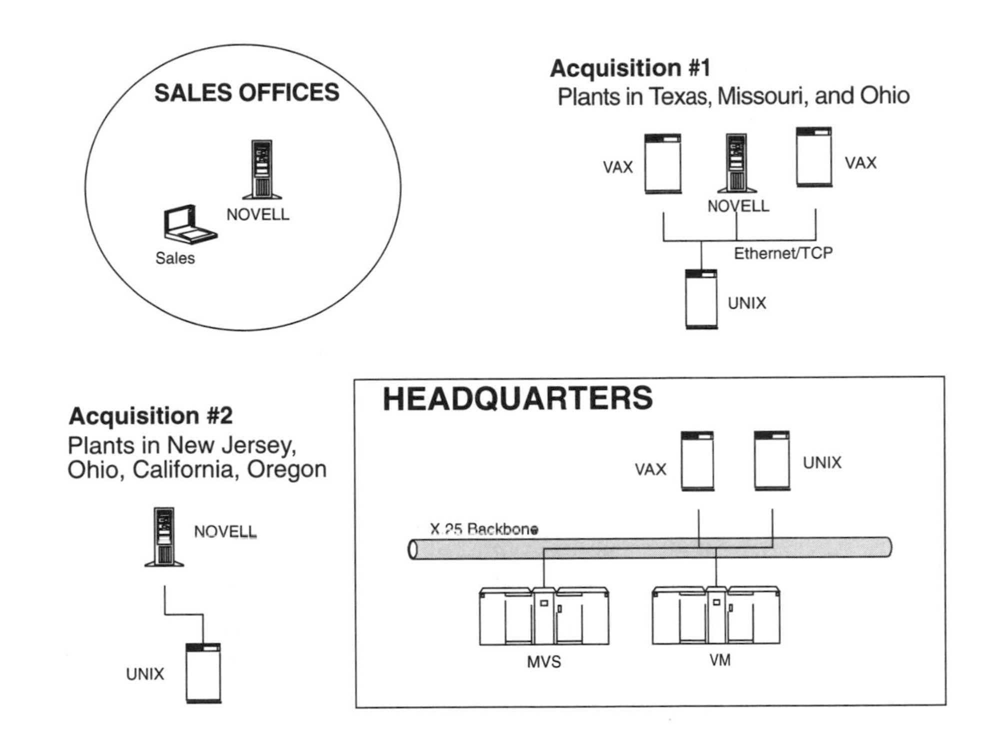

Figure 2.8: *Incompatible infrastructures can arise through business acquisitions*

Though incompatible systems have allowed separate business entities to be effectively managed and grow over the years, they still are typically focused on less than the entire enterprise. Further, they have no common architecture. This orientation poses a problem to those who are required to analyze the business as a whole, because they need to view data across functional boundaries and, more than likely, across architectural boundaries.

As if these complications weren't enough, outsiders have data that is important to you. Corporate data may be combined or compared to overall industry data to determine how well a product, a market, or an entire company is faring against the competition. Data warehouse users require this data along with the internal data to spot trends, improve operations, or increase competitiveness. Examples of external sources of data include the following.

- Purchasing-trends and market-research reports (A.C. Nielson, IRI, and JD Powers)
- Demographic and credit reports (Dun and Bradstreet, Equifax, and TRW)
- Popular business journals (*Wall Street Journal, Barrons, Business Week, Forbes,* and *Fortune*)
- Industry newsletters
- Technology reports

Though internal data sources may appear to be complicated, external data sources will pose additional challenges that may be more complicated in the long run. These issues include legal referencing of data sources, orderly usage and entry of data, frequency of data updates, and the unstructured format of the data.

You must trace data from the capture point through the process to the ultimate data source, and store the reference information in a *metadata repository*. Metadata is data about data. Metadata describes the structure, content, and source of data within a data warehouse. Metadata plays an important role in all data warehouse implementations and will be the place where all data, internal and external, are defined and registered for use within a data warehouse. This metadata is a valuable source of information that will assist the development team and users throughout a data warehouse's processes from data transformation through the data access areas of a data warehouse. Metadata can be considered a data warehouse's equivalent of a library's card catalog system—a corporate card catalog.

Remember, don't just look inside for data; data providers exist in most industries to provide valuable data to assist your company in better understanding how you stack up against the competition. You must search out this data and marry it with your internal data to provide your users with a complete understanding of how they can gain competitive advantage. When a proper data source is located, log all relevant information into your metadata repository. This procedure gives you a management tool for versioning data and for managing the data warehouse's data feeds as the warehouse and company evolve.

Clearly Define Unique Subjects

It is the business of thought to define things, to find the boundaries; thought, indeed, is a ceaseless process of definition. It is the business of art to give things shape. Anyone who takes no delight in the firm outline of an object, or in its essential character, has no artistic sense.... He cannot even be nourished by art. Like Ephraim, he feeds upon the East wind, which has no boundaries.

—*Vance Palmer*

Every business has subject areas, which are of great importance to it, as well as key business measures. These subjects and business measures must be contained and defined within a data warehouse. Each of these subject areas and business measures must have a unique definition that is standardized across the company and organized around a standardized time dimension. Within data warehouse implementations, the following are common subject areas.

- **Product** What the company sells to its customers
- **Geography** Locations where the company sells its products
- **Customer** To whom the company sells its products

Within data warehouse implementations, the following are common key business measures.

- **Sales** The total dollar amount of product revenue, often discussed and measured in terms of budgeted sales and actual sales.
- **Expenses** What has the company spent to generate sales for a given time period? Much like sales, expenses are often measured in terms of budgeted expenses and actual expenses.
- **Profit/loss** The dollars remaining after expenses are subtracted from sales.
- **Employee turnover** The percentage of employees who have left the company and require replacement.

One of the most important data definition exercises that will occur within your data warehouse project is defining these high-level subjects and key business measures, along with their related information. The challenge will be defining and documenting these subject areas and key business measures in business terms so that they are uniform across the enterprise. You must not deliver overlapping or confusing definitions of subjects and measures.

These definitions allow you to ultimately map the meaning to its actual data source within internal or external data; that is, provide users of the data warehouse with information valid within a given subject area. Your sponsor or steering committee should provide leadership and assistance in these definitions from a business end, while you will be required to complete the definition within the technology.

Upon conclusion of this data definition exercise, you and your team will be able to answer the following questions.

- What is a customer?
- What is a product?
- What is a geographic area?
- What is a sale?
- What is an expense?

As illustrated in Figures 2.3 and 2.4, these uniform definitions and implementations will be utilized across subject-oriented data warehouses and become the standard access mechanisms into a data warehouse. Getting the unique definition correct initially dramatically improves your ongoing success rate as you proceed with additional subject-oriented data warehouse implementations. Your project plan should include phases for defining what subjects and key business measures will be included in the scope of the project, acquiring the related information for each subject and business measure, and planning for updating and maintaining this information. This planning is essential for the success of your data warehouse.

Force the Use and Reference of All Decision-Oriented Data Matter

What is there that confers the noblest delight? What is that which swells a man's breast with pride above that which any other experience can bring to him? Discovery! To know that you are walking where no others have walked; that you are beholding what human eye has not seen before; that you are breathing a virgin atmosphere. To give birth to an idea, to discover a great thought—an intellectual nugget, right under the dust of a field that many a brain-plough had gone over before. To find a new planet, to invent a new hinge, to find a way to make the lightnings carry your messages. To be the first—that is the idea.

—Mark Twain

Information is a deceptive thing. Think for a moment about how many meetings you have attended in which a presenter was full of unsourced information. Finding data that supports your position, your need, or your desire has become a way of selling individual points. How are people getting this information? There are many ways, though it should be noted that numbers can be bent to support even the weakest business cases.

The early implementations of decision support systems with which we were involved typically involved extracting large amounts of data from mainframe sources and placing them in spreadsheets. Users then manipulated the data to support their causes, placed it in a graphic, and went to their meetings. Of course, this data would enrage some meeting attendees and spark the curiosity of others. Either way, a majority of the meeting was spent discussing the source of the data rather than the business issue itself. Even from a tools perspective, if a tool appeared to make the acquisition of data easier, the user must have it! The content was unimportant—access, manipulation, and presentation were.

In one specific consulting engagement, the company project leader placed a justification for a data warehouse solely on the time that would be saved by eliminating the sourcing discussions. The project leader sold his management on the fact that of most 90-minute meetings, 45 minutes or more were spent understanding the source of the data within presentations or reports.

A data warehouse gives you a way to alleviate the numbers games played in many businesses today. If you complete all of the items discussed in this chapter, you will have a data warehouse that has credible data. All reports should be sourced. Upon implementing a data warehouse for a given business area, all sources should be the data warehouse. If this is not true, you should be able to obtain the source from a report; and if it is important to the business, expand the data warehouse to include the new data source.

Therefore, your sponsor and steering committee should begin to establish a policy throughout the company that makes all reports and presentations that draw on informative data reference their source. An action such as this does two things. First, it forces better use of the warehouse for continuous improvement of quality and content. Second, it makes those unaware of such a valuable resource aware.

Summary

Planning is a crucial aspect of data warehouse development, because most of the strategic decisions associated with design, implementation, and promotion of deliverables are determined by this planning. Specific techniques and instructions for individual data warehouse development steps are discussed in detail throughout this book.

Prior to commencing your data warehouse project, it is critical that the items discussed in this chapter are scrutinized and followed. It has been our experience that failure to follow each of these items will contribute to the demise of your project. Following these items will not guarantee success, but it will certainly place you on the correct path toward success. Again, prior to beginning a data warehouse project, make sure that you attend to the following issues.

- Obtain management commitment
- Begin with a manageable project
- Clearly communicate realistic expectations
- Assign a user-oriented manager
- Use proven methods
- Design based on queries, not on transactions
- Only load data that is needed
- Define the proper data source, or system of record
- Clearly define unique subjects
- Force the use of, and reference to, your data warehouse

Keeping these tips in developing a successful data warehouse in mind, we now move to Section II, in which we build the foundation—that is, the architecture—for your data warehouse project. Chapter 3, Planning a Data Warehouse Architecture, starts us on this journey with a discussion that focuses on defining, developing, and evaluating an effective architecture.

SECTION II

Architecture: Building the Required Foundation

3

Planning a Data Warehouse Architecture

The physician can bury his mistakes, but the architect can only advise his clients to plant vines.

—*Frank Lloyd Wright*

With the emergence of data warehouses, organizations need a way to manage transition in a cost-effective and practical manner. This process is particularly difficult when facing the complex task of integrating established operational application technologies with the newly established data warehouse technologies. The structure that ties everything together is called an *architecture*.

The areas of system architecture planning and definition have been extensively documented and discussed over the years. Architecture planning and definition is the process of mapping an overall enterprise mission to information system goals and objectives. It has been our experience that most companies do not take the proper time for the painstaking effort required to properly map these business requirements to a system architecture. Committing to the wrong architecture is extremely costly, not only in money, but in costly disruption of your enterprise's normal activities. It can be a setback with profound business impact.

For example, imagine the impact of an improper architecture in the following noninformation systems scenario. Imagine you told a home builder you wanted a custom-built house. When discussing your needs, the builder discovered you required more storage space than your current residence offered. Now, suppose the builder made the assumption that more storage space meant more closets, not a basement. The builder proceeded with this design and built a slab house for you. Upon completion, you discovered the ghastly mistake—you wanted a basement! Upon notifying the builder that more storage meant a basement, the builder gave you an estimated price for the fix. How costly and difficult will it be to put a basement in this house? How does that cost compare to designing the house properly from the beginning? If the builder had produced a blueprint, showed the planned house and detailed the assumptions, and reviewed everything with you, there would have been no surprises. The house would have been built the right way from the beginning, laying the proper foundation from the beginning of the project.

Data warehouses are no different. Architecture-based development provides a comprehensive basis for integration. The definition of an architecture in the initial phase of a data warehouse project is critical. You first need to develop an architecture, then proceed with the development effort. A proper framework will be delivered by an architecture, providing a set of balanced methods—an approach, a methodology for defining the data, and application and technology aspects of the data warehouse. The architecture will define standards, quality measures, general design, and support techniques for a project. The architectural definition process greatly enhances the success rate of data warehouse projects.

Building an architecture for a data warehouse requires the data warehouse team to do the following.

- Understand the existing information technology architecture
- Understand the high-level information problem, especially the data model and business priorities
- Map current operational data (and the systems that maintain it) to the required subject areas

An architecture paves the way for a stable, useful, and extensible data warehouse. However, by itself, neither will an architecture improve the quality or flexibility of existing operational systems nor solve any of the data quality problems in existing databases. Fixing those problems requires systems to be upgraded and an overall operational systems architectural plan. A successful data warehouse certainly helps to clarify requirements for improvements to existing systems, though implementing those improvements is another effort. In this chapter, we investigate the concepts behind building your data warehouse architecture.

Architecture Defined

Architecture has many meanings among people who develop and use computer systems. Here is a literal definition of architecture.

ar·chi·tec·ture *(är'kĭ-tĕk'cher)* A style and method of design and construction; an orderly arrangement of parts.

With regard to a data warehouse, an architecture facilitates the creation of a data resource that is accurate, shareable, and easily accessible throughout an enterprise. An architecture provides a blueprint that explains how the vision, goals, and objectives of a data warehouse will be delivered. The components of this architecture include shared data, technical infrastructure, and reusable program logic. Such an architecture offers several key benefits to an enterprise, including the following.

- **More consistent data** As common data standards and models become widely used, data consistency will become the norm within your enterprise. A good data architecture employs consistent data standards and models that are fully inventoried.
- **Simplified application development** By intelligently designing and implementing a cohesive approach to how an enterprise creates, accesses, and modifies data, the time to implement new applications or change existing ones will be greatly reduced.
- **Business responsiveness** The integration of data, applications, and technology architectures will leverage an enterprise's ability to respond to business needs in a high-quality, consistent, and timely manner.

To build a data warehouse, you must establish the proper architecture first, not after development has begun. Your data warehouse architecture should be established and accepted in principle by the entire enterprise prior to proceeding with development. Without acceptance and support, further development efforts that target an integrated enterprise data warehouse will inevitably fail.

Developing an Architecture

The development process involves extensive research and discussion around the content of the architecture. The foundation of the architecture will be formulated through many reviews of organizational architectures with representatives from all business areas. Many standard models can assist in developing your own enterprise architecture, including those from technology-oriented organizations such as International Business Machines, Digital Equipment Corporation, Apple, and Sybase.

These frameworks typically define architectural components, or individual architectures, which will logically segment the overall architectural definition. These components typically include applications, data, and technology. Often, architectures can also be expanded to include the organizations and business functions that support an overall enterprise. Each of these individual architectures should have its own subarchitecture, which describes its individual support of the overall business and overall architecture.

You need to determine for your organization which individual architectural components are most critical to determine. In this book, we strongly focus on an architecture that includes subdefinitions for applications, data, and technology. We also venture into the support organization because, within most companies, data warehousing redefines certain aspects of the overall information support organization.

As with any other major development effort, architectural development requires thorough planning prior to its initiation. The major deliverable from the planning process is a project work plan that specifies the phases and tasks necessary to develop and implement individual architectures.

Prior to the commencement of planning, you should obtain the support and commitment from your executive sponsor and other management that is actively monitoring data warehouse activities. The terms *support* and *commitment* imply the allocation of personnel, budget, and time to complete the vision proposed by the architectural development effort.

Create a Vision

As companies grow into national or world leaders within their discipline, their business processes and structure continue to evolve. This business evolution drives support organizations to change. Traditional Information Systems organizations were based on a functional organization; however, in the 1990s many corporations have realized that it may be more effective to formulate cross-functional project teams.

These new cross-functional teams are becoming more commonplace and are required if you are to create an enterprise data warehouse. The overall goal behind creating these multidisciplinary, cross-functional business management teams is to drive the evolution of support systems within a business, thus allowing the personnel of a company to obtain the information and support that they need to legitimately perform their job.

As a business evolves, so do support systems. Within each of these systems, developing a vision is important. The vision will assist development and support personnel by allowing them to focus on improving the process and, in the long run, the business. In the late 1980s, manufacturing organizations began to set new visions with concepts of *just-in-time* and *made-to-order* processing.

The just-in-time vision dramatically changed business models. Suppliers could better support those selling their products by quickly delivering inventory replenishments as distributors required. This fundamental business change allowed significant business improvement. Some of those benefits include the following.

- Distributors have less cost in inventory
- Suppliers and distributors can manage smaller warehouse space
- Because it costs less for distributors to set up operations, suppliers could expand their distribution base
- Business planning improves, because the supply and demand lines are better understood
- Suppliers' production lines increase capacity due to the increased demand created by distributors

The 1980s and 1990s have been an era of technology growth. The made-to-order vision assisted companies in better utilizing and leveraging technology to reduce their expenses and improve product quality. This vision, much like the just-in-time vision, assisted in changing business models.

Within previous business models, companies stockpiled inventory and fed that to their distributors. New inventory was not produced until the old was depleted. The made-to-order process changed all of that. Now, a product waits for consumers to define how it should be built. This allowed for more customization and less inventory stockpiles. Also, because inventory stockpiles are reduced, a business can incorporate changes in technology at a more rapid pace, allowing its products to improve as technology improves. And as technology gets cheaper, so do products. Do you remember the price of early calculators? Calculators today are more advanced and nearly disposable, because most cost very little compared to the past.

These visions allow enterprises to trim costs, improve customer satisfaction, and increase revenues. Information systems have begun to take on similar characteristics. The key to developing information systems is to utilize a made-to-order process that utilizes standardized, readily available components that integrate architecturally across a corporation. The assembly process eradicates the old way of custom manufacturing a system for a user. Data warehousing is a specialty system that easily adapts to this concept and vision.

Data warehousing addresses a problem that users currently experience, lack of data from which to make informed decisions. The vision of a data warehouse should be one that helps an employee get the job done more effectively. Many times, data warehouses and other report-oriented systems get in the way of the user's decision-making process. Therefore, the vision of your data warehouse should be driven by the user's requirements and have a strong business-oriented focus. Data warehouses are built to support business decision making, not to automate specific business processes. As a result, the most important element in building a data warehouse is a clear understanding of the kinds of decisions the business needs to make and of the information required to support those decisions.

In characterizing most report-oriented systems today, users often state that the current systems provide no "usable" reports. It should be the vision of the data warehouse team that their deliverables strive to assist users in their job, in effect building a system that provides users with the following.

- **User driven reports** Users can characterize the type of information that they want in their reports on their own and have the system produce efficient reports
- **Business gauges** Users can define a control panel filled with gauges that constantly monitor their specific business measures
- **Exception-based reporting agents** Report agents automatically notify users when an exception occurs, allowing them to take corrective action

This type of vision produces an information system that helps users perform their job more effectively. The system becomes part of their process rather than inhibiting the process. The positive reaction you get from users is amazing when you admit your previous mistakes, such as today's reporting systems are nearly useless for monitoring the key performance measures to which users are held accountable.

The vision discussed above states that: Today, you must download and merge multiple reports to get useful information; early implementations of a data warehouse will begin to deliver more standard reporting mechanisms and better ad hoc reporting capabilities on a unified data source; and the ultimate goal of a data warehouse will, in three to five years, become an intelligent system that works for the user, much like an automated assistant or agent. This type of vision will help you gain the respect and support of your user community, allowing you to leverage their extensive business knowledge and improve on deliverables as well as time lines.

Adopt a Methodology

Methodology, much like architecture, has many meanings among people who develop and use computer systems. Here is a literal definition of methodology.

meth·od·ol·o·gy (mèth'e-dòl'e-jê) A body of practices, procedures, and rules used by those who work in a discipline or engage in an inquiry; a set of working methods.

Most architectural methodologies provide a process for defining, constructing, and integrating the major architectures that support application development efforts, including data, applications, and technology. These methodologies include all of the tasks and activities that must be performed, as well as the information that must be captured, for you to successfully define and implement a new architecture. You want to select a methodology that allows you to create a computing environment that supports multiple cooperating applications, including your legacy operational systems and the data warehouse. The key areas that are addressed by most architectural methodologies include the following.

- **Data architecture** Data architecture is the organization of the sources and stores of business information throughout an enterprise
- **Application architecture** Application architecture defines and supports the software process for implementation of required business functionality
- **Technology architecture** Technology architecture is a computing infrastructure that enables data and applications to successfully and seamlessly interact throughout an enterprise

The methodology that you select should allow you to take these three individual architectures (data, application, and technology) and integrate them into a single environment, because the interaction and interdependencies of these individual architectures are keys to implementing an enterprise architecture that supports business improvement.

The methodology that your organization adopts for delivering a data warehouse architecture provides an outline for the project work plan and team training sessions. This work plan defines the required steps along with their purpose, deliverables, source documents, procedures, guidelines, roles, responsibilities, and effort estimates.

It would be wise to select your support tools during this phase of the planning process. The ability to automate a majority of the planning and monitoring activities now exists. When searching for such tools, verify that they support your methodology and provide adequate facilities for reporting. The reporting options should include selectivity, sorting, ad hoc query, and export facilities. This functionality provides adequate reporting for analysis and the ability to extend internal models utilized by the supporting tool set.

Assemble an Architectural Team

A core team should be brought together to adapt the architecture to the enterprise environment. While the methodology will provide your team with the general structure for the architecture, the team will perform the actual research and formulation of the architectural content. These activities include clearly defining the special needs of the enterprise and researching approaches utilized by other leading companies. The team composition, including roles and responsibilities, is detailed in Table 3.1.

Table 3.1: *Architectural team roles and responsibilities*

Role	Responsibility
Project Manager	The project manager manages the day-to-day activities of a project and its members. On a regular basis, the project manager produces status reports and evaluates the completion dates, percentage of work completed, and issues that may be blocking successful completion. The project manager should be held accountable for all deliverables.
Business Analysts	Business analysts provide a user perspective and business knowledge to the team.
Individual Component Architects	A team has a minimum need for a data, an application, and a technology architect. Because technology has expanded, this area may involve a further breakdown. If your enterprise has a network specialist, this is typically the first expansion in the area of technology. Each of these architects provides expertise in an area of specialization.
Tool Suite Administrator	Because a data warehouse is the land of tools, the architectural team requires a person who oversees the installation, preparation, and use of tool suite products.

When formulating your team, strive for a balance of skills and the participation of noninformation systems personnel. A highly effective data warehouse architectural committee should contain a 50–50 balance between information systems and noninformation systems personnel. This allows the committee to avoid second guessing what the business people do and need.

An extended review team of architects from other departments within an enterprise should be assembled to review the findings of the architectural team. The extended team's focus is to guarantee support and implementation across the enterprise. Other potential participants on the team include your executive sponsor (or the sponsor's delegate) and an outside consultant.

Define the Project Scope

When people refer to a data warehouse, they tend to express a strong desire for an *enterprise data warehouse*. Therefore, the architectural planning process should clearly define what *enterprise* means. Because the aim of a data warehouse is to enable an entire enterprise to share data, the term enterprise should include all areas that need to share substantial amounts of data. This sharing of data should encompass the constant access and use of the data warehouse, not simply periodic consolidation of data.

Be aware of the risks when the scope of your architecture is too narrow or too broad. A scope that is too narrow, such as a single department, results in an architecture that is incomplete and lacks the fortitude to support other areas of the business. On the other hand, a scope that is too broad, such as the entire enterprise, places your project team under a crunch in which you will ultimately not have enough time or resources to get sufficient detailed definitions of the architecture completed, making the architecture invalid and perhaps useless.

A good scope equates to a business unit or division, such an organization includes all business functions as well as responsibility and control for the bottom line. With this type of scope, economic benefits and justification of an architectural development effort can be established.

Define Business Goals and Objectives

Within the business goals and objectives section of your architectural plan, you should clearly state the project goal. The goals and corresponding objectives should clearly state and document the business rationale driving the data warehouse initiative. You should also clearly define the uses of the warehouse throughout the enterprise and how the business will benefit from such an application. It is important to define these goals and objectives in simple, concise, nontechnical language. Be precise about what will be accomplished.

Sample Goal

Here is a sample goal: To build a data warehouse that links information throughout the company and organizes this information into user-friendly subject areas (such as location, product, and customer) and business measures (such as on-time shipments, on-stream time, and plant cycle time), allowing users widespread and easy access.

Sample Objectives

1. Define a scaleable architecture that will allow the enterprise to start with small, high-impact warehouse deliverables and ultimately grow to an enterprise-wide warehouse of information.
2. Develop a logical data model so that the warehouse content is intelligible to users, allowing them to be less dependent on Information Systems personnel in the production of business-specific information.
3. Implement the data warehouse through small, highly effective, and subject-oriented data warehouse projects to provide the business with rapid deliverables and rapid return on investment.
4. Implement an easy-to-use front-end query tool suite, including ad hoc query, decision support, and executive information tools that support the spectrum of users who require access to the data warehouse.
5. Develop the proper user training to transform the reporting process from an information systems-dependent reporting approach to a user-driven reporting approach.

Prepare a Work Breakdown Structure

The architectural team's work breakdown structure is the project schedule and the plan for all team activities. It is critical for all architectural work to be completed on time. Without a detailed work plan, a project will likely fall behind schedule, and architecture planning is not immune to this. A well planned architectural engagement leads to quality deliverables and avoids the cancellation of future efforts related to the data warehouse. Steps for the planning and development of an architecture are illustrated in Figure 3.1.

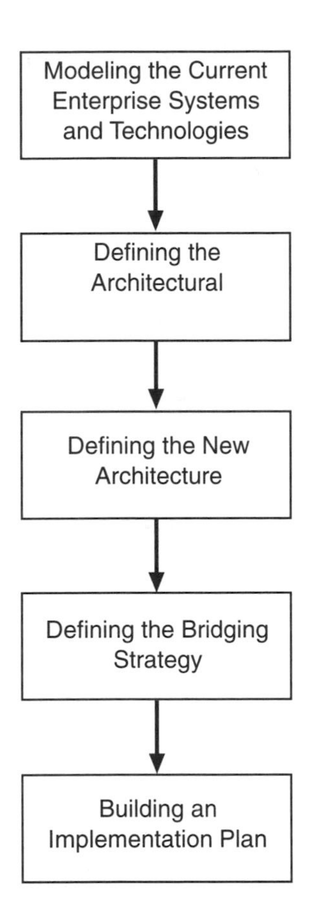

Figure 3.1: *Steps for architecture planning and development*

Obtain Management Commitment

To implement an architecture, several steps must be executed. In each of the steps, management commitment is of utmost importance. Obtaining management commitment is a risky phase of the planning process, so be prepared.

You need to know what must be said and how to say it. Typically, management commitment is not obtained in one session. This is a process that you must present several times to the primary and secondary decision makers. The initial presentations will be conducted to prepare and educate the decision makers on the purpose of your activities and the benefits that the business will derive from these activities. These must be executive-level presentations, typically the summary material that is appropriate for management.

You should rehearse your presentations with the architectural team and work out every aspect of each presentation. The diverse composition of the team will assist you.

You may also want informal meetings with the business executives and decision makers to best determine their opinions with regard to the scope, goals, objectives, benefits, and critical success factors of your project. You must be sensitive to corporate culture and politics within these sessions. Seek the advice of others, including mentors and political allies who have been successful in the past.

Upon presenting your material to executives, listen carefully to their feedback and directly answer their questions. You will be required to resolve all issues and concerns about funding, schedules, and required resources. After all issues have been satisfactorily resolved, it is time to obtain approval to proceed with the project.

Evaluating the Current Architecture

An architect should live as little in cities as a painter. Send him to our hills and let him study there what nature understands by a buttress, and what by a dome.

—John Ruskin

Any major technology initiative must take into account the existing computing infrastructure. If a project team had a blank slate on which to develop systems, life would be infinitely easier. But this rarely, if ever, occurs. An architecture must enable the business to migrate to new technologies in a controlled fashion with minimal disruption. Therefore, be aware of the requirement to integrate new data warehouse systems with critical legacy applications.

To support legacy system integration, a firm understanding of the current environment is crucial. Legacy systems greatly impact the development of a new architecture. The problems inherited by legacy systems and their infrastructure include the following.

- Systems that have data that cannot be accessed without significant application customization and development
- The lack of a proper knowledge base for supporting and integrating the components of the system
- The draining of computing resources, including equipment and people

These problems aside, legacy systems are the backbone of the information systems that keep the company running and, therefore, every precaution must be taken to avoid disrupting their operation.

Modeling the Existing Enterprise

When documenting existing technologies, your efforts should focus on clarifying the data, application, and technology areas of the current information systems. It is also important to define the support organization behind these existing systems and technologies. This phase will shed new light on the business processes and what has been done—or not done—historically to support them. Your team will find answers to questions such as the following.

- What business functions are integral to the enterprise?
- What information is required to support these business functions?
- Where are the business functions performed?
- How often are the business functions performed?
- Who performs the business functions?
- What is required to improve the performance of the business functions?

The information that is gathered during this phase should be captured and stored in an organized and automated fashion. This will more than likely be the first time an evaluation of this magnitude has been conducted in your company. Though the information that you gather in this phase is highly summarized, it is a strong foundation from which future analysis can be performed. Formal collection of this data will assist future efforts, including your own subject-oriented data warehouses, as they progress through their development cycles. Upon completion of this phase, your team will have produced a set of models that define the current enterprise systems and technologies, as well as how they fundamentally support business processes.

Surveying Current Systems and Technology

When evaluating the current enterprise architecture, the team should inventory each of the business functions required within the scope of the data warehouse. These functions will then be modeled and allocated to application systems and subsystems. The resulting set of models will define the relationships and interdependencies among these application systems.

Because most Information Systems organizations are organized based on business function or application support, you will typically not find a single organization that understands the whole enterprise. Therefore, you need to schedule individual interview and review sessions with each of the support organizations to capture all relevant system information. The best candidates for this interviewing and data gathering exercise include application support groups in the Information Systems department of your company as well as "super users" of the application systems and business-oriented user representatives, who are often found in business system liaison groups.

The facts and information that you capture during these sessions will provide valuable insight into the enterprise's current architecture, if one exists. The information that you capture for each system should include the following.

- The official name of the application system.
- The business function or department that is supported by the application.
- A solid definition of how the system automates the business function that it supports.
- The overall system status; that is, where it is in its life cycle: planned, under development, implemented, or being phased out.
- The organization or person responsible for maintaining the application; and the number of people involved.
- The specific support personnel who will be important for data access: project manager, data administrator, database administrator, systems administrator, and business manager.
- The technology that is utilized to support the system, including hardware platforms, network or communication platforms, and software.
- Supplemental system documentation that will assist in the architectural evaluation, such as data models, data layouts, system flow diagrams, and process models.
- Other technical information about the system, such as: Is it batch or on-line? Is it operational 24 hours per day, seven days per week; or is there planned downtime? What kind of batch processing schedule does it have? Is the system at maximum utilization?

Sample data-collection forms have been provided in Appendix D.

Modeling the Application Architecture

It is often easier to start your architectural analysis with the applications that support the business, because they are more readily understood than the data associated with these systems. You will quickly determine what data sources need to be analyzed in the data architectural phase based on the focus of the applications. Within each application, try to capture information about the systems in general as well as their relationship to other systems so that a high-level map of the application architecture can be built. A hypothetical map of major application systems and their relationships is depicted in Figure 3.2.

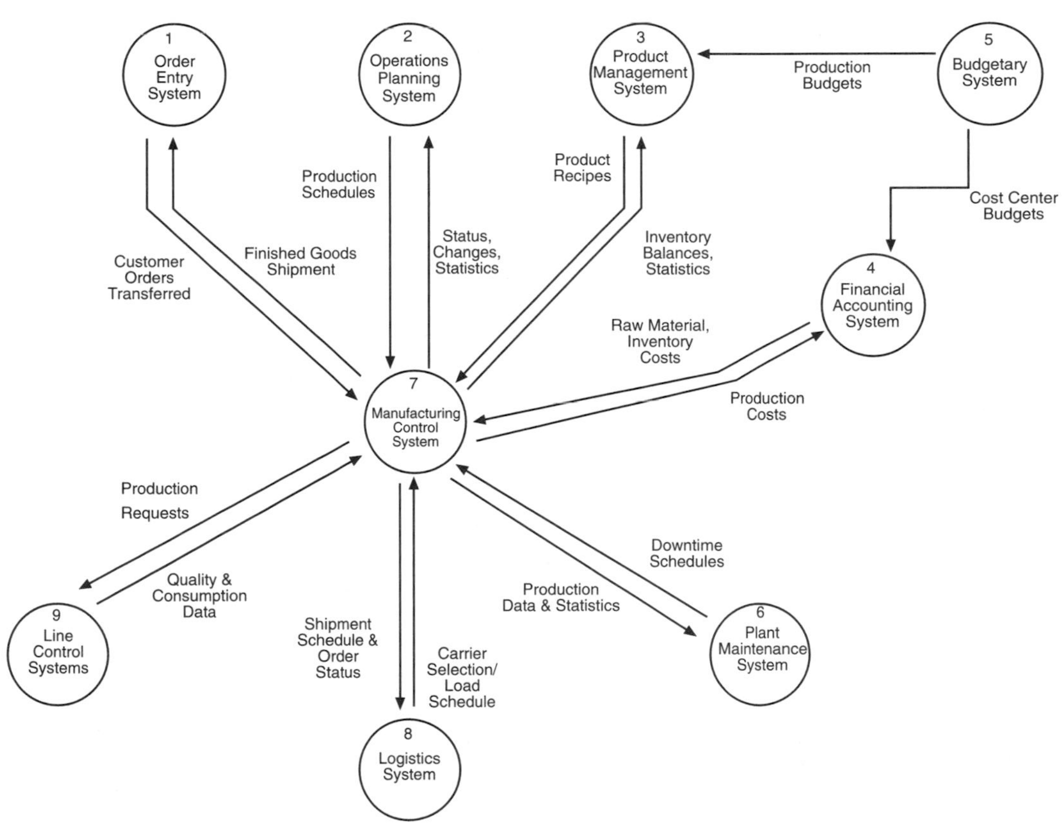

Figure 3.2: *A manufacturing enterprise's high-level application architecture*

The information that is gathered should allow you to build a comprehensive application index, defining the major enterprise systems and the business functions that they support. This data will become relevant for the data warehouse in the area of subject definition. Table 3.2 suggests a possible enterprise application index.

Table 3.2: *Typical enterprise application index*

System	Business functions supported
Accounting	General ledger Accounts payable Accounts receivable Fixed assets
Logistics	Distribution Shipment planning Carrier procurement
Manufacturing control	Product costing Formula management Production management Materials management Quality certification Scheduling Purchasing Shipping Receiving
Operational planning	Demand forecasting Production planning Capacity planning Master scheduling
Order entry	Customer orders Finished goods inventory Billing and credit Complaints
Product management	Product mix optimization Customer mix optimization Product management New product development

Process modeling is a far more complex technique than described here. The data warehouse, being a data driven environment, seldom requires a detailed process model; process modeling can, in fact, become a hindrance to your project efforts. In many environments, a process model is invaluable; a data warehouse architecture is not one of them.

You should guard against getting too involved in detail process modeling activities. A high-level process model suffices and provides great value to a corporation. The global process model is an outstanding tool for business planning and cultivation of information systems. These models assist in an enterprise's operational automation of business processes as well as in uniformly defining where data entities should be integrated. The greatest values that are provided to a data warehouse project include the following.

- A definition of the major application systems and their value to the corporation.
- An understanding of the systems that have automated business functions and their overall scope. Understand that companies often have several order processing systems, each of them automating a similar set of business functions. However, these systems are limited in scope by location or type of order.
- An understanding of the type of data controlled by operational systems.
- A definition of the opportunities for integrating processing schedules, including data warehouse loading activities.

Modeling the Data Architecture

A data warehouse is a data driven application, and the architectural team should ensure that a sound, pragmatic logical data model is defined for the business area covered by the architectural effort. Therefore, if no data model exists, the team should develop one.

Without a proper understanding of the current data within an enterprise, the data warehouse team will continuously find holes in its development plan and incur delays while it evaluates a new information source. It is wise to conduct this research prior to commencement of any subject-oriented data warehouses as it will ultimately save time in your development efforts. Data modeling focuses on the information that is important to the enterprise and the relationships among informational entities.

The Entity Relationship Diagram

Entity relationship diagrams (ERD) are the charts most frequently associated with data modeling. The ERD is a conceptual representation of real world objects and the relationships among them. ERDs typically define information in a system by grouping items into logical entities. Figure 3.3 illustrates sample high-level data utilizing ERD.

High-Level Data Model
utilizing the
Martin Entity Relationship Diagram's
Method and Symbols

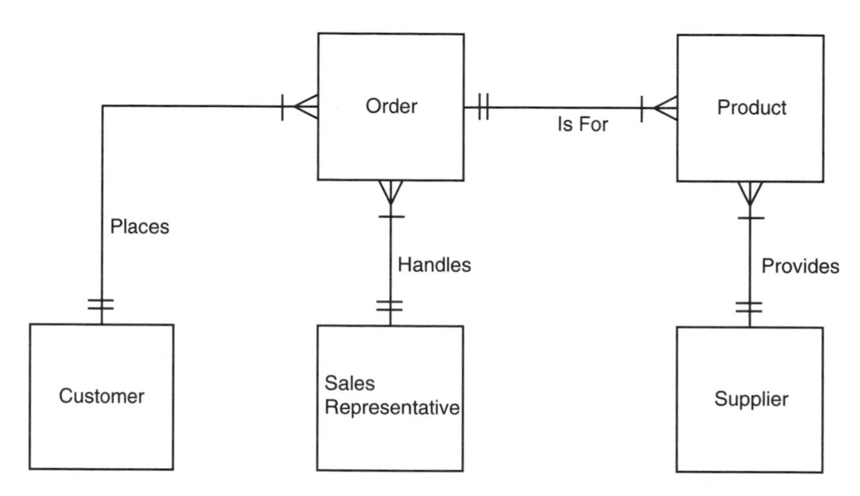

Figure 3.3: *Sample entity relationship diagram*

Entities represent the major subject areas managed by a given application and business process. An entity is a logical grouping of related data items. Some typical entities include the following.

- Orders
- Products
- Employees
- Inventory
- Invoices
- Customers
- Accounts
- Suppliers

Relationships document the association between two entities typically providing greater detail about how data flows and what is contained within data entities.

Relationships display information such as which data entity is the master of the relationship and which is the detail, as well as whether the relationship is required or optional. Relationships typically are labeled with verbs or actions to allow the reader of an ERD to visualize an entity-to-entity action, such as in the following examples.

- A *customer* places one or more *orders*
- An *order* is for one or more *products*
- A *sales representative* handles one or more *orders*
- A *supplier* provides one or more *products*

When developing a high-level, enterprise ERD, try to abstract the entities to their highest level. Therefore, entities such as *orders*, which could decompose into *order heading information* and *order line item information*, should at this point be defined simply as *orders*. Remember to organize your architectural ERD along logical business functions. During the development phases of subject-oriented data warehouses, you will spend more time with the details associated with each entity. At this point, you are gathering information to assist you in assimilating what exists, not trying to gather low-level details.

During this analysis, you will likely find nuances associated with the data such as overlapping entities, or entities that merely provide a different state of a second entity. For example, a sales prospect may be thought about as a variant of a customer entity. A prospect who has yet to purchase anything from your company is not yet a customer. However, upon purchasing merchandise, the customer data is now filled with the prospect information. Therefore, when developing a lower-level understanding of the data, it often helps to understand the relationship among entities by construction an entity life cycle model, which clarifies the various states an entity passes through from the time the enterprise becomes aware of the data managed by the entity until the entity is destroyed.

The CRUD Matrix

Along with the data entities and their associated relationships, it also is important for you to understand the birth and death events for each major data entity. A birth event of a data entity occurs when the item is captured. A death event occurs when a data entity is formally retired, archived, or removed from an information system.

Birth and death events of data entities are of critical importance to a data warehouse. As you will learn in later chapters, each subject area is highly sensitive to creation and destruction dates. No data should ever, within reason, be removed from a data warehouse. In operational systems, data is removed because smaller databases allow the operational systems to perform better and the focus of these systems are not historical in nature. A data warehouse, as described earlier, is historical and requires a comprehensive view of an enterprise over time. Therefore, data will be entered and time stamped within a data warehouse upon its creation within the operational systems. The data will also be time stamped in the data warehouse upon deletion within operational systems.

For example, when a customer first purchases product from your company, an order entry system would probably record this as a birth event. Within the operational system, the customer's first order would capture all of the relevant data about that customer: whom to bill, where to ship, whom to contact, and how much discount to provide. However, operational systems may have a business rule that states that customers who have not purchased product from the enterprise in more than 24 months should be moved to an inactive status, and if the time between purchases exceeds 36 months, they should be removed from the system. Now, suppose you want to report information on customer behavior during the last five years. Should we see this customer? The answer is typically yes. A data warehouse gives you a snapshot of how the company appeared during each of those five years, and the customer subject area is typically important. Therefore, the data warehouse should state the date on which the customer in essence became a customer, and his or her last purchase date. Other demographics about the customer may also be maintained, such as active or inactive status.

A highly effective tool for capturing this type of information is a CRUD Matrix. CRUD stands for *C*reate, *R*eference (or *R*ead), *U*pdate, *D*elete. The matrix maps data entity events to systems, including when an entity is created, read, updated, or deleted. A CRUD Matrix matches data entities with application processing. When building a CRUD Matrix, try to document the significant business function to data entity events and avoid over-documenting events that occur infrequently.

The most significant events are creation and deletion events, because they impact the time stamping mechanisms maintained in a data warehouse. Update events also are significant; however, they are less significant than creation and deletion events. The significance of defining creation and deletion events of a given entity lies in the data quality and integrity issues behind creating a data warehouse as a single source for reality. If you discover—and you will—two separate systems that think they own a birth event, data integrity is a potential problem. The same is true for deletion events. Therefore, when this conflict occurs you should try to resolve it as soon as possible and determine where the most valuable source of data exists.

When performing this task, remember that at this time we are performing high-level analysis. Consensus and compromise apply to this task. There can literally be thousands of potential data usage relationships, and you have little time to dwell on particular issues and relationships. After all, dirty data and data quality are justification points for data warehouses. Issues in these areas should be noted and provided as feedback to those who control the data input aspects of the information systems. Your focus is on finding the proper data source to feed the data warehouse; you will be unable to fix all of the operational system problems within the scope of your project.

A sample CRUD Matrix appears in Table 3.3. In it, the letters C, R, U, and D in the right-hand columns represent Create, Reference (or Read), Update, and Delete, respectively.

Table 3.3: *A sample of CRUD Matrix entity-to-function relationships*

	Customer	Order	Product	Sales Representative	Supplier
Order entry	CRUD	CRUD	R	RU	RU
Operations planning		CRUD		CRUD	
Product management	R	R	RU		R
Budgetary system	R	R	R	RU	R
Financial accounting	RU	R	RU	R	R
Manufacturing control	R	RU	CRUD		R
Logistics	R	RU	R		RU
Line control		RU			

Modeling the Technology Architecture

Technology architecture defines the major technologies and platforms that provide an environment for the applications that are managing data. Technology platforms provide the means to collect data from suppliers, to store and process data, and to transport and deliver data to customers. In a plumbing analogy, data and information are water, and the technology architecture are pipes, fittings, and valves.

During this phase, the team should define all of the platforms that currently support the applications and data previously modeled. This model is similar in nature to the data and application models; that is, it should be conceptual in nature while detailing the technology infrastructure. This approach includes identifying the types of clients and servers that are currently utilized by users of the information systems. The models should also include a definition of the connectivity approach utilized by the enterprise; that is, the various network strategies and interconnectivity among remote sites. This interconnectivity is depicted in Figure 3.4.

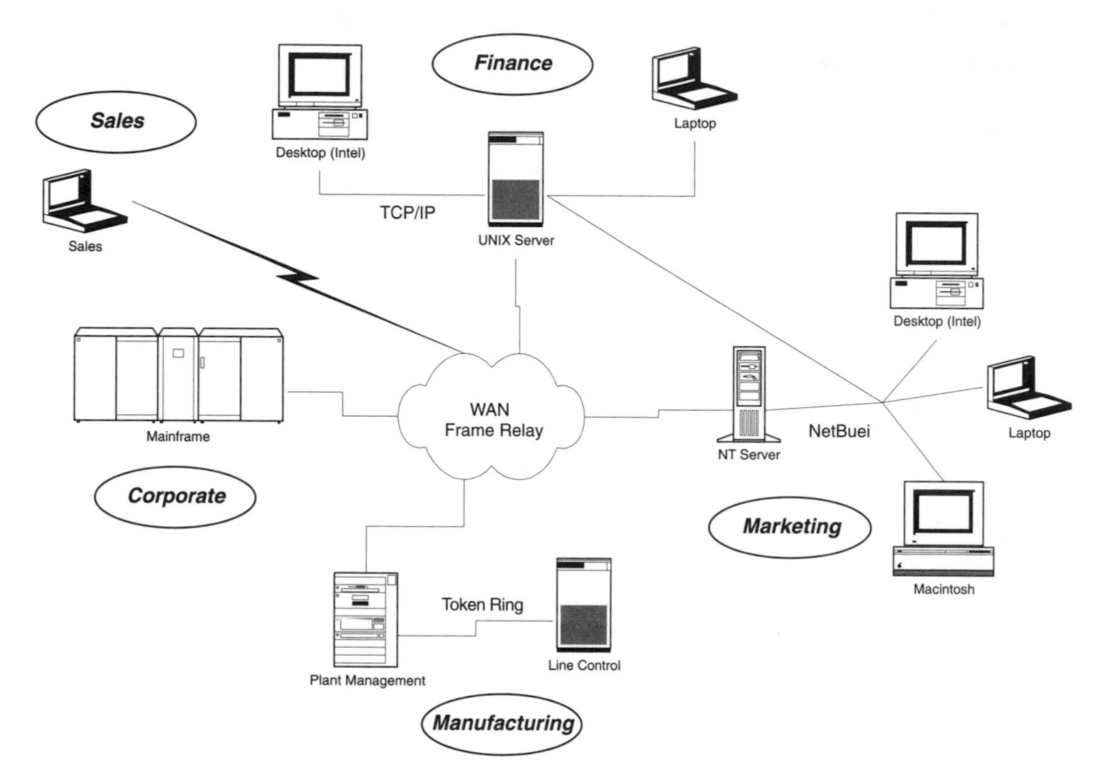

Figure 3.4: *A high-level technology architecture*

Mapping Database Technologies

It is important that the data warehouse architecture team capture all information that will be relevant to establishing the proper foundation from which to build a data warehouse. This includes a need to better understand the system software that manages current corporate data resources as well as the methods of interconnecting the disparate data resources. Your team should evaluate each of the major application systems and determine how the data resource is being managed. Most enterprises have a minimum of five major database vendors, and many enterprises will exceed 10 database management systems.

Table 3.4 demonstrates documenting of applications and their associated database management systems, or the technique used to manage the associated data resource. Each of the application systems is listed in the first column, including order entry, operational planning, and product management. The additional columns assist the architectural team in understanding the database management system that houses and controls the data resource that is potentially required by the data warehouse. For this example, the database management systems include DB2, IMS and VSAM from IBM, RDB from Oracle (formerly from Digital), and Btrieve. As well, a column provides for other data resources that may be used within individual systems.

Table 3.4: *Data store mapping*

Applications	DB2	IMS	VSAM	RDB	Btrieve	Other
Order entry	✔	✔				
Operational planning					✔	
Product management			✔			
Financial accounting	✔		✔			
Budgetary					✔	✔ (Excel and Lotus)
Logistics		✔				
Manufacturing		✔		✔		
Plant maintenance				✔		

When building your data warehouse architecture, the systems that feed the data warehouse through the back-end process will require an ability to access the data resources of the identified application systems. Connectivity is important for the processing of operational data within back-end data warehouse processes. When capturing information related to the database management systems utilized by the application systems, the architectural team should also gather information such as the following about each of the database management systems.

- Is the database vendor still a viable corporation?
- What is our support arrangement with the database vendor?
- Does the enterprise have a development or run-time license for the database products?
- What communication protocols are supported for client/server connectivity?
- What compiler technology is supported?
- What standard data manipulation language is utilized by the database?

Summary

A data warehouse must support a new kind of user—subject matter experts, who have been characterized as impatient decision makers. Their impatience grows from a limited business window in which decisions must be made: They need just-in-time information. These users require a system that allows them to perform their job better. They will constantly return to a data warehouse for more information. These target data warehouse users require a system that strongly supports their need for iterative analysis of the data collected from operational data sources. The key to providing the information required by a business in a timely fashion is a proper foundation—that is, an architecture.

In a data warehouse environment, an architecture allowing a more flexible make-to-order process means that your enterprise will have standard data, utilities, and processes for managing the information assets; that is, the corporate knowledge base. You will no longer be required to start from scratch when building or revising information systems. All users requiring a specific kind of data will use the same data, thereby eliminating the inefficiencies and inaccuracies caused by redundant, nonstandard data.

Quality of information must be planned. Without planning, most tasks will fail. Within your data warehouse project, make sure you start with a strong architecture planning effort. Within this planning, you will establish a vision, goals, objectives, and critical success factors. You also will be evaluating what the enterprise currently has in place. Clearly understanding in-place operational systems, data stores, and technologies allows your architectural effort to leverage and account for the legacy systems that will feed the new data warehouse. You will not be able to develop an architecture without this information, and this information will be invaluable as you begin to document the details of your planned architecture.

Understanding the past will lead you to the future. A proper architecture provides the foundation to deliver quality data and allows you to achieve the information system mission established by your enterprise. To deliver the architecture, make sure to plan and document the components that will formulate that foundation. The information you gather during your investigation and planning of an architecture will make it easier to deliver the architectural blueprint and defined technologies for implementing your data warehouse, as discussed in the chapters that follow.

4

Building an Architectural Blueprint

The job of buildings is to improve human relations: Architecture must ease them, not make them worse.

—Ralph Erskine

Data warehousing provides users with an information framework that represents a comprehensive model of a business. To deliver an effective data warehouse, companies must deal with the complexities of their current enterprises. Generally, a business will require its data warehouse to support the following.

- **Rapid response** Users need to analyze large amounts of data to make business decisions. The users are often faced with a limited window of time in which to perform this analysis to make timely business decisions and to react quickly to changing market conditions.
- **Complex analysis** Business analysis involves determining the answers to some extremely complex questions, often requiring iterative analysis of data. Business users typically issue queries that invoke multiple conditions, summarizations, and complex subqueries, which places increased demands on a database.

- **Dynamic business environment** Users need the flexibility to access information in a wide variety of ever-changing ways to resolve specific business problems quickly. As a business environment changes, users need to view and analyze data in complex and ever-changing ways. This often involves the ability to cross-correlate different subject areas and business measures.

Prior to addressing the building of a data warehouse architecture, let us review what an architecture is. In Chapter 3, Planning a Data Warehouse Architecture, we defined architecture as a style and method of design and construction that provide an orderly arrangement of overall system parts.

With regard to a data warehouse, an architecture facilitates the creation of a data resource that is accurate, shareable, and easily accessible throughout an enterprise. This architecture provides a blueprint that explains how the vision, goals, and objectives of a data warehouse will be delivered. The components of this architecture include shared data, technical infrastructure, and reusable program logic—the items that will deliver the content required by users to make informed decisions. These architectural components explain factors such as what business functions will be supported and which decisions-making functions will be enabled by a data warehouse.

Architecture Requirements

The architectural definition process begins with clearly understanding functional business requirements. The architectural team begins by translating business requirements into goals that fall into one of the individual architectural areas of data, application, or technology. The architectural analysis is primarily business-oriented, addressing the means for applying technology to an enterprise and defining the factors that exist within a business that can—and more than likely will—affect the outcome of an architectural implementation. The process of mapping requirements ensures that the delivered architecture will meet the needs of a business. The documentation resulting from this phase assists the development staff in understanding the best way to implement a data warehouse.

The following are samples of data warehouse system business requirements.

- Data from multiple divisions in an enterprise must be integrated for reporting purposes without integrating legacy operational systems.

- A regulatory reporting requirement spans multiple business cycles with data up to 20 years of age.

- An enterprise must quickly respond to changes in the marketplace, including new markets, new competitors, and new customers. However, the corresponding information is currently inaccessible.
- Data to assist business units in performing more effective target marketing campaigns is needed.
- The majority of users are mobile and need to be disconnected from an information source. However, the system must support these users and allow them to obtain the data required to perform their job.

Each of these requirements provides important details that assist in defining the technology that will be utilized to implement a final solution. The architectural requirements help to define the answers to physical implementation issues like: *Will the warehouse be centralized or distributed?* The impact of not defining this type of architectural information is enormous, forcing the development team to replace the current underpinnings with products that support the undiscovered requirements. Within individual architectures, the team will need to define factors such as those listed in Table 4.1.

Table 4.1: *Individual architecture requirements*

Architectural area	Requirement details
Technology	Geographic support required (dispersed or centralized) Availability Resiliency Communication bandwidth and transmission Network service Security and authentication Disconnected computing On-line and off-line data storage Client and server processing
Data	Data synchronization Latency tolerance Local and other read-only copies of data Optimization of queries Static versus dynamic optimization and access Data size Integration of multiple formats Partitioning Data quality

(continues)

Table 4.1: *(continued)*

Architectural area	Requirement details
Application	Timing requirements (example: within five days of the close of accounting) Critical interfaces (example: this depends on successful completion of BOM process) User sophistication, analytical experience, or computer literacy Design tools Business function sharing Software configuration management Testing tools Development environment (examples: APIs and GUIs) User tool suite (examples: executive information system [EIS], decision support system [DSS], data mining, ad hoc reporting, standard reporting, application development, and product reporting)

Defining Individual Architectures

At this stage of the process, the architectural team begins to identify potential technology components, such as hardware and software, that might serve the enterprise's needs. Beginning to analyze these factors at this stage of the project safeguards an architectural team against defining an architecture that is too complex to be built in acceptable time frames, and in essence assists in keeping a project on track.

When defining the individual architectures, the team analyzes what the data warehouse system is required to do—fleshing out the structures and functions, and beginning to build models for the new architecture. From these models, the team can specify the functional requirements and gain concurrence from the user community that the resultant data warehouse will, in theory, achieve the established goals. It is important to note that this phase defines what the system needs to do rather than how to do it.

The purpose of this phase is to refine the gathered requirements and transform them into individual architectures. Your focus should be on the requirements to extract relevant data from operational data sources and on how best to provide quick access to this data via the data warehouse. An architecture, such as the one shown in Figure 4.1, should begin to formulate. Requirements should be grouped into more detailed technology areas, such as replication agents, loading processors, data scrubbing, data transformation, and connectivity. The overall architecture that is developed by the team will provide a context for all future systems development activities.

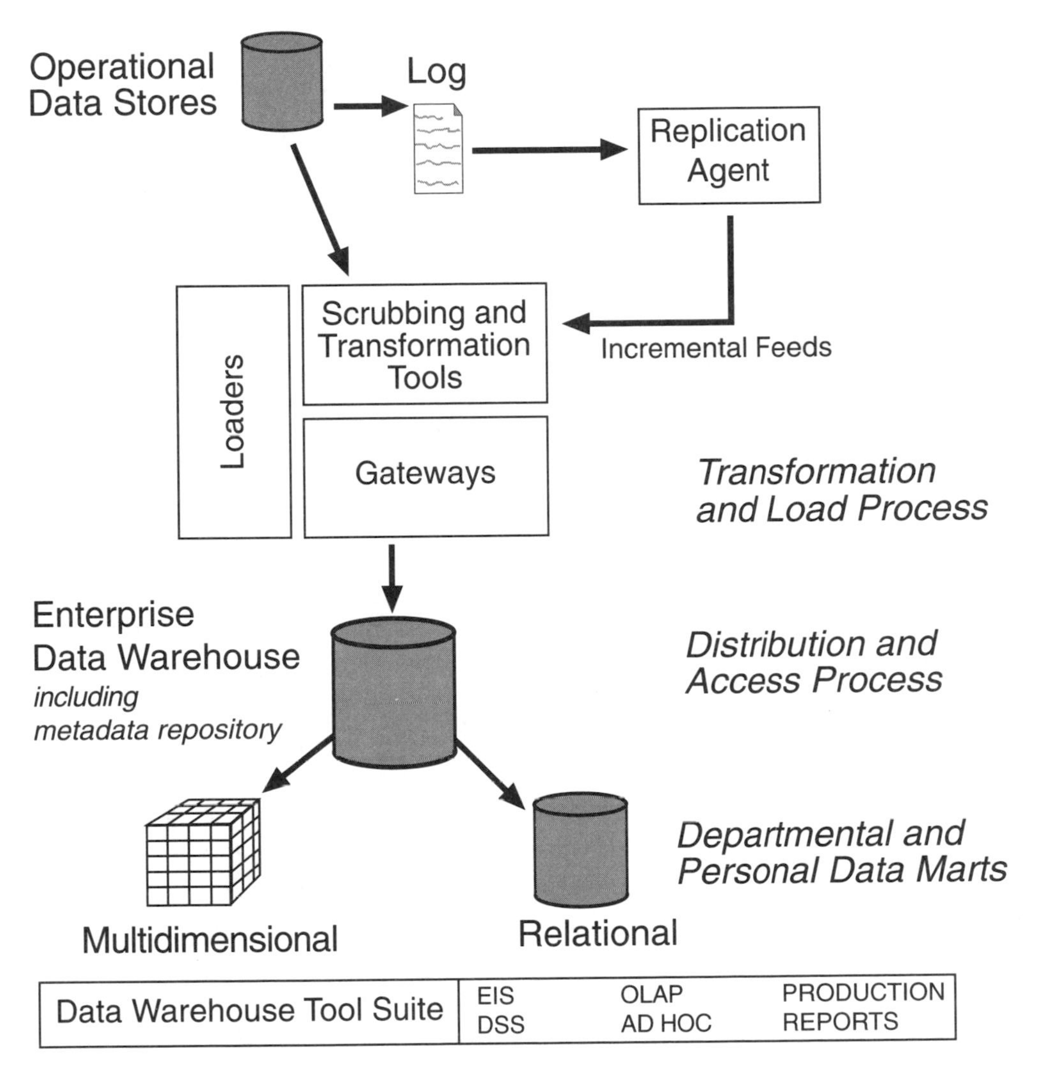

Figure 4.1: *Data warehouse architectural requirement areas*

The target architecture shown in Figure 4.1 fits the needs of most enterprises. This target architecture will be valid for you if you are in a large or small enterprise; if you are in a vertical industry such as banking, insurance, government, manufacturing, or retail; or if you are in a primarily centralized mainframe shop or a highly distributed, client/server shop.

Data Architecture

A target architecture contains a myriad of data components. The most important of these components are the operational data stores (input sources) and the data warehouse (target sources).

You will notice that a data warehouse is presented in Figure 4.1 as a network of databases. The subcomponents of a data warehouse will include the enterprise data warehouse, the metadata repository, departmental and personal data marts, and multidimensional data stores. These subcomponents are documented separately, because the architecture should present a logical implementation. It is the job of the data warehouse implementation teams to determine the proper way to physically implement the recommended architecture. This suggests that the implementation may well be on the same physical database rather than separate data stores as shown in Figure 4.1.

Metadata

A crucial area of a data warehouse environment is metadata, data that describes the data. Within a data warehouse, metadata describes and locates data components, their origin (which may be either the operational systems or the data warehouse), and their movement through the data warehouse process. The data access, data stores, and processing information will have associated descriptions about the data and processing—the inputs, calculations, and outputs—documented in the metadata.

This metadata should be captured within the data architecture and managed from the beginning of a data warehouse project. The metadata repository should contain information such as that listed next.

- Description of the data model
- Description of the layouts used in the database design
- Definition of the primary system managing the data items
- A map of the data from the system of record to the other locations in the data warehouse, including the descriptions of transformations and aggregations
- Specific database design definitions
- Data element definitions, including rules for derivations and summaries

It is through metadata that a data warehouse becomes an effective tool for an overall enterprise. This repository of information will tell the story of the data: where it originated, how it has been transformed, where it went, and how often—that is, its genealogy or artifacts. Technically, the metadata repository will also improve the maintainability and manageability of a warehouse by making impact analysis information and entity life histories available to the support staff.

Volumetrics

The volume of data that will be processed and housed by a data warehouse is probably the biggest factor that determines the technology utilized by the data warehouse to manage and store the information. The volume of data impacts the warehouse in two ways: overall size and ability to load.

Too often, people design their warehouse load processes only for mass loading of the data from the operational systems to the data warehouse. Don't fall into this trap! When defining your data architecture, you should architect a solution that allows mass loading as well as incremental, or delta, change loading.

Mass loading is typically a high-risk area no matter what database provider you select; the database management systems can only load data so fast. Mass loading also forces downtime, and we want our users to have access to a data warehouse in a nearly 24-hour by seven-day environment. Therefore, when attacking this issue you should clearly define what it takes to do the mass load, but focus more of your energy on determining how volatile the data is and what the incremental data loading strategy should be. How will you load the deltas to operational data, and at what frequency?

Gathering information to assist in determining the best responses to these questions should not be difficult. During the architectural planning and discovery process, you listed the major data sources and relevant contacts. The individuals who manage the data assets of the company can provide valuable insight into what transaction activity occurs within their databases on a daily basis. We tend to request information based on two factors, growth and volatility.

The *growth* factor is important because it defines how quickly the data will grow over time. In a relational, SQL world, this is understanding how many *insert* statements occur—that is, the number of birth events for major subject areas.

The *volatility* factor determines other transaction types that occur on the data, allowing you to determine which tables contain relatively static data and which tables are hot spots of activity, containing highly dynamic data. In a relational, SQL world, this is understanding the *update* statement patterns.

A sample of volumetric data gathering for operational growth and volatility data is presented in Table 4.2.

Table 4.2: *Operational data growth and volatility*

Data entity	***Current rows***	***Growth (rows/day)***	***Volatility (trans/day)***	***Projected annual rows***
Orders	797,508	300	100	900,000
Customers	398,754	150	3,500	450,000
Sales representatives	3,543	nil	18	4,000
Products	2,577	2	1	5,160
Suppliers	1,302	20	10	2,604

Upon gathering the growth and volatility information about major data entities, you can calculate annual projections and begin to determine the size impact that each entity will have on the data warehouse. Notice that, in Table 4.2, *orders* and *customers* are the most volatile data sources. The chart indicates that 50,000 new customers are added per year, and that nearly a million orders are processed each year. The *sales representative* data source is the closest to static data listed in Table 4.2. Each of the columns shown in the table contains relevant data, allowing you to fully calculate the projected annual rows for a data entity. The Current Rows column allows you to understand the activity up to the point in time where you are measuring the data. The Growth column indicates how many rows are added (in SQL terms, *inserted*) into the data entity. The Volatility column indicates how many rows are modified (*updated*) within the data entity. The Projected Annual Rows is a calculated column derived by multiplying the Growth column by the number of business days in a year. This column should be evaluated in relation to the Current Rows column to gauge the reliability of your calculation. Another way to calculate the Projected Annual Rows is to take the Current rows column and divide it by the represented business days for which data has been captured. This number of rows can then be multiplied by the number of business days within a year to determine the Projected Annual Rows.

It is important to obtain this information from raw data sources. However, you should match the raw number against estimates from your business users. Most users can quote major numbers, such as *total number of active customers, orders per year, shipments per year,* and *total number of sales representatives employed.* These numbers often are discussed during the business planning process to determine how to establish the infrastructure supporting the business and how to allocate funds to support that infrastructure.

A data warehouse, unlike operational systems, takes these row counts and multiplies them based on a time variable. For example, if an enterprise wants to maintain information about orders for five years, the data warehouse in our example must manage five million orders and their associated entities.

The information that you derive from this exercise will assist you in planning load cycles and server configurations. Some data that is very volatile may require loads as frequently as hourly, while static data may only need to be loaded on a monthly, quarterly, or annual basis. These determinations are made in conjunction with the strategies you implement for capturing individual changes to operational data stores.

Upon completion of this discovery phase, you will be able to assemble a comprehensive loading process schedule to assist in establishing processing requirements and other technology-oriented tasks for managing the data transition process.

Transformation

A data architecture needs to provide a clear understanding of transformation requirements that must be supported, including logic and complexity. This is one area in which the architectural team will have difficulty finding commercially available software to manage or assist with the process. Transformation tools and standards are currently immature. However, with the rapid growth in the data warehousing market, this situation is bound to change soon. Many tools that currently occupy this space are those that were initially developed to assist companies in moving applications away from mainframes. These tools did not succeed within that market and viewed the data warehouse market as their savior.

Operational data stores are vast and varied. Many data stores are unsupported by these transformational tools. The tools support the popular database engines, but do nothing to advance your effort with little-known or unpopular databases.

It is often better to evaluate and select a transformational tool or agent that supports a good connectivity tool, such as Sybase's Omni family of products or Information Builder's EDA/SQL, rather than one that supports a native file access strategy. With an open connectivity product, your development teams can focus on multiplatform, multidatabase transformations. Additionally, products such as Sybase's Open Server can assist with point solutions for unsupported data structures.

Data Synchronization

Within your transformation architecture, make sure to determine the best way to synchronize data from legacy data stores to the data warehouse. Your synchronization architecture should focus on standardization of transformation language, staging platform, communication strategy, and support strategy. The synchronization process between a data warehouse and operational data stores can take on various architectures. Each of these synchronization options involves components on the legacy server and the data warehouse server. The primary difference in each of these synchronization techniques is the level of control and sophistication that exists. Also, a cost is associated with obtaining greater control and sophistication.

We examine three synchronization options in the following sections.

Synchronization Option 1: Batch File Transfer

In the batch file transfer synchronization option, client workstation applications do all of their processing against the data warehouse. The data warehouse is treated by the client workstation application as though it were the only version of the data. The legacy operational database continues to be updated on a transaction basis via operational systems. The data warehouse is updated by the operational database on a periodic, batch basis. In this architecture, a batch program extracts data from the operational database and transfers it to the data warehouse via a file transfer capability. A batch program in the data warehouse server later applies this data to the data warehouse database. A depiction of this synchronization option appears in Figure 4.2.

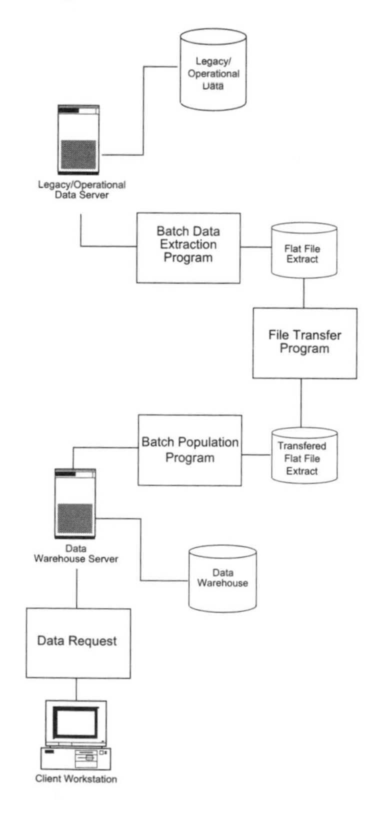

Figure 4.2: *Flat file transfer synchronization*

Synchronization Option 2: Batch Processing Through a Gateway

Most initial data warehouse implementations utilize a data warehouse system infrastructure that implements a batch synchronization architecture in conjunction with gateway access. This option allows legacy systems to supply the data warehouse with decision support data and allows the data warehouse to off-load the current operational systems for analytical and historical reporting needs. Figure 4.3 shows this synchronization option.

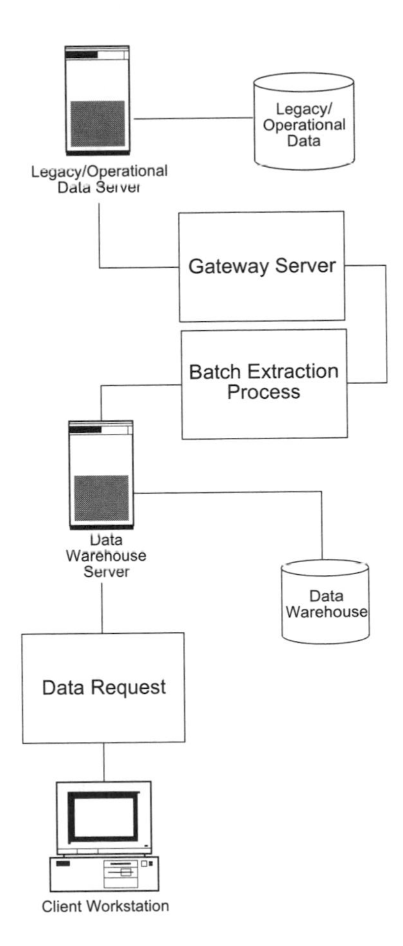

Figure 4.3: *Batch synchronization through gateways*

Synchronization Option 3: Replication

The final synchronization option, replication, is a distributed architecture in which the data warehouse and legacy databases are treated as current by different applications during the same processing periods. The data is replicated from one of the databases to the other using replication technology. In this architecture, a client application updates data in the transaction database server, and the replication technology queues and "dequeues" the transaction information for updating the data warehouse. This architecture should be viewed as a long-term, strategic implementation plan. This architecture offers enormous flexibility for deployment of applications, which are re-engineered while reducing the cost of the infrastructure through reuse of current hardware and software. The replication synchronization option is illustrated in Figure 4-4.

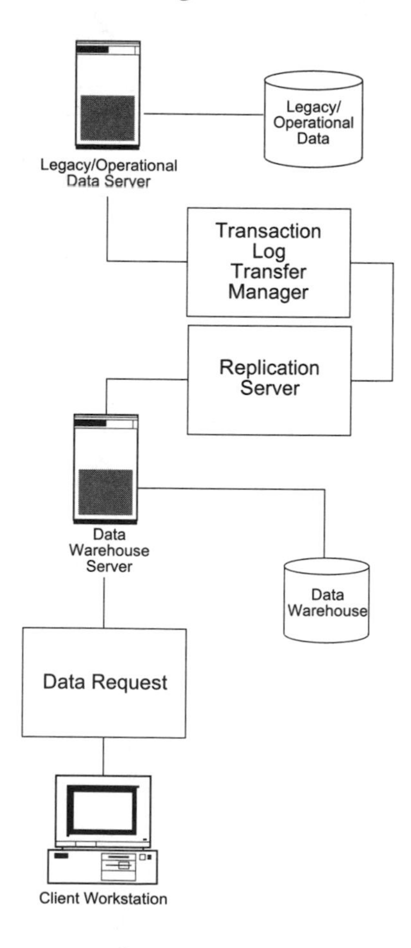

Figure 4.4: *Replication agents*

Replication technology has advanced immensely in the 1990s, and can now greatly assist in the data warehouse loading processing. Not all database management systems support the concept of replication, but many modern relational databases now have the ability to be replicated. The primary requirement in this area is the reduction of mass loading within a data warehouse, allowing the processing of incremental changes. If you can utilize replication technology, you will avoid the need to make any modifications within the source database or source application to capture daily transactions to drive daily transformation requirements.

Replication technology, such as Sybase's Replication Server, minimizes the disruption to your operational environment, because it retrieves its information from database logs, not actual data records. This forces you to incur some latency with regard to the transfer of data modifications from the operational environment to the data warehouse environment. However, this technique offers two benefits: avoiding disruption of the transaction window within the operational systems and avoiding potential locks on the data record.

It is best to select a replication technology that permits you flexibility in how the replication occurs. Again, the operational environment dictates many of the restrictions for platform use, data access windows, and batch scheduling. Replication technologies allow you to almost have your cake and eat it too.

Architecture Tip 1: You should establish a replication technology that provides an unintrusive data warehouse agent—such as a Log Transfer Manager—to assist in the data warehouse loading and transformation processing. This type of technology minimizes the impact and interruptions that may occur on operational systems.

Data Cleansing

Aside from finding tools to automate the transformation process, your team should evaluate the complexity behind data transformations. Most legacy data stores lack standards and have anomalies that can become nightmares for your development staff. Again, tools are evolving to assist you in automating transformations, including complex issues such as buried data, lack of legacy standards, and noncentralized key data. We briefly discuss each of these issues in the following sections.

Buried Data

Often, legacy systems utilize composite keys to uniquely define data. Though these fields appear as one in a database, they represent multiple pieces of information. Figure 4.5 illustrates buried data by showing a vehicle identification number that contains many pieces of information.

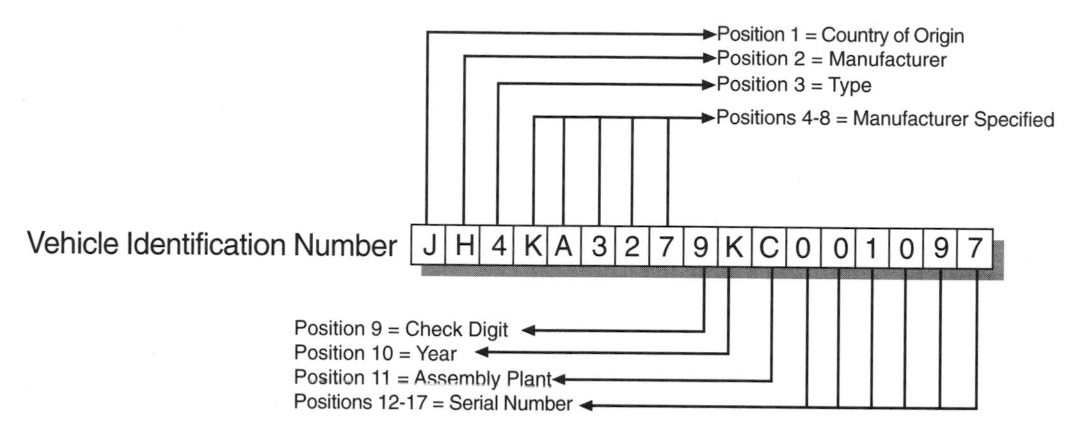

Figure 4.5: *Data problems—buried data*

Lack of Legacy Standards

Items such as descriptions, names, labels, and keys have typically been managed on an application-by-application basis. And as suggested by Figure 4.6, in many legacy systems such fields lack clear definition. As you will note in this illustration, data in the name field is haphazardly formatted. Finally, application software providers may offer user-oriented fields, which can be used and defined as required by the customer. Depending on your company, you will find various levels of quality in these types of fields.

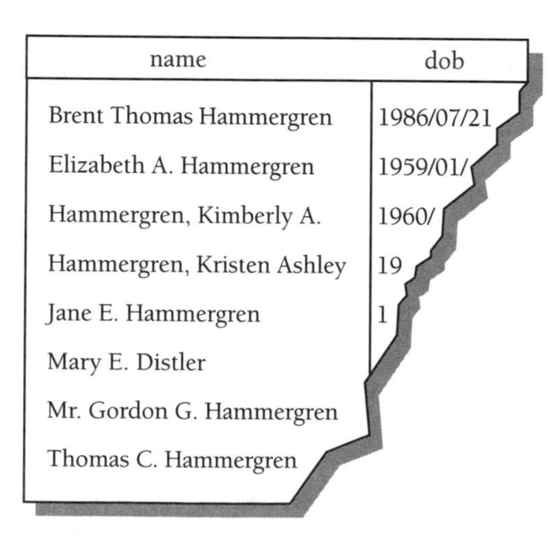

name	dob
Brent Thomas Hammergren	1986/07/21
Elizabeth A. Hammergren	1959/01/
Hammergren, Kimberly A.	1960/
Hammergren, Kristen Ashley	19
Jane E. Hammergren	1
Mary E. Distler	
Mr. Gordon G. Hammergren	
Thomas C. Hammergren	

Figure 4.6: *Data problems—no legacy standards*

Noncentralized Key Data

As companies have evolved through acquisition or growth, various systems took ownership of data that may not have been in their scope. This is especially true for companies that can be characterized as heavy users of packaged application software and those that have grown through acquisition. Notice how the noncentralized *cust_no* field varies from one database to another for the hypothetical company represented in Figure 4.7.

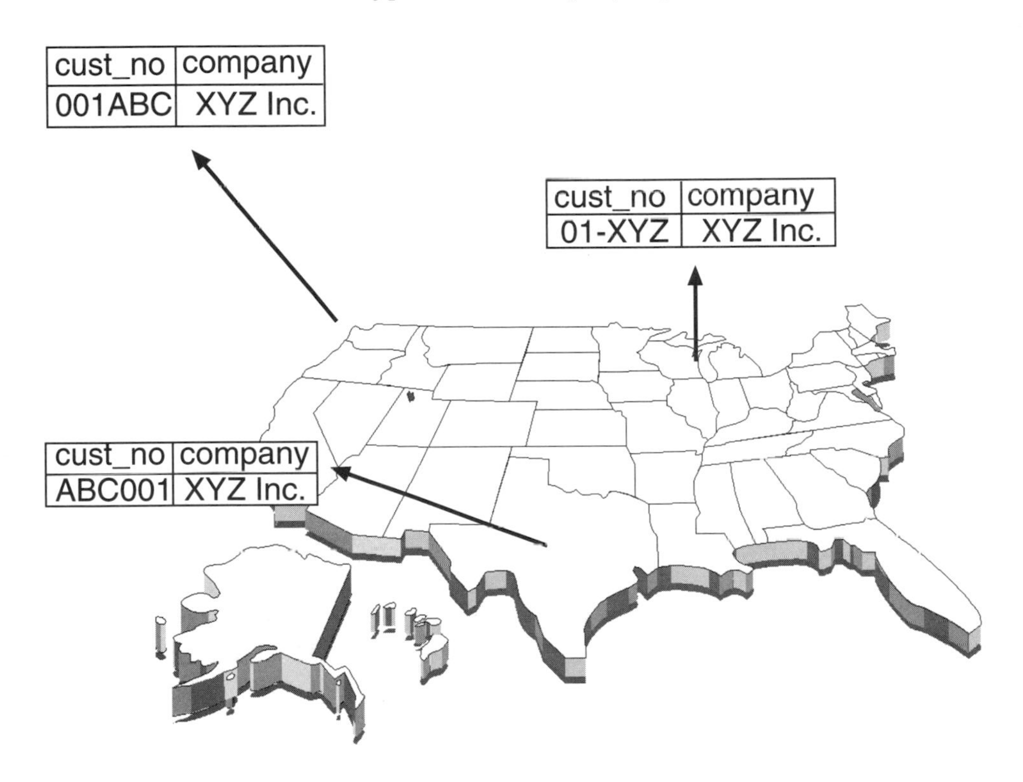

Figure 4.7: *Data problems—Noncentralized key data*

Concluding Thoughts About Transformation Architectures

The ultimate goal of a transformation architecture is to allow your development teams to create a repeatable transformation process. Depending on the complexities that you face within your data, you may be unable to find tools to automate the transformation process. Tools that are currently available lack the industrial strength required by most diversified enterprises. However, this will change in time, so you should formally review such tools on a regular basis. Therefore, make sure to clearly define your needs for data synchronization and data cleansing. A sense of the requirements in these areas will allow you to best define the proper transformation architecture.

Data Architectural Requirements

The volumetric numbers discussed early in this chapter will assist you in better determining the requirements for a data warehouse, including scaleability, connectivity to operational data, and replication for incremental loading. However, until you begin to design the physical structures of a data warehouse, these numbers will only provide you with gauges, not final estimates. The requirements placed on a data warehouse revolve around several characteristics, such as those discussed next.

- **Subject-oriented data** Data that is contained within a data warehouse should be organized by subject. For example, if your data warehouse focuses on sales and marketing processes, you need to generate data about customers, prospects, orders, products, and so on. To completely define a subject area, the back-end processing may require you to draw upon data from multiple operational systems. To derive the data entities that clearly define the sales and marketing process of an enterprise, you might need to draw upon an order entry system, a sales force automation system, and various other applications.
- **Time-based data** Data in a data warehouse should relate specifically to a time period, allowing users to capture data that is relevant to their analysis period. Consider an example in which a new customer was added to an order entry system with a primary contact of *John Doe* on 2/17/96. This customer's data was changed on 4/19/96 to reflect a new primary contact of *Jane Doe*. In this scenario, the data warehouse would contain the two contact records shown in Table 4.3.

Table 4.3: *Time variant data*

customer_id	contact_id	last_name	first_name	time_stamp
199602170005	001	Doe	John	02/17/1996
199602170005	001	Doe	Jane	04/19/1996

- **Update processing** A data warehouse should contain data that represents closed operational items, such as a fulfilled customer order. In this sense, the data warehouse will typically contain little or no update processing. Typically, incremental or mass load processes are run to insert data into the data warehouse. Updating individual records that are already in the data warehouse will rarely occur.

- **Transformed and scrubbed data** Data that are contained in a data warehouse should be transformed, scrubbed, and integrated into user-friendly subject areas.
- **Aggregation** Data needs to be aggregated into and out of a data warehouse. Therefore, computational requirements will be placed on the entire data warehousing process.
- **Granularity** A data warehouse typically contains multiple levels of granularity. It is normal for the data in a data warehouse to be summarized and contain less detail than the original operational data; however, some data warehouses require dual levels of granularity. For example, a sales manager may need to understand how sales representatives in his or her area perform a forecasting task. In this example, monthly summaries that contain the data associated with the sales representatives' forecast and the actual orders received are enough data; there is no requirement to see each individual line item of an order—hence, the summarized data. However, a retailer may need to wade through individual sales transactions to look for correlations that show people tend to buy soft drinks and snacks together. This need requires more detail associated with each individual purchase. The data required to fulfill both of these requests may exist, and therefore the data warehouse might be built to manage both the summarized data to fulfill a very rapid query and the more detailed data required to fulfill a lengthy analysis process.
- **Metadata management** Because a data warehouse pulls information from a variety of sources and the data warehouse teams will perform data gathering on current data stores and new data stores, you should require that storage and management of metadata can be effectively done throughout the data warehouse process.

Application Architecture

An application architecture determines how users interact with a data warehouse. The front-end process of data warehouses ranges from a controlled, standard reporting environment to a highly dynamic, ad hoc, tools-driven environment. To determine the application architecture that is best for your company, evaluate the users and classify their skill set. Technology and budget also have a say in your ultimate deployment. However, for defining the architecture, you should define the *what*, not the *how*, of the application architecture. Within a standard architecture, these user categories will assist you in determining the proper tools to outfit their reporting and analysis needs. A sampling of user category definitions are listed in Table 4.4.

Table 4.4: *User category definitions*

User category	Definition
Power users	Technical users who require little to no support to develop complex reports and queries. These users tend to support other users and analyze data throughout the entire enterprise.
Frequent users	Less technical users who primarily interface with the power users for support, but sometimes require the Information Systems department to support them. These users tend to provide management reporting support up to the division level within an enterprise, a narrower scope than for power users.
Casual users	These users touch the system and computers in general infrequently. They tend to require a higher degree of support, which normally includes building predetermined reports, graphs, and tables for their analysis purposes.

Tools Criteria

Tools must be made available to users to access a data warehouse. These tools should be carefully selected so that they are efficient and compatible with other parts of the architecture and standards. These tools must accommodate all users, and no tools fall into the silver-bullet category. Therefore, realizing that no one tool will fill all users' needs, you must define the criteria for multiple types of tools. Figure 4.8 suggests the relationship between data warehousing tools and an application architecture. We discuss several of the tools depicted in this figure next.

Data warehouses require specialty tools to be successful. Much like the transition that companies made to office automation products, data warehouse tool suites are becoming more and more popular. If you evaluate office automation products, you will quickly realize that you can perform spreadsheet-like functions in a word processor, word processing in a spreadsheet, presentations in a word processor, or databases in a spreadsheet. However, tools in office automation suites are specifically designed for spreadsheet, word processing, presentation, and database tasks. It makes sense that you buy all of them and use the right tool for the right job. With the boom in the personal computing industry, these tools have become economically priced to allow everyone to purchase a complete suite. Data warehouse tools are beginning to display similar separation; no one-size tool fits all. When selecting your tool suite, you will find unique requirements for the following (and potentially more) tasks.

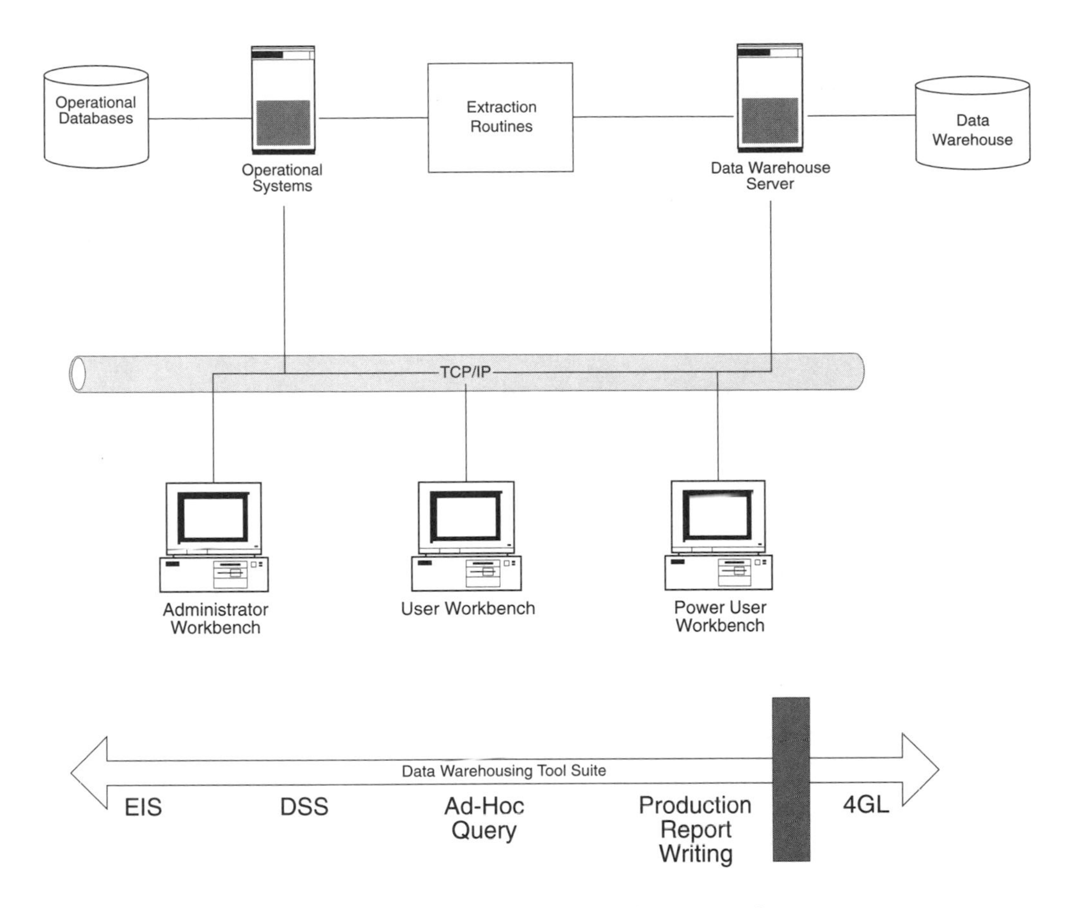

Figure 4.8: *A tools suite for an application architecture*

- **Executive information systems (EIS) and decision support systems (DSS)** These tools transform data into information and present that information to users in a meaningful and usable manner. These tools support advanced analytical techniques and free-form data exploration, allowing users to easily transform data into information. The "E" in EIS previously stood for Executive. But while these tools still exist in today's market, the "E" now should be characterized more as Everyone's, as in Everyone's Information System. EIS tools tend to give their users a high-level summarization of key performance measures to support decision making. These tools fall into the big-button syndrome, in which an application development team builds a nice standard report with hooks to many other reports, then presents this information behind a big button. When the user clicks the button, magic happens. Maps appear with regions colored, raised, and blinking alerts. Clicking a region drills down and reveals a graphical representation of a summary forecast and actual numbers. Buttons link to relevant news articles, and so on. While EIS tools traditionally targeted executives, DSS tools targeted more technical knowledge workers, who required more flexibility and ad hoc analytical capabilities. DSS tools allow users, as one vendor put it, "to tiptoe through their data." This phrase characterizes the more free flowing, analytical style that knowledge workers utilize to browse their data, transforming it into information. These tools avoided the big-button syndrome. However, these DSS tools traditionally have worked off a highly summarized data extract, which often is placed in a proprietary, multidimensional database.

- **Ad hoc query and reporting** The purpose of EIS and DSS applications is to allow business users to analyze, manipulate, and report on corporate data using familiar, easy-to-use interfaces. These tools conform to presentation styles that business people understand and with which they are comfortable. Unfortunately, many of these tools have size restrictions that do not allow them to access large data stores or to access data in a highly normalized structure, such as a relational database, in a rapid fashion; in other words, they can be slow. Therefore, users need tools that allow for more traditional reporting against relational, or two-dimensional, data structures. These tools offer database access with limited coding and often allow users to create read-only applications. Ad hoc query and reporting tools are an important component within a data warehouse tool suite, because they off-load some types of application development to the user, lowering the cost of Information Systems operations. However, their greatest advantage is contained in the term *ad hoc*. This means that decision makers can access data in an easy and timely fashion.

- **Production report writers** A production report writer allows the development staff to build and deploy reports that will be widely exploited by the user community in an efficient manner. These tools are often components within fourth generation languages (4GLs) and allow for complex computational logic and advanced formatting capabilities. Data warehouses are not immune to requiring standard reports, which are typically built by Information Systems departments. The production report writer is utilized by these developers and the finished product is deployed to users. It is best to find a vendor that provides an ad hoc query tool that can transform itself into a production report writer. However, these vendors are few and far between.

- **Application development environments (ADE)** Application development environments are nothing new, and many people overlook the need for such tools within a data warehouse tool suite. However, you will need to develop some presentation system for your users. The development, though minimal, is still a requirement, and we advise that data warehouse development projects standardize on an ADE. Ease of use and rapid application development (RAD) via iterative prototyping are the hallmarks of this group. These tools have been very popular in targeted environments, such as Microsoft Windows, offering little portability. Examples include Microsoft Visual Basic and Powersoft PowerBuilder. This situation is quickly changing, and many of these tools now support the concept of cross-platform development for environment such as Microsoft Windows, Apple Macintosh, and OS/2 Presentation Manager. However, the trend appears to be driving the tool set to support, at a minimum, Internet browsing capabilities as well as application partitioning, as demonstrated by Powersoft PowerBuilder 5, Forte, and Dynasty tools. Every data warehouse project team should have a standard ADE in its arsenal.
- **Other tools** Though the tools just described represent minimum requirements, you may find a need for several other specialty tools. Many new marketplaces are arising to support the mentioned concept of tiptoeing through your data. These additional tools include on-line analytical processing (OLAP), data mining, and managed query environments.

You should begin to characterize the minimal set of available tools to access the content of your data warehouse and how those tools will be managed. If you characterize your users and investigate their needs, you will find that specific tools are required by user type. Some users will require all tools—the entire data warehouse tool suite—while others will only require one tool or access to only standard reports.

Data Warehouse Tool Suite Requirements

The tools that you make available to users have specific requirements that will allow you to perform a more focused search based on capabilities or user needs. Samples of these requirements include the following.

- **Quick response time** Many databases and database tables are quite large. Many tools require the return of an entire result set of a query to the client workstation prior to display of data. These tools will typically be slow. Also, some tools work great when they access only one database table; however, when you join two or more tables, they die. Benchmarking tools during your prototype phases allows you to better evaluate if you in fact are buying a tool that will perform in your environment. What is quick response time? You need to define this, because different users have different expectations from a second to a day.

- **Time slicing** Because some reports take additional time, the ability to submit queries that will be time sliced by the server or that can execute in the background will add great value to the user. Background processing should allow the user to continue work within the tool, including the ability to create additional requests against the data warehouse.
- **File transfer** Users will want the ability to load data into a spreadsheet, presentation, or word processing document—or even into a local database—without assistance from the data warehouse development team. Again, this type of functionality can assist in off-loading processing cycles from the main data warehouse server and can add value to the process. However, remember the golden rule of forcing users to reference where the data was sourced. Users who take data and give it new life beyond a simple analytical model (in other words, who download data in January and continually update the local data until December without ever accessing the data warehouse) should be severely reprimanded.
- **Report scheduling** Similar to time slicing, the user should be able to submit reports on the server when they realize that the reports will run over long periods of time. If a user has an understanding that he or she is asking for a lot of data, or if a given time period is exceeded during a report, the user should be prompted to place the report in a batch schedule to be run at off peak hours or overnight. Upon completion, the report could be delivered via an e-mail interface, a personal file extract, or another, more optimal method than waiting on line for the results.
- **User designed report formatting** Users will require the capability to easily design and create their own reports. This requirement typically encompasses graphs, forms, multiple query result placements, and presentations. Many reporting tools offer style sheets or templates that allow users to easily prepare these types of reports on their own.

At this point, your application and tools architecture should begin to flesh out. Answers will be developed to questions such as: What classifications of tools are required? How will they correlate to user classifications?

You will be able to map need to class; however, you should remember that these tools are continuously upgraded. You should define the *what*, not the *how*. Do not fall into the trap of overcommitting too soon to a tool from a given vendor. You need to define the capabilities and some potential technologies—the *what*. Your development project teams should choose the tools that allow them to implement most effectively—the *how*.

Technology Architecture

It is in the technology architectural section of your blueprint that you begin to define the hardware, software, and network topology that will support the implementation of your data warehouse. The goal of a technology architecture is to provide a technical platform that is performance engineered, scaleable, portable, maintainable, supportable, and cost effective. This architecture is composed of three major components—clients, servers, and networks—and the software to manage each of them. Let's now look at each of these components separately.

- **Clients** The client technology component comprises the devices that are utilized by users. These devices can include workstations, personal computers, personal digital assistants, and even beepers for support personnel. Each of these devices has a purpose in being served by a data warehouse. Conceptually, the client either contains a lot of software to access the data warehouse (this is the traditional client in the client/server model and is known as a "fat" client) or it contains very little software and accesses a server that contains most of the software required to access a data warehouse. The latter approach is the evolving Internet client model known as a "thin" client and "fat" server.
- **Servers** The server technology component includes the physical hardware platforms as well as the operating systems that manage the hardware. Other components, typically software, can also be grouped within this component, including: database management software; transaction processors (though these are really not needed in data warehousing); application server software; gateway connectivity software; replication software; and configuration management software.
- **Networks** The network component defines the transport technologies needed to support communications activity between the clients and the servers. This component includes requirements and decisions for wide area networks (WANs), local area networks (LANs), communication protocols, and other hardware associated with networks, such as bridges, routers, and gateways.

The Data Warehouse Blueprint

The architectural planning process deliverable, or data warehouse blueprint, should include clear documentation of the following items.

- **Requirements** What does the business want from the data warehouse?
- **Architectural blueprint** How will you deliver what the business wants?
- **Development approach** What is a clear definition of phased delivery cycles, including architectural review and refinement processes?

The blueprint document essentially translates an enterprise's mission, goals, and objectives for the data warehouse into a logical technology architecture composed of individual subarchitectures for the application, data, and technology components of a data warehouse, as shown in Figure 4.9. Business requirements are mapped to architectural requirements, which in turn are mapped to technology-rich product requirements.

An architectural blueprint is important, because it serves as the road map for all development work and as a guide for integrating the data warehouse with legacy systems. When the blueprint is understood by the development staff, decisions become much easier. The real worth of an architecture is to give context to all system development activities. In other words, you will define the *hows* so that they withstand the test of time.

The blueprint should be developed in a *logical* sense rather than in a *physical* sense. For example, in home building, all houses have exterior finishes. It is required; it is logical. The physical implementation can be different for the same architecture—aluminum siding, vinyl siding, brick, wood siding, or stucco. For the database components, you will state things like, "The data store for the data warehouse will support an easy-to-use data manipulation language that is standard in the industry, such as SQL." This is a logical architecture-product requirement. When you implement the data warehouse, this could be Sybase SQL Server, Sybase MPP, Sybase IQ, or another database product. However, the logical definition allows your implementations to grow as technology evolves. If your business requirements do not change in the next three to five years, neither will your blueprint.

However, if you had placed a physical implementation component in your blueprint, you might be forced to change it even though business requirements had not changed. An example of this scenario is stating that the data warehouse should be implemented utilizing Digital Equipment Corporation' CMOS VAX Processor running VMS 4.1. Three to five years ago this may have been state of the art. Is it today?

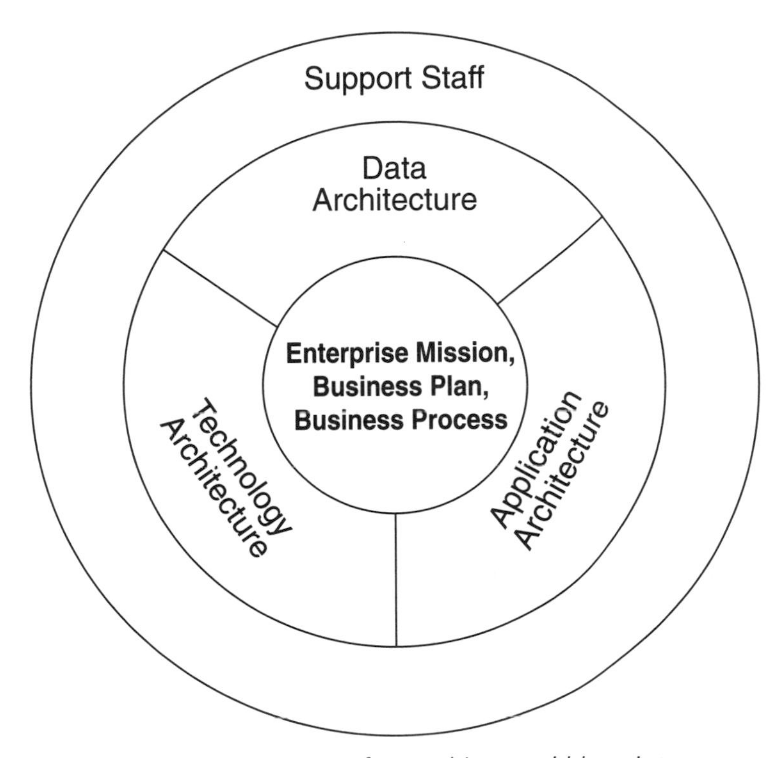

Figure 4.9: *Areas of an architectural blueprint*

The blueprint should present an integrated architecture that includes the following concerns.

- Client components
- Server components
- Hardware
- Operating system
- Connectivity protocol
- End user tools (EIS/DSS, ad hoc query and reporting, OLAP, and data mining)
- Client development tools (production report writing and application development environment)
- Database management software

- Warehouse management software
- Server development tools (production report writer, extraction, migration, maintenance, and assembly)
- Metadata repository
- Connectivity tools
- Scheduling software
- Information distribution (propagation, replication, and routing)
- Archival tools
- Transformation tools (cleansing, scrubbing, summarization, aggregation, data enhancement, data enrichment, data merging, data formatting, and data splitting)
- System and process management (resource governors, security, schedulers, purging, archiving, performance monitoring, connectivity, data storage, metadata storage, multimedia needs, and auditing)
- Large volume data loading
- Software for backup and recovery of large data sets
- System fault resilience
- Security
- Text and document storage and retrieval
- Multimedia and video storage and retrieval
- World Wide Web and other Internet interfaces

Each of these architectural components should be compatible and proven to formulate the basis for the technology architecture, as shown in Figure 4.1.

Summary

To deliver what is required in a data warehouse, you must establish a solid foundation of technology infrastructure; that is, an architecture. An architecture is critical to the overall success of a data warehouse. This architecture clearly defines what the data warehouse will contain, for what purposes, at what level of granularity, and with what level of retention.

Most enterprise data warehouses start with smaller, subject-oriented data warehouses that inevitably will connect. This means that, over time, you will build the enterprise data warehouse through smaller, iterative phases. Without a proper architecture, the interconnectivity required by the data models, tools, and underlying technologies will not occur.

The architecture that you define for your data warehouse should allow for an Information Systems development philosophy that allows systems to be built utilizing components. These components improve the overall quality of a system by offering shared data and reusable program logic within the technical infrastructure. With this type of standardization, support for data warehousing systems will be well defined and efficient: No more square pegs will be built to fill round holes.

An architecture offers the following characteristics.

- **Shorter lead time** The architecture clearly defines how components plug into or interface with other components of a data warehouse system. The only required lead time will be for the assembly process.

- **Flexibility** Within a data warehouse, prefabricated parts can and will be added or removed as necessary.

- **Less expensive to produce** Costs are cut with the shorter lead time, the simplified development process, and the higher reliability of the parts or components of a data warehouse.

- **Less expensive to maintain** With well-defined standards established at the beginning of a process, the ability to add technical components or improve the quality of components is greatly enhanced.

This architecture is the foundation that will support user requirements and should be logical in scope. With a logical definition, the architecture will be flexible and support technology swings in the market without requiring massive change. The only time that you will be required to change your logical architecture is when business or user requirements are dramatically modified.

The physical deployment and implementation of an architecture depends on current best-of-breed technologies, allowing you to physically map the technology at any point in time. If requirements have not changed, the architecture should not change even though, at any point in time, the physical implementations may be different.

When working on your architecture, make sure to attend to the following.

- Focus on strategic use of technology for managing data within your enterprise. This data should be viewed as an asset, and therefore managed like other assets of value to the enterprise.
- Build models of the business that explain the business and assess the impact of changes on the business. These models will assist in understanding areas that may benefit from a data warehouse as well as those in which risk may be high.
- Focus on delivering an architecture that complements the long-range business plan of your enterprise. Scaling up to the enterprise data warehouse should focus on how the business is growing and on what strategic information is required to assist executives.
- Eliminate complex and costly interfaces among incongruent systems.

After your architecture is completed, you can easily assess the benefits and impact of new subject-oriented data warehouses being added to the data warehouse as well as the addition of new tools to assist in the management and accessibility of the warehouse. From a business point of view, your Information Systems staff will also be able to easily analyze the impact of business changes such as mergers, acquisitions, new products, and new lines of business. New systems can be developed faster and at a lower cost with a proper architecture in place. This architecture benefits the enterprise through common data, common code, and shortened requirements phases within new development projects.

The architecture will also assist you with overall project planning—the work breakdown structure and project team composition defined within the project plan, which is discussed in the following chapters.

SECTION III

Managing the Process

5

Project Life Cycle and Management

Some great men owe most of their greatness to the ability of detecting in those they destine for their tools the exact quality of strength that matters for their work.

—*Joseph Conrad*

A data warehouse is a single source for key performance measurement and historically significant corporate information. All of the entities contained in a data warehouse are interconnected; therefore, the processes that comprise a data warehouse should also be interconnected. Decisions that are required within the project management space of development will rely on these interconnections. These stated items will lead to an iterative development methodology. The process is meant to quickly deliver, in an iterative fashion, the subject-oriented data warehouses required by the target audiences.

The four stages of the information packaging methodology, as shown in Figure 5.1, are as follows.

1. Architecture and system planning
2. Analysis and design

3. Implementation
4. Deployment

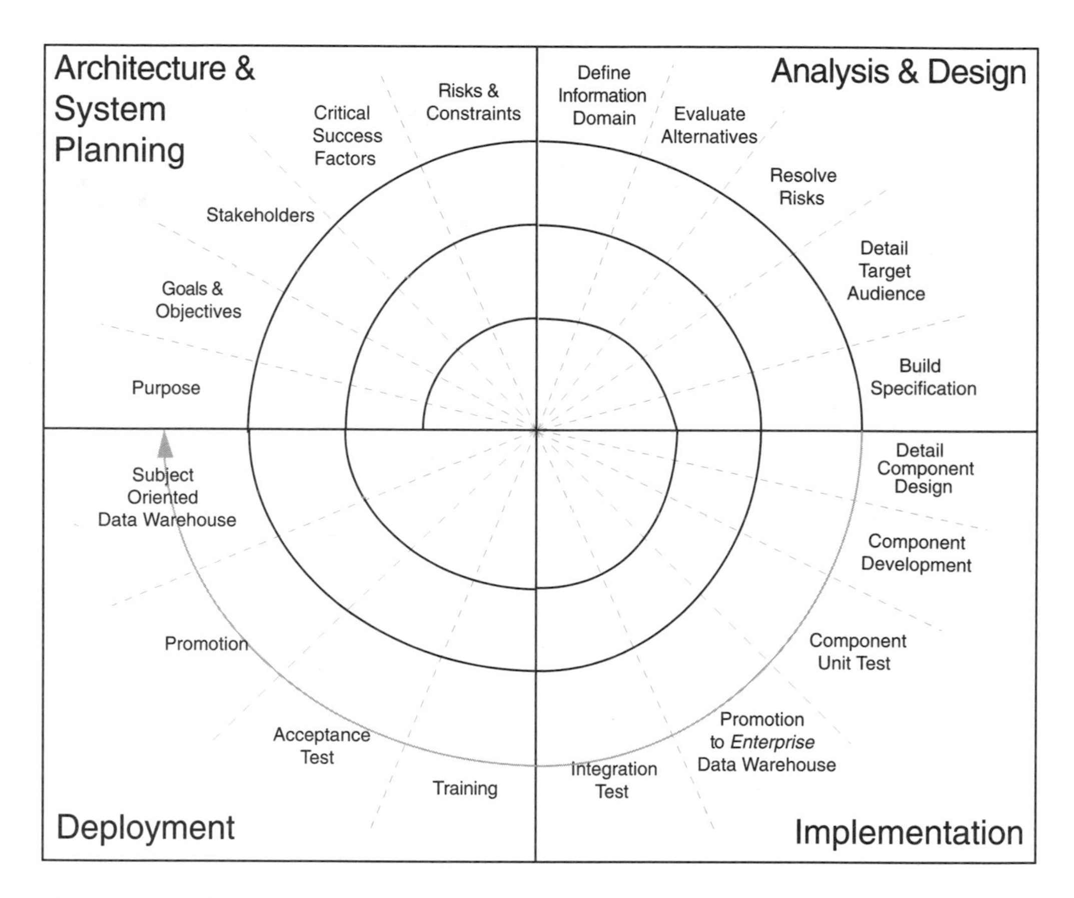

Figure 5.1: *Information packaging—spiral development for data warehousing methodology*

The development flow cycle between these four stages—planning, analysis and design, implementation, and finally deployment—is depicted in Figure 5.2.

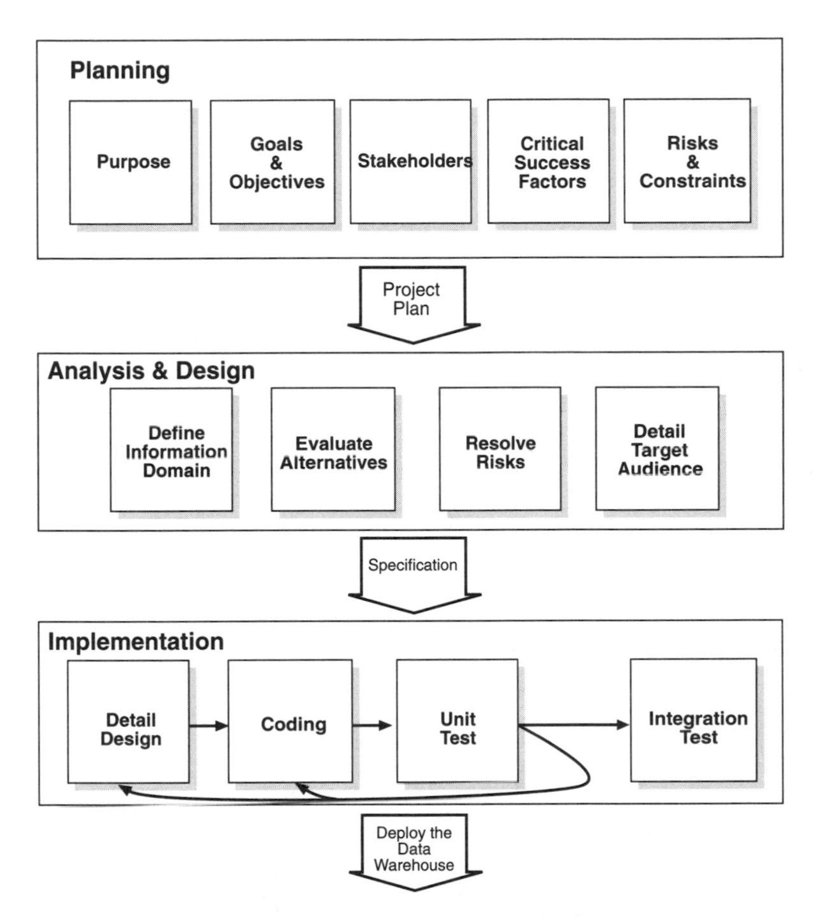

Figure 5.2: *Development cycle flow*

The goal of this methodology is to overcome potential weaknesses in the development staff, purpose definition, design, or implementation. These potential weaknesses will not disappear through the use of a methodology, but the methodology will compensate and allow the implementation team to counter the inevitable problems that arise in development situations. Thinking about your own development projects, does anyone really understand the complete system requirements until some part of the system is implemented, prototyped or clearly modeled? The spiral development approach assists you in more rapid delivery and discovery cycles, which allows your development staff to avoid lengthy development cycles that miss the requirement. A rapid feedback cycle develops in association with a rapid delivery cycle, which in turn assists in educating the development staff on how best to meet the data warehouse users' needs.

The first subject-oriented data warehouse that you implement should be built upon the architecture defined within the architectural phase discussed in Section II of this book. One of the goals of initial data warehouse development, aside from building a usable subject-oriented data warehouse, is to flush out all problems within the proposed architecture. This initial implementation will be a far cry from the data warehouses that are often discussed in trade journals today; however, the intent is to utilize an iterative development approach for building an enterprise data warehouse. Starting small enables you to lay the groundwork for a successful, ongoing warehouse strategy. This initial project will verify or upgrade the required network computing infrastructure to support a corporate-wide implementation.

Architecture Tip 2: The architectural phase and architectural review are outside the development scope. However, they should not be forgotten, because they are the foundation of a proper enterprise data warehousing strategy. Would you build your house without a foundation or blueprint? Data warehouses should be built upon the proper foundation.

Architecture and System Planning

The architecture and system planning phase of a data warehouse development effort allows a project's scope to be set, assisting the project management staff in sizing the time and effort required to deliver a subject-oriented data warehouse, or subsystem of a enterprise data warehouse. Within the business scope, it is important to state the business domain that will be covered by your project, namely: the business functions supported; the decision making enabled; and the stakeholders or key organizational personnel who have the most to win or lose by the implementation of a data warehouse.

Planning Tip 1: The planning process is one in which you must remember that the most important single factor in determining the final delivery date is the date on which a project begins.

The architecture and system planning phase provides several key deliverables described in the following sections. These deliverables include a purpose definition, goals and objectives, stakeholder identification, critical success factors, and risks and constraints.

Purpose Definition

The purpose statement is an articulation of the scope and reason for the subject-oriented data warehouse that is being planned. The project must clearly define a purpose that all developers understand and use as their boundary for development. For example, the purpose might be to deliver an information source that allows brand management personnel to monitor and clearly determine whether promotions are successful and disclose the factors that lead to their success.

Goals and Objectives

The goals and objectives flow from the purpose statement, and define the specific accomplishments desired from the development effort. Typically, you will be defining business-oriented objectives. For example, the goal might be: The data warehouse will provide comparative reporting capabilities for promoted versus nonpromoted shipments by geography, product, and manufacturer over time, allowing users of the data warehouse to compare themselves against the competition.

Technology oriented goals and objectives may also be included within your project's purpose statement. These typically include items such as building a subject-oriented data warehouse to verify the planned architecture and verify the architecture's requirements. Within this type of technical goal, you would work out any inconsistencies in the defined architecture and fix them before later projects and implementations.

You may also include certain operational-oriented goals. These goals allow you to better define the organization, standards, and methods you will use to support the data warehouse. An example here might be to gain an experience base and to define and develop the new support structures that permit long-term data warehouse development.

Stakeholder Identification

Stakeholders are the individuals who will benefit the most or be impacted the most by the delivery of the data warehouse. For this purpose, the stakeholders become the target audience, and you will need to gather significant information on them to best determine their needs. This information includes the audience's background, interests, job responsibilities, success measures, and all other detail helpful to shaping the information that will be delivered in the data warehouse. All of this information may not be complete at any specific time during the development process. However, a good collection system should be cultivated during the planning phase. Note, this data will be dynamic and change over time.

Therefore, a good collection system should allow the development team to identify stakeholders and manage any changes during the entire data warehouse development effort.

Critical Success Factors

The critical success factors of a data warehouse project should be clearly documented. This benefits the development team and company management in determining whether the development effort was a success. Much like the data warehouse initiative allows the business to better understand the key performance measures of the business, the data warehouse project should clearly define what success is. It is important that projects state what will be viewed as successful. For example, a data warehousing project typically views the following as criteria required for success.

- **One version of reality** The data warehouse will provide the enterprise with the ability to pull together information from a variety of sources at regular intervals to construct an integrated view of business activities—one version of reality of the business. This source may reside on different servers and be stored in a variety of relational and legacy systems. To be valuable for decision making, it must be transformed into a consistent view and distributed where needed. That is, the data must be placed within a target data warehouse environment. After the data has been placed in the data warehouse, support for open industry standard APIs should be provided to allow a high degree of interoperability and connectivity.
- **Quick and easy user access** To gain value from this information, rapid response to requests for information is crucial. The information must be delivered quickly, because data warehouse applications are becoming less batch oriented and more interactive. The result is no longer a report or presentation, but a strategic decision on which millions of dollars may ride. The tools that access a data warehouse must cross a reporting continuum that includes executive information systems, decision support systems, ad hoc queries, and production reporting.
- **User driven, not IS driven** The data and reports that are produced from a data warehouse should be what the users want and need—not what the Information Systems department wants to give the users. A major goal should be one that has the development staff filling the data and pushing data access and presentation tasks out to the users. In essence, get out of the report writing business that haunts all of us. If you build your warehouse properly, this is achievable.

- **Controllable** We want to provide users with everything they want, but do we also want to be able to control these deliverables? We don't want to, we need to! Control is a nebulous word, but in this context we mean controlling the processes of loading, the access methods, the security, and in general the system. Users want information and they want access from their tools to data, but they don't want to take this system away from us. As well, the data is a valuable asset of the corporation, so specific controls must be placed on this asset so it stays in the hands of the corporation, not of the competition.

If these items are successfully implemented, the project team will deliver to users the ability to use and integrate best-of-breed products throughout the data warehouse. This allows the company and users to choose the best vendor for each warehouse component, allowing a tailored solution to unique business requirements. At the same time, an infrastructure for flexible data distribution, including support for heterogeneous data and platforms, should be defined to allow the company to derive full value from its data warehousing investment.

Risks and Constraints

Every project has the potential for success or failure. Failures tend to stem directly from risks outside the project team's direct control. Each risk area should be completely defined prior to the project's full implementation. Within the analysis and design phase, the project team should build a contingency plan for each defined risk, determining how best to avoid any impact of it to the project.

Risks should be documented and communicated to all parties, especially the stakeholders, so that the stakeholders can assist in controlling the factors that minimize the risk. Risks fall into two areas: technical and business. Here are some examples.

- If you realize that certain expense issues will impede your ability to acquire proper resources such as equipment in time to begin development, this should be noted. You should then build an action plan for obtaining management commitment to extend your expense budget or lift the restriction prior to project commencement.
- If your project team doesn't have a great deal of experience with data warehousing, you will incur significant risk. You should document this and build a contingency plan for utilizing outside consultants and training programs to increase the knowledge base on which the data warehouse will be built.

- In many projects, division of control arises as a problem. Matrix-managed organizations have benefits; however, control is not one of them. Typically, the resources required to develop and implement a data warehouse project are obtained from multiple internal organizations. Without ultimate control over the budget and scheduling of these resources, you will incur significant risk, because the controlling entity may determine that the resource must be reassigned to its original organization prior to completion of its data warehouse tasks.
- Two huge risks that may stall commencement of a data warehouse project are lack of a user-organization sponsor and lack of a direct executive sponsor. These factors will force the data warehouse project to be driven by technologists, which means the project is destined to fail.
- An often overlooked risk is the transition that many organizations have made to an Information Systems buy versus build strategy. When Information Systems organizations migrate their applications portfolio outside the parent company, the focus on how best to manage and develop systems is lost. You should evaluate when the last large system was developed and deployed; and if it is not equivalent in scope to the data warehouse, you may be at risk. An organization that has lost its ability to develop in-house projects should seek the advice, knowledge transfer, and training of outside consulting firms.

All projects have problems at different points during their life cycle. These problems arise without warning and include budgetary freezes, team or resource reallocation, and loss of personnel. If these items are known before a project begins, define them as risks and build a contingency plan to avoid any major impact.

Your risk assessment process should be continuous throughout the project. When performing this assessment, you will define the risk and recommend an action plan to alleviate any impact based on the risk item. You hope that the item never occurs; but if it does, you need to be prepared. Within the spiral methodology shown in Figure 5.1, risks are identified within the planning phase. The assessment and contingency planning will be completed in the analysis and design phase.

Planning Tip 2: Remember that the initial plan is a starting point from which you will determine the size of a project. Managing this effectively means not overcommitting resources by negotiating major time or cost cuts within tasks. Until you reach final agreement on time, resources, and cost, the project plan will not be solidified.

Analysis and Design

The analysis and design phase of a data warehouse development effort better defines the details of a project's scope. The project management team begins to develop detailed answers to *what, how,* and *who* questions, such as the following.

- What information will be contained within the data warehouse?
- What alternatives are available for delivering the desired information and results to the user?
- How will the risks identified in the architecture and system planning phase be resolved and addressed to minimize their impact on the overall project?
- Who is the target audience?
- What details do we know about the target audience?

Answers to each of these questions and more will then be placed within the project's specification document. This document will assist the developers in delivering what is required for the development cycle.

Information Domain

Information domain refers to the data that provides users with their required business intelligence in the areas of subjects and measures. This information includes data that is presented to the users as well as supporting data that is required to deliver the requirements but is not presented to the users. The definition of the information domain provides the development team with information and knowledge that is required for them to do a good job. Your analysis should define the following.

- What data is required by the users?
- What supporting data will be required by the subject-oriented data warehouse?
- What business knowledge will the development team require to successfully deliver data to the users?
- Might any background information, such as current systems or potential outside data providers, provide the data?
- What is the plan for updating and maintaining the data?

The answer to these and many other questions will assist you in properly defining the overall requirements of a data warehouse development effort. To fully deliver the information domain, you need to attend to the following.

- Define overall requirements
- Document existing systems of record and systems environment
- Identify and rank the candidate applications that will utilize the data within the data warehouse
- Build a transition model that identifies dimensions, facts, and time stamping algorithms for extracting information from operational systems and for placing them in the data warehouse

The logical models that were built within the architectural phase provide an excellent starting point for your analysts. Those analysts will be able to take the previously collected logical models and contacts to begin delivering more detailed information on the source applications; that is, the *systems of record*. You will also be required to work with business executives and business analysts to determine what portion of this information is valuable for the data warehouse—in other words, what data is required to run the business. The business analysts and user community will be able to further define requirements such as the level of data granularity, the level of aggregation, the frequency of data loading, and the number of time periods to maintain.

The quality of the information domain affects the users' perceptions of the data warehouse's overall quality. Inaccurate or incomplete information hinders a data warehouse's ability to satisfy users. The users must assist the design team in validating that the information domain is accurate, updated, and complete. This will be done through a series of review tasks in which the design team gradually obtains more detailed information about the user requirements and proceeds to document and present them to the users for verification. Additional periodic checks should be scheduled throughout the development process to validate the requirements.

Verifying the accuracy, currency, and completeness of an information domain is a difficult task. The verification process requires that the analyst develop adequate knowledge of the subject matter and user base to make a judgment with regard to the information domain.

Alternative Evaluation

Every time you begin a development project, you should evaluate available alternative solutions. Questions, as shown next, should be asked at the start of a data warehouse development and continuously during the project. New products and solutions will evolve, and someone else may develop a data warehouse solution that accomplishes the objectives of your project for your audience in a more cost effective manner.

- Is the purpose already accomplished elsewhere within the enterprise's information systems?
- Does a publicly available software product solve the entire problem, or is it a partial solution?
- Are incomplete solutions available in either of the above places? Are they 50 percent, 60 percent, 70 percent, or more of the overall required system?

Risk Resolution Planning

As noted in the planning section of this chapter, risk assessment and resolution planning occur within the analysis and design phase. Here, you need to assign a seasoned software professional to lead a team in formulating a plan to alleviate and avoid any of the previously defined risks.

For example, we had a project that was delivered by a remote and highly mobile project team. Because they were quite a distance from the project site, we made sure to define mother nature as a risk. To address this risk, we implemented a remote development strategy. Mother nature gave us very bad weather, but the impact on the project was minimal because we had built a virtual office concept from the beginning to avert this risk. This contingency plan allowed us to fend off potential problems that the weather imposed, assisting us in achieving the goals and objectives set for the project. Resources were able to work from home when the snow made travelling hazardous.

The project management team must assign sufficient priority and resources to complete a risk assessment and contingency plan. If the proper resources and time are not assigned to this effort, the risks may greatly impact the project team's ability to successfully deliver the required software components and applications.

Target Audience Information

Information about the target audience is crucial for a successful data warehouse. The data warehouse analysts should define the target audience and the specifics of information that are important to them.

An adequate description of the users, needs and wants should be developed. Such documentation will greatly assist in the overall development process. For example, a developer may want to provide information to "brand managers who are interested in promotional success rates." Although this is a generalization, it serves as a valuable guide for developing many of the elements in data warehouses. One effective way of defining your audience is to generate a knowledge chart, as shown in Figure 5.3, that maps high-level user organizations with data warehouse components such as subject areas and measures. This chart is a building block that will be compiled and developed over the entire data warehousing process. You will continue to flesh out additional details of the information domain and users as well as their security and access needs.

Target Audience

Information Domain	Plant Management	Production	Material Management	Plant Accounting	Process Engineering	Business Groups	Corporate Controller/Accounting	Manufacturing Management	Sales Planning	Distribution & Logistics	Quality Assurance	Customer Service
Inventory Locations	O	A	K	A	A	K	K	A	K	A	A	
Customer				K		O	A		A	A	K	A
Product	A	K	K	A	K	A	A	O	A	A	A	A
Process Line	A	A	K	K	O		K	A		K	A	
Shipment Methods	K			A	A	K	K		A	O		A
Process Events	K	K			O			K		A	A	
Capaign Status	A	A	K	A	K	K	K	A	O	K	K	K
Lot	A	K	O	A				K			K	A
Conformance to Schedule	K	O			K	A		K			K	
Cycle Time	K		O					K		K		
First Pass Prime	K	O			A			K				
Disposition Prime	K	O			A			K				
On Stream Time	K	O			K	K		K	K			
On Time Shipments	K		O			K					A	
Inventory Transactions	K		O	A					K			
WIP Inventory	K		O	A					K			
Rework Savings	K	O						K	A			
Transition Index	K	O	A						K			

LEGEND
O = The user organization owns the information
A = The user organization requires access to the information
K = The user organization occasionally needs to know the data

Figure 5.3: *Knowledge chart defining the requirements of target audiences in relation to information domains*

To complete the chart, list the information domain data associated with subject areas and key performance measures in the rows of the chart. Then, take the defined user constituencies and place them in the columns of the chart. At each intersecting cell of a user and an information entity, place a letter defining how or if the user will require the data.

Specification Assembly

As a data warehousing project proceeds, specifications should be built for each component defined within the information domain. These components should include those that are presented to the user and those that are required to compile the information required by the user. The detail designs behind these specifications evolve in concert with the development process. The primary purpose at this point is to provide a valid reference point for detail design activity and acceptance testing criteria.

The specifications refine the goals and objectives in more specific terms. The detailing of these statements includes adding a layer of constraints, business rules, and other requirements. It also includes mapping them to the architectural components of the data warehouse. These requirements may restrict or further describe what the data warehouse development effort will offer and how it will be presented to the user.

For example, a specification might take the following objective statement and map it as in Figure 5.4: *The data warehouse provides comparative reporting capabilities for promoted versus nonpromoted shipments by geography, product, and manufacturer over time, allowing the users of the data warehouse to compare themselves to the competition.*

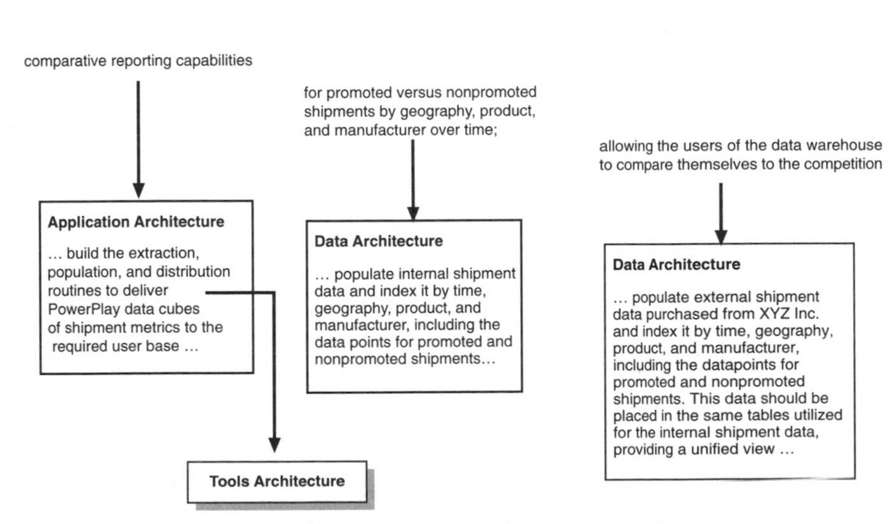

Figure 5.4: *Sample specification mapping*

A specification acts as a guidebook for the implementers who create the actual data warehouse components. The specification should fully document the applications, data, and technology components (including tools) to utilize in delivery of the distinct data warehouse parts. The specification should also identify any restrictions based on standards, guidelines, or policies previously defined for the project.

After completion, the specifications provide a baseline reference for developing detail designs, and system and acceptance tests. Precise tracking and disciplined change control must be implemented from these specifications. As the system evolves and requirements are modified, you should refer back to these documents and reevaluate the impact of any modifications. After the development effort is concluded, you will also be able to utilize these documents for testing purposes. Every test should be correlated with both the specifications and the requirements so that every required function is tested.

Analysis and Design Tip 1: All project objectives and requirements for a data warehouse and associated data marts should be mapped to one or more components within the standard architecture. If the mapping cannot occur, the architecture or the requirements are incomplete.

Implementation

We keep coming back to the global statement that a data warehouse is a user driven system. Users strongly associate implementation aspects of a data warehouse with its *look and feel*. This is a front-end focus. The development team must also focus on the back-end and mid-tier process of a data warehouse to guarantee consistency and performance. A good design accounts for all of the previously defined elements—the purpose, goals, objectives, success factors, risks, constraints, audience, and information domain—and combines them to produce a plan for properly implementing a data warehouse.

Throughout the development process, the development team will gain a better understanding of the data warehousing process and user requirements. Very practical issues are involved in the implementation of a data warehouse, such as how the user will access the information, from which the development team will gain a sense of judgment and experience. This allows the team to begin delivering the ultimate data warehouse. Staff members will evolve a sense of design and development into an art form required by the users.

A successful data warehouse implementation requires interlocking development processes to guarantees that all elements work in concert and harmony to provide the user with the proper system. The analysis and design process was greatly influenced by the knowledge of what is possible within the data warehouse. The implementation process begins to focus on the best way to physically implement the design.

Detail Design

Most individuals, users and technical staff, can only handle and process manageable quantities of information at one time. Your detail design work should be broken into manageable chunks that allow the design team to deliver components that will not overwhelm users. The detail design of data warehouse components involves several tasks, including the following.

- **Packaging the information** Your detail design needs to crystallize the needs of users and complete the model for the data, including the dimensional hierarchies and business measures required to deliver the required business intelligence. These detail designs will specify access mechanisms and further define standardized data structures.
- **Mapping data structures to operational data stores** The information package will proceed to map to the operational data sources in a corporation. These maps and data definitions should be placed in the metadata repository. As the map evolves, so will the transformation logic required to deliver data to the warehouse.
- **Detailing physical requirements** The rules and configuration management information will be physically defined to the data warehouse metadata repository. These items include factors such as business rules or constraints, distribution or replication requirements, indexes, and partitioning strategies.
- **Build user applications** Depending on the choices made within the architecture, the detail plan will need to define the applications and tools that will be utilized by the user to access the newly placed data in the warehouse.
- **Determining quality tasks** It is important to define the data integrity process in your detail design. This allows the development process to begin performing data validation so that the resultant information package contains the right data.

It is important to realize that no silver bullet can solve the data warehousing dilemma. You will find vendors offering tools for automating design and delivery mechanisms will make promises that border on the absurd. There is no replacement for the experience that your development teams will gather within the detail design process and the lessons they learn in earlier projects. Structure and standards from the onset—that is, doing it right—is the best way to guarantee future successes for your data warehouse team.

Code

Coding is probably a misnomer here. But it is used to signify that your resources will be physically implementing the system. This means the following.

- The database administrator will build or modify the physical data structures that house the new data and that are populated in this development cycle
- The development resources will build the transformation routines and integration logic to move data from the source to the warehouse, massaging the data as required along the way to fully populate the data structures
- The administrative staff will also begin to automate the extraction, movement, and transformation processes as well as other administrative tasks such as backup and recovery schemes

The desired outcome of these tasks is to build a component, subject-oriented data warehouse that can be integrated into the overall enterprise data warehouse architecture and released to the users.

Unit Testing

After individual components have been built, the process of testing them commences, as shown in Figure 5.5. Unit testing verifies single programs, stored procedures, and other modules in an isolated test environment. Unit testing is often done by the development resource person who produced the code, because he or she best understands what the component does. The project management staff must be aware of this, because developers are biased and understand all too well what the component being tested is supposed to do. Those who create system faults are typically the least likely to recognize them. While this poses a negative aura around this process, unit testing generally yields the highest number of detected problems within all testing techniques.

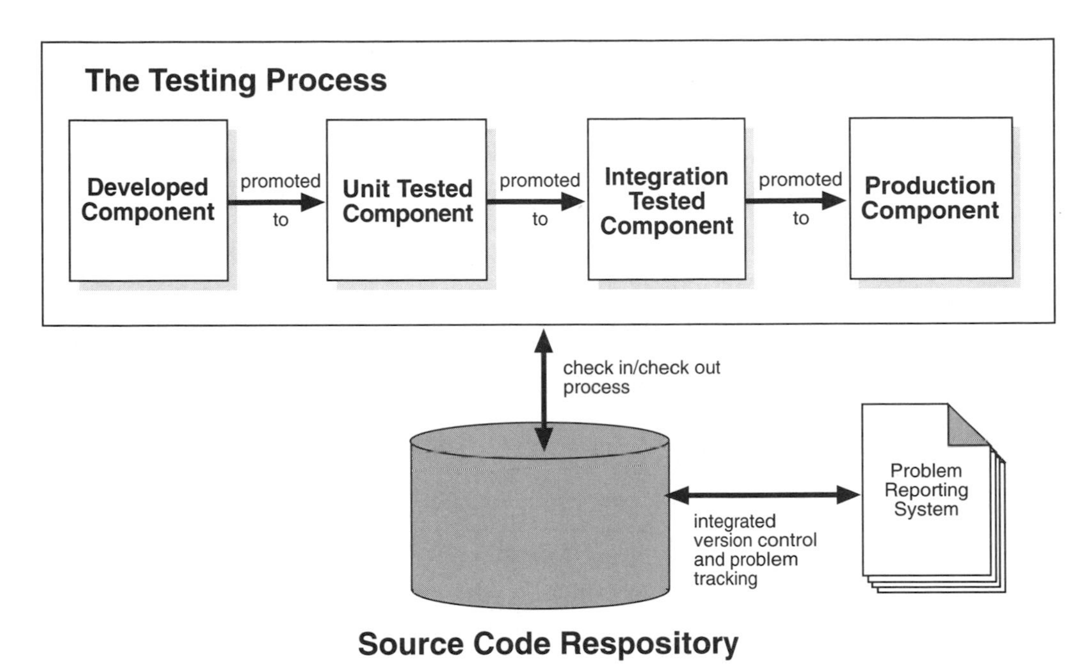

Figure 5.5: *Automation of testing, problem tracking, and version control*

Integration Testing

Integration tests take the individual components and verify their interfaces with other components of the overall data warehouse system and subsystems. As opposed to unit testing, which is typically done by the programmer, integration testing should be done by a dedicated quality assurance team.

The test team should take completed data warehouse components and perform extensive function and regression tests. Functional testing verifies that the components in fact have been built to deliver the functionality defined in the external specifications. Regression testing incorporates previous test cases, executing these items to verify that the new functional component has not adversely affected the items that are currently in the production system.

Each of these testing techniques should be utilized to gather data on the quality of all delivered components, as shown in Figure 5.5. Testing should fully exercise the system and determine if it is ready for release to users. Effective test planning and execution starts with the overall development plan that defines the functions, roles, and methods for all components within a data warehouse. Each testing scenario should be carefully controlled and recorded so that errors resulting from the test can be reproduced. The test results should then be detailed and retained for further use by the development staff. Problems always occur in development projects. The testing phase and testing team should be targeted to detect and uncover any deficiencies that will hinder the development project from achieving its objectives. After a component is fully tested, it is ready to be deployed.

Architecture Tip 3: Quality obviously is important; the guaranteed pursuit of quality should be too. Therefore, be sure to design an automated quality system in your architecture so that you can automate the testing process and more efficiently perform your integration testing.

Deployment

After a data warehouse is built, you must guarantee success by formally defining a deployment strategy. This includes the concepts of training users, obtaining their acceptance and feedback, and generally promoting the availability of the data warehouse throughout the enterprise.

The constantly increasing and changing needs of users and the flood of localized systems make launching a data warehouse a difficult task. However, you need to leverage your steering committee and executive sponsor to gain and keep the attention of your users through this last, critical phase.

Training

Training users how to use your delivered components is extremely important to the overall acceptance and usage of a data warehouse. Your user community has grown accustomed to receiving data in various reports, spreadsheets, extracts, and locally developed systems. This will be the first time they have a system that allows them to go to one place to receive all of this information. The training should focus on the following points.

- An introduction to data warehouse concepts
- A users' view of the data model
- Where the data that populates the data warehouse has been obtained
- How users access the data warehouse
- How any standard reports or applications that you have provided will assist users in obtaining warehouse information

- A clear definition of the tools and the type of analysis each tool provides
- How to utilize the tools provided in the architecture

Training should be provided by seasoned trainers, not the development staff. Educators have a way of communicating with and understanding the needs of their students that developers may lack. The course should be conducted close to the users' environment and should include ample exercises that demonstrate how the data warehouse delivers the users' requirements.

Acceptance

Acceptance testing validates that the system or a component of the data warehouse system matches the users' requirements. In an acceptance test, you should validate that the software can be installed and operated effectively within the users' environment. It is also advisable to conduct usability tests with the users. Usability tests involve simple observation of members from the target audience using a data warehouse in their own setting. Areas that are important to observe include the following.

- How users interact with the components of the data warehouse
- How users accomplish their work with the data warehouse
- Whether the data warehouse fails to meet the users' needs in accomplishing their work
- How the data warehouse might be expanded or better service users

If possible, videotape the usability testing sessions and interviews. This may be difficult, depending on the size of the enterprise. Larger companies should try to develop a usability lab in which video equipment can be hidden from users to make them more at ease. Smaller organizations may require additional time to allow users to develop comfort with the camera. Either way, videotaping is an effective tool for providing feedback to your development staff.

Acceptance tests clearly define any shortcomings that exist in the delivered components as well as provide valuable feedback for the development staff in the areas of usability, content improvement, accuracy of data, and required alternate views into the data warehouse. And, yes, the video can also provide positive feedback to the development staff. Often, we forget that happy users motivate a development staff. If we clearly specify the requirements and deliver what users wants, they will display a satisfying image on the video from which the development staff can glow with pride. These positive videos may also provide support to the project management team in justifying spending associated with subsequent data warehouse development phases.

Deployment Tip 1: A system is not complete until it is fully accepted by the user community. Only the user can say, "Done!"

Promotion

The main goal of promoting the completed components of a data warehouse is to keep users informed about data warehouse content. During the promotion of a new data warehouse, it is important to obtain skills in areas such as public relations and mass communication. Because a data warehouse is a dynamic environment involving additional development cycles, you may want to develop a standard promotional forum that is continually upgraded to keep users informed.

At times—primarily during the introduction of new components for a data warehouse—users will experience information overload. So, make sure to build the proper infrastructure to give users an educational continuum and to give developers ongoing feedback. Forums such as Lotus Notes discussion databases, e-mail, Usenet newsgroups, and World Wide Web sites are prime targets for such forums.

Formal Review

The corporate data warehouse architecture team should reconvene after each completed data warehouse development project to determine if the architecture is in fact valid and working. More than likely, a majority of the architecture will be viewed as sound, while several improvements may be noted. This should be further documented within the standard-bearer document and enforced in further development efforts. And, importantly, it should be retrofitted to the current implementation of any subject-oriented data warehouse or the initial project to constitute a standard. A course to transfer the knowledge and standards regarding the process and architecture should be developed to guarantee future successes.

Summary

We have entered an era in which an entire market cycle can begin and end in 18 months. Competition is global, customer loyalty is fleeting, and the window of opportunity is narrow. In this business climate, the advantage goes to the company that can most quickly sift through massive amounts of information—historical, geographic, across business units, and across product lines. Information on how to respond to a product opportunity, a competitive threat, a trade imbalance, or a political challenge can be mined from the data contained across the various departments within an organization.

Extracting this information from a morass of data means redefining the very concept of decision support. Managers need to operate in discovery mode, constructing their queries on the fly. Overnight batch reports are no longer adequate, because even a simple question about pricing can lead to more detailed queries about the enterprise's operations, such as the following.

- What products did our competitors advertise?
- Where are we losing market share?
- What is our tolerance for a price differential versus that of our competition?
- Are volumes for store brands increasing or decreasing?

The ability to quickly ask follow-up questions allows a manager to better understand the business environment before making a critical decision. The thirst for interactive access to information coupled with the promise of rapid response has become the focus of today's data warehouses.

A data warehouse's evolution is iterative in nature. You won't get the data warehouse right on the first pass. Business analysts and executive users will discover new information that they need as they become proficient in using a data warehouse. Therefore, it is important to develop a project management and life-cycle philosophy in which you will deliver smaller projects at a more rapid pace than in traditional systems development. The spiral information packaging development methodology is recommended for delivery of data warehouse components, or subject-oriented data warehouses, because it achieves such results. Within this methodology, you should work in four primary disciplines.

- **Architecture and systems planning** Within the planning phase, you define your development and provide a comprehensive plan on its proposed delivery.
- **Analysis and design** During the analysis and design phase, you further specify and gain users' concurrence on the development effort deliverables.
- **Implementation** During the implementation phase, you build the components to be placed in the data warehouse system and architecture.

- **Deployment** Upon completion of development and testing, you deploy the system to the user community with a lot of training and a little flair. This phase should guarantee usage of the corporate knowledge base.

Following an entire development cycle, the architecture team should reconvene and perform a review of the architectural blueprint. Did the architecture withstand the users' requirements? Do areas of the architecture require enhancement? Could new technologies improve the architecture? Answers to these and other questions allow the architecture team to keep the architecture up to date and capable of delivering the corporation's information requirements.

Because a data warehouse is a dynamic environment based on constantly changing data and business processes, the development process is never complete. You will continue to develop additional components for your data warehouse. As you will see in Chapter 6, Formulating a Project Team, you may want to develop a strategy that allows your development team to clone itself and proceed with multiple development cycles in parallel, or you may choose to have one focused team. Either way, after you complete your first subject-oriented data warehouse, it will be time to proceed to the next.

6

Formulating a Project Team

Any consideration of the life and larger social existence of the modern corporate man ... begins and also largely ends with the effect of one all-embracing force. That is organization—the highly structured assemblage of men, and now some women, of which he is a part. It is to this, at the expense of family, friends, sex, recreation, and sometimes health and effective control of alcoholic intake, that he is expected to devote his energies.

—*John Kenneth Galbraith*

One of the most difficult concepts for management to recognize is that the course of developing software in new areas is a human-intensive process. As the development process evolves, people learn new skills and find different ways to solve problems. Enterprises often feel that their problems are unique. However, it has been our experience that most companies face similar problems—and most of these problems have been solved before, often within the same organization. Software professionals need a higher degree of assistance in areas including the following.

- Controlling requirements and project scope
- Planning a project and individual tasks
- Managing a project's timing process, including interdependencies
- Resolving system design issues
- Coordinating the change-management process

In the process of developing software, people are the most important ingredient. Leadership is required to stabilize and standardize the development process. Most projects require a stable management team with the conviction to deliver upon long-term requirements and improvements to business systems and infrastructure. This management team sets challenging goals, monitors the progress, and insists on performance.

Better people clearly do better work. You want to formulate the best team possible for your data warehouse projects. However, realize that you have several factors against you when trying to formulate your project teams. Superior skill sets in any specialized area are in short supply. You need to realize that talent is a relative term. Therefore, you should place a strong focus on gaining a team with a mix of maturity, attitude, and skill.

- Maturity provides the team with proper leadership and support, guiding the team to do better work than at present.
- Attitude is everything. Those professionals in the software industry who view themselves as experts and no longer in need of training are worth little to your project. You need individuals who believe that anything is possible and can be implemented. As well, these individuals should have the attitude that life is a continuum of educational experiences and that they still have much to learn.
- A key skill for your project team is knowledge of the application area supported by the subject-oriented data warehouse being constructed. When this knowledge base is coupled with proper design techniques, a quality deliverable results.

Knowledge Cloning

When you begin the process of developing data warehouse solutions, your development process will be immature. Even after following the framework and guidelines within this book, your process will not be solidified until you have been through the process and develop your organization's way of delivering data warehouses. You should therefore start your first project with a foundation team that will be the experience base for future projects. This team will be split and cloned over time to expand the knowledge of how to build, in rapid progression, your data warehouse and how to groom the development process to your enterprise. Figure 6.1 illustrates the concept of project knowledge cloning.

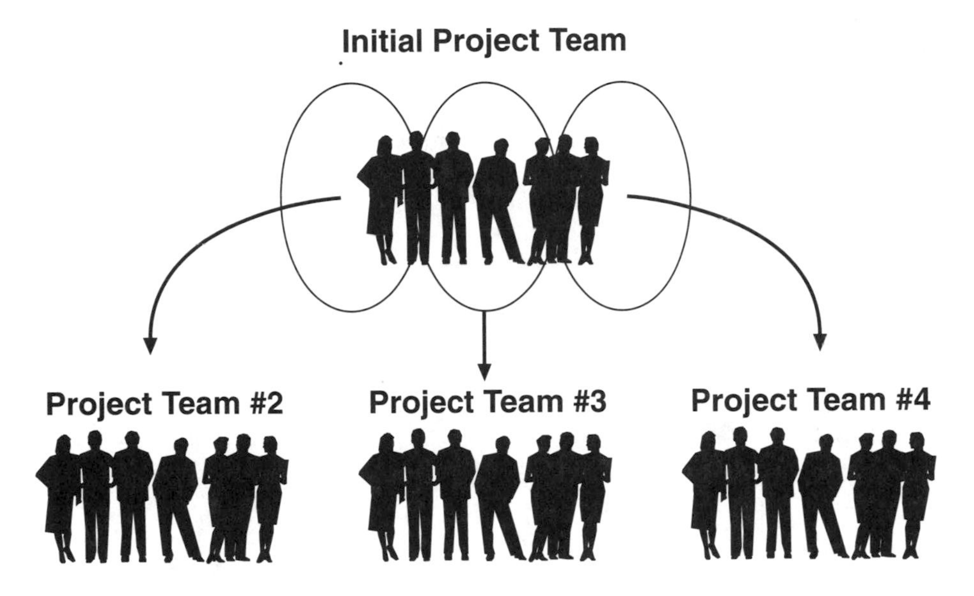

Figure 6.1: *The project knowledge cloning process*

While the need for dedicated resources to improve the development process may seem obvious, it is surprising how often organizations avoid allocating such resources. A matrix-style organization in which managers rely on borrowing or reassigning their people as needed has become commonplace. However, it is key to build and clone a strong knowledge base throughout an organization when entering into such a new technology. This knowledge cloning pays off by improving the software development process in areas such as planning, automation, testing, training, and quality.

Planning Tip 3: It is nearly impossible to build a "dream team" with any sort of staying power. Be sure to define a longer-term strategy that supports the needs of your initial team. Satisfying your goals and your people's goals enhances your ability to succeed.

The Project Management Team

From our experience, each project requires a focused project management team. The role of any project management team is to ensure that the project is successfully completed.

This management team must verify the meaning of success and completion within its individual projects. This management team is mandated with the tasks of properly planning, designing, and monitoring the progress of a data warehouse development effort until its completion. The foundation for this project management team is a commitment to discipline.

Commitment is fundamental to the success of any software development effort and is met by committed people—not by plans, reviews, standards, procedures, or tools. The people in this core management team utilize these components to make their commitment; this will become their system for managing future projects. Their management system will then formalize how natural conflicts between the projects and line or staff organizations are resolved.

The core project management team consists of highly skilled personnel in focused roles. Because the best software people are always overcommitted, you should guarantee that these individuals will focus on making your enterprise successful at data warehousing. This guarantee means that, while you may not have the overall best resource for a task, you will have a focused team that provides the best focused skill set. The primary core team consists of a project manager, an architect, and a database administrator. We examine the responsibilities and the desirable background for each of these team members in the next sections.

Project Manager

The project manager is in essence the team leader. With this role, the project manager manages the day-to-day activities of the entire project team and is accountable for all deliverables. The project manager is required to provide the discipline for managing successful projects. Thus, the manager coordinates and provides detailed plans, tracking systems, and periodic reviews of the project at both the technical and management levels. A technical background generally helps, but is not essential. It is, however, essential that the project manager be capable of understanding how technology can solve the business requirements of users. As stated in Chapter 2, What Factors Drive a Successful Data Warehouse Project?, the project manager and other core project team members are required to visualize the desires and needs of users and guide the project team to that end. The responsibilities of a project manager are many and varied, including the following.

- Resource management
- Project plan development

- Project team selection and composition
- Project and task estimating
- Work breakdown structure development
- Scheduling and interdependency management
- Project tracking
- Resource coordination
- Project status communication
- Conflict resolution

Ideally, a project manager will have the following experience and educational background.

- Project management and conflict resolution
- Interviewing skills
- Business systems analysis and design
- Decision support system analysis and design
- Fundamentals of Structured Query Language (SQL)
- Relational database design and modeling techniques
- Client/server system design
- Graphical user interface design
- Quality management systems and testing

Lead Architect

The lead architect is essentially the technical project manager and lead designer of the overall system. While this role is often overlooked when formulating project teams, we view this person as a critical component of a successful project management team. The lead architect is required to provide the best implementation of technology to support the business' requirements. This person should be technically competent and have a good working relationship with the project manager. The compatibility between your project manager and lead architect is a key ingredient to successful delivery of the required systems. If these two individuals do not effectively communicate and work as a team, you will seldom accomplish the required level of commitment. Therefore, the project manager should be highly involved in the selection process of a lead architect. Responsibilities of a lead architect include the following.

- Develop business conceptual model
- Design system architecture
- Work with individual team members to deliver data and process models
- Work with the business analyst to develop a logical design
- Verify all physical designs
- Develop test plans
- Direct and coordinate quality control and quality assurance
- Handle technical design and prioritization of enhancements and changes

The experience and educational background of a lead architect should include the following.

- System architecture planning and development
- Business systems analysis and design
- Decision support system analysis and design
- Fundamentals of operating systems such as UNIX, MVS, and Microsoft Windows
- Fundamentals of Structured Query Language (SQL)
- Relational database design and modeling techniques
- Relational database performance and tuning
- Client/server system design
- Client/server system performance and tuning
- Graphical user interface design
- Quality management systems and testing

Database Administrator

The database administrator (DBA) is in charge of the enterprise data model developed for a data warehouse. It is critical that the model be built and cultivated from the beginning. This person develops a set of comprehensive standards to which each individual development team adheres. Because a data warehouse is a data driven technology, you would be remiss not to include a database expert on your core project management team. Among the responsibilities of a database administrator are the following.

- Develop data standards
- Design data model
- Work with the business analyst to develop logical data design
- Verify all physical data designs (tables, columns, triggers, stored procedures, data access techniques, indexes, data placement, and so forth)
- Technical design and prioritization of data enhancements and changes

A database administrator should have experience and an educational similar to the following.

- Business systems analysis and design
- Decision support system analysis and design
- Fundamentals of operating systems such as UNIX, MVS, and Microsoft Windows
- Fundamentals of Structured Query Language (SQL)
- Relational database design and modeling techniques
- Database management and administration
- Relational database performance and tuning

Executive Sponsor

Having the proper sponsor is critical for the success of a data warehouse. The project sponsor must be a high-level executive within the company who controls a majority of the business processes affected by the data warehouse. Examples of the proper sponsor include the vice president of sales, vice president of marketing, vice president of manufacturing, and vice president of operations. This person will become the driving force to correctly complete your project. He or she gives the project credibility beyond a traditional development project. Support by an executive delivers a strategic vision and the respect of the entire organization to a data warehouse, assisting you in accessing information that would be difficult to receive without this support. This information may come from interviewing someone who typically would not see you, from documents that are viewed as strategic to the company, or from general insight of what the company views as strategic. Your project's sponsor allows you to apply a sense of urgency with those from whom you need to obtain information, thus avoiding unnecessary delays.

The Steering Committee

It is wise to establish a steering committee composed of leaders or business analysts from targeted user communities. This steering committee is a high-level, decision-making authority with guidance or direction from the executive sponsor. Some sponsors actively manage steering committees, while others manage through delegation. Either way, both the sponsor and the steering committee provide the required user backing to make your project successful.

A steering committee should comprise three to five members of the user community, typically business analysts who support the management of the business function for which you are developing the data warehouse. The committee's role is to provide the project with direction and guarantee that the project obtains all of the required resources to achieve the project's goals. From a high level, this committee assists the project manager in the decision-making process. It in essence is the consumer who is paying the bills for the development effort you are undertaking. In this role, the steering committee must manage a high-level agenda that includes creating policies and procedures for change control and resolving issues outside the development process. This team and the sponsor should meet with the project management team on a regular basis to assist in guiding the project to a successful completion.

The Project Resource Pool

A resource pool that allows a flexible deployment of resource people to critical projects should be established in addition to the project management team. These resources, as shown in Figure 6.2, should be trained in the standard development process and should begin to develop an overall understanding of data warehouse applications development. These resources may initially be allocated to a team and, upon completion of their individual tasks, be quickly reassigned to another team to begin its development work. These resources should align themselves with the specific disciplines required to build a successful development team, including foundation, content, application, and implementation. We look at each of these resources separately in the following sections.

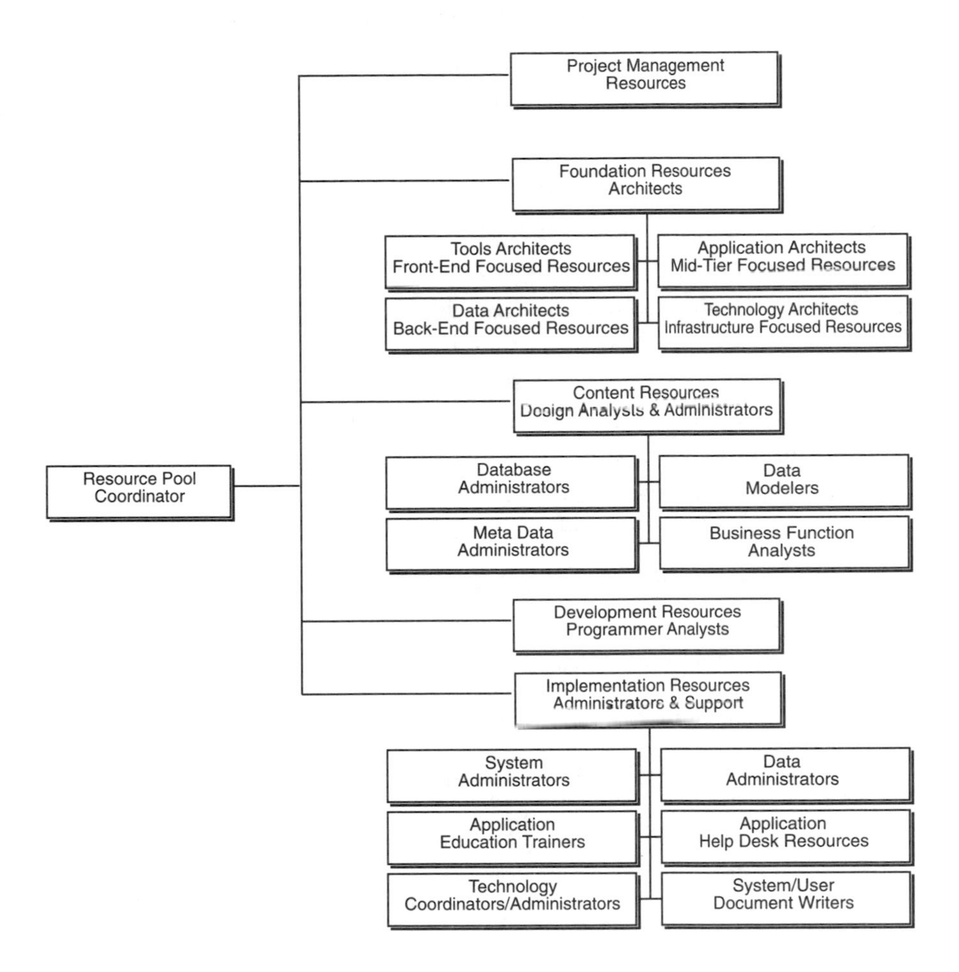

Figure 6.2: *Project resources pool*

Foundation Resources

The foundation resources should be composed of an architect pool. Though the project management team will contain a lead architect, we recommend that you cultivate and develop architects with expertise in primary data warehousing areas. The individuals who are responsible for these areas include the following.

- **Front-end architects** focus on the applications and tool sets utilized by users to access a data warehouse. Their tasks control the user interface, access patterns, and look and feel of client-side processing involved with a data warehouse.
- **Mid-tier architects** focus on the middle-tier processing requirements of a data warehouse, which include tasks such as data transformation, data merging, and other process-heavy deliverables. Their experience provides smooth integration of legacy systems and front-end data access components.
- **Back-end architects** focus on legacy data store access requirements and other server-side components of a data warehouse. These tasks include connectivity, data manipulation, replication technologies, and global data dictionaries deliverables. The experience of back-end architects provides the link to existing systems and to how best to access these systems. These architects should have a comprehensive knowledge of the data assets within the company, allowing the team to best determine where a subject or measure entity should be obtained. Depending on the size of your enterprise and data warehouse needs, these positions may be merged with those of the mid-tier architects.
- **Technology architects** focus on the technology infrastructure to support the roll out and deployment of a data warehouse. Their roles include tasks for system, network, and communication as well as software component selection.

Responsibilities of foundation resource personnel include the following.

- Develop individual architectures
- Assist in overall system architecture
- Deliver individual models (data, process, and technology)
- Integrate architecture components
- Provide physical designs for individual architectures
- Develop test plans for individual architectures
- Direct and coordinate quality control and quality assurance for individual architectures

The experience and educational requirements for foundation resources should focus on the following.

- Planning and development for individual architectures

- Business systems analysis and design
- Decision support system analysis and design
- Fundamentals of operating systems such as UNIX, MVS, and Microsoft Windows
- Fundamentals of Structured Query Language (SQL)
- Design and modeling techniques for individual architectures
- Performance and tuning for individual architectures
- Quality management systems and their testing

Content Resources

Content resources are composed of design analysts and administrators. These resources are tasked with designing and delivering the content of a data warehouse. They work closely with the project management team and coordinate the activities of the development resources to guarantee deliverables in a standard manner. The resources in this category include database administrators, data modelers, metadata administrators, and business or function analysts. We look at each of these roles separately in the sections that follow.

Database Administrators

Database administrators provide data definition expertise. These DBAs are the corporate guideline and standards custodians for the data managed by an enterprise. Their responsibilities include the following.

- Maintaining the corporate data model
- Creating and enforcing data standards and guidelines
- Supporting modeling sessions
- Conducting reviews of database physical models and implementation

Database administrators should have the following experience and educational background.

- Decision support system analysis and design
- Fundamentals of operating systems such as UNIX, MVS, and Microsoft Windows

- Fundamentals of Structured Query Language (SQL)
- Relational database design and modeling techniques
- Relational database performance and tuning
- Physical database management and administration

Data Modelers

Data modelers own the overall database design rules. In smaller organizations, the database administrator is tasked with data modeling responsibilities. But as an organization grows, the two responsibilities diverge. Data modelers have these responsibilities.

- Conduct logical database design reviews
- Conduct physical database design walk-through
- Assist developers with database design issues
- Maintain SQL coding standards
- Assist system and database administrators with tuning, design, and control extracts

The experience and educational background of data modelers should include the following.

- Decision support system analysis and design
- Fundamentals of Structured Query Language (SQL)
- Relational database design and modeling techniques
- Relational database performance and tuning

Metadata Administrators

Metadata administrators are the owners of the data warehouse metadata repository. The metadata repository contains information on current data warehouse database definitions as well as historical operational data designs and transformation data mappings. Currently, most organizations do not have such a role; this role is typically merged with the role of the database administrator. However, as more subject-oriented data warehouses are brought on-line in an enterprise, the need for a repository manager grows. It is advisable to begin segmenting these responsibilities to best manage your growth. Candidates for this position include object managers and former repository or librarian employees. The responsibilities for metadata administrators include those that follow.

- Versioning of metadata
- Data sourcing
- Data quality

Metadata administrators should have the following experience and educational credentials.

- Fundamentals of Structured Query Language (SQL)
- Librarian, object management, and version control systems and techniques

Business or Functional Analysts

Business, or functional, analysts provide the project team with business knowledge and perspective. These resources typically evolve from analysts who previously supported a user organization or executive in the formulation of business data. These resources are abundant in most large organizations, though migrating them into a development role may be difficult. Business analysts are the brain trust behind current decision support systems. Therefore, user organizations must see the value of releasing management control of this resource to the data warehouse project team. The responsibilities of business analysts include the following.

- Provides support and detail for the project team
- User requirements definition
- Logical design of user requirements

Business analysts should have the following experience or educational credentials.

- Fundamentals of Structured Query Language (SQL)
- Fundamentals of business systems design
- Fundamentals of decision support system design
- Fundamentals of graphical user interface design

Development Resources

Development resources are the builders of a data warehouse. They take specifications from the design specialists and physically implement them. The largest contribution of development resources to the design of the system involves identifying design deficiencies. Other than that, they specifically need to develop the subsystems and components that have been designed by the architects and content specialists. Responsibilities of development resources staff include the following.

- Assist designers with deficiencies in data design, process design, and project standards
- Assist the project management team (primarily the database administrator and architect) in defining coding standards
- Develop and unit test program logic, including user interfaces, reports, screens, and menus
- Assist the system administrator with the application-specific areas of system management, including batch schedules and process tuning
- Identify physical database design deficiencies and develop alternatives
- Work with quality personnel to resolve any defects arising in application program modules

Development resources should bring the following experience or educational requirements to their role.

- Fundamentals of operating systems such as UNIX, MVS, and Microsoft Windows
- Fundamentals of Structured Query Language (SQL)
- Relational database performance and tuning, including coding proper access mechanisms such as stored procedures
- Client/server system performance and tuning
- Graphical user interface design
- Specific tools training as required (such as PowerBuilder, C++, Impromptu, and PowerPlay)

Implementation Resources

Implementation resources are tasked with supporting and servicing the deployed data warehouse and associated architectural environment. These resources function as the organization that trains users how to use what has been developed for the data warehouse. They also are the organization that assures that the data warehouse is operational.

Technology Administration

The technology administration team supports and maintains the data warehouse environment, which includes the functions of a help desk and the technology coordinator for the data warehouse user tool set. Technology administration oversees the administration, installation, preparation, and use of the tool set for accessing the data warehouse.

The technology administration team also is the logical owner of the production data warehouse. With these responsibilities, technology administration personnel focus on delivering high-quality, integrated data and the associated repository of metadata. The metadata must have information on current operational database definitions as well as historical data or prior designs and metadata versioning. The technology administration has the following responsibilities.

- Help desk and support
- Technology coordination and vendor support
- Software distribution
- Workgroup computing supplies
- Hardware and software installation
- Configuration management
- Network administration
- Systems administration
- Data administration

Training and User Documentation

The training and user documentation organization should focus on delivering proper information to users about how best to utilize the system and obtain support. The responsibilities of this team form a short list, as follows.

- User documentation
- Training of users

Consultants

Consultants may be used from time to time, primarily to fill holes in the resource pool. However, early in the evolution of your enterprise's data warehouse strategy you may desire to seek the advice of a consultant to assist in the proactive and positive commencement of the project. Consultants are available in a wide range of skill, including technology guidance and methodology direction. These consultants can assist you in supplementing or cultivating your enterprise's talent in areas such as quality of deliverables and preparation of reports and presentations (especially to executives). Consultants can assist in and ensure your success through support, training, and mentorship.

Planning Tip 4: Hourly rate should not be a decision criterion for selecting resources from the world of consulting. Experience and ability to stand behind a project far outweigh the hourly cost. Your consultants should be held accountable. Make sure their company guarantees their work.

Project Work Flow

After a project team is assembled, the work flow follows a relatively traditional pattern, as shown in Figure 6.3. Designs, specifications, and standards will be developed within the core project team. From this team's lead, additional project development teams will follow, implementing a common set of practices shaped within your enterprise. The work of these teams will be completed and passed along to the project implementation team, which will be responsible for the successful roll out and deployment of data warehouse technology. Their tasks include documentation, training, and continual support of the user community.

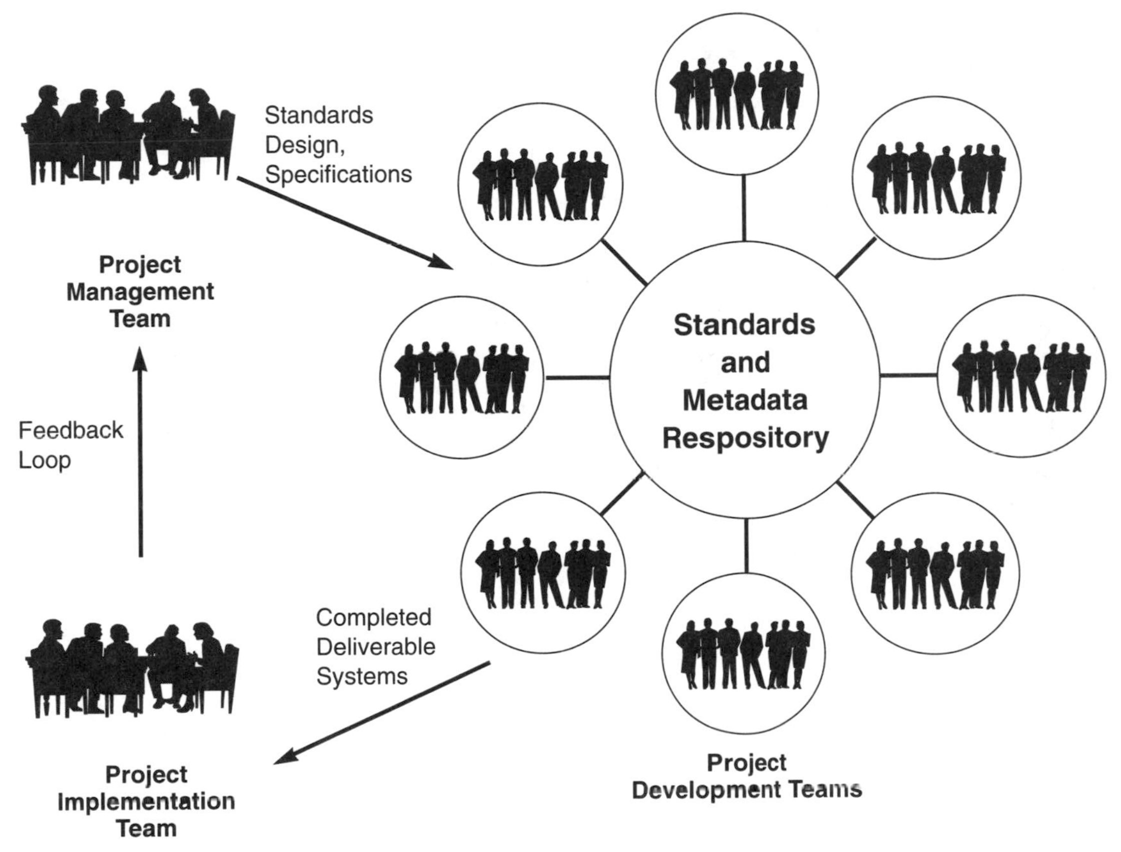

Figure 6.3: *Development work flow*

Summary

Data warehouse teams need the following attributes to thrive.

- *Continuity* is required so that the experience in working together is not thrown away after a project is completed.
- *A common purpose* inspires each member to contribute.
- *Goals and deadlines* let a team know what to do and when to finish.

- *A common fate* The three musketeers said it best: “One for all, and all for one.” You should motivate each team member with the knowledge that everyone is rewarded if the team succeeds, and everyone loses if it fails.
- *Good communication* permits all-important quick feedback.

Your first data warehouse effort should be built with your best people, a sort of dream team of development resources. Following the first successful implementation, these team members should be split into multiple subject-oriented data warehouse teams. These additional teams can begin parallel development efforts on additional subject-oriented data warehouses to quickly expand the coverage of an overall data warehouse. The experience base of these teams becomes a mentorship pool that allows you to continue to grow your own development resources with minimal ramp-up time.

After your team has been established, it is time to get into the details of building and delivering a data warehouse. This subject is covered next in Section IV.

7

Data Gathering: Information Usage Analysis

Listening to someone talk isn't at all like listening to their words played over on a machine. What you hear when you have a face before you is never what you hear when you have before you a winding tape.

—*Oriana Fallaci*

As we stated in earlier chapters, building a data warehouse is largely different than building a transaction system. The difference becomes very notable within the data gathering phase of a development effort. The center of all good development is a solid, coherent, and comprehensive design specification. Most developers will tell you that gathering data requirements for a data warehouse is a nebulous process: The users can neither concretely define what they want, nor concretely define the process of getting the information they want. This leaves most analysts in a quandary. How can you properly build something that the user cannot fully define?

The Dimensional Nature of Business Data

Even more than previous chapters, this one presents some powerful concepts that need to be absorbed and understood before moving forward to later chapters. A majority of data warehouses today are working with dimensional data; business data by nature is dimensional. The techniques that follow in this book will greatly assist you in understanding how to model and package this dimensional business data for your data warehouse implementations.

Dimensionally Mapping User Requirements

While at Cognos Incorporated, we were exposed to a unique concept of data gathering referred to as dimension mapping, or information packaging. This technique is the cornerstone of the methodology utilized within this book to develop and deliver data warehouses.

Information packaging, as shown in Figure 7.1, focuses on the dimensional nature of business data. For example, if you were a sales manager for cola products within the Midwest, you might want to understand key measurement data about your area. Figure 7.1 breaks out the information package, often referred to as a data cube, for the following business dimensions.

- Time Period = January
- Product = Cola Drink
- Geography = Cincinnati

This data cube allows you to better understand how well cola drinks sold in the Cincinatti territory during the month of January. As you can see, three dimensions are associated with this data—time, product, and geography—hence the statement that business data tends to be dimensional.

This book extends this technique to be less proprietary to the Cognos technologies and therefore more open to other implementations of data warehouses and decision support databases. This more open technique is what I refer to as the *information packaging methodology*. The information package diagram has proven to be an effective communication tool between technical staff and data warehouse users.

An information package diagram is a common, consistent, and coherent design and communication tool. This diagram conveys the right information at the right time to those who understand its purpose. It models a user's required *information package*. The information package diagram technique is a productive way to define and communicate user business query requirements, or information package requirements. The information package diagram assists us in performing the following tasks.

- Defining the common subject areas utilized within a business, such as time, customer, geography, and product
- Designing key business measures that can be tracked to determine how a business is performing and operating
- Deciding how data should be presented to the user of a warehouse
- Determining how the user aggregates, or rolls up, data along common hierarchies
- Deciding how much data is actually involved in a given user analysis or query
- Defining how data will be accessed, what its entry points are, where the user wants to go, and how the information package will be navigated
- Establishing data granularity
- Estimating the size of a warehouse
- Determining the frequency of refreshing the data within a data warehouse
- Formulating how information should be packaged for distribution to the user

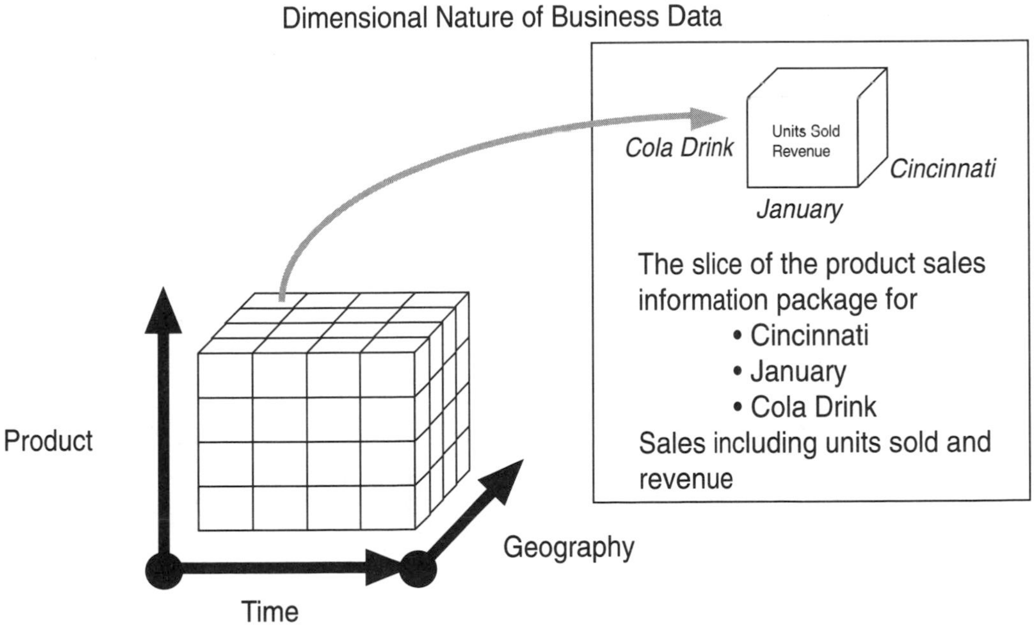

Dimensional Nature of Business Data

Units Sold
Revenue
Cola Drink
Cincinnati
January

The slice of the product sales information package for
• Cincinnati
• January
• Cola Drink
Sales including units sold and revenue

Product
Time
Geography

Figure 7.1: *The dimensional nature of business data*

This chapter focuses on the steps involved in preparing and interpreting user information requirements through information package diagrams. In Figure 7.1 you saw data within three dimensions—time, product, and geography. However, you will notice in Figure 7.2 that six dimensions are defined—time, location, product, age group, economic class, and gender. As previously stated, most if not all business data is dimensional. However, gathering and presenting more than three dimensions traditionally has been a difficult task. The information package diagram simplifies this task and allows you to design and communicate multidimensional information packages to developers and users alike. However, prior to jumping into the information package diagram, let us regress and define some terms that are required for fully understanding this requirements gathering technique.

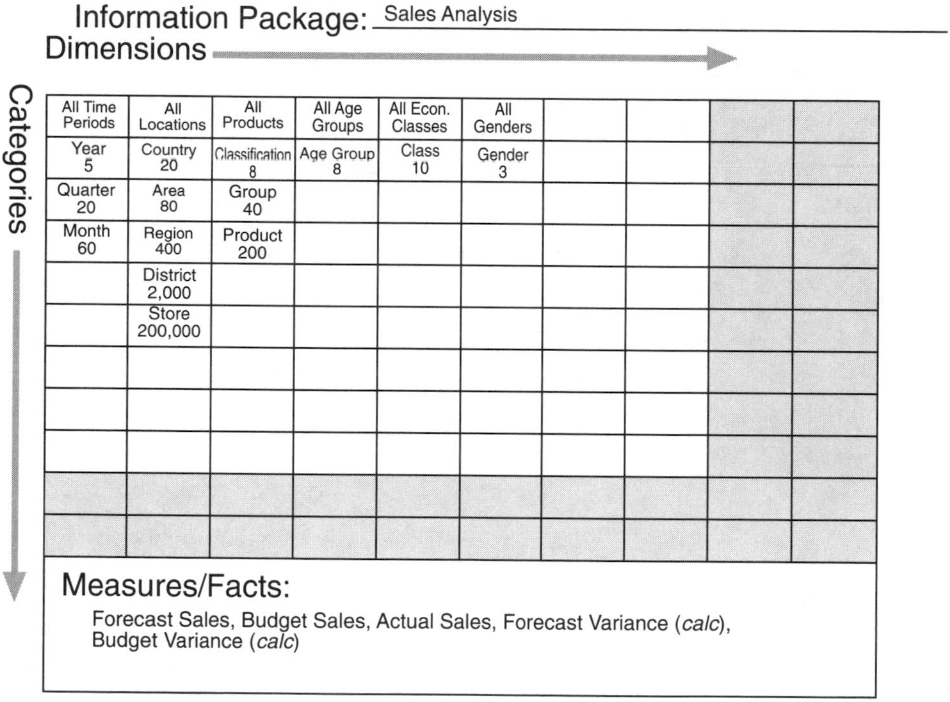

Information Package: Sales Analysis

Dimensions →

Categories ↓

All Time Periods	All Locations	All Products	All Age Groups	All Econ. Classes	All Genders				
Year 5	Country 20	Classification 8	Age Group 8	Class 10	Gender 3				
Quarter 20	Area 80	Group 40							
Month 60	Region 400	Product 200							
	District 2,000								
	Store 200,000								

Measures/Facts:

Forecast Sales, Budget Sales, Actual Sales, Forecast Variance (*calc*), Budget Variance (*calc*)

Figure 7.2: *Sample information package diagram for sales analysis*

Terminology

In the following sections, we define several terms that are useful for our current discussion. These terms are: *dimension, multidimensional, aggregate, category, detail category, drill down and drill up, and measures.*

Dimension

A dimension is a physical property, such as time, location, or product, that is regarded as a fundamental way of accessing and presenting business information. Consider two examples.

- **The time dimension** comprises all days of the year, the weeks of the year, the months of the year, and possibly multiple years
- **The location dimension** comprises all cities in which your company has offices, the districts that contain those cities, the regions that contain those districts, and the countries that contain those regions

A dimension typically acts as an index for identifying data. We commonly think of standard reports that present rows and columns as two dimensional. A manager who is evaluating a budget may look at a two-dimensional spreadsheet containing accounts in the rows and cost centers in the columns. The intersecting point between the rows and columns, or a cell, contains relevant numeric information about the specific cost center and account, such as product development's salary budget.

Multidimensional

It logically follows from the discussion in the previous section that multidimensional is a term that refers to information that is defined as, or accessed by, several dimensions. In a geometric world, the easiest description of a multidimensional entity is a cube. The cube has three specified dimensions: width, height, and depth.

Surprisingly, most business models are actually represented in a multidimensional view. The budgetary example described in the definition of dimension contains two dimensions, cost center and accounts. In reality, this example is missing a very important dimension, time. Most financial analysts evaluate their data with a minimum of three dimensions. Pick up a publicly traded company's annual report. Turn to the pages that give the overview of performance. You see information about how the company has performed over time, typically three to five years. You see graphs and charts representing important business measures, such as sales revenues, expenses, profit, stock performance, and earnings per share, tracked over multiple dimensions, such as time product, and division.

An information package diagram provides a technique for modeling user information in a multidimensional space. This design provides a visual representation of the business analyst's mental model of their information package. This diagram provides you with a solid design that is both simple and fast. If you think of a Rubik's Cube, solving the puzzle is similar to the way a business analyst moves through multidimensional data. Each analyst has a different way to twist and turn the cube until the desired result is found, much in the way that different people have different ways to solve the puzzle.

Aggregate

A dictionary defines aggregate as: *To gather into a mass, sum, or whole; to amount to; total.* With regard to a data warehouse, aggregation refers to the concept of rolling up data within a dimensional hierarchy. Each dimension contains many levels that, in turn, can present the user with a rolled-up version of data. For example, in the locations dimension, all districts add up to a total region.

Aggregates and aggregation provide a valuable type of computation within a decision support system or data warehouse. Most users want to see aggregations not only in one dimension, but across dimensional boundaries. Because dimensions are indexes into numerical business measures, this goal is possible. For example, a regional sales manager may want to see all sales figures, forecast and actual, for each district by product line. For this aggregation, the sales figures must be summarized for each of the cities within the district by product line to present to the user.

Category

A category is a division specifically defined in a dimensional hierarchy that provides a detailed classification system. This discrete member of a dimension is used to identify and isolate specific data. For example, *Cincinnati* and *Central Region* are categories within the location dimension. Similarly, *January* and *Quarter 1* are categories within the time dimension.

Detail Category

A detail category is the lowest available level of detail within a dimension. For example, if the time dimension contains information about time periods that include year, month, and day, day is a detail category; the value of *1996/11/19* is an instance of the detail category.

Drill Down and Drill Up

Drilling down and drilling up are navigational techniques for users to further analyze detail information (down) or aggregate the data to another summary level (up) within a dimension. The navigational paths are set up within the dimensions. If you view the categories within a dimension, they formulate a hierarchy of valid data points. For example, when viewing information based on the location dimension, users might start by viewing the data organized by country. They could then drill down on the Western Region, and further drill down to the state of California. Drilling up works in the opposite manner. If users were viewing information organized by state, they could drill up to region, then drill up again to a country view.

Measures

A measure (also referred to as a key performance measure, a fact, a key business measure or indication) is a device that measures business information along dimensions. Measures are typically quantities, capacities, or money that are ascertained by comparison with a standard. These data points are used for the quantitative comparison of business performance. For example, product revenues in dollars, wasted raw materials in pounds, new minority hires as a count, or plant up time in hours are measures.

Gathering Requirements

In gathering requirements for a data warehouse, you want to interview users to better determine their information requirements—the type of data they use, how they use it, and what they would like to do with it in the future. The information that you obtain within these user interviews will become the basis of your overall design.

Preparing for the Interviews

A data warehouse is highly driven by the user community; the users are your customers. To ensure success, make sure that your core design team (project manager, architect, and database administrator) participate in the interview process. Depending on your experience with user sessions, you may want to include a consultant who specializes in the area of decision support or data warehousing. The consultant should provide valuable insight to your design team, and potentially assist in gathering your requirements quicker.

Preparation for the interviews is important. You will require input from the key personnel in the user community. You will do yourself and your team a large favor by being well prepared and optimizing your visit with the users. Remember, their time is valuable to the enterprise. After all, they are making strategic and tactical decisions that are worth millions of dollars to the company. Your senior sponsor or steering committee should be able to assist you in obtaining interviews with individuals whom you may otherwise be unable to contact or schedule time with.

Based on the stature of these individuals, you need to give them plenty of advanced notice and reminders to guarantee their active participation. When notifying these individuals, stress the importance of their involvement and the objectives of the interview. Within the objectives, state the agenda, what you expect from them, and any materials you want them to bring, such as sample reports that they currently find helpful.

It sometimes is also of value to publish the interview schedule for all interviewees. This helps in two ways. First, those interviewed will notice others who, politically or otherwise, give the targeted individual motivation to be involved. Second, it provides interviewees with a way of rescheduling if a time conflict arises, because they know who else is involved and when.

You should be able to schedule two to four interviews in a day. Make sure to allocate enough time to capture your ideas and summarize them on paper between interviews. In the early going, you probably want to schedule closer to the two in a day. As you gain momentum, move to four each day. The interviews will typically last one to two hours. The people you want to interview include the following.

- Executives who are either sponsoring the data warehouse project or closely involved in the focused business area
- Key managers who report to the executives from the business area of focus
- Business analysts who prepare reports for the managers and executives
- Anyone recommended by the executives, managers, or analysts

It is often beneficial to start at the top end of the organization chart. The lead executive can give you an amazing amount of insight as to the business process and what he or she expects from the organization. This information can assist your following interviews from a content and flow perspective.

Analysis and Design Tip 2: Preparation for user interviews is important. You will require input from the key personnel in the user community. Do yourself and your team a large favor by being well prepared and optimizing your visits with users. Remember, their time is valuable to the enterprise. After all, they are making strategic and tactical decisions that are worth millions of dollars to the company.

What to Ask in Interview Sessions

Depending on the interviewee, your questions will differ. Obviously, you will ask different questions of an executive than of a lower-level employee. However, you want to gain answers to the following questions from all interviewees.

- Their positions in the organization.
- How their performance is measured; that is, what factors determine success and failure?
- What impacts these performance measures? What data or information do the interviewees currently receive to assist them with understanding the key indicators? (Get data or report samples if interviewees have any.)
- Upon getting the information, what is done with it? How is it processed? Is the information complete, or is it entered in a spreadsheet for further processing? Merged with another report or other information?
- To whom do they distribute the information or analysis results that are derived from this data?
- How do they analyze the data? For what are they looking? How long does it take to find?
- How long does the entire analysis process take? What decisions result from the analysis?
- What is the method of distribution of the information? A report? Paper? E-mail?
- What types of information are they currently lacking to complete their analysis?
- How do they fill these information gaps today?
- What level of detail is required for them to analyze the data?
- What is the source of the report from which the information is derived? Who is responsible for the creation, maintenance, and distribution of the report?
- If they could get 20 business questions answered on a regular basis, what are they and how would they prioritize them?

If the individual is higher in the organization, you also will begin asking questions such as the following.

- What are the business unit's objectives? How do these roll up into the corporation's objectives?
- What is required to meet these objectives? What are the critical success factors? What are the risks that would impede the corporation's ability to make these objectives?

- With regard to the previously-mentioned 20 business questions, what is the financial impact of the answers to these questions? Rank on financial impact. Rank on importance.
- How do the interviewees perform comparisons to the corporation's competition?
- Do they purchase outside data? From whom? Who else has data that the corporation has not purchased? Why did the corporation select the data providers? How do the data providers distribute information?

Additional Questions

Additionally, you may choose to ask questions that target available information sources as well as destination data warehouse content. These questions revolve around areas such as the following.

- Current information sources
- Subject areas within the business
- Key performance measures or facts important to the business
- Frequency of usage
- The user community

Depending on the position of the interviewee, you may want to include a smattering of these types of questions. A sampling of questions in these areas follows.

Current Information Sources

The current information sources line of questioning allows you to define existing data origins from which users are already obtaining information. Your line of questioning allows you to quickly target these information sources as potential input for your data warehouse.

- What essential information is currently delivered in existing reports or in downloads?
- Does this information contain the right amount of detail? Too much or too little detail?
- Which operational areas generate data and information about important subject areas?

- Are these operational areas supported by computer systems?
- What is the business assessment of the quality, reliability, consistency, and integrity of data held in these computer systems?

Subject Areas

The subject area line of questions assists you in defining what is important to the business in terms of subjects. You will find that, depending on the position of the individual you are interviewing, various subject areas and dimensions clearly define their realm of data, making it easy for you to package their information. These questions focus on how data within the data warehouse will be indexed, or how the user will analyze, navigate, and filter the data that is contained in the key performance measures of the business.

- Which dimensions or subject areas are most valuable for analysis? Do the dimensions have natural business hierarchies?
- Are there natural business partitions for decision making?
- Do geographical locations need only their local information to make sound business decisions?
- Are certain products sold only in certain areas?

Key Performance Measures and Facts

The key performance measures line of questions, much like subject areas, varies depending on the interviewee. These questions allow you to determine how the business defines success for the individuals you are interviewing. These indications are typically parameterized by the subject areas or dimensions you uncovered within the subject area line of questioning, and completes the information package requirements for a given interviewee.

- How is the performance of the organization currently monitored in the business environment?
- What critical success factors are monitored within the organization?
- How do the key measures roll up?
- Are the measures evenly split when they are averaged in a roll-up?
- Are all markets measured equally?

Information Frequency

The information frequency line of questions allows you to determine from your interviewee the sensitivity of time with regard to information packages. All information packages will be time based; therefore, each interviewee should be able to provide valuable insight as to the frequency requirement of each information package you define.

- How often does the interviewee need to be updated with this data? What is the relevant time frame?
- What is the timeliness requirement for the information in the data warehouse?
- When analyzing data, how is it compared over time?

User Base

The user base line of questioning assists you in defining who should be able to see the data and what capabilities the user possesses. Again, these questions will allow you to better isolate who needs the information packages that are defined for the data warehouse.

- What business is the organization in?
- What is the business' strategy?
- What is its mission statement?
- Who is the customer, or business user, for the data warehouse?
- Do all users require the same information? What are the special cases? Clearly define the categories of users.

General

You also want to develop a set of general questions. These questions assist in validating previously asked questions or further detailing general information about the business with which you are unfamiliar.

- What are the areas of business operations?
- How closely do these business areas work together to achieve business results?
- What are the most critical business queries that the data warehouse is expected to satisfy?
- What are the customers' requirements for business use data?

- What is the highest level of data summarization with which the business can work?

Modeling Information Requirements

Although plenty of design techniques and methodologies allow you to build a data warehouse, no one way will necessarily work best at all times. Therefore, as a developer you might consider varying approaches, or a blend of approaches, to deliver your detail designs. We summarize these approaches in the following sections.

- **Bottom-up modeling** Bottom-up modeling involves identifying the specific elements of data that your users currently utilize, then grouping them into broad dimensions and measures. Sometimes, we hear this technique referred to as *data grouping*. The bottom-up method is the one in which most database administrators and developers are most comfortable. This is a detailed process that at times can force developers to lose focus of what the users wants. Bottom-up modeling tends to ignore many important data sources—those that are external to existing operational systems. The benefit of this technique is that the designer is working within a known universe, a comfort zone that can lead to quick productivity.

- **Top-down modeling** The top-down modeling technique begins from the users' point of view by interviewing them and determining their information requirements. This technique assumes nothing, and is viewed by many to take too long and to produce frustration for the technical members of a data warehouse team. However, this technique takes into account all information sources and how the business is impacted by them. One benefit of top-down modeling is that the designer can develop information packages along a common theme or business area. The information package diagram is an excellent tool for top-down modeling and provides an information packaging template that provides consistency among your implementation staff.

When designing a data warehouse, you will find yourself utilizing a blended method that typically involves both top-down and bottom-up techniques. Your own personal modeling techniques will begin to take shape as you experience the process several times and find value in certain techniques. The remainder of this book discusses the information packaging methodology modeling technique, which is closely aligned with the top-down approach. Like many aspects of system design and development, these techniques are an art unto themselves. For you to become truly comfortable, you must make your own art.

Analyzing Interview Results

Your interviewing sessions should target the information that the data warehouse needs to address. These interviews should define a clear information need for the users. For example: *Users of the data warehouse need to see product revenues detailed by demographic information, including age group, gender, location, and economic classification over the last five years. The product revenues should be presented in budget, forecast, and actual figures.*

The interview sessions should disclose the information users require on a day-to-day basis. Users typically will pinpoint data that should be included in the data warehouse as well as data that should be excluded. Remember, we do not want to create a data junk yard of unnecessary data. Design your data warehouse on a need-to-know basis. The smaller the data warehouse is, the better it will perform and the easier it will be to manage.

When analyzing the information to design your data warehouse, use multiple information package diagrams. Don't try to cover all possible information requests with one information package diagram. Creating different diagrams, each tailored to suit a particular information request or information package, allows you to build a data warehouse that performs better and provides a higher degree of user satisfaction.

In your analysis, determine the highest and lowest levels of information that the data warehouse requires. This information assists you in understanding the necessary degree of data granularity in the data warehouse structures and overall structure of the database.

Analysis and Design Tip 3: The data granularity required by the user is typically one detail level lower than the decision point. For example, if a sales manager is only interested in quarterly variance of forecasted revenue to actual revenue because the selling cycle is 90 days and all decisions are based on the selling cycle, you want to deliver monthly variance figures within the data warehouse. By delivering this next layer of detail, you support the process of investigation required by the manager, his or her analysts, or the personnel within his or her organization, who are typically asked for the reasons behind a change in trends. Though the ultimate business change might be made based on quarterly statistics, monthly trends information provides insight when variances occur.

When analyzing the results of your interviews, be sure to key off user-oriented keywords that assist in defining the information packages. Words such as *by* and *over* assist you in defining dimensions and measures within information package diagrams.

Analysis and Design Tip 4: Users tag key information with common, *user-oriented keywords* such as *by* and *over.* These keywords give additional meaning to data requirements and allow you to easily package the information required by users into the proper structure. For example, a manager may desire to see product sales information by month, by geography, and by product over the last five years. The tag *by* assists in defining the dimensions of month, geography, and product. The tag *over* assists in defining the content of the time dimension, or how many months are required to fill the information request.

Using these earlier tips, we can easily break down the information request as follows: *Users of the data warehouse need to see product revenues detailed by demographic information, including age group, gender, location, and economic classification over the last five years. The product revenues should be presented in budget, forecast, and actual figures.*

From the user's information request, we can extract the following words to derive the required measures and dimensions for the information package: *need to see product revenues...product revenues should be presented in budget, forecast, and actual figures.* This transforms into the following points.

- **Measures** include actual revenue from product sales, budgeted revenue from product sales, and forecasted revenue from product sales
- **Dimensions** include products that are sold

Extracting the remaining requirements from the user's information request, we can complete the information package definition as follows: *detailed by demographic information, including age group, gender, location, and economic class.* This transforms into the following definition.

- **Dimensions** include age group, gender, and economic class of the customer, as well as the location of the sale to the customer

Finally, the last fragment assists us in the user's information request as follows: *over the last five years.* This transforms into the following.

- **Dimensions** include time periods for five years

Analysis and Design Tip 5: Data warehouses contain data that is fundamentally dimension and measure oriented. Begin to listen and dissect your users' comments into dimensions (subjects) and measures (facts).

Building Information Package Diagrams

An information package diagram presents the conceptual definition of the users' required information package. A blank information package diagram is shown in Figure 7.3. Note the line at the top of the information package diagram, which you use to write the information package's description. You may choose to enter a summary description, detail description, or both to identify what the information package diagram describes. From there, you work with users to further define and describe the proper packaging of data warehouse information.

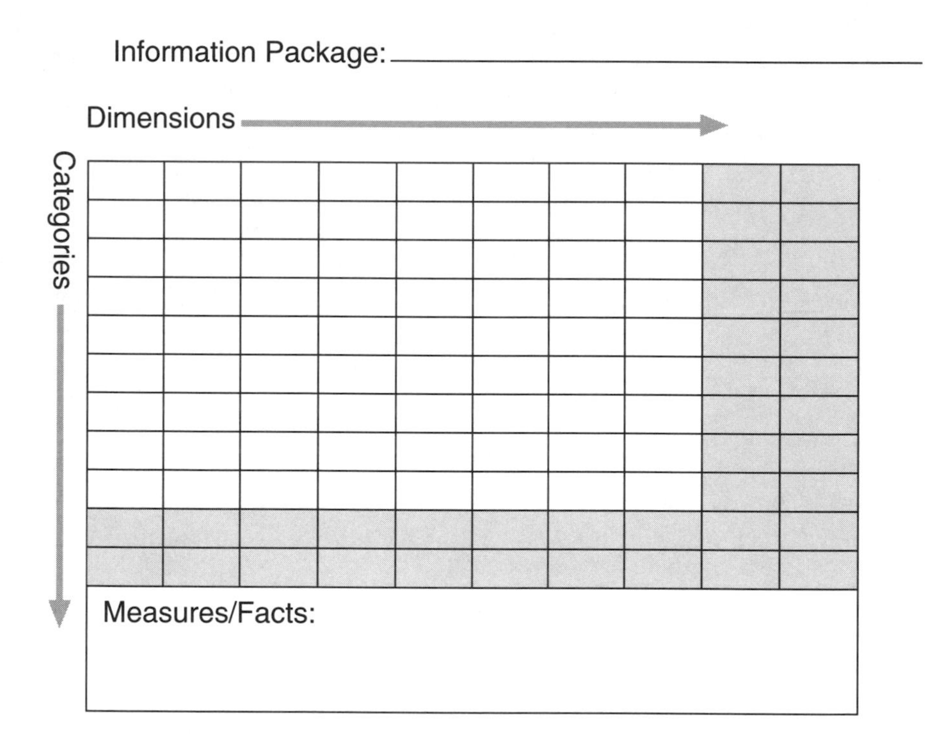

Figure 7.3: *A blank information package diagram*

Defining Key Performance Measures

A key to building successful information packages is guaranteeing that users can have multiple performance measures from which to report. Combining measures with dimensions provides an extremely useful model that allows users to gain significant insight into their business and its trends. For a measure to be valid, there must be some way of relating it to each dimension. When we get to the physical implementation, we will further verify this type of relationship. However, you may want to begin your investigation now. If a given measure is only valid or referenced by certain dimensions, you may want to complete multiple models on separate information package diagrams. In implementing information packages on a relational database, we can perform SQL *join* logic to bring the information together at a later date.

On your information package diagram, write the names of the measures your users need in the box at the bottom, as shown in Figure 7.4. When considering the measures, think about derived or calculated measures. Often, after initial design users will request that you include precalculated measures. When considering these special forms of data, determine how they might impact key performance measures, and specifically if they will further inform the user. Here are two examples of precalculated measures.

- Forecast Variance = Forecast Revenue – Actual Revenue
- Budget Variance = Budget Revenue – Actual Revenue

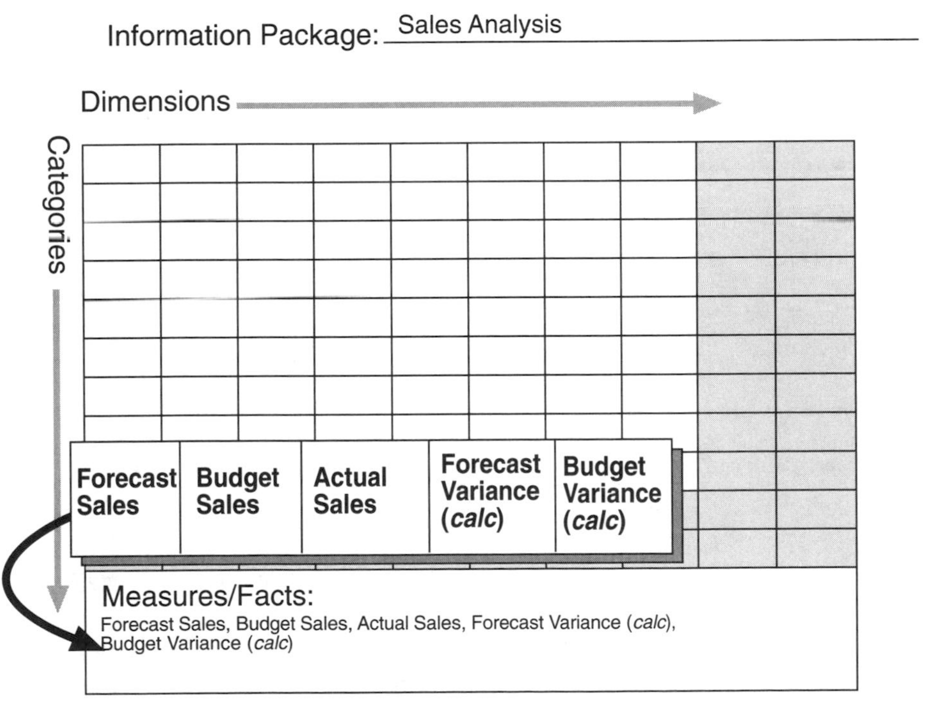

Figure 7.4: *Placement of business measures on an information package diagram*

Defining Dimensions

The dimensions can now be placed on the information package diagram, as shown in Figure 7.5. Remember, the dimensions are the high-level paths that the user requires to gain access to the measurement data. Each dimension presents a uniform access path into the information contained in the data warehouse. These dimensions also typically define a complete subject classification, or grouping of data, that will be used as reference material to support the key business measures. When defining dimensions, be careful to cover only the primary paths for the information; do not try to cover all of the possibilities.

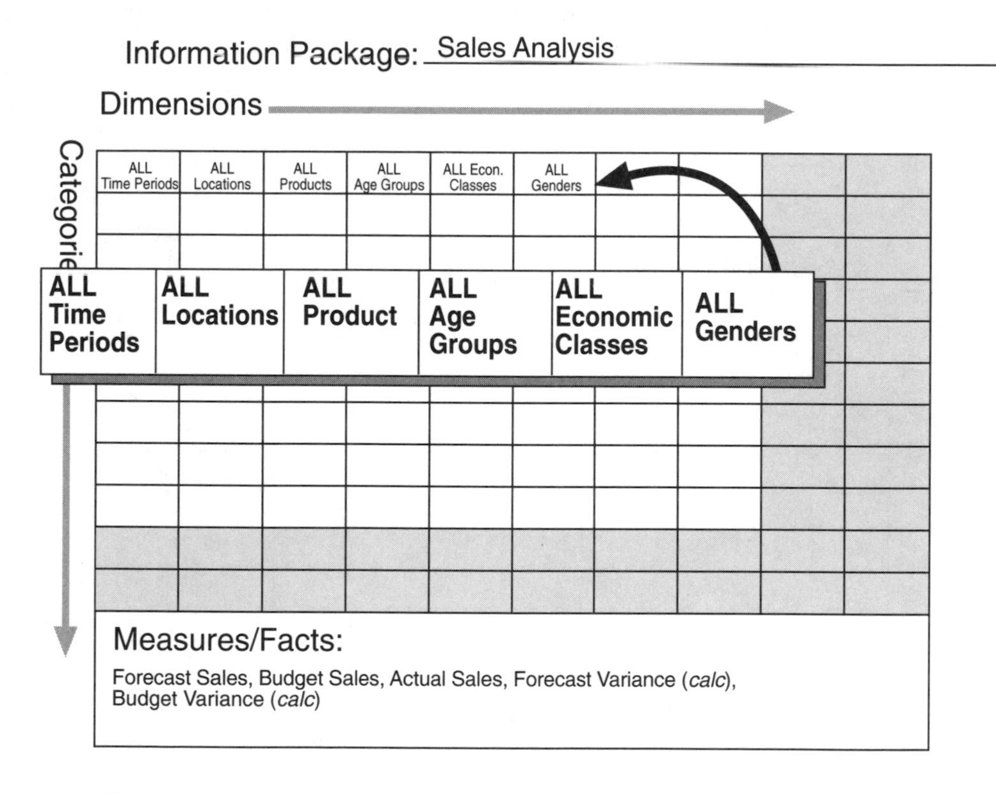

***Figure 7.5:** Placement of dimensions on an information package diagram*

Each of the dimensions is written in a column of the first row of an information package diagram. The categories of a dimension occupy the cells of the dimension's column. To designate that this row contains the high-level dimension definition, utilize the word *ALL*. Example: *ALL Time Periods and ALL Locations.*

Analysis and Design Tip 6: When working with an information package diagram, try to minimize your access paths, or dimensions. This helps the user by simplifying the manner in which the data is obtained. Keep the number of dimensions within a reasonable number, such as under 10. This is not a fixed limit, and many information models require a larger number of dimensions. However, usability is hampered when you exceed this number. Usability should be the number one focus of your warehouse project. The shaded areas on the information package diagram remind you of this usability tip.

Defining Categories

Categories provide the detail information for a given dimension. Often, these details are referred to as the aggregation levels or the hierarchy of the dimension. This is because the information that comprises a dimension is typically hierarchical data that summarizes, or aggregates, upward.

Following the definition of your key dimensions, you need to further define how the user will navigate to the detail information, or how the data will be aggregated. On the information package diagram, detail categories are contained within the cells in the dimension's column.

Analysis and Design Tip 7: The relationship between category levels and a dimension should be contained under a 1:10 ratio. This assists the user in navigating and understanding the data. This is not a fixed limit, and many information models require a larger ratio between dimensions and categories. However, usability is hampered when you exceed this number. Usability should be the top focus of your warehouse project. The shaded areas on the information package diagram remind you of this usability tip.

As shown in Figure 7.6, you should place the category's name and an estimate for the number of data points represented by that category. These numbers assist in many areas, including usability and data sizing. You should keep the ratio of categories between levels reasonable. If the numbers becomes too high, you may want to insert an artificial level within the dimension hierarchy to refine navigation for the user.

Figure 7.6 shows reasonable ratios: five years to 20 quarters, or a 1:4 ratio between levels. It also shows 20 quarters to 60 months, or a 1:3 ratio between levels. On the other hand, figure 7.7 shows an unreasonable ratio between locations, 1:3,000. To correct this situation, an artificial category has been placed in the hierarchy to allow the user to navigate customers via an alphabetizing system. Inserting the alphabetizing category might reduce the ratio to 1:115, a much more reasonable number.

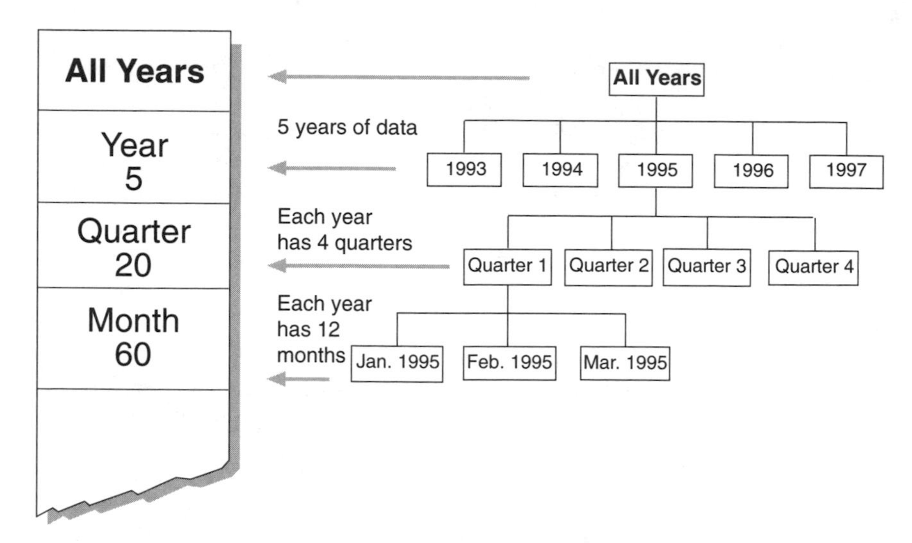

Figure 7.6: *Defining detail categories for a time dimension*

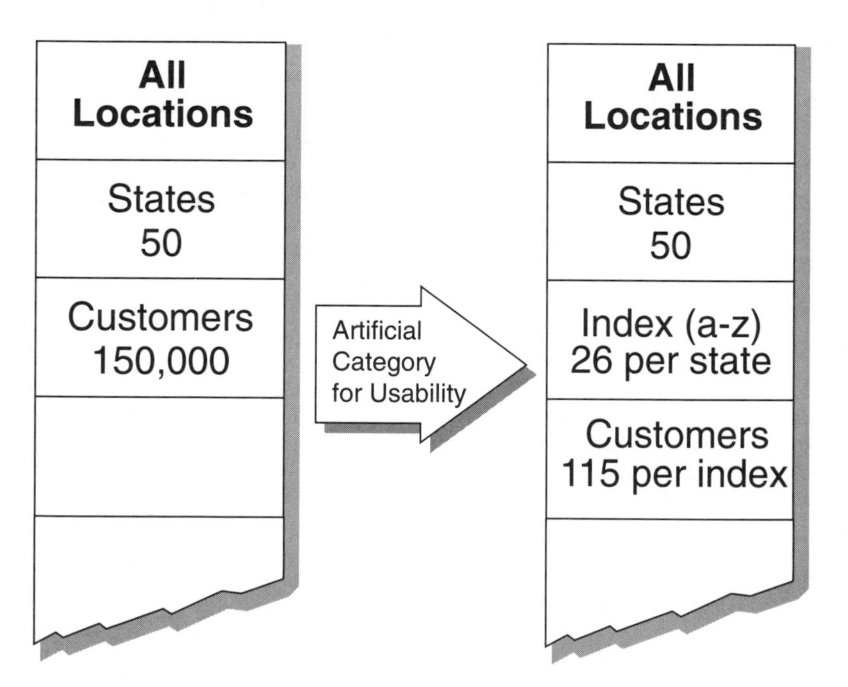

Figure 7.7: *Inserting an artificial category for usability*

Analysis and Design Tip 8: If you get in a situation in which you exceed a reasonable ratio between category levels, you can place an artificial category in your information package that logically organizes the category level into a manageable ratio. A ratio between category levels that exceeds 1:150 should be further analyzed for applying this tip. This is not a fixed limit, and many information models require a larger ratio between category levels. But, usability is hampered when you exceed this number. Usability should be the number one focus of your warehouse project.

Category level ratios also play a key role in assisting you with sizing the data contained and managed in an information package. While gathering the information about how many potential values exists for a category, you should obtain information on the density of the rows that the information package defines. Density is a term often used with multidimensional databases to refer to the percentage of possible combinations for data compared to the actual data. If a relatively high percentage of dimension combinations exists, the data is referred to as *dense*. When a relatively low percentage of the dimension combinations exists, the data is referred to as *sparse*.

For example, an antique shop that contains products such as chairs, tables, books, pictures, artwork, and other rare collectibles is unlikely to sell all products within a given month. It follows that the intersection of time and product dimensions will be sparse, because many products in the inventory will not be sold each month. On the other hand, a grocery store with food products such as bread, vegetables, fruits, and snacks is likely to sell all products within a given month, turning over its inventory. The grocery store will therefore have a *dense* relationship between time and product dimensions, because each product will be sold in a month.

Performance is greatly impacted by the size of an information package, because the size is a direct reflection of the number of data rows that must be read or scanned to obtain a result. Depending on how dense the data is that your information package diagram represents, you may choose to take action to minimize performance implications. These actions occur during the physical implementation of the data warehouse and include either utilizing software (indexing technology) or hardware (parallel processing) to minimize performance impact. Each of these activities is discussed later in this book.

Analysis and Design Tip 9*:* Try to insert the numbers that represent the unique occurrences of a category value within your category cells. These numbers assist you in understanding the volume of potential data and the relationships on types of data that could greatly impact the size of your warehouse. This data assists you if you need to split an information package in the future.

Figure 7.8 demonstrates a completed information package diagram. Each dimension has been listed in the column headings. The cells that comprise a column are filled with their associated category title and the number of unique occurrences that will potentially exist in the information package. At the bottom of the information package diagram, the key measures or facts that are important to the user are also listed. This information package, as stated early in this chapter, represents business data in a dimensional—or more specifically, multidimensional—fashion. Someone who desires to analyze the data can now look across six dimensions (time, location, product, age group, economic class, and gender) and evaluate business measures (forecast sales, budget sales, actual sales, and their associated variances).

Information Package: Sales Analysis

Dimensions

Categories

All Time Periods	All Locations	All Products	All Age Groups	All Econ. Classes	All Genders
Year 5	Country 20	Classification 8	Age Group 8	Class 10	Gender 3
Quarter 60	Area 80	Group 40			
Month 60	Region 400	Product 200			
	District 2,000				
	Store 200,000				

Measures/Facts:

Forecast Sales, Budget Sales, Actual Sales, Forecast Variance (*calc*), Budget Variance *(calc)*

Figure 7.8: *Placing categories on an information package diagram*

The detail required by users for proper analysis and reporting of the data will determine how many categories you define. It isn't necessary that the levels within each dimension be perfectly balanced. By *balanced* we mean that every dimension is represented with even hierarchies that provide the same level of detail. For example, a time period dimension that is represented by a hierarchy made up of year, quarter, and month would be balanced if each measurement was represented down to the month. This is often not the case. In fact, it is quite typical that the data is unbalanced. For example, the business may desire the measurement data to be represented to the month for two trailing years; but three years prior to that it be represented only to the quarterly level. Make sure to capture the potential levels required and make sure to document any anomalies along the way. They may become more important as you near physical implementation of your data warehouse.

Sample Dimensions

To assist you in defining your own information packages, we have included some high-level sample dimensions. Figure 7.9 demonstrates a sample location dimension. Within this figure, you see the location represented as a dimension as well as a hierarchy. The translation from a hierarchy to the dimension occurs when you name the hierarchy level, or category, and place it in the appropriate cell of the dimension column. Therefore, Figure 7.9 represents the location dimension and the top node of the dimension is referred to as *All Locations*. This label is transferred to the column heading of the dimension, or level 0. The first level of the dimension hierarchy represents countries. There is an assumption in Figure 7.9 that this dimension represents approximately 10 countries, such as the USA. This figure further represents the second level of the dimension hierarchy to be an area, such as *Eastern Area* or *Western Area*. This geographical boundary is further subdivided into the regions that comprise an area for the third level of the dimension hierarchy. The fourth level includes the districts, and so on.

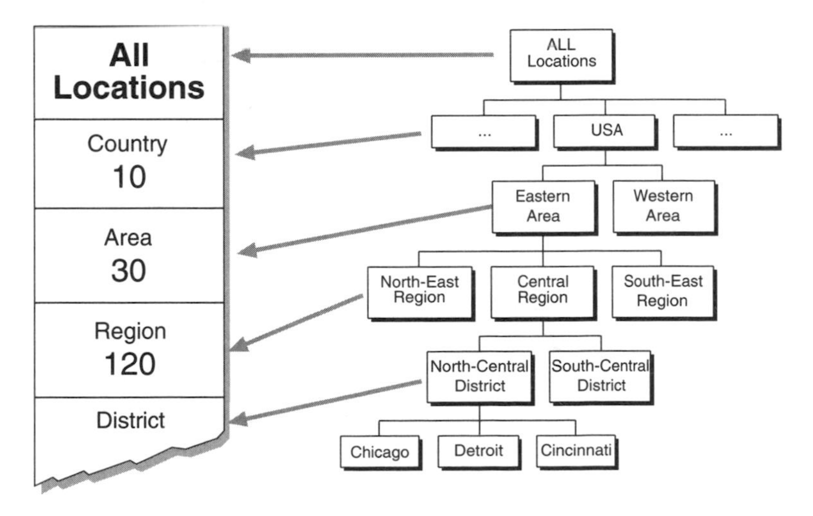

Figure 7.9: *Sample location dimension*

Another common dimension for businesses is the product dimension. Most businesses want to measure their effectiveness within given markets based on the products that they sell to those markets. Figure 7.10 shows a sample product dimension and product hierarchy. The translation of a hierarchy to a dimension column of an information package diagram that we described also applies here. The top level of the hierarchy and dimension labels the contents as *All Products*. From there, this figure demonstrates the product family level as the first level within the hierarchy, for example *Bottled Beverages*. These products are then represented within a product or a group of products. The second level of the data shown in Figure 7.10 displays the bottle size as a way of grouping the bottled beverages, such as *8 ounces* or *16 ounces*. Finally, the sample product dimension shows the products within these bottle size groups as *Cola* and *Uncola*.

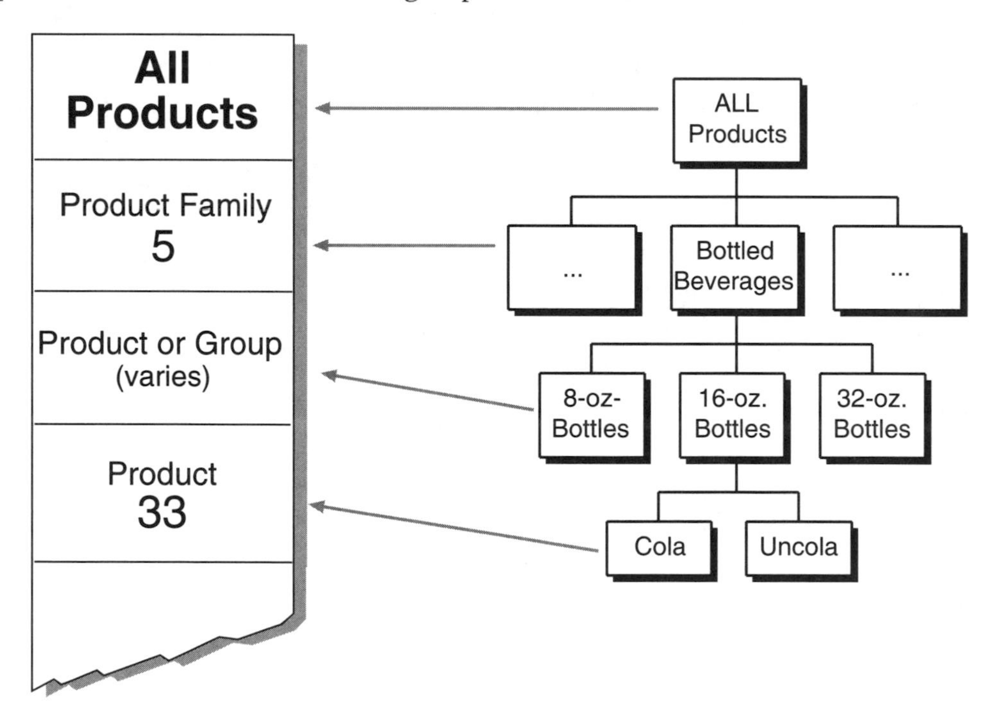

Figure 7.10: *Sample product dimension*

As a final example of defining dimensions, Figure 7.11 demonstrates a demographic dimension. Demographics are the characteristics of human populations and population segments, and are typically utilized to identify consumer markets. This figure demonstrates a demographic that shows the age characteristics of the information package. The translation rules described earlier for locations and products also apply here. Other demographics might include sex, income brackets, and level of education, to name a few.

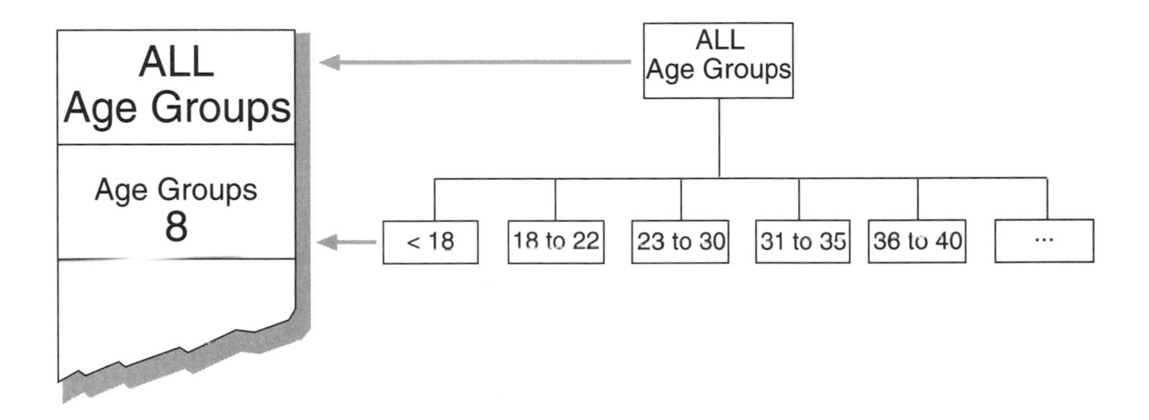

Figure 7.11: *Sample age group dimension*

Potential Issues with Information Packages

As with any requirements-gathering technique, information package diagrams are not always perfect. You should try to capture a definition of the information package that is as clean and consistent as possible, then proceed with the design work. Three common data inconsistencies are listed next, with brief explanations of their solutions.

Unbalanced Hierarchies

Dimensions are not always balanced. Example: Your user wants two years of data to the month level of the time dimension followed by the previous five years of quarterly detail and five additional years of annual detail, as illustrated in Figure 7.12. This is acceptable, and in many ways good. These types of definitions reduce the overall number of detail rows within your fact tables, which decreases the overall size while improving the overall performance of your data warehouse. However, the physical data definitions will be impacted. You need to validate that all relationships among the dimensions and the measures are valid to proceed with such a definition.

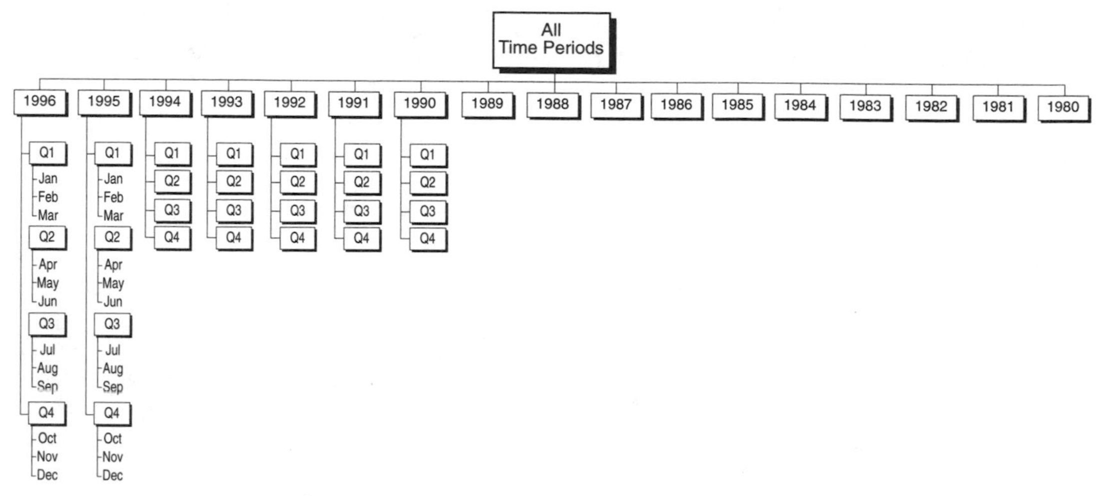

Figure 7.12: *Unbalanced dimension hierarchy*

Multiple Access Paths

Often, users request relative categories. These are categories that change in definition relative to the moment that the information is queried. Again, the best example involves time periods. The definitions that we have shown for time comprise a clean hierarchy of year to quarter to month. Now, let's say that your user desires to see multiple definitions of the data, such as month to date, quarter to date, year to date, or last 90 days.

When you gather the information, you may want to note these special definitions in the free space at the bottom of the dimension column. Document the primary access path in the information package diagram; this is the access path that will be predominately used. However, other access paths should be defined either on the information package diagram or in a separate document, as shown in Figure 7.13. These multiple access paths will be important during physical data definition.

Another example, which often occurs in sales analysis, is redefining the location dimension by physical geography as well as by management structures. In this situation, it may not initially be clear whether this will be two separate dimensions or the same dimension with multiple access paths. Document this and move on. Research for other information packages may resolve the issue. If, after you complete all of your information package diagrams, this has not been resolved, experiment with giving the data separate dimensions versus multiple access paths. Let the user be the ultimate judge through the user interface.

Artificial Categories

Artificial categories are typically used to break up data and to add aggregations. They must be highlighted, because the transformation process must accommodate the insertion of the data warehouse required data. The example shown in Figure 7.7 demonstrates this data inconsistency.

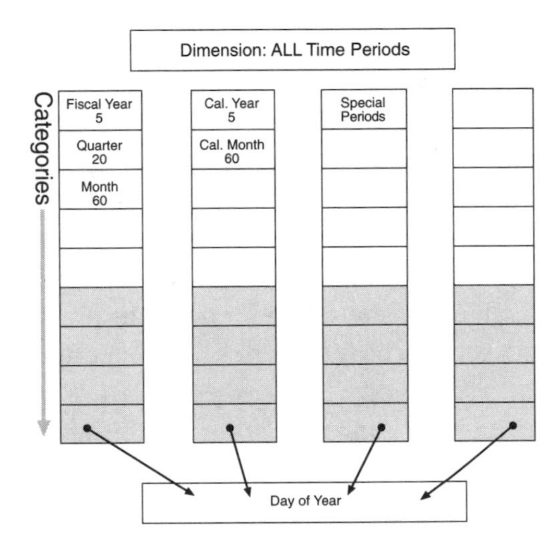

Figure 7.13: *Multiple access paths for the time dimension*

Summary

Prior to moving to the following chapters in this book, make sure you have absorbed the concepts of an information package and how this package is modeled through an information package diagram. An information package diagram is a common, consistent, coherent design and communication tool. The information package diagram conveys the right information, at the right time, to those who understand its purpose. It models a user-required information package. The information package diagram provides a productive requirements-gathering technique that defines and communicates user business query requirements.

During information usage analysis, you strive to gain a clear understanding of the users' information package requirements and the decision making process facilitated by an information package. The definition of this information package requirement is documented and defined in an information package diagram. This diagram defines the subject areas and the key performance measures important to a business. The definitions include dimensions, categories, and measures.

Analysis and Design Tip 10: When analyzing information to design your data warehouse, use multiple information package diagrams. Don't try to cover all possible information requests with one information package diagram. Creating several different information package diagrams, each tailored to suit a particular information request or information package, allows you to build a data warehouse that performs better and provides a higher degree of user satisfaction.

It is important to investigate information requests in detail. Too often, we in Information Systems focus on delivery—what the users are asking for—without asking questions such as *why* and *how*. The fundamental theme of data warehouse analysis and design is to build a consistent, coherent model of the information used by an organization.

During user interviews, inquire about where the users are currently getting their data. This discussion is often an eye opening experience. Sometimes, you will find the information is being obtained from everywhere except the reports that your Information Systems department has been delivering. Other times, you will find a key report that can assist in your development process.

A data warehouse should provide managers with factual information. If users are taking data, entering it into their own spreadsheets, and manually maintaining it outside the data warehouse, the facts may be distorted. Decisions would be made on data that has taken on a life of its own; understanding how this data is maintained is important.

Analyze business queries in detail because the creation of a good data warehouse depends so strongly on its intended purpose and target audience. These requirements will formulate the information packages that will be the core data in your data warehouse. Each of these information packages will be defined in an individual information package diagram, and the data warehouse will require many information packages. Therefore, you will have many information package diagrams after you have analyzed users' information requirements.

After you have the required documentation, your project can proceed to the next level of development, including tasks such as the following.

- Finalizing subject areas
- Finalizing facts and measures
- Finalizing dimensions and hierarchies
- Determining granularity, data summarizations, and aggregations

8

Building a Data Model

Where do architects and designers get their ideas? The answer, of course, is mainly from other architects and designers, so is it mere casuistry to distinguish between tradition and plagiarism?

—*Stephen Bayley*

Prior to diving into the building of a data model, let us review what is required by a data warehouse. First, we discussed a vision. The short term vision included the following.

- **User-driven reports** Users can characterize the type of information that they want in their reports on their own and have the system efficiently produce those reports.

Then we discussed requirements, which included the following.

- **Rapid response** Users have a need to analyze large amounts of data to make business decisions. The user is often faced with a limited window of time in which to perform this analysis to make timely business decisions and react quickly to changing market conditions.

- **Complex analysis** Business analysis involves finding the answers to extremely complex questions, often requiring iterative analysis of data. Business users typically issue queries that invoke multiple conditions, summarizations, and complex subqueries, which place increased demands on a database.
- **Dynamic business, environment** Users need the flexibility to access information in a wide variety of ever-changing ways to resolve specific business problems quickly. As the business environment changes, users need to view and analyze data in complex and changing ways. This often involves the ability to cross-correlate different subject areas and business measures.

The vision and requirements will, in many ways, dictate data design. Let's look at the four areas of vision and requirements we have just discussed from this perspective.

- **User-driven reports** Data structures must be understandable in user terms so that users can easily create their own reports without assistance. This leads us to some denormalization and preaggregation of measurement data within data structures, eliminating the nasty concepts of SQL, such as table joins and *group by* aggregation functions.
- **Rapid response** Tables containing the details of key measurement data may include millions of rows. The data structures need to provide a facility for narrowing a result set to a manageable number of rows that can easily be digested by any user. We need to build tables that surround measurement data and assist in the minimizing of result set rows for any query. Remember, these queries may not be clearly defined.
- **Complex analysis** Data structures need to accommodate the users' need to perform complex analysis while maintaining the simplicity already discussed. Users typically need to take the results of one query and use them to formulate a second query, and so on. Data structures may assist here, but this problem is normally placed in the client software from which the user requests the data. However, it should be noted that some intelligence is required within data structures and database engine to minimize the risk of what we refer to as "meaning-of-life queries." These queries tend to be run-away queries in which the user simply has asked for too much data. Therefore, the data model should safeguard against this, again with peripheral tables to assist in narrowing the scope of any result set.

- **Dynamic business environment** This is a big issue that will drive and define your architecture. Because a data warehouse evolves, how do you best insulate users from additions while giving them the benefit of the added data? Typically, this dilemma is solved through multiple means, but standardizing the way data is presented in user-oriented terms versus data processing terms greatly assists. An adaptable architecture with flexible data structures and well adapted standards for naming each of these structures and standards is key to delivering this objective. Also, technologies such as a relational database management system allow you to dynamically add entities to a data warehouse without requiring user applications to change. This approach provides the expandable, scaleable, plug-and-play environment required by an enterprise data warehouse.

Star Schema Design

Data warehouses are best modeled utilizing a technique known as *star schema* modeling. The star schema is optimized for query-based activities versus traditional database modeling techniques such as normalized schema models. Normalized schema models contain natural entities and their associated relationships. However, they provide an irregular structure for query processing and user comprehension. By contrast, star schema models define data entities in a way that supports the decision makers' view of the business as well as the data entities that reflect the important operational aspects of a business. This is because a star schema contains three logical entities: dimension, measure, and category detail entities. A star schema is optimized to queries and therefore provides a database design that is focused on rapid response to the users of a system. Also, the design that is built from a star schema is not as complicated as traditional database designs. Hence, the model also will be more understandable by users of the system. Users will be able to better understand the navigation paths available to them through interpreting the star schema. This logical database design's name hails from a visual representation derived from the data model: It forms a star, as shown in Figure 8.1.

Within the information packaging methodology, the information package diagrams described in detail in Chapter 7, Data Gathering: Information Usage Analysis, provides the conceptual basis for a logical star schema and allows it to be easily generated. The star schema defines the join paths for how users access the facts about their business or the information packages defined in information package diagrams.

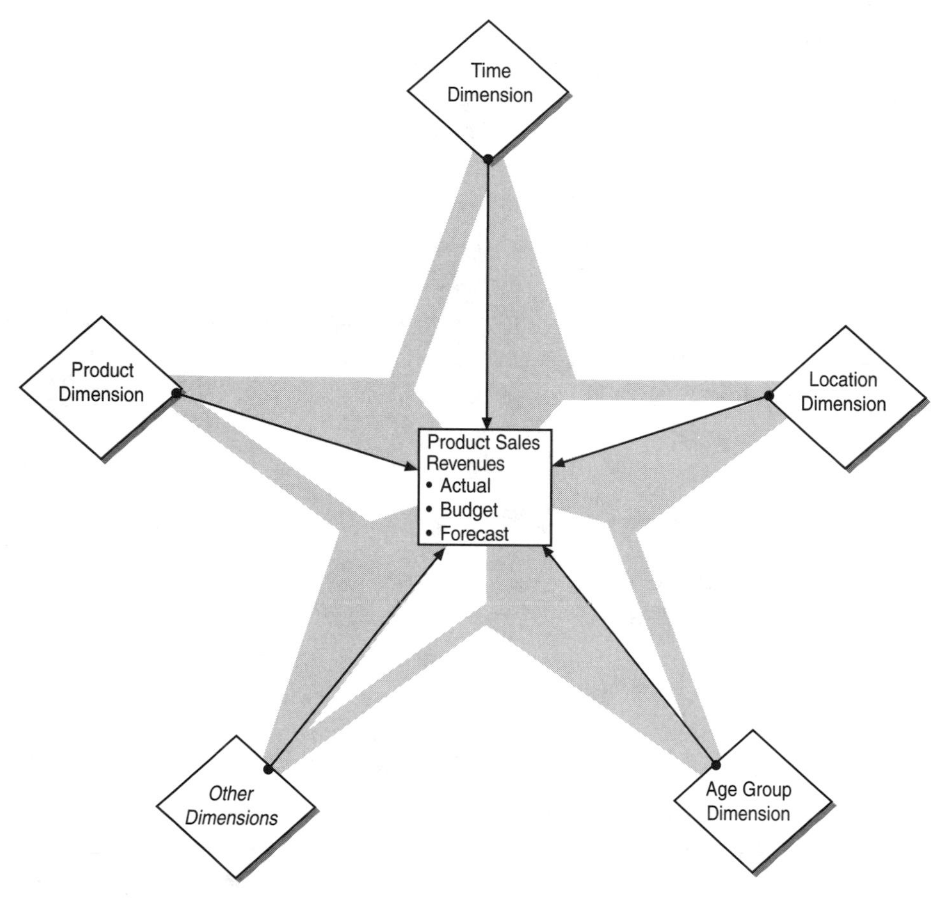

Figure 8.1: *A star schema design*

The optimization originates from the information package diagram, or conceptual understanding of what the user wants. When defining information requirements through an information package diagram, we focus on manageable information packages information and usability. The true power of a star schema design is to model a data structure that allows filtering, or reduction in result size, of the massive measure entities during user queries and searches. A star schema also provides a usable and understandable data structure, because the points of the star, or dimension entities, provide a mechanism by which a user can filter, aggregate, drill down, and slice and dice the measurement data in the center of the star.

Entities Within a Data Warehouse

A star schema, like the data warehouse it models, contains three types of logical entities: measures, dimensions, and category details. Each of these subjects is discussed separately in the next sections.

Measure Entities

The information package diagram represented in Figure 7.8 is a good starting point for understanding a measure entity. In Chapter 7, we defined a sales analysis information package. Within a star schema, the center of the star—and often the focus of users' query activity—is the measure entity, the low-level contents of the information package modeled within an information package diagram. A sample of raw measure data is showing in Figure 8.2.

month	branch	product	sales forecast	sales actual	variance
199601	CINCINNATI	COLA	2000000	1900000	-100000
199601	DETROIT	COLA	1500000	1550000	50000
199601	CLEVELAND	COLA	1250000	1050000	-200000
199601	CINCINNATI	UNCOLA	250000	1000000	750000
199601	DETROIT	UNCOLA	250000	750000	500000
199601	CLEVELAND	UNCOLA	250000	350000	100000

Figure 8.2: *Measure entity data*

The data contained in a measure entity is factual information from which users derive "business intelligence." This data is therefore often given synonymous names to measure, such as key business measures, facts, metrics, performance measures, and indicators. The measurement data provides users with quantitative data about a business. As stated earlier, this data is numerical information that the users desire to monitor, such as dollars, pounds, degrees, counts, and quantities. All of these categories allow users to look into the corporate knowledge base and understand the good, the bad, and the ugly of the business processes being measured.

The data contained within measure entities grows large over time and therefore is typically of greatest concern to your technical support personnel, database administrators, and system administrators. As an example of data's potential for growth, imagine the largest retail store's cash register receipts within one of these entities. It could happen, and probably will happen in coming years, but that is a lot of data.

Dimension Entities

Dimension entities are much smaller entities compared to measure entities. The dimensions and their associated data allow users of a data warehouse to browse measurement data with ease of use and familiarity. These entities assist users in minimizing the rows of data within a measure entity and in aggregating key measurement data. Both of these tasks are required to fulfill a user's information request. In that sense, these entities filter data or force the server to aggregate data so that fewer rows are returned from the measure entities. Within a star schema model, the dimension entities are represented as the points of the star, as demonstrated in Figure 8.1 by the time, location, and product dimensions. Figure 8.3 presents a sampling of dimension data and a hierarchy representing the contents of a dimension entity.

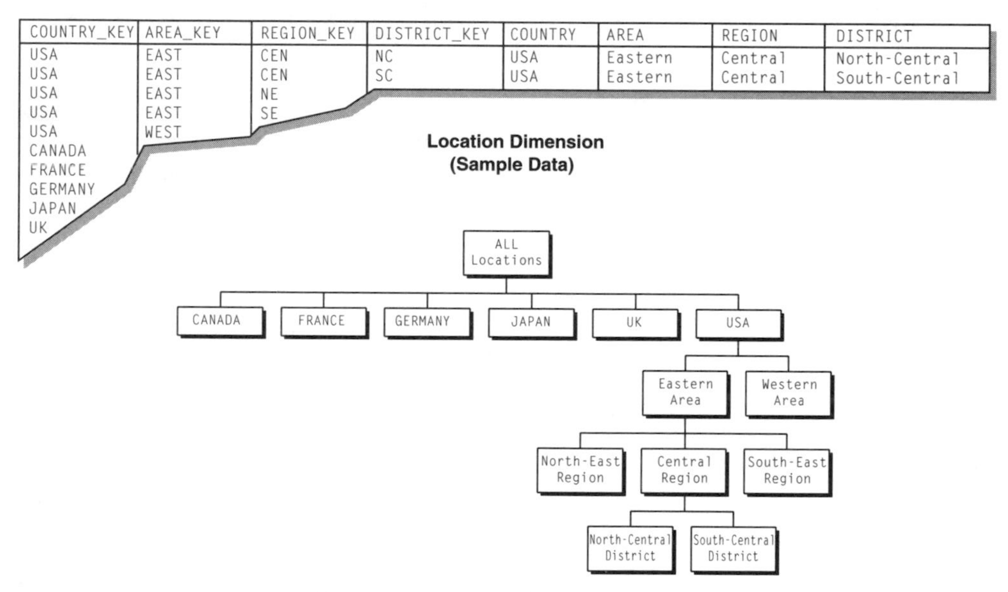

Figure 8.3: *Dimension entity data*

Category Detail Entities

Within an information package diagram, each cell in a dimension is a category and represents an isolated level within a dimension that might require more detail information to fulfill a user's information package requirements. Those categories that require more detail data are managed within category detail entities. These entities have textual matter that supports the measurement data and provides more detail or qualitative information to assist in the decision making process. Figure 8.4 demonstrates the need for a client category detail entity within the All Clients dimension.

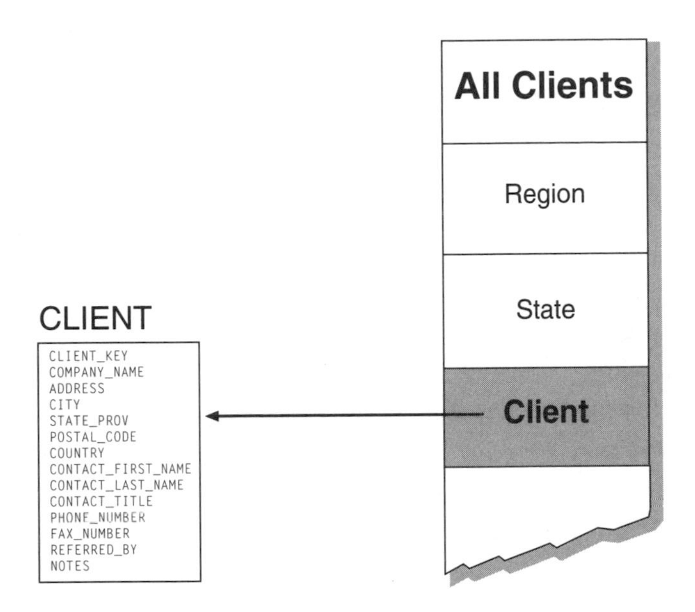

Figure 8.4: *Category detail entity data*

Navigating an Information Package

Dimension entities assist users in navigating a data warehouse and provide key access paths into the data managed by the measure and category detail entities. If you analyze users' navigational habits, measurement data is the key to the business intelligence contained in a data warehouse; therefore the measure entities are the primary entities on which users focus.

As stated earlier, dimension entities are the axes on which users organize, summarize, or dissect the facts measured within measure entities. These structures give meaning to the measurement data, allowing users to obtain more intelligent quantitative data to add to their analysis. So, users utilize dimension entities to navigate measure entities and ultimately gain their business intelligence.

Warehouse Navigation Example

In the next several sections, we look at a detailed example of an information package that supports an automobile dealership's service manager. We discuss the business need that drives the information package, the important entities that provide the information to users, the star schema design considerations for the resulting information package, and the functionality provided by the information package that allows the users to make intelligent business decisions.

For purposes of this example, assume that you are a service manager at a major General Motors dealership. As service manager, you must be aware of all recalls, frequently occurring problems, and general mechanical information to keep customers happy after they have purchased a vehicle. Let us further assume you have noticed a high incidence of Camaro Z-28s and Corvettes returning with chipped paint—specifically those that were painted pearl white. You were curious but not overly concerned, and maintained a closer eye on this apparent problem. There had been no recall, so maybe it was just your imagination.

But now, crisis arises! A consumer is infuriated. She had returned her car seven times for the same chipped paint problem and is threatening to sue your dealership if the problem is not corrected. At this point, you tap the corporate knowledge base and begin to wade through all of the data to get more facts on the case. Your knowledge base contains the following.

- A time dimension for all model years of cars
- A product dimension that has make, model, and trim package (sometimes referred to as series)
- A component or part breakdown dimension that discusses the assembly of the car
- A supplier dimension that provides information on who supplied what components for the car
- A defects dimension that provides common problems
- A measurement, which is basically a counting operator for the sum of the dimensions

To fully discover the impact of the current problem, you focus on an isolation technique within the product dimension. You want all sports vehicles, which includes Camaros and Corvettes. You want the component dimension to be isolated on pearl white paint. From there, you may want a report on the number of incidents of chipped paint from the problems dimension. This too will be an isolation filter on the measurement data. These three items have filtered a large amount of the data contained within your data warehouse.

Now you want to see the data. You may want to see, over time, the occurrences of chipped paint problems by model of car, controlling the axes in which the data is displayed. You see that the last two years contain a significant jump in paint chipping for cars with pearl white paint. Again, you isolate the time dimension for those years and begin to focus on the suppliers of paint for that time period. You find that the chipped paint problem is isolated to one specific supplier. You now have facts and knowledge to begin solving the consumer's problem.

Let's recap the activities to this point.

1. Isolate product dimension on sports vehicles—Camaros and Corvettes
2. Isolate component dimension on pearl white paint
3. Isolate problem dimension on chipped paint
4. Graph the count measure over time and model
5. Noting the increased incidence in the last two years, isolate time dimension on last two years
6. Graph the count measure on supplier and model

Drill Down

Isolation activity, such as that in our current example, typically occurs in a drill-down operation. Users select the dimension on which they want to focus and drill down into the dimension hierarchy until they find the data they want. Isolation and drill down performs several critical functions. First, it reduces the number of measurement rows that must be returned. Second, it guides the query processor in how to aggregate the data, providing the proper counts of vehicles that were impacted on the criteria.

Slice and Dice

The slice-and-dice functionality provided by data structures is demonstrated in items 4 through 6 of the preceding list. You first requested that the data be presented by time and model. You then isolated on the time dimension through a drill-down or filtering technique, and changed the presentation of the data to supplier and model. Here, you swapped the time and supplier dimensions to present the data properly and continued with your analysis. This technique of changing presentation coordinates is referred to as a slice-and-dice operation.

Make the Decision

We now have the problem detailed with facts and have a way of knowing who else in our customer base might incur this chipped paint problem in the future. But can we make a decision on how to solve the problem? After all, money is involved and someone will be forced to pay—the customer, the supplier, or the dealership. Do you have enough information to determine which party? As well, do you have enough information to provide advance notice to those valued customers who have purchased this defective product? What will you tell them? Should you ignore the problem and hope it does not occur again? Or do you tell the affected customers and fix the problem, building loyalty for future business?

These are tough questions that involve a lot of money. To better answer them, additional information is required. This information is not numerical or quantitative. You need additional information that is more textual, more legal, and more qualitative.

Fortunately, your data warehouse contains not only dimensions and measures, but also hooks to other, verbose data sources such as a legal library—that is, category detail entities. As the service manager, prior to making any further decision you want to look at the contracts between the supplier and the manufacturer, the dealer and the manufacturer, and the dealer and the customer. You may then find that the supplier offers a three-year warranty against items such as chipped paint in its standard agreement. Now you have the business intelligence that allows you to make the right decision. You notify the supplier and arrange a recall. You then notify all affected customers and schedule the repainting of their vehicles.

Optimize Navigation

This example shows a typical scenario for user navigation through a data warehouse. Each entity has a purpose. The design of the data warehouse led us to an optimal design that flows in the same way the users think. This design has been derived through the conceptual model—information package diagram and the logical model—star schema. As shown in Figure 8.5, the resulting information package entities allow users to navigate the information from the points of the star (the time, product, component, problem, and supplier dimensional entities) to the center of the star, which contains the defect measurement data. The functionality provided by the resultant design allows users to isolate on a fact—the supplier providing poor quality paint. After the fact is clear to the users, they can proceed to compile the additional data that is required to make an intelligent business decision. The supporting category detail information navigation is similar to that utilized to discover the facts. The star schema design allows users to traverse the center of the star, or defect measure entity, back out to the supporting information within the category detail data, the legal repository.

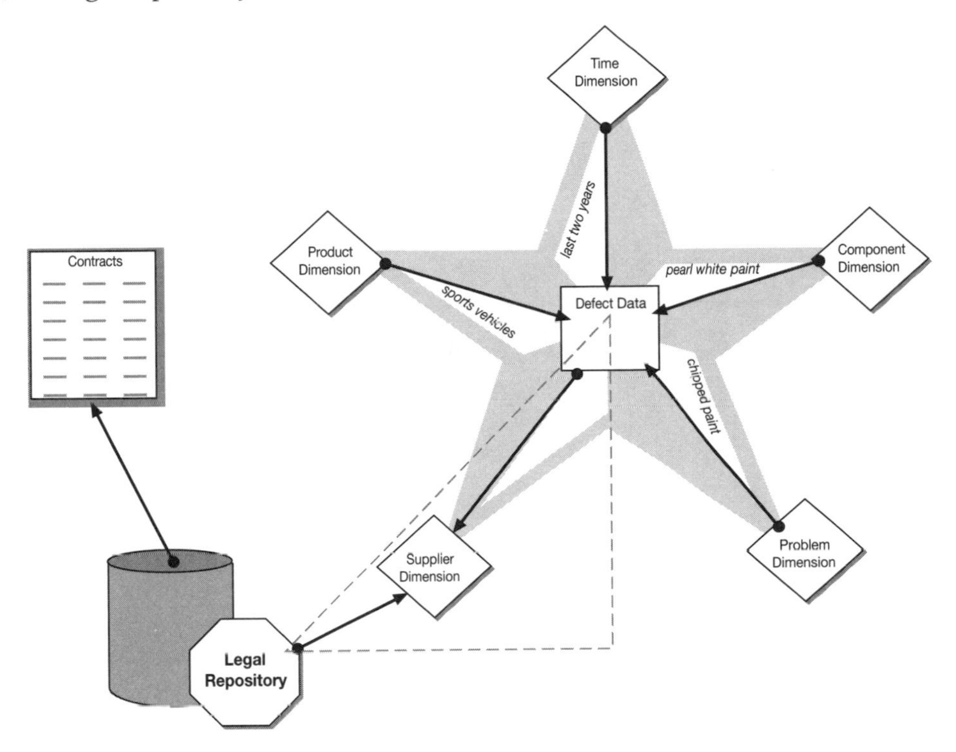

***Figure 8.5:** User navigation optimized with star schema*

Graphically Representing Entities in a Data Model

Each entity in your star schema performs a specialized function. It is important to graphically represent each entity within your data model. However, traditional data models do not graphically depict anything, they simply organize the information into entities (boxes) and relationships (arrows); no significance is placed on how the entities are drawn graphically. When detailing a data model in our information packaging methodology, we utilize the graphical symbols depicted in Figure 8.6 for each mentioned entity.

These symbols show common characteristics for the entities that they represent. You will find in modeling a star schema that a business has many common dimensions, measures, and category details. As a result, the stars begin to collide and overlap. This problem makes it difficult to present a star schema at the enterprise level. However, with an information package diagram, a conceptual model of user requirements, the star schema model for logically depicting the data models, and common entity characteristics, you can simplify your data models for analysis purposes. With these graphical representations, your project team and sophisticated users can visually understand the information package managed by a data warehouse, its associated entities, and the functions of each entity.

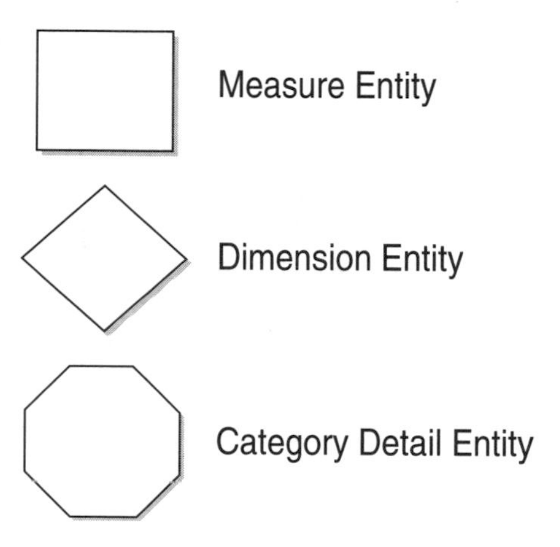

Figure 8.6: *Symbols for graphically representing data warehouse logical entities*

Measure Entity Attributes

A measure entity is represented by a rectangle and is placed in the center of a star schema diagram, because it is the most obvious entity and the focus of a majority of query activity. Though the transformation from an information package diagram to a star schema presents a logical data model, these entities typically become physical entities in a data warehouse. A measure entity represents a set of related facts and often corresponds to a real-world transaction or an event such as a shipment or sale. The measure entity typically represents a summary level of a real-world transaction and is related to just one point in every associated dimension. Characteristics of a measure entity include the following.

- Provides a primary focus for quantitative data, business measure data, or factual data
- Contains numerous access paths, dimensions, or pointers into the measurement data
- Encompasses relatively normalized data

- Comprises the lowest categories in each dimension and the measures from an information package diagram
- Can grow to become very large tables
- Will be the heart and soul of analytical activity

Dimension Entity Attributes

Dimension entities are utilized by users of a data warehouse as navigational aides to filter and aggregate data within measure entities. To graphically represent these entities, we use the traditional flowchart symbol for filtering indicated in Figure 8.5, because a major function of a dimension entity is to restrict the result set rows returned from user query activity. But dimension entities also form a common link between entities of a data warehouse, including measure-to-measure relationships and measure-to-category detail relationships. Characteristics of a dimension entity include the following.

- Represents the dimensional hierarchy
- Has primary foci of navigation and filtering measure entities
- Encompasses relatively denormalized entities
- Contain codes, or keywords, and their related description for an entire dimensional hierarchy
- Maps to the columns of an information package diagram
- Will typically be small tables if physically implemented
- Provides the gateway to a data warehouse
- Is often utilized to fill pick lists, such as list boxes or combo boxes, within front-end graphical applications

Category Detail Entity Attributes

Category detail entities, like measure entities, typically translate into a physical database table. These entities map relatively cleanly to transaction database structures and may in fact be mapped that way to a data warehouse in situations in which the transaction database can support query loads. (This circumstance is infrequent, however.) A category detail entity corresponds to a real-world entity, such as a customer, store, or market. These entities contain data that provides more qualitative information to users and assists in supporting the decision making process. The stop sign symbol is used to graphically depict these entities, because users typically flow through the dimension entities to get the measure entity data, then stop their investigation with supporting category detail data. Some common attributes of a category detail entity are as follows.

- Contains data for reference and support information to complete the intelligence of measurement data
- Provides data that is more qualitative
- Maps closely to transaction structures
- Typically contains normalized data structures
- Is represented by an individual cell, or a category, on an information package diagram
- Typically contains a medium amount of data rows—less than measure entities and more than dimension entities
- Contains descriptive, or qualitative data—not merely numbers

---

Implementation Tip 1: To give a more descriptive meaning to your star schema models, utilize graphics that communicate a clear meaning for each entity in the model. Recommended graphics are rectangles for measure entities, diamonds for dimension entities, and stop signs for category detail entities.

Translating Information Package Diagrams into Star Schemas

Now, we will put everything together and begin translating the information package diagram into a star schema. First, let's review the information package diagram produced in Chapter 7, Data Gathering: Information Usage Analysis. Our user interviews uncovered the requirement for providing the information package that follows. This information was then translated into the information package diagram displayed in Figure 8.7

Users of the data warehouse need to see product revenues detailed by demographic information, including age group, gender, location, and economic classification over the last five years. The product revenues should be presented in budget, forecast, and actual figures.

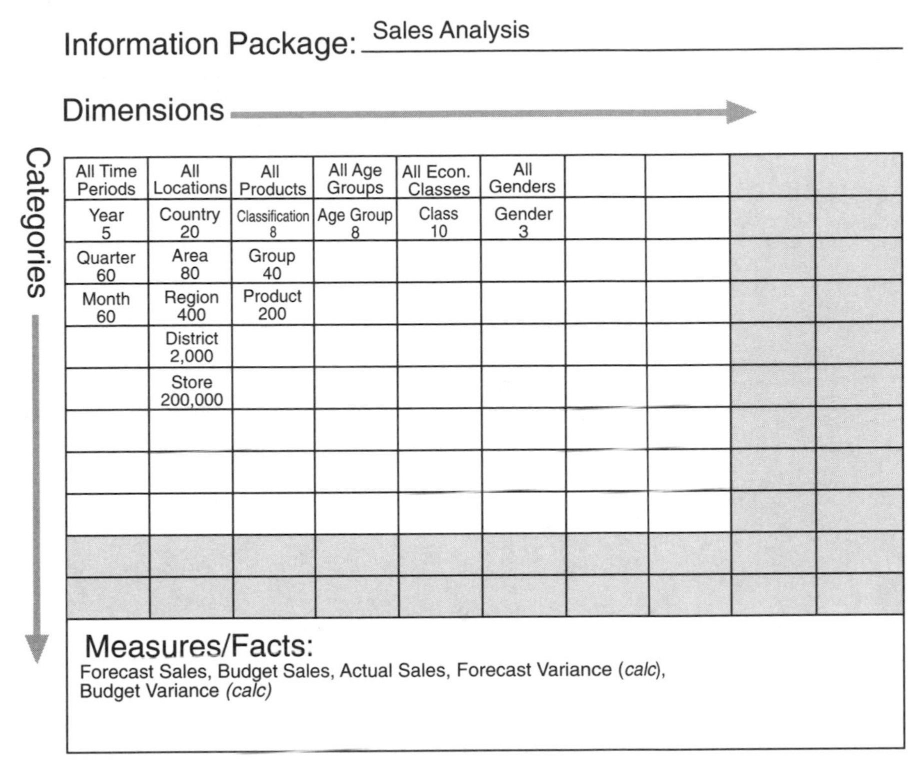

Figure 8.7: *Information package diagram ready for translation into star schema*

Defining the Measure Entity

When placed in the star of a star schema, each information package diagram represents one complete star and information package. The measure entity is placed in the middle of the star. See Figure 8.8 for a depiction.

To define the logical measure entity for each information package diagram, take the lowest category, or cell, within each dimension along with each of the measures and make them columns in a logical data entity, as illustrated by Figure 8.9.

Implementation Tip 2: Measure entities are composed of the keys to the detail, or lowest level, category in each dimension of an information package diagram. Each column must relate to all measures on the information package diagram. At this point, determine whether you will store calculated measurements. It is wise to estimate the overhead of users calculating the measurement data each time they access an information package versus the additional storage space and processing time required to precalculate the measurement data.

Figure 8.8: Measure entity placement on a star schema diagram

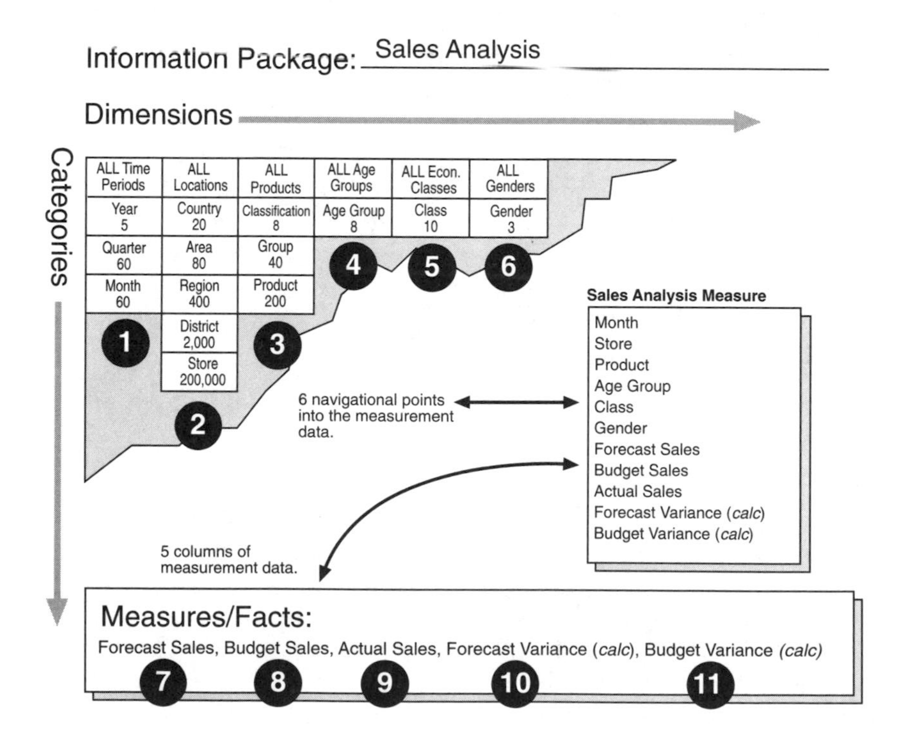

Figure 8.9: Measure entity translation from an information package diagram

Defining Dimension Entities

Each dimension entity, or column, of an information package diagram is a dimension entity that is placed on the periphery of the star of a star schema, symbolizing the points of the star. See Figure 8.10.

Following the placement of the dimension entities, you want to define the relationships that they have to the measure entity. Because dimension entities always require representation within the measure entity, there always is a relationship. The relationship is defined over the lowest-level detail category for the logical model; this is the last cell in each dimension. These relationships possess typically one-to-many cardinality; in other words, one dimension entity exists for many within the measures. For example, you may hope to make many product sales (*Sales Analysis*) to females (*Gender*) within the star illustrated in Figure 8.10.

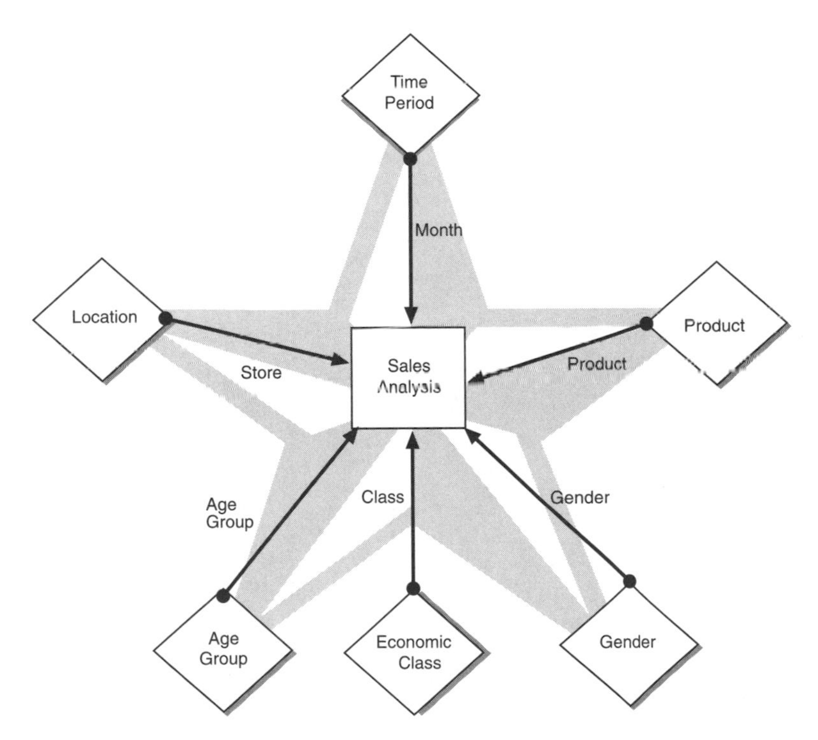

Figure 8.10: *Star schema relationships between dimension and measure entities*

To define the logical dimension entities, take each cell in the information package diagram and make it a column in the logical data entity. These logical data entities will be further transformed into physical database entities, as will be discussed in Chapter 9, Database Design. Dimension entities may span information package diagrams, so at this point make sure that you consolidate on a standard definition per dimension entity. (For more information on this topic, see the "Unique Entity Definitions" section later in this chapter.)

Figures 8.11 through 8.16 present further detail on transforming an information package diagram into logical data entities and their associated attributes that are represented within the star schema. These figures present the methodical nature of this transformation. Within each figure, the logical data represented within a cell of the information package diagram transforms itself into a column, or attribute, of the logical dimension entity.

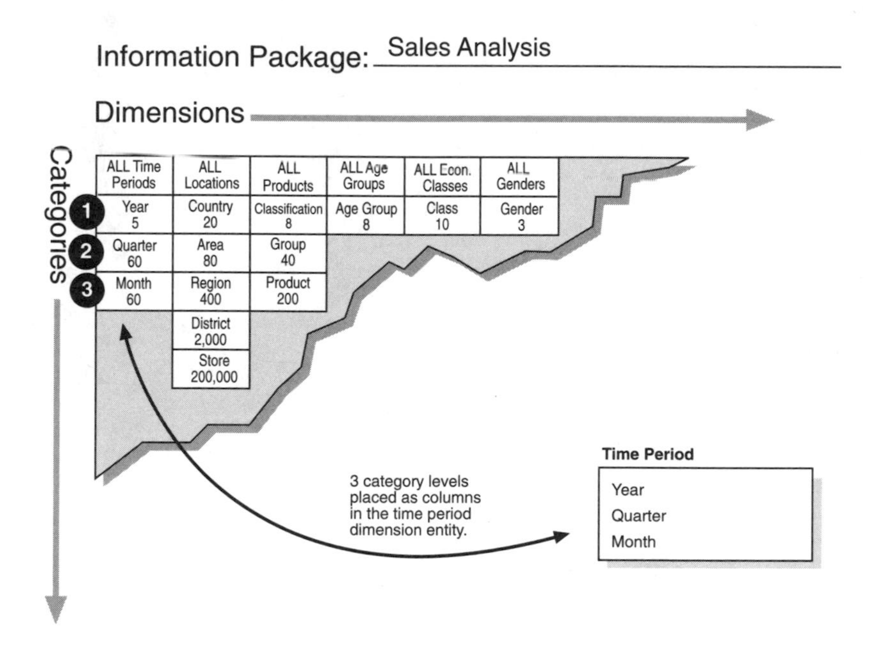

Figure 8.11: *Time period dimension entity translation from an information package diagram*

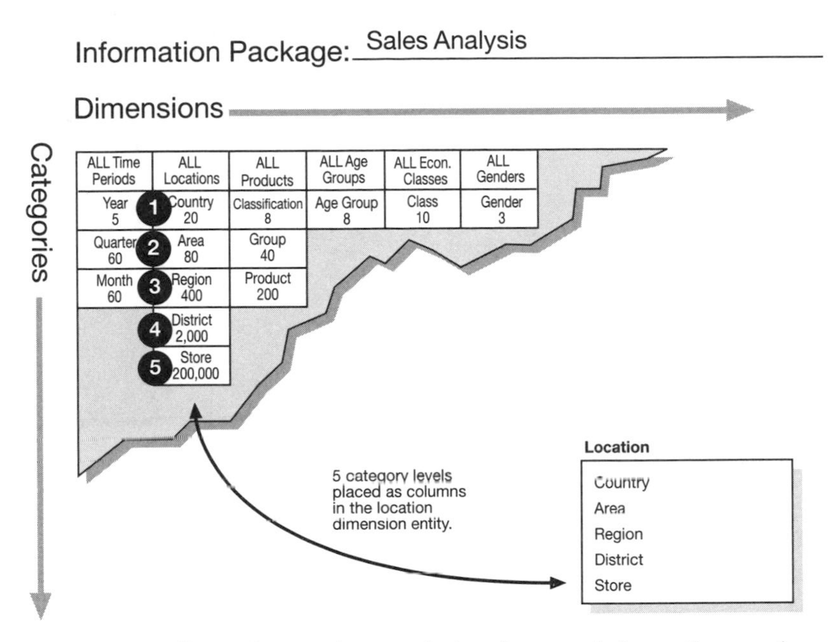

Figure 8.12: *Location dimension entity translation from an information package diagram*

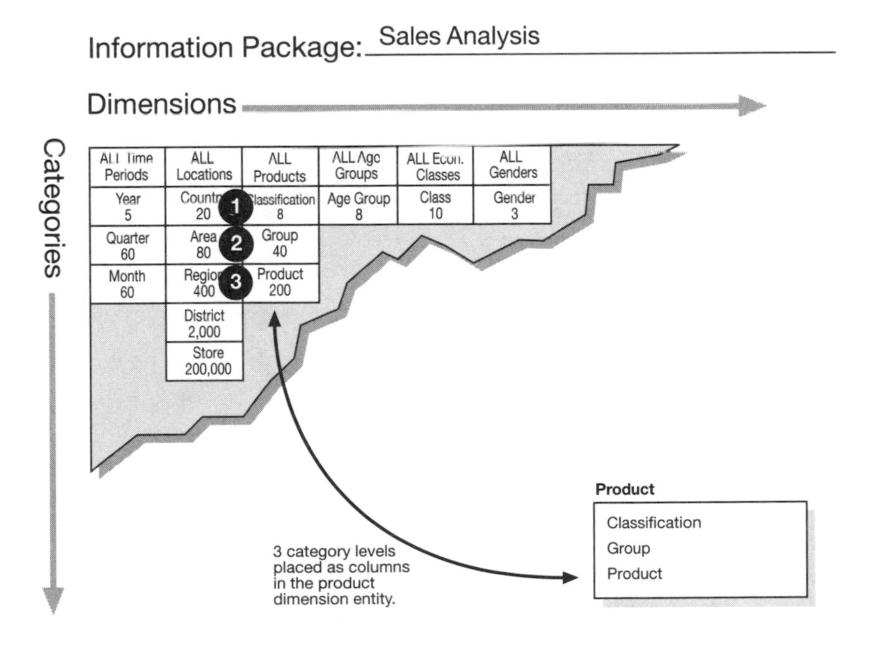

Figure 8.13: *Product dimension entity translation from an information package diagram*

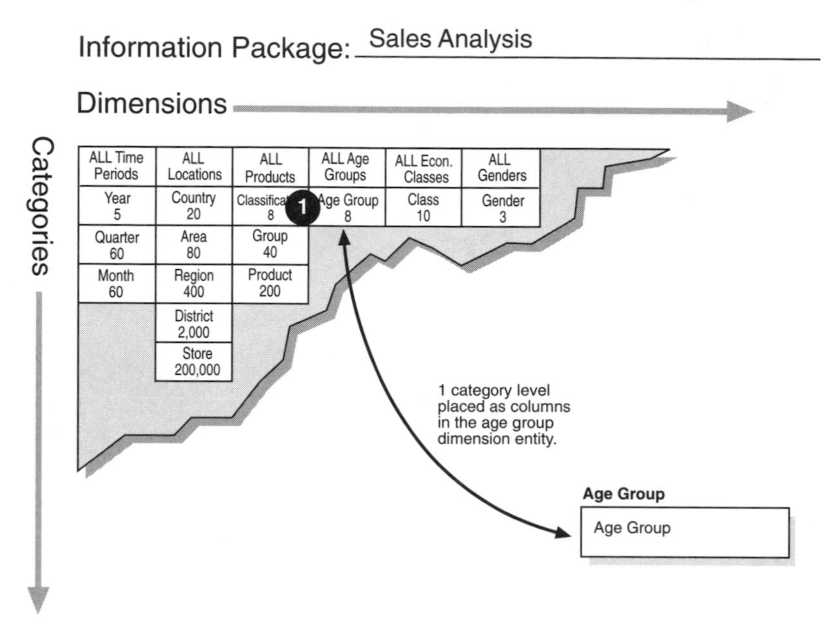

Figure 8.14: *Age group dimension entity translation from an information package diagram*

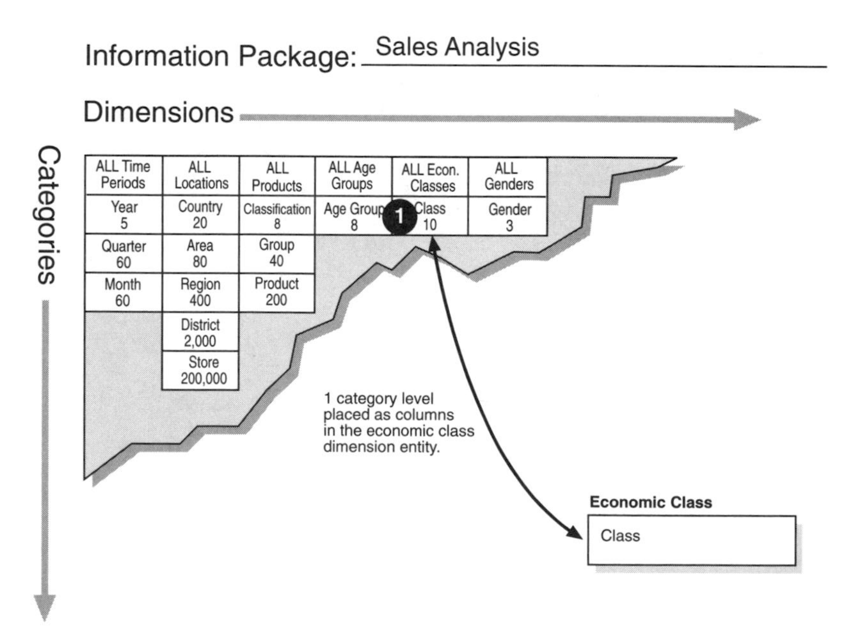

Figure 8.15: *Economic class dimension entity translation from an information package diagram*

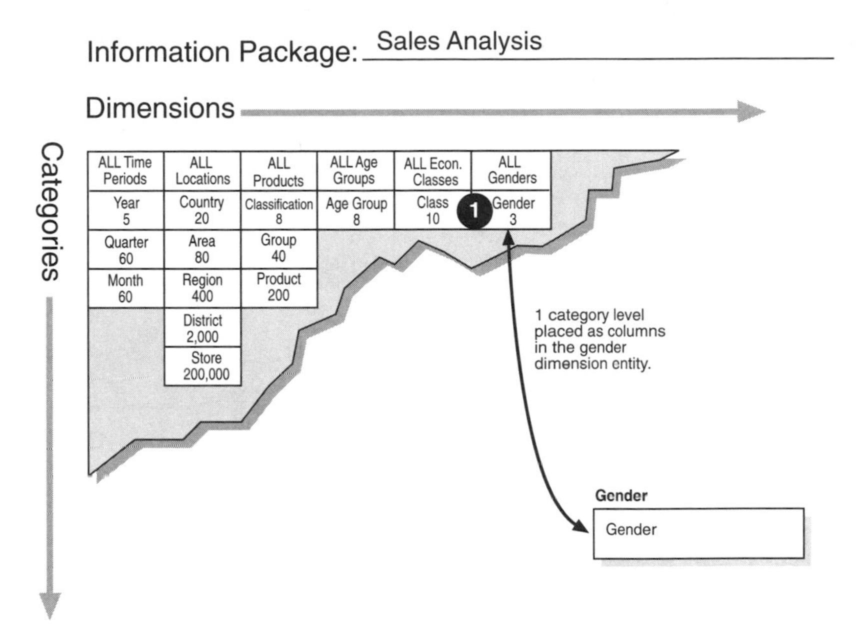

Figure 8.16: *Gender dimension entity translation from the information package diagram*

Implementation Tip 3: Dimension entities are placed on the points of a star schema and have a relationship that projects inward to the center of the star. The relationships between dimension and measure entities is one to many; one dimension entity instance relates to many measure entity instances. Dimension entities are logical in nature and are the most denormalized of the three major data warehouse entity structures.

Extending a Star Schema: The Snowflake Schema

The star schema model simplifies the logical data model by organizing data entities in a more optimal fashion for analytical processing. In a simple star schema, a central entity—the measure entity—is surrounded by dimension entities for navigation. However, it is more likely that you will have additional relationships extending off the points of the star. This extended schema begins to take on the appearance of a snowflake, and is therefore referred to as a *snowflake schema.*

The final step in defining the logical model transforms the star schema into one of these snowflake schemas. Each individual cell of an information package diagram must be evaluated and researched to determine if it qualifies as a category detail entity. If the user has a requirement for additional information about a category, this formulates the requirement for a category detail entity. These entities become extensions of dimension entities, as suggested by Figure 8.17.

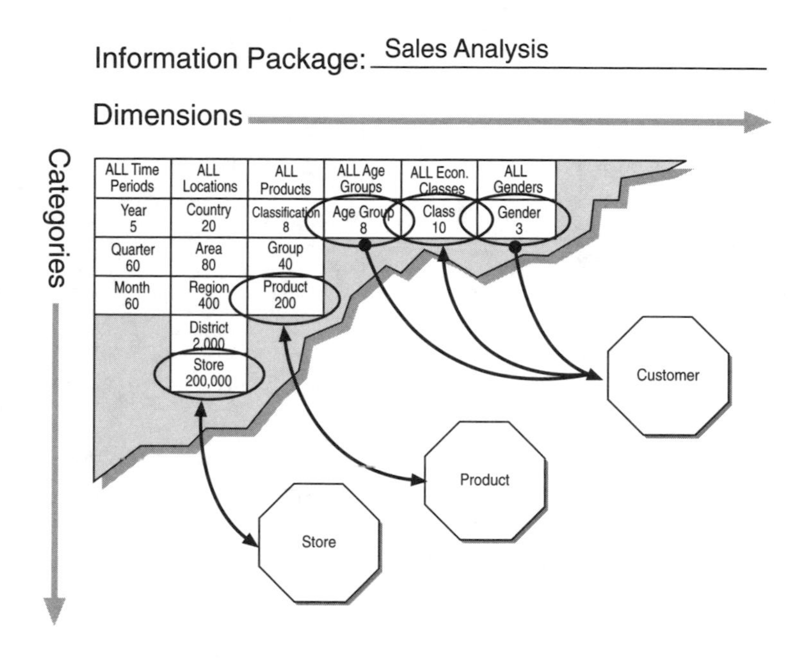

Figure 8.17: *Category detail entity translation*

In our information package diagram, we need to see more detail information about data such as store, product, and customer categories. These entities, when added into the current star schema, now appear as shown in Figure 8.18. Notice how it has taken on a snowflake look.

Implementation Tip 4: Category detail entity definitions contain information that enhances and adds qualitative data to the measurement, or quantitative data. The category details transform your star schema diagram into a snowflake schema, because of the branching effect that the category details deliver to the star schema. (Note: Some industry gurus have different meanings for snowflake schemas. The type we discuss here is controlled and will not be a detriment to your implementation.)

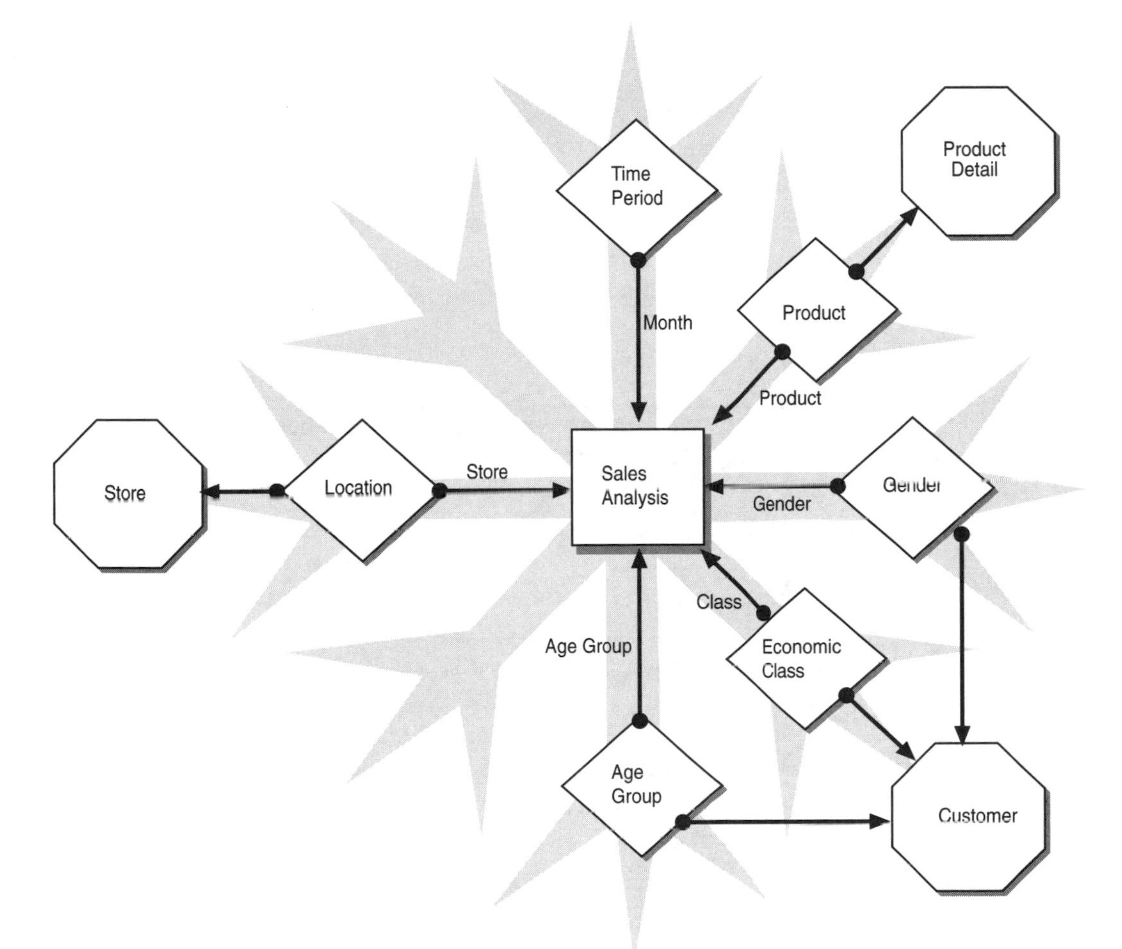

Figure 8.18: *Snowflake schema*

Unique Entity Definitions

While the examples in this book focus on one specific information package diagram—primarily to discuss theory and concepts—in reality you will have many information package diagrams for each subject-oriented data warehouse. A data warehouse project might be composed of 20 or more information package diagrams. When analyzing these individually, you will begin to see overlaps within dimensions. This is good.

As indicated in Chapter 2, What Factors Drive a Successful Data Warehouse Project?, you should find a high degree of similarity with the analytical techniques used by the management personnel within different business areas. This will make future subject-oriented data warehouses much easier, because you not need fully design and develop every entity within the data warehouse; instead you can reuse the entities from previous subject-oriented data warehouses. Defining these unique entities also assists in the usability aspects of the data warehouse. Users begin to understand what is meant by a customer, a product, or a location.

To assist you in clearly defining unique data warehouse entities, a matrix mapping the entities to information packages managed by a data warehouse such as shown in Figure 8.19 should be completed.

Information Package ➡ Data Warehouse Entities	Sales	Marketing Analysis	Quality Analysis	Supplier Performance
Time Period	X	X	X	X
Locations	X	X		
Channels	X			
Business	X			
Performance	X			
Markets		X		
Product	X	X	X	
Margin Ranges		X		
Departments			X	
Customer	X			
Buyer				X
Vendors				X
On Time/Late Range				X

Figure 8.19: *Data warehouse entity to information package cross-reference matrix*

You can refer to the master entity matrix of standard and unique entities presented in Figure 8.19 in the future to help maintain the unique entity definitions across a data warehouse. If you have multiple entities with the same definition but different meanings, you should further analyze these entities. Again, this could mean that there really should be two different entities, or it could mean that the detail level data is the same with different aggregation levels—that is, multiple access paths.

In areas in which multiple information package diagrams reference a given entity, realize that it is valid to have differing levels of detail managed by entities within a data warehouse. For example, all of the information packages in Figure 8.19 utilize the time period dimension. Quality requires time period dimension data down to the day level, while the remainder of the information packages require time period dimension data down to the month level. This is fine. Figure 8.20 shows how the data model associated to this example might appear. The key to validating the entity required to manage the time period dimension is that, in both situations, the requirement definition means time; the only difference is that one goes to another detail category level.

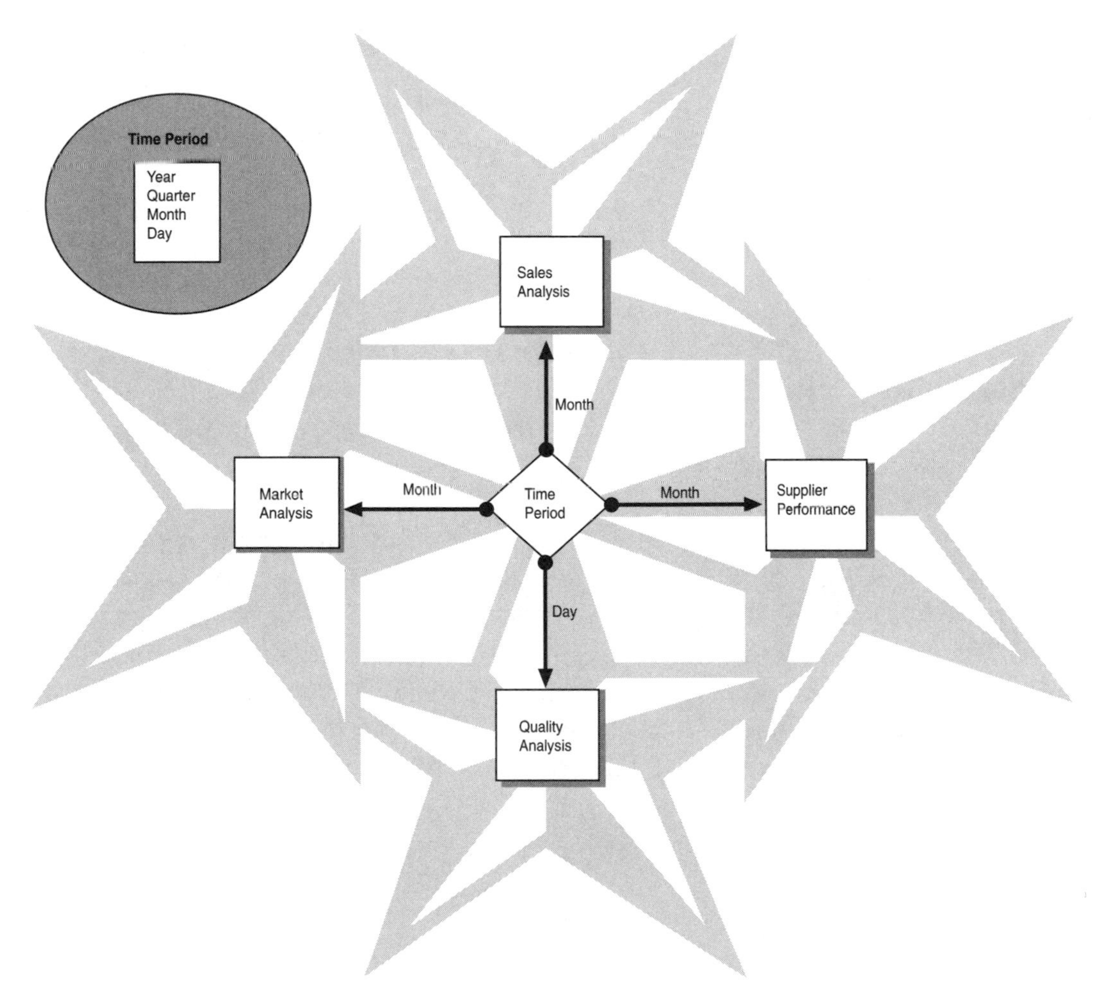

Figure 8.20: *Resolving unique entities*

Implementation Tip 5: It is important that you uniquely and clearly define all entities in your data warehouse: *What is a Customer? Product? Region?* You also should realize that it is okay for different measure entities to require the same dimension entity to provide relationships at differing levels of category detail: *A Time Period relates to Measure Entity 1 at the month level, while Measure Entity 2 relates at a day level.* Remember, a relational database, which you typically utilize to implement a data warehouse, allows you to join tables with various entity columns. Therefore, you can take the Month column and join it from the Time Period dimension entity to the Month column within Measure Entity 1. You can also join the Date column from the Time Period dimension entity to the Date column within Measure Entity 2. Month and Date are both time periods and will be contained within the same entity even though they provide us with different levels of detail.

An Additional Information Package Definition

You may have noticed some interesting concepts that would enhance the current requirements of the information package we have been discussing. Our original information package diagram that has been converted into a star schema is beginning to develop an additional "information package." The topical subject area is demographics.

Look closely at the model shown in Figure 8.21. In the lower-right corner, the potential for more information is beginning to take shape. Our guess is that the users would have defined a demographics information package diagram. But if they had not, this gives you an excellent opportunity to expand their knowledge base and to give them more intelligence.

Demographic information can be valuable to sales and marketing professionals. This type of data will either indicate what type of a market exists or what type of customer your products have attracted. Therefore, if users want to better understand the customer base or a specific constituency within the customer base, the necessary queries would be easy with a proper information package. For instance, if you want to know how many men between the ages of 36 and 40 have an income between $40,000 and $50,000, a simple, yet powerful query such as shown below could be issued for the data warehouse represented by Figure 8.21.

```
select count(*) from CUSTOMER where GENDER_CODE = 'M'
and ECON_CLASS_CODE = '40-50' and AGE_GROUP_CODE = '36-40'
```

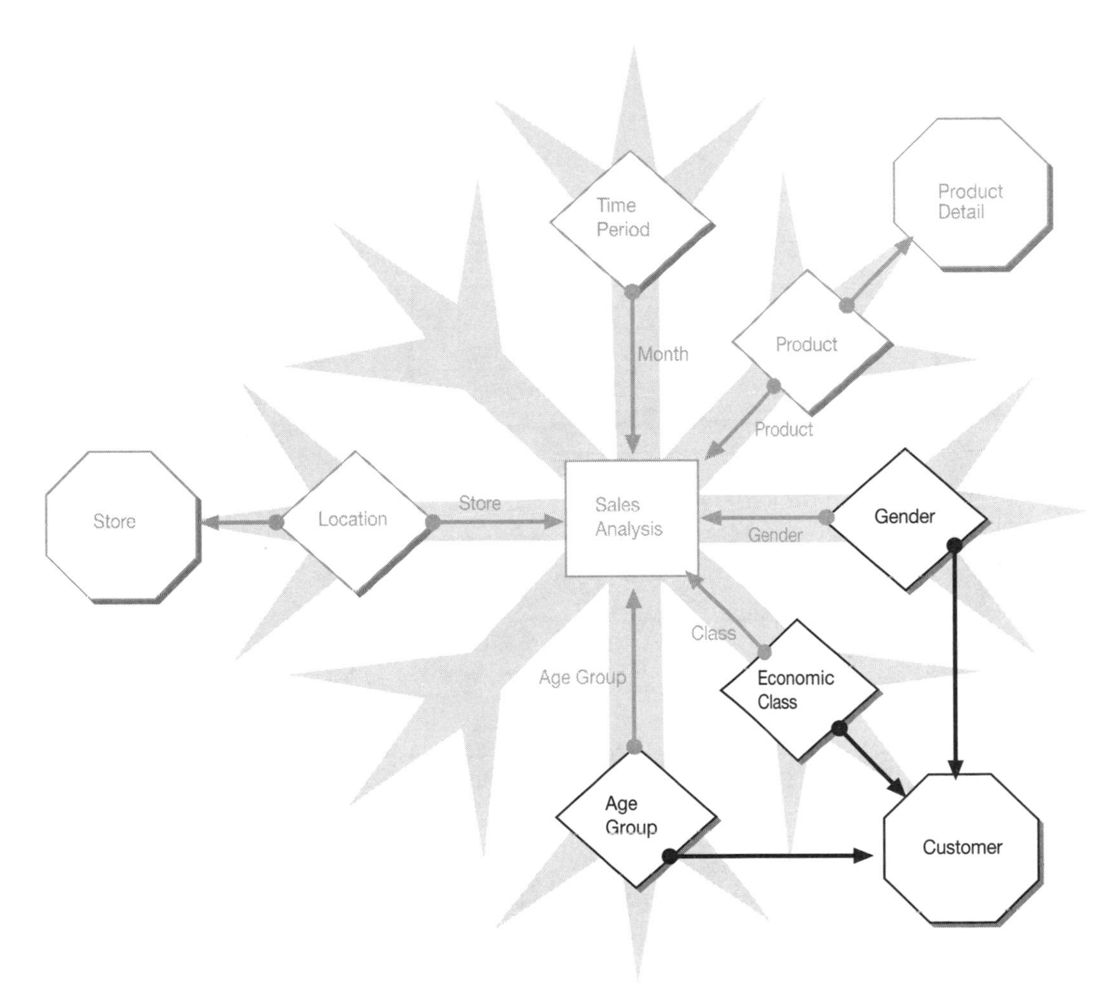

Figure 8.21: *An emerging additional information package*

However, if you also look closely at the figure, you notice that the *Customer* entity is a category detail, as denoted by the stop sign graphic. As you transform an information package diagram into star schema models and further transform the star schema into a physical database, you will note overlap of functionality that will require some decision making by the modeling and implementation teams. Specific design answers will come from better understanding of how users will access the data. The information package diagram for demographic information would likely contain a very shallow model that includes many dimensions that only go down one level, as shown in Figure 8.22.

Information Package: Customer Demographic Data

Dimensions →

Categories ↓

ALL Time Periods	ALL Locations	ALL Age Groups	ALL Economic Classes	ALL Genders	ALL Occupations	ALL Education	ALL Marital Status	ALL Dependents	ALL Rent/Own
Year 5	Country 20	Age Group 8	Class 10	Gender 3	Occupation 100	Education 6	Marital Status 5	No Children 12	Home Status 2
Quarter 20	Area 80				Title 10,000				
Month 60	Region 400								
	District 2,000								
	Store 200,000								
	Customer 20,000,000								

Measures/Facts:

Counts (*calc*)

Figure 8.22: *Customer demographic information package diagram*

The size of the customer base represented in Figure 8.22 was based on an estimate of 100 regularly monitored customers per store. In this case, we have a entity that will potentially have 20 million rows. Therefore, we may choose to split this subject into a category detail entity with corresponding data such as name, address, and phone number, and a measure entity with only customer numbers and key attributes. The measure entity would more than likely be smaller without the larger text fields and allow for quicker computation. The star schema representation resulting from the splitting of the customer data of this information package is shown in Figure 8.23.

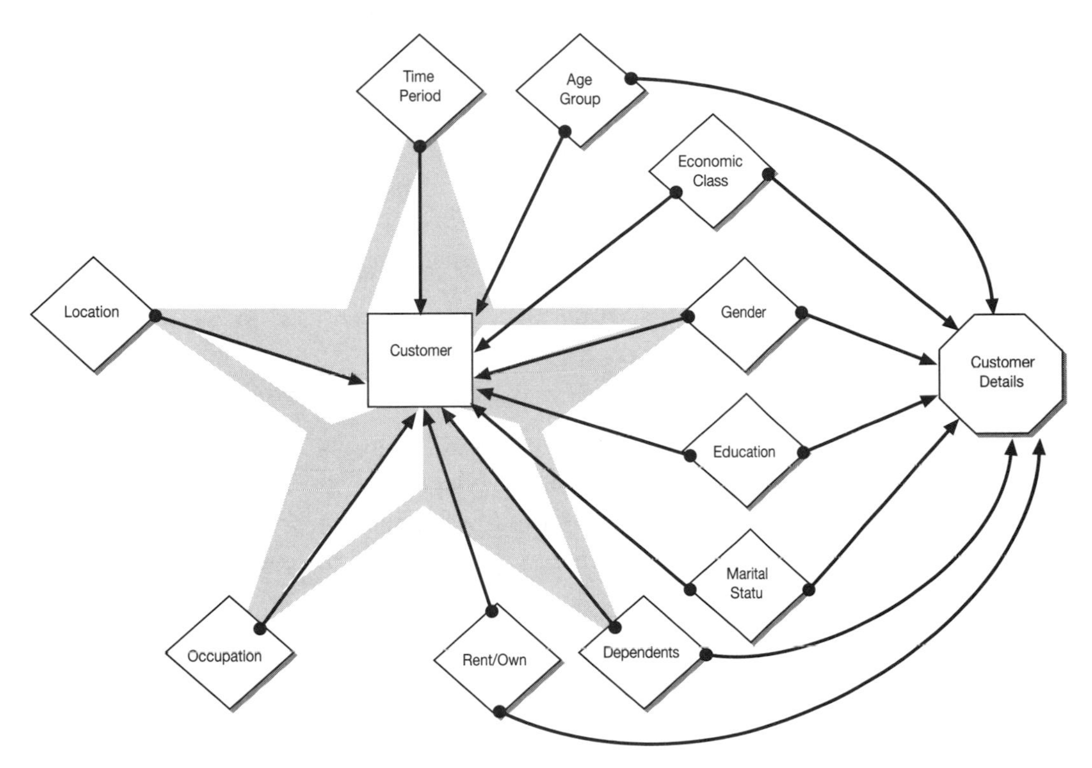

Figure 8.23: *Customer demographic star schema model*

Summary

The star schema modeling technique is the preferred, if not the required, technique to logically model your data warehouse. This technique has close links to relational database query processing and decision-support query processing logic, allowing you to build and develop highly performance-oriented data structures within your data warehouse. As well, star schemas easily translate from our information package diagramming techniques.

When decomposing your information package diagrams into star schemas, you define three types of logical data entities: measure, dimension, and category detail. The information package diagram delivers the requirements for the information package requested by users. The entire contents of a single information package diagram is represented by a set of these three entities. The star schema allows a data warehouse to deliver functionality that has either been established as requirements or is the vision of the data warehouse project, as described next.

- Dimension entities make it easy for users to traverse data structures, allowing them to easily build their own *user-driven reports*.
- The structures are query literate, and therefore have been designed to deliver *rapid response*. The techniques of an information package diagram and a star schema help to minimize joins as well as the volume of result sets; therefore, performance prevails.
- Slice-and-dice and drill-down concepts are built into the design structures. They enhance the user's capability to perform *complex analysis*. Also, the dimensions that assist in navigating data allow for uniform data objects to span multiple measure entities; and with SQL, users can perform complex, cross-measure analysis.
- Because a star schema provides a standard for design, the system can easily expand within a *dynamic business environment*. Many of the entities can be reused as additional subject-oriented data warehouses are brought on line, and the consistency inherent in the design allows users to easily adapt as the system grows.

9

Database Design

Design in art is a recognition of the relation among various things, various elements in the creative flux. You can't invent a design. You recognize it in the fourth dimension. That is, with your blood and your bones, as well as with your eyes.

—*D. H. Lawrence*

A data model is typically a representation of the data structure that is used in some segment of a business. Data models become part of the overall data architecture in a company. These data models are particularly useful in documenting the data resources within the organization. The models provide a basis for planning and designing new information systems, or in the case of a data warehouse, subject-oriented data warehouses. The ultimate benefits derived from the information packaging methodology we are utilizing here are as follows.

- **Data consistency and availability** A stable, integrated data structure results in consistent data that can support any user need for data, because the data definitions are shared by all of the users. The data can be easily accessed as needed. Even though your enterprise may go through organizational changes or experience employee turnover, the data remains stable. The result is data documentation for the entire data warehouse.

- **Cost-effective systems development and maintenance** Perhaps the most significant benefit is cost-effective systems development and maintenance. Data models act as a neutral buffer between applications and the databases that are developed. When properly built, the models are independent enough that changes to the design through the model can expedite a revamping of internal interfaces. This process results in better systems design, because the systems are based on a stable data structure.

Level of Refinement

Within this book, we have focused on an information packaging methodology that presents several different levels of the data models that are developed during the development process of a data warehouse. Each level is essentially a refinement or more detailed version of the previously developed data model, as shown in Figure 9.1.

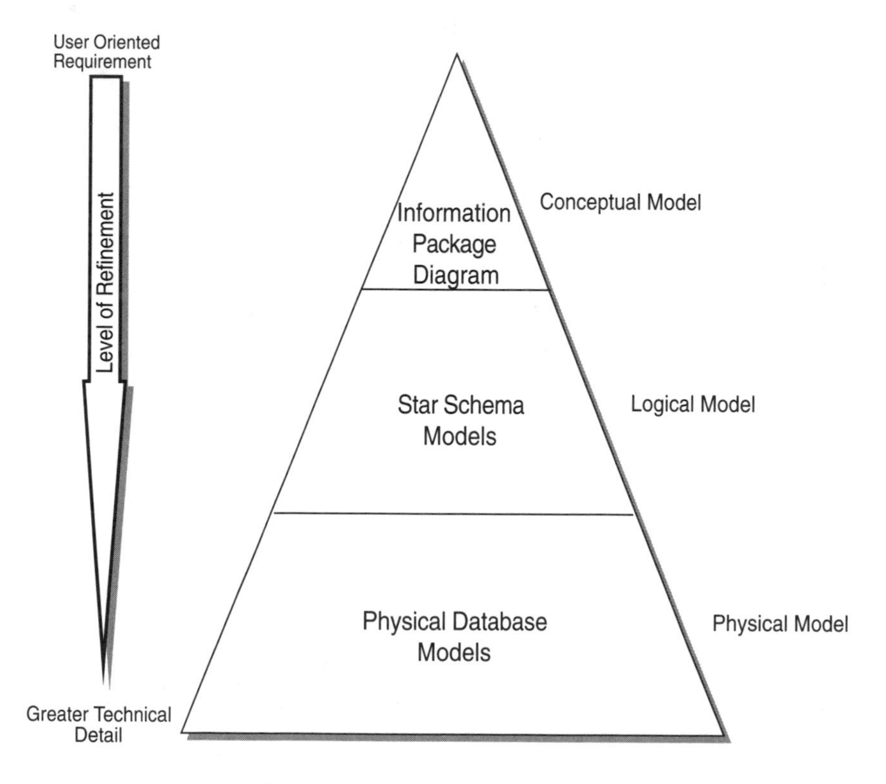

Figure 9.1: *Data model refinement*

By working through multiple levels of detail during the design, your project team will build in quality and deliver subject-oriented data warehouses that more closely align with what the users have requested. Some of the other benefits include the following.

- **A more precise representation of data** The refinement of data models continually provides a more precise representation of the data that is involved in delivering a data warehouse.
- **Planning for project deliverables** At this time, enough analysis has been completed to begin planning complete implementation and deployment schedules. These models will verify, and in many ways guarantee, that the data models and their associated subject-oriented data warehouses will be successfully integrated and reused.
- **Discovery and validation** The refinement of data models also is the beginning of working on an overall integration of an enterprise data warehouse. The greater the detail, the better the understanding of what the future environment will consist of. This process will also assist in the discovery and validation of previously developed work breakdown structures and activity plans.

The Information Package Diagram

The first and highest, or most generalized, level of a data model is its information package diagram. This model focuses on the information packaging requirements of users. An information package diagram defines the relationships between subject matter and key performance measures. And though an information package diagram has a highly targeted purpose, it provides only a generalization of what it really takes to place data in a data warehouse. You can generalize information package diagrams as providing a focused scope for user requirements, yet only delivering a data model that lacks the proper depth for implementation. Because information package diagrams do target what the users want, they are effective in communication between the technical staff and the user organization for flushing any inconsistencies between the requirements and what will be delivered. Figure 9.2 presents an information package diagram.

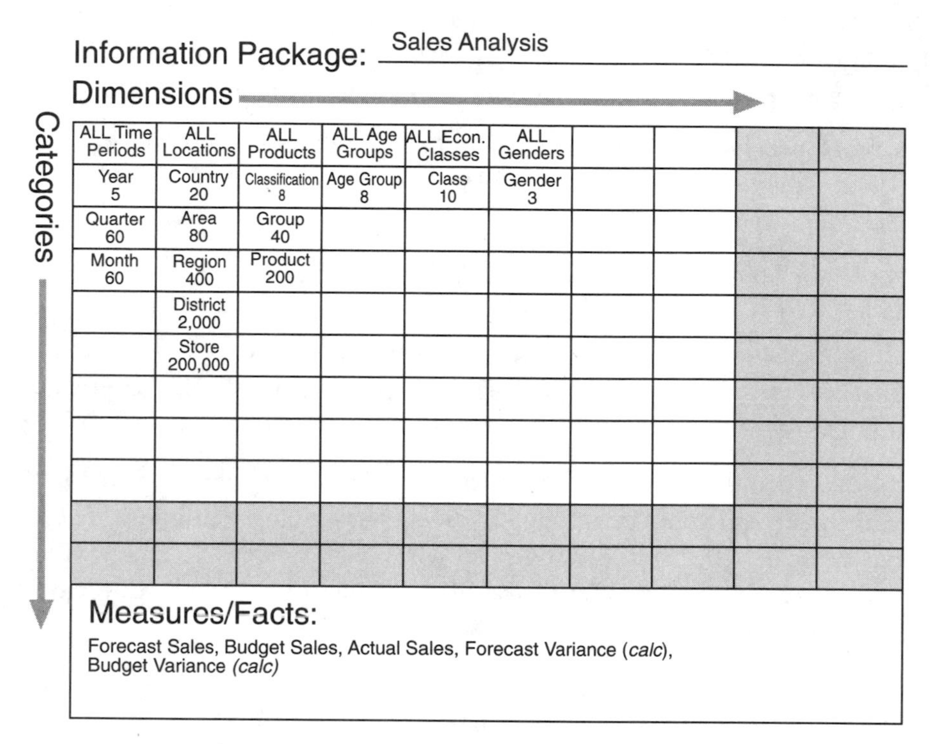

Figure 9.2: *An information package diagram*

The Star Schema Data Model

The second level of a data model is the star schema, which adds some refinement to the ultimate data structures. Entities are defined and characterized with specific purposes to assist users. These entities are characterized as follows: measure entities with fact based content, dimension entities with navigational content, and category detail entities with subject descriptive content. Also, a star schema begins to define attributes, or columns, that are contained in each of the major entities, and the relationships among those entities. A star schema data model provides more depth in preparation of fully defining the physical data entities. Again, this design is worked through the user community to flush the process of decision-oriented data and the requirements for additional supporting data from the original information package diagram. The star schema representing the information contained in Figure 9.2's information package diagram is presented in Figure 9.3.

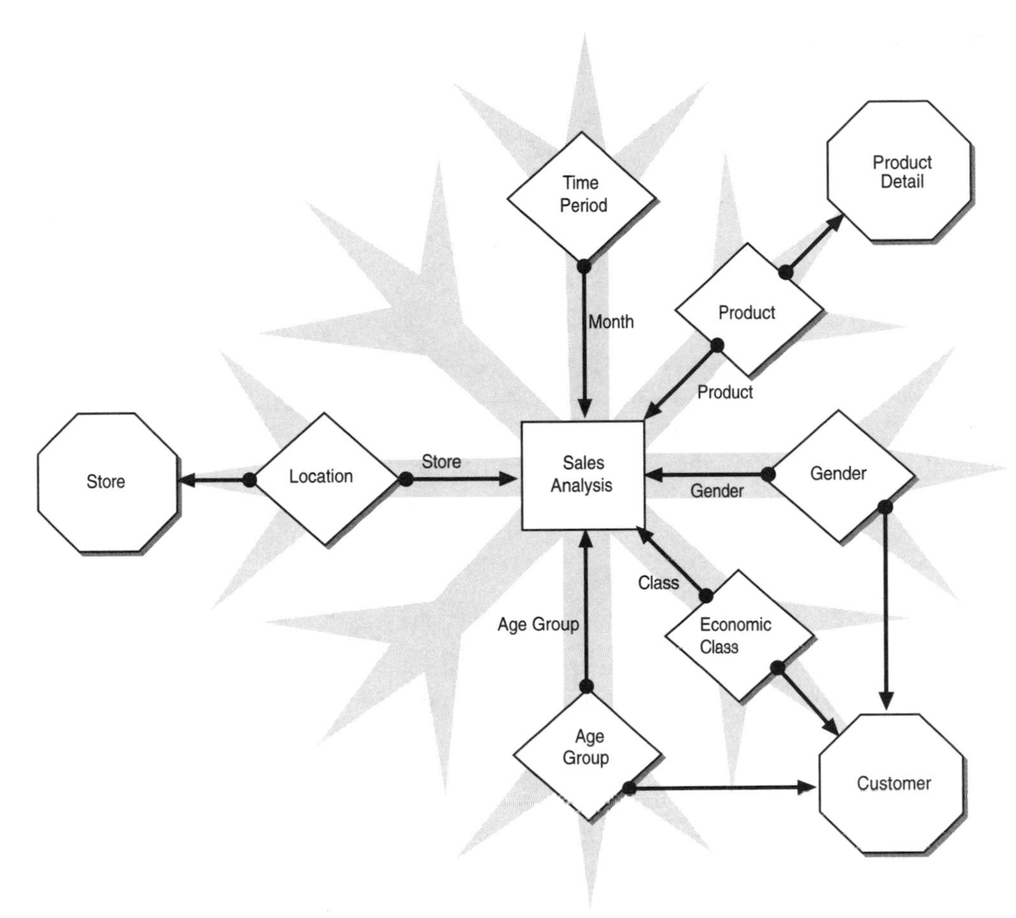

Figure 9.3: *The star schema for the information package diagram in Figure 9.2*

The Physical Data Model

The third level of a data model is a fully attributed data model, which becomes part of an enterprise's data architecture. The star schema data model should be used as a foundation for physical database design and implementation, because it specifies what data should be included and the relationships among the entities. This data model represents an information package in the greatest amount of depth and detail.

Implementation Tip 6: Be sure to follow the complete refinement process when modeling your data; that is, from information package diagram through star schema to physical data model. This is a key part of the process that should be strictly followed to assist in the overall quality of a data warehouse and the components managed by the data warehouse.

Building the Physical Data Model

The following sections describe the translation of a star schema into a physical data model. Though we primarily cover this information in summary fashion, this is the most traditional part of the data development process. We have conducted similar designs and models since the early information centers in the mainframe days and since the introduction to decision support systems that were deployed on the early relational database management systems of the mid-1980s.

Defining Data Standards

Prior to defining your first physical entity, relationship, or column, you should clearly define naming conventions that provide meaningful and descriptive information about the represented component. In general, your standards should adhere to the following guidelines.

- **Complete words** Because data will be accessed by users, you should attempt to use complete words wherever possible. When abbreviations are required, try to utilize standard and well-known abbreviations. Example: *OrdNo* is better represented as *OrderNumber* or *ORDER_NUMBER*.
- **Character case** Lowercase? Uppercase? Some database management system vendors recommend a specified case standard. But whatever you do, be consistent throughout. If you introduce the concept of mixed case, you may provide a more readable name, but one that is technically difficult to enforce. Example: Which do you find more readable: *order_number, ORDER_NUMBER,* or *OrderNumber*?
- **Underscores versus hyphens** Underscores improve the readability of any component name and should be the standard. If you utilize a data source that does not support underscores as a valid character, a hyphen is the next best thing. However, consistency is again an overriding factor for your decision here; use one of these characters to improve the readability of component names, not both. Example: *first_name*, *first-name*, or *firstname*.
- **Domains** When possible, create a list of common data definitions for components that represent similar data. Examples: Dates, Time, Time Stamps, Elapsed Time, Codes, Names, Descriptions, Pounds, Currency (Cost, Revenues, and so forth).

It is important to publish and enforce these guidelines throughout a data warehouse. The enforcement should be placed in the hands of those who oversee object management, such as the database administrator or object administrator.

Architecture Tip 4: Standards should be defined for each of the components or pieces of the data warehouse, including the following.

columns	constraints	databases	devices
datatypes	defaults	security groups	indexes
logins	rules	segments	servers
stored procedures	tables	triggers	information packages
views	standard reports	users	catalogs
domains	relationships		

Defining Entities

The star schema has us well on the road to defining the common entities for any given subject-oriented data warehouse. When defining the entities, you want to verify them and completely define their properties. This allows you to physically implement the entities within your chosen database management system.

Verifying Entities

When you transfer entities from a star schema to a physical model, you need to ask questions to verify if the entity is part of another entity, or one that can stand on its own. Here are some typical questions you need to ask.

- Can the entity be described?
- Does the entity have columns, or attributes, relevant to the user requirements?
- Are there several instances of this entity? (If there is only one instance of an entity, it may need to collapse into another entity or multiple entities.)
- Can one entity instance be separated or identified from another? (If not, they may be the same entity.)
- Does the entity refer to or describe something else, such as another entity? (In this case, it might be a column within that entity versus an entity that can stand on its own.)

Entity Properties

Now that we have defined the fundamental building blocks of a data model—including the entities, the relationships, and some of the columns—we need to examine the refinement of these items more specifically. Let's identify and define the properties of the data by looking at key and nonkey columns, and at data characteristics.

Key and Nonkey Columns

Data columns may provide key facts about an entire row in a given data entity. If the data uniquely identifies a row or is a common access path for users, the column may qualify to become a key. In query-oriented systems, keys and indexes assist in retrieval of data. However, they also introduce overhead to the database management system, so use care when defining such attributes.

- **Primary key** A primary key is a column or set of columns whose values can be used to uniquely identify instances of an entity. For example, the key to an order is typically an ORDER_NUMBER, which uniquely defines all of the associated data that is managed by that order.
- **Alternate key** An alternate key is a column or set of columns that is designated as a preferred or common means of accessing the instances of a given entity. For example, the primary key to a customer table might be CUSTOMER_NUMBER, while an alternate key might be CUSTOMER_NAME. CUSTOMER_NAME does not guarantee uniqueness of the instance of a customer; therefore, a number is typically generated by the operational system to uniquely represent the customer. However, users of the system are more likely to remember the name of a customer, so we should provide them with that way to access the data.
- **Foreign key** A foreign key is any column or group of columns within an entity whose values exist as primary key values in a parent entity. When verifying an entity instance's relationships at the key level, the value of the primary key must be present in the instance of the foreign key and vice versa. Example: In an order entry system, the order is typically represented by ORDER_HEADER and ORDER_LINE entities. ORDER_HEADER is typically referred to as the parent entity and ORDER_LINE as the child entity. ORDER_NUMBER is a primary key within ORDER_HEADER, because it defines a unique occurrence of an order. ORDER_NUMBER is considered a foreign key in the ORDER_LINE entity, because it defines the relationship between ORDER_LINE and ORDER_HEADER. Each ORDER_LINE must contain an ORDER_NUMBER, because without an ORDER_HEADER instance, an ORDER_LINE instance should never exist.

- **Nonkey data** A column that is not part of a primary or alternate key is referred to as nonkey data. This data is primarily used to further describe the instance of an entity. Example: On an order, you would typically not provide a key for a line item's units sold. However, this data gives further explanation to what a customer ordered.

- **Null values** If a column of data is contained within either a primary or alternate key, it may *not* contain a null value. Null refers to a column that has no value and is therefore unknown by the system. A null value allows you to distinguish between a deliberate entry of zero, or blank, and a nonentry.

Data Volumetrics and Update Frequency

Each entity contained in a data warehouse must be evaluated with regard to the volume of information processed and the frequency of update. This information becomes valuable during the transformation process discussed within Chapter 10, Data Extraction and Cleansing. You should build a chart, as shown in Table 9.1, that clear defines the following for each entity.

- Volumetrics, including the number of expected rows and growth patterns
- Update frequency

Accurate figures may not always be available for these characteristics, so you should model the figures based on existing systems.

Table 9.1: *Entity volumetric and update frequency chart*

Entity	Volumetrics	Update Frequency
COUNTRY	Low volume; approximately 20 rows	Whenever a reorganization occurs with the field sales force
AREA	Low volume; multiple of COUNTRY; approximately 80 rows	Whenever a reorganization occurs with the field sales force
REGION	Low volume; multiple of COUNTRY and AREA; approximately 400 rows	Whenever a reorganization occurs with the field sales force
DISTRICT	Low volume; multiple of COUNTRY, AREA, and REGION; approximately 2,000 rows	Whenever a reorganization occurs with the field sales force

(continues)

Table 9.1: *(continued)*

Entity	Volumetrics	Update Frequency
STORE	Low volume; multiple of COUNTRY, AREA, REGION, and DISTRICT; approximately 200,000 rows	Monthly, though tied to the other territory information; stores are added periodically, so to avoid missing a store, we will refresh monthly
LOCATION	Low volume; dimension entity that is impacted any time COUNTRY, AREA, REGION, DISTRICT, or STORE changes	Monthly; see note on STORE
TIME_PERIOD	Low volume; contains the calendar of approximately 100 rows	Annually load the new calendar
PRODUCT	Low volume; approximately 200 rows; dependent on PRODUCT_DETAIL	Monthly; see note on PRODUCT_DETAIL
PRODUCT_DETAIL	Low volume; approximately 200 rows	Monthly; in this example, we show a potential specialty store that manages only about 200 products; however, because some new items could be added monthly, we load at that frequency
ECONOMIC_CLASS	Approximately 10 rows: < $20,000 $20,000 to 30,000 $30,000 to 40,000 $40,000 to 50,000 $50,000 to 60,000 $60,000 to 70,000 $70,000 to 80,000 $80,000 to 90,000 $90,000 to 100,000 > $100,000	Static data

(continues)

Table 9.1: *(continued)*

Entity	Volumetrics	Update Frequency
GENDER	3 rows: male; female; unknown	Static data
AGE_GROUP	Approximately 10 rows: < 18 18 to 22 23 to 30 30 to 35 36 to 40 41 to 55 56 to 70 > 70	Static data
CUSTOMER	Each STORE has approximately 100 regularly monitored customers	Monthly, because the volume of data is relatively low and changes are periodically made, we load at that frequency
SALES_ANALYSIS	High volume; will contain all transactions for purchases at the store level; if the database were 100% dense, the potential is for 576,000,000,000 total rows with a monthly transaction volume of 9,600,000,000. This dense number would assume that, every month, every store sold every product to every age group for every economic class and gender. The odds of this are low, but this upper limit assists in planning.	Daily; though data is rolled up to the monthly level, transactions are stored to the daily level to avoid a large batch job at the end of the month, a time period that is volatile in an operational system environment

Entity Characteristics

It is important to fully identify the characteristics of each individual entity within a data warehouse. These characteristics are important for final implementation and deployment of the actual data, including the concepts of fragmentation and data access. Entity characteristics include the following.

- Individual columns of distinct data items

- Key attributes
- Valid range of data values
- Integrity constraints placed on the data
- Type and size of the data

These characteristics can be mapped to each entity utilizing a table like the one in Table 9.2, which is associated with the SALES_ANALYSIS entry found in Table 9.1.

Table 9.2: *Entity characteristics for the SALES_ANALYSIS entity in Table 9.1*

Columns	Key Attributes	Valid Range of Values	Integrity Constraints	Type and Size
TIME_PERIOD_KEY	Primary key; foreign key	Month for last 5 years from TIME_PERIOD entity	A row can't exist without time period key	char (6); YYYYMM format
STORE_KEY	Primary key; foreign key	Valid store key from STORE entity	A row can't exist without a store key	char(6)
PRODUCT_KEY	Primary key; foreign key	Valid product key from PRODUCT entity	A row can't exist without a product key	char (6)
AGE_GROUP_KEY	Primary key; foreign key	Valid age group key from AGE_GROUP entity	A row can't exist without an age group key	char(6)
ECON_CLASS_KEY	Primary key; foreign key	Valid economic class key from ECON_CLASS entity	A row can't exist without an economic class key	char (6)
GENDER_KEY	Primary key; foreign key	Valid gender key from GENDER entity	A row can't exist without a gender key	char (6)
FORECAST_SALES		Positive dollar amount		money (float)
BUDGET_SALES		Positive dollar amount		money (float)
ACTUAL_SALES		Positive dollar amount		money (float)

(continues)

Table 9.2: *(continued)*

Columns	Key Attributes	Valid Range of Values	Integrity Constraints	Type and Size
FORECAST_VARIANCE		Positive or negative dollar amount		money (float)
BUDGET_VARIANCE		Positive or negative dollar amount		money (float)

Tools to Automate the Definition

Plenty of tools are available in today's software marketplace to assist you with maintaining your data warehouse data model. The one that we utilize to continue with our examples is SDesignor from Powersoft Corporation. When selecting a tool for managing your data model, make sure that the tool contains items such as those that follow. We look at each of these items separately in following sections.

- Logical data modeling
- Domain management
- Physical data modeling
- Data definition language generation
- Reverse engineering of legacy data models
- Native database support
- Complete reporting

Architecture Tip 5: Your data warehouse standards should be developed prior to tool selection. Try to find the tool that most matches your standards and continually monitor available tools to find the tool that is best for your standards. *Do not build your standards based on tools. Over time, tools change and your standards will be left in the dark ages, or at least at the previous generation of tools.*

Logical Data Modeling

Your logical modeling process will not be too closely aligned to any given database management system. The separation of a logical definition from the native database management system allows you to begin compiling the required model of enterprise data sources without being concerned with physical attributes. These attributes will be further cultivated after a logical model is ready to be transformed and implemented into a physical model. Figure 9.4 demonstrates the logical model for Figure 9.3 as modeled in SDesignor.

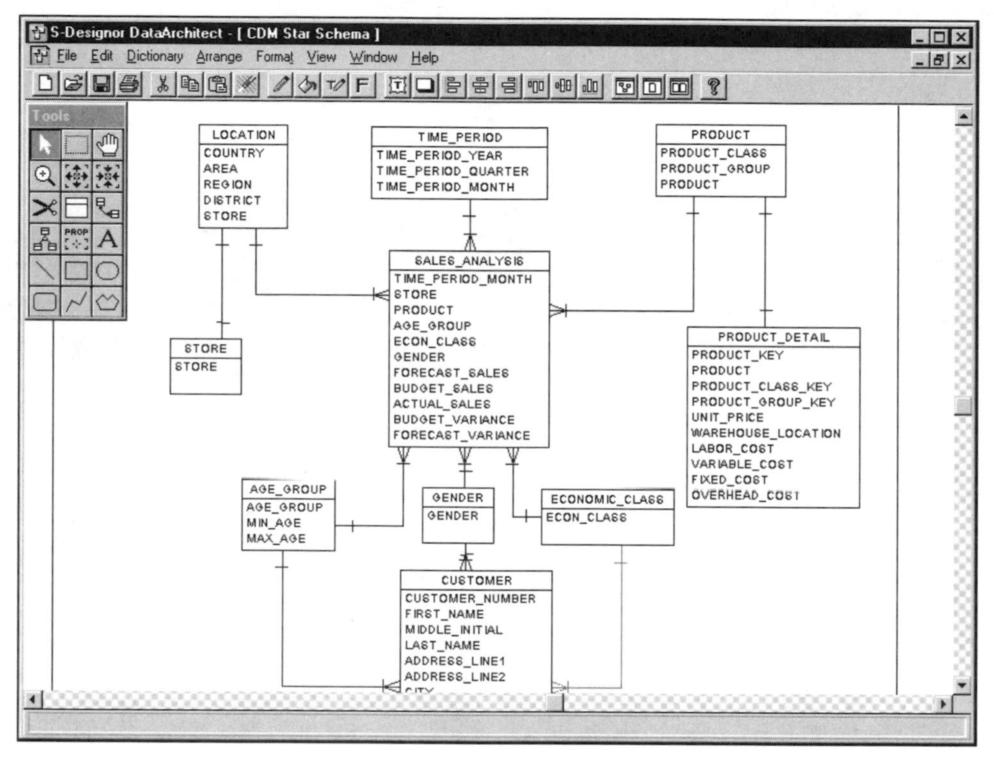

Figure 9.4: *SDesignor logical data model for the star schema illustrated in Figure 9.3*

Domain Management

Domain definition and management assists you in enforcing your standards. If you can characterize a set of common data types for your data warehouse, such a facility allows you to standardize how the data is physically implemented. As changes are required, such as increasing the size attribute, you can simply modify the domain, and all items that utilize the domain adjust to reflect the change. Figure 9.5 provides a list of domains that have been defined within our SDesignor model.

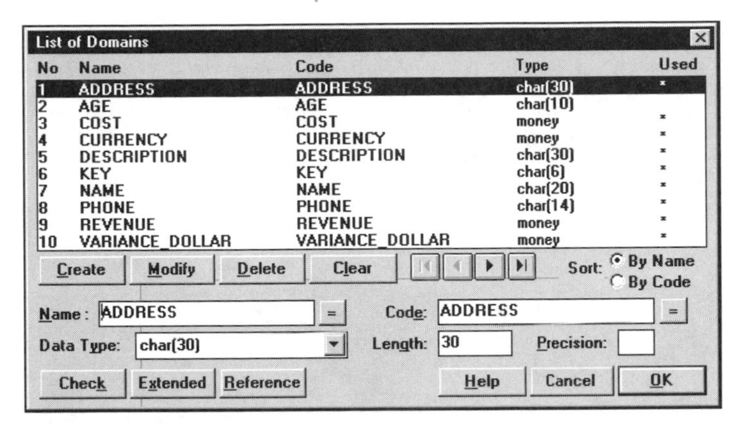

Figure 9.5: *Domain management*

Physical Data Modeling

Each database management system vendor has various nuances, so it is good to build a model that shows how you have accommodated physical implementations of your data model. During the physical modeling of your database, you make key decisions about which entities will be transformed from the logical definitions to the physical database. This physical data model is shown in Figure 9.6.

If you look closely at Figure 9.7, you will note that one such transformation has occurred with regard to the small demographic tables. Recall that these tables help to characterize our customer base and its buying trends. When you physically implement these data sources, you must take reasonable precautions in the area of performance: Don't overly analyze the data, just be reasonable. In looking at the demographic tables, there would be only approximately three genders (*male, female, and unknown*), 10 economic classes, and 10 age groups. These tables, though valuable to the overall system, are too costly to maintain as individual tables. The cost is not in maintenance; it is the cost to users, who would be required to perform three additional joins to retrieve the demographic information. The resolution to this issue is to merge the entities and populate all permutations into one demographic table. The number of rows that will be contained can be calculated by figuring the overall permutations for the three entities, as indicated below. This is a maintainable table—still small, but we now incur only one join versus the previous three.

```
3 genders * 10 economic classes * 10 age groups = 300 rows
```

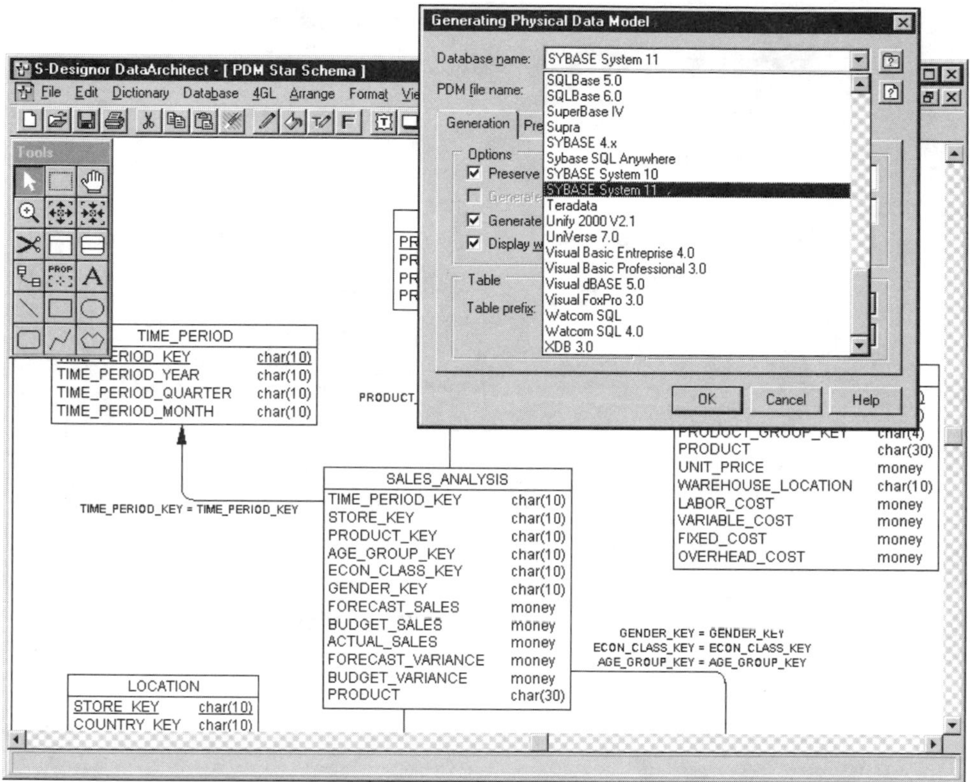

Figure 9.6: *Physical data modeling based on a native database management system*

This is yet another example of the denormalization that occurs in the physical implementation of a data warehouse. This denormalization greatly assists the performance of the overall system by reducing the server-based overhead required to obtain all of the relevant detail information that the users require. With the addition of this table, you should also note that the other tables have gone away; this is basically a merger of the three demographic tables. We still have the customer table for additional information, which we don't want to necessarily denormalize, because it may be an infrequently queried table. In Figure 9.7, the three separate data items of GENDER_KEY, ECON_CLASS_KEY, and AGE_GROUP_KEY have been retained within the index. This circumstance involves another design decision that needs to be made as you transform your logical data model into a physical data model—whether to maintain and index over multiple columns, or to use a synthetic key. A synthetic key is one that is essentially derived either by the developer or the system to uniquely identify the occurrence of a row.

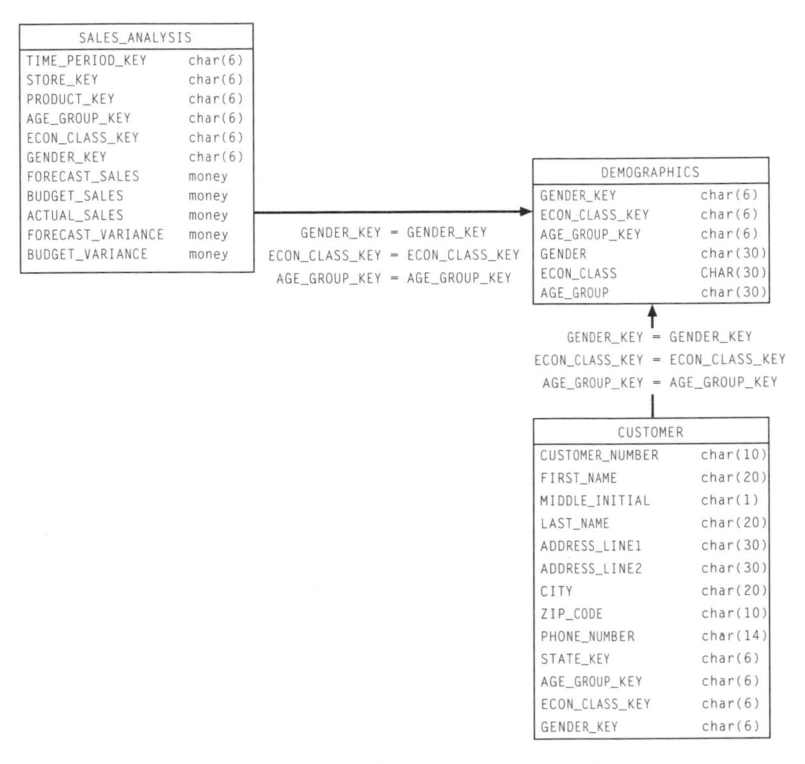

Figure 9.7: *Merging demographic data*

In this instance, we replace the three data items with a single data item (DEMOGRAPHIC_KEY) that represents a single permutation of three values (GENDER_KEY, ECON_CLASS_KEY, and AGE_GROUP_KEY). Synthetic keys often simplify the processing logic and overhead within a database management system and may be the best alternative for an ad hoc query front-end application. However, the natural data items may be a better implementation for applications that are more rigid and fixed. These keys can be given meaning and allow a front-end application to avoid table joins or other associated overhead—or avoid confusion associated with providing users with data from more than one database table.

For example, if the GENDER_KEY column is maintained in the DEMOGRAPHICS and SALES_ANALYSIS table, the developer can fill a list box with the values for GENDER_KEY and issue a query only against SALES_ANALYSIS, because most users will understand *M*, *F*, and *U* as valid genders. If a synthetic key is utilized, a DEMOGRAPHIC_KEY value of *0020* might represent the GENDER of *male*, AGE_GROUP of *30* to *35*, and ECONOMIC_CLASS of *40K to 50K*. In this situation, users will be unable to determine that *0020* performs all three of these filters. Therefore, the query will require the DEMOGRAPHICS and SALES_ANALYSIS tables, which creates the overhead of a join within a query. Decisions like these need to be made as you translate your model from a logical design to a physical design. Memory, disk space, and processing power of the resources within an architecture ultimately impact these decisions.

Data Definition Language (DDL) Generation

Most database management system vendors still require a scripting language, typically SQL, to generate a physical database. You want a tool that understands your database management system, and that can generate and manage the DDL required to build your database. SDesignor provides an elegant generation facility as shown in Figure 9.8. Upon selecting the options within this figure, SDesignor generates an SQL DDL file as shown in Figure 9.9.

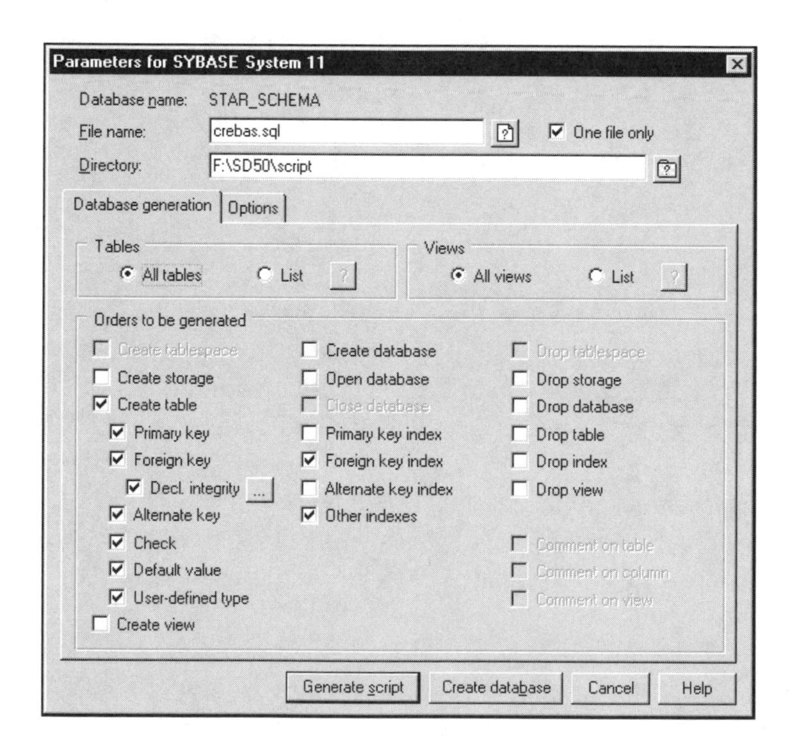

Figure 9.8: *Generation of database*

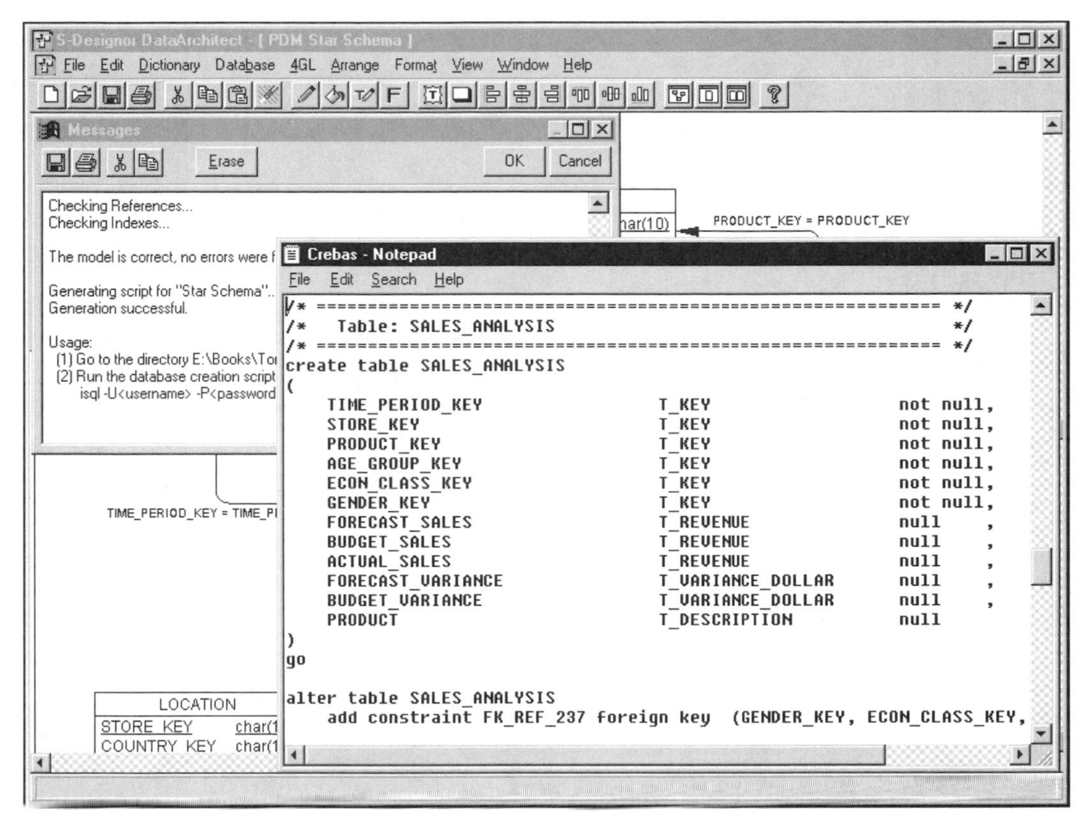

Figure 9.9: *Generation of native DDL*

Reverse Engineering of Legacy Data Models

As stated in the logical data model section earlier in this chapter, you want to be able to attach to existing data structures and populate their current data models. Typically, the reverse engineering process involves attaching to the database management system or reading a script file to generate a physical data model. Figure 9.10 demonstrates the reverse engineering facility found in SDesignor. From this physical model, you can migrate up to a logical model, which will assist you in merging system models to build an enterprise data model.

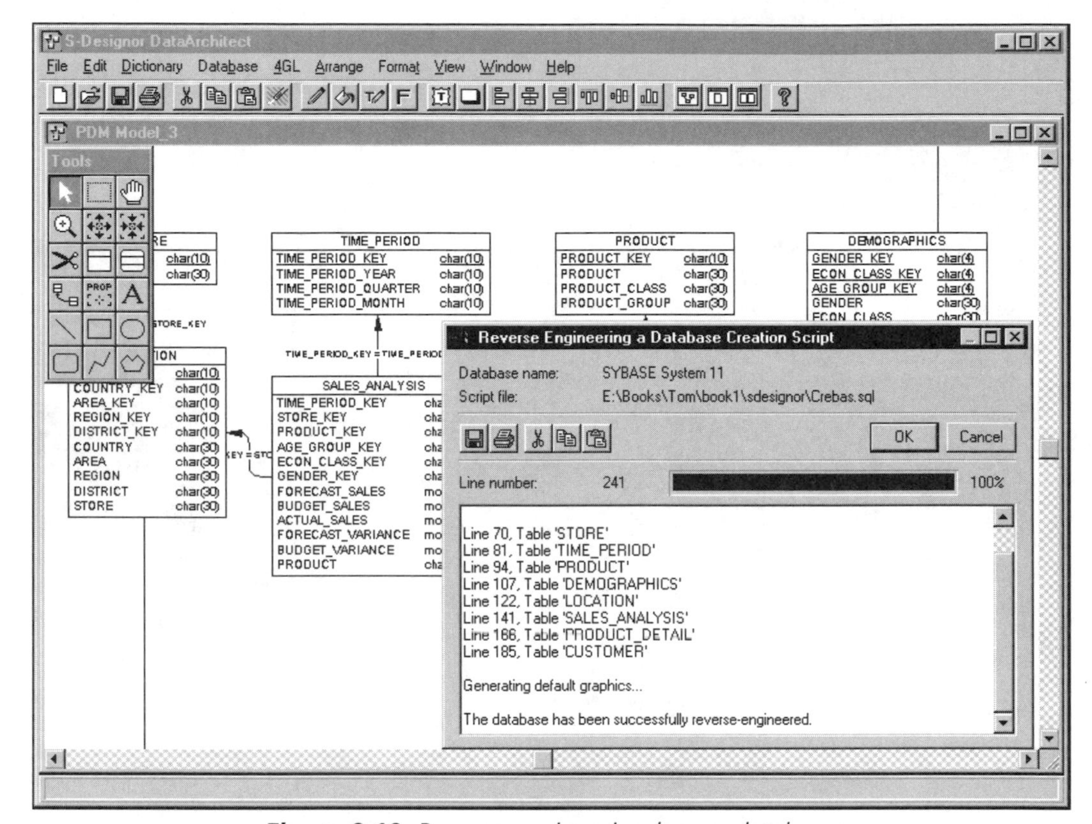

Figure 9.10: *Reverse engineering legacy databases*

Native Database Management System Support

As we stated in above sections, it is important to be able to work with native database management system support. This ability ensures that the proper syntax is generated for an optimized physical data model. Without it, you have a bland script requiring a high degree of rework, relegating the data modeling tool to a documentation-only tool. There are too many tools to settle for one that does not support your native data structures.

Complete Reporting

To avoid maintaining reams of paper documentation, ensure that your data modeling tool maintains relevant information about the objects being managed and that it has the ability to produce well designed documentation. The reporting capabilities should also allow the export of reports to common word processor formats, such as Rich Text Format (RTF). This feature allows you to merge your data model documentation with other documents for a data warehouse and overall architecture. SDesignor provides such a capability, as shown in Figure 9.11.

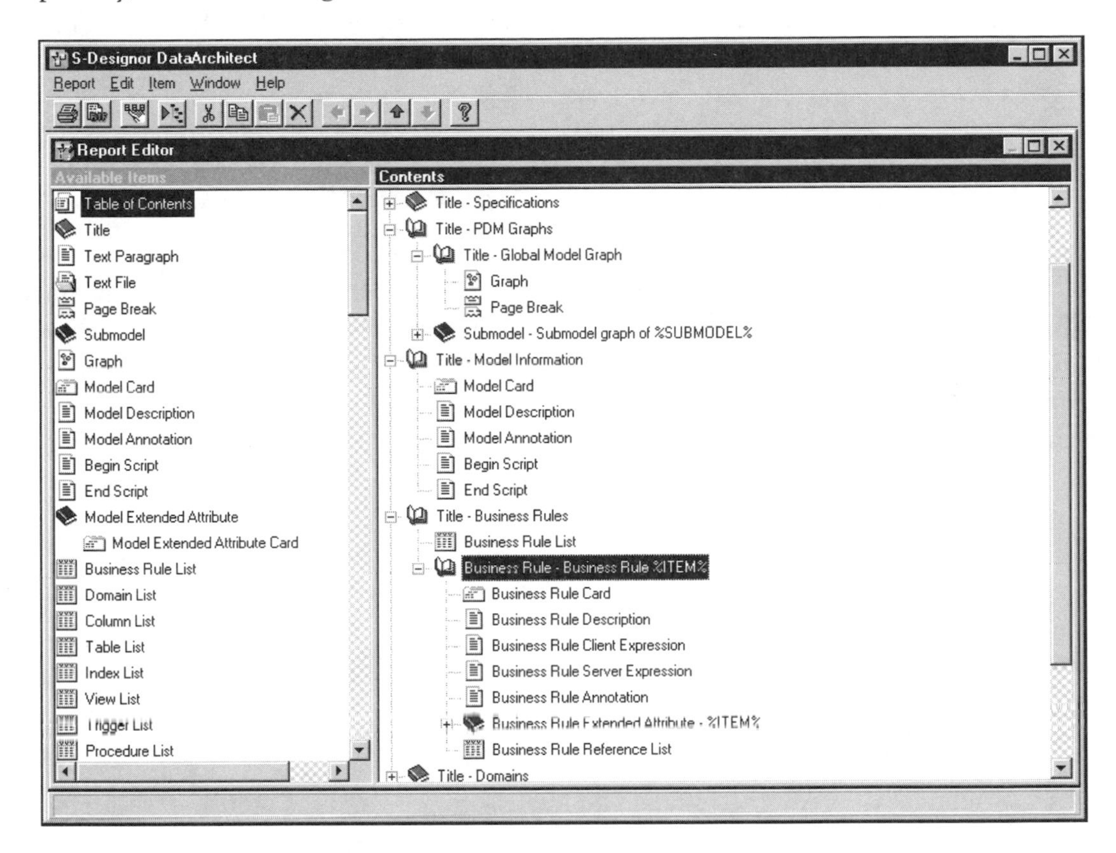

***Figure 9.11:** Complete documenting capabilities provided by SDesignor*

Architecture Tip 6: A data modeling tool should at a minimum support the following: logical data modeling; physical database modeling; automatic generation of the native, physical data definition language for your chosen database management system; domain management; reverse engineering of legacy data models; native database management system support; and complete reporting capabilities for impact analysis and documentation. Don't settle for less.

Implementing a Data Model

The final step in the process of defining your data model is to transform the entity definitions and associated characteristics into your tool of choice. This process allows you to proceed at a more rapid and automated pace for delivering the required data warehouse to your users. If you have charted each of your entities as discussed earlier and as shown in Tables 9.1 and 9.2, and have properly selected a tool as discussed earlier, the entry process should be short and sweet. With the tool able to generate the proper structures for your target database management system, you are well on your way to success.

A Closer Look at a Physical Data Warehouse

Now that a physical data model is present, let's take a closer look at what has been populated for each entity by type (measure, dimension, and category detail), as shown in Figure 9.12. The data that has been placed in the data model includes that which has been derived from the information package diagram as well as additional information viewed as important from the interview research you conducted. Therefore, while you may have an information package diagram that is nearly identical to the one in this book, the physical data model may be totally different. (We hope that yours will be more robust and complete.)

Measure Entity Attributes

Remember that the characteristics of a measure entity include the following.

- Provides the primary focus for quantitative data, business measure data, or factual data
- Contains numerous access paths, dimensions, or indexes into the measurement data
- Involves relatively normalized data
- Composed of the lowest categories in each dimension and the measures from the information package diagram
- Can grow to be large tables
- Will be the heart and soul of analytical activity

After thorough analysis of these attributes, the physical measure entity that has been created includes the foreign keys for the relationships among the measure entity and all associated dimension entities, as well as the facts that were highlighted within the information package. These relationships among the measure and dimension entities include the following, which we have represented as SQL *join* logic.

```
WHERE TIME_PERIOD.TIME_PERIOD_KEY = SALES_ANALYSIS.TIME_PERIOD_KEY
WHERE LOCATION.STORE_KEY = SALES_ANALYSIS.STORE_KEY
WHERE PRODUCT.PRODUCT_KEY = SALES_ANALYSIS.PRODUCT_KEY
WHERE GENDER.GENDER_KEY = SALES_ANALYSIS.GENDER_KEY
  AND ECONOMIC_CLASS.ECON_CLASS_KEY = SALES_ANALYSIS.ECON_CLASS_KEY
  AND AGE_GROUP.AGE_GROUP_KEY = SALES_ANALYSIS.AGE_GROUP_KEY
```

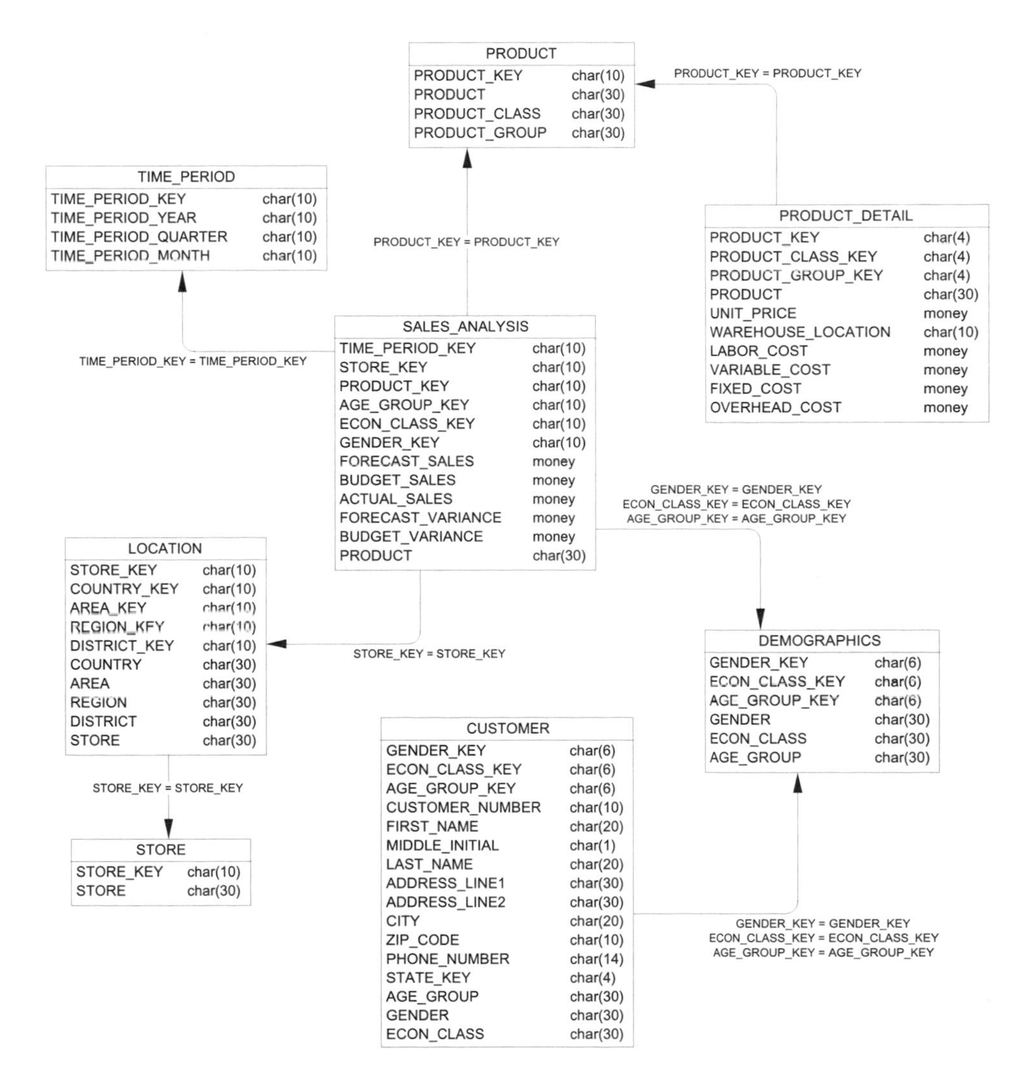

Figure 9.12: *A data warehouse physical model*

The largest assumptions that have been made in this physical implementation of a measure entity are that STORE_KEY and PRODUCT_KEY are unique and therefore they do not require their additional dimension hierarchy keys to locate the associated measure information. If this were not true, you would simply have a more complex, compound key joining these tables, similar to the one utilized by the DEMOGRAPHICS table. The columns within the SALES_ANALYSIS table that are foreign keys are therefore the following.

```
TIME_PERIOD_KEY
STORE_KEY
PRODUCT_KEY
GENDER_KEY
ECON_CLASS_KEY
AGE_GROUP_KEY
```

In addition to the foreign key items, numerical information is included in the measure entity physical definition. These data columns are documented at the bottom of the information package diagram, as seen in Figure 9.2, and include the following.

```
FORECAST_SALES
BUDGET_SALES
ACTUAL_SALES
FORECAST_VARIANCE
BUDGET_VARIANCE
```

Dimension Entity Attributes

As previously discussed, the characteristics of dimension entities include the following.

- Has a primary focus of navigation of the measure entities
- Involves relatively denormalized entities
- Contains codes, or keywords, and their related description for the entire dimensional hierarchy
- Maps to the columns of the information package diagram
- Will typically be small tables, if physically implemented
- Serves as the gateway to a data warehouse
- Is often utilized to fill graphical pick lists, such as list boxes or combo boxes, in front-end applications

Dimension entities are logical and not guaranteed to translate directly into a physical database table. The physical change of the gender, economic class, and age group demographic dimension entities in the previous examples demonstrates this concept. By producing a denormalized merger of the demographic dimension entities, we produced a better performing physical entity.

You need to evaluate each of your dimension entities to determine whether it should be physically realized. For example, questions similar to those asked for the demographic dimension entity may be asked of the location dimension entity: *Should country, area, region, district, store, and location be in separate tables, or in denormalized, merged location dimension entities?* Some people feel that dimension entities should always be realized. This type of thinking drives a physical model that has the following characteristics.

- Directly maps to a star schema
- Is clearly easier for users to understand and navigate
- Provides dimension entities that provide a data integrity check for a measure entity, because measurement data should not have an association with its associated dimension entities

If we look closely at the LOCATION entity, we see that it possesses the following columns.

```
COUNTRY_KEY
COUNTRY
AREA_KEY
AREA
REGION_KEY
REGION
DISTRICT_KEY
DISTRICT
STORE_KEY
STORE
```

The preceding LOCATION dimension entity illustrates the denormalization concepts that we discussed earlier in this book. Each level in the hierarchy has an associated key and description. This allows us to retrieve all of the data for the complete hierarchy without requiring a relational join and its associated overhead. With dimension entities, a data warehouse access tool can navigate and filter the measures by presenting users with descriptions, with which they are familiar, while behind the scenes the tool can filter the data with the keys, with which the database is more optimized. The keys reduce overhead, because the measure entity can contain smaller data than the descriptions. The descriptions are maintained centrally, so we can optimally change descriptions without affecting the measure entity. The keys stay the same, while the descriptions change.

Figure 9.13 shows a sampling of how this data structure might look. Notice the repetition or denormalization of country, area, region, and district. All of these descriptions would traditionally be placed in other database tables. However, such an implementation would force a five-way join to obtain the hierarchy and a six-way join to match the analysis data. This is overhead we avoid through our implementation.

COUNTRY_KEY	COUNTRY	AREA_KEY	AREA	REGION_KEY	REGION	DISTRICT_KEY	DISTRICT	STORE_KEY	STORE
USA	USA	EAST	EASTERN	NE	NORTH-EASTERN	NWEN	NEW ENGLAND	BST1	BOSTON STORE 1
USA	USA	EAST	EASTERN	NE	NORTH-EASTERN	NWEN	NEW ENGLAND	NSH1	NASHUA STORE 1
USA	USA	EAST	EASTERN	NE	NORTH-EASTERN	NY	NEW YORK	MAT1	MANHATTEN STORE 1
USA	USA	EAST	EASTERN	NE	NORTH-EASTERN	NY	NEW YORK	MAT2	MANHATTEN STORE 2
USA	USA	EAST	EASTERN	MA	MID-ATLANTIC	CAR	CAROLINAS	NMB1	NORTH MYRTLE BEACH STORE 1
USA	USA	EAST	EASTERN	SE	SOUTH-EASTERN	FLA	FLORIDA	WB1	WALTON BEACH STORE 1
USA	USA	EAST	EASTERN	SE	SOUTH-EASTERN	FLA	FLORIDA	TB1	TAMPA BAY STORE 1
USA	USA	EAST	EASTERN	SE	SOUTH-EASTERN	FLA	FLORIDA	MIA1	MIAMI BEACH STORE 1
USA	USA	EAST	EASTERN	SE	SOUTH-EASTERN	FLA	FLORIDA	MIA2	MIAMI BEACH STORE 2
CAN	CANADA	WEST	WESTERN	BC	BRITISH COLUMBIA	VAN	VANCOUVER	BCV1	VANCOUVER STORE 1

Figure 9.13: *Sample data from a location dimension entity*

The decision to physically realize all of dimension entities is heavily influenced by the database management system's optimizer. An optimizer that recognizes dimension tables and builds the correct join sequences rewards a strategy of realizing these entities.

If a dimension entity is only used for one information package when you go through your physical implementation, you may want to collapse it with your measure entity. If the dimension entity is used with multiple information packages, you may want to collapse it with an associated category detail entity. However, keeping dimension entities separate on an initial implementation allows you to perform better description, or label maintenance. If descriptive data is stored within measure or category detail entities in a denormalized design, substantial overhead will be associated with changing a descriptive label. The dimension entity will isolate the denormalized data in a relatively small database table, which decreases the overhead associated with any change in descriptive label data. You should weigh these physical design issues against the potential overhead of increased SQL *join* logic that would be required with separation of tables into dimension, measure, and category detail entities.

Remember that these entities are utilized by users of a data warehouse as navigational aides to filter and aggregate data within measure entities. Therefore, a front-end application may initially load data from these dimension entities and never utilize them again. These entities also form a common link between measures of a data warehouse, including measure-to-measure and measure-to-category-detail relationships. Users are more familiar with the descriptions of these entities than with the keys, but we may still want to manage these entities with keys and descriptions to optimize query behavior.

Category Detail Entity Attributes

Category detail entities, like measure entities, typically translate into a physical database table. These entities contain data that provides more qualitative information to users and assists in supporting the decision making process. Remember that their common attributes include the following.

- Provides data for reference and as support information to complete the intelligence of measurement data
- Contains data that is more qualitative
- Maps closely to transaction structures
- Involves typically normalized data structures
- Is represented by a cell, or category, on the information package diagram
- Typically contains a medium amount of data rows—less than measures and more than dimension entities
- Contains descriptive or qualitative data, not merely numbers

CUSTOMER and PRODUCT_DETAIL entities are two that have been detailed out and included in the current data model. Both of these entities, which are displayed in Figure 9.14, are interesting because they will probably evolve into their own information package diagram. Note that the CUSTOMER entity has a lot of demographic data that will be of interest to people performing functions such as target marketing and product development. The PRODUCT_DETAIL entity contains various cost information that will be important to those who monitor the profitability of a company.

Implementation Tip 7: Data warehouse entities should be driven by users' query behavior. To this end, dimension entities assist users in navigating and filtering measure entities, and proceed to allowing users to focus on data in category detail entities.

PRODUCT_DETAIL	
PRODUCT_CLASS_KEY	char(6)
PRODUCT_GROUP_KEY	char(6)
PRODUCT_KEY	char(6)
PRODUCT	char(30)
UNIT_PRICE	money
WAREHOUSE_LOCATION	char(10)
LABOR_COST	money
VARIABLE_COST	money
FIXED_COST	money
OVERHEAD_COST	money

CUSTOMER	
CUSTOMER_NUMBER	char(10)
FIRST_NAME	char(20)
MIDDLE_INITIAL	char(1)
LAST_NAME	char(20)
ADDRESS_LINE1	char(30)
ADDRESS_LINE2	char(30)
CITY	char(20)
ZIP_CODE	char(10)
PHONE_NUMBER	char(14)
STATE_KEY	char(6)
AGE_GROUP_KEY	char(6)
ECON_CLASS_KEY	char(6)
GENDER_KEY	char(6)

Figure 9.14: *PRODUCT_DETAIL and CUSTOMER category detail entities*

Summary

The level of refinement that produces a final data warehouse physical database design has us building three separate models that provide greater detail each step of the way. We start with an information package diagram, which gives us a definition that is highly understood by users and relatively incomplete for a database administrator. Through our research, analysis, and design we transform this information package into a star schema, and finally produce a database management system's specific physical data model.

You should proceed with your projects utilizing this set of refinements to the data model. You will discover many areas where improvements can be made to the data model along the way, such as the demographic dimension entity merger we discussed in our refinements. These techniques are important and will assist your team in becoming better information packagers—a requirement for the architects and designers of a data warehouse. Too often, designers try to take the short route to the final deliverable and lose much value-added information along the way.

Though entity relationship modeling has played a part in this process, it should not be the first and only part. The concepts of information packaging methodology will build the required data architecture and functionality for your data warehouse. The information packaging diagram technique of data gathering and star schema modeling design technique provide consistency in design as well as a set of standardized communication tools that will make your warehouse more cost effective and easier to develop and maintain. Remember, this is the users' system, not yours. To cut directly to design techniques that have been developed over the years for transaction processing systems rather than data warehousing systems will not benefit anyone—your development team or users.

There is no simple way to transform an entity relationship model into a multidimensional model or design. Decision support systems and traditional business analysis require the multidimensional aspects found in such a model. Therefore, remember the steps of refinement for information packaging methodology listed here.

1. Build a conceptual model of your information packages with information package diagrams. These diagrams are completed based on your interview sessions with users and the executives overseeing the business area covered by your subject-oriented data warehouse.

2. From the information package diagrams, begin to unify your three major warehouse entities—the measure, dimension, and category detail entities. You should guarantee in this step that you clearly distinguish entities and do not deliver overlapping information. The delivery vehicle for these logical data models is the star schema design. Clearly build each star on a graphical entity map utilizing symbols to define and distinguish the entities and their operational characteristics. A rectangle defines a measure, a filter symbol defines a dimension entity, and a stop sign defines a category detail entity.

3. From the star schema design, transform your multidimensional model into a physical database model. It is wise to pick one of the many standard data modeling tools available in today's marketplace to assist you in automating this process. It is key that you work from a data modeling tool that natively supports your data warehouse architecture and delivers productivity for ongoing maintenance of an enterprise data model.

10

Data Extraction and Cleansing

Information is the oxygen of the modern age. It seeps through the walls topped by barbed wire, it wafts across the electrified borders.

—*Ronald Reagan*

The data model that we produced in Section 4, The Process, just gives us a data store that users can easily navigate; it gives us no firm way to load a data asset. At this point, we basically have a house with no furnishings, and no moving company. We have proceeded to this point in a methodical manner. Too often, development resources want to retrieve the operational system data models and begin dumping the operational data into the data warehouse. (*"Let's see what they use and how they use it."*) These data junk yards fail, because the key "user-driven" ingredient is lacking; little to no thought has been given to how users want the data. The information packaging methodology discussed in this book assists your team in avoiding this approach.

The construction of a data warehouse begins with careful attention to an overall architecture and data model, and with their sizing components. It is key that the correct architecture is firmly in place for supporting the activities of a data warehouse. After the architecture is in place and the data model is developed, the builders of a data warehouse can figure out which data they want to access, in what form, and how it will flow through an organization. And as stated earlier, the architecture—specifically the data architecture—is more important than the tools that are used.

This phase of a data warehouse project will deliver the goods. This is where data is extracted from its current environment and transformed into the user-friendly data model managed by a data warehouse. Remember, this is a phase that is all about quality. A data warehouse is only as good as the data that it manages, so you need to focus your project team on the overall principles of quality. Time is not the most important element when it comes to data warehousing. A user would readily accept a delay in your project rather than accept bad data. If you are working with systems that are 10 to 15 years old, you may face some unknown data quality problems in redundancy and inconsistency. Be aware of these issues and plan accordingly.

Managing Corporate Data Assets

The process of managing corporate data has evolved over time. It is a job filled with peril, because all users want something to fit their specific need, while those managing the resources are trying to centrally control and unify the data asset. This process has evolved into "how to manage the data architecture," when in the past it was simply "database administration." We can often segment this task into individual components that comprise the overall management of the data asset. This process is illustrated in Figure 10.1, and includes the following.

- Operational aspects of data entry and data processing
- Access requirements for operational data
- Extraction requirements for warehoused data

Operational Processing

Operational processing of data takes many forms. But for simplicity, we have narrowed it down to two primary functions: data entry and data processing. We cover each of these functions separately in the following sections.

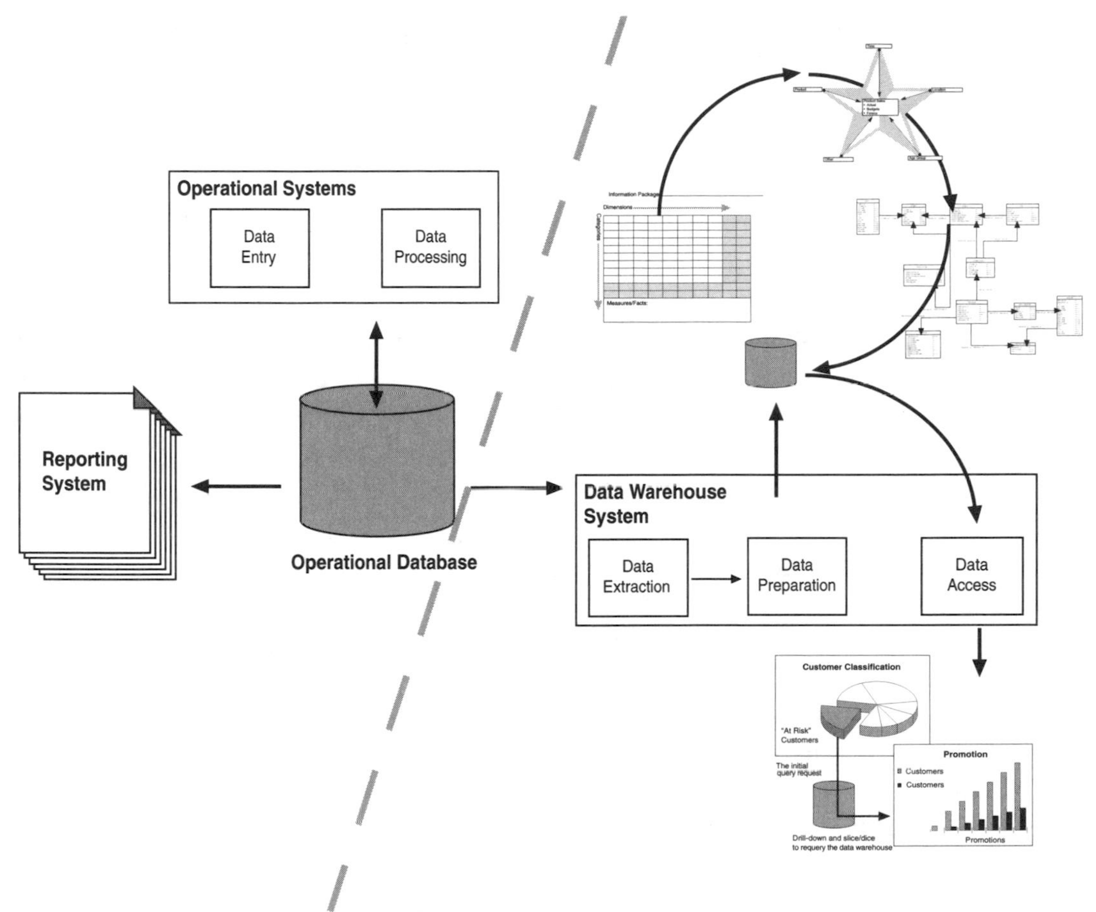

Figure 10.1: *Management of data assets*

Data Entry

Data entry is the process of capturing and recording raw data from various functions, including users keying the data, scanning the data, and real-time acquiring the data. Typically, we have built systems that perform editing and value-checking at the time of data entry. This has caused many data quality problems. In recent years, with the onset of programmable database management systems, data validation and quality have begun to migrate to servers. However, we are far from standardized on these principles.

It is wise to have your data capture systems record several items at the time of data capture, including: who performed the initial data entry; time stamping when the data entry occurred; and performance of any data validation, including checking data standards. If these items in fact existed on most operational databases, the process of extracting and cleansing the data would be infinitely easier. However, our experience is that most operational systems provide little to no data auditing of this nature. These items allow for an extraction process that scans and determines the who, what, where, and how of the data. This type of information permits an extraction algorithm based on time and function for populating data warehouse tables. Any design input that you have on the operational side should include these items, because they make your job easier.

Data Processing

Data processing is typically a system process that is often referred to as batch systems. These systems apply business logic to the data entered in the data entry process, with the result of an updated operational database. This update can be done on a continuous or deferred basis.

Again, these processes are mostly historical in nature. For systems requiring support of an enormous transaction load, these processes are quite common. For systems that require a lesser transaction load, these processes are embedded in the data entry processes or data capture systems. In the three-tier architectures that have recently been developed, this logic is housed and maintained by an application server.

These applications, much like data entry systems, should update the data in a fashion that allows extraction procedures to understand: who, what system, or what source updated the system; and when, with a time stamp, the system was updated.

The design of these operational systems is typically predetermined, as more corporations buy applications rather than build their own. However, we highly recommend that you interject your comments to those making the decisions on either acquisitions or reengineering of operational systems. You should clearly state that audit information is required for all data components that would include information to assist in the data extraction process, namely the following.

- Who performed the update?
- What system or component performed the update?
- When was the data entered into the system?
- When was the data modified in the system, including logical deletions?
- What was affected by the update?

These requests will become more obvious as we define the extraction process. Your specifications will clearly map to these types of items.

Implementation Tip 8: Become the leader in your company in driving an auditing standard for all operational systems, and data stores in general. This eases the process of extracting data from operational data stores and of loading the cleansed data into data warehouse data stores.

Operational Access

The function of operational access mechanisms is to allow other systems to gain access to the data managed by operational databases. These requesting systems may or may not be able to directly read the operational database.

If the requesting system has the capability of reading the data store, obviously real-time access is the desired objective. If the requesting system cannot read the data store directly, the requirement includes a query facility that allows the requesting system to send a query request along with its format requirements and to receive the results in a response transaction.

Operational data access systems have expanded enormously over the years, primarily due to the lack of adequate reporting systems and data warehouses. The land of the data extract evolved to feed user spreadsheets. How many resources and people, and how much software and hardware, have your company invested in the extraction world? A data warehouse should has a goal to nearly eliminate frivolous extracts to users. Some data extracts will still be required; however, synchronization routines or data feeds to synchronize supporting systems with data consistent to an enterprise will more than likely be the only required extracts.

Operational data access systems provide an alternative for data warehouse extraction routines. The extraction processes that your development team creates may simply fit into a data architecture as another operational access routine. However, data warehouse processing typically is restricted to the dedicated hardware for a data warehouse. This may impact your strategies for connecting to operational data stores. Also, the onset of replication technology has introduced another way to access operational data, reading the log of an operational data store. Too often, data warehouse extraction forces lock in either the operational environment or an expansion of a transaction window. As we will discuss later, replication technologies can overcome these issues and produce a low overhead alternative for capturing and accessing changes to an operational system.

Extraction Processing

Extraction processing is key to the success of a data warehouse. Remember: garbage in, garbage out. In an extraction process, data will be formatted and distributed to sources requiring shareable data from the operational environment. This obviously includes shipping data to a data warehouse. The metadata repository is instrumental in this process.

It is the job of a metadata repository to define and explain data sources and data standards. Therefore, translation processes that execute on operational data should place the data in standard data formats as defined in the metadata repository. For example, a legacy operational system may store name information in a 20-character field; however, the domain standards that have been set for future information systems state that the name domain will be stored in a 30-character field. The extraction process should read this domain definition from the metadata repository and transform or fix the legacy data to conform to the new standard prior to passing the data to other systems, such as a data warehouse.

Instead of creating multiple copies of shareable data, the extract processing should define a uniform, standard, single copy of data that is passed to requesting systems such as a data warehouse. This avoids additional overhead that may occur within the extraction processing. Too often, you will find great resistance within the Information Systems community to allowing the data warehouse extraction process to exist without the elimination of something. This is because batch windows on most operational systems are out of control and near to exceeding the allotted nightly time window. So, be careful to design the most optimal method for your extraction, and if possible determine other processes that will be eliminated after the data warehouse is delivered.

The processing of an extract is actually driven by an individual situation. The basis of design for any extract is determined by application requirements, data volume, and data volatility. You should have these items well documented by the time you request your data. The data requirements of a data warehouse are clearly defined in the data model; data volume is clearly defined in the information package diagram; and volatility charts provide details of the volatile nature of the data. Therefore, if you follow the procedures in this book, you should be well prepared to go to the glass house and request your data.

In most instances, you will want incremental changes sent to your extraction routines. As stated earlier, the way of determining the deltas, or changes, within operational data is through time stamp identification. Therefore, when possible you will simply build transactions as of the last extraction. This processing is done by comparing the extraction time stamp data in the metadata repository against the operational data store's time stamping data auditing mechanism. When this is not possible, additional methods must be defined, standardized, and developed. Some of these methods include the following.

- Inserting logic into an application that creates a file of changes as those changes occur
- Developing a file comparison algorithm that produces the differences
- Creatively accessing and utilizing a database log

Extract Specifications

The extraction portion of a data warehouse is a traditional process design. There is an obvious data flow, with the inputs being operational systems and the outputs being the data warehouse. However, the key to the extraction process is what happens to cleanse the data and transform it into usable data that the user can access and make into business intelligence.

Therefore, techniques such as data flow diagrams may be beneficial to defining extraction specifications for your development staff. One important input to such a specification may be the useful reports that you collected during user interviews. Often, we have experienced the ability to take a standard report or two, and utilize the data access logic in these programs to place the data represented in the report in a data warehouse. Typically, the two largest problems that users had with the report are the following.

- It contained too much data. It was created for everyone to use, but the users only required three pages of data.
- The presentation of the data was incorrect. There was only one presentation style, but the user wanted graphics or subtotals to appear before the detail report items.

If you are so lucky as to land on such a report, you may simply utilize the logic in the report's source module to guide you through the process of data compilation.

On-Time Shipment Example

To demonstrate the extract process specification, we will utilize an on-time shipment example. The specification should be self-contained, much like the information that supports users. The specification becomes the sole document explaining the process and concepts that derive the information package of on-time shipments. This packaging technique draws upon various resources, including your data models and metadata repository, to drive the developed logic to an optimal solution. Throughout the on-time shipment example, we refer to items that are documented in the figures and tables. Also, the syntax that we utilize in this example is Sybase's Transact-SQL. We assume that you have some preliminary understanding of Transact-SQL or industry-standard SQL.

Within your specification, be sure to include information which fulfills a table of contents such as the following.

```
1. Introduction
 1.a. Purpose
 1.b. Scope
 1.c. Information Package Diagram
 1.d. References
2. Process Overview
 2.a. Legacy Entities
 2.b. Data Warehouse Entities (including Star Schema and Physical Data Model)
 2.c. Data Flow Diagram
 2.d. Processing Notes
3. Detail Processes Information
 3.a. Individual Process (for each step in the process)
 3.a.1. Source Inputs
 3.a.2. Filter and Join Criteria
 3.a.3. Sorting and Aggregation Criteria
 3.a.4. Target Outputs
 3.b The next process…
```

On-Time Shipment Information Package Diagram

For the example in the preceding listing, shipment data will be monitored over a five-year period. Obviously, your ability to ship finished product on time to your customers will determine, to some degree, customer satisfaction and supplier performance.

Customer satisfaction is key, because this is the ultimate revenue source for the company. If you consistently ship product late, the business may be able to take several actions, including the following.

- Change estimation procedures
- Increase inventory levels, but only if you are selling standard products
- Modify how you ship product to a customer

Monitoring shipment methods will assist in determining where the problem lies—in your process or in the shipment process. Therefore, the dimensions that will be key in this information package include the following.

- **The time dimension** for five years, down to the monthly level. The time period will also monitor the production calendar so that users can better understand, based on calendar year or business year, if shipping is impacted. Typically, during the fourth quarter companies become extremely efficient at shipping product.

- **The location dimension** allows us to further define our analysis on a plant-by-plant basis. Some factors could arise from facilities from which products are shipped. One plant may be more efficient than another. From there, you can investigate the reasons. Is it a more modern facility? Does it have more capacity? Does it have better management procedures? Does it just have better people?

- **The product dimension** allows us to analyze the data for any individual product that we manufacture. Again, are shipping problems isolated to an individual product, or do they involve all products? This clearly is a factor that impacts our overall decision making process. We would not want to change shipping procedures for all products if we only had problems with one.

- **The customer dimension** allows us to determine if shipment problems are isolated on regional boundaries (such as someone not doing paper work properly), or if they are in fact global problems. This also allows for continuous monitoring of shipment performance to a customer who has complained in the past. We will be able to isolate that customer's shipment records and show how we have improved the process of shipping to him or her, hopefully changing the customer's opinion and attitude toward our company.

- **The shipment method dimension** allows us to monitor different shipment methods. Is the rail system better than trucking? This allows us to understand how our outside suppliers of shipping services are performing and, more importantly, how they are impacting our business.

- **The measurement data** includes how many shipments are made. This may assist us in understanding why shipments were late if we saw a dramatic increase in shipments for a problem month. There are also the metrics of what percentage shipments were on time or late. These metrics are basically calculated numbers that we have determined will always be queried. Therefore, we will preaggregate them for users. The alternative is to incur a calculation for each query. The two percentage items will be important to users. And, based on the simplicity of the percentage equation, we will probably store the data definition rather than the raw data for this information.

An information package diagram and star schema for our on-time shipments example are illustrated in Figures 10.2 and 10.3, respectively.

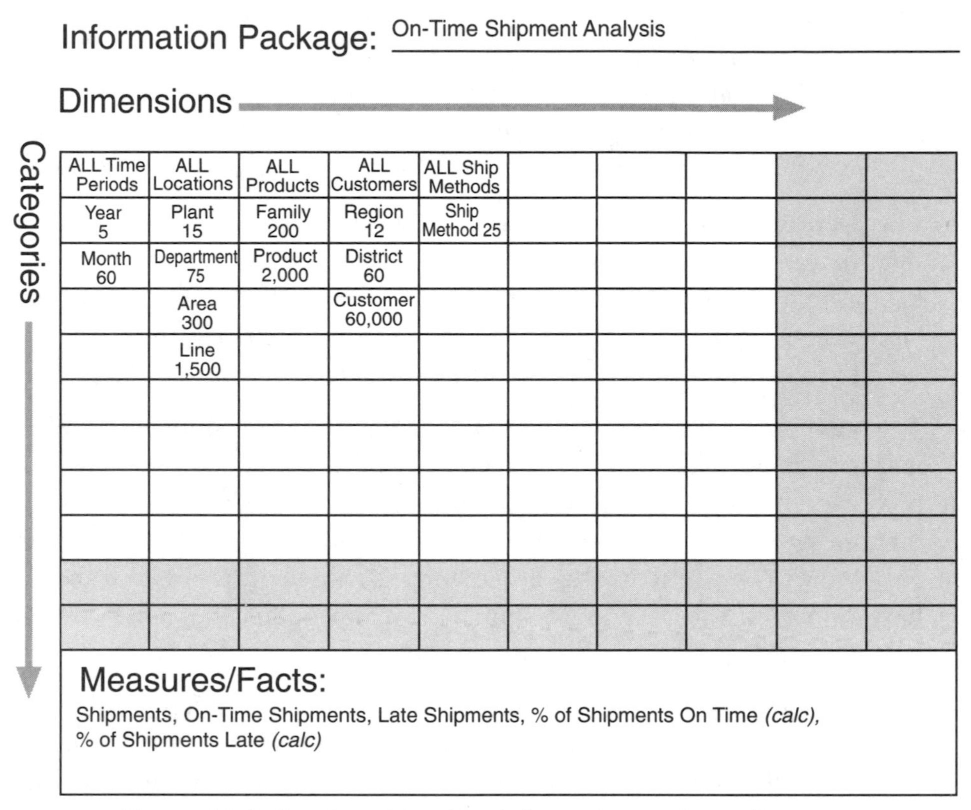

Figure 10.2: *On-time shipments information package diagram*

On-Time Shipment Data Flow Diagram

The extraction process specification can be easily documented utilizing traditional data flow diagrams. The purpose of a data flow diagram is to define at a lower level of detail the processes and components that make up an extraction process. These diagrams show detail that identifies the information flows and data stores that will be utilized to exchange or drive data processing tasks. Figure 10.4 illustrates a data flow diagram for our on-time shipment example.

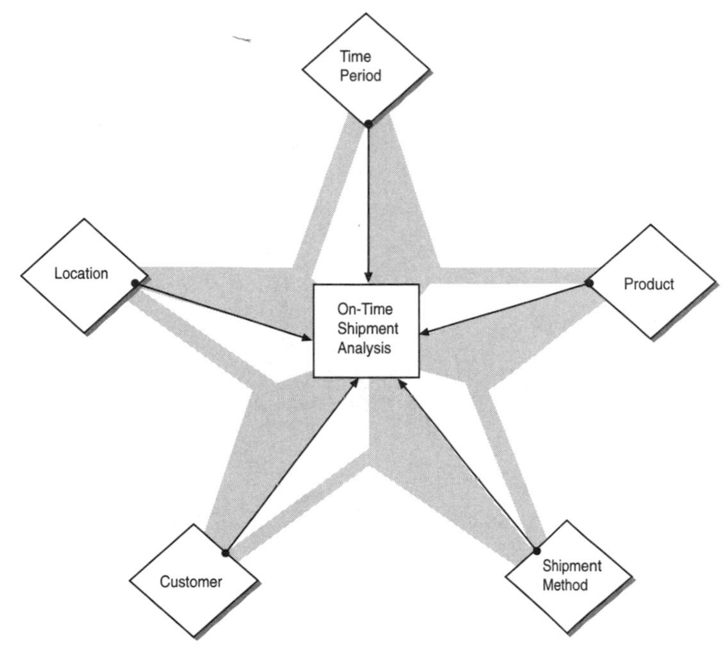

Figure 10.3: *On-time shipments star schema*

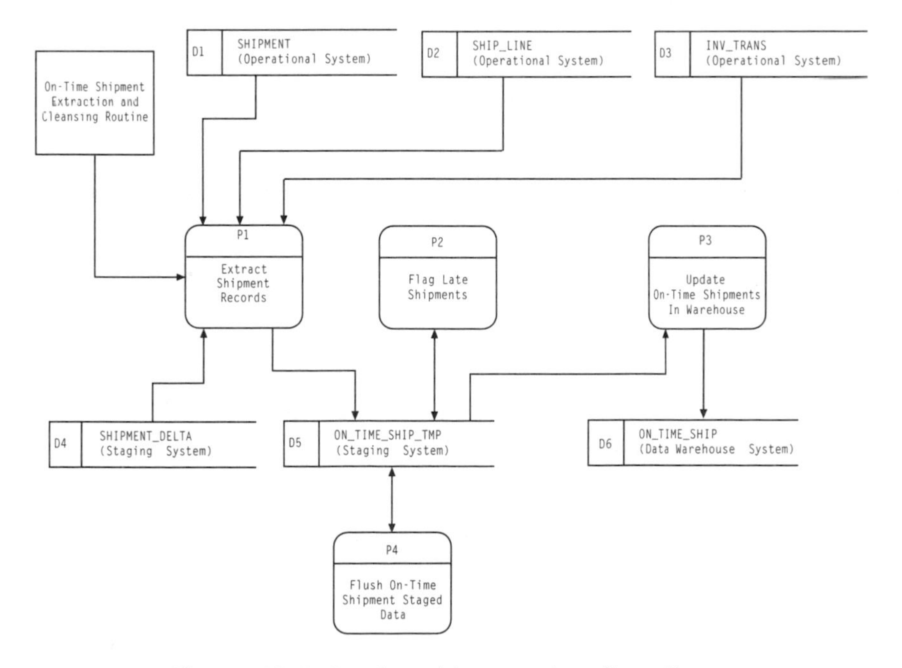

Figure 10.4: *On-time shipment data flow diagram*

The technology architecture drives how theses extraction processes and data flow diagrams are designed. The best technology architecture is one that provides a common and consistent repository and syntax across data structures, including legacy systems and the data warehouse. We have found that a tool such as Sybase OMNIConnect effectively provides this consistency in a technology architecture. Similar tools are on the market from IBM, Information Builders, Oracle, and others. However, Sybase OMNIConnect provides a more robust and open solution for this required connectivity middleware.

When attempting to build extraction components, you want your tool of choice to provide the following functions.

- Transparent read/write access to all of your data stores
- Location transparency, so that you can process on the operational platform, the warehouse platform, or staging platform without requiring coding modifications
- Heterogeneous joins across data structures, including across multiple system data structures
- Standardized coding techniques for all extraction processes, which assists in management and maintenance of extraction sequencing and schedule

On-Time Shipment Process Definitions

From a data flow diagram, documentation should be developed detailing each component. The detailed process descriptions allow you to provide development staff with a connect-the-dots implementation plan. This should include defining the following points.

- **Source tables for the input of the extraction process** Within your definition, be sure to include the platform, database, and tables that will be utilized for input parameters. Table 10.1 illustrates the documenting of these source tables.

Table 10.1: *Process P1 (from Figure 10.4)—source tables for the extraction process*

Platform	Database	Table Name
VAX/VMS	MCS *(Manufacturing Control System)*	SHIPMENT
VAX/VMS	MCS *(Manufacturing Control System)*	SHIP_LINE
VAX/VMS	MCS **(Manufacturing Control System)**	INV_TRANS

- **Filter and join criteria** Because our discussion is in the context of a relational connectivity tool like Sybase's OMNIConnect, define how the answer sets will be formulated. Within this definition, the specific column and its parent table should be defined, along with the operation or operator that will be utilized in the filtering of the data and the value on which the operation will be performed. This step helps to consolidate data in a consistent format for placement within the data warehouse. Often, legacy systems utilized techniques such as coded record structures in which one file housed multiple definitions of a record. A code determined the record layout that should be used. You will want to make sure you are getting the right data and using the right data layout for the input data. Table 10.2 demonstrates how to document filter and join criteria. A simple table that presents the compound conditions, the table name and column involved, the filter or join operation to be performed, and the comparison values will assist developers in building the correct syntax to extract the data for any process.

Table 10.2: *Process P1 (from Figure 10.4)—filter and join criteria for the extraction process*

Compound Conditions	Table Name Column	Filter or Join Operation	Comparison Value
	Join over the primary index for SHIPMENT, SHIP_LINE, and INV_TRANS		
AND (	SHIPMENT.SHIPMENT_STATUS	equal	'50'
OR	SHIPMENT.SHIPMENT_STATUS	equal	'90'
) AND	SHIPMENT.SHPMNT_NBR characters 1 and 2	not equal	'CI'

- **Sorting or aggregating criteria** These criteria are important, because they define the proper level of granularity. With regard to on-time shipments, we are only interested in seeing monthly shipment numbers for each customer, product, plant, and shipment method. This may include all of the shipments, but on the other hand it might return one row that represents thousands of shipments. Table 10.3 presents the proper sequencing of the result data by defining the column and its associated table name that will be sorted, the ordering of the data, and whether a SQL *group by* clause will be needed for aggregations.

Table 10.3: *Process P1 (from Figure 10.4)—sorting and aggregating criteria for the extraction process*

Table Name.Column	Order	Group
SHIPMENT.SHPMNT_NBR	ascending	yes

- **Target or projected column definitions** Within this part of the specification, you define all manipulation, calculation, and general cleansing that must take place on data prior to its placement in the target environment. Important information includes the result or target column name, the source column or source calculation, and a brief process description to assist in understanding the calculation or cleansing details. See Table 10.4.

Table 10.4: *Process P1 (from Figure 10.4)—target column definitions for the extraction process*

Result Table Name.Column	Source Table Name.Column	Description/Notes
ON_TIME_SHIP_TMP.SHIPMENT_NBR	SHIPMENT.SHPMNT_NBR	Shipment number
ON_TIME_SHIP_TMP.SCHED_SHIP_DATE	*Calculated:* convert SHIPMENT.SCHED_SHIP_DT from Julian date to Gregorian date	Scheduled ship date
ON_TIME_SHIP_TMP.ACTUAL_SHIP_DATE	*Calculated:* convert SHIPMENT.DATE_SHIP from Julian date to Gregorian date	Actual shipment date
ON_TIME_SHIP_TMP.ACTUAL_NET_WT_SHIP	SHIPMENT.NET_WT_ACT_SHIP	Net weight of the actual shipment
ON_TIME_SHIP_TMP.SHIPMENT_STATUS	SHIPMENT.SHIPMENT_STATUS	Shipment status
ON_TIME_SHIP_TMP.QTY_TO_SHIP	*Calculated:* SUM(SHIP_LINE.QTY_TO_SHIP)	Quantity that was to be shipped
ON_TIME_SHIP_TMP.SHIP_LINE_STATUS	SHIP_LINE.SHIP_LINE_STATUS	Shipment line item status
ON_TIME_SHIP_TMP.CONT_CODE	SHIP_LINE.CONT_CODE	Container code
ON_TIME_SHIP_TMP.DAY_OF_WEEK	*Calculated:* convert SHIPMENT.SCHED_SHIP to determine the day of the week	Day of the week scheduled to ship

(continues)

Table 10.4: *(continued)*

Result Table Name.Column	Source Table Name.Column	Description/Notes
ON_TIME_SHIP_TMP.DAYS_LATE	*Calculated:* SHIPMENT.DATE_SHIP - SHIPMENT.SCHED_SHIP	Number of days the shipment was late
ON_TIME_SHIP_TMP.ITEM_NBR	SHIP_LINE.ITEM_NBR	Item number
ON_TIME_SHIP_TMP.ITEM_SPEC_NBR	SHIP_LINE.ITEM_SPEC_NBR	Item spec number
ON_TIME_SHIP_TMP.LATE_FLAG	NULL	Based on calculations within P2; the shipment may not be late even though there are days late (see adjustment calculations in P2)

Loading Data

The specification discussed in the preceding sections allows the development staff to adequately map the logic required within a SQL statement. Remember, this example is utilizing Sybase's standard SQL syntax, Transact-SQL. The resulting module is a stored procedure. The SQL syntax mapping is depicted in Figure 10.5.

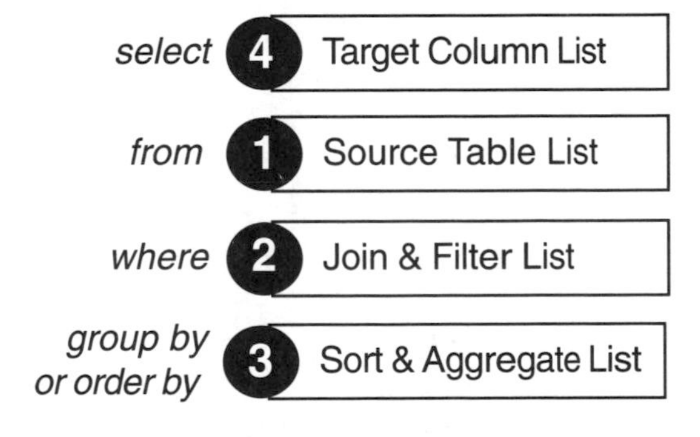

Figure 10.5: *Specification to SQL select map*

You may find it interesting to find that the mapping of the specification illustrated by Figure 10.6 is to an SQL *select* statement. We had two reasons for the mapping to a *select* statement.

- First, if you are loading into a staging area, you will want to utilize bulk copying concepts such as the SQL *select into* statement. This approach allows you to parse the source data and place it into a staging area with one statement.
- Second, you may want to utilize SQL *cursor* logic, which allows you to perform specific logic on each row of a result set. In this situation, you may be selecting the data as shown, then performing row-at-a-time conversion to the data. The results of this process would then be processed in an *insert* or *update* statement.

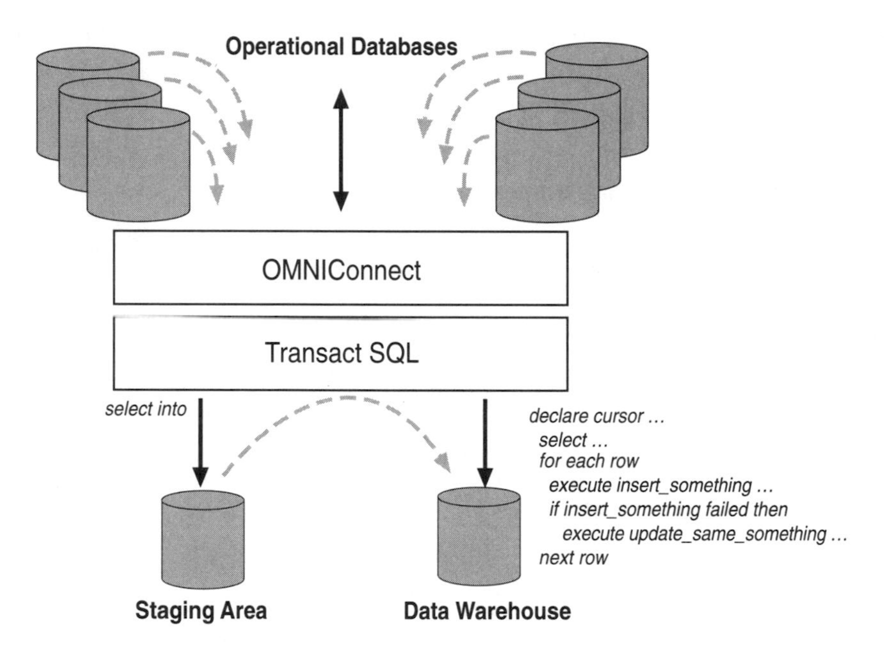

Figure 10.6: *Processing extracted data*

Multiple Passes of Data

It is important to realize that even productivity tools such as Sybase's OMNIConnect and other set-oriented tools are unable to complete everything in one pass of data. Our on-time shipment example could potentially be done in one pass; however, the operational staff for a production system may have told you to get your data and move on—no calculating, no processing, just get what you need and get off the machine. More complex extractions require you to pull data from multiple systems and merge the resultant data while performing calculations and transformations for placement into a data warehouse.

The sales analysis example that we carried through the data modeling phase in the previous chapters might be such an application. We may be obtaining budget sales information from a budgetary system, which is different from the order entry system from which we get actual sales data, which in turn is different from the forecast management system from which we get forecast sales data. In this scenario, we would need to access three separate systems to fill one row within the sales analysis measure table. So, be aware that the extraction and loading process is easier if you break it into smaller processing units and let the tools within your architecture, such as Sybase's OMNIConnect, work for you rather than against you.

Staging Area

Creating and defining a staging area assists your cleansing process. This is a simple concept that allows you to maximize up-time of a data warehouse while you extract and cleanse the data. You simply utilize a temporary work space—a staging area—to manage transactions that will be further processed to develop data warehouse transactions. In SQL Server, this might be *tempdb*. However, you may want to define a permanent staging area to assist in things such as checkpoint restart logic and replication agent management.

Checkpoint Restart Logic

The concept of checkpoint restart has been around for many years. The concept originated in batch processing on mainframe computers. This type of logic states that if we have a long running process that fails prior to completion, you restart the process at the point of failure rather than at the beginning. You should implement similar concepts in your extraction and cleansing logic. Within the staging area, define the necessary structures to monitor the activities of transformation stored procedures. Each of these programming units has an input variable that determines where in the process it should begin. Therefore, if failure occurs within the seventh procedure of an extraction procedure that has 10 steps, assuming the right rollback logic is in place you would only require that the last four steps (steps 7 through10) be conducted.

Data Loading

After data has been extracted, it is ready to be loaded into a data warehouse. In the data loading process, cleansed and transformed data that now complies with the data standards is moved into the appropriate data warehouse entities. Data may be summarized and reformatted as a part of this process, depending on the extraction and cleansing specifications and the performance requirements of the data warehouse. After the data has been loaded, data inventory information is updated within the metadata repository to reflect the activity that has just completed.

Data loading will most likely occur during a batch window period during which utilization and access by users is not required. This period will typically be late evening or early morning hours. However, with an architecture defining the staging area and technologies such as replication, there should be an ability to perform real-time updates via asynchronous extraction and loading. This situation is typically not a requirement for data warehouses, though real-time updating of the staging area is a real requirement.

The loading of data should utilize a standard methodology and common utilities. These factors provide the most efficient manner of loading a data warehouse, while minimizing the need for custom-developed utilities. Depending on the nature of an extraction or transformation process, some customized loading may have to be performed. This should not be the norm, but the possibility should be reviewed closely by the architecture team as a case arises for the best possible solution.

Implementation Tip 9: Just because SQL is a set-oriented language does not mean that everything can be easily and most efficiently done in one pass of data. Remember the policy of keeping things simple; simplicity often, but not always, equates to efficiency. Many cleansing and load processes require more than one pass at data. Design your load modules with your eye on the future and your mind in the past. That is, don't forget things such as checkpoint restart logic, which optimized batch jobs of old. These techniques can bridge to the future and optimize your loading process.

Optimize Extractions with Replication Agents

Replication technology has begun to emerge as a viable solution to many problems that previously hindered the implementation of distributed data sources. Specifically, the concepts of data placement within a distributed data environment are beginning to be mastered by replication technologies. Replication is simply defined as the process of creating and maintaining associated copies of original data at distributed sites.

Typically, a replication architecture involves a publisher of data and a subscriber of data. The publisher is the original, or controlling, source. If we utilize a CRUD diagram as discussed earlier in the book to represent the publisher, it would be characterized as the source that *c*reates and *d*eletes data; or more easily stated, it controls the capturing and purging of data from a corporation. A subscriber, on the other hand, is a system that needs access to the data, but only from a reference data perspective. In other words, subscribers are *r*eaders within a CRUD diagram of the specified entities.

The concept of replicating data may on the surface appear to be simple. However, upon complete investigation you will find that these architectures have evolved to solve some complex problems with a simple interface. Replication is more than just copying data from one site to another. A complete replication architecture accomplishes the following.

- Provides reliable replication that is not exposed to problems such as system failures
- Delivers consistent data that adheres to all data integrity rules
- Optimizes the delivery process to reduce the latency between the capture or modification of data and the resultant delivery of replicas

These objectives are high-level items for guiding your selection of a replication agent. Additionally, the replication system that you choose should be easy to administer, provide an architecture that allows for as many of your data sources as possible to be replicated, and be independent of location.

How Does Replication Work?

For purposes of this discussion, we refer to implementations utilizing Sybase's Replication Server, though each database management system vendors as well as transaction processing monitor vendors and other third parties may provide you with a replication solution.

Sybase's Replication Server provides the capability for individual servers to publish data and for others to subscribe to the replicas. Sybase's replication technology offers an enormous benefit to the overall performance and management of replication, because it allows us to simply monitor the log activity of a given publisher to provide the required replica information. This contrasts with some other replication technologies that work from an actual data record image within the transaction window. The approach provided by Sybase provides a great benefit to our extraction processing. We can now trap data changes without changing the application logic or increasing the transaction window. Both of these characteristics will be greatly resisted in most organizations as too costly or unachievable. The processing flow works as follows, and is illustrated in Figure 10.7.

1. The operational system changes the data
2. The change is committed to the operational database

3. Upon completion of the commit, the transaction is logged to the operational database's log
4. The Log Transfer Manager component of Replication Server recognizes the data change
5. The Log Transfer Manager obtains the data that has been subscribed (which can be partial data)
6. The Log Transfer Manager sends the transaction to Replication Server
7. Replication Server distributes the transaction to subscribers
8. The subscriber receives the Replication Server transaction and processes it as a transaction

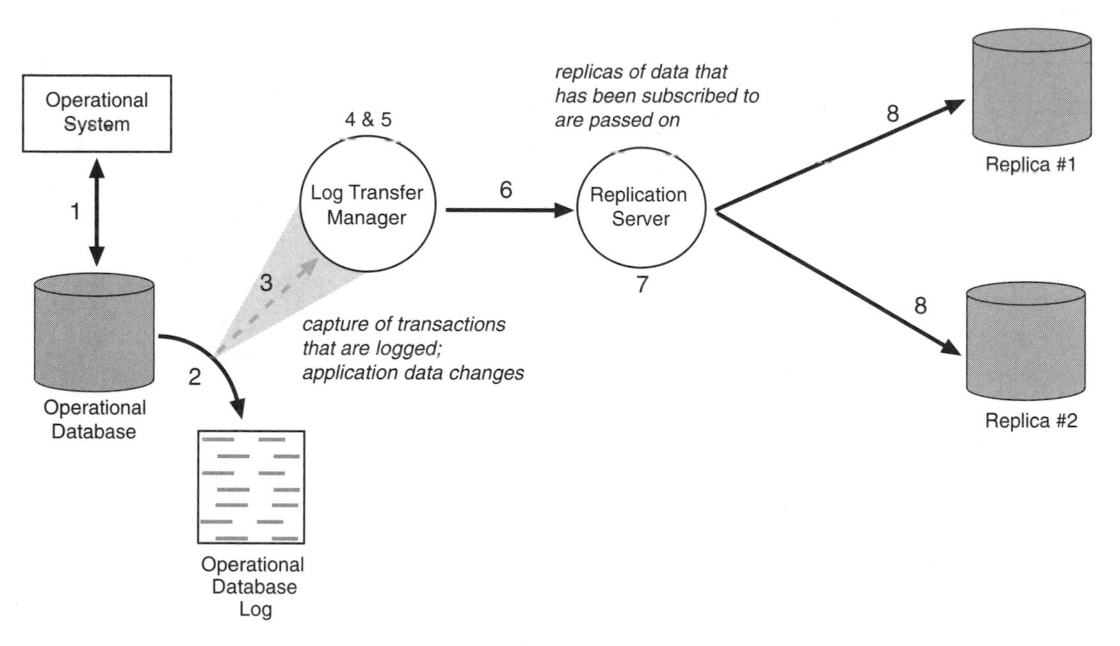

Figure 10.7: *Sybase Replication Server processing*

Sybase's Replication Server offers many benefits, one of the greatest of which is its overall architecture. This technology can be mapped to heterogeneous sources with relative ease, because it is based on the Sybase Open Client/Open Server architecture. Several off-the-shelf replication agents for heterogeneous data sources allow you to easily integrate this component into your overall data architecture.

How Can the Extraction Process Use Replication?

The extraction process is sensitive to loading volumes, or the number of rows from the operational data store that must be transformed and placed into a data warehouse. When you design your extraction processes, you must cover two situations: mass loading and incremental loading.

Mass loading is relatively easy to handle. The extraction process grabs all of the operational data and refreshes the data warehouse. However, this does not account for many things.

- **Volume considerations** The volume of some data sources prohibits a pure mass loading concept; or probably better stated, it forces you to surround the data warehousing problem with expensive software and hardware to handle the processing of large volumes of data.

- **Historical content considerations** A data warehouse is meant to provide a historical perspective to the data assets of an enterprise. The mass loading concept typically correlates to a refreshing of data, which means that data may be inadvertently purged from a data warehouse if it is purged from an operational data store. This conflicts with the overall goal of a data warehouse system to provide historical context.

- **Optimization of resources** The resources that surround operational and data warehouse systems, such as a network, processors, and memory, will be thoroughly saturated if the only loading strategy implemented is mass loading.

The solution to this loading dilemma is to develop an extraction and loading process that can perform incremental loads. When possible, each of the Transact-SQL stored procedures that were discussed for loading data warehouse entities will be triggered off a shadow key table.

A shadow key table is a database table, typically stored within a data warehouse's staging area, that contains replicas of the keys and associated modification information for an associated table within an operational database environment. This technique provides a way for a data warehouse to subscribe to the source of the data, and capture the information associated with daily transactions that have transpired on that data: What changed? How did it change? And so on. This type of information allows us to apply selective logic in our loading process to reduce the overall volume of data, in essence optimizing a data warehouse's loading process.

Selective logic assists in optimizing the load in several ways, as listed here.

- It utilizes keys from the data source, so we can perform indexed reads versus table scans on a data source, thus minimizing access time and overhead to the source system.
- It permits no transaction window increase. If we implement shadow tables in an operational system either through code or other database triggering devices, we increase the time to commit transactions. Reading the log for information assures that the transaction is already committed prior to any work being done by a process that in fact has no bearing on the transaction. This nonintrusive way of capturing changes will please your application support staff.
- If an application has not been written with a time stamping algorithm (most legacy systems we have encountered lack this), you still can perform incremental processing.
- Because more than just the key can be replicated, you may reduce the need to access the original data source through subscribing to more of the data. This circumstance allows all changes to be sent to the staging area for further processing, again maximizing resources by minimizing the overall query load.

However, like all new technologies, replication won't fit in every environment. Therefore, you will probably incur a mixed environment for your data loading in which you utilize the best available strategy. The ranking of these implementations is as follows.

1. Replication of operational transaction information
2. Time stamping of operational data
3. Triggering of operational transaction information into shadow key tables

If none of these options are available, you should still look to minimize the burden of mass loading, which can have an overall impact on the cost and content of a data warehouse. An inability to implement incremental strategies for data loading forces an enterprise to spend more money on hardware and software to throw at the resource problems; otherwise the company must suffer having less data within its data warehouse. Neither option is appealing.

Implementation Tip 10: Replication technologies can be extremely useful for the data warehouse loading process. Search for the least intrusive method of trapping data modifications within operational systems. These systems can ill afford an increase in the transaction window or code revisions. A good replication technology that monitors a data store's log file delivers this least intrusive solution.

Data Distribution

The process of data distribution can be similar to the job of a newspaper delivery person. After the newspaper is printed and made available to a central distribution center, the delivery person goes to individual subscribers and provides them with their own copies of the newspaper. The concept is the same in a data warehouse. Systems feed off a centralized data warehouse. The data warehouse subsystems must be provided with properly sourced data from the extraction, cleansing, and loading processes.

A set of standard utilities in the overall architecture should be implemented to support this distribution concept. Again, today's modern replication software can be invaluable in this area. However, you may find that there is no one clear cut solution for your data distribution problem. Therefore, make sure that your utilities can work in harmony within the allotted time window for performing the distribution of the data and for making it available to all users. These utilities hold the burden of physically moving data from a data warehouse to data consumers, which could include users, standard reports, multidimensional analysis systems, or departmental data marts.

Technology and data architectures should guarantee that a data distribution system accomplishes the following.

- Ensures that data distribution occurs in a timely and efficient manner
- Ensures that only data that has been ordered is delivered
- Establishes proper and required service level standards
- Gathers data to provide statistical evidence that the service level standards are being achieved

Extraction Processing Standards

To achieve consistency within your extraction processing environment, a comprehensive set of standards is required, similar to the data standards discussed in Section 4, The Process. These standards will ease coding, facilitate debugging, and simplify maintenance of the back-end processing managed by a data warehouse system. The success of this methodology, as within other methodologies, is the enforcement and adherence to overall standards. Therefore, proper enforcement personnel must be defined within a data warehouse management structure.

The recommended strategy for implementing your extraction processing is a programmable database management environment that supports server-based logic, stored procedures, and replication technology to reduce the volume of data loads. This strategy requires that the database management system vendor provides adequate facilities for connecting to your operational data stores and a common syntax standard that operates on each of these data stores.

A stored procedure is simply a collection of SQL statements that are precompiled, stored in a database under a given name, and executed as one unit. Stored procedures have evolved over the years with relational database management systems and are now the common technique for implementing a programmable database and optimizing performance. Common processes that are implemented as stored procedures include business rules such as data validations, referential integrity checks, and frequently used queries. Stored procedures offer a modular development technique that is focused on reuse of program logic while providing a layer of abstraction between the database management system and the application development environment, including user data presentation.

Stored procedures typically run faster than the same group of commands executed interactively. Therefore, implementation of store procedures also offers performance benefits. These benefits are derived from the reduction of overall network traffic, because the execution logic merely references the name of the stored procedure and any required input parameters. From there, the server executes multiple requests without further prompting from the client application. Prior to the implementation of stored procedures, a client application was required to call the database server for every SQL statement that was desired in a transaction. Therefore, an application executing a transaction that requires an *insert* of data followed by a *select* that feeds an *update* can be executed within one stored procedure versus three separate client requests. Note that stored procedures can call other stored procedures. Therefore, a client request can trigger a series of server-oriented activities in one network packet.

Standards should be established within stored procedures for defining the individual components. Many of these standards will be driven by current data standards, because SQL statements contained within stored procedures will reference those data items. However, you will also be required to define the standards for the following objects.

- **Stored procedure names** The names of stored procedures are typically only visible to development staff. Therefore, meaningful naming conventions that help to define the purpose of a stored procedures should be developed. For an example, consider *pAction_object*, whose elements are described in Table 10.5. Therefore, the incremental loading process for on-time shipments might be named as *pn_ON_TIME_SHIPMENT*.

Table 10.5: *Stored procedure naming standards for pAction_object example*

Element	Description
p	Defines this object as a stored procedure
Action	Defines what the stored procedure's primary processing is, such as: d—Delete i—Insert s—Select u—Update n—Incremental load m—Mass load
object	Defines the objects affected by the stored procedure

- **Parameter names** Stored procedures can receive input parameters as well as define output parameters. These parameters should be named according to good programming conventions, again focusing on the content, data type, and purpose of the defined entity. You may want to utilize a well-established standard for these values, such as Hungarian notation.

In addition to naming conventions and standards, recognize that stored procedures are code modules. Therefore, explicit standards for the development of code must also be defined for your development team. Examples of these items include the following.

- **Return codes** Because stored procedures are simply modular code that is managed by a server rather than a client, good communication regarding processing and execution between code modules is needed, including use of return codes. A common set of return codes should be developed to define what has transpired and any further activities that should occur based on the status of execution, such as messages and aborting of a process. All stored procedures should return a status code that indicates completion of the process, with or without errors.
- **Documentation blocks** Each stored procedure should provide some common documentation to improve its management and maintenance. This documentation block should include items such as the name of the procedure, a brief description, parameters used by the stored procedure, return codes (including result sets and processing status codes), and modification history. Here is an example.

```
/****************************************************
 ** PROCEDURE NAME: pn_ON_TIME_SHIPMENT
 **
 ** DESCRIPTION: This procedure performs the
```

```
 ** incremental load process for the on-time
 ** shipment data warehouse information package.
 ** This procedure accomplishes the following.
 ** 1 - Extracts data from the MCS
 ** (Manufacturing Control System) on the
 ** plant-based VAX/VMS machine utilizing
 ** Sybase OMNIConnect
 ** 2 - Stores the data in the data warehouse
 ** staging area
 ** 3 - Processes the on-time shipment calculations
 ** that flag shipments as either late or on time
 ** 4 - Places the data within the data warehouse
 ** 5 - Purges the staging area
 **
 ** RETURNS
 ** ——-
 ** Result Sets - none
 **
 ** Status Codes
 ** '4' - Row count of zero
 ** '8' - Invalid Action code
 ** '16' - An error occurred
 **
 ** MODIFICATION HISTORY:
 ** Author Date Comments
 ** T. Hammergren 12/01/96 Initial Build
 **
*****************************************************/
```

- **Code comments** Develop a standard that requires adequate comments for the source logic. This standard should state that no more than a specified number of lines of code can be written without a comment. This again improves the management and maintenance tasks of stored procedures.
- **Error checking** Global variables *@@error* and *@@rowcount* should be checked after each SQL statement. The *@@error* variable indicates whether a statement was successfully executed or an error was detected. The *@@rowcount* variable indicates the number of rows affected by the execution of a SQL statement. This may be important for guiding further processing within a stored procedure. Also, if you perform nested stored procedure calls, check the return status code to verify that execution either completed successfully or aborted with an error status.
- **Passing parameters by name** When passing parameters to a stored procedure, pass them by name rather than by positional reference.

- **Do not use "*" in place of all columns** Explicitly state all desired column names within a *select* column list. Do not use "*select* *. ..." Following this rule enhances maintainability of a system.

To guarantee that the standards you develop are easily adopted, you may want to purchase a generation tool for stored procedures, or simply define stored procedure templates from which all stored procedures evolve.

Summary

A data warehouse consists of a set of storage facilities containing shareable data for use by reporting and decision support processes. Data is moved to a data warehouse in a structured extraction process that accesses operational data, transforms the data into proper data warehouse format, and distributes the data to sites requiring replicas.

The notion of a single, logical enterprise data environment begs the question of the number of physical operational data stores and physical data warehouses. The architecture that is defined for a data warehouse should accommodate the number of physical data stores and their underlying technology, making them as transparent as possible to the overall data warehouse processes. If this architecture is provided, the process of data extraction and cleansing is greatly simplified. Connectivity tools from vendors such as Sybase offer enormous flexibility in this area. The benefits derived from standardizing on such a connectivity platform include more consistency within the transformation process and the ability to standardize on a process definition.

Process models can be used to describe a complex systems such as the data extraction and cleansing process. Because a data warehouse is primarily a data-driven system, process modeling is typically not required in an architecture definition. Within an overall data warehouse system, two fundamental processes occur.

- A transformation process from each data source feeding the warehouse
- A query processing process

Process model diagrams become useful when the development of transformation processes from operational data stores to a data warehouse are further detailed. Process modeling covers the practices and techniques utilized to capture a representation of a business activity. The process model defines the following tasks.

- Steps in the process

- Order of the steps
- Reference to the data used and affected by the process
- Business rules that govern the process
- Transformations that can occur within the process

These models assist development staff in evaluating system requirements, providing a visual communication medium and a basis for the physical design or implementation of a system.

Because the extraction and cleansing process is a development effort, traditional development standards such as process modeling are utilized to successfully implement a data warehouse and its associated processes. It should be the job of the central data warehouse support team, especially the database administrator, to ensure that the extraction and cleansing process that loads a data warehouse conforms to the overall architecture. This conformance includes the following goals.

- All data that is loaded into a data warehouse conforms to corporate data standards. These standards should be published and available through a means such as a metadata repository or an electronic manual.
- Any time data warehouse data is modified, the inventory information for that data area is updated to reflect the changes and logged within the metadata repository. Remember, the repository gives us the life history of any entity.

11

Publishing and Accessing Data

Utility is our national shibboleth: The savior of the American businessman is fact and his uterine half-brother, statistics.

—*Edward Dahlberg*

Knowledge is power. This statement is true if your entire organization is knowledgeable; the statement is false if only a few key executives are knowledgeable. Bureaucratic ways of the past are collapsing all around us. The organizations that are succeeding today are *intelligent organizations*. This type of enterprise thrives on the brilliance of all of its employees and their abilities to make wise choices. Therefore, corporations are realizing that one of the most powerful and potent assets they possess is their employees' brain power.

We like to think of a data warehouse as food—food to feed the employees' brains. Data—past, present, and future—is meaningless without the brain; with it, the corporate knowledge base is brought to fruition.

Today, the whole nature of work is changing. It is changing from unskilled work to knowledge work. Even in factories, most jobs now involve technical knowledge instead of unskilled assembly line work. Machines are now doing the mindless routine work, so employees can spend more of their time and ability focused on innovation to see what the customer really wants and to assist in reshaping the business to meet these demands. Intelligent organizations trust all of their employees to make decisions that used to be made by the chain of command.

For example, all of us have heard stories about levers above assembly line workers within a manufacturing facility that allow any worker to stop the assembly line if something is wrong. Companies are beginning to place more faith in every employee and make the employees more accountable and responsible in their own right—not just the managers. The justification for this change in accountability is the premise that the average employee is better at making smart choices and decisions than managers from the old school of bureaucratic thinking realize.

To become more successful at allowing employees to be responsible and accountable, those employees must have access to information—an ability to tap into the corporate knowledge base. Each employee needs to be able to touch the data that directly impacts his or her accountable area, as well as some supporting data. We used to laugh when we set up data warehouses or decision support databases when mid-level managers shuddered at the word that certain reports were going to management. Those managers were in fear of their jobs, afraid that the boss was using the data to somehow crucify them for poor performance.

Today, it is possible to allow the entire chain of command to view the same data on which analysis and decisions are performed. Conversations are about the same factors, they just get into more detail the further down the chain of command you go and more summarized the higher up the chain of command you go. Workers can only make good decisions if they are given good information. Top management must give employees instant access to the data they need to become knowledge workers.

Access Tools: Pay Now or Pay Later

Multiple types of tools can be provided to users for accessing a data warehouse, as shown in Figure 11.1. Some impressive tools allow users to do a lot as long as they understand the concepts and principles of SQL—specifically the *select* statement. This type of tool tends to restrict the population who can utilize the data within a data warehouse. Organizations should ask themselves if these tools meet the goals and objectives of their data warehouse. *Do I really want my users to be technical? Will this make my company more competitive?*

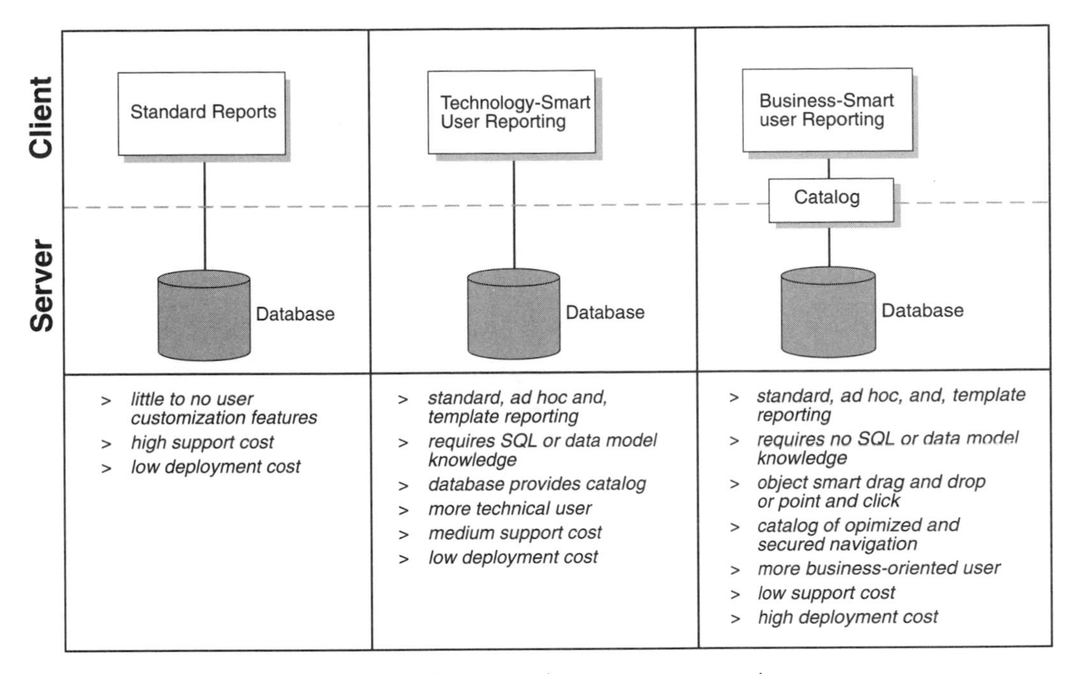

Figure 11.1: *Query tool spectrum comparison*

More sophisticated tools offer a more productive way to access the data within a data warehouse. These tools offer the user predefined business subjects, allowing controlled, yet optimized access paths into a data warehouse. Ad hoc reporting is still available in these tools; however, to assist in performance and security, the join strategies and access maps are stored in a catalog outside the warehouse and tool. Database administrators no longer are forced to continually tune and map the entities, views, and queries in a data warehouse. Database administrators do their work, much like the work involved in view definition, in the tool's catalog, which guarantees performance for user queries.

If performance continues to be an issue, other user tools allow the computation, query, and expression engines to reside on a different server or on multiple servers, as shown in Figure 11.2. This multitiered architecture includes an additional layer to provide centralized control of resources and security. The centralized process assists in more consistent performance that is not dependent on the client device.

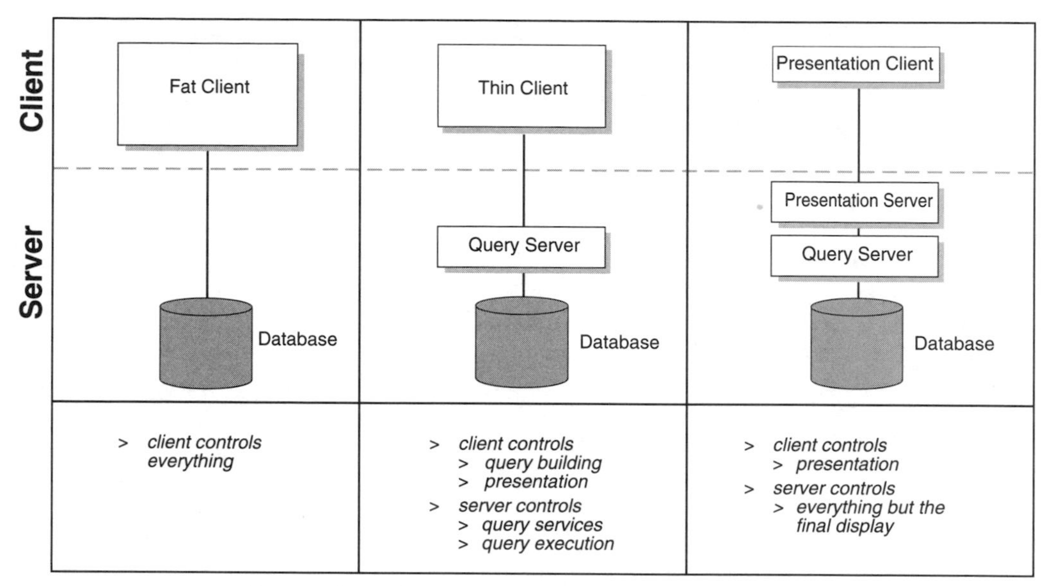

Figure 11.2: *Processing separation of query tools*

As someone focusing on the data warehousing process, you are required to recommend the best alternative for making your user base intelligent with the ability to access the data warehouse. The tools will have specific architectures and focus. With regard to architecture, you must decide if you want to allow split processing among shared application servers and clients, or to allow all of the processing to occur on the client or server.

The split processing decision is based somewhat on the resources that are at your disposal as well as on the behaviors of the user base you are supporting. A fat client scenario may require you not only to deliver a reporting tool to your users, but also to upgrade their personal computers, including random access memory, hard drive, operating system, and application software. The architectural part of your data warehouse should have determined these requirements; however, we often find that people forget that client-side software includes a cost of more than just the software. Fat client tools are good for users who need to detach from the corporate network—those who are remote or mobile.

On the other end of the spectrum are Internet and intranet solutions, which offer a thin client with a big server. This solution is viable for users who are connected via a network or high-speed backbone, but it is not very efficient for remote and mobile users.

The middle of the road is a split architecture that off-loads the need for a larger client. However, the tools involved in a split architecture tend to lose some flexibility for the user, such as the ability to detach and go mobile. Regardless of what you choose from this architectural perspective, you must also look at the overall capabilities for your users to manipulate and display the results of their queries.

In the area of tools, data warehouses require a suite much like office automation. Why? A suite can better map to the individual requirements of a user community with the type of user accessing a data warehouse. In office automation, tool suites have become the norm. Some users need to do word processing. You can do this in a spreadsheet, but a word processor better maps to the users' needs. Comparable situations are true with presentation and spreadsheet software. Much of the functionality of each tool is represented in the others; however, focus is lacking, and implementing user requirements is much more difficult with an unfocused tool.

Within a data warehouse, you find similar functional breakdowns. To best determine the required tools, it helps to have a firm understanding of your user community and its individual requirements. Though some of this work is application specific, much of it should be completed by the architecture team prior to the development and deployment of a tool suite. That team should bear in mind that your data warehouse tool suite and office automation tools should work in harmony.

Types of Users

The types of users that you may be required to support can vary greatly, from an executive who requires a system that offers focused reports with REALLY BIG BUTTONS directing the user to those reports, to an analyst who wants freedom and access to do everything. It is important to characterize the traits and requirements of each user constituency so that you can fit the constituencies with the proper tools to accomplish their associated tasks. An example of user categorization documentation is presented in Table 11.1.

Table 11.1: *User categorization*

Type of User	Information Requirements	Tool
High-level decision maker (executive)	Standard reports on key measurement data personalized for needs	Production report writer or spreadsheet interface tool; executive information system

(continues)

Table 11.1: *(continued)*

Type of User	Information Requirements	Tool
Technical-oriented user (analyst)	Complex analysis, including statistical analysis, drill down and slice-dice, graphics, ad hoc querying, and freedom of access to entire data warehouse	Executive information system; multidimensional database; statistical analysis and data mining capabilities—basically an entire warehouse tool suite
Business-oriented user (knowledge worker)	Point and click graphical reporting, standard report, and view customization	Decision support, ad hoc query, and reporting tools

User Needs

The users of a data warehouse desire to better understand how a business is running and what can be done to improve the business. These items are the heart and soul of the requirements discussed by many executives, managers, and analysts. These users are often compensated based on the overall success of a business.

You must continually tell your development team these tidbits and that users are more interested in the business aspects, not the technology aspects of a data warehouse. This means that your team should strive to provide access to data in a simple, nontechnical, and nonthreatening manner. Therefore, you should pay close attention to how a data warehouse's user interface is built and what the overall content of the tool suite includes. In doing so, bear the following points in mind.

- **Behavior patterns** The behavior patterns of your key users will assist you in understanding how to deliver a proper user interface to them.
  - Are they users who frequently utilize a personal computer? Or do they avoid personal computers?
  - Do the users frequently access data? Or do they require data on time boundaries, such as at the end of each month, quarter, or year?
  - Do the users have a support staff that provides the information to them? Or are they hands-on individuals who want the ability and freedom to access and manipulate data on an as-needed basis?
- **Content and granularity** The content of users' data requests is critical for defining how a data warehouse is presented.

    - Do the users only look at summarized data? Or do they require detail information to transaction levels?
    - Do they desire a blank sheet of paper from which they build a report? Or do they want reports sent to them based on their standards? Or do they want a standard report that allows them to further manipulate and perform discovery work?
    - How low do they go with regard to the dimensional level of data? Do they start high, then work their way down? Or do they start low and work their way up the data?

- **Equipment to access** The available resources that you have to deploy a data warehouse user interface may limit how the data warehouse is delivered to the user community.
    - Are the users equipped with personal computers? Do they have Microsoft Windows workstations? Do they have Macintosh workstations? Do they only have access to terminal-based applications?
    - Can you control the tool that they use? Or must you support whatever tool users request?
    - What are the typical configurations of the users' computing devices? How much memory? How much disk space? Are they connected to a LAN?
    - What do users typically run on their workstations simultaneously? Do they frequently have their complete office automation set of products open and active? How much of the resources is consumed by these products? What does that leave you for data warehouse applications and tools?

Information Delivery Techniques

Based on current technologies, you may also be restricted to the technique that is utilized to deliver information. There are currently many ways for delivering information, which include the following.

- **Paper-based reports** Hardcopy reports are dated and typically not desired by those who use them. Paper-based reports tend to be organized database dumps that force users to manually filter the data. The users typically have someone rekey the data into a spreadsheet so they can perform analysis, which interjects a quality risk. These reports also lack a timely delivery mechanism. Therefore, they should be avoided. However, this approach may be the only means for delivery in some organizations. If that is true for you, you will have to live with it for the time it takes you and your team to convince management that there is a better, more efficient, and economical way to deliver data.

- **Automated, indexed paper reports** Many companies have automated paper-based reporting to overcome the delivery time problem. This technique merely makes these reports more accessible for on-line users; however, the content still matches that of an organized dump of a database. Still, you may find that some generations of workers have become attached to their reports and continue to want them. The optimization technique that works best for these reports is to take a final printout and index the content of the report. This way, users can easily scan the contents of the report and directly locate the pages that interest them. You may also want to provide an extraction capability based on these indexes so users can electronically transfer the important portions of the report to the most effective work environment. This technique will assist you in overcoming the obstacles that are inherent in hardcopy reports—a delivery mechanism and timely deliver. Again, the concept of low flexibility and too much information are housed in these types of reports. They also should be avoided if at all possible.
- **Parameter-driven reports** Building report templates with common content is a better technique that is more advanced than the two previously discussed techniques. Parameter-driven reports allow users to dynamically build reports based on a fill-in-the-blank approach. The down side to this technique is similar to any ad hoc style reporting in that users will run the report more times than probably is necessary. The benefit of such a technique is that you can almost build reporting objects with a high degree of reuse and allow the user to specify the desired content. Often, you can use more modern tools with older tools to deliver such a solution. Reports can utilize an older, server-side reporting tool that produces results and passes them to the users' office automation package. The office automation package will likely allow the reports to include more modern graphic and calculation capabilities. Also, the office automation tool can isolate any major calculations to a specific user's work environment, reducing the impact to the overall system.
- **Starting-point reports** We often refer to starting-point reports as brainstorming launch pads. They are canned reports that you offer to the user community; however, they are presented within a fully functioning ad hoc reporting tool. This way, users can customize and investigate data as much as they want. Many decision support systems have offered this solution over the years, and it has proven effec-

tive for knowledge-based workers, such as business analysts and managers. All users of such systems start from the same information point; however, they can further investigate factors that may influence the data in different paths. For example, a brand manager may be interested in market share information and the promotions that affected that market share, while a sales manager may be more interested in the quantity and margin trends based on where the product was located in a given store. Each of these individuals looks at the same data, but the brand manager is more focused on the promotions that were run by his or her company and competitors. A sale manager may be more concerned with the location of the product—whether it was on the correct shelf, in the correct isle, at the correct height, and so forth.

- **Ad hoc reporting tools** Of course, we would love to have all of the user base fully accept responsibility for developing the reports that satisfy their own needs. However, this is a dream that will likely never come true. Nonetheless, we recommend that you try to deliver a strategy that mixes the concepts of starting-point reports and ad hoc reporting tools. Try to begin guiding the behaviors of users and to begin to deliver tools that offer ease of use. You may get lucky and find that the analysts within the user community will take the lead and responsibility for delivery of the starting-point reports to other users. This will lift an enormous burden off your development team. However, be fairly warned that not all user-access tools are created equal; and while it is a sad statement, you typically get what you pay for. So, those users who are excited about the tool that they found on sale for $49.95 at their local computer store may cost you more in support costs than the tool is worth. Though we want users to take more of the reporting responsibility, there must be some control and performance orientation to the tools that are delivered.

Application Framework

A data warehouse is as much an application as it is a database. People often use the terms Executive Information System (EIS) or Decision Support System (DSS) to describe how users access a data warehouse. Whatever you call your system, it must surround a set of tools and interfaces that provide the ultimate access points between your users and your data warehouse. EIS, DSS, data mining, OLAP, ad hoc reporting, business intelligence—everyone has a term—the fact is that your system will contain a little of each of these concepts. We will simply refer to your deliverable here as an *application framework*.

Guidelines for Building Your Framework

The framework that you build to deliver the user to a data warehouse should follow some specific user interface guidelines, such as those that follow.

- **Consistency** You should strive for consistency by providing sequences and actions that are similar in comparable situations. This consistency should extend to the standards that you follow for terminology in dialogs, prompts, error messages, menus, and help screens.
- **Error handling** The system should provide comprehensive error handling. As much as possible, design your system so users cannot make a serious error. If an error is made, try to have the system detect the error and offer simple, concise mechanisms for handling it—including the ability to undo what caused the error.
- **Feedback** Offer informative feedback for every operation. For frequent and minor actions, the response can be modest, such as a line of text on a message line or even a delayed message like the ToolTips found in Windows 95 applications. However, infrequent activities should provide substantial feedback and guiding mechanisms that lead users through the process and make it easy, much like the Wizards in many Windows 95 applications.
- **Shortcuts** You should enable shortcuts for the more technically knowledgeable and frequent users of a system. As users become more aware of the capabilities within the tools to which they have access, they want to reduce the number of interactions with the framework and increase interaction with the live tools. Quicker paths to the tools and the data should be built into a framework, and users should be encouraged to investigate and utilize these shortcuts. These characteristics reduce the amount of application code that a data warehouse project team must write and—better yet—maintain.

Direct Manipulation

No single system has all of the admirable attributes or design features desired by a user community. Building a system with all of the desired features may be impossible. However, the concept of direct manipulation is a feature that gains the enthusiastic support of users and provides for the guidelines described in the preceding section.

Following are a series of examples to demonstrate the applicability of direct manipulation to decision support applications. People talk of data warehouse access and data manipulation in various ways: wading through data; mining data; and data discovery. Whatever term you use, this access and manipulation basically allows users to focus on the content of a data warehouse, not on how to operate data warehouse applications that provide access to the data warehouse. Remember, we want users to focus on business, not technology. Your framework and the tools that are used to create your framework will guide users' ability to focus on business.

The tools that are used in these examples are Cognos' PowerPlay and Impromptu, two tools that were built with the user in mind and that provide an elegant solution in the data warehouse arena. These tools eliminate a large number of the technical barriers of many tools today and offer a business-oriented view of a data warehouse—more specifically, the ability to perform direct manipulation of data itself.

Reporting Examples with Impromptu

Impromptu provides an easy environment for users to create standard and ad hoc reports. This environment allows users to exploit direct manipulation to explore a data warehouse without the need to know or understand the underlying data structures. After data has been retrieved, users can continue their investigation by pointing, clicking, and dragging on the active report and data to refine, filter, sort, and format the desired results. Though Impromptu fills the traditional two-dimensional reporting space that most query and reporting tools share, many advanced features allow data warehouse support staff to be more at ease in allowing users to explore data warehouse and create reports to their heart's content.

Creating a Simple Report and Filtering Unwanted Data

In this example, users want to create a simple report that shows the products that are available to sell and the margin yielded through sale of these products.

Users select the data that they desire on the report by opening folders that contain data items that are related and relevant to each other, as shown in Figure 11.3. The folders are contained in an Impromptu catalog and represent a logical grouping that an administrator has established for an individual user or group of users. To carry out this task, they perform the following operations.

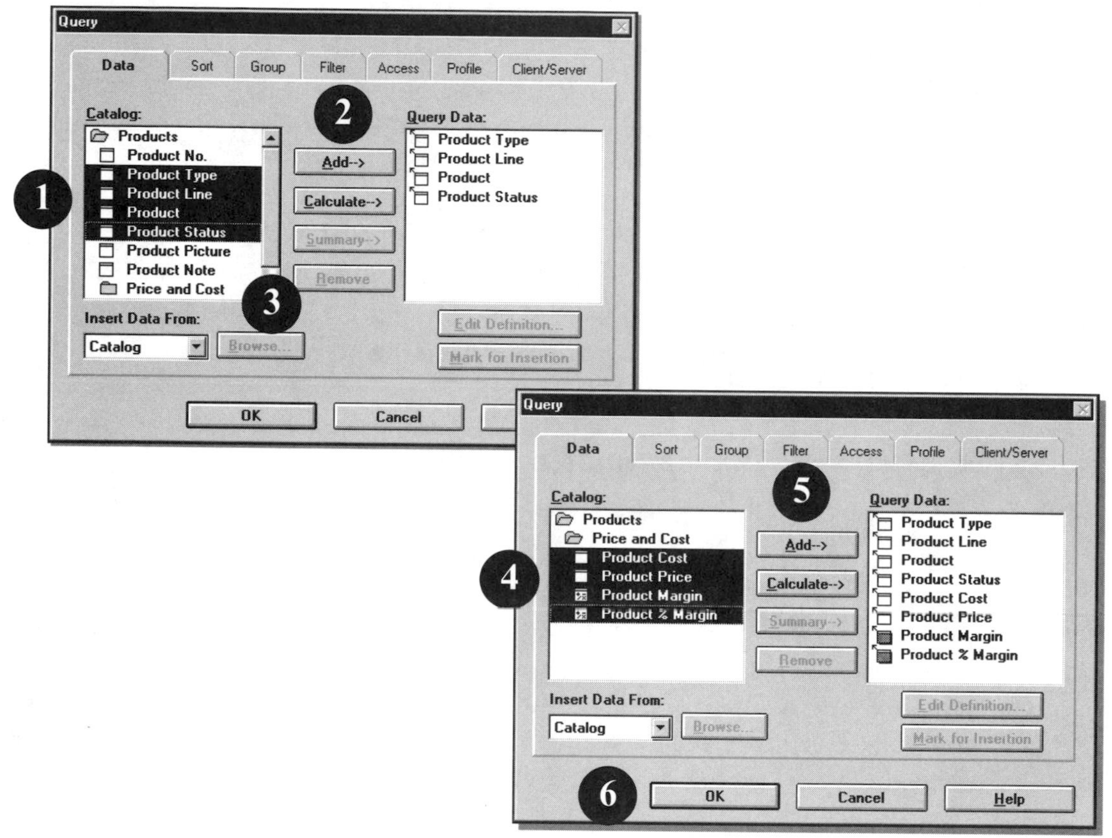

Figure 11.3: *Selecting data for a report with Impromptu*

The first folder opened was the product folder, from which the user selected several items through the following steps.

1. Highlight the data columns
2. Click the Add button
3. Open another folder with price and cost information
4. Select additional data items to include in the report
5. Click the Add button
6. Click the OK button

These steps produce the results shown in Figure 11.4.

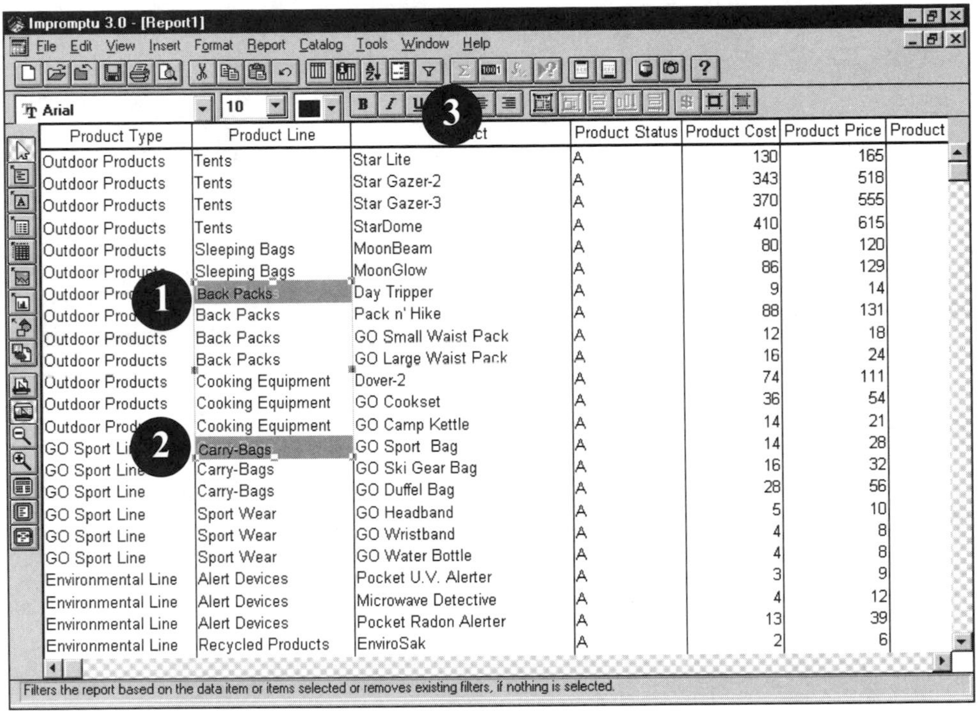

Product Type	Product Line	...ct	Product Status	Product Cost	Product Price	Product
Outdoor Products	Tents	Star Lite	A	130	165	
Outdoor Products	Tents	Star Gazer-2	A	343	518	
Outdoor Products	Tents	Star Gazer-3	A	370	555	
Outdoor Products	Tents	StarDome	A	410	615	
Outdoor Products	Sleeping Bags	MoonBeam	A	80	120	
Outdoor Produ...	Sleeping Bags	MoonGlow	A	86	129	
Outdoor Pro...	Back Packs	Day Tripper	A	9	14	
Outdoor Pro...	Back Packs	Pack n' Hike	A	88	131	
Outdoor Products	Back Packs	GO Small Waist Pack	A	12	18	
Outdoor Products	Back Packs	GO Large Waist Pack	A	16	24	
Outdoor Products	Cooking Equipment	Dover-2	A	74	111	
Outdoor Products	Cooking Equipment	GO Cookset	A	36	54	
Outdoor Prod...	Cooking Equipment	GO Camp Kettle	A	14	21	
GO Sport Li...	Carry-Bags	GO Sport Bag	A	14	28	
GO Sport Lin...	Carry-Bags	GO Ski Gear Bag	A	16	32	
GO Sport Line	Carry-Bags	GO Duffel Bag	A	28	56	
GO Sport Line	Sport Wear	GO Headband	A	5	10	
GO Sport Line	Sport Wear	GO Wristband	A	4	8	
GO Sport Line	Sport Wear	GO Water Bottle	A	4	8	
Environmental Line	Alert Devices	Pocket U.V. Alerter	A	3	9	
Environmental Line	Alert Devices	Microwave Detective	A	4	12	
Environmental Line	Alert Devices	Pocket Radon Alerter	A	13	39	
Environmental Line	Recycled Products	EnviroSak	A	2	6	

Filters the report based on the data item or items selected or removes existing filters, if nothing is selected.

Figure 11.4: *Direct manipulation for filtering data in an Impromptu report*

Filtering Data with Direct Manipulation

Suppose users only want to see back packs and carry bags. With the direct manipulation techniques offered inside the Impromptu package, users simply follow these steps, as shown in Figure 11.4.

1. Select a displayed value of *back packs*
2. Select a displayed value of *carry bags*
3. Click the Filter button to tell Impromptu to filter the result set according to the selected data

After following these three steps, users receive the results in a report as shown in Figure 11.5.

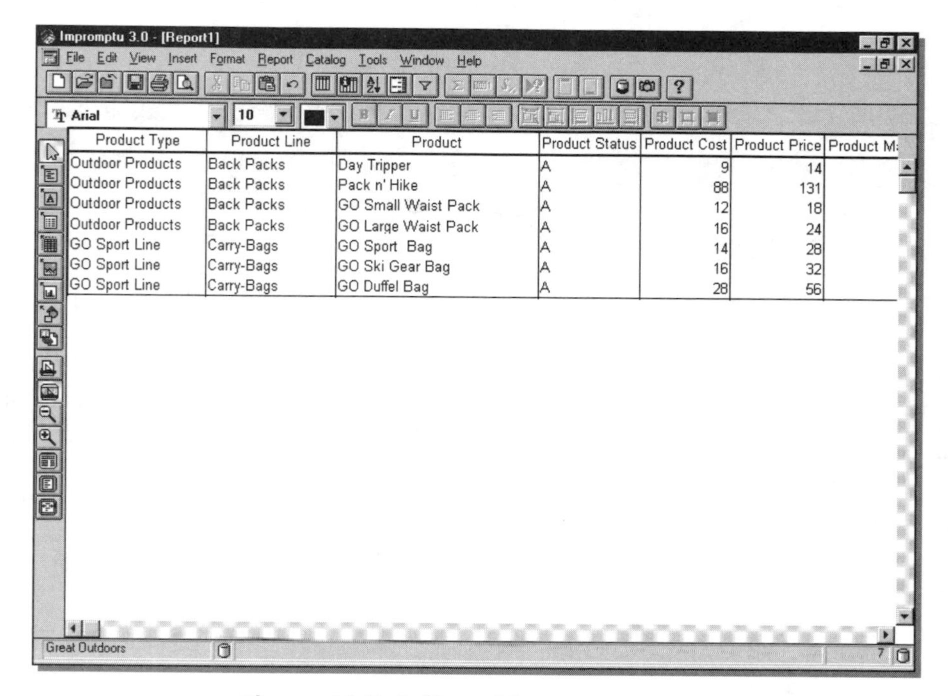

Figure 11.5: *A filtered Impromptu report*

These direct manipulation techniques can be extended to include more complex filters, logical grouping of data, sorting of data, aggregation functions, and formatting functions. Of course, Impromptu allows more technical users to fill in traditional dialogs and optimize the process. However, for novices or users who infrequently perform reporting tasks, this tool provides a flexible and unintimidating interface into their data world. Point and click, drag and drop, utilizing the mouse or pointing device more effectively than the keyboard—all of these techniques are advancements that you should try to offer your user community in bridging the technology-to-business gap that exists today.

Filling a Report Template and Sorting the Results

In this example, users create a report based on a template provided by the development staff. The template has been built to perform sales analysis with regard to the margins attained by selling a product. To carry out this task, users perform the following operations, as shown in Figure 11.6.

1. Users select the folders that contain the data items they desire

2. The data items are added to the report either by dragging the item into the template column list or by clicking the Add button
3. After users have all the fields they need, the OK button is clicked to indicate that they are done with their selections

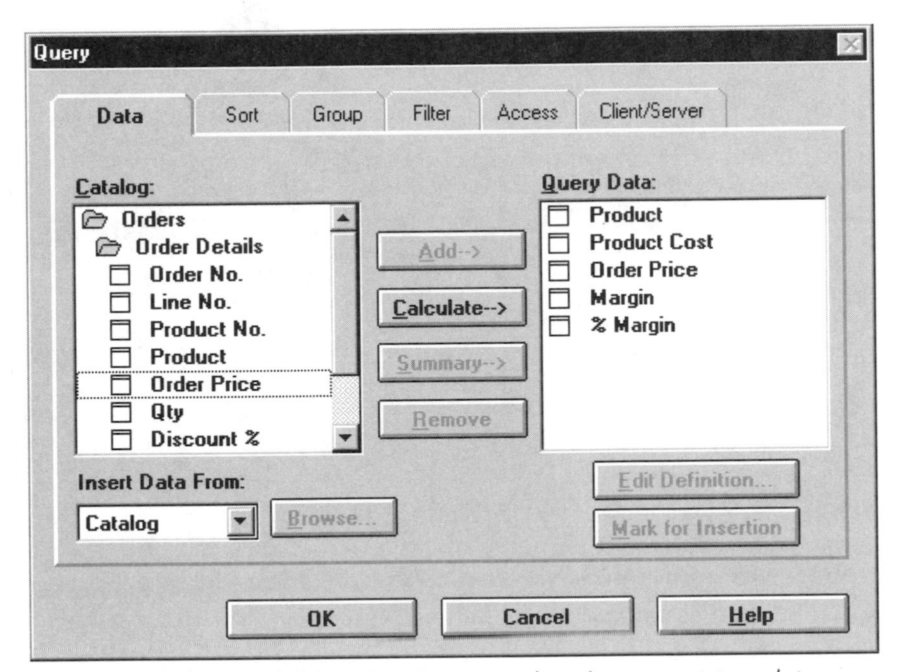

Figure 11.6: *Selecting data items to place in a report template*

After the preceding steps, the template is filled as shown in Figure 11.7.

Sorting Results with Direct Manipulation

If users want to change the order of data within a report, they use simple direct manipulation techniques. The steps involved in this process are listed next, as shown in Figure 11.7.

1. Select the column or data that users want sorted
2. Click the Sort button

After following these steps, users now have a report as showing in Figure 11.8, which presents the products in descending order based upon margin by sale.

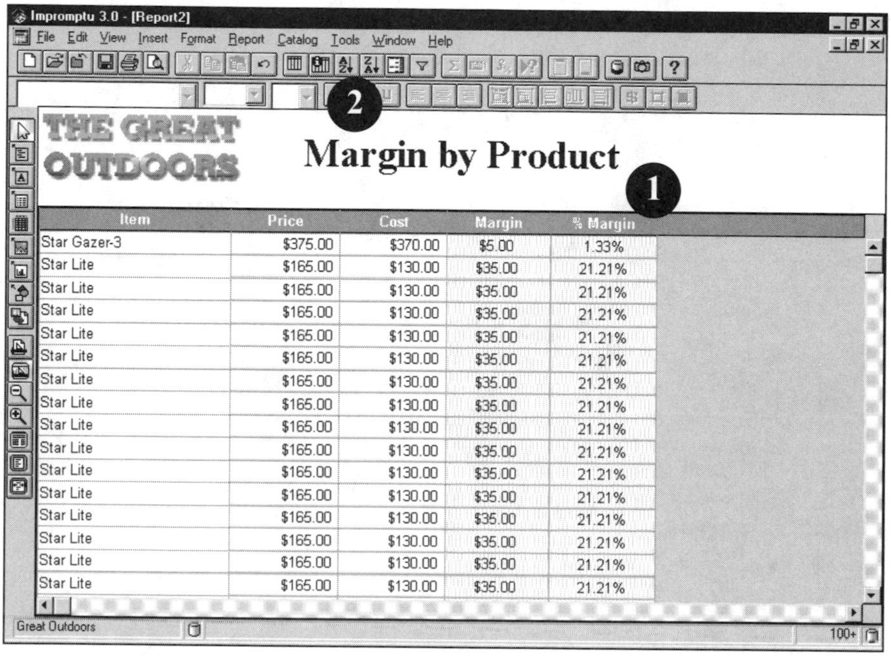

Impromptu 3.0 - [Report2]

File Edit View Insert Format Report Catalog Tools Window Help

THE GREAT OUTDOORS

Margin by Product

Item	Price	Cost	Margin	% Margin
Star Gazer-3	$375.00	$370.00	$5.00	1.33%
Star Lite	$165.00	$130.00	$35.00	21.21%
Star Lite	$165.00	$130.00	$35.00	21.21%
Star Lite	$165.00	$130.00	$35.00	21.21%
Star Lite	$165.00	$130.00	$35.00	21.21%
Star Lite	$165.00	$130.00	$35.00	21.21%
Star Lite	$165.00	$130.00	$35.00	21.21%
Star Lite	$165.00	$130.00	$35.00	21.21%
Star Lite	$165.00	$130.00	$35.00	21.21%
Star Lite	$165.00	$130.00	$35.00	21.21%
Star Lite	$165.00	$130.00	$35.00	21.21%
Star Lite	$165.00	$130.00	$35.00	21.21%
Star Lite	$165.00	$130.00	$35.00	21.21%
Star Lite	$165.00	$130.00	$35.00	21.21%
Star Lite	$165.00	$130.00	$35.00	21.21%
Star Lite	$165.00	$130.00	$35.00	21.21%

Great Outdoors

Figure 11.7: *Sorting a report through direct manipulation*

Again, direct manipulation allows users to customize the report without being required to understand commands or which dialog box to use. Users simply select data and click an operator button to perform a task. This is not the most optimal method for querying, but it simplifies the process enough to make it less intimidating to novice or less frequent users—directly reducing the cost associated with training. After user becomes more familiar with the tool, they can use more advanced, shortcut methods to more efficiently and quickly produce the same results. (All of the filtering and sorting that we have illustrated can be done within the dialog box from which the user selected the data items, so this could be a single-step process.)

The following is the SQL *select* statement that was utilized by Impromptu to display the report shown in Figure 11.8. Of course, this code is lacking the format characteristics of the report, but notice how the users selected familiar data items and got a report. This SQL statement contains calculated items, join conditions, and *order by* clauses. This is not an overly complex SQL statement; however, no user would code this statement.

```
select T1."PRODUCT" as c1,
 T1."PROD_COST" as c2,
 T2."PRICE" as c3,
```

```
 T2."PRICE" - T1."PROD_COST" as c4,
 ((T2."PRICE" - T1."PROD_COST") / T2."PRICE") as c5
from "ORDRDETL" T2,
 "PRODUCT" T1
where (T2."PROD_NO" = T1."PROD_NO")
order by c1 asc,c5 desc
```

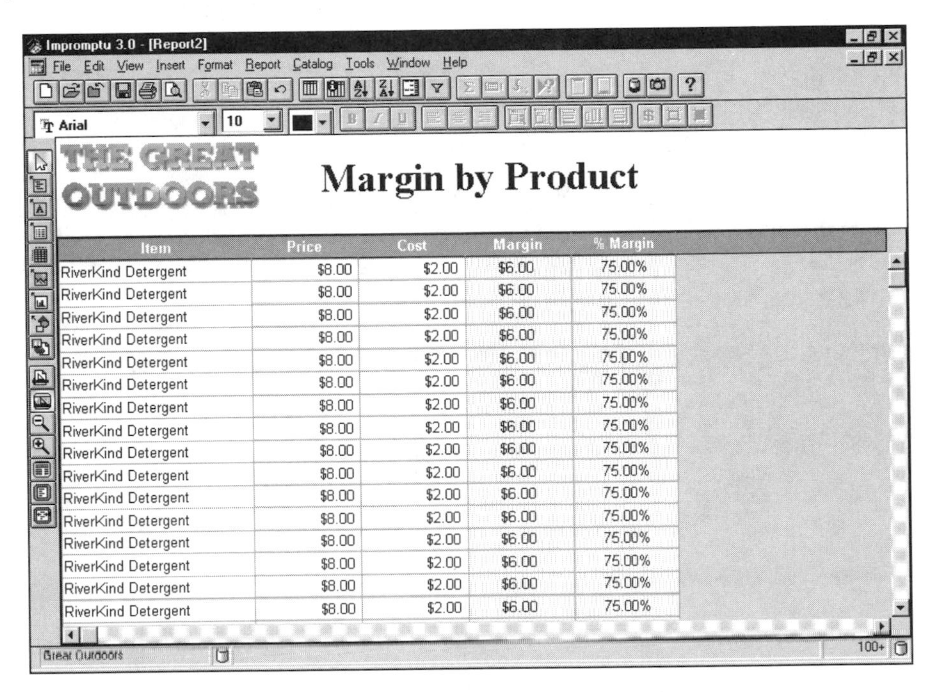

Item	Price	Cost	Margin	% Margin
RiverKind Detergent	$8.00	$2.00	$6.00	75.00%
RiverKind Detergent	$8.00	$2.00	$6.00	75.00%
RiverKind Detergent	$8.00	$2.00	$6.00	75.00%
RiverKind Detergent	$8.00	$2.00	$6.00	75.00%
RiverKind Detergent	$8.00	$2.00	$6.00	75.00%
RiverKind Detergent	$8.00	$2.00	$6.00	75.00%
RiverKind Detergent	$8.00	$2.00	$6.00	75.00%
RiverKind Detergent	$8.00	$2.00	$6.00	75.00%
RiverKind Detergent	$8.00	$2.00	$6.00	75.00%
RiverKind Detergent	$8.00	$2.00	$6.00	75.00%
RiverKind Detergent	$8.00	$2.00	$6.00	75.00%
RiverKind Detergent	$8.00	$2.00	$6.00	75.00%
RiverKind Detergent	$8.00	$2.00	$6.00	75.00%
RiverKind Detergent	$8.00	$2.00	$6.00	75.00%
RiverKind Detergent	$8.00	$2.00	$6.00	75.00%
RiverKind Detergent	$8.00	$2.00	$6.00	75.00%

Figure 11.8: *Results after sorting the template report*

Multidimensional Analysis Examples with PowerPlay

PowerPlay provides multidimensional capabilities that allow users to analyze and report on the data within a data warehouse. This environment launches users into a data cube and allows them to directly manipulate the presentation of data along any of the provided dimensions within a variety of different display formats. Because these dimensions have been defined to PowerPlay, the product aggregates and presents the data in different summarized levels of a business, allowing users to twist and turn the data cube until they have thoroughly analyzed it.

The heart and soul of PowerPlay is direct manipulation. Users literally are presented with the data cube and asked to manipulate it instead of the traditional reporting schemes in which users must explain how to present, access, and filter data—all before they get any results.

The following examples use similar data to what we saw within the Impromptu examples. However, you will immediately notice the analytical nature of PowerPlay versus the reporting nature of Impromptu.

We enter the data cube in an exploratory mode, as shown in Figure 11.9. Notice that PowerPlay immediately graphs the first measure, quantity sold, against the first two dimensions within the cube, time and product. The dimensions that users can manipulate include time periods, products, sales representatives, customer types, and margin ranges. The measures can be altered among sales, quantity sold, and cost. Notice how we have not done anything vaguely similar to a *select* statement with a *where* condition, which you will see in most report writers. Users are simply presented with data. The dimension titles are the closest we come to a data model in this elegant interface.

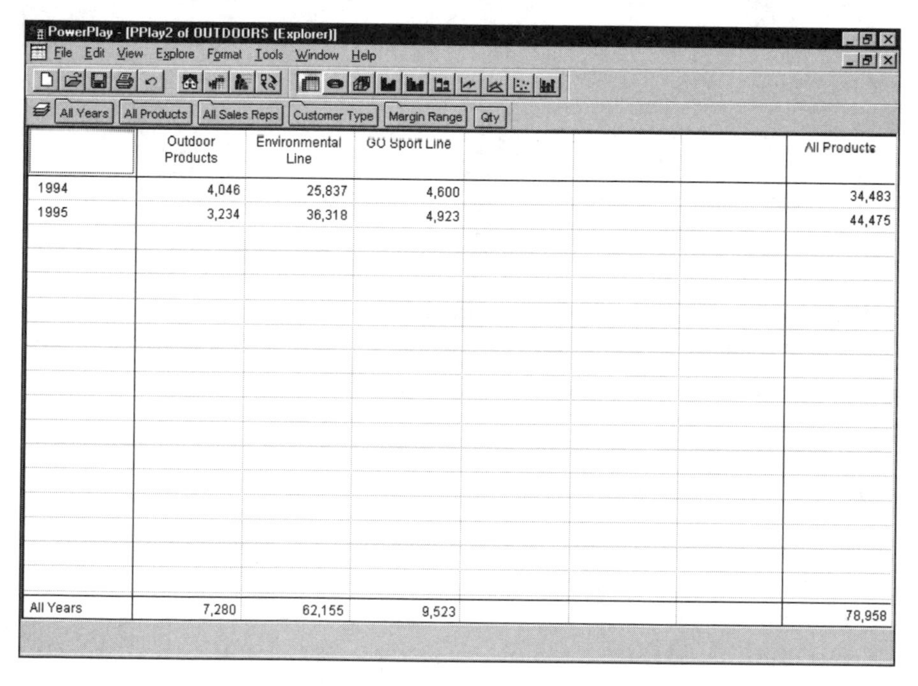

Figure 11.9: *Initial PowerPlay exploration view of data*

Drilling Down to Discover

Our first direct manipulation example in PowerPlay involves the concept of drilling down, a relatively easy concept to understand. Users want to get more detailed information for data already present; they therefore want to drill down to the next detail layer. In PowerPlay, users are guided to where they can drill through subtle changes in the cursor. Basically, any data item is fair game for drill down. PowerPlay presents us with an appropriate cursor when the mouse moves over data. We want to drill down on the time dimension of 1995 and on the environmental line of products. We can do this in several ways in PowerPlay. One way includes double clicking the mouse on 1995, then double clicking environmental line. The shortcut is to go to the cell representing the intersection between 1995 and environmental line of products, then double clicking. This tells PowerPlay to expose the details of that intersection point. The result of this drill down activity is presented in Figure 11.10.

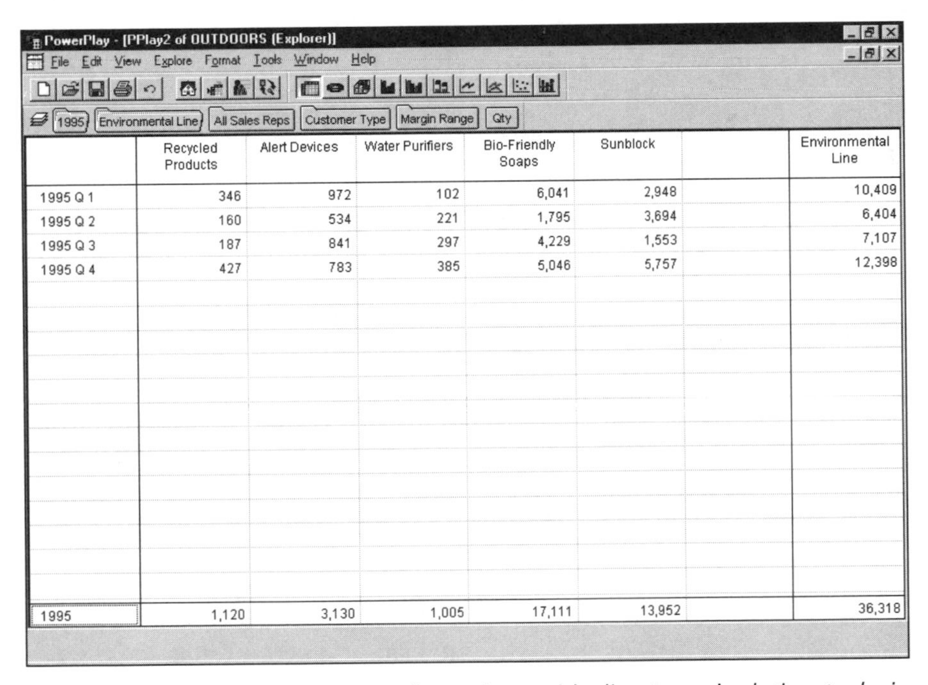

	Recycled Products	Alert Devices	Water Purifiers	Bio-Friendly Soaps	Sunblock	Environmental Line
1995 Q 1	346	972	102	6,041	2,948	10,409
1995 Q 2	160	534	221	1,795	3,694	6,404
1995 Q 3	187	841	297	4,229	1,553	7,107
1995 Q 4	427	783	385	5,046	5,757	12,398
1995	1,120	3,130	1,005	17,111	13,952	36,318

Figure 11.10: *Drilling down on two dimensions with direct manipulation techniques*

Slicing and Dicing to Isolate

The ability to isolate on any given dimension and further investigate the data in other dimensions is what provides the true multidimensional analysis required to analyze business data. In the sample database, we will tell PowerPlay to isolate on the product dimension utilizing Bio-Friendly Soaps, then to slice and dice the dimensions so that we are presented with the data by time and customer type. This is done by drilling down on the

Bio-Friendly Soap product and simply dragging the customer type dimension folder on the dimension line to the column headers. In performing such an activity, PowerPlay produces the results shown in Figure 11.11.

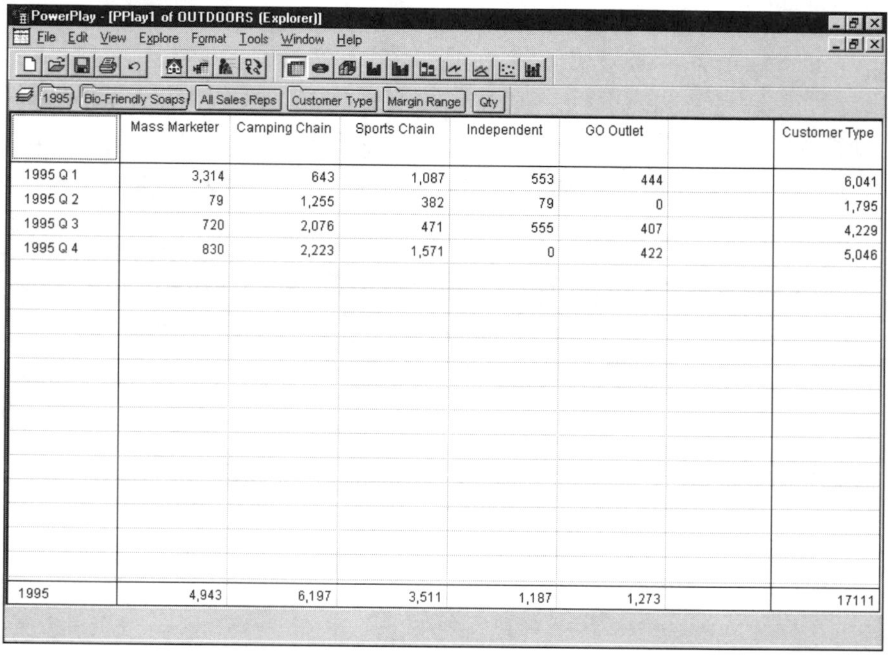

PowerPlay - [PPlay1 of OUTDOORS (Explorer)]

File Edit View Explore Format Tools Window Help

1995 | Bio-Friendly Soaps | All Sales Reps | Customer Type | Margin Range | Qty

	Mass Marketer	Camping Chain	Sports Chain	Independent	GO Outlet	Customer Type
1995 Q 1	3,314	643	1,087	553	444	6,041
1995 Q 2	79	1,255	382	79	0	1,795
1995 Q 3	720	2,076	471	555	407	4,229
1995 Q 4	830	2,223	1,571	0	422	5,046
1995	4,943	6,197	3,511	1,187	1,273	17111

Figure 11.11: *Slicing and dicing a data cube*

Again, we are directly manipulating a data cube to see the data in different angles along different dimensions. (Remember the earlier analogies and references to Rubiks Cube.) We can also manipulate the final display of this information to better understand the numbers, as shown in Figure 11.12. Here, we simply asked PowerPlay to format the data as a pie chart so that we could visualize the data and better understand where the Bio-Friendly Soap has been selling during the time period.

The tools in these examples, Cognos' PowerPlay and Impromptu, allow users to directly manipulate data, which provides a true "information at your fingertips" approach. Direct manipulation can be appealing to novices or intermittent users, because it simplifies the learning cycle. Direct manipulation is also good for frequent users, because they are essentially working on the problem solving or information discovery tasks, not the compilation and formatting tasks offered in many common reporting tools. In essence, concepts like direct manipulation assist you in delivering a data warehouse application framework that is very usable.

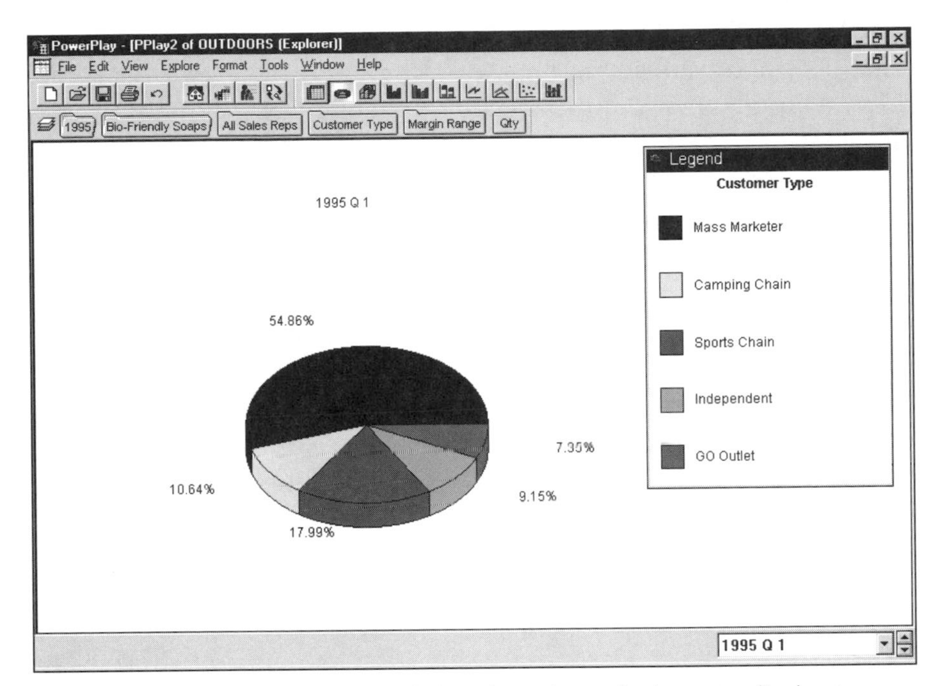

Figure 11.12: *Graphically visualizing data through alternate display types*

Measurable Factors for Usability

The following list will help you to gauge how usable your application framework is. These items should be tested with your user community to understand the impact that the overall solution you provide will have on your organization. You should develop a set of benchmark tasks that are associated with the requirements the users defined and have the users utilize the tool to solve the problems contained in the benchmark. Such a usability test will greatly assist your team in delivering a proper solution to your user community.

- **Time to learn** How long does it take typical users in the target community to learn the application, the reports, and their applicability to solving information requirements? How long does it take users to access and use the data warehouse with a relevant set of data to solve a relevant information task or decision problem?
- **Rate of errors by users** Error making is a critical component of system usage and therefore deserves extensive study. How many and what kind of errors are made by the users of the data warehouse in some benchmark tasks that are involved in gathering information?

- **Speed of performance** How long does it take to carry out the benchmark set of tasks? How long does it take for users to have enough knowledge to make a decision? Does the application framework respond quickly to fulfill user's rapid-fire questioning?
- **Retention over time** How well do users maintain their knowledge of the system after an hour? A day? A week? Retention may be closely linked to time to learn, and is also based on frequency of use. User testing plays an important role here, so make sure to perform these tests with a cross-section of your user community.
- **Subjective satisfaction** How much did users like using the system? This can be ascertained by interview, written survey, or directly videotaping testing sessions. You want to determine overall satisfaction and allow users to provide free-form comments and feedback on how to improve the system.

Deployment Tip 2: The users' interest is in the information contained and managed by the data warehouse. Therefore, make sure to choose or build a deployment environment that is composed of tools and applications that support the business first—techie stuff much later, if at all.

Delivering the Goods

No matter what, the coordinator of a data warehouse faces an immense job when deploying a data warehouse. This individual is required to provide access and customized reports to a large user community with vastly differing reporting needs. These differences include the volume of reporting, the diversity of reporting, and the access strategies involved with both of these items. The challenges of providing adequate facilities and resources to support users and giving them timely solutions to their information needs are demanding.

The key to successful deployment is a good architecture that provides flexibility while reducing the requirement for fixed and standard reports. If you can build your data warehouse in an easy-to-understand manner and provide your users with the proper tools to access the data, you will achieve a high user satisfaction rating.

Delivering such solutions also raises internal information systems issues along the lines of performance, security, and ongoing support of the user community. The key to delivering such solutions is insulation. If you insulate the user from being required to understand technology such as data structures, join strategies, networks, and other highly technical things, you will be able to solve their problems. To some database administrators, this means creating a lot of security schemes on top of views in their relational database. To those who have successfully deployed data warehouses, the abstraction is even higher than that.

A Layered Approach

Creating an environment that is safe for the corporation and the user alike can be done with several modern tools that target the decision support, OLAP, and data mining marketplaces. These tools address the security and access issues with catalogs that are managed outside a native database.

At a minimum, the application framework provided to users must eliminate the presentation of technology-oriented concepts. For example, the technical concept of joining two or more tables is foreign to users. This types of technology concept increases the learning curve for deployment of a data warehouse and potentially introduces the risk of users not accepting the delivered solution. These concepts also prove to be technically risky.

Most data access and query tools that allow users to perform joins have no intelligence with regard to optimizing the join. Therefore, users can easily make mistakes and create meaningless queries with simple point-and-click tools. We often say that the tools of today can assist the knowing in creating fabulous systems quickly, but they also can assist the unknowing in creating the biggest nightmares—just as quickly. Exposing concepts like data navigation and join strategies to users introduces danger into a peaceful query environment. Users can easily create a Cartesian product, which is a set of all pairs of elements (x, y) that can be constructed from given sets X and Y, such that x belongs to X and y to Y. These types of queries are a database administrator's worst nightmare. Then again, this is the beauty of SQL—ease of use and flexibility.

So how is the issue associated with presenting join dialogs to users addressed? One way is for database administrators to constantly work on establishing views that control the join strategies. Does this eliminate the join dialog in a data access tool? No, the user can simply access two views and do the same damage. The best way to control such activities is through creation of a controlled access catalog from which all queries are populated.

To demonstrate this concept, we will build a user query utilizing two tools on opposite ends of the control spectrum—one with limited control, Microsoft Query, and one with considerable control, Cognos' Impromptu. You may be able to easily try this example yourself, because it uses the Northwind database provided with Microsoft Access.

We will simply execute a query that accesses the Order information. This data is contained within the ORDER and ORDER_DETAIL_EXTENDED tables. We will report on the numerical information that is associated with sales, including ORDER_DATE, REQUIRED_DATE, SHIPMENT_DATE, PRODUCT_NAME, UNIT_PRICE, QUANTITY, FREIGHT, DISCOUNT, and EXTENDED_PRICE.

Microsoft Query Example

Microsoft Query utilizes a data model query selection process, whereby users select tables and define the columns in a report. If the users do not realize that they need to define a join between the two tables in our example, the query runs away and finally returns an error after formulating a Cartesian product as shown in Figure 11.3. Notice that the error returned from the query is quite misleading with regard to the true problem, stating only that it could not return all rows.

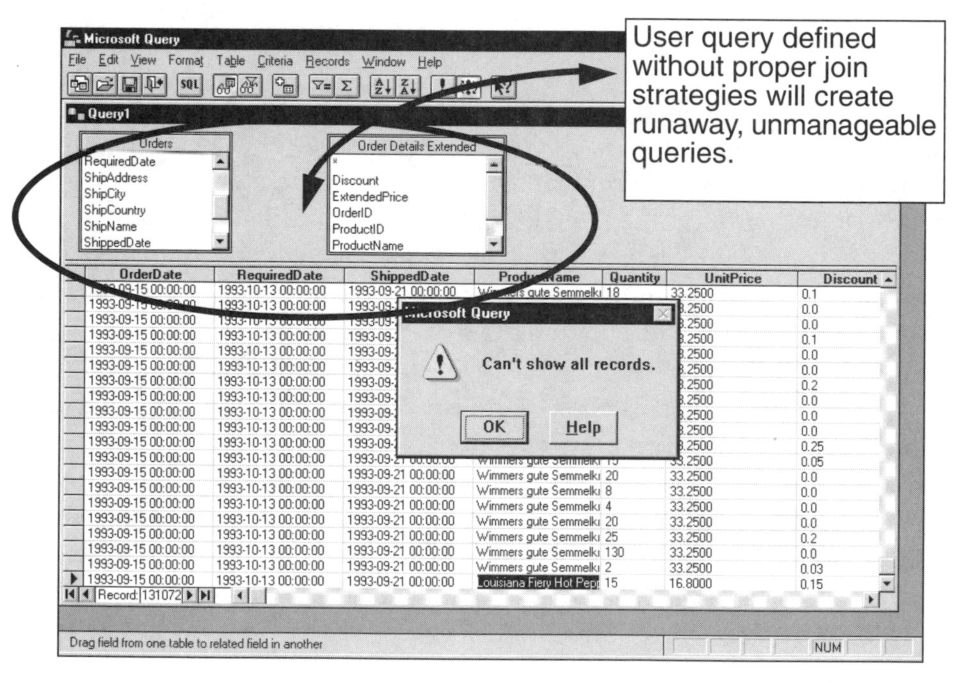

Figure 11.13: *Microsoft Query producing a Cartesian product*

With a proper join strategy over the correct columns, this query returns 2,155 rows, as shown in Figure 11.14. Questions to ask in tools selection: Is it intuitive to users that a join is required to receive correct data? Do you feel that your support staff can handle the required support for such a tool?

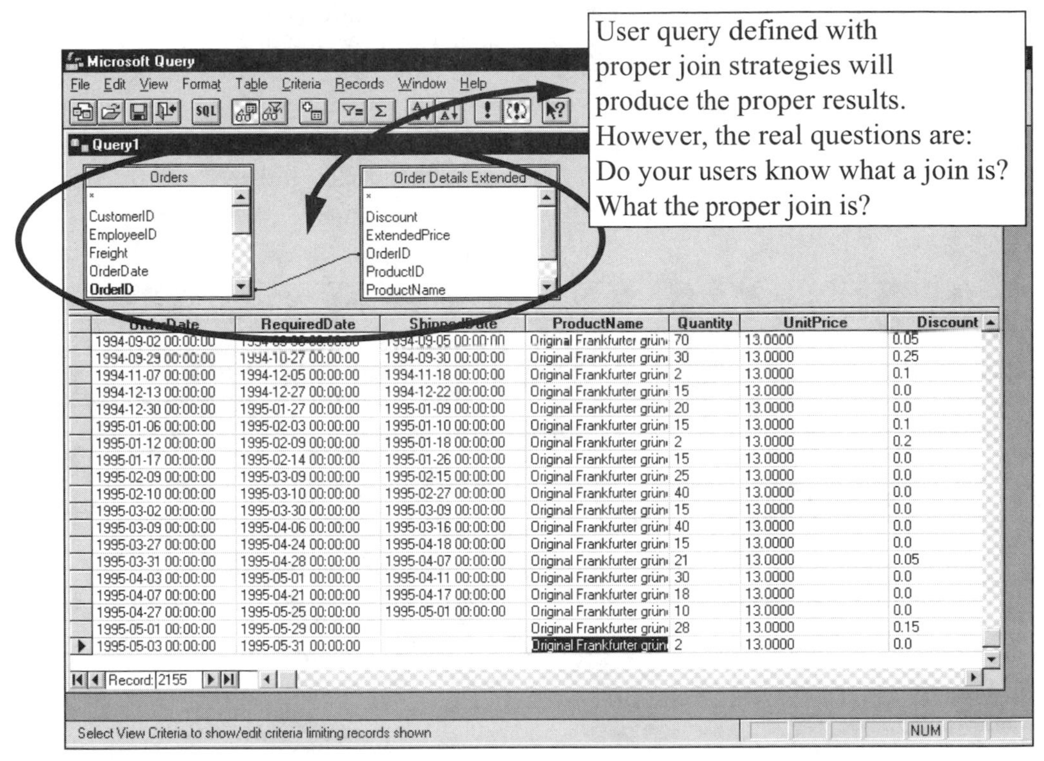

Figure 11.14: *Microsoft Query after using a proper join strategy*

Cognos' Impromptu Example

Cognos' Impromptu and similar tools enable you to greatly simplify the training, support, and performance of your users' queries. This simplification is due to a catalog-driven reporting engine. You administratively define how you want users to view data—typically mapping an underlying database to a view that matches the business' view of information. This catalog also defines the join strategies to utilize between database tables. Users never see a join dialog, and proper tuning of queries can be administered. The result is simple, yet powerful user querying of a data warehouse. This catalog also allows administrative staff to further control items such as the following.

- **Security** By user class, folder, field, or value
- **Resource utilization** By balancing the client/server load, restricting database queries, and controlling costly queries

- **Performance** By predefining base-level join strategies, storing filter conditions to narrow result sets, and allowing data caching to the local device

The result is a fast, yet easy-to-use environment to which your users will quickly adapt. The same query run in the previous section in Impromptu is shown in Figures 11.15 and 11.16. Notice the absence of Cartesian products and misleading result sets. Users receive only what they requested.

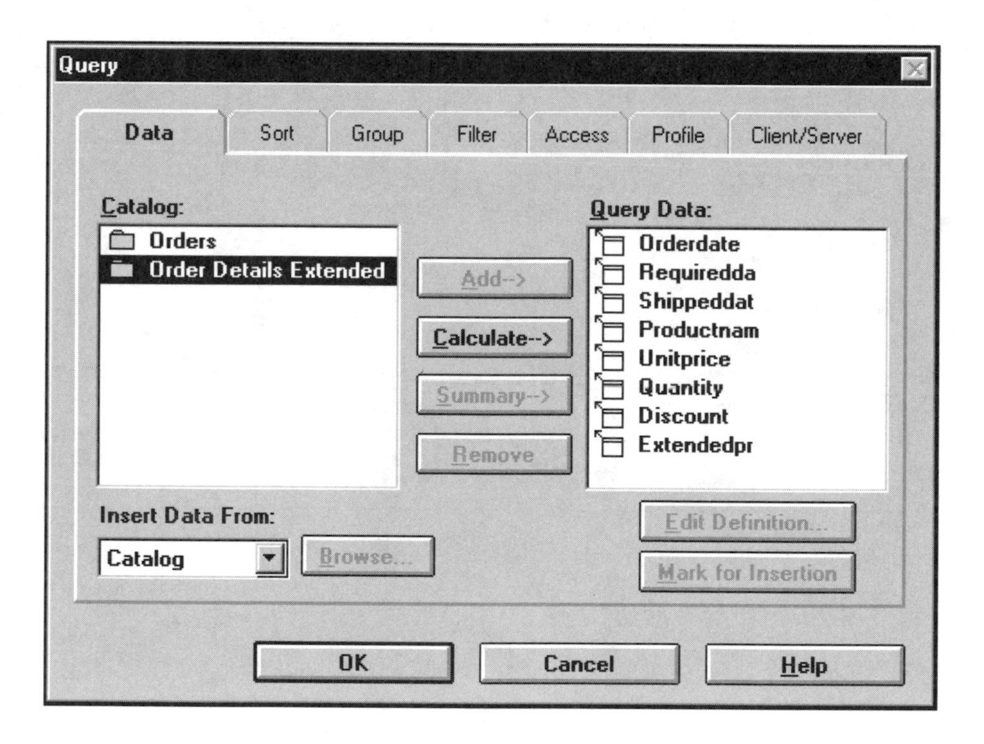

Figure 11.15: *Users select reporting columns from a catalog in Impromptu*

Impromptu comes in an administrator package as well as a user package. The administrators define the folders, or logical data groupings, along with naming conventions and other features contained in an Impromptu catalog. This type of tool relieves administrative personnel of the ongoing task of view maintenance that is required in many data warehouse implementations. The interface for administration is similar to the query interface, offering both the administrative staff and users a quick learning curve. Figure 11.17 demonstrates how a join strategy is defined between two tables in Impromptu Administrator.

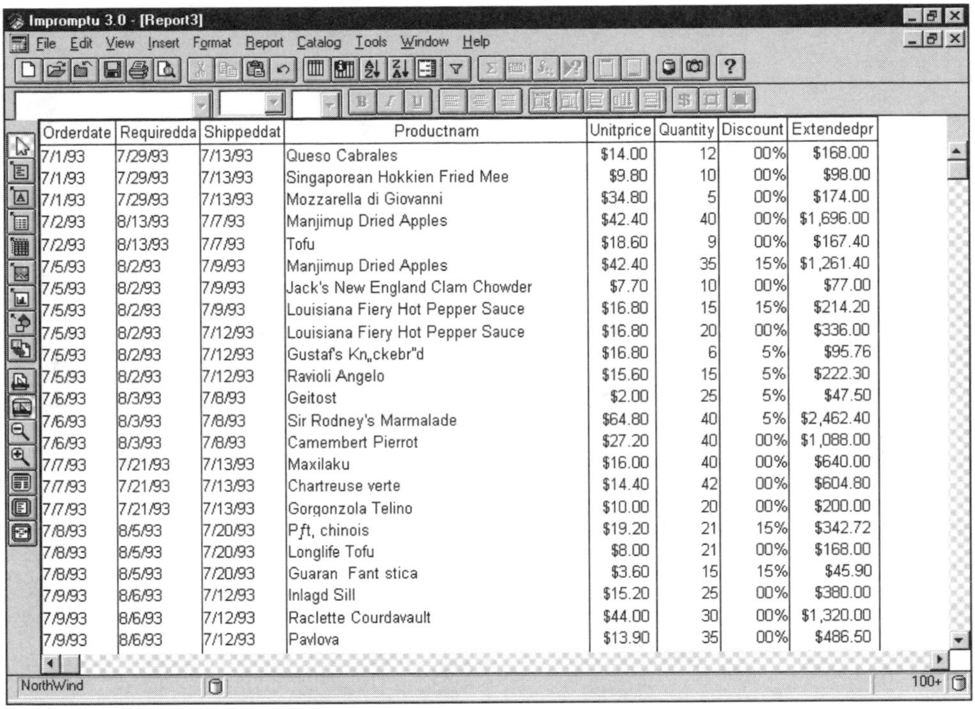

Impromptu 3.0 - [Report3]

File Edit View Insert Format Report Catalog Tools Window Help

Orderdate	Requiredda	Shippeddat	Productnam	Unitprice	Quantity	Discount	Extendedpr
7/1/93	7/29/93	7/13/93	Queso Cabrales	$14.00	12	00%	$168.00
7/1/93	7/29/93	7/13/93	Singaporean Hokkien Fried Mee	$9.80	10	00%	$98.00
7/1/93	7/29/93	7/13/93	Mozzarella di Giovanni	$34.80	5	00%	$174.00
7/2/93	8/13/93	7/7/93	Manjimup Dried Apples	$42.40	40	00%	$1,696.00
7/2/93	8/13/93	7/7/93	Tofu	$18.60	9	00%	$167.40
7/5/93	8/2/93	7/9/93	Manjimup Dried Apples	$42.40	35	15%	$1,261.40
7/5/93	8/2/93	7/9/93	Jack's New England Clam Chowder	$7.70	10	00%	$77.00
7/5/93	8/2/93	7/9/93	Louisiana Fiery Hot Pepper Sauce	$16.80	15	15%	$214.20
7/5/93	8/2/93	7/12/93	Louisiana Fiery Hot Pepper Sauce	$16.80	20	00%	$336.00
7/5/93	8/2/93	7/12/93	Gustaf's Kn„ckebr"d	$16.80	6	5%	$95.76
7/5/93	8/2/93	7/12/93	Ravioli Angelo	$15.60	15	5%	$222.30
7/6/93	8/3/93	7/8/93	Geitost	$2.00	25	5%	$47.50
7/6/93	8/3/93	7/8/93	Sir Rodney's Marmalade	$64.80	40	5%	$2,462.40
7/6/93	8/3/93	7/8/93	Camembert Pierrot	$27.20	40	00%	$1,088.00
7/7/93	7/21/93	7/13/93	Maxilaku	$16.00	40	00%	$640.00
7/7/93	7/21/93	7/13/93	Chartreuse verte	$14.40	42	00%	$604.80
7/7/93	7/21/93	7/13/93	Gorgonzola Telino	$10.00	20	00%	$200.00
7/8/93	8/5/93	7/20/93	Pƒt, chinois	$19.20	21	15%	$342.72
7/8/93	8/5/93	7/20/93	Longlife Tofu	$8.00	21	00%	$168.00
7/8/93	8/5/93	7/20/93	Guaran Fant stica	$3.60	15	15%	$45.90
7/9/93	8/6/93	7/12/93	Inlagd Sill	$15.20	25	00%	$380.00
7/9/93	8/6/93	7/12/93	Raclette Courdavault	$44.00	30	00%	$1,320.00
7/9/93	8/6/93	7/12/93	Pavlova	$13.90	35	00%	$486.50

NorthWind 100+

***Figure 11.16:** Resultant Impromptu query*

Cognos' PowerPlay Example

Cognos' PowerPlay provides an even better interface for true decision support analysis. This interface contains no joins, no selects, no data columns—just direct manipulation of the real data in an information package. PowerPlay, like Impromptu, requires administrative support to initialize data structures, which allows for its flexibility. However, after the data structures are implemented, users have little opportunity for errors.

PowerPlay's administrative tool is known as the Transformer, depicted in Figure 11.18. This tool allows an administrator to define multidimensional data cubes off a data warehouse, from which users perform business analysis. These data cubes are in essence personal or workgroup-oriented data marts—an extraction provided to users for optimized analytical work, including the ability to work independently of a data warehouse in a mobile environment.

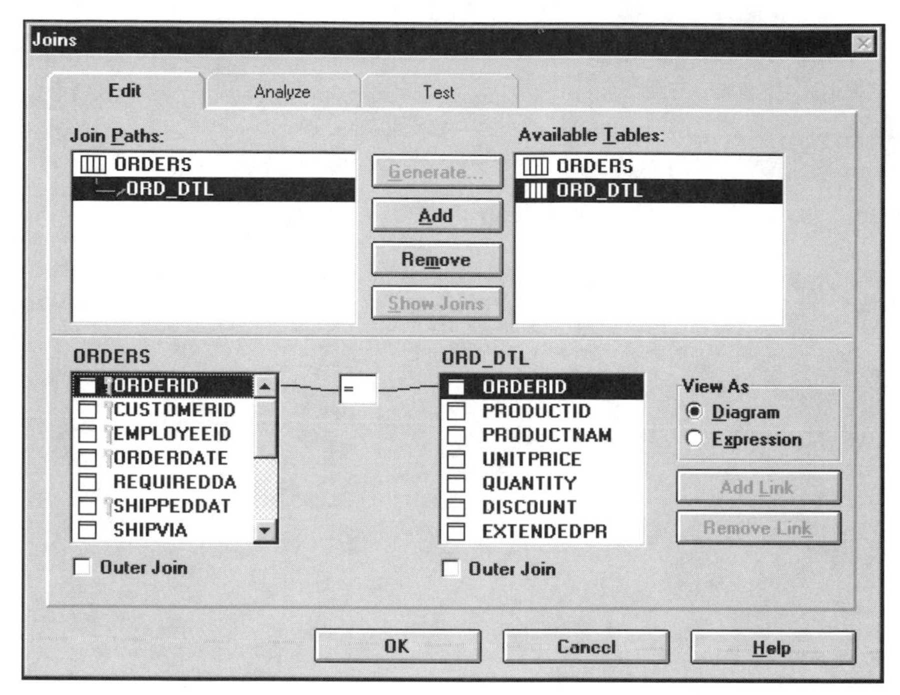

Figure 11.17: *Impromptu Administrator join definition*

The mechanism to obtain data and build a multidimensional data cube can be Impromptu or another query tool. A PowerPlay multidimensional view is illustrated in Figure 11.19. The Transformer provides a unique facility that allows an administrator to visualize data in the dimensions of a data cube, then create a centralized repository of data cubes. These data cubes can be stored in a variety of methods, including a proprietary format (such as formats of Cognos' PowerPlay or Arbor Software's Essbase) or an open format within a relational database (such as Sybase SQL Server or Oracle).

Application Layer Content

Your final delivery mechanism should allow for complete access to your enterprise's data warehouse environment. This system should be built around an architecture that consists of data, technology, and application components. Your data warehouse tool suite is the foundation from which your application framework is delivered to access various data stores, such as the enterprise data warehouse, local data marts, and multidimensional data analysis data stores. A detailed data warehouse application framework is illustrated in Figure 11.20.

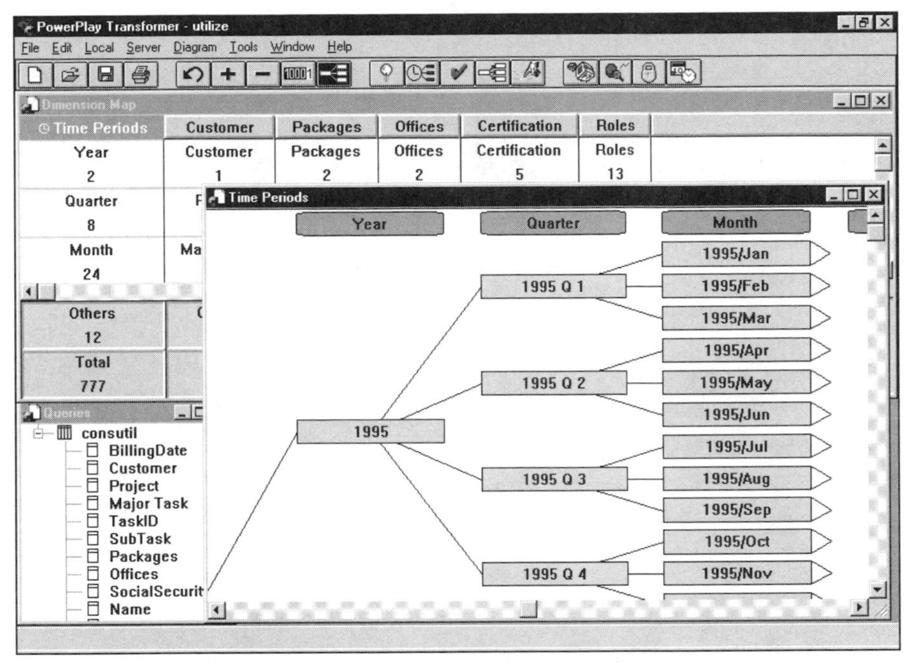

Figure 11.18: *PowerPlay data transformation*

PowerPlay - [PPlay1 of ONTIMESH (Explorer)]

File Edit View Explore Format Tools Window Help

Orderdate | Requiredda | Shippeddat | USA | Productnam | Quantity

USA — Layer 13 of 13

	1993	1994	1995	Orderdate
Konbu	10	0	252	262
Tarte au sucre	120	55	181	356
Chang	25	130	139	294
Chai	38	5	137	180
Scottish Longbreads	11	101	135	247
Raclette Courdavault	40	106	130	276
Alice Mutton	71	165	125	361
Rh"nbr„u Klosterbier	6	167	124	297
Sir Rodney's Scones	0	24	115	139
Pavlova	31	154	110	295
Inlagd Sill	0	80	105	185
C"te de Blaye	20	55	95	170
Gnocchi di nonna Alice	122	184	80	386
Guaran Fant stica	0	18	79	97
Flotemysost	60	84	71	215
Chef Anton's Gumbo Mix	12	4	70	86
Productnam	1707	4541	3082	9330

Figure 11.19: *PowerPlay multidimensional view of quantity by location, product, and time*

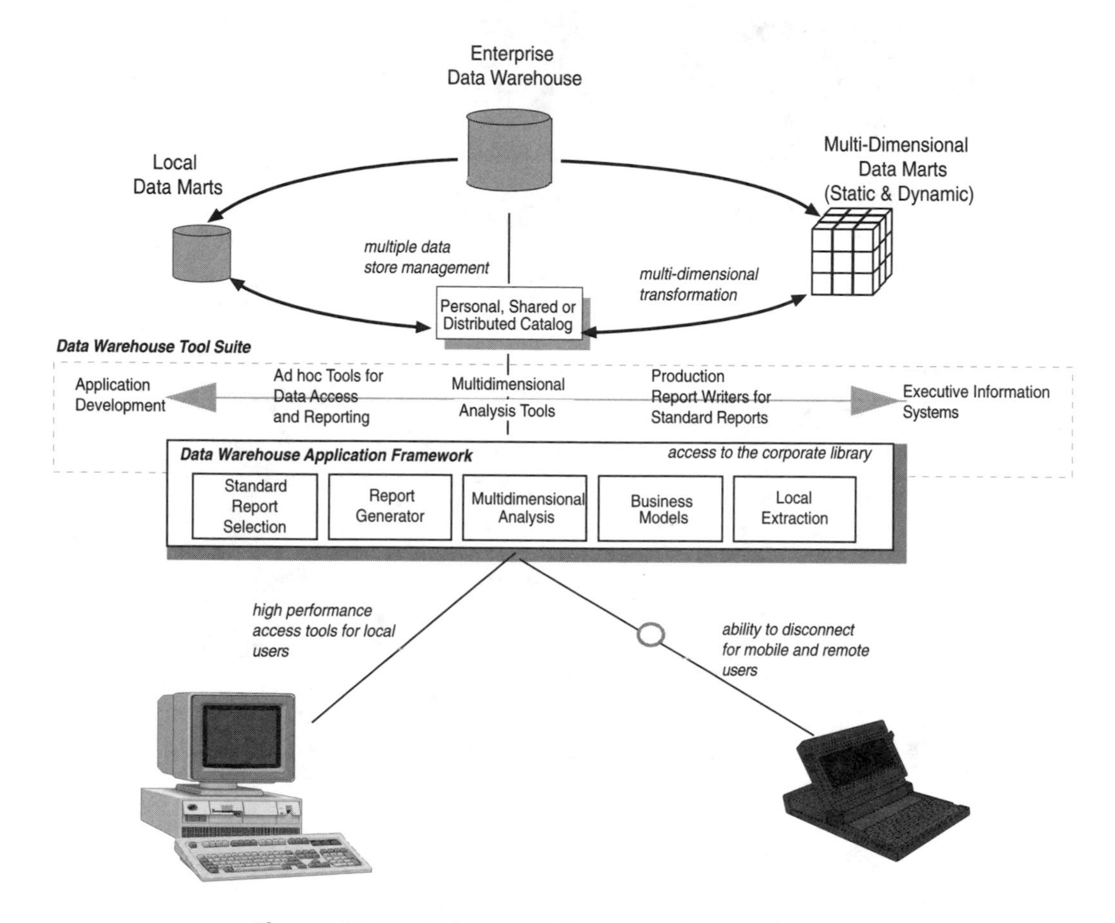

Figure 11.20: *A data warehouse application framework*

Great care should be taken to validate your framework, which should include or account for the following items.

- Data and database
    - **Centralized log-on and log-off processing** Minimize the number of logins required per user
    - **Database links** Connect to required information sources
    - **Data dictionary** Provide definition of terms and sources
    - **Aggregator** Provide roll-up capability to new subtotals
    - **Integrator** Link to other, disparate systems that support the data warehouse
    - **Data reduction tools** Provide statistical and pattern matching tools

  - **Data management tools** Provide proper administration of the data warehouse

- Application and analytic logic
  - **Corporate report library** Provide standard business reports
  - **Report generator** Produce request for data based on user parameters
  - **Drill down** Include the ability to drill down through data hierarchies
  - **Dimension and measure definition** Provide on-line help with examples
  - **Exception reporting** Provide reports that offer comparisons to expectations
  - **Measure creation** Include an ability to define and save new measures
  - **Private libraries** Store own reports
- User interface and control
  - **Report selection** Choose report from library
  - **Parameter selection** Offer a simple, intuitive selection for numerous choices
  - **Filter** Change display and remove from display
  - **Highlighter** Annotate reports
  - **SQL tool** Create own complex queries
- Presentation
  - **Internal tools** Offer reports, graphs, email, and more
  - **External tools** Translate to personal productivity tools
  - **Advanced formatting** Provide presentation tools

Deployment Tip 3: In the area of tools, it is unfortunate but true that *you get what your pay for.* Don't be penny wise and pound foolish when deploying tools to your user community. The more sophisticated the tool is, the more productive the user will be and the less burden will be placed on your development team.

Summary

The data warehousing tools supporting users allow many users to navigate corporate data stores. Access includes ad hoc, interactive, repetitive querying. All of this functionality is provided without impacting mission-critical operational systems. Within a given session, users can issue query upon query in an iterative manner to explore trends, pinpoint or discover problems, and evaluate business opportunities. This information allows users to make better decisions in a more rapid fashion, allowing the company to become more competitive. To make your organization succeed, create an informed environment for widespread knowledge. To make your organization more intelligent, share the business intelligence from the corporate knowledge base with everyone. This freedom of information will begin to allow everyone to unite around a common vision of responsibility and accountability. Put the intelligence of every employee to work through maximum use of the information in your data warehouse. Every person can, and will, make a difference in the future. The sooner you get started, the further you will be ahead of your competitors and the faster your enterprise can be viewed as a truly intelligent enterprise.

When building a technical solution that will spread knowledge throughout your organization, it is important to understand the distinction between the applications framework provided by a data warehouse and the tool set that delivers this framework. The framework delivers a set of required capabilities to the users of a warehouse. The capabilities that the users derive from the framework are delivered by individual tools, or by tools working together with one another as well as with administrative resources provided by warehouse administrators.

The tools that support a data warehouse application framework may—and more than likely will—change over time. However, these changes should not change the applications framework except to enhance and improve it.

Great care should be used to provide the users of a data warehouse with a complete solution that covers the spectrum of their data access and reporting needs. However, you must realize that users have little to no desire to learn technical nuances of database management systems. Therefore, selection of tools should focus on those that totally insulate users from constructs such as table joins. Giving your users power from a tool does not mean that they should learn how to code; it means they will have power to explore data without learning technology. Up to this point in the book, we have discussed the concept and the compelling case for developing a data warehouse, then proceeded methodically through all of the essential steps required to implement a successful data warehouse project and make it accessible to users. In the next chapter, we document and address major problems and issues that are common to such projects with the goal of helping you to avoid or at least minimize them in your own situation.

12

Avoiding Production Obstacles

Any solution to a problem changes the problem.

—*R. W. Johnson*

Many obstacles arise during any information system development project, and data warehouses are no exception. However, some of these obstacles can either be avoided or eliminated with common sense solutions. The focus of this chapter is to define several common obstacles that arise in data warehouse development projects or during their implementation. We hope that, by documenting these items, we will provide you with a reference for quickly solving the obstacles.

Data Integration

Much of this book has been focused on integrating operational data to provide the uniform corporate knowledge base. However, two items often are difficult for an implementation team: application package software integration and external data integration. With a properly defined architecture, these two sources of data should be as easy as the rest; but in leading data warehouse projects, these two areas can pose problems in overall deployment and implementation of a data warehouse. We examine each of these subjects separately in the next two sections of this chapter.

Application Package Software Integration

Growth in the applications area of the software market includes applications that support both nonstrategic and strategic areas of businesses. For example, applications are widely available to support payroll, financials, human resources, sales, manufacturing, and other areas of businesses. As companies find it more viable to purchase business solutions from vendors offering applications packages, data warehouse teams continue to be forced to integrate applications that were never intended to communicate with each other.

The main task for applications-oriented companies is to quickly develop a consolidated repository of all application data sources. Data administrators are now managing multiple data stores with no uniform standards and often conflicting standards. These standards include naming conventions, items not exposed frequently to users, and data issues that are exposed to users. For example, think in your company of the true definition of a customer. Customer service, sales, and order management systems may have different definitions of a customer. Worse, related data and process of a customer is unintelligible across systems.

A data administrator's role is to minimize this redundancy while adequately supporting business requirements. Key to solving this growing problem is a strong metadata repository. Traditionally, data models have evolved from a design process that was owned by the company, as shown in Figure 12.1.

When outside applications are brought into companies, an enormous learning process must be undertaken. You do not go through the logical and physical design process; you simply receive the data definition language (DDL). So, you do not fully appreciate or understand how you got to the data model that has physically been implemented. On top of that, you face the following issues.

- You inherit the database or database format of the application provider
- You lose reusability and must introduce redundancy of data
- You violate corporate standards

There is no true solution to these problems. The best advice is to become more involved in the package selection process and to develop a comprehensive repository for all application databases. When evaluating application packages, your data warehouse administrator should be brought in to evaluate the ability to support the business through the data warehouse. Remember, application packages will improve business efficiencies—that is, reduce expenses. A data warehouse will assist in discovering revenue generating opportunities and areas that could further reduce expenses. Both objectives should be evaluated when understanding the impact of an application package purchase. You should require the following from your application provider.

- A complete data model
- Training for your data administration staff on the data model and data flow of the application
- Complete business rule documentation
- An open database environment
- An ability to extend and reuse the database
- Well-defined data standards

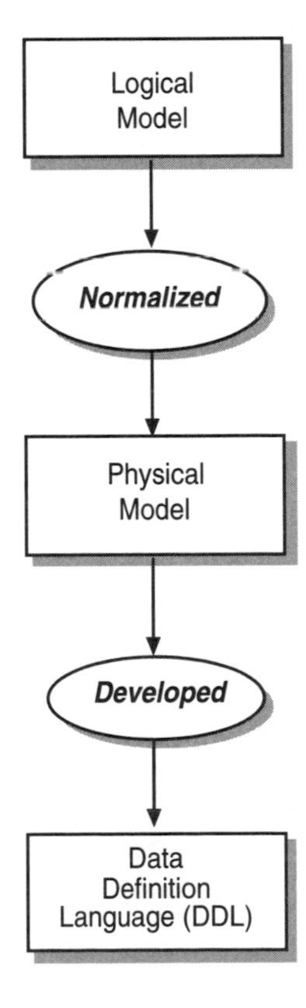

Figure 12.1: *Data model evolution*

It should be specifically noted that the application software packages that your enterprise implements are extremely important to an overall data warehouse effort. Packaged applications are a source of data for a data warehouse. With this importance, your organization must realize that an intimate understanding of the packaged application's data model for these applications is critical to your success.

Implementation Tip 11: Application packages should not be hard to integrate into your overall data warehouse strategy. However, often they are difficult to integrate due to your company's low technical knowledge in data management with regard to the application. Guarantee that your development team receives adequate documentation and training on any in-house applications that will provide data to a data warehouse.

External Data Integration

Though packaged applications have been developed by an external entity and the true data model is initially an unknown, the data and associated administration are owned by your company. Hence, an externally developed application manages internally developed data. However, the success of most companies in leveraging data is the ability to easily integrate external data.

External data is critical in many industries, such as the consumer packaged goods industry. This data is derived from a number of sources, including vendors such as A.C. Nielson, IRI, IMS America, and Sami Burke. The structures of their data are similar in nature to the structures you will create utilizing the techniques described in this book. The question is: What is best with regard to integrating the external data? A metadata repository should be intimately involved in this task of defining external data—from where it came, when it is refreshed, how it is refreshed, and so on.

Depending on the external data provider, for a cost you can obtain the data in a predefined format. The biggest issues you face with these companies is contractual, not technical. These companies in fact have been delivering data in a multidimensional format for years, so the data should integrate nicely into your data warehouse. One technical decision you need to make is whether you want to place this data in the same fact tables as internally supplied data or in separate fact tables that will ease your maintenance and loading processes. It is important to remember that we have defined a common set of subjects to which all fact tables relate. If external data and internal data are provided to similar levels of granularity, it may be acceptable to merge the two sets of data. However, depending on the frequency and format of the updates provided by your external vendor, you may find it better to separate the data. Whichever way you proceed, make sure that the subjects that you have defined don't conflict with the subjects your supplier has defined.

Try to have your supplier provide data in your standard format. If they provide you flat files from which your load processing will work, you will be able to control all of these aspects. However, the data volume that can be produced by these vendors can be enormous, and the amount of maintenance tends to be in line with the volume. So you may want to contract with the provider to offer the data in a clean format to expedite your loading process.

Note that external data providers have business-savvy sales people and tend to have their own tool. Watch out, or your users will quickly gravitate to these savvy salespeople and you will find your architecture compromised. Unless these external tools are generally applicable to your overall architecture and can access your data, avoid implementing them.

Integrating Disparate Operational Systems

One kind of a data warehouse—an operational data store—can make it easier for companies to integrate diverse applications and disparate data sources. The operational data store provides a consistent set of near-current operational data that can be a feeder system to a data warehouse. Within this book, many of the staging area concepts can be managed either from within a temporary, flexible environment of a data warehouse or from within an operational data store. Companies that look to widely implement packaged applications may be more prone to needing an operational data store that consolidates and improves the quality of data, both in operational systems and in a data warehouse. Figure 12.2 presents the integration of an operational data store into an overall data warehouse architecture.

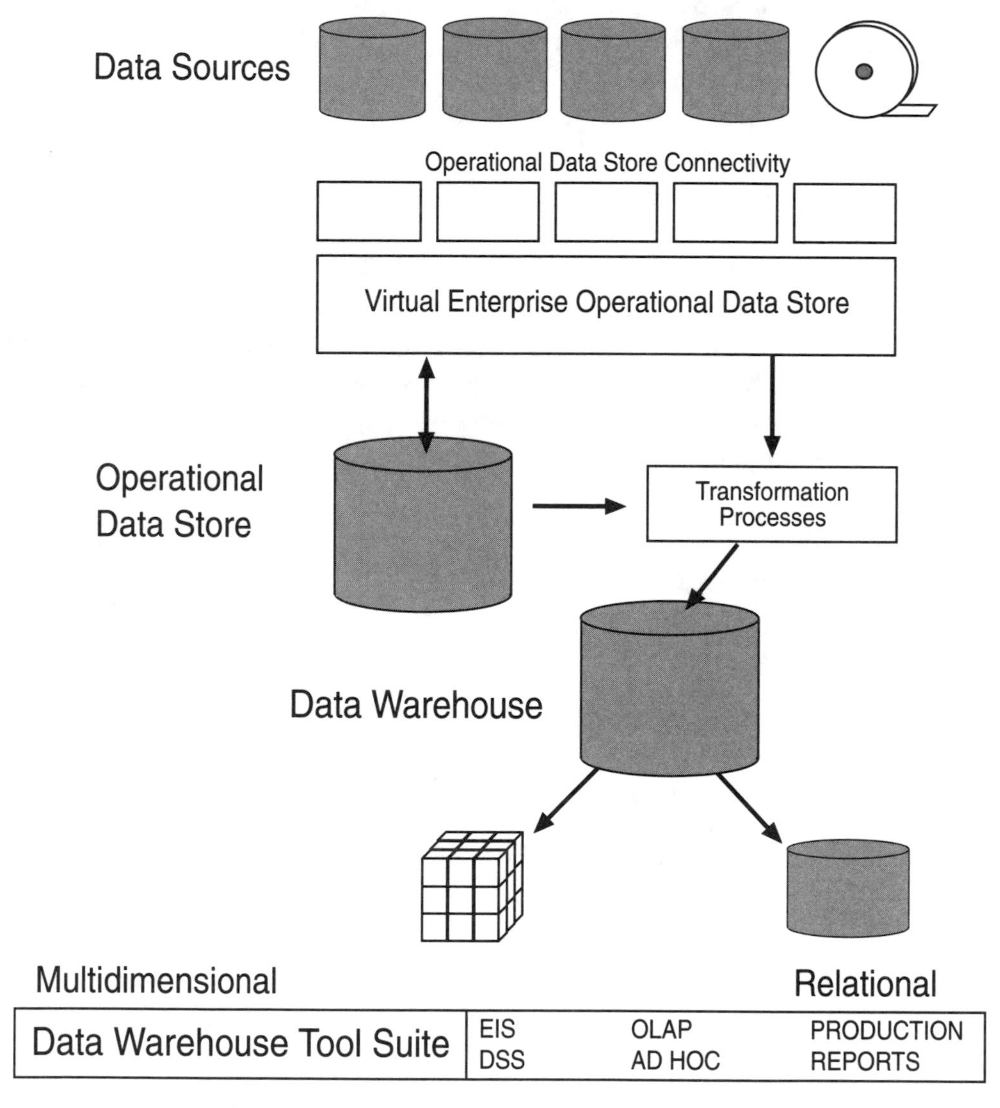

Figure 12.2: *An integrated operational data store*

Constant Tuning Required

A data warehouse manages and organizes a large volume of operational data for informational and analytical processing. The heart and soul of most data warehouses today is a relational database management system in which the data for the data warehouse is stored. When users place their demands on a data warehouse for information to better understand the answers to critical business questions, technological factors often cause dissatisfaction.

The number one problem for data warehouses and the management of data warehouses is performance. For proper performance to be delivered, database administrators often find themselves forced to constantly tune a database and its associated user queries. This doesn't have to be the case. As explained in Chapter 11, Publishing and Accessing Data, tools are available today, such as Cognos' Impromptu, that ease the tuning burden. Typically, the tuning problem is associated with a bad join or *where* condition within a user query *select* statement. Data warehouse systems issue queries that span a performance range of interactive, ad hoc queries requiring near-real-time response to complex analysis queries that are submitted for processing and expected to incur long response times.

Decision support activities such as drilling down and drilling up force a database engine to perform various aggregation calculations, and can force queries to scan an entire or large part of a fact table. Computational aspects of these queries include joins, group bys, sorts, and aggregation functions. Special technologies are now available to assist in this area of decision support tuning. Options include an optimized front-end tool such as Impromptu, a dedicated support person or organization for continuous tuning such as a database administrator, a targeted middleware component such as Sybase IQ, or a parallel server component such as Sybase MPP. The decision for solving these tuning problems will be resolved through a software solution, such as Sybase IQ; or a hardware solution that is supported by software, such as Sybase MPP. In the following sections, we examine Sybase IQ and Sybase MPP.

Solving Tuning Problems with Software—Sybase IQ

Sybase IQ is a software tool that is designed to assist and optimize decision support system queries to allow organizations to more readily develop interactive data warehouses. Specifically, Sybase IQ's design goal is to increase the speed of decision support queries performed against large amounts of data stored in Sybase SQL Server and other databases utilizing a current hardware infrastructure.

Traditional Indexing

Traditionally, relational database management systems such as Sybase SQL Server, Informix, and Oracle have utilized a variation on a B-tree architecture for their indexes, as shown in Figure 12.3. These indexing techniques assist a database management system in locating and identifying the data pages that physically contain the values requested in a given query. The B-tree approach to indexing minimizes the amount of index data that a database management system must browse to retrieve the data requested by a user or an application. As shown in Figure 12.3, to select a customer with the name of *Hammergren*, the database management system performs the following steps.

1. Start with the top index and determine that *Hammergren* is less than L
2. Based on that determination, navigate the index structure to the left
3. Compare *Hammergren* against the index pointers at this level, E and *I*
4. *Hammergren* is greater than E and less than *I*, therefore follow the appropriate index path
5. Reevaluate the index structure at this new level, *F* and *H*
6. *Hammergren* and *H* are a match, therefore retrieve the data page associated with this index

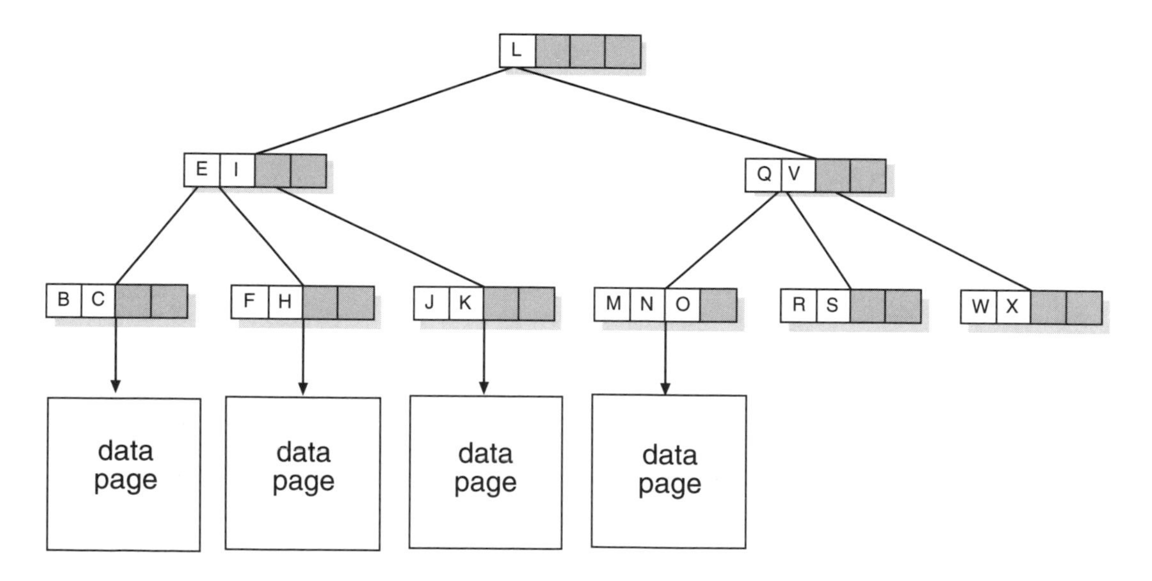

Figure 12.3: *B-tree indexing*

This type of indexing is highly effective for situations in which a small number of rows must be retrieved. However, based on this data structure you are typically limited to the number of data columns that are indexable. Columns that contain data with few values, such as the gender of an employee, are not good index candidates for this structure, because the overhead is too costly. Also, these structures tend to work well only for simple queries, such as: "Select all customers in the state of Ohio."

Sybase IQ Indexing

Sybase IQ has introduced a patent pending indexing technology that Sybase refers to as *Bit-Wise* indexing. This technique for indexing data has been shown to be quite effective for mid-sized data warehouses; that is, warehouses to a few hundred gigabytes. Unlike B-tree structures, Sybase IQ indexes provide fast access for larger result set retrieval and allow values such as gender to participate as an effective index. Sybase IQ has also created an environment in which index searches can be performed in parallel or evaluated concurrently with each other.

Sybase IQ is a good fit for applications with the following characteristics.

- Ad hoc queries
- A need to query many fields
- Tables in query require a large number of indexes, something that is impractical in most RDBMSs
- Data tables that are large in both height and width
- Query activity demonstrates a large number of table scans

Sybase IQ does *not* fit well in applications with the following characteristics.

- Low query volume
- Smaller tables that lack height
- Low number of indexes that are manageable by a RDBMS
- Tables with adequate resources and that can be memory cached by an RDBMS
- Real-time update requirements

Sybase IQ can integrate easily into an existing client/server environment due to its architecture, which is based on the Sybase Open Client/Open Server model. The Sybase IQ architecture is illustrated in Figure 12.4.

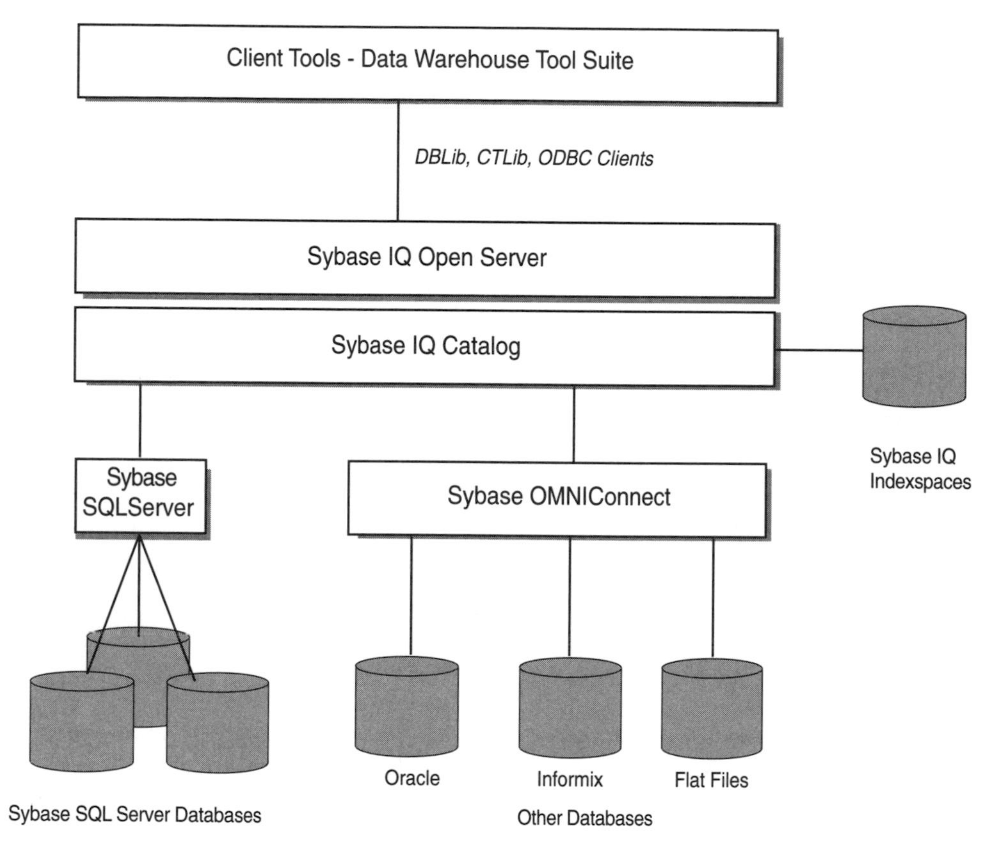

Figure 12.4: *Sybase IQ architecture*

An important factor with a technology such as found in the Sybase IQ architecture is cardinality of data values. Cardinality describes the relationship between two items. In an entity-relationship diagram, cardinality is used to better define a relationship between tables, such as a one-to-many relationship. An example of this is ORDERS related in a one-to-many fashion to ORDER_LINE; or in English terminology, each order has many line items. Cardinality in Sybase IQ refers to the relationship between a data column and the values contained within that column. This is important, because cardinality is a specification for the defining of a given index within Sybase IQ. Figure 12.5 presents the cardinality for many of the dimension entities that have been previously discussed.

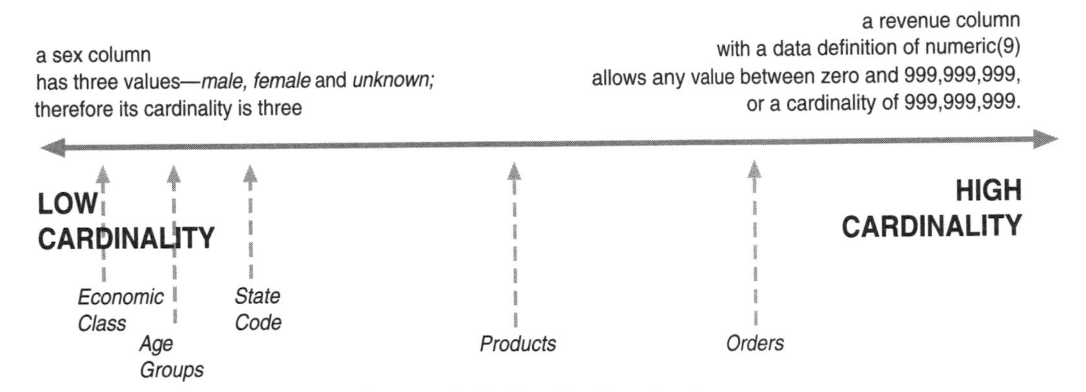

Figure 12.5: *Cardinality of values*

The indexing capabilities of Sybase IQ revolve around five specific index types managed by the Bit-Wise algorithms. The appropriate index is selected based on two important criteria, the cardinality as shown in Table 12.1, and the type of query, as shown in Table 12.2.

Table 12.1: *Sybase IQ index selection based on cardinality*

Index Type	Cardinality	Examples	Comments
FASTPROJECTION			Should create on all columns in the index set you intend to query. Designed for ad hoc joins, SQL *like* operations, and intercolumn comparisons
LOWFAST	Less than 500	Marital status, sex, and state	
LOWDISK	Less than 1,000	State, product code, and time period	Seldom used, this is similar to LOWFAST, yet takes less disk space but requires more computing resources.
HIGHGROUP	Greater than 500	Employee number	Ideal for aggregates and range searches; more suitable for queries with *group by* clauses.

(continues)

Table 12.1: *(continued)*

Index Type	Cardinality	Examples	Comments
HIGHNONGROUP	Greater than 500		Ideal for aggregates and range searches.

Table 12.2: *Sybase IQ index type selection by query type*

Type of Query	Index Type Recommended	Index Type Not Recommended
select projection list	FASTPROJECTION	HIGHGROUP or HIGHNON GROUP
Aggregate columns with argument *avg* or *sum*	FASTPROJECTION, HIGHNONGROUP, LOWFAST, or HIGHGROUP	LOWDISK
Aggregate columns with argument *min* or *max*	FASTPROJECTION, LOWFAST, or HIGHGROUP	LOWDISK
Aggregate columns with argument *count*	FASTPROJECTION, HIGHNONGROUP, LOWFAST, or HIGHGROUP	LOWDISK
Arguments *count distinct*, *select distinct*, or *group by*	FASTPROJECTION, HIGHGROUP, or LOWFAST	HIGHNONGROUP
where clause calculations	FASTPROJECTION	LOWDISK
where clause *like* argument	FASTPROJECTION	
where clause ad hoc join columns	FASTPROJECTION or HIGHGROUP	HIGHNONGROUP
where clause range queries	FASTPROJECTION, HIGHGROUP, or HIGHNONGROUP	LOWDISK or LOWFAST
Columns used in a joined index set	FASTPROJECTION, HIGHGROUP, or LOWFAST	HIGHNONGROUP
If field doesn't allow duplicates	FASTPROJECTION, HIGHGROUP, LOWFAST, or LOWDISK	HIGHNONGROUP

Implementing Sybase IQ

Sybase IQ utilizes a data definition language (DDL) that is similar to the standard SQL database DDL. This language allows you to define the proper structures for IQ to store indexed data and populate data structures. As noted earlier, Sybase IQ is able to access many different types of data, including Sybase SQL Server, Oracle, and flat files. Therefore, this product offers a lot to any data warehouse environment regardless of whether it utilizes Sybase products.

Indexing for an information package diagram and its associated measure entities is demonstrated in Figure 12.6. As discussed in Chapter 8, Building a Data Model, a measure entity is derived from the lowest-level category from each dimension (items 1 through 6 in Figure 12.6) and from each of the measures (items 7 through 11). Each of the columns of a measure entity can be indexed. Figure 12.6 presents a chart describing the potential index types to be utilized based on the cardinality of the associated data column.

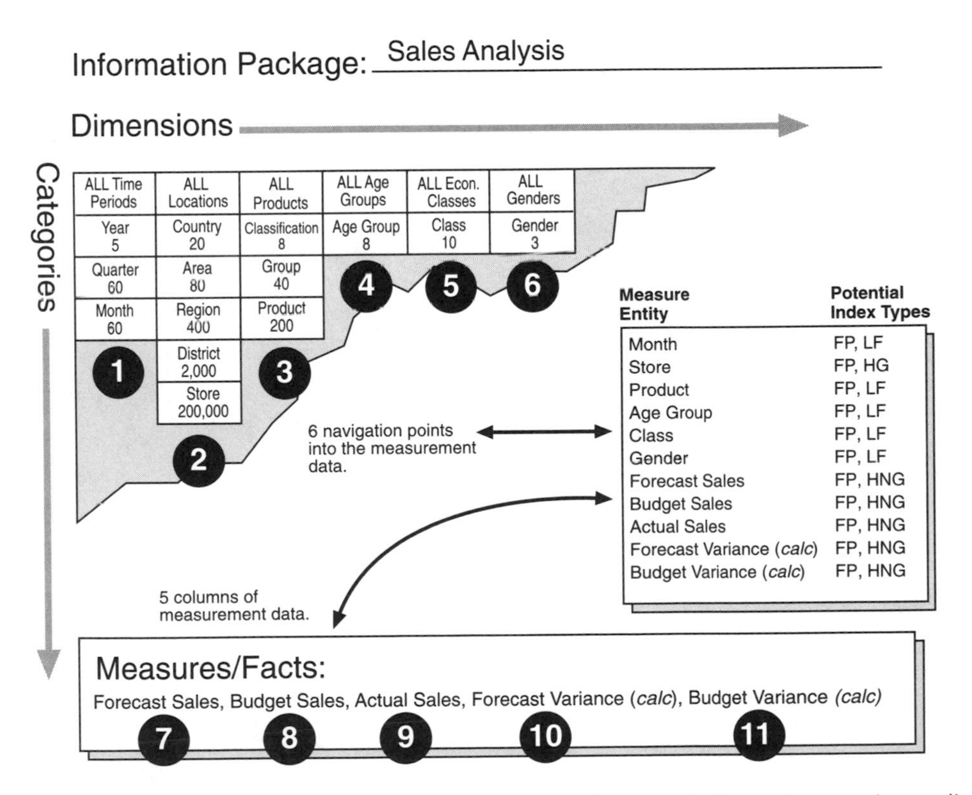

Figure 12.6: *Sybase IQ index selection and translation from an information package diagram*

On top of standard indexing features, IQ allows you to define prejoins and index them. Therefore, in our samples of star schemas, you would more than likely build a joined index set between your dimension entities and measure entities, as shown in Figure 12.7. This optimizes searches through fact tables to provide the much needed descriptive information that is contained in navigational entities. As well, the join strategies between subject detail entities and navigational entities, or direct joins to the measure tables, may also be indexed.

It is important to note that, because Sybase IQ is an open-server, add-on product to the Sybase database management family, it works with the hundreds of tools that support Sybase SQL Server. This means you gain incremental performance without changing the front-end environment and without disrupting your users—an important concept in implementing a server-oriented performance solution.

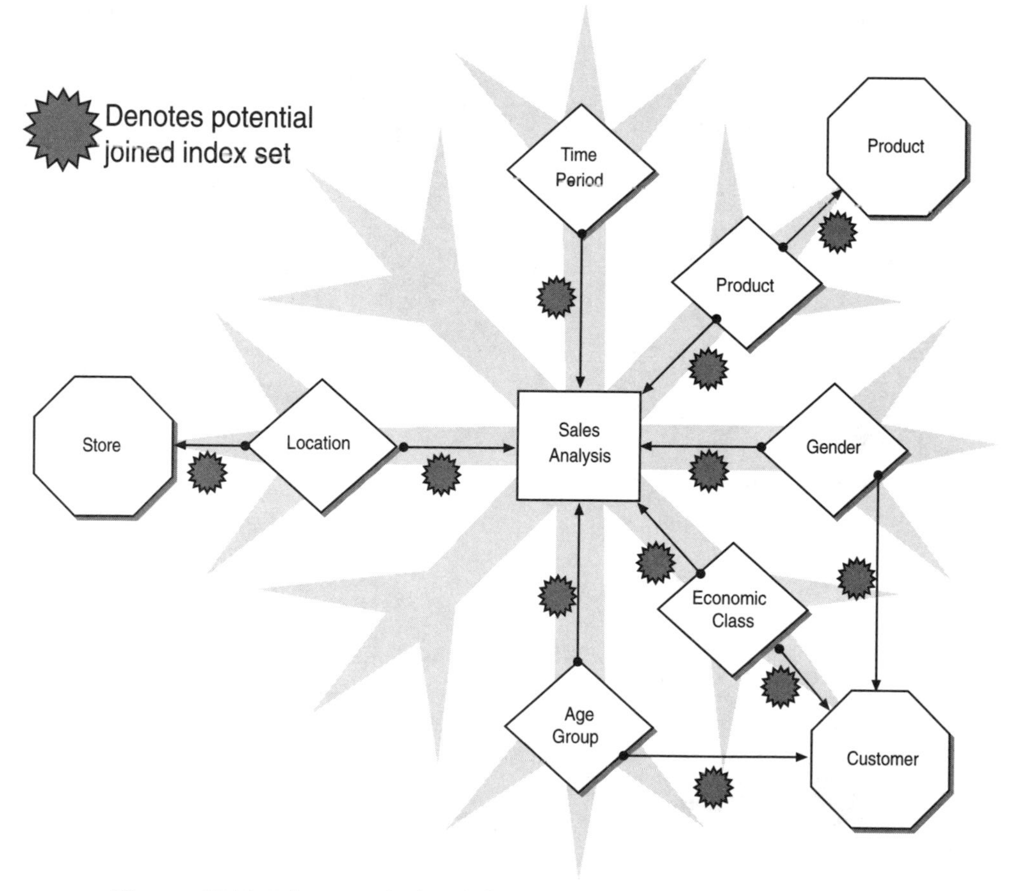

Figure 12.7: *Sybase IQ index definition derived from the star schema*

Solving Tuning Problems with Hardware—Sybase MPP

Massively Parallel Processing (MPP) is a technology that has been introduced in the hardware and software marketplaces to improve the scalability of very large processes and databases by removing inherent architectural issues with older processing technologies. MPP technology solves tuning problems through hardware; hence, more processing power and more software that takes advantage of this hardware architecture. This type of technology is tremendous at increasing scalability, performance, and throughput for a specific set of applications, including data warehouses. However, it is much more expensive and therefore limited in its applicability to many companies.

Parallel Architectures

Prior to discussing the Sybase MPP product, it is important to understand the available parallel architectures that are actively marketed by vendors today. These architectures include shared memory, shared disk, and shared nothing architectures. Parallel processing can mean different things based on the architecture on which the technology is built. Therefore, in best understanding your situation, clearly define architectural requirements prior to believing a vendor's claims of parallel processing capabilities. Here is a description of each of these types of architectures.

- **Shared memory architecture** is a configuration in which multiple processors share common memory resources. See Figure 12.8.

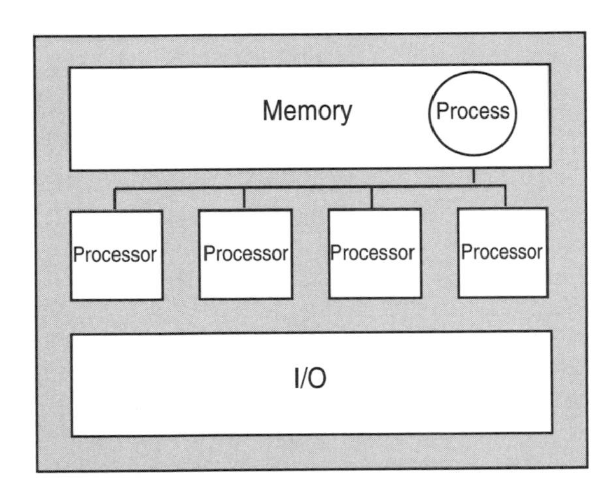

Figure 12.8: *Shared memory architecture*

- **Shared disk architecture** is a configuration in which a high-speed interconnect is placed among multiple machines that are configured with local memory and processors. Each of these machines shares common disk resources via an interconnected network. See Figure 12.9.

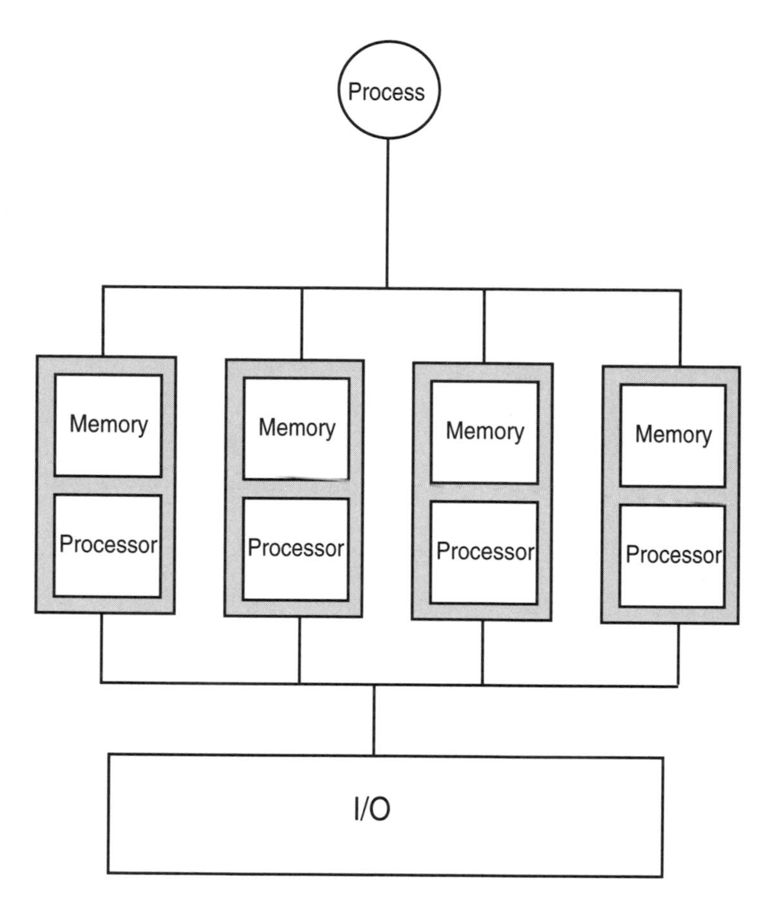

Figure 12.9: *Shared disk architecture*

- **Shared nothing architecture** is a configuration in which all resources are independent of the parallel process. There is clear ownership and delineation among memory, I/O, operating system, and disk resources. See Figure 12.10.

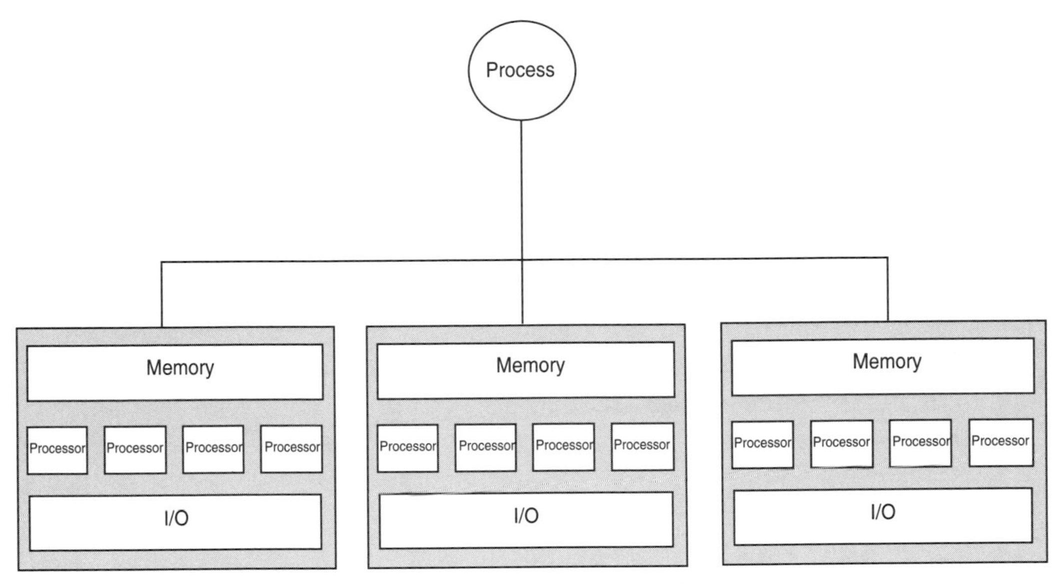

Figure 12.10: *Shared nothing architecture*

Parallel Processing

Another factor in determining the fit for a parallel solution is what type of processing occurs. MPP solutions provide two major aspects of parallel processing: data fragmentation and query decomposition. We next discuss each of these subjects in separate sections.

Data Fragmentation

Data fragmentation involves the partitioning of data in some fashion: vertical fragmentation, horizontal fragmentation, or schema fragmentation. The concept for each of these topics is relatively straightforward.

- **Vertical fragmentation** involves splitting a table vertically, or by columns. To recompose data that has been vertically fragmented, you simply join over the common key. This type of fragmentation assists in splitting large columns, such as blobs, or frequently unused columns into their own tables with a one-to-one relationship between them. This process reduces the overall size and management burden associated with frequently versus infrequently used data. Figure 12.11 demonstrates vertically fragmented data in items 1, 1a, and 1b. Item 1 is a complete set of data that has been physically fragmented into 1a and 1b. This fragmentation occurs horizontally or by representing different columns in separate tables that relate to the same key—for example, Customer Demographic Data in partition 1a and Customer Contact Data in partition 1b. Each of these entities contains the Customer Key to which the associated columns relate; a complete picture of a Customer cannot exist without the data managed in both tables.

- **Horizontal fragmentation** involves splitting a table based on rows, typically with a range of values. To recompose data that has been horizontally fragmented, you simply perform a union of all fragments. This type of fragmentation is utilized to store locally important data closer to the user, thereby reducing network queries. Figure 12.11 demonstrates horizontally fragmented data in items 2, 2a, and 2b. Item 2 is a complete set of data that has been physically fragmented into 2a and 2b. This fragmentation occurs horizontally, or by representing the same columns fragmented by value—for example, the New York Sales Data in partition 2a and the California Sales Data in fragment 2b.

- **Schema fragmentation** involves splitting one schema across multiple distributed systems. You can obtain the complete data for one table from that specific server, or join across multiple servers to build a projection. This type of fragmentation is utilized to separate smaller, static tables from those that are more volatile and grow larger. Figure 12.11 demonstrates schema fragmentation in item 3. The *select* syntax is clearly referencing tables that are managed by two separate nodes, node1 and node2. In Sybase Transact-SQL, this syntax is mapped by referring to the *database.table.column* when naming any column. The database reference is to a separate database with its own controls and operating procedures. This separation of tables along database lines represents a fragmented entity within an overall schema.

The overall objective of fragmentation is to optimize data by location or content in preparation of query activity. This issue is another key aspect that must be fully understood when someone states they have a parallel processing database: What partitioning schemes are supported?

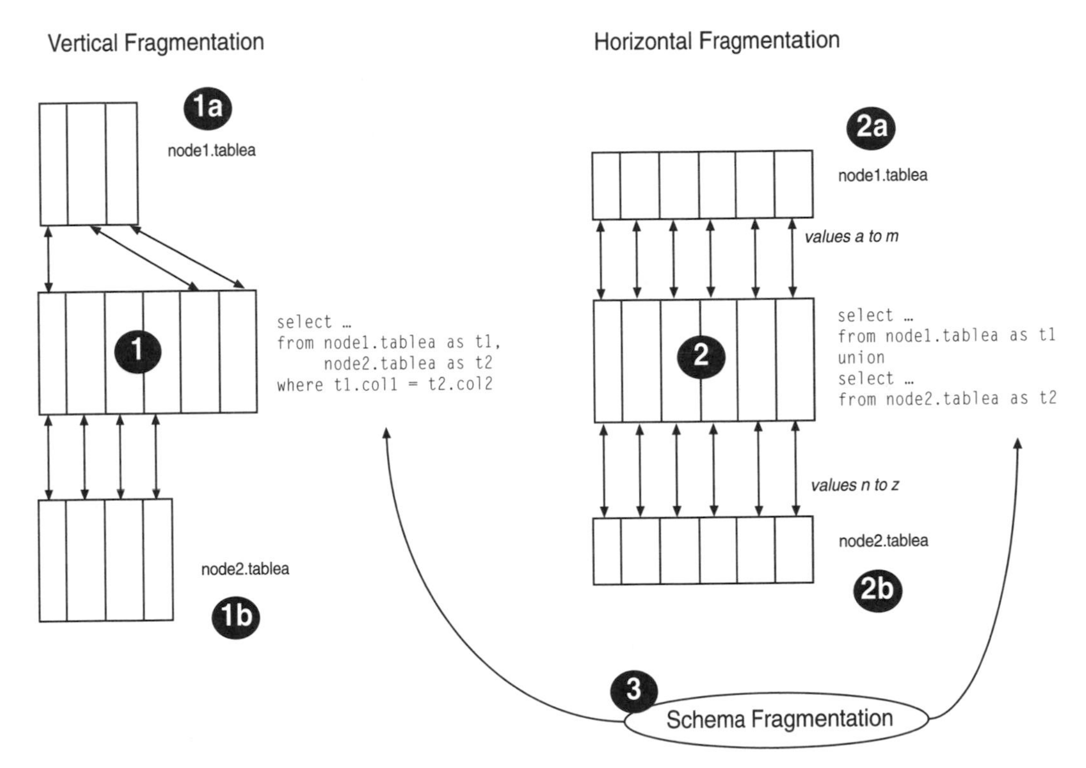

Figure12.11: *Data fragmentation*

Query Decomposition

Query decomposition is the process of splitting a single SQL request into multiple, independent processes that can simultaneously execute, as shown in Figure 12.12. This concept is where the speed and scalability of parallel systems are derived. If you can break down a process or throw more processing power at it, you often can achieve faster results. Much like in project management, if you have a project that is estimated to require six programmer months, can you get it done in one month with six programmers? Or in one day with 180 programmers? Some processes just cannot be shortened in duration. However, this is yet another consideration when discussing parallel processing databases.

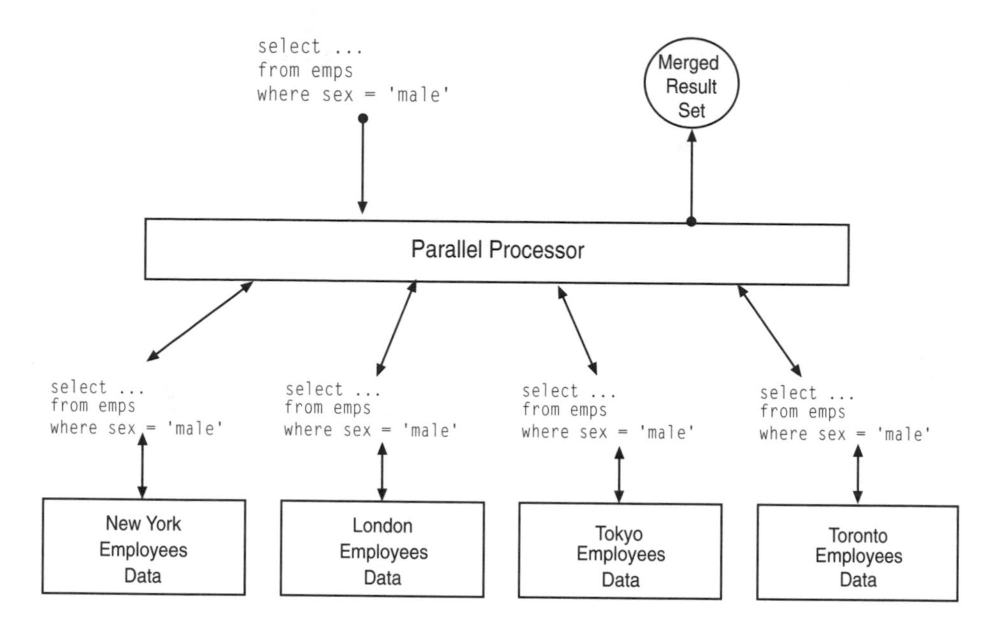

Figure 12.12: *Query decomposition*

The Sybase MPP Architecture

Sybase's MPP product uses a shared nothing architecture. This assists implementers in avoiding the shortcomings of other architectures, such as I/O bottleneck and lack of processing resources. Parallel processing databases should become important to you when your data approaches 250GB. Smaller data warehouse do not require this much horsepower; however, they could utilize some of the features in their smaller architectures.

Sybase MPP is built on the native Sybase Open Client/Open Server architecture and offers a highly scaleable, plug-and-play solution for those who require the ability to scale up their warehouse to a large size. The components of Sybase MPP include those described in Table 12.3.

Table 12.3: *Sybase MPP components*

Component Server	Base Architecture	Comments
Control Server	Open Server	The front-end processor for Sybase MPP
Schema Server	SQL Server	Controls the global data dictionary or schema

(continues)

Table 12.3: *(continued)*

Component Server	Base Architecture	Comments
Split Server	Open Server	Primarily used to handle joins within a parallel processor
DBA Server	Open Server	The process that works with the Schema Server to provide the brains behind Sybase MPP
SQL Server	SQL Server	The individual data stores managed by Sybase MPP

Sybase MPP Processing a Data Request

The sequence of events that Sybase MPP utilizes to process an individual SQL request is depicted in Figure 12.13. The following steps correspond to the numbers in the figure.

1. The client application signs onto the Sybase MPP Control Server using an Open Client request
2. The request is passed from Control Server to the Sybase MPP DBA Server using an Open Client connection
3. The DBA Server works with the Sybase MPP Schema Server to parse the client request
4. The Sybase MPP Parallel SQL Compiler compiles and optimizes the SQL request
5. Stored procedures are sent from the PSQL Compiler to the participating SQL Servers
6. The individual participating SQL Servers load the PSQL plans into memory for execution and are initiated by the Sybase MPP Control Server
7. Upon completion of the user request, the results are returned to the client application via the Control Server

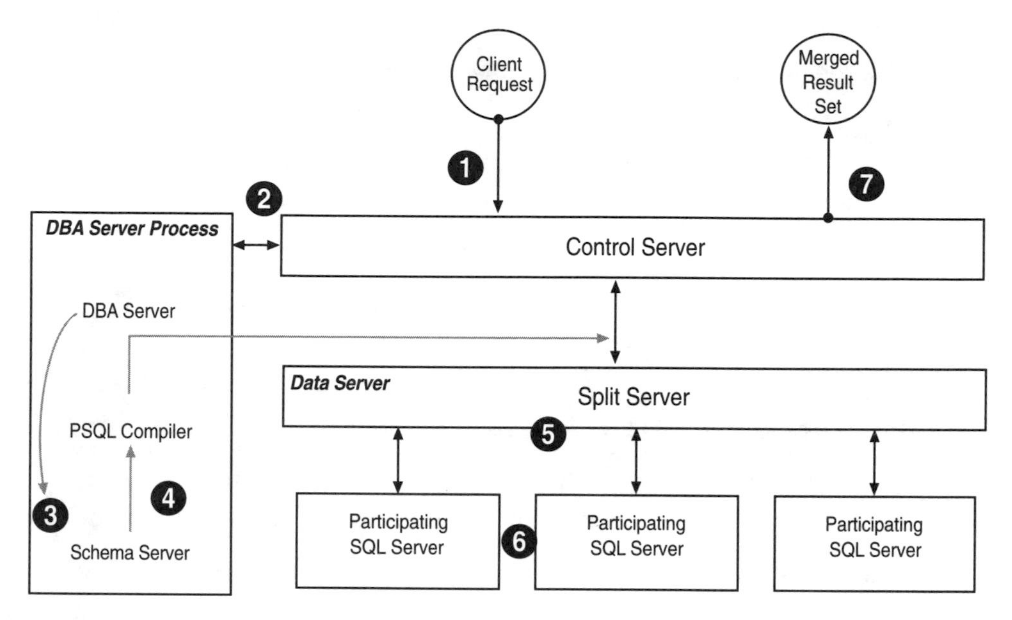

Figure 12.13: *Sybase MPP processing*

Sybase MPP is a good fit for applications with the following characteristics.

- Large table scans
- Large result sets
- Large sorted result sets
- Large aggregations
- Raw data that is greater than 500GB
- Rapid, unpredictable growth rate (greater than 50 percent per year)
- Very large Decision Support Systems (DSSs)

Sybase MPP does *not* fit well in applications with the following characteristics.

- Operational requirements of seven days per week, 24 hours per day
- No predictable join paths
- Limited ability or definitions available for fragmentation of the data

Implementing Sybase MPP

The information package methodology described in this book provides you with valuable information on how best to implement a Sybase MPP data warehouse. Namely, the information package diagram provides adequate sizing estimates and dimensions that assist in narrowing the overall size and scope of measure entity implementations. These tools should be used to their fullest extent and become the guiding light to clearly defining the best fragmentation and partitioning strategies. After being fragmented, entities such as a measure entity easily work in a parallel scheme to your users' advantage.

Architecture Tip 7: When choosing components of your architecture, choose products and tools that provide building blocks and expansion, or scalability options, in the future, The components you select also should involve little to no disruption to your users when scaling or expanding. You should not be required to purchase all of your architectural components and tools in the beginning.

Resource Governors

Resource governors are another confusing area from which many marketers drive their product sales. A resource governor is a component that places controls and limits on the utilization of resources. For example, a query that will run for three hours could be placed in a batch queue instead of utilizing on-line resources. Some database management system products come with resource governors, while others such as Sybase IQ have little to no need for resource governors, because they are a general-purpose implementation of the concepts behind resource governors.

It is important to determine the real need for a resource governor in your circumstances. Typically, the lack of database-oriented smarts for run-away queries is the reason. But if you develop your warehouse properly, your resource governor can do a lot more for you.

A nice facet about the Sybase product set is the fundamental architecture from which it has been built. Sybase's Open Server is a powerful offering that allows your development staff to perform many miraculous things without compromising your overall architecture. We often recommend the Sybase technologies for data services, fundamentally because of Open Server. This product fills a void if you are missing connectivity software to a less than popular legacy data source. It also can assist you in fronting a SQL Server application to control the activity and security aspects of an application.

Resource governors and data warehouses are highly compatible technologies. You may want to deploy such a technology as your user base increases. A resource governor allows you to better manage sharable resources and avoid the high cost of allowing users to really ask the meaning-of-life queries that many tools allow through their limitless join dialogs. A resource governor written in Open Server can query a database optimizer and request numerous pieces of information about what will transpire should the query be allowed to proceed. You can, in turn, build some intelligence into your metadata repository that classifies access periods and processing parameters for individuals or groups of users. Depending what a user has requested, you may want to send the request into an overnight batch queue and mail a response when the query is completed. Of course, proper communication with the client application is required in this situation. But in your user interviews, you will find that users would rather receive a long-running request at a known time than wait hours for a response. Therefore, when building your architecture and data warehouse, make sure to understand the overall processing requirements. You can easily build your own custom resource governor to control the schedules of queries as well as to avoid queries that dramatically affect others on the system.

Security

Security is another pickle that you will often find hampers your ability to fully implement a data warehouse. It is key for your development team to flesh out an early security scheme and stick with it. Often, people begin to desire security by value and by field, as well as other complex schemes for implementing a data warehouse. If you can avoid these approaches, do. If you can't, try to build a security system that does not produce an enormous amount of overhead when implemented throughout your data warehouse.

Again, a technology like Sybase's Open Server can be extremely important in this area. However, if implemented incorrectly this feature may also become a major system bottleneck. Open Server, as discussed in the preceding section, allows you to simulate a SQL Server and trap any activity or request of a database prior to execution. You can, therefore, implement an Open Server that traps calls to a data warehouse and applies whatever special security features that are required prior to passing the data request to the data warehouse. An example of this might be inclusion of a security code in the *where* condition of a SQL *select* statement. This allows you to implement a client application that passes general SQL *selects* to the data warehouse. These *selects* are trapped by your Open Server, and the security *where* condition is appended to the *where* clause of the SQL statement without the tool or user knowing it occurred.

Architecture Tip 8: Look for impossible things in your vendor community, things you think can't be done—then have your vendor prove that it *can* be done. However, make sure to pay for the proof with something like a money-back guarantee. If you pay for a service, the vendor will realize you are serious and may assign more talented resources to your account than if you want a freebie proof.

Summary

Certainly, more obstacles than those that we have outlined in this chapter arise. However, the obstacles discussed in this chapter are the largest obstacles that typically block a development process. You should make sure that your architecture team is intimately involved in the decisions that obstacles such as these bring forth. Creating solutions for data warehouse obstacles for only a single data mart, or smaller implementation of an overall enterprise, will lead to disaster within your overall architecture. Therefore, simply selecting a way to globally solve an issue without the commitment of the architects is a mistake that you will live to regret. With a defined plan and a proper architecture in place, few obstacles will arise that you cannot solve.

In the Epilogue that follows this chapter, we take off our instructor's hat and put on a prophet's hat long enough to peer into the future of data warehousing. While premised significantly on conjecture and speculation, we hope this material will prepare you for some of the exciting advances that are now on the horizon and that promise to make your data warehouse projects even more useful.

Epilogue

Bring On the Future

It is possible to believe that all the past is but the beginning of a beginning, and that all that is and has been is but the twilight of the dawn. It is possible to believe that all the human mind has ever accomplished is but the dream before the awakening.

—*H. G. Wells*

The data warehouse market and many of our Information Systems departments have been far too technology oriented through their initial boom years. In the near future, we hope we will begin to see vendors, developers, and data administration personnel provide more consumer-friendly solutions. These future solutions will allow systems such as data warehouses to actually become assistants to their users. Currently, many of these systems simply get in the way and are required only to provide detail information to the management of a company—not to the common employee.

As will become obvious, the information in this epilogue is only conjecture and speculation. However, we feel a duty, as we believe you should, to continue to pursue and push the technologist in new, and in many ways more appealing, areas. Technology is breaking out of its roots and branching quickly into the consumer marketplace. You now walk into the store where you purchase a washer or stove and see a computer. The technology boom has made computing a consumer-oriented business. Games, home accounting packages, home designers, recipe managers, wine cellar management, tax preparation—the list describing how computers have invaded our everyday life goes on and on. Yet, are they helping or hurting—are those entrenched within the computer craze dysfunctional?

Only future generations will be able to answer that question. It is obvious that high-tech companies are getting better at understanding users. The users of today and tomorrow typically have less technology knowledge, but want a device that will make them more productive. As we discussed in Chapter 1, The Data Warehouse Market Explosion, our lives are driven by data. Therefore, data warehouses will also begin to undertake a consumer-oriented edge. People will want to access and use information within knowledge bases to make wiser decisions. To accomplish this goal, many advances need to occur. The vendors, developers, and administrators of data warehouses and associated products need to begin to shape their environment to accept these novices into our world. And they need to begin to build tools that help users within their processes, not tools that get in the way and are a nuisance. We want to discard the image of *you can't live with 'em; you can't live without 'em* when we think of data warehouses.

The remainder of this chapter explores anticipated advances in three areas: the vendor community, the developer community, and finally the data management community.

Vendor Community Advances

Performance and usability are keys to a data warehouse, and to that end vendors will continue to make advances in these areas. We already are beginning to see large performance gains with the onset of indexing technologies, such as Sybase IQ; and generalized parallel systems, such as Sybase MPP. We are seeing enormous gains in the area of access with the explosion of the Internet, specifically the World Wide Web, and the associated browsing tools from Netscape and Microsoft.

So what is lacking? The answer is, a lot. The users of technology have traditionally focused on the OLTP (on-line transaction processing) nature of systems that were required to make a company operate efficiently—probably better stated: How do we get the data into the computer? The shift in recent years has begun to dramatically indicate advances in the future will be in data access—probably better stated: How do we get the data out of the computer? The underlying technologies need to understand better how users query data, how users present data, and how systems should manage and distribute data. This focus will force vendors to expand and enhance their current technologies in many areas. We discuss here a few of these technologies that we think are critical.

Connectivity

Because all of us seem to have many databases and will continue to have them—*its a myth to think any one company can survive with one database*—we require connectivity software that can easily tap into any format of a databases and efficiently operate on that data. In reality, this is a mid-tier database management system without any physical data store. Many people would say this exists in products such as Sybase OMNIConnect or IBI EDA/SQL. The problem is that these tools often are unable to support large numbers of users and are less than optimal in their current implementations. The performance attributes and optimization techniques of these products need to be dramatically improved during the coming years to make them mainstream.

Performance

The concept of performance has haunted and will continue to haunt the vendor community. The personal computer on which we are working is more powerful than the machine on which we worked when we were graduated from college and is infinitely smaller. But, we will feel it is slow in many areas. Performance is perception, and until we can respond to users in near-real-time with our systems, we still have performance problems. The vendor community needs to continue to advance the ability to access large fact tables within data warehouses, better deliver on compression technologies, and advance the cause of parallel processing within a share-nothing environment.

Data Access

The ability to support a large number of users accessing a very large data table is one that is displeasing to many database administrators. Vendors are addressing such problems with indexing products, more intelligent data caching, and parallel processing. However, many of these solutions are essentially throwing more hardware and software at a problem that may be better solved within the architecture of a database management solution. This solution includes not only the physical data stores, but more importantly the connectivity solutions that exist in the middleware marketplace. The more data that we accumulate, the more access that will be required. Therefore, scalability has yet to be solved by any vendor (though their marketing departments will claim they have). Systems of the future require much greater access than ever before. Therefore, look for middleware components that currently offer connectivity to begin to provide optimization techniques that allow for heterogeneous parallelism, heterogeneous indexing capabilities, and increased capabilities for large numbers of user to access large data banks. In essence, the optimizer needs to better understand underlying design techniques and optimize the access strategies around which they are built, such as star schemas and star schema joins.

Compression

The data forms with which users will perform queries in the future will expand to include more rich, multimedia formats as text, images, audio, and video. This data matter provides additional insight to historical information and in many ways is a current requirement that cannot be filled based on the lack of a solution. Hardware and software alike are problems in this area. However, the future will see better management of such data forms and advancement in data compression techniques. This compression will make it more effective to allow users to access these data sources; however, the compression will not be limited to multimedia data stores. Improvements will also become more dramatic with our current data—both numbers and text. This compression will allow more data to be passed and filtered with less overhead, hence improving the overall access and performance of systems such as a data warehouse.

Parallel Processing

Britton-Lee, Teradata, and other vendors offered parallel processing technology in the middle to late 1980s. Yet today this is the cornerstone of some database vendor's marketing strategies—as if they invented something new. The fact is, parallel processing has been around for a long time and is now becoming affordable to the masses. Every database vendor has its own slant on why its version of parallel processing is better than the next—and yes, we have our opinion. In the future, we need a true share-nothing parallel processing tool. Again, it is our belief that this will exist in a middleware, connectivity tool. However, it is obvious based on current database vendors' marketing pushes in this area that physical data stores will also offer this technology, as will hardware processors.

What does the future require? We need a parallel processing engine that supports all of these concepts in harmony. This type of an adaptive architecture would allow us to deploy information systems such as a data warehouse that would provide parallelism across networks, processors, memory, disk controllers, and databases (physical data stores). All aspects of infrastructure could be utilized and optimized for parallel processing activities. We would have intelligent software that figured out the optimal way to give us a near-real-time response.

Design Tools

Most current design tools offer little assistance in designing a data warehouse. CASE tools of old and the current data modeling tools have not taken full advantage of the graphical environments on which they have been built. Each offers a relatively bland graphical-oriented display. An entity is a box. A system is a circle. A process is a box with round corners. An interface is a shadowed box.

The design tools of the future need to take the concepts of modeling to new heights. As shown in this book, your graphic design renderings can provide meaning by defining symbols that give the reader of the diagram more information, such as the true function of that entity. This will be difficult for general purpose systems; however, for specialty systems such as a data warehouse, this market will expand dramatically. We need a whole suite of design-oriented tools to assist in the data modeling aspects of a data warehouse (star schema) as well as in the integration of processing-oriented aspects (loading and transformation)—and it would be nice to have one tool provide the complete modeling aspects of the data warehouse process.

Administration Tools

The administration process is one that currently has been neglected because of so many other weaknesses. Few vendors have taken a leadership role in this area. However, the concepts of administration of a data warehouse will begin to emerge as a large need as more and more data warehouses are deployed. Currently, the systems are small and seemingly manageable. In the future, as we expand and begin supporting more remote and mobile users, outside parties, heterogeneous data stores, Internet and intranet access, and the plethora of software required to deliver such a solution, administration tools will begin to offer more flexibility and intelligence. This will include tools in the areas of configuration management, help desk, data structure optimization, resource governors, backup and restore, process management, and others. These tools will benefit from other advances in areas such as user interfaces and direct manipulation, delivering simplicity to the administrator who currently struggles with the requirement of being a jack of all trades and master of none.

User Access Tools

Having spent a good deal of our career in this area, we have to claim a great deal of disappointment in the vendor community. Maybe it is because of the near-monopoly vendors such as Microsoft have on user interfaces, but this area is truly weak and neglected. A few vendors have been shining in this area; however, we still lack a great marketplace that provides tool suites for data warehouses—much like the office automation solutions available today. Interfaces such as those found in NextStep—so called object-oriented interfaces—are what we need.

Think of your own environment. If you have an application and a query tool executing on users' workstations, how many sign-on dialogs do they see? Typically, the answer is at least two. We need better access tools that incorporate the concept of a tool suite. Different users have different techniques and desires for analyzing data. As you will see in the next section of this epilogue, we discuss our ideas for user interfaces; however, additional tool advances are needed. The tools of today typically offer little to no understanding of the overall environment in which they execute. There are fat clients and obese clients, but no truly distributed or parallel processing systems offered in this space with adequate user interface capabilities. The users' access space needs to focus on the concepts of authentication, resource and infrastructure utilization, and human interfacing techniques. The future of these tools is exciting, because advances in the interface world such as voice recognition and virtual reality will become more readily usable in the next three to five years. And should vendors like Cognos and Micro Strategies continue to develop the interplay between their tools and the heterogeneous infrastructures they support as well as the depth of their product lines, we may not be far from a tool suite market.

By offering these and many more features, vendors will continue to pursue this ever-expanding market. The net result will be the ability for enterprises to deliver integrated decision making to the expanding user population.

Developer Advances

When designed properly, interactive systems with user-friendly interfaces such as data warehouses generate considerably more enthusiasm among users than systems with improper, or nonuser-friendly designs. We must begin to cultivate our development staffs to better design and deliver these interactive systems. A sophisticated simplicity much like that found in today's computer game market is required to bridge the gap between a user understanding the tool and a user becoming immersed in the tool.

If you look at the game market, probably your most profound discovery is that no one is afraid of the games. Child, parent, or grandparent simply grabs the control stick and goes at it or with wild enthusiasm. Before long, you hear them express positive feelings, such as the following.

- The ease at which they learn the system
- How they expand their knowledge to advanced levels in the system
- How they master the system
- How confident they are that they can continue performing tasks within the system
- How much they enjoy the system
- How eager they are to show others how to use the system
- A growing desire to explore other, more powerful aspects of the system

Along with these system-oriented concepts, users of game systems tend to retain their mastery of the system over time. Wouldn't it be nice if the user components of our systems provided as much joy, enthusiasm, and knowledge retention? They can, and in the future they will. You may want to begin molding your development staff in this direction now. Doing so allows your developers to begin to deliver systems that lower your overhead associated with training and increase the retention of the content and capabilities of systems by your users.

The questions then revolve around how to begin this training process for cultivating a new breed of developer. Our response is to establish common ways of expanding the minds of your development staff. Developing information systems is a fast-paced, stress-oriented profession. It is difficult to cultivate the creative side of any individual under these circumstances, but good managers find ways. An hour here, an hour there placed strategically in the schedule and you too can attain this seemingly impossible dream. So, get your own project management thinking cap out and conjure ways to better utilize the time you have with your staff.

The techniques for this educational process are not very traditional. Typically, we educate our staffs by sending them to a school on a related subject area. This way is easily justified and often fills a quota for Human Resources. We need to be more compassionate and creative within these educational experiences; after all, many of these creative technicians are borderline geniuses. Begin scheduling advanced practice seminars in which your staff explores other technology areas, plays games, and watches videos. The specific techniques that we offer here may sound crazy; but they offer two things, relief from stress and burnout, and an educational environment.

Explore Other Software Packages

Have your staff explore software packages that are remote from their focus. Often, we get so tied up in solving our own problems that an experience outside the mainstream, daily drudgery may provide better knowledge retention in our key people. Areas that focus on direct manipulation techniques, multiple dimension visualization, and virtual reality provide rich user interfaces that can teach our designers a thing or two.

Many three-dimensional software packages have offered flexible user interfaces for years. Take, for instance, the mature CAD (computer aided design) packages, the newer technologies such as mapping software, or the emerging technologies such as virtual reality and its spin-offs such as VRML (Virtual Reality Modeling Language).

CAD Software

For years, computer aided design systems have assisted in the design and specification process to build automobiles, machine tools, aircraft, and buildings. Users of these systems interact with the model, which is composed of many standard components. The software that manages the models and components can assist its user in further understanding the design. The intelligence produced by CAD packages includes items such as voltage drops, fabrication costs, and manufacturing problems or inconsistencies.

These systems are complex and flexible in their implementation. Few CAD packages today require users to communicate through cryptic syntax or commands. You simply use the cursor and graphic-oriented commands to directly manipulate the model. These direct manipulation techniques and the associated intelligence provided by the software, not the user, are areas that can enhance a data warehouse's implementation and interface.

Process and Facility Control Software

Process and facility control software provides a basic strategy that eliminates the need for complex commands that must only be recalled in once-in-a-year emergency conditions. This software typically offers a schematic of a plant's facilities and provides its users with problem solving by analogy. This is done through linkages among real-world items such as colors and gauges, which become indicators that define when problems such as high temperatures and low pressure arise. Upon notification, users can obtain a more detailed view of the troubled component by drilling down on the hierarchical structure of individual sensors, valves, and circuits to continue their evaluation process. These user interface metaphors and the exception handling are additional concepts that would greatly benefit users of a data warehouse.

Play Some Video Games

The question of how to train your developers on the techniques utilized within game software is an easy one—one that actually may not cost you time on the job, but might be conducted on employees' time. The answer to the question is: Purchase some modern computer games for your employees!

The designers of these games provide stimulating entertainment and an intriguing lesson in the factors of interface design. These interfaces provide a strong attraction that is in marked contrast to the anxiety and resistance displayed by users when they utilize current information systems.

We should begin to push our developers to build systems that address the following issues.

- Users will be able to learn simply by watching someone else use the systems for 30 seconds. User interface goals should be established in the area of retention in training. A few minutes to become a competent novice and a few hours to become an expert should be the goal.
- Learning should be by analogy. Commands should become physical actions, with the results presented immediately on the screen—no syntax to remember and therefore no syntax error messages to interpret. For example, if you move your player in an incorrect direction in a game, the visible display makes it apparent that nothing can be done. To correct this action, users simply reverse their movement—no error messages are presented, only visual clues.
- Continuous feedback should be built into the systems, allowing users to make their own subjective judgments about how they are mastering the systems. For example, games have a continuous display of scores, fuel levels, and comparisons to those who proceeded them; users feel confident that they are mastering the system when they approach the high score list.

Of course, the computer game of today is also not viewed by its user as work and therefore we cannot totally compensate for the user's attraction to the game. However, developers can learn techniques for improving the human interface to their computing systems. Our information systems will probably not present entertainment value or surprise events to challenge users, and most systems will not place their users in competition.

Watch Some Flicks

Along with games, you may want to introduce a monthly science fiction movie event. Many motion picture houses have developed high-tech solutions without realizing it. These movies are beacons to how the future of technology might evolve. Look back at movies such as 2001: Space Odyssey, Star Trek, Buck Rogers, and Star Wars. If you are saying to yourself that we have gone too far with this comment, that this recommendation lacks credibility, look closely at what these movies can teach us.

- How about voice recognition interfaces?
- How about holograms and holodecks?
- How about large visualization data banks?

Who can forget scenes such as Doctor McCoy, who travels back in time and tries to communicate with a personal computer by picking up the mouse and talking into it—only to become frustrated, realizing that the only way to interface with this *primitive* device is the mouse and keyboard. Or another scene from Star Trek in which the Enterprise is in danger of being destroyed and the holodeck recreates the building and architecture of the ship so that the engineers can better understand how to fix the problems on board. Then again, who can forget Hal, the voice-automated computer and how out of control it became by trying to do too much, by trying to automate too many tasks that required the human mind. These movies are astounding in the visualization of what technology could do for us—the good and the bad. The point here is to get a development staff focused on new and better ways to improve the interfacing technologies through which our users currently suffer.

Developer Advances Summary

If a data warehouse and its components ever truly deliver on the vision of helping users and become a corporate knowledge base, the users' method of communication needs dramatic improvement. Think of the impact of the Macintosh, CAD, and games. These interfaces were dramatic at their point in time. Certainly, we can improve our user interfaces to be more consumer oriented and less technology oriented so every user can benefit, not just a few. So get some popcorn, reserve a conference room, and spend an afternoon brainstorming—for the hour and a half to two hours it takes to watch a movie and the two hours you will spend to analyze their technology advances that could be utilized in your environment.

Who knows, you could be the first company to place a brand manager in a holodeck so he or she could visualize the effects of a promotion. What were people's reaction as they walked by your product? Was it located properly in the store? Where were the competitor's products? Did the competitor have a similar promotion?

Or you could be the first company to provide a voice-automated data bank for a medical team, such as surgeons who have limited use in their practice for a device requiring yet another hand. Or you could deliver a product to your sales force that pours over previous buying trends and promotional indicators to automate the building of a draft sales plan for your sales force, taking past knowledge and assisting them in increasing their sales in the future. Who are the decision makers? What makes them buy quicker? What products do they like? Dislike? When do they buy more from you? What season? What month? From what channel? What is their typical order size? How does this compare with competitors? Are the competitors more aggressive in their buying habits? Should you inform them of this?

Data Management Advances

We wish data management advances were as cool as user interfaces or other developer advances, but this information is less visual. However, the discussion of data management is a must for data warehouses and bringing the future. We need to begin focusing the energies of our data administrators and database administrators on optimal strategies for managing the data architecture within a company. This will more than likely involve a sophisticated strategy of connectivity software.

As companies continue to purchase prebuilt applications, the control they have over physical data stores slips further and further away. After all, the business aspect of an application is its focus, not necessarily the technology. Therefore, ways of tapping into that data source and the ability to own the middle layer of an application, or the I/O interface modules, is key to the success of a data architecture. Many new technologies will evolve from vendors, staking claim to the universal database that understands everything data oriented—numbers, text, audio, video, and so on. However, until these vendors can manipulate the application providers into delivering their technology solely on this database, you will require a heterogeneous solution.

A strong mid-tier processing component that allows you to manage your enterprise data architecture as one logical data store is the best answer available today and in the near future. However, these types of technologies require better optimization techniques and network strategies than are currently offered. The ability for these software packages to utilize spare cycles on processors that are idle and additional intelligence must be cultivated prior to offering these software components as mainstream products. This is not an easy task, because the leading connectivity vendors tend also to be database vendors. They need to better understand how to manipulate the optimizers of underlying databases, or physical data stores, so that the two optimizers do not work in conflict. But database vendors have shown a great lack of communication in these strategic areas.

So what is the lesson in all this? Teach or have your data architecture team become well versed in optimization and data storage techniques. Let them understand the software and hardware aspects of data management. Many technology advances over the years have eluded these people, and they get caught off guard when a package or vendor claims a better way and the user buys it. RAID, WORM, CD-ROM, clustering, parallel processing—all of these techniques have been strongly marketed over the years; however, does your data architecture team understand them? Train your people, even on technologies that are not implemented in your shop. Get involved with the university community to understand what research is being conducted. And most importantly, develop a visionary staff who look to advance the data resources of your enterprise. All too often, the keepers of the data are pessimistic and shoot down any new ideas as unmanageable in the current environment. You need visionaries who will not be so quick to dismiss technology, but who can see the technology's benefits for the future architecture of a data warehouse.

Summary

Information is key, which we hope the quotations contained within this book have shown you. Two of the most profound quotations in our opinion have been the following.

Knowledge in the form of an informational commodity indispensable to productive power is already, and will continue to be, a major—perhaps the *major—stake in the worldwide competition for power. It is conceivable that the nation-states will one day fight for control of information, just as they battled in the past for control over territory, and afterwards for control over access to and exploitation of raw materials and cheap labor.*

—Jean François Lyotard

Information is the oxygen of the modern age. It seeps through the walls topped by barbed wire, it wafts across the electrified borders.

—Ronald Reagan

Keeping our user base informed and providing them with knowledge is becoming increasingly important in delivering success in the form of competitive advantage to our enterprises. Among interactive systems that provide equivalent functionality and reliability, those that emerge and dominate the competition are those that provide the most appealing and enjoyable user interfaces. The users of these systems are presented with a natural representation of the task and valid actions. And through the use of direct manipulation techniques, they can freely and easily utilize the system. These systems are easy to learn, easy to use, and easy to retain. If we want to advance the data warehouse concept and continue its current explosive growth, we must deliver easy, yet powerful systems—that is, *sophisticated simplicity*.

Offering such interfaces to our user community allows us to more readily integrate novices. These users will acquire a simple subset of commands, then progress to more elaborate operations within a system. These actions are rapid, incremental, and reversible. The actions tend to be performed as physical actions, not as complex syntactical actions. The results of such actions are immediately visible, and the concept of error processing is visually built into a system rather than through cryptic messaging.

However, be fairly warned that direct manipulation and similar techniques will not ensure the overall success of your system. Poor design, slow implementation, and inadequate functionality undermine user acceptance of any system. Therefore, research needs to be done to refine your understanding of the contribution each feature provides to the overall system. Standard techniques for development and delivery of such systems is still required. Techniques as offered in this and other books should be adopted and adapted to your enterprise.

Data warehousing requires information packaging experts! From there, your researchers and designers should begin to free themselves and think visually toward the future. Proper allocation to the research function should be scheduled so that your staff begins to develop new techniques to advance your systems. Past commands and operations that were tedious will quickly become accessible through lively, enjoyable interactive systems that reduce learning time and increase speed, performance, and user satisfaction.

Upon achieving such lofty goals, you will have transformed your enterprise and built the corporate knowledge base—being one of the first to offer your users a completely integrated decision-making environment!

As we conclude this book, we wish you good luck. Keep pushing the technology envelope!

Appendix A
Sample Information Packages

The following information package models have been derived from various data warehouse implementations. This book has sought to teach you the fundamental theories behind the design and implementation of successful data warehouses using the information packaging methodology. In doing so, it primarily focused on the fundamental aspects of the modeling techniques. This appendix presents several examples in various industries with many targets. You should examine each of these examples for applicability to your specific business. Each example provides the following elements.

- A brief narrative of the purpose behind the information package
- A sample information package diagram covering business requirements
- Sample questions that will be answered by the information package
- A sample star schema demonstrating the dimension, measure, and category detail entities

Within these examples, the dimensions may change in overall content, and measurements may be added to the analysis. However, the models themselves provide a good foundation for beginning the information package modeling process.

Automotive: Product Defect and Quality Analysis

As discussed in the earlier chapters of this book, understanding the product problems that exist in your offered products can alleviate a great deal of pain and suffering throughout your organization and customer base. Figure A.1 presents an information package diagram that models the service problem by tracking data for an automotive group. This model assists in defining which products have problems. The problems can be identified based on the given component that is incurring the problem. Also, suppliers can be tagged to the items that are defective. The star schema for this information package is presented in Figure A.2.

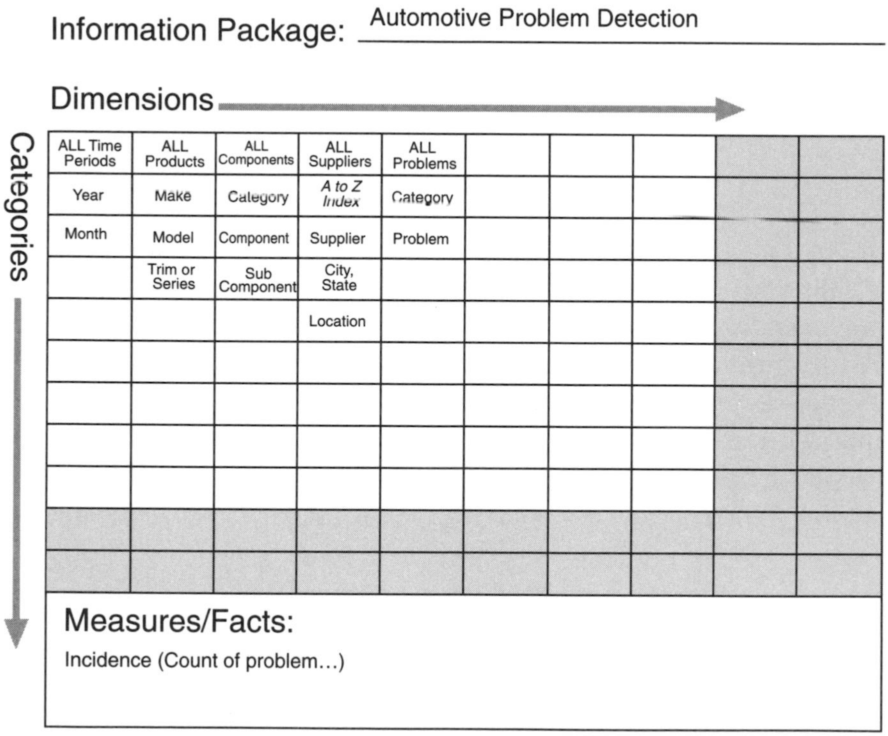

Information Package: Automotive Problem Detection

Dimensions

Categories

ALL Time Periods	ALL Products	ALL Components	ALL Suppliers	ALL Problems
Year	Make	Category	A to Z Index	Category
Month	Model	Component	Supplier	Problem
	Trim or Series	Sub Component	City, State	
			Location	

Measures/Facts:

Incidence (Count of problem...)

Figure A.1: *Automotive product defect and quality analysis information package diagram*

This information package allows for flexible analysis, including the ability to determine the following.

- Which suppliers offer the best quality components?
- Which products offer the lowest quality and require immediate focus?
- Which components seem to cause the largest number of problems?
- What types of problems are more likely to occur over time as the product ages?
- Which suppliers have been improving their quality levels over time, and which have been getting worse?

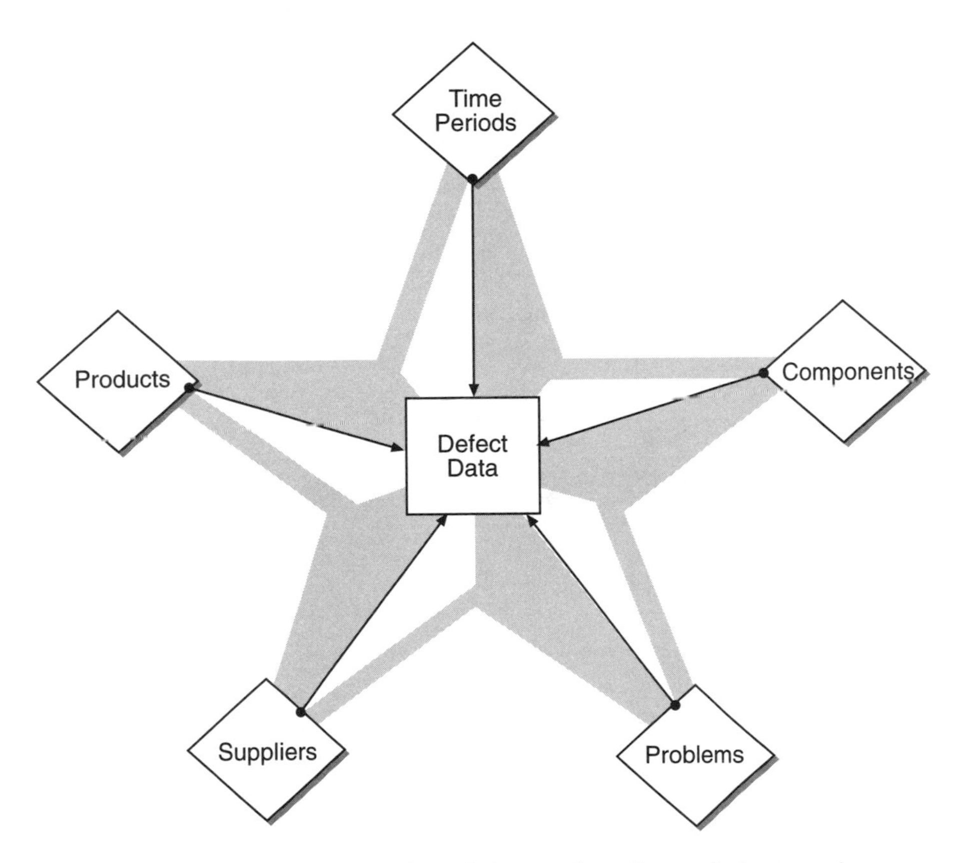

***Figure A.2**: Automotive product defect and quality analysis star schema*

Brand Management: Promotional Analysis

Promotional analysis and other forms of marketing and sales analysis have driven the data warehouse market to where it is today. Therefore, your company may have a similar need as shown in this information package. Typically, brand managers want to drive a consumer's desire for their product in many ways, such as promotions. These promotions can include items such as coupons, newspaper advertisements, give-aways, and display specials. To evaluate the overall effectiveness of such promotions, brand managers typically are interested in analyzing data for the products represented, the promotions offered, and the locations where the promotions ran. This type of information offers enormous insight to the overall effect (positive or negative) of a given promotion or campaign. The information package diagram for this data mart is presented in Figure A.3. The associated star schema is presented in Figure A.4.

NOTE: In competitive marketplaces such as the consumer packaged goods industry, this data is often combined with external data offered by IRI and Neilson to determine if a competitor's promotion was more effective during similar time periods.

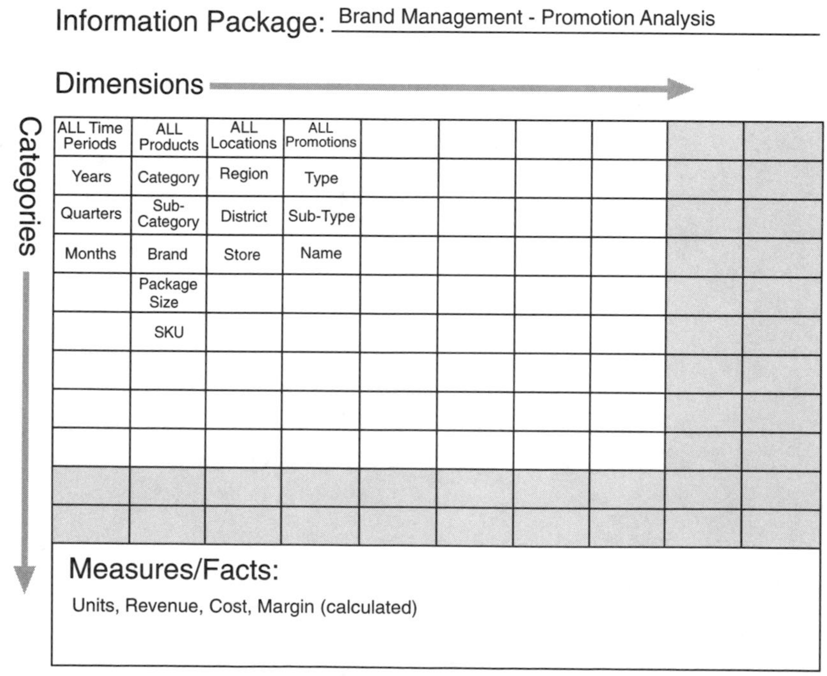

Information Package: Brand Management - Promotion Analysis

Dimensions →

Categories ↓

ALL Time Periods	ALL Products	ALL Locations	ALL Promotions
Years	Category	Region	Type
Quarters	Sub-Category	District	Sub-Type
Months	Brand	Store	Name
	Package Size		
	SKU		

Measures/Facts:

Units, Revenue, Cost, Margin (calculated)

Figure A.3: *Brand management and promotional analysis information package diagram*

This type of model allows a brand manager or other financial analyzer to evaluate the answers to questions such as those that follow.

- Was a promotion profitable?
- What was the cost of developing the brand name over time?
- Was the promotion more successful in some locations than others?
- Based on historical data, how long does it take to build a brand name?
- Is the time to achieve name recognition decreasing or increasing?
- Does the product appear to have a seasonal trend; and if so, do promotions assist in altering such trends?

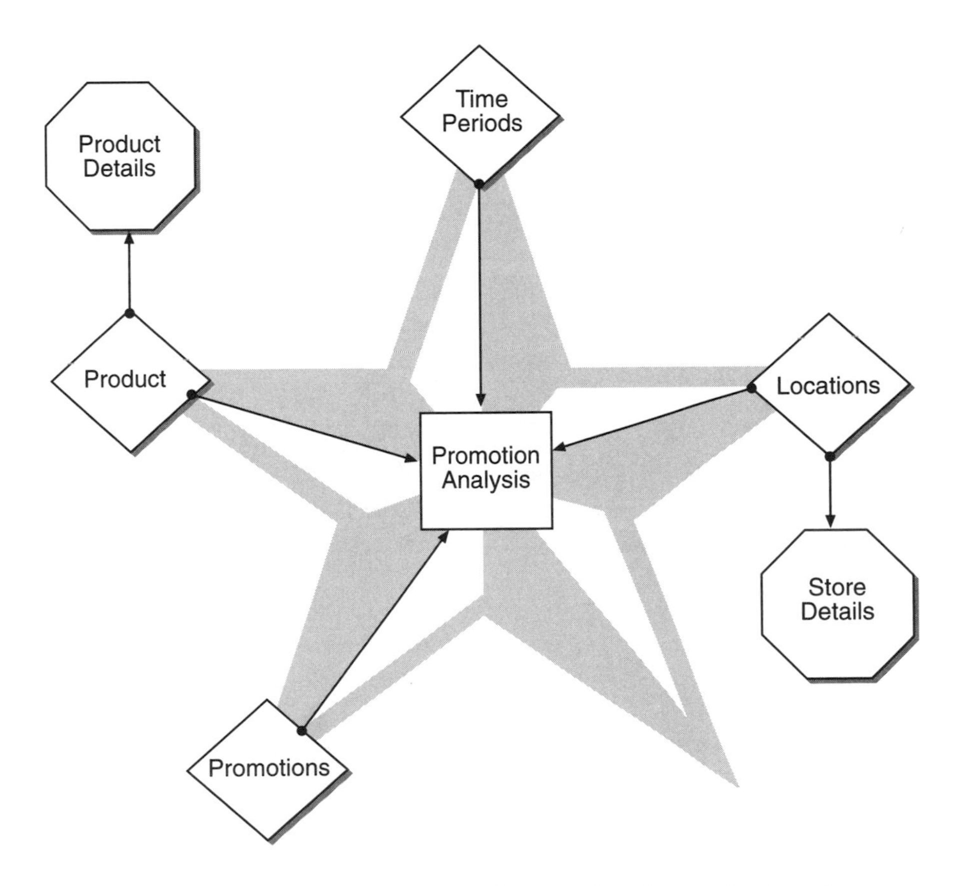

Figure A.4: *Brand management and promotional analysis star schema*

Consulting Services: Expense Analysis

Of course, all companies want to grow through revenue increases. However, it is important in industries such as consulting services to adequately manage expenses that are incurred internally versus those that are only required based on your customer's needs and therefore paid by the customer. As a manager, typically the areas of interest include the individual consultant and the associated management chain; the projects that are active as well as a historical perspective of similar projects for planning purposes; and the types of expenses incurred. The information package diagram for this data mart is presented in Figure A.5. The associated star schema is presented in Figure A.6.

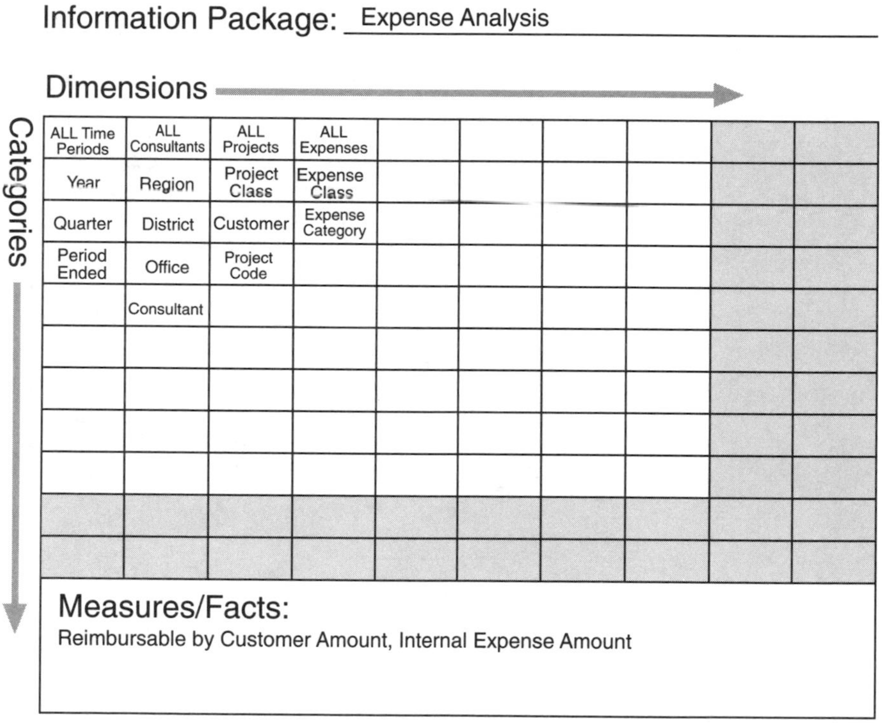

Information Package: Expense Analysis

Dimensions

Categories

ALL Time Periods	ALL Consultants	ALL Projects	ALL Expenses
Year	Region	Project Class	Expense Class
Quarter	District	Customer	Expense Category
Period Ended	Office	Project Code	
	Consultant		

Measures/Facts:
Reimbursable by Customer Amount, Internal Expense Amount

Figure A.5: *Consulting services and expense analysis information package diagram*

This information package assists the user in answering questions such as those that follow.

- What percentage of total expenses is incurred by a customer?
- Are expenses rising? By how much?
- What are typical expenses for a project of a certain class?
- Are there any expense deviations among customers with similar projects?
- Are certain consultants abusing expenses?
- What class of project incurs the highest expenses?
- For which categories of expenses do we need to control better or plan?

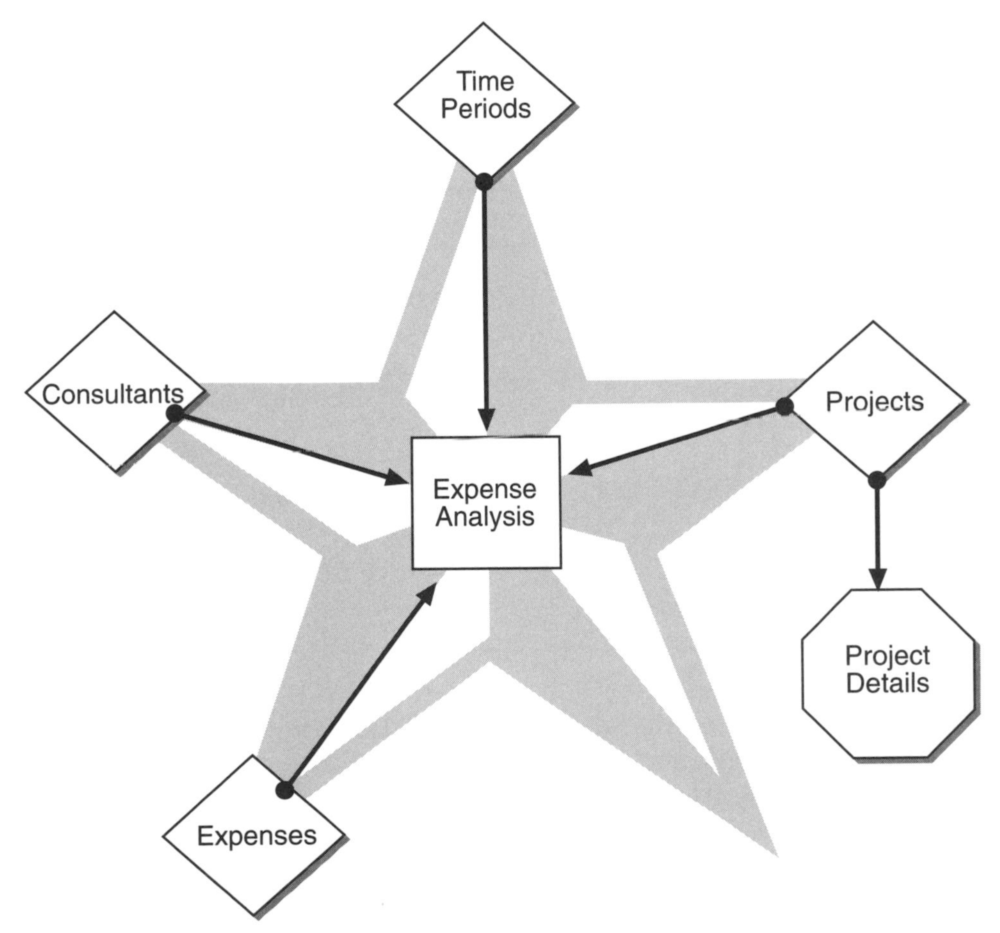

Figure A.6: *Consulting services and expense analysis star schema*

Consulting Services: Utilization Analysis

In the services industry, it is important to examine the various aspects that drive the success of a business. The following model is driven from a consulting services company whose areas of interest include customers, consultants, and service packages. With regard to the customers, it is important to better understand the project assignments and associated tasks with which the firm is involved. With regard to the consultant, it is important to understand the marketable attributes of these resources, such as their office location, certifications, and skill set or role as requested by the customer. The performance measurements that are key to the overall business include the utilization factor—or how often the consultant is billable and doing customer work—and the rate that was paid for such work. The information package diagram for this data mart is presented in Figure A.7. The associated star schema is presented in Figure A.8.

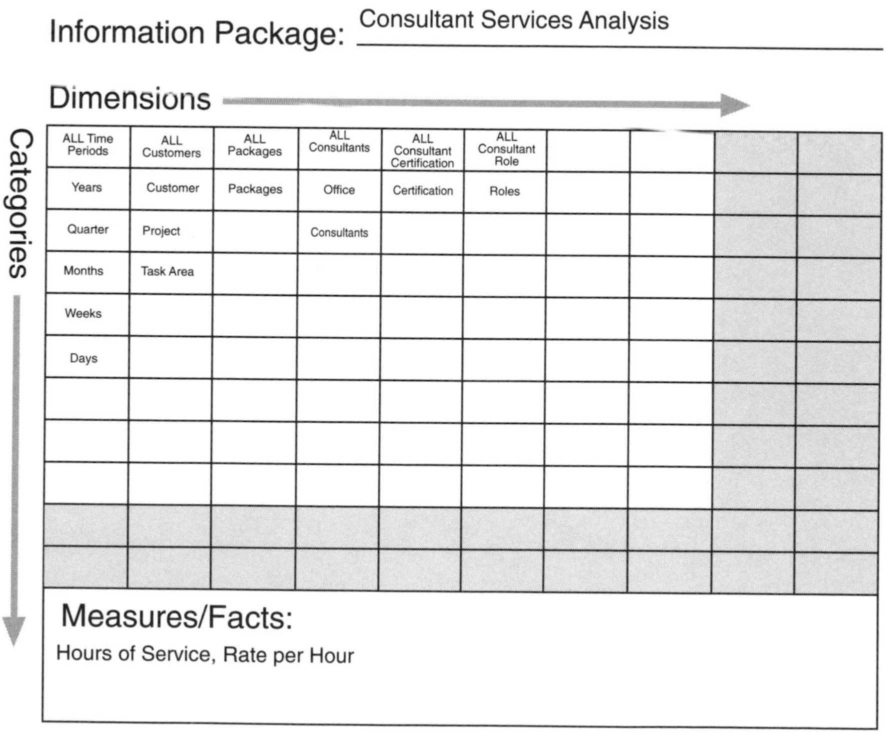

Information Package: Consultant Services Analysis

Dimensions →

Categories ↓

ALL Time Periods	ALL Customers	ALL Packages	ALL Consultants	ALL Consultant Certification	ALL Consultant Role
Years	Customer	Packages	Office	Certification	Roles
Quarter	Project		Consultants		
Months	Task Area				
Weeks					
Days					

Measures/Facts:

Hours of Service, Rate per Hour

Figure A.7: *Consulting services and utilization analysis information package diagram*

This type of data allows a consulting manager to evaluate many aspects of the overall business, including those that follow.

- If location affects billing rate or utilization percentage of the consultants
- Which packages are and are not successful
- If customer trends in utilization and rate sensitivity indicate that customers are using more certified consultants, and in what roles
- If certification alters the utilization and billing rate of a consultant
- Which customers are buying services from you, what services, and in what volume
- If specific roles are decreasing in popularity, whether you should retrain your consultants

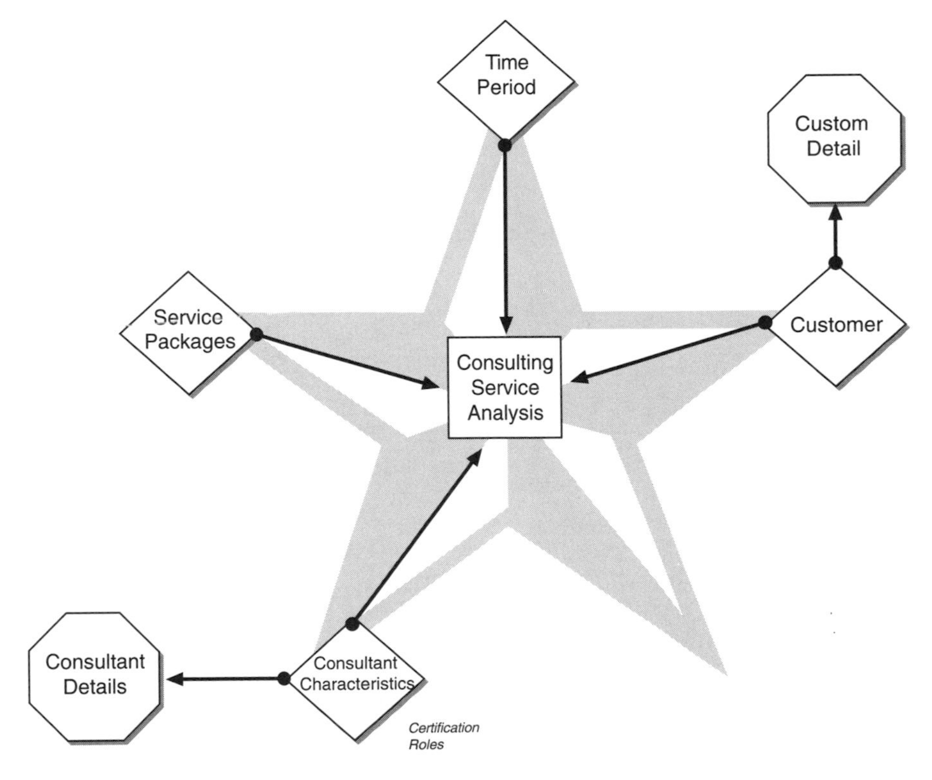

Figure A.8: *Consulting services and utilization analysis star schema*

Financial: Account Analysis

Financial managers are constantly monitoring their accounts and searching for anomalies in the data. Traditionally, access to such data was difficult and data quality was compromised when financial managers took report data and entered it in their own spreadsheets. From these local data sources, a financial manager could build proper models necessary to understand the current state of affairs. A data warehouse offers enormous value to the financial managers of most, if not all, companies. The following information package is for monitoring accounts by profit center over time. This model allows managers to determine what the financial conditions are with regard to the original budget versus the actual data and short-term outlook. The information package diagram for this data mart is presented in Figure A.9. The associated star schema is presented in Figure A.10.

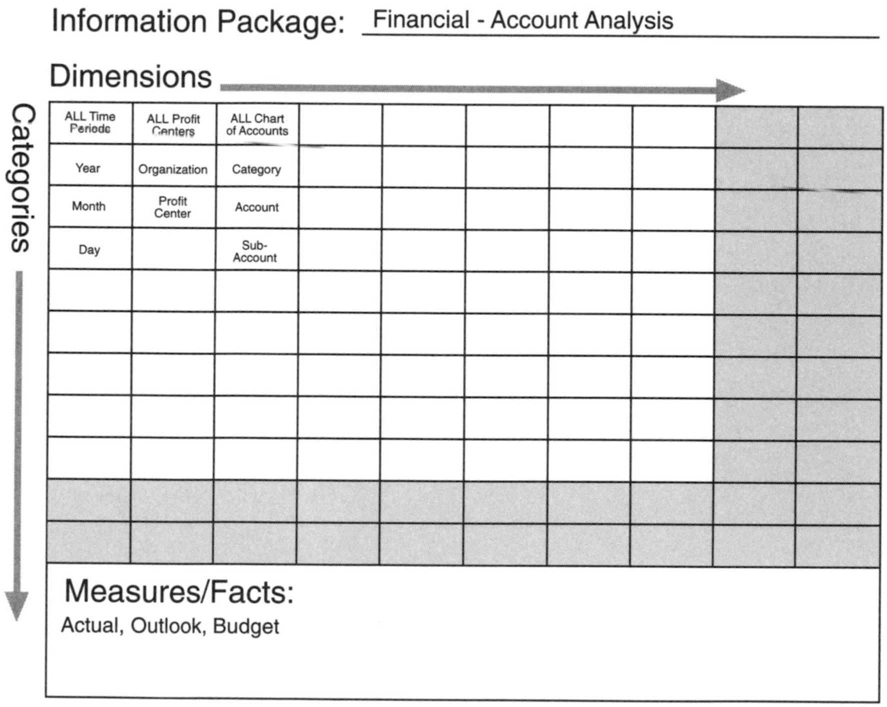

Information Package: Financial - Account Analysis

Dimensions

Categories

ALL Time Periods	ALL Profit Centers	ALL Chart of Accounts
Year	Organization	Category
Month	Profit Center	Account
Day		Sub-Account

Measures/Facts:
Actual, Outlook, Budget

Figure A.9: *Financial and account analysis information package diagram*

This information model assists users in answering questions such as the following.

- How is the business doing when actual data is compared to the budget?
- How does the outlook of the accounts compare to the budget?
- Where may the company incur risk due to account management and poor budgeting practices?
- Which profit centers and organizations have a good handle on their budgets, and which don't or need assistance?

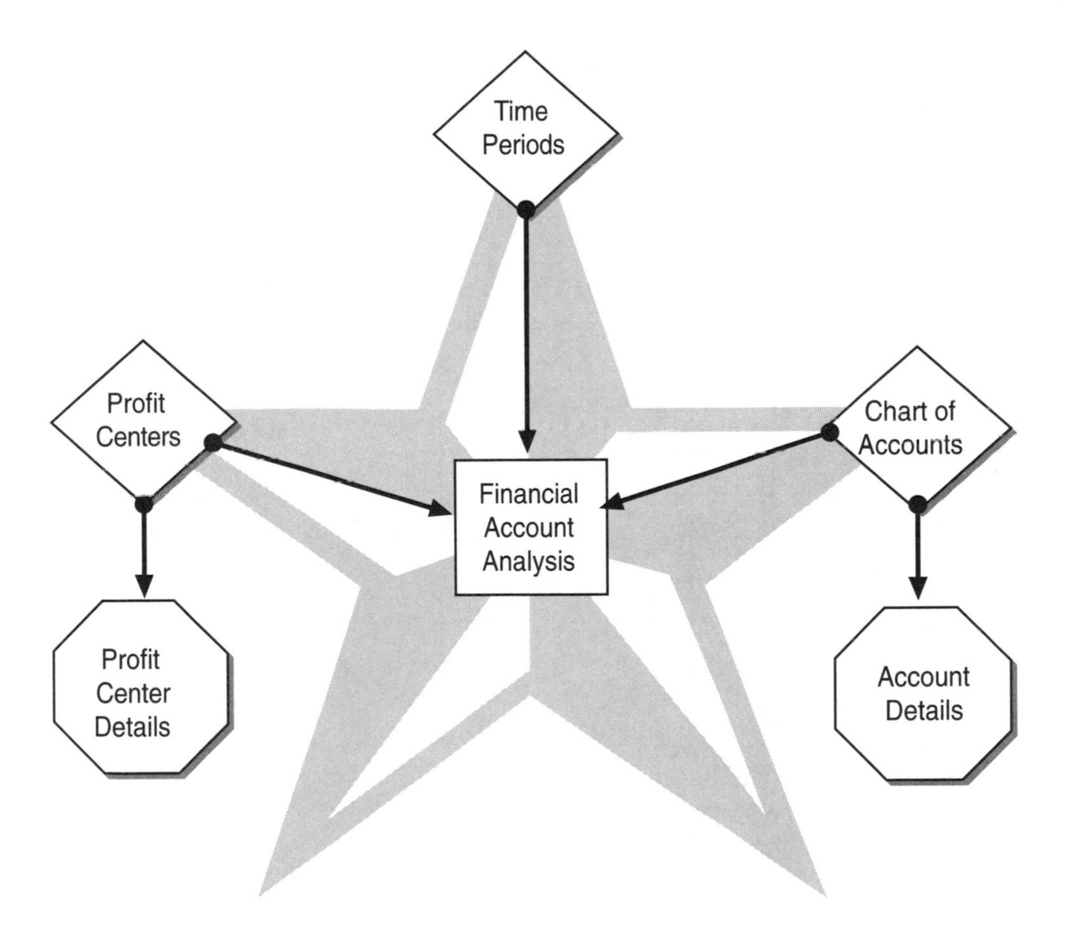

Figure A.10: *Financial and account analysis star schema*

Financial Services: Loan Analysis

In the financial services industry, such as banking and lending institutions, it is important to analyze the exposure for loans to clients. The specific example shown here is for a company that focuses its lending on student loans. These loans are provided through the lending institution to specific institutions and guaranteed by a limited number of guarantors. The loans can be characterized by several attributes, including loan type, disbursement method, loan status, and risk rating. To ease the interface with users, notice the index categories that have been added. Remember that this is a conceptual specification that should help the database development team and the front-end development team. Notes on the information package diagram assist both groups in better partitioning and presenting data. The information package diagram for this data mart is presented in Figure A.11. The associated star schema is presented in Figure A.12.

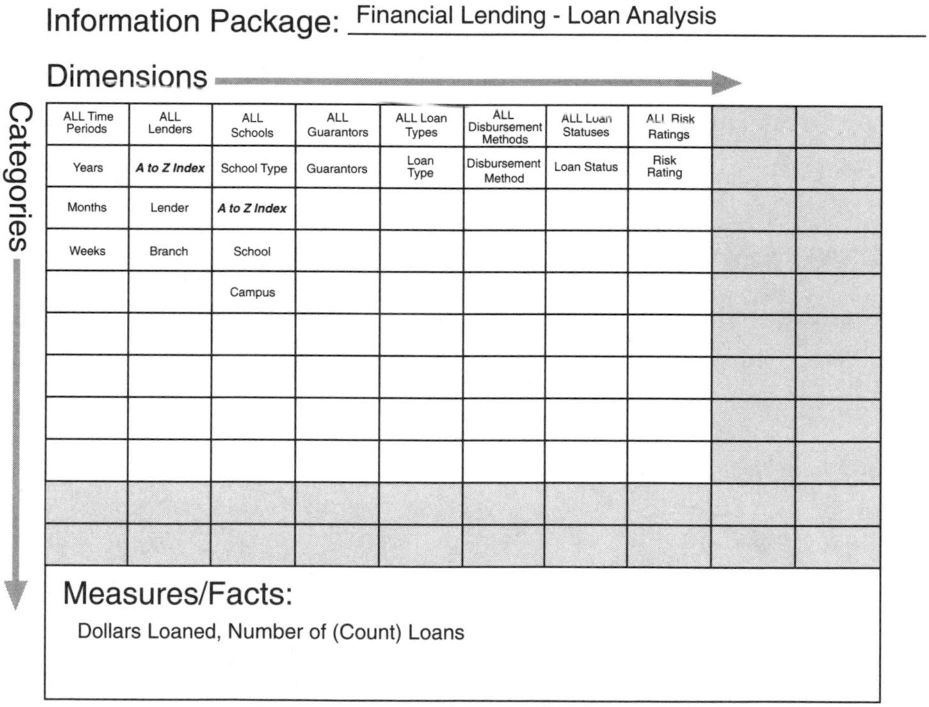

Information Package: Financial Lending - Loan Analysis

Dimensions →

Categories ↓

ALL Time Periods	ALL Lenders	ALL Schools	ALL Guarantors	ALL Loan Types	ALL Disbursement Methods	ALL Loan Statuses	ALL Risk Ratings		
Years	***A to Z Index***	School Type	Guarantors	Loan Type	Disbursement Method	Loan Status	Risk Rating		
Months	Lender	***A to Z Index***							
Weeks	Branch	School							
		Campus							

Measures/Facts:

Dollars Loaned, Number of (Count) Loans

Figure A.11: *Financial services and loan analysis information package diagram*

This information package diagram allows its users to answer questions such as those that follow.

- How many dollars have been loaned by institution?
- Which guarantors are exposed with a high amount of loaned dollars?
- What is the average loan value at a given school?
- What are the most popular types of loans?
- How are the moneys distributed across loan risk ratings?

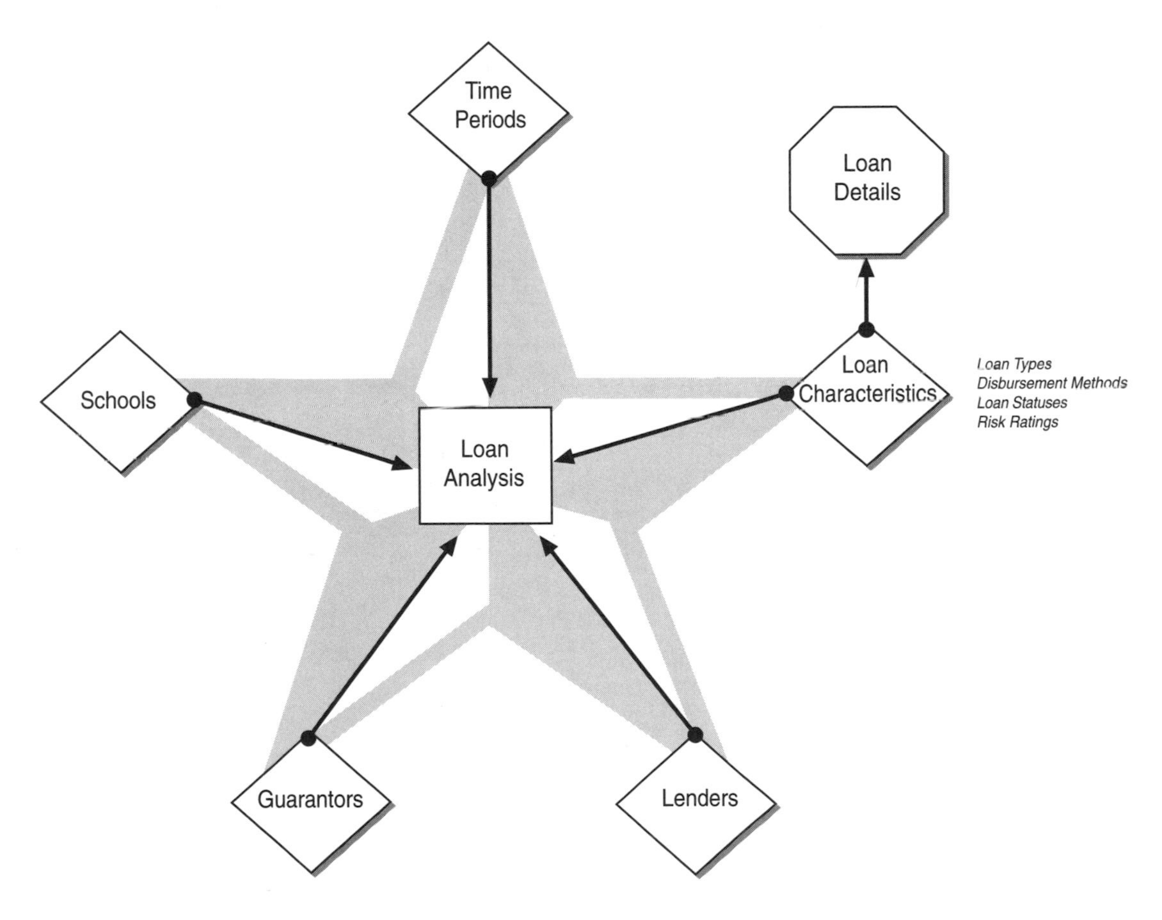

Figure A.12: *Financial services and loan analysis star schema*

Health Care: Service Utilization

The health care industry has been under enormous pressure during the past years. These pressures have forced Information System professionals in these organizations to produce quicker and more accurate reporting. The managed care and insurance industries have been converging on a better understanding and management of costs associated with care. This information package allows their users to better understand and measure the popular areas of service by department as well as the duration of incidents by diagnostic related groups (DRGs). The information package diagram for this data mart is presented in Figure A.13. The associated star schema is presented in Figure A.14.

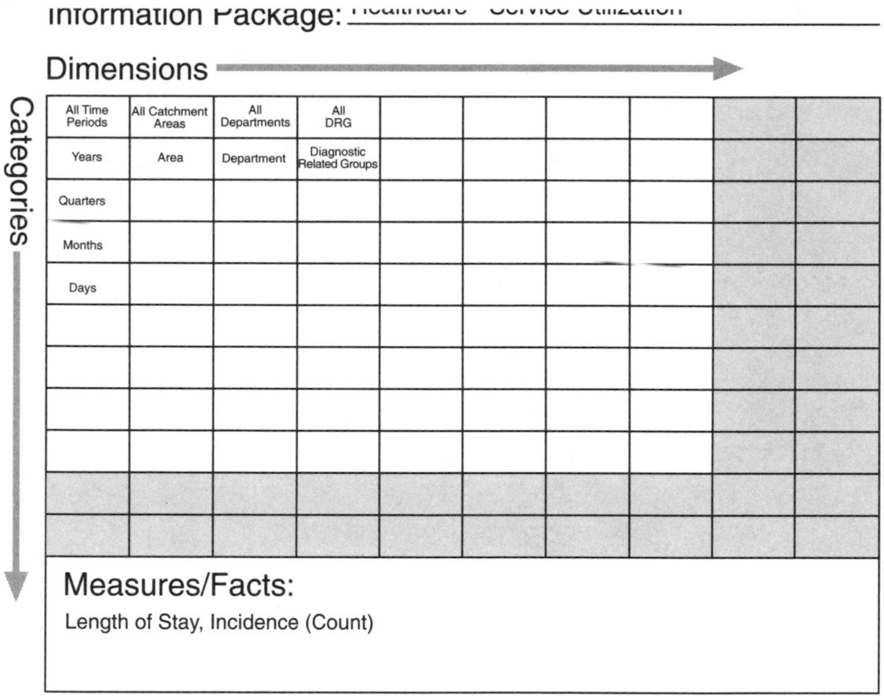

Information Package:

Dimensions

Categories

All Time Periods	All Catchment Areas	All Departments	All DRG
Years	Area	Department	Diagnostic Related Groups
Quarters			
Months			
Days			

Measures/Facts:

Length of Stay, Incidence (Count)

Figure A.13: *Health care and service utilization information package diagram*

This information package allows users to answer questions such as those that follow.

- Is the length of stay increasing or decreasing by DRG?
- What DRGs do we incur the most? The least?
- What are the top 10 procedures performed by year? Is our focus changing or growing?
- What procedures appear to be growing? Shrinking?
- What staffing mix might be required?
- What is the average length of stay for the top 10 procedures?
- What procedures require the least length of stay? The most?

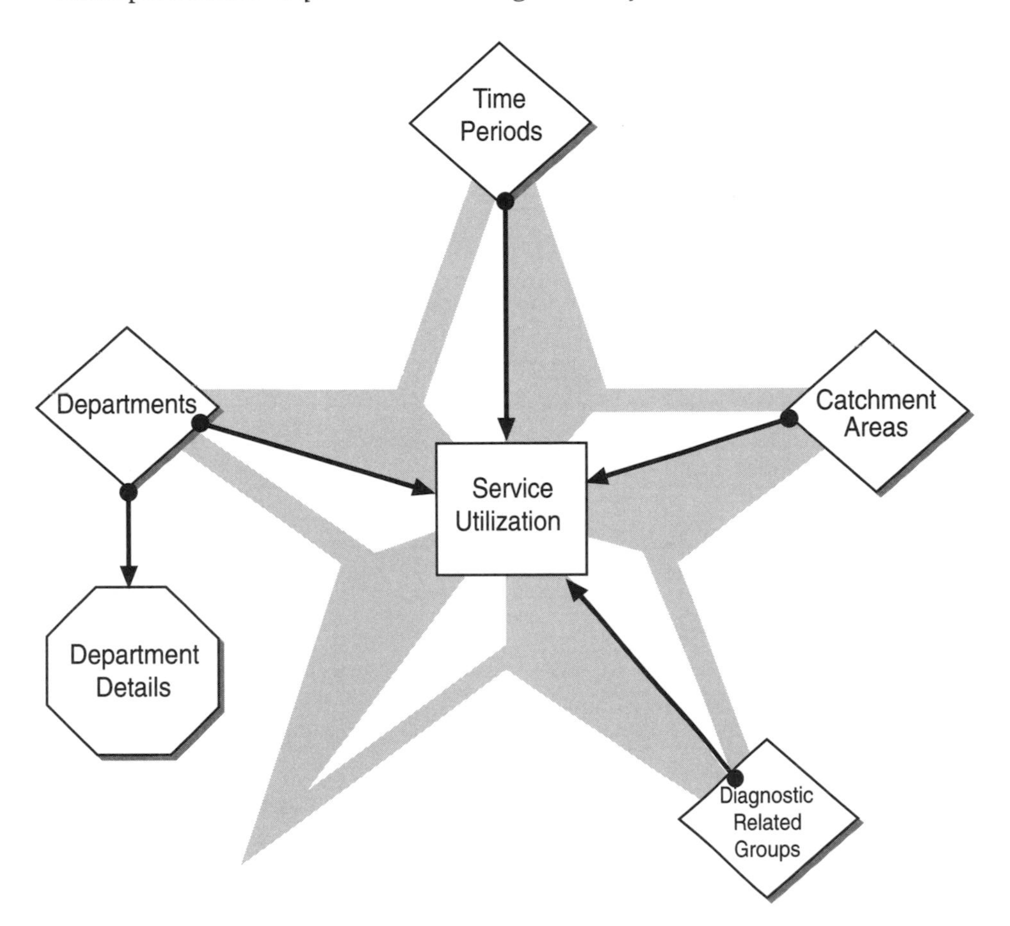

Figure A.14: *Health care and service utilization star schema*

Human Resources: Employee Downtime and Turnover

Today, many companies are trying to regain employee loyalty. With this focus, human resources departments are requesting information with regard to employee downtime (sick leave, vacation, and so forth) and turnover (terminations and both voluntary and involuntary separations). Human resources managers want to assist others in the organization in retaining the highest quality personnel possible. The following information package model was defined to monitor related information. It offers a monthly view of data, such as available work days downtime, and active and terminated employee counts. The information package diagram for this data mart is presented in Figure A.15. The associated star schema is presented in Figure A.16.

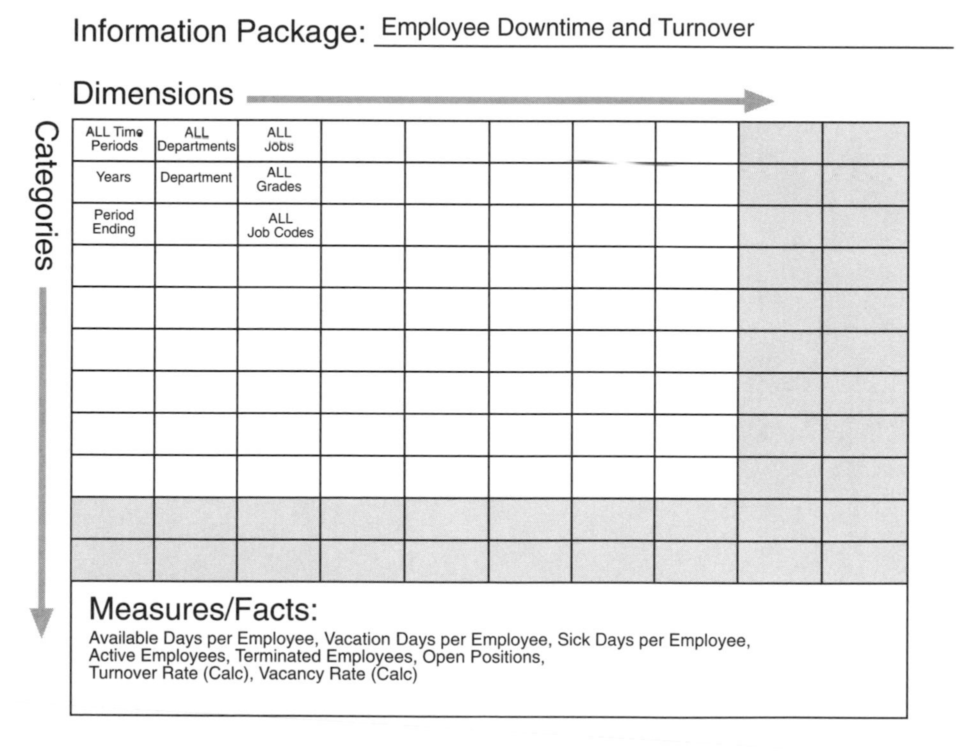

Figure A.15: *Human resources and employee downtime and turnover information package diagram*

This information package helps human resources management and other users answer questions such as those listed here.

- What are the turnover and vacancy trends by department?
- Are certain departments more susceptible to turnover than others?
- In which jobs is it the most difficult to retain employees?
- Which jobs show a high tendency for sick time? For vacation time?
- Which departments are slow to fill vacancies?

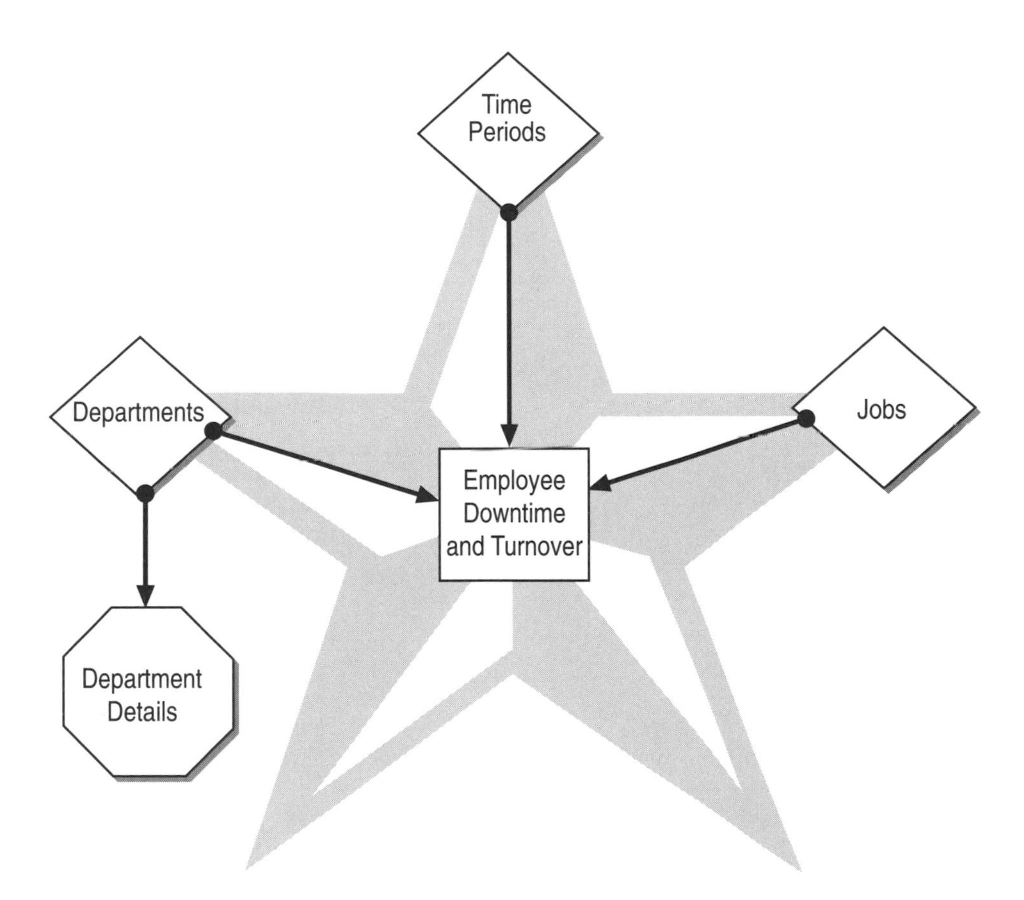

Figure A.16: *Human resources employee downtime and turnover star schema*

Human Resources: Payroll Benefits Analysis

Another important aspect of human resource management is benefits administration. Good benefits packages attract quality people, while packages lacking in quality cause quality people to look elsewhere. Companies want to offer competitive and diverse benefit packages to their employees; however, this is a growing cost area because of recent increases in health care costs and insurance. The following information package model was built to better understand what benefits are being used by employees as well as to understand the incurred cost per employee. The information package diagram for this data mart is presented in Figure A.17. The associated star schema is presented in Figure A.18. The demographics entity in the star schema is shaded because it is a merged dimension entity, created from all the individual dimension entities that describe an employee.

NOTE: This model could be enhanced by adding demographic data and outside benchmark data.

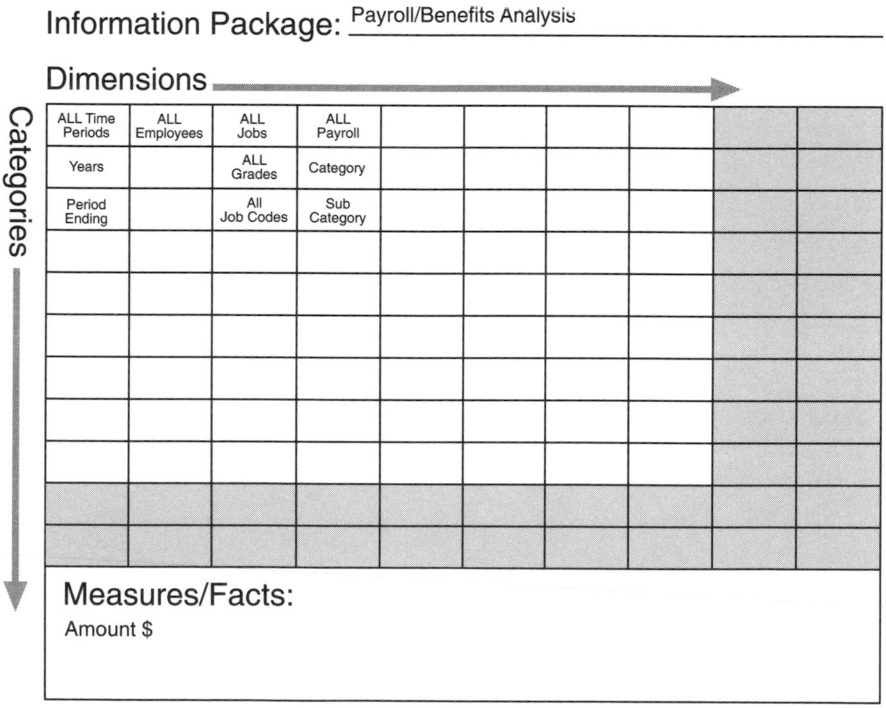

Information Package: Payroll/Benefits Analysis

Dimensions →

Categories ↓

ALL Time Periods	ALL Employees	ALL Jobs	ALL Payroll
Years		ALL Grades	Category
Period Ending		All Job Codes	Sub Category

Measures/Facts:

Amount $

***Figure A.17**: Human resources and payroll benefit analysis information package diagram*

This information package model assists users in better answering questions such as those that follow.

- What contribution is required by employees to get benefits? Has the contribution trend been increasing or decreasing?
- What are the top 10 payroll deductions used by employees?
- Do deductions fall in line with job classifications? Are some positions more prone to accept certain benefits?
- What benefits are not utilized? What are the bottom 10 benefits according to utilization?

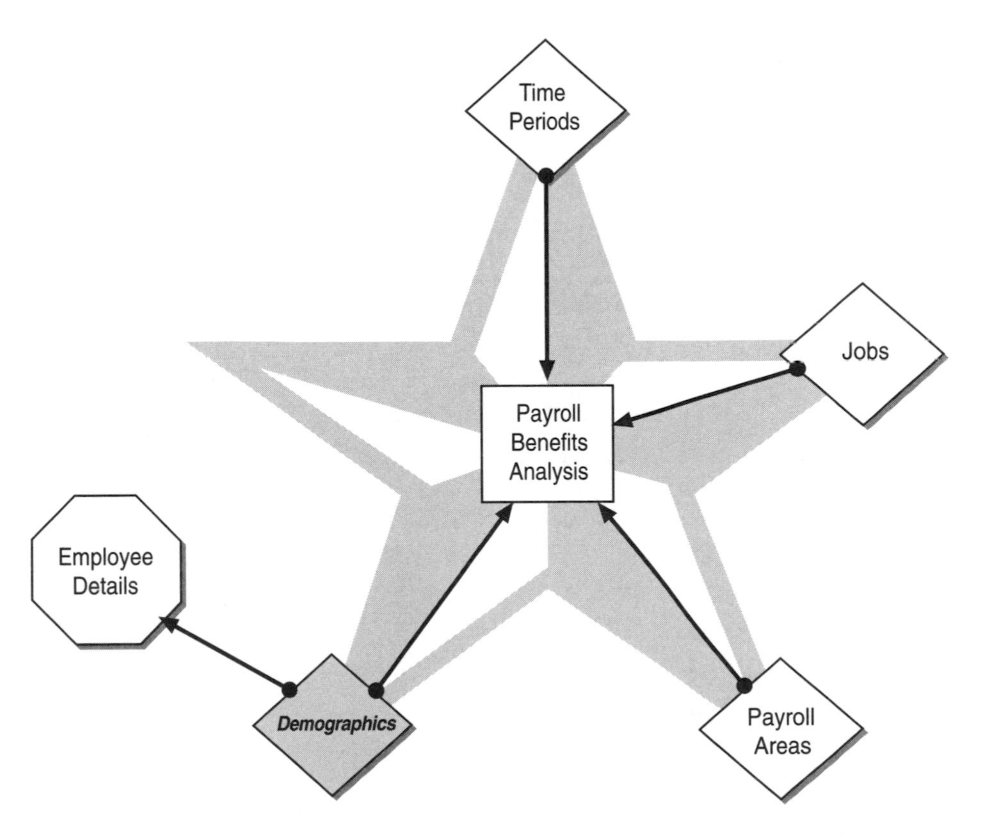

Figure A.18: *Human resources and payroll benefit analysis star schema*

Manufacturing: Cycle Time

Cycle time is a key business measure, because a dramatic reduction in cycle time can greatly increase a company's competitiveness and profitability. Many managers today monitor cycle time more closely than other standard cost reduction programs.

This model assists a process manufacturing company in better understanding its cycle time and the overall process of manufacturing its products. This data is monitored by product, processing line, and phase within process. The information package diagram for this data mart is presented in Figure A.19. The associated star schema is presented in Figure A.20.

Note: This model could be greatly enhanced by including external benchmark data on cycle time, allowing managers to understand how favorably they compare to their competition and the marketplace in general.

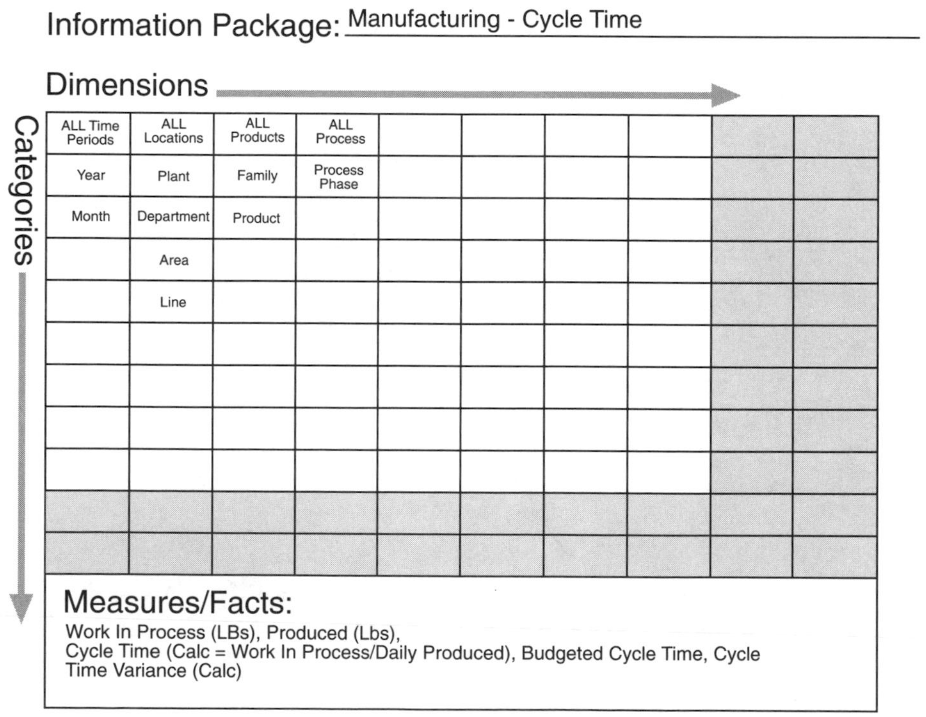

Information Package: Manufacturing - Cycle Time

Dimensions →

Categories ↓

ALL Time Periods	ALL Locations	ALL Products	ALL Process
Year	Plant	Family	Process Phase
Month	Department	Product	
	Area		
	Line		

Measures/Facts:

Work In Process (LBs), Produced (Lbs),
Cycle Time (Calc = Work In Process/Daily Produced), Budgeted Cycle Time, Cycle Time Variance (Calc)

Figure A.19: *Manufacturing and cycle time information package diagram*

This information package model allows users to answer questions such as the following.

- Which products have the longest cycle time? The shortest?
- Does the facility (processing line) have any impact on the cycle time of a product?
- Which part of a process incurs the longest duration?
- Are trends in cycle time decreasing? Increasing? For all products? For some products?
- From where are shrinkages in the cycle time coming?

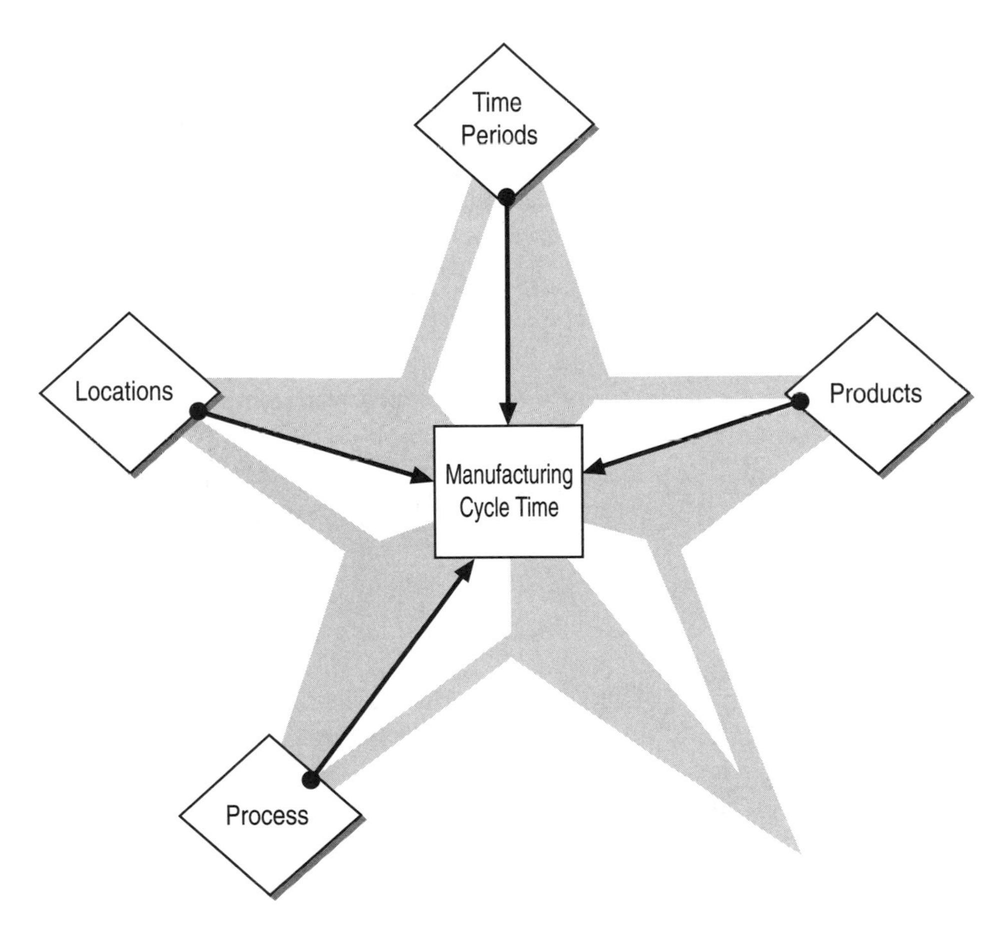

Figure A.20: *Manufacturing and cycle time star schema*

Manufacturing: Inventory Transaction Analysis

Inventory is another of area for significant business improvement. We recently bought a pair of gym shoes and asked the clerk what was available in size 15. He said we had to pick the shoes and he would check them. After about the tenth pair selected without finding a size 15, we felt frustrated. If the shoes had been stored by size, then by manufacturer, and then by style, the clerk could have told us that there were only two pairs in the desired size. Instead, we had to try 200 or so pairs of shoes to find the two pairs.

Inventory is important: You can improve many things in your business by understanding inventory. The shoe dealer could improve customer satisfaction, and probably employee satisfaction. In the example captured in Figures A.21 and A.22, the manufacturing company can begin to improve the manufacturing process by better understanding its inventory and associated transactions. This information package model contains an inventory location dimension, a product dimension, and a transaction dimension. The information package diagram for this data mart is presented in Figure A.21. The associated star schema is presented in Figure A.22. The Purchase Order Details entity in the star schema is shaded and unconnected in this logical diagram because multiple entities will be required to fulfill this requirement. These entities should be developed and realized in the physical database model of the information package.

Information Package: Manufacturing - Inventory Transaction Analysis

Dimensions

Categories

ALL Time Periods	ALL Locations	ALL Products	ALL Inventory Transactions
Year	Plant	Family	Inventory Transaction
Month	Department	Product	
	Area		
	Inventory Location		

Measures/Facts:
Amount (Lbs)

Figure A.21: Manufacturing and inventory transaction analysis information package diagram

This information package assists users in answering questions such as those that follow.

- What is the frequency of specific inventory transactions?
- How often is a product taken from and placed back into a bin?
- What are the timings of inventory transactions by product?
- Is there a clustering effect of inventory transactions?
- Based on inventory transactions, could we reorganize bin locations to improve the process?

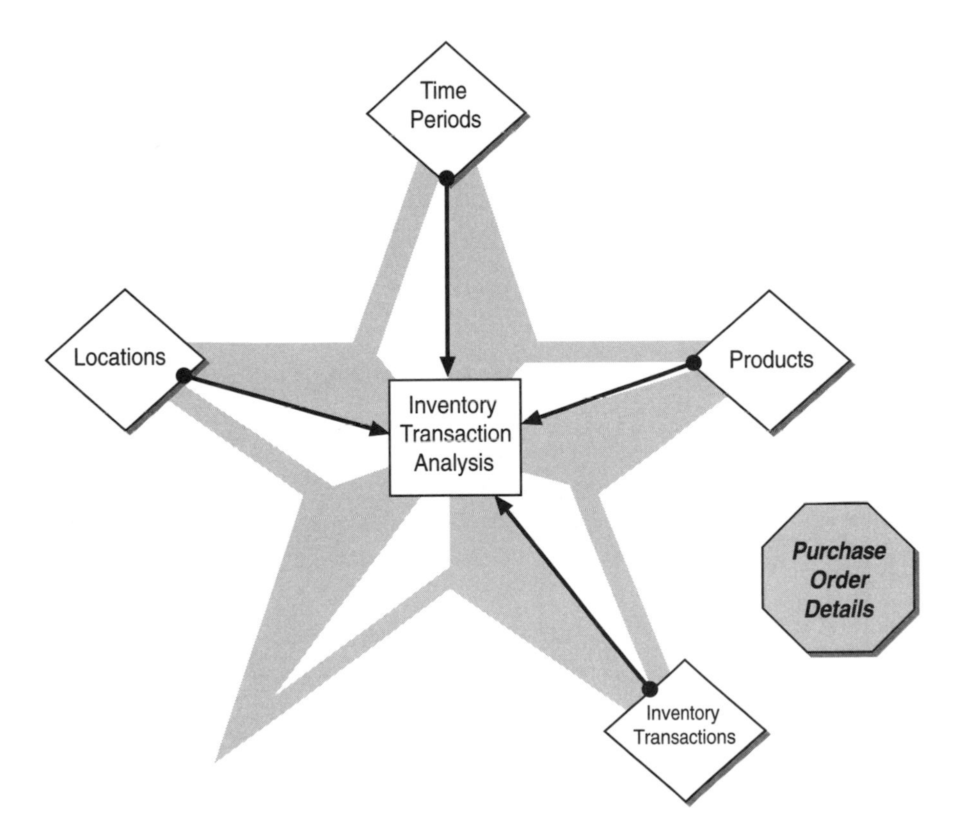

Figure A.22: *Manufacturing and inventory transaction analysis star schema*

Manufacturing: Labor Hour Analysis

Often, the cost of humans is more than the cost of the entire process of manufacturing a product. Therefore, information packages that allow users to better track how and where labor hours are used assist in better managing a process and developing a product. The information model in this section tracks labor hours by cost center, product, and production phase. The information package diagram for this data mart is presented in Figure A.23. The associated star schema is presented in Figure A.24.

Information Package: Manufacturing - Labor Hours

Dimensions

Categories

ALL Time Periods	ALL Locations	ALL Products	ALL Process	ALL Types of Labor
Year	Plant	Family	Process Phase	Labor Category
Month	Department	Product		Labor Type
	Cost Center			

Measures/Facts:
Hours

Figure A.23: *Manufacturing and labor hour analysis information package diagram*

This information package allows users to track the hours of a manufacturing process and to answer questions such as those listed here.

- Which cost center incurs the most overtime hours?
- Which plant is most efficient in labor hours? The least?
- Which product has the most labor hours? What is the process breakdown of hours? Can this process be optimized?
- What is the trend by product for labor hours?
- What is the seasonality of labor hours?

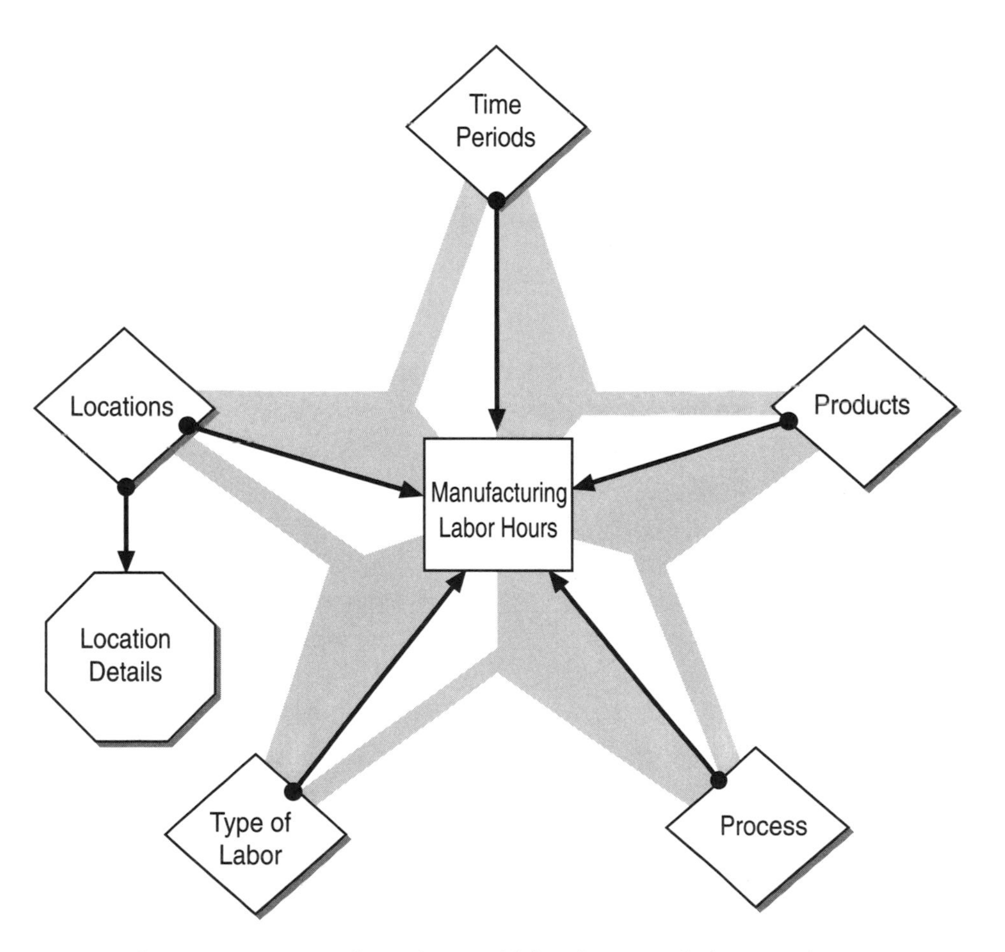

Figure A.24: *Manufacturing and labor hour analysis star schema*

Manufacturing: On-Time Shipment Analysis

Customer satisfaction, customer referrals, and overall quality often are measured in a company's abilities to ship product on time. Many items can control the overall ability of a company to deliver product on time. Some of these items include the plant, production facility, and shipment method. The information package diagram for this data mart is presented in Figure A.25. The associated star schema is presented in Figure A.26.

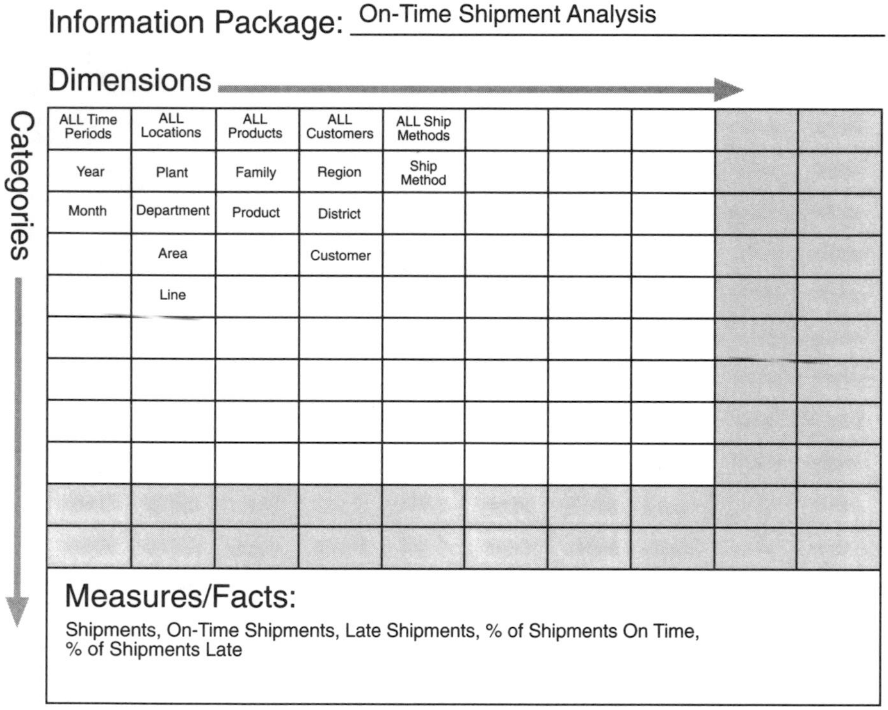

Information Package: On-Time Shipment Analysis

Dimensions →

Categories ↓

ALL Time Periods	ALL Locations	ALL Products	ALL Customers	ALL Ship Methods
Year	Plant	Family	Region	Ship Method
Month	Department	Product	District	
	Area		Customer	
	Line			

Measures/Facts:

Shipments, On-Time Shipments, Late Shipments, % of Shipments On Time, % of Shipments Late

Figure A.25: *Manufacturing and on-time shipment analysis information package diagram*

With this information package, users can answer questions such as those that follow.

- What percentage of shipments is on time?
- Who are the top 10 customers who receive late shipments? Are they receiving shipments from the same or different plants? Using similar or different shipping methods? During the same or a different time period?
- Are on-time shipments affected by the season? Are they better during the summer or winter?
- Which products are typically late? Which plants are typically late? What areas in the plant are typically associated with shipments that are late? What shipment methods are typically late?

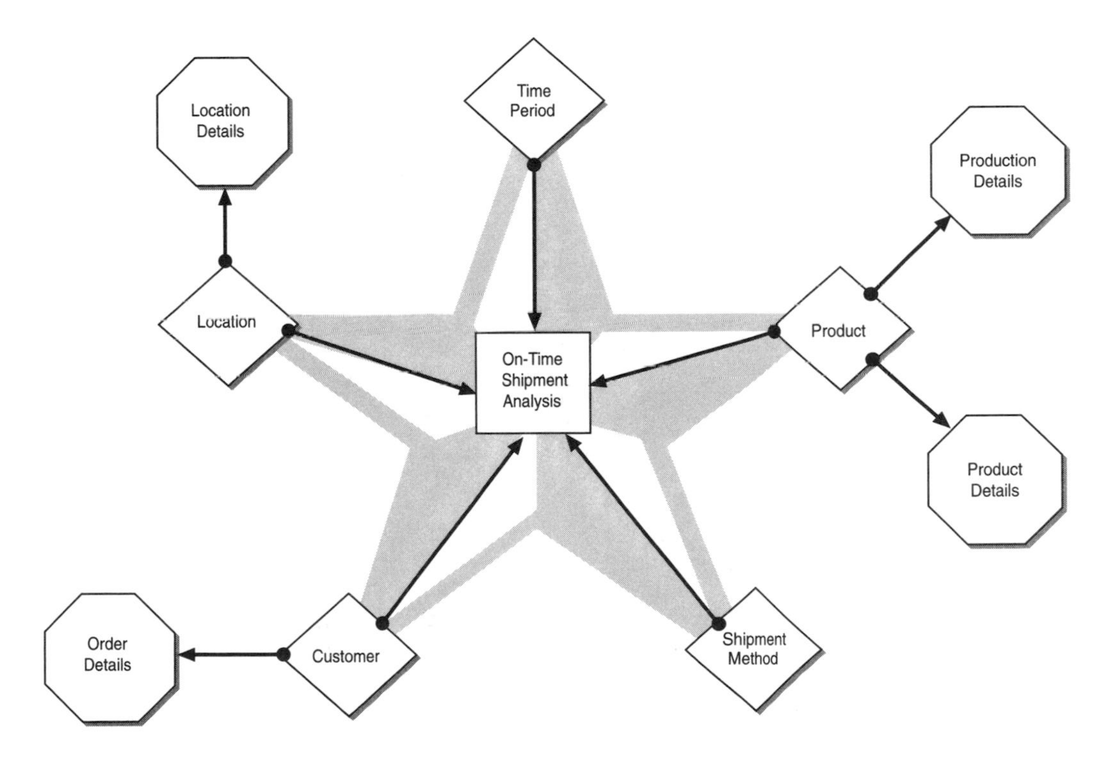

Figure A.26: *Manufacturing and on-time shipment analysis star schema*

Manufacturing: Product Costing Analysis

Knowing margins of products is of extraordinary value to management of most manufacturing companies. However, not all managers need to understand the overall impact of margins and solely focus on product cost factors of any given product—and more importantly, on controlling those costs. The following information package, presented in Figure A.27, shows the minimum amount of information required to assist users with product costing issues. The associated star schema is presented in Figure A.28.

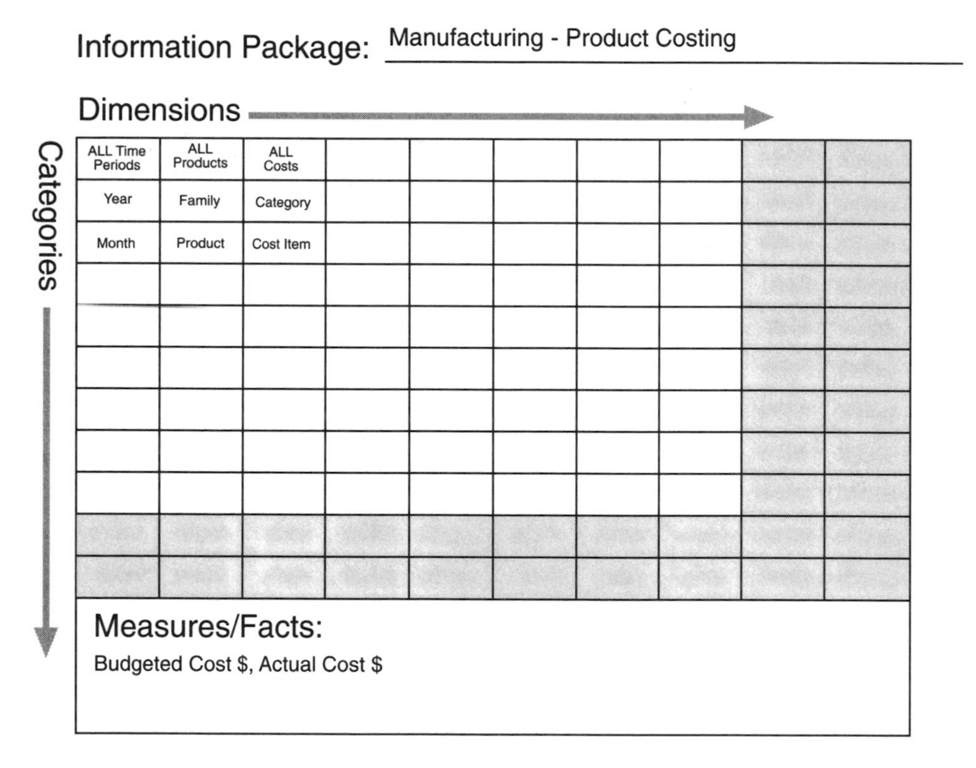

Figure A.27: *Manufacturing and product costing analysis information package diagram*

This information package allows users to obtain answers to questions such as those that follow.

- Which cost items appear to be out of control, potentially requiring new contracts and so forth?
- Are some cost items on the rise? Declining?
- If users need to control the overall cost of a product, which areas should be their prime foci?
- Are costs seasonal or continuous?
- Which products cost the most to produce? Would it be wise to outsource some of the product manufacturing process? Would this alleviate some of the cost burden?

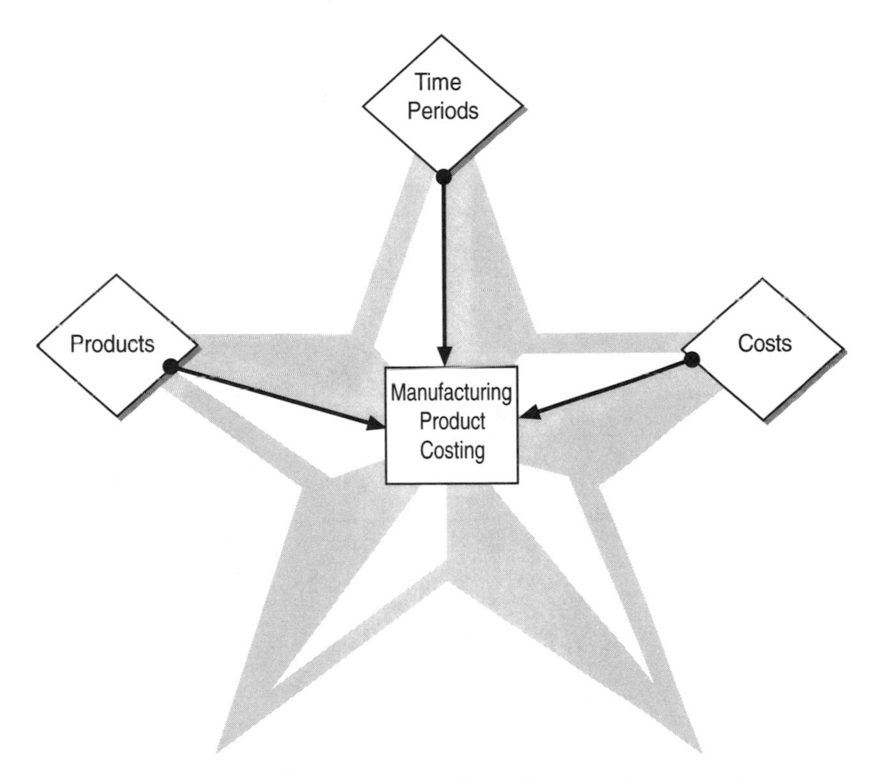

Figure A.28: *Manufacturing and product costing star schema*

Manufacturing: Supplier Performance

Supplier performance is similar to on-time shipments. However, supplier performance is yet another factor that may cause problems in your company's ability to deliver on-time shipments to your customers. Therefore, like on-time shipment monitoring, the monitoring of supplier performance is an important factor in controlling the overall success of a business. The following information package model focuses on the key areas for analyzing supplier performance, such as: areas that receive and often store raw materials; the raw materials; buyers who prepare the contracts for raw materials; suppliers who provide raw materials; and methods by which deliveries are shipped. The information package diagram for this data mart is presented in Figure A.29. The associated star schema is presented in Figure A.30. The Contract Details entity is not attached to the overall star schema due to the need for multiple physical entities to fulfill the Contract Entities. These entities should be developed in the physical database model.

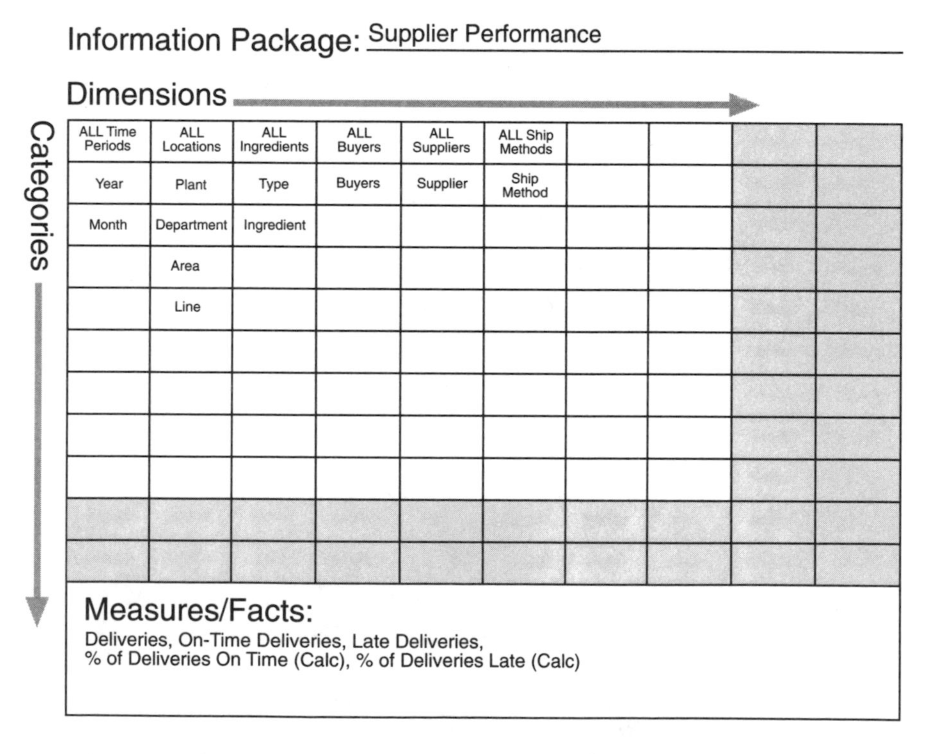

Figure A.29: *Manufacturing and supplier performance information package diagram*

This information package model helps users answer questions such as those that follow.

- Who are the most reliable suppliers? Who are the least reliable suppliers?
- Which products are at greater risk due to supplier reliability?
- Which plants have the worst supplier reliability? Which buyers were associated with these deals? Which suppliers?
- Which shipment methods are the most reliable? The least reliable?
- Is reliability improving or declining?
- Which raw materials are the least reliable? Most reliable?

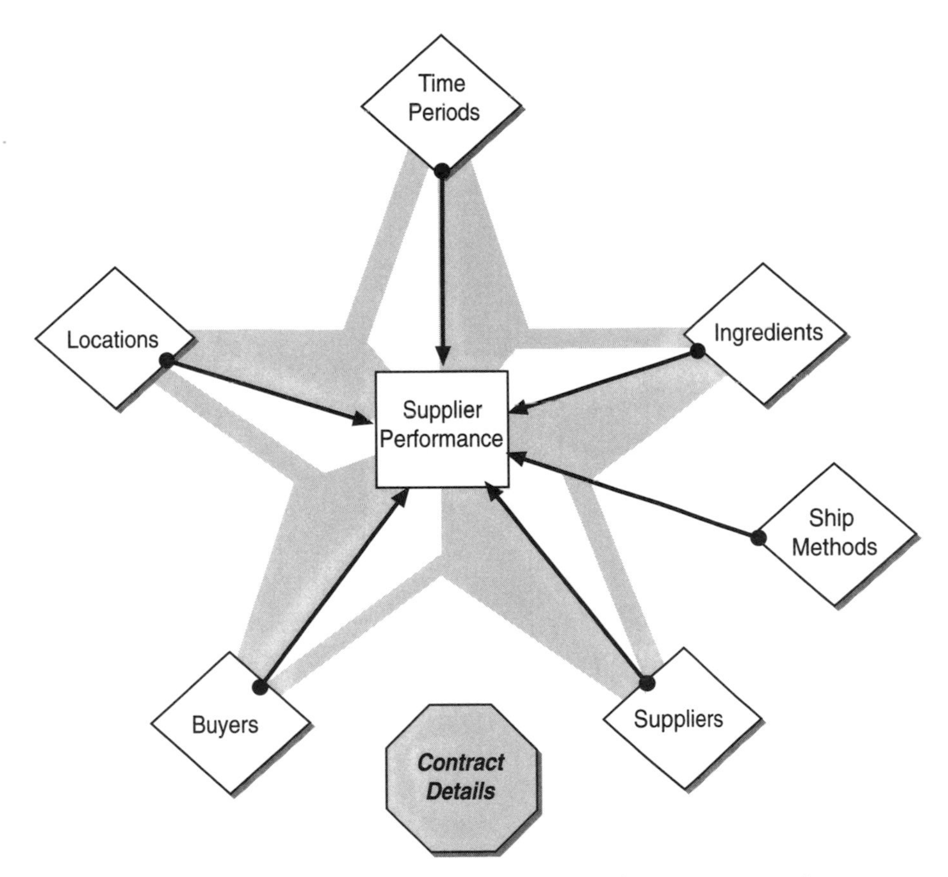

Figure A.30: *Manufacturing and supplier performance star schema*

Product Management: Market Analysis

Market analysis assists companies in better understanding the buying public. This data traditionally is obtained from external sources. However, some larger companies have their own market research teams that, through various techniques, gather market data to assist the marketing departments and product management departments in understanding who and what can be sold. This information model is primarily a factless model, meaning there is no raw data other than the ability to count the dimensions or data in the category detail entity. That is, there are no dollars, pounds, units, and so forth. Therefore, users of this system can slice and dice the information cube along certain demographic boundaries to understand what the buying public looks like and how that public has changed over time. However, these queries will be performed off an entity that is structured more like a category detail entity than a measure entity—hence a factless model. The information package diagram for this data mart is presented in Figure A.31. The associated star schema is presented in Figure A.32.

Information Package: Market Analysis

Dimensions →

Categories ↓

ALL Time Periods	ALL Geography's	ALL Sexes	ALL Ages	ALL Incomes	ALL Children	ALL Marital Status	ALL Home
Years	Geographic Locations	Sex	Age Range	Income Range	Number of Children	Marital Status	Own/ Rent
Quarterly							

Measures/Facts:

Number of ... (Count)

Figure A.31: *Product management and market analysis information package diagram*

This information package assists its users in answering questions such as the following.

- What is the average income range of the known marketplace?
- Is income affected by age? By number of children? By marital status? By home ownership?
- Do certain geographical areas attract married couples? Widowers? Single people?
- For targeted geographic locations, what does the average person look like? What sex is this person? In what income range is this person? Does this person own a home or rent an apartment? Do this person have children? How many?

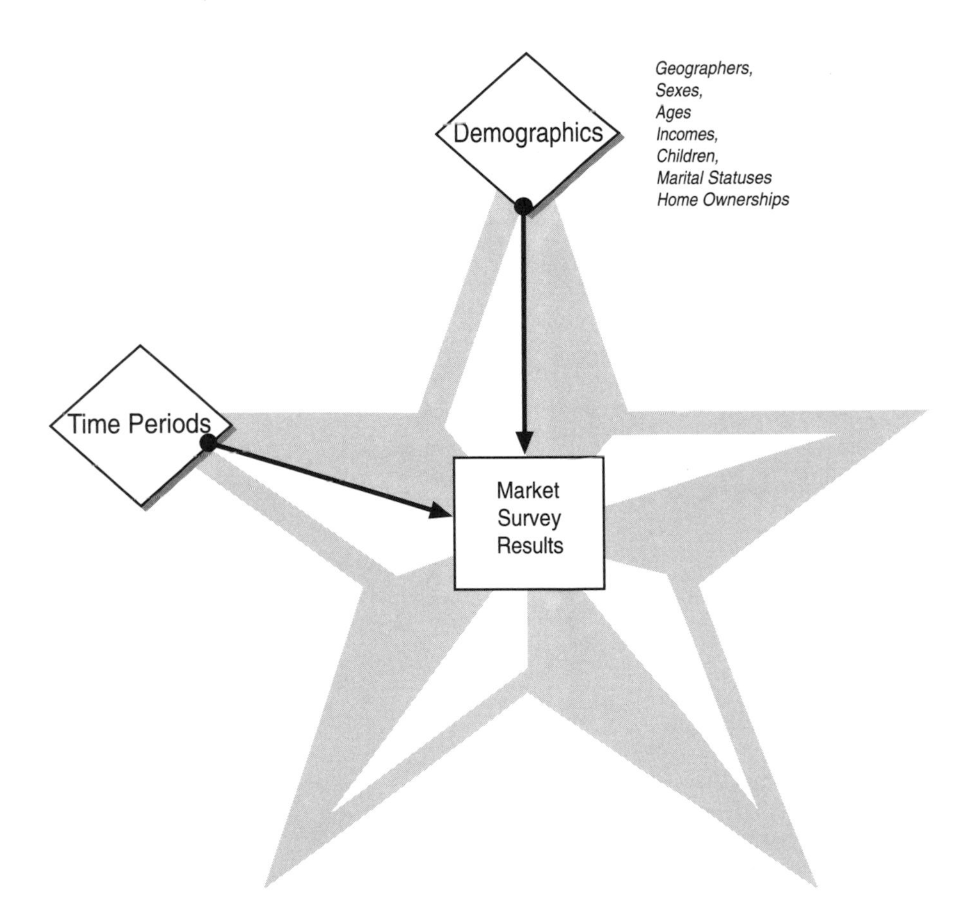

Figure A.32: *Product management and market analysis star schema*

Sales: Customer Demographic Analysis

Customer demographics are similar to market analysis demographics except that this information represents the constituency to which the company has successfully marketed and sold. This is similar to the supply versus demand concepts that were discussed with on-time shipments and on-time deliveries. The market analysis example showed the available population to which can be sold, while this information package shows the market to which have successfully sold and will continue to sell. This is a more focused set of data that allows marketing and sales personnel to build programs and promotions to effectively increase the recurring revenue stream. Again, this is a data source that is only targeted at counting those who match a set of navigational filters (counts). The information package diagram for this data mart is presented in Figure A.33. The associated star schema is presented in Figure A.34.

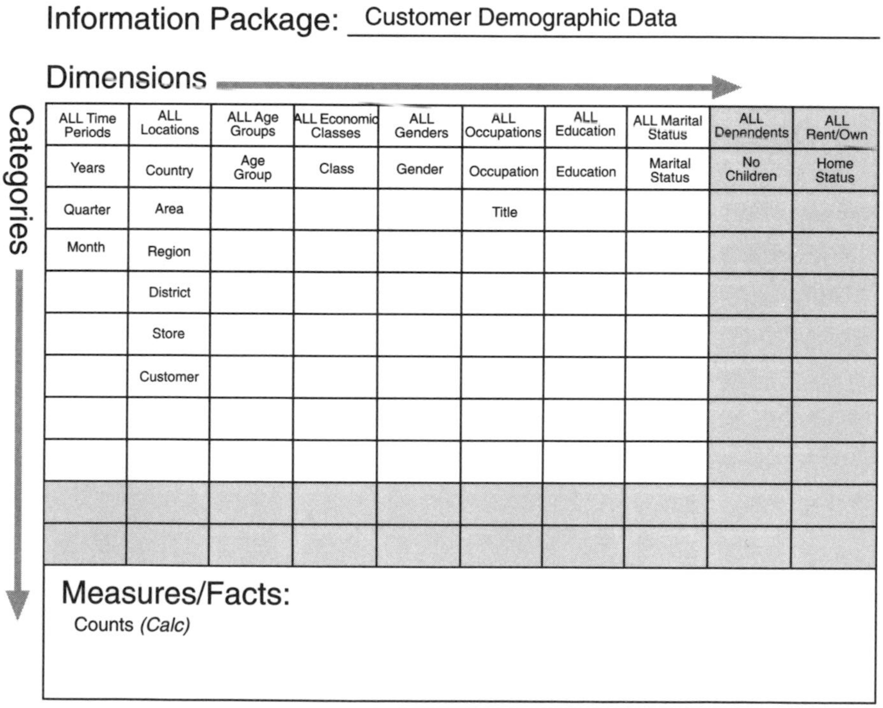

Information Package: Customer Demographic Data

Dimensions →

Categories ↓

ALL Time Periods	ALL Locations	ALL Age Groups	ALL Economic Classes	ALL Genders	ALL Occupations	ALL Education	ALL Marital Status	ALL Dependents	ALL Rent/Own
Years	Country	Age Group	Class	Gender	Occupation	Education	Marital Status	No Children	Home Status
Quarter	Area				Title				
Month	Region								
	District								
	Store								
	Customer								

Measures/Facts:
Counts *(Calc)*

Figure A.33: *Sales and customer demographic analysis information package diagram*

This information package model assists users in answering questions such as the following.

- Which market segments have been most receptive to sales of a company's products in the past? Which have been least receptive?
- Rank the top 10 markets last year and compare with previous years. Is the trend changing? If so, how?
- Which market segments are growing? Shrinking?

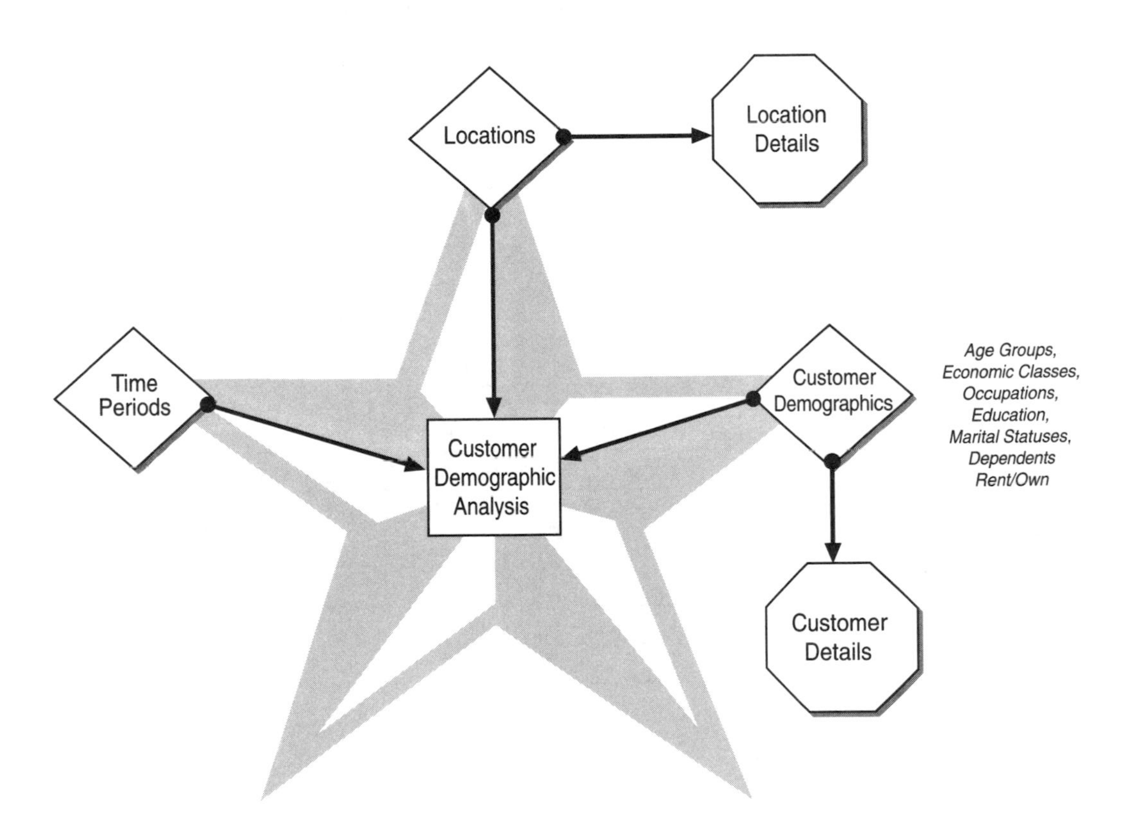

Figure A.34: *Sales and customer demographic analysis star schema*

Sales: Pipeline Management Analysis

Sales pipelines are forecasting tools used by sales organizations to assist in understanding what is coming down the pipeline and when. This information package assists sales personnel and management in better understanding where the revenue stream stands. The data is characterized by sales channel, available product mix, sales territories (accounts), status of an account (open, closed, and so forth), probability of the deal closing (typically a percentage), phase in the pipeline (qualified, developed, committed, or other), and the source of the lead (such as an ad in *XYZ Magazine* in the December issue). The information package diagram for this data mart is presented in Figure A.35. The associated star schema is presented in Figure A.36. Additional detail information are required in the star schema to support the deal details. This likely will involve many physical entities built into the physical database model.

NOTE: This information package could be enhanced by linking deal information as shown in the star schema.

Information Package: Sales Pipeline Analysis

Dimensions →

Categories ↓

ALL Time Periods	ALL Sales Reps	ALL Products	ALL Accounts	ALL Account Status	ALL Probability of Sale	ALL Pipeline Phase	ALL Lead Source
Years	Channel	Product	State	Status	Probability	Phase	Group
Quarter	Area	Manufacturer	City				Source
Month	Region	Platform	Account				
	District						
	Branch						
	Sales Rep						

Measures/Facts:
$ Value

Figure A.35: *Sales and pipeline management analysis information package diagram*

This information package helps users answer questions such as those that follow.

- What does the revenue stream appear to be over time?
- Where is the pipeline weak? Strong?
- What are our best sources for leads? Has the trend changed over the years?
- What product mix currently comprises the closable business? What products are excluded?

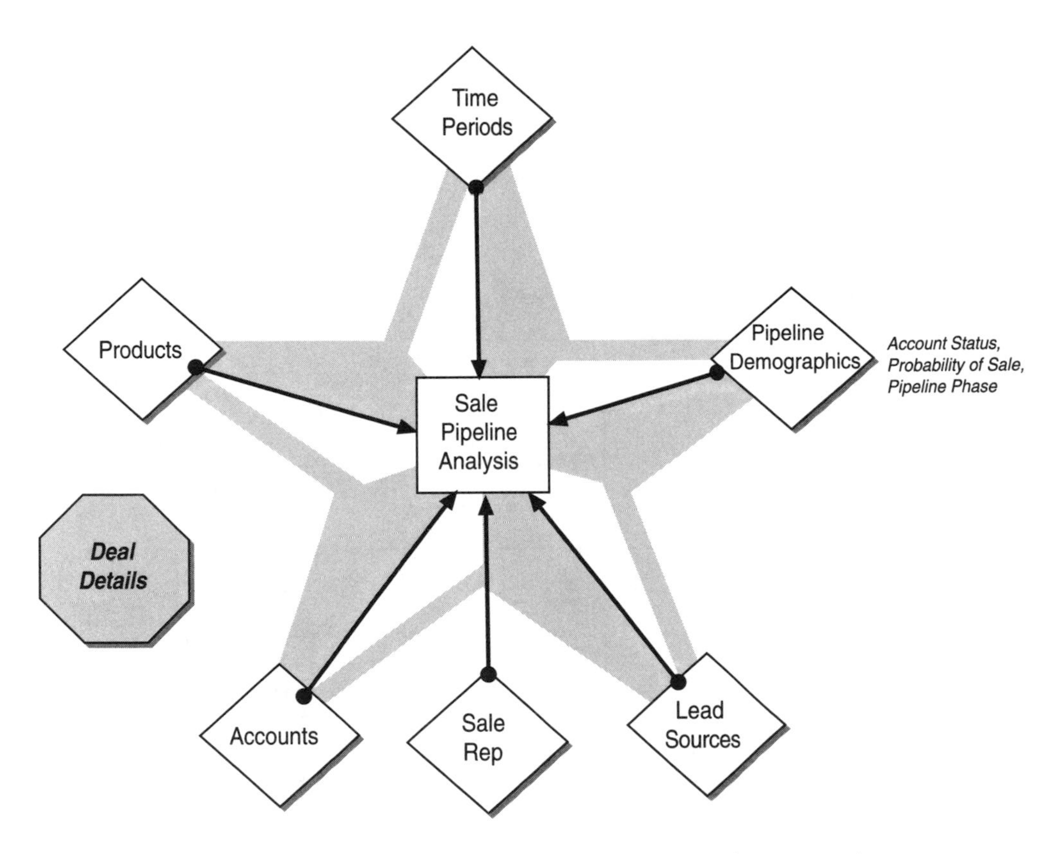

Figure A.36: *Sales and pipeline management analysis star schema*

Sales: Sales Analysis

Sales analysis in general is an important activity no matter what your business is as this represents the lifeline of a company. Therefore, sales analysis is a common information package and often one of the first subject-oriented data warehouses deployed. This is an example of a sales analysis information package focused on store sales for products broken down by consumer demographics. The comparative measures here include: what the company expects (budgeted revenue); what the store expects (forecasted revenue); and what really happened (actual revenue). This example offers three very different looks at the same thing, revenue or sales dollars. The information package diagram for this data mart is presented in Figure A.37. The associated star schema is presented in Figure A.38.

Information Package: Sales Analysis

Dimensions

Categories

ALL Time Periods	ALL Locations	ALL Products	ALL Age Groups	ALL Economic Classes	ALL Genders
Years	Country	Classification	Age Group	Class	Gender
Quarter	Area	Group			
Month	Region	Product			
	District				
	Store				

Measures/Facts:

Forecast Sales, Budget Sales, Actual Sales, Forecast Variance (*Calc*), Budget Variance (*Calc*)

Figure A.37: *Sales analysis information package diagram*

This information package assists users in answering questions such as those that follow.

- Which country is closest to achieving its budgeted sales? Which area? Which region? Which district?
- What are the top stores that are overachieving their budgets? Their forecasts?
- What are the top stores that are underachieving their budgets? Their forecasts?
- For those stores that are underachieving, is this their history or just a bad year? For those overachieving, is this their history or a good year?
- Are certain market segments behind budget? Is this a universal trend or limited to product and geography mix?
- Which products are overachieving? Underachieving?
- Do certain products sell better during specific months? Quarters?

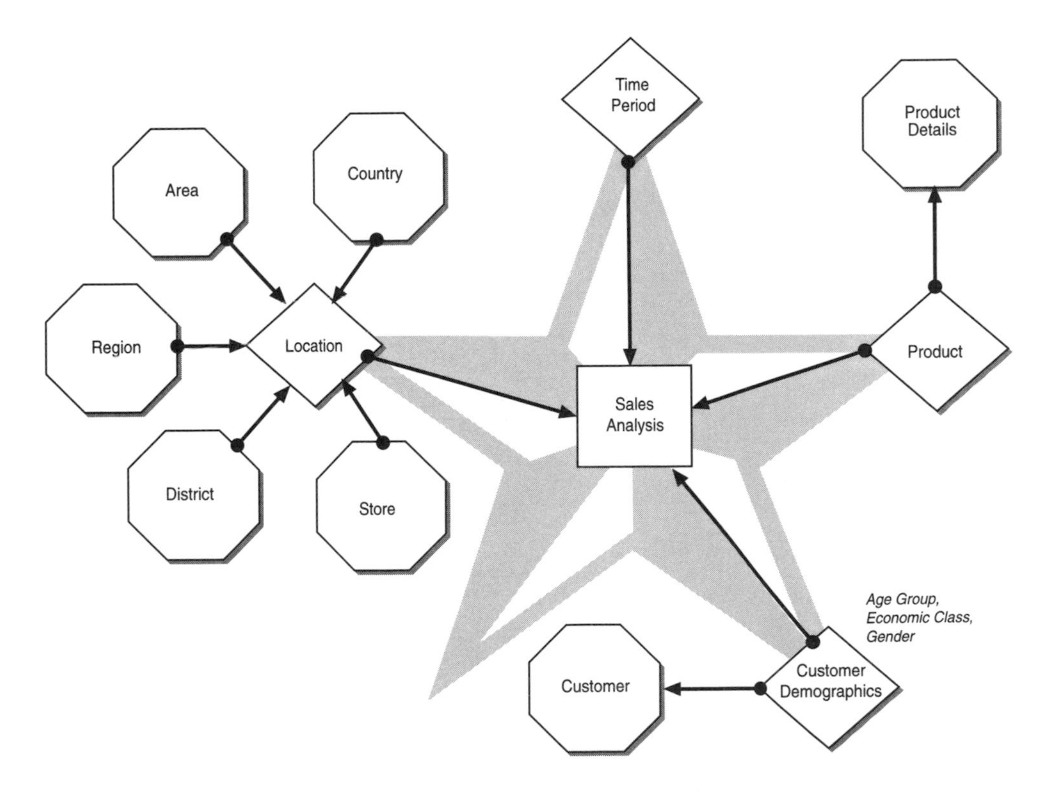

Figure A.38: *Sales analysis star schema*

Sales: Software Product Sales Analysis

This is another information package that focuses on sales analysis. Based on the importance of sales to the key metrics in a company, we want to provide you with several examples of how information packages could change based on the marketplace. Here, we look at software product sales. The important dimensions include: ever-present time, location, and product as well as channels, types of sales (renewal license, new license, consulting, education, and so forth), and platform (Intel—Windows; Hewlett Packard—UNIX, and so forth). This information package is similar to the other sales analysis packages, but with a few additional dimensions or modifications to the standard dimensions. The information package diagram for this data mart is presented in Figure A.39. The associated star schema is presented in Figure A.40.

Information Package: Software Product Sales Analysis

Dimensions →

Categories ↓

ALL Time Periods	ALL Locations	ALL Channels	ALL Sales Types	ALL Platforms	ALL Products				
Year	Country	Channel	Sales Type	Machine Type	Product Family				
Quarter	Area		Sub Type	Sub Type	Product				
Month	Region								
	District								

Measures/Facts:

Revenue

Figure A.39: *Software product sales analysis information package diagram*

This information package allows its users to answer questions such as those that follow.

- What products are currently the best sellers? Worst sellers?
- To which platforms are we selling better? Selling worse?
- Which district, region, area, or country is producing the most revenue?
- What are the trends within channels? Is indirect working better than direct?
- What is the breakdown of all revenue by type of sales? How does this compare historically? What are the trends?

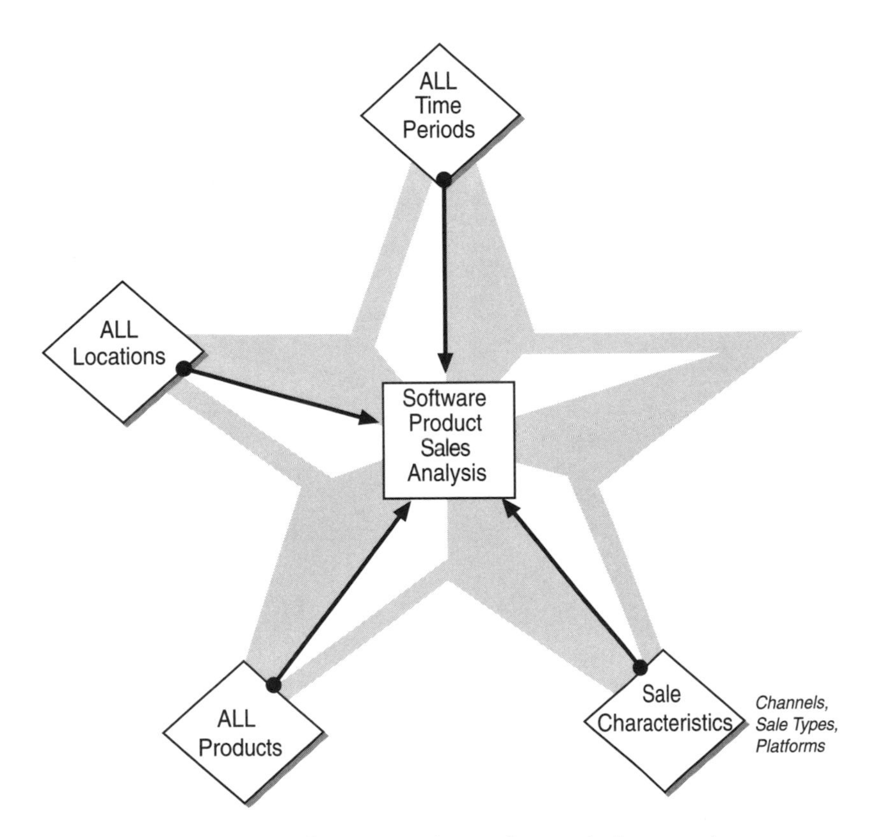

Figure A.40: *Software product sales analysis star schema*

Sales: Telecommunication Product Sales Analysis

Another example of sales analysis is shown here for telecommunications industry product sales. The important dimensions include: the ever-present time, location (customer), and product (which appears in the information package under the category of Project within the Customer dimension) as well as business units, types of sales (win-back, new business, and so forth), pipeline information, and confidence rating. This information package is similar to the other sales analysis packages, but with a few additional dimensions or modifications to the standard dimensions. The information package diagram for this data mart is presented in Figure A.41. The associated star schema is presented in Figure A.42.

Information Package: Telecommunication Product Sales Analysis

Dimensions →

Categories ↓

ALL Time Periods	ALL Customers	ALL Business Unit	ALL Sales Types	ALL Sales Status	ALL Confidence
Year	Region	SBU	Sales Type	Pipeline Location	Confidence of Sale
Quarter	Branch	Group		Status	
Month	Sales Area				
	Account				
	Project				

Measures/Facts:

This Month Revenue, Next Month Revenue, Next Year Revenue

Figure A.41: *Telecommunication product sales analysis information package diagram*

This information package allows users to answer questions such as those listed here.

- How much business have they won back from the competition?
- How does the win-back business trend compare with new business?
- Are we cannibalizing our own business? Has voice mail eliminated waiting calls?
- How strong is the current pipeline? How does that compare with previous years?
- Which customers have the most pipeline activity?
- Which branches have the best balance in revenue between this month and next? This year and next?

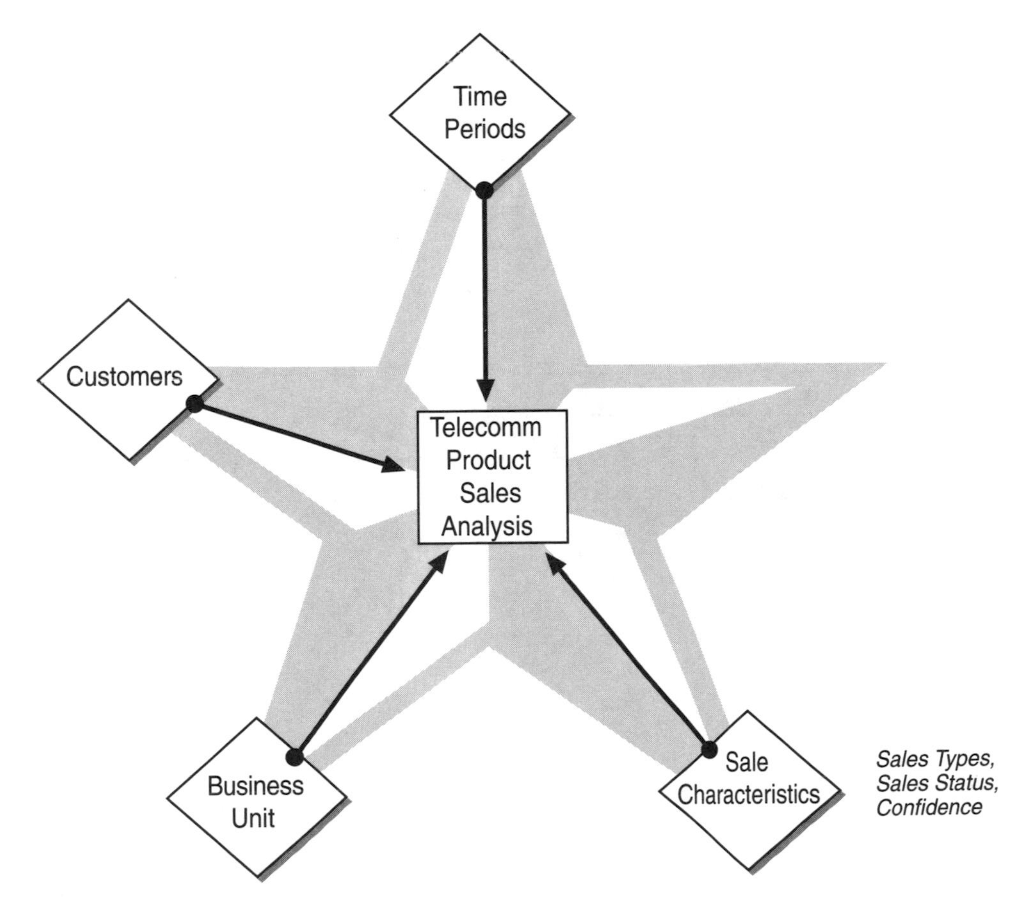

Figure A.42: *Telecommunication product sales analysis star schema*

Service Center: Call Analysis

Managing a service center is a critical component to the overall success of many businesses. After all, your employees will be working with your customers—your installation base—who we hope will provide referrals for new business. Your installation base comprises the people who can convince skeptical prospects that your company is a great place to do business. The information package diagram for this data mart is presented in Figure A.43. The associated star schema is presented in Figure A.44.

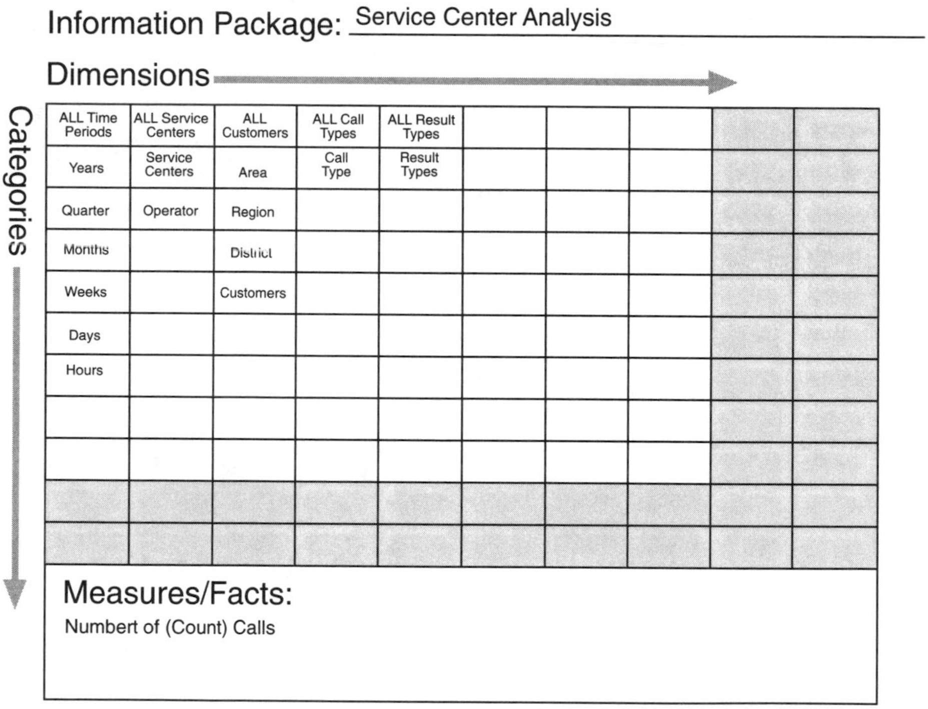

Information Package: Service Center Analysis

Dimensions

Categories

ALL Time Periods	ALL Service Centers	ALL Customers	ALL Call Types	ALL Result Types
Years	Service Centers	Area	Call Type	Result Types
Quarter	Operator	Region		
Months		District		
Weeks		Customers		
Days				
Hours				

Measures/Facts:

Numbert of (Count) Calls

Figure A.43: *Service center and call analysis information package diagram*

To analyze how users are doing with their customers, the following might be some of the questions requiring answers.

- Who is calling?
- How frequently are they calling?
- About what are they calling?
- What transpires as a result of the call?
- What are the busiest times for calls?
- Who typically responds best to each type of call?

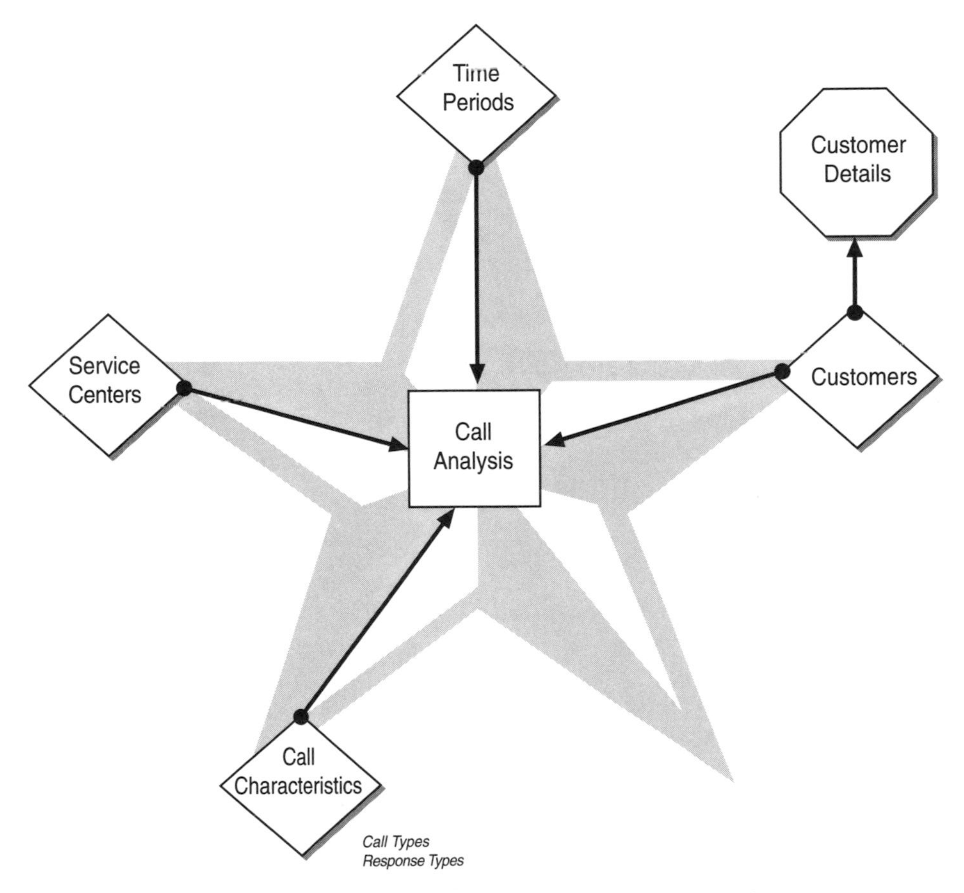

Figure A.44: *Service center and call analysis star schema*

Summary

This appendix will assist you in defining your own information packages. While the content of your information package may be different, these examples give you working models to assist in better implementing the information packaging methodology for your data warehouse project. These example information packages provide you with a good foundation for modeling your business requirements.

Appendix B
A Sample Subject-Oriented Data Warehouse

This appendix provides you with a complete subject-oriented data warehouse sample. The model is based on a fictitious consulting services company that desires to analyze its consultant utilization. Many goals have been established for the company, but for the business unit that will utilize this subject-oriented data warehouse, the four top goals are listed here in order.

1. Increase consultant utilization to 70 percent
2. Increase the general consulting business to 20 percent of the overall business
3. Increase the Dayton office contribution to 35 percent of the overall unit's business
4. Increase the average rate per hour for each consultant to $115/hour

The users of this subject-oriented data warehouse have requested the ability to monitor these goals, and more specifically to be able to analyze the following data.

- The billable status of each consultant
- The factors that could impact the billable nature of consultants, namely their industry certifications and the roles that they are able to fill

- The service packages that are offered as promotions
- Their customer projects by task

The consulting services company wants to be able to analyze this data over time down to the individual day on which a billing occurs. The key measurements are the rate at which the consultant bills and the hours of service provided.

Architecture

The architecture on which this data warehouse is implemented includes the following, as illustrated by Figure B.1.

- A layer to insulate the transformation and loading processes from operational data stores. This layer is known as the *virtual enterprise database*, and allows the development staff to easily utilize the native facilities in Sybase Transact-SQL to access legacy data, stage the data into a temporary working area of the data warehouse, convert and transform the data, and load the data into the data warehouse. This virtual environment supports various legacy data stores including, but not limited to Oracle, Informix, DB2, IMS, VSAM, and RDB.
- The actual data warehouse, which is implemented on Sybase SQL Server. Depending on the load rates seen initially from user access, Sybase IQ may also be implemented to provide an optimal indexing strategy and to avoid costly query activity such as large table scans.
- A data access layer, managed by Sybase Open Client, the native (and the recommended) connectivity component for Sybase SQL Server.
- A data warehouse tool suite composed of the Cognos end user tools of PowerPlay, Impromptu, and Portfolio.
- Other tools not listed here are Sybase system management facilities, including SQL Server Manager, SQL Server Monitor, and Backup Server.

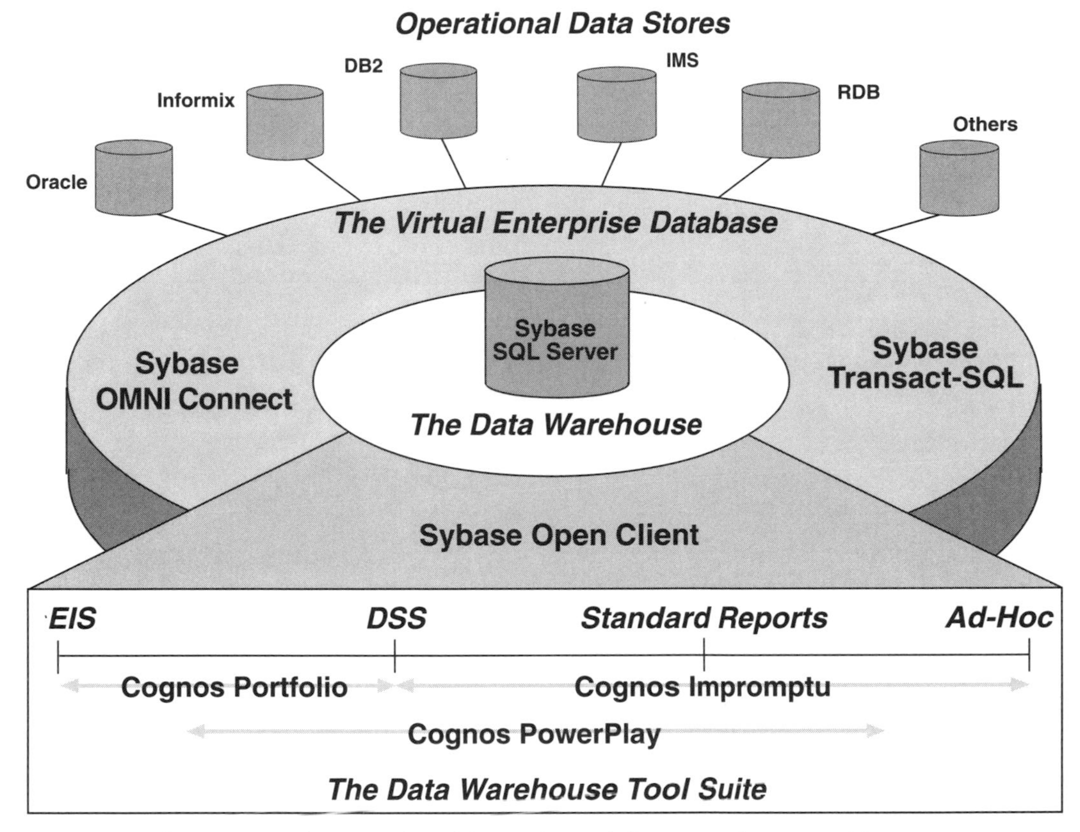

Figure B.1: *The sample subject-oriented data warehouse architecture*

Data Architecture

A data architecture contains many components. To recap, the process of defining a data architecture follows an information packaging refinement technique that produces an information package diagram, a star schema, then physical database structures that will house the information package data. We look at each of these concepts individually in the next three sections.

Information Package Diagram

An information package diagram builds a relevant information package based on user requirements—the goals and objectives discovered during interview sessions. The business entity in our example requests that the subject-oriented data warehouse track the following data—entities that are presented in the information package shown in Figure B.2.

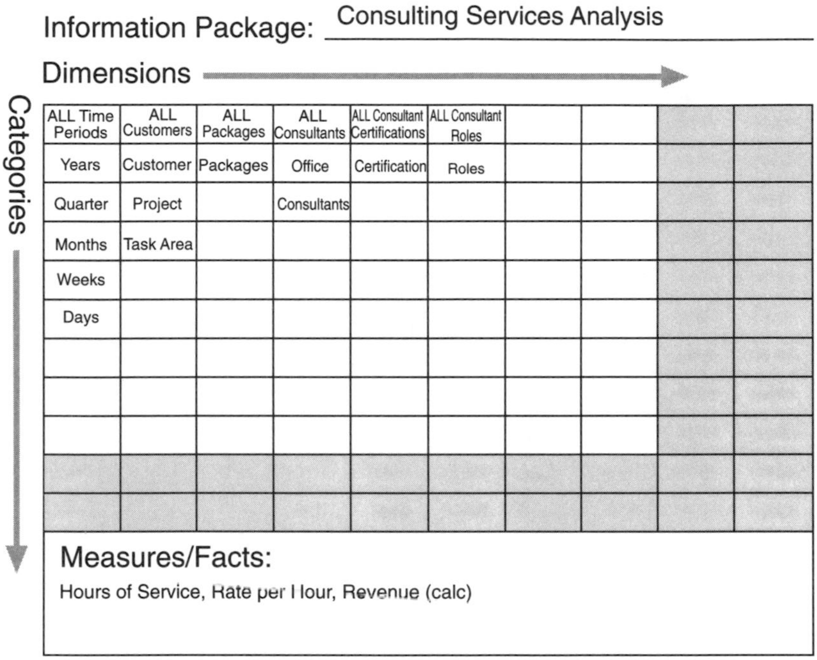

Information Package: Consulting Services Analysis

Dimensions →

Categories ↓

ALL Time Periods	ALL Customers	ALL Packages	ALL Consultants	ALL Consultant Certifications	ALL Consultant Roles				
Years	Customer	Packages	Office	Certification	Roles				
Quarter	Project		Consultants						
Months	Task Area								
Weeks									
Days									

Measures/Facts:

Hours of Service, Rate per Hour, Revenue (calc)

Figure B.2: *Information package diagram for the example data mart*

The information package in Figure B.2 provides data associated with the following user requirements.

- **Time periods** For the last two years, track the billable days and allow for aggregations at weekly, monthly, quarterly, and yearly levels.
- **Customers** For each customer project, track the individual task assignments billed to the customer and allow for aggregates by task, project, and customer.
- **Packages** Track billable services for all engagements based on each promotional software consulting package.
- **Consultants** Track all billable resources and consultants by their office, allowing the system to aggregate data based on consultant, office, or everyone.
- **Certifications** Track many industry standard certifications and determine if there is an impact on the billable rate and percent utilization based on a consultant's certifications. Therefore, this is a demographic of the consultant.
- **Roles** When performing a service for a customer, the consultant is asked to perform a role. Therefore, this too is a demographic of the consulting work.

- **Measures** Though this data may contain many measures, the two that have been requested are hours of service and rate per hour. These metrics allow users to determine if they are attaining the business' goals and objectives—and if so, how.

Star Schema

The information package diagram is then refined, beginning the process of defining data entities. The star schema is the preferred, if not required method for the conceptual data model. The information package diagram provides the requirements for the star schema and yields three primary entity types, which are listed next.

- **Measure entities** This is the transaction-oriented data that is placed in the center of the star schema. This entity contains the keys or pointers into the data measures, or facts. Within the star schema, we use a rectangle to represent this table. When employees view the star schema, they know that all rectangles are measure entities, and therefore understand the entities' purposes and common attributes.
- **Dimension entities** Dimension entities are the paths into the facts. These entities are highly denormalized data structures that assist the front-end development team build selectors, or filters, to narrow the data within the large measure entities. These entities also help the user navigate the subject-oriented data warehouse and measurement data. When these entities are placed in the star schema, they are represented as diamonds, the traditional filter flowcharting symbol. This graphic represents the dimension entities, because its primary purpose is to filter the data within the measure entity to which it points. This graphic also assists viewers of the star schema in understanding the purposes and common attributes of the defined entities.
- **Category detail entities** Additional support data for the measure entities are stored within a category detail entity. This is typically data to complete the discover process. Users typically enter the subject-oriented data warehouse through the dimension entities, filtering the measurement data to find a business trend and then connect back to the category detail data upon completing their discovering within the measurement data. Because this is typically the last stop to completion, a stop sign symbol is used to describe these entities in the star schema model. Like the other entities, this symbol tells reader of the star schema the common attributes and functionality available by the objects it represents.

To define a star schema, we further analyze the information package diagram cell by cell. The entire information package diagram with its lowest level categories becomes the measure entity. Each column potentially becomes a dimension entity. And each cell has the potential to become a category detail entity. For this subject-oriented data warehouse, the star schema is defined by seven entities, as shown in Figure B.3. These entities include a utilization measure entity, time period dimension entity, customer dimension entity, package dimension entity, consultant dimension entity, consultant demographic dimension entity, customer category detail entity, and consultant category detail entity.

Physical Database

The final refinement of a data architecture is the physical data structures, the entities, and their relationships, which will be implemented in the database management system. The information package diagram was refined into a star schema, and the star schema will be placed into physical database structures. This physical definition of a subject-oriented data warehouse will be merged into an overall data warehouse in which data entities will be reused among information packages. Figure B.4 presents the first cut of our physical data structures represented in an entity relationship diagram (ERD).

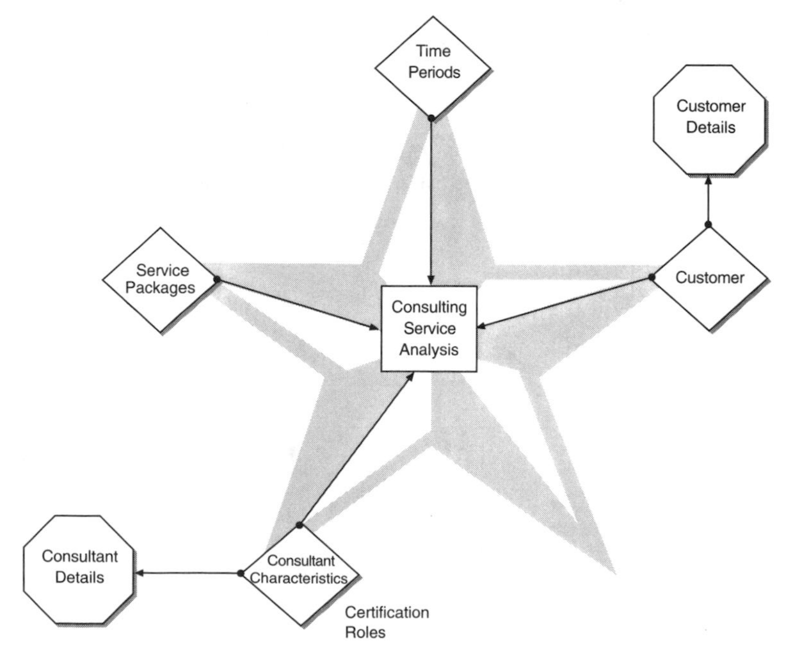

Figure B.3: *Star schema design for the example data mart*

Application Architecture

The data architecture, discussed in the previous section, properly places data in a data mart. The application architecture provides a visualization capability to the users of the data warehouse. An application architecture is typically composed of a suite of user tools, predefined applications, and predefined reports. For this example, we have chosen Cognos user tools—Portfolio, PowerPlay, and Impromptu—which are discussed in the following sections.

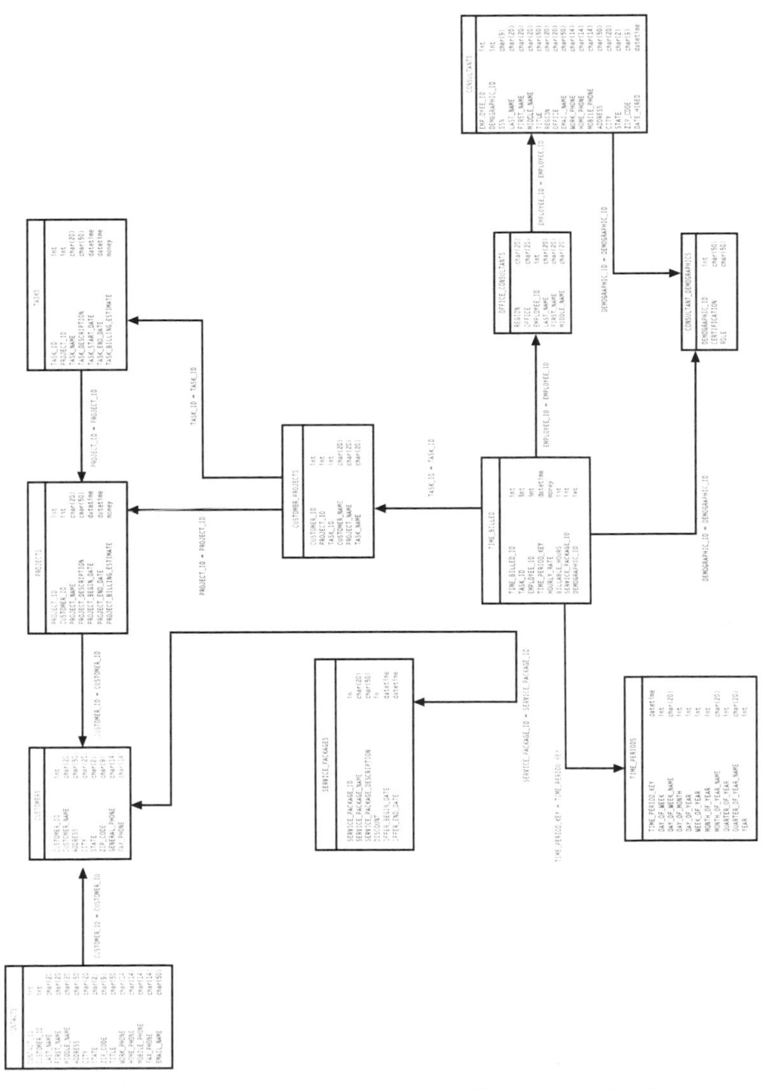

Figure B.4: *Entity relationship diagram of the example data mart*

Cognos Portfolio

Cognos Portfolio offers an excellent packaging tool for distributing your data warehouse information to executives and other users alike. This tool allows reports and other OLE-compliant documents to be placed in one central briefing book, or portfolio, to be distributed as if they were standard reports. However, the objects in the briefing book are live! This means that users can double click any of the reports to immediately launch PowerPlay or whatever tool created the package. This way, users can further analyze the data, while the corporation can project a standard message with the distribution. The following example shows the utilization reports, emphasizing the four annual goals for this operational unit, which were listed at the beginning of this appendix.

Figure B.5 presents the data related to highest-priority goal, achieving a 70 percent utilization rate for all consultants. This is the first report presented in the Cognos Portfolio application that has been built to focus on the company goals. This report reminds the user of the goal and provides adequate data to allow the user to understand whether the goal is being achieved. Additional information is also provided that further explains the impact of the utilization on the overall business, namely the rate at which the consultants are billing and the revenue they have earned the company.

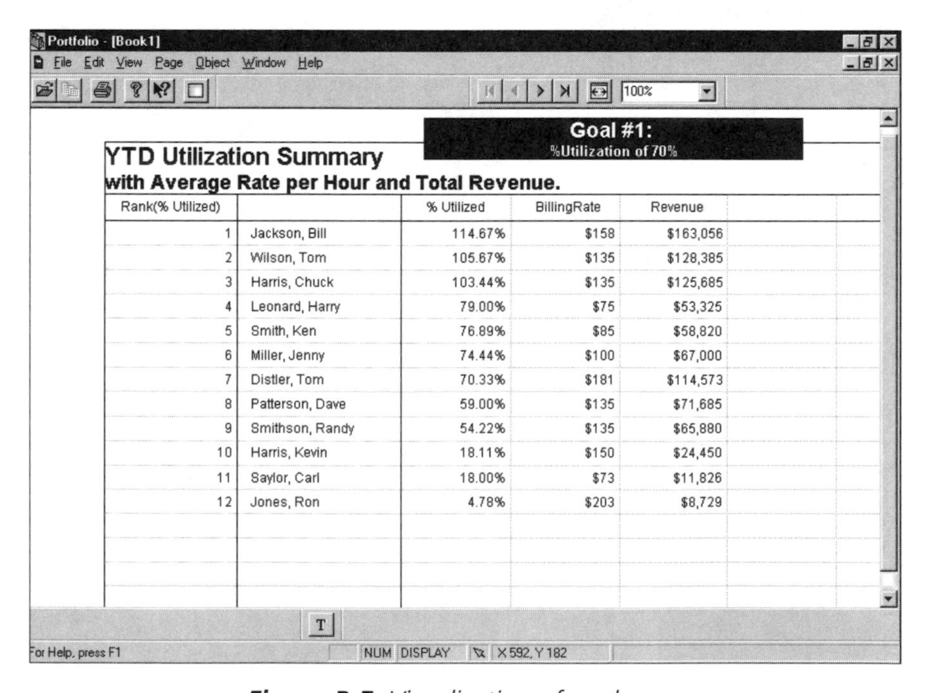

Rank(% Utilized)		% Utilized	BillingRate	Revenue
1	Jackson, Bill	114.67%	$158	$163,056
2	Wilson, Tom	105.67%	$135	$128,385
3	Harris, Chuck	103.44%	$135	$125,685
4	Leonard, Harry	79.00%	$75	$53,325
5	Smith, Ken	76.89%	$85	$58,820
6	Miller, Jenny	74.44%	$100	$67,000
7	Distler, Tom	70.33%	$181	$114,573
8	Patterson, Dave	59.00%	$135	$71,685
9	Smithson, Randy	54.22%	$135	$65,880
10	Harris, Kevin	18.11%	$150	$24,450
11	Saylor, Carl	18.00%	$73	$11,826
12	Jones, Ron	4.78%	$203	$8,729

Figure B.5: *Visualization of goal one*

Figure B.6 presents goals two and three side-by-side within Cognos Portfolio. A pie chart is used to better visualize the data associated with these goals. In Figure B.5, the numbers were important to provide additional information. Here in Figure B.6, the pie chart allows users of the system to visualize the percentage breakdowns as a piece of the overall business. As in the previous report, this report presents the relevant data as well as the goals that are desired by the business—increasing general consulting to 20 percent of the overall business and increasing the Dayton operations to 35 percent of the overall business.

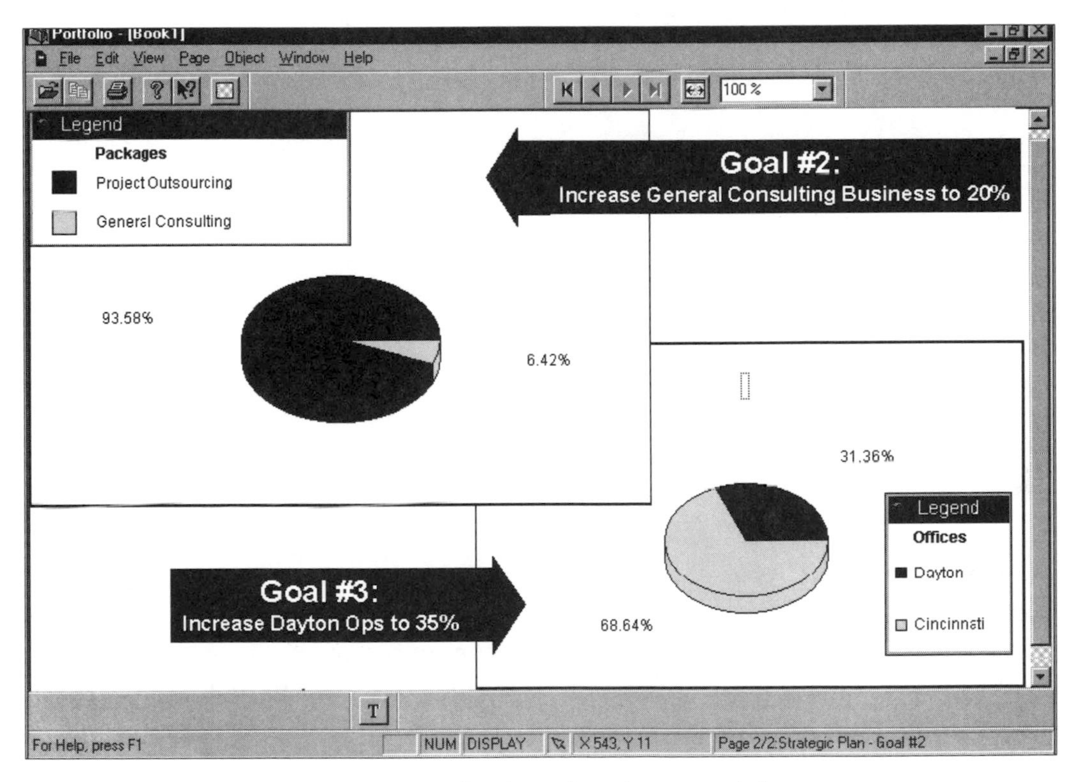

Figure B.6: *Visualization of goals two and three*

Figure B.7 provides detail data associated with the fourth goal, which is to develop an average billable rate of $115/hour. As in Figure B.6, Figure B.7 presents two reports in a single slide. These reports are complementary and provide users with relevant information to determine if the company is achieving the fourth goal.

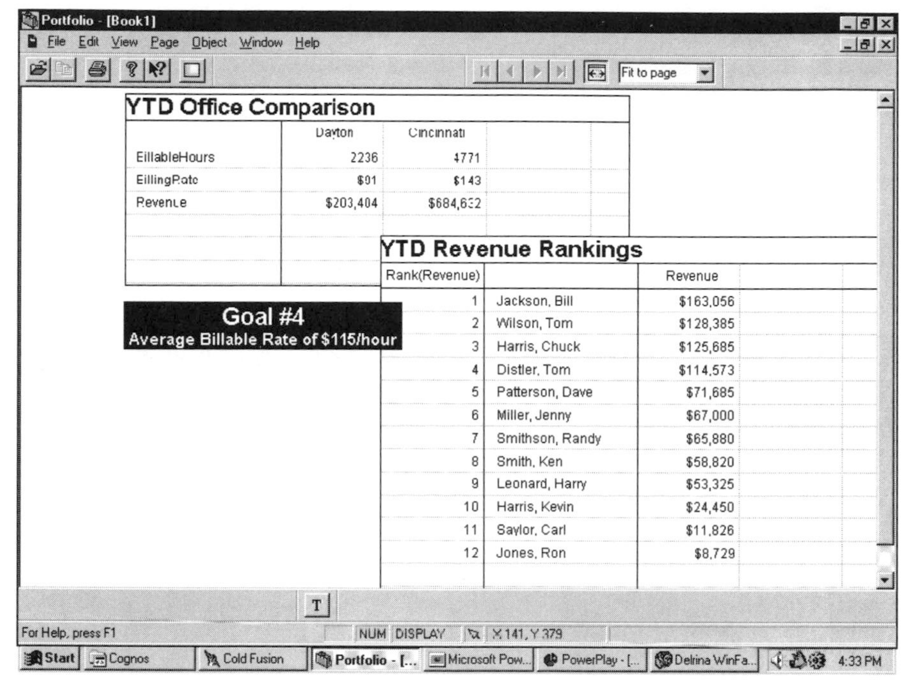

Figure B.7: *Visualization of goal four*

Cognos PowerPlay

Cognos PowerPlay offers users an ability to easily wander through their information package, or data cube. The focus of this tool is on the users' ability to explore, analyze, and interpret business information. Therefore, the interface places them directly in the data, not in a query-oriented tool. As you will see in the following reports, users can twist and turn the cube's dimensions in a free-form way, allowing them to look at the data from many different angles. This massaging of the data includes drill down, drill up, and slice-and-dice capabilities. There is also a plethora of display formats, including but not limited to cross tab reports, bar charts, line charts, and pie charts.

In Figure B.8, we start with a report that filters the data as follows.

- **Time** The time period dimension, which includes data only for this year to date (YTD). This data is displayed in the columns and is summarized at the quarterly level.
- **Customer** The customer dimension to the Sales Force Automation Project and the major project tasks included within this project. This data is displayed in the rows.

- **Packages** All of the offered consulting packages.
- **Consultants** All of the offices and associated consultants.
- **Certifications** All of the available certifications.
- **Roles** All of the roles performed during the consulting work.
- **Measure** The time and roles display the number of billable hours within the filtered result set.

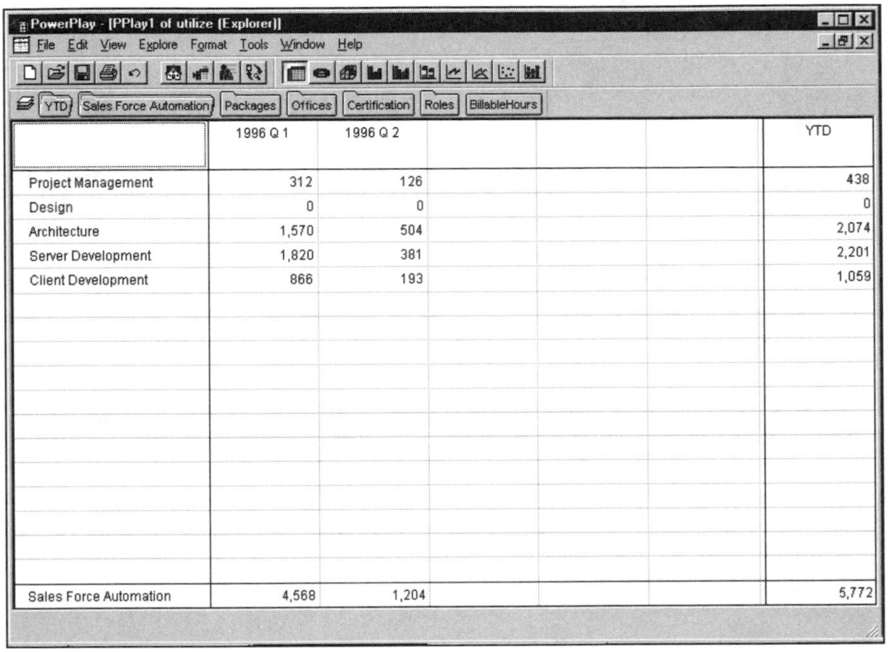

PowerPlay - [PPlay1 of utilize (Explorer)]

File Edit View Explore Format Tools Window Help

YTD | Sales Force Automation | Packages | Offices | Certification | Roles | BillableHours

	1996 Q 1	1996 Q 2	YTD
Project Management	312	126	438
Design	0	0	0
Architecture	1,570	504	2,074
Server Development	1,820	381	2,201
Client Development	866	193	1,059
Sales Force Automation	4,568	1,204	5,772

Figure B.8: *An ad hoc report formulated in Cognos' PowerPlay*

The categories can be easily selected through direct manipulation on screen or with the category selection dialog shown in Figure B.9.

The display for any report can also be easily modified to show either the numeric values as shown in Figure B.8 or the percent values of the row, column, or layer. This feature can significantly improve the readability of the information package. In Figure B.10, we see the quarterly percentage of billable hours by project task for the Sales Force Automation Project. This report presents the consulting utilization data filtered for the current year-to-date numbers for the Sales Force Automation Project by time period and project task.

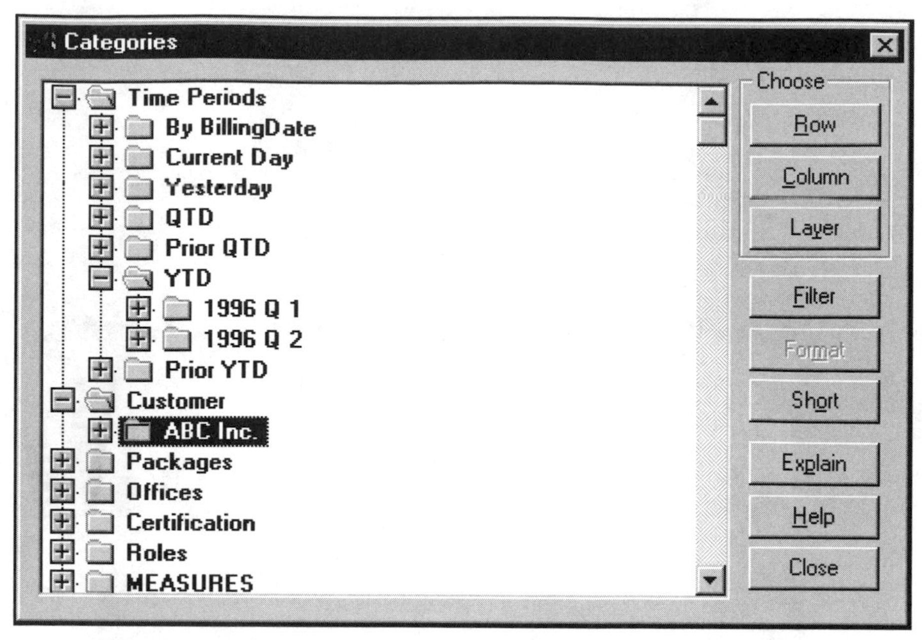

Figure B.9: *The Category Selection dialog of Cognos' PowerPlay*

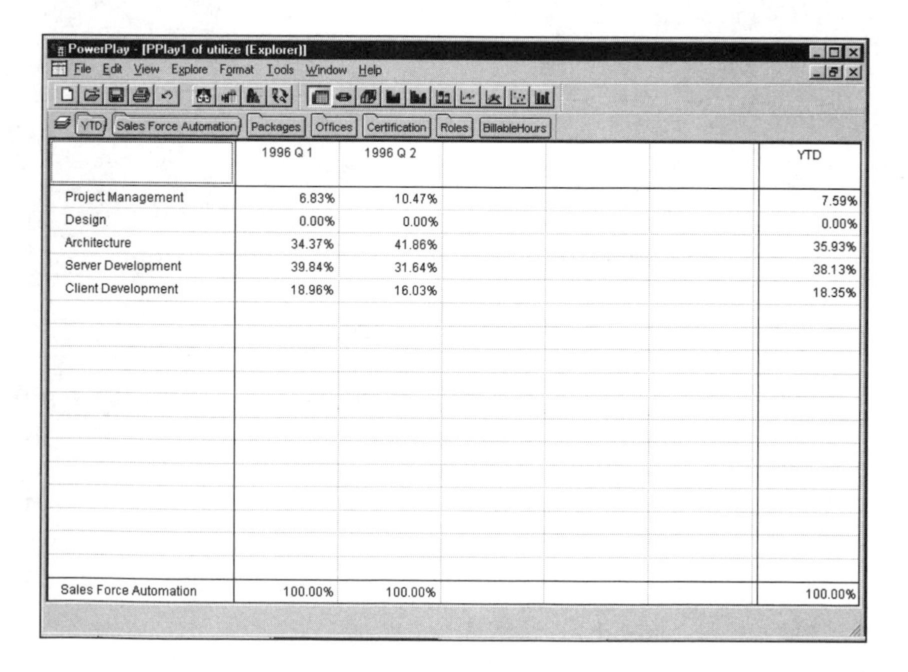

	1996 Q 1	1996 Q 2	YTD
Project Management	6.83%	10.47%	7.59%
Design	0.00%	0.00%	0.00%
Architecture	34.37%	41.86%	35.93%
Server Development	39.84%	31.64%	38.13%
Client Development	18.96%	16.03%	18.35%
Sales Force Automation	100.00%	100.00%	100.00%

Figure B.10: *A Cognos' PowerPlay report presenting filtered consulting utilization data*

Presentation styles can also be easily modified, again to assist users in better visualizing the data. It is often said that a picture is worth a thousand words, so your user interface should allow users to easily visualize data through more graphical presentation. Figure B.11 changes the view of data to display the following filtered result set.

- **Time** The year-to-date time filter is set for the graph
- **Customer** All customers are placed in the graph
- **Packages** All packages are placed in the graph
- **Consultants** All consultants are placed in the graph
- **Certifications** All certifications are placed in the graph
- **Roles** The roles are the slices of the pie graphs

Figure B.11 presents the visualization of the consulting utilization data in a pie chart in Cognos' PowerPlay. This information has been filtered to include only the current year's billable hours data for all customers, all service packages, all offices, all certifications, and all roles. The billable hours are broken down by roles in the pie chart so managers can visualize the role's utilization as a percentage of all billable hours.

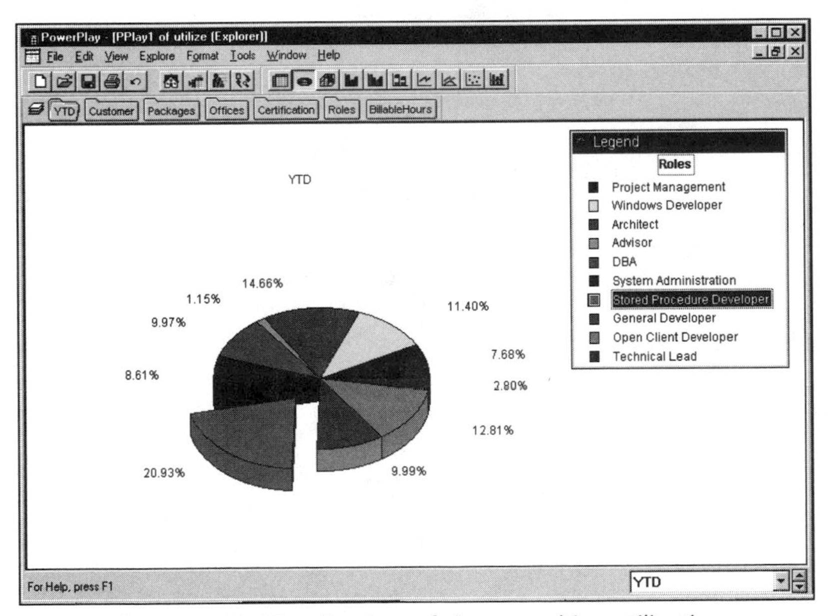

Figure B.11: *Visualization of the consulting utilization data in a pie chart in Cognos' PowerPlay*

We can now slice and dice this graph, exchanging the time dimension with the offices dimension. The report in Figure B.12 isolates on the YTD figures for the Cincinnati office by role. If you look closely, you see the business intelligence present itself. In the previous pie chart, notice that the largest slice is Stored Procedure Development. However, the Cincinnati office displays a different picture. Its largest slice is Architecture. However, within the Cincinnati office the different disciplines are relatively evenly distributed, much like the entire unit's graph.

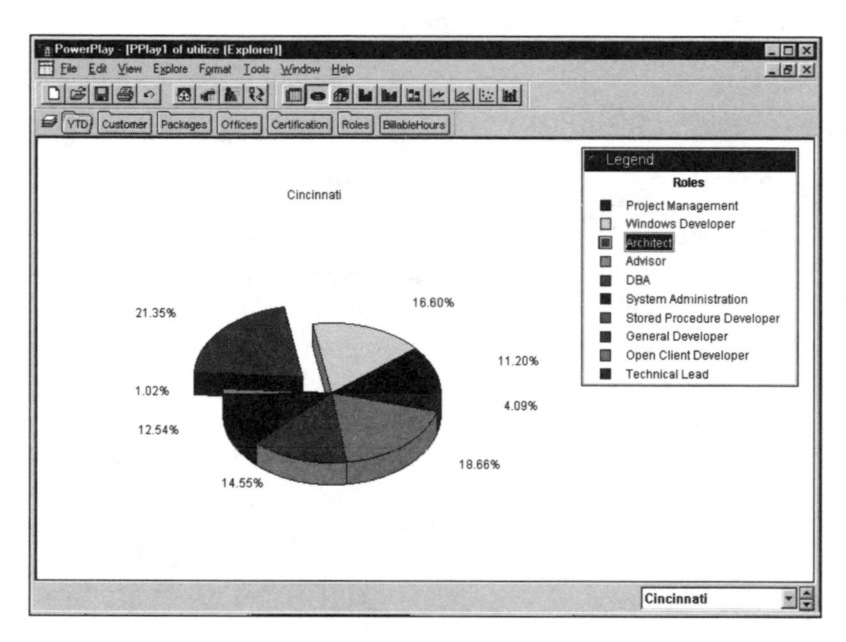

Figure B.12: *Report on consulting utilization data for the Cincinnati office isolated on the Architect role*

We can continue this line of investigation and further notice that the Dayton office, as depicted in Figure B.13, is heavily skewed toward a few disciplines—a clear indication of a start-up and something that should be closely monitored, as was shown in the unit's overall goals. Less roles have billable hours, and the Stored Procedure Development role dominates.

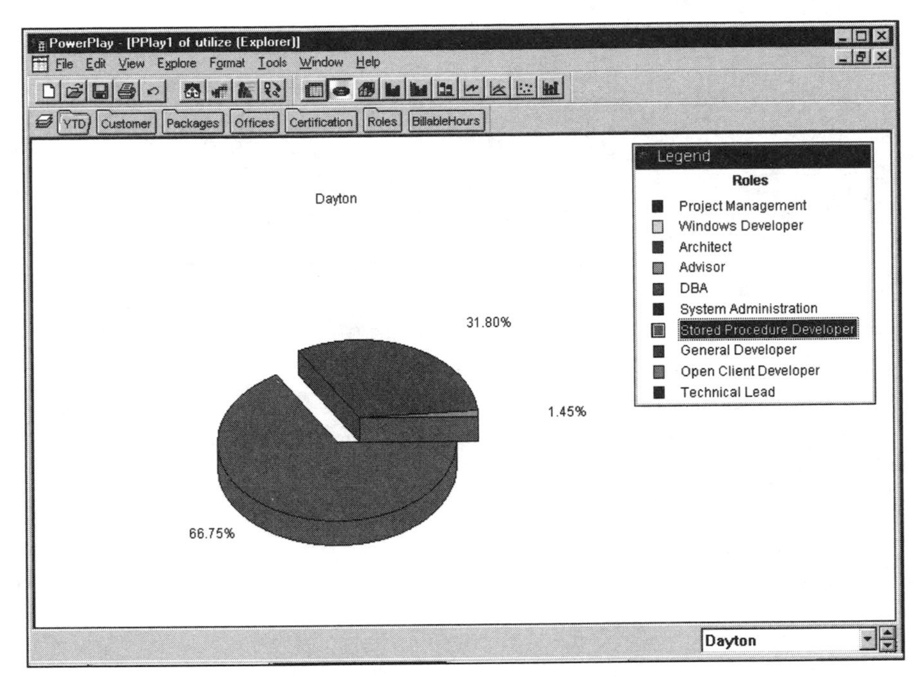

Figure B.13: *Report on consulting utilization for the Dayton office shows a very different picture than for the Cincinnati office shown in Figure B.12*

Cognos' Impromptu

Cognos' Impromptu is a tool for individuals who need to build more traditional reports, as shown in Figure B.14. Often, these users have little to no need to understand database structures or how to communicate with databases. As discussed in the main part of this book, Cognos' Impromptu is one of the best-of-breed interactive query and reporting tools available today for delivering such reports.

Impromptu offers great flexibility for the user as well as the administrator of a data warehouse. As you will see in the following reports, the user can be presented with subject-oriented data warehouse information organized very similarly to an information package diagram and star schema. This consistency makes for easier support and documentation of your final subject-oriented data warehouse. The queries that are built from such data architectures are optimized based on a catalog that the administrator creates.

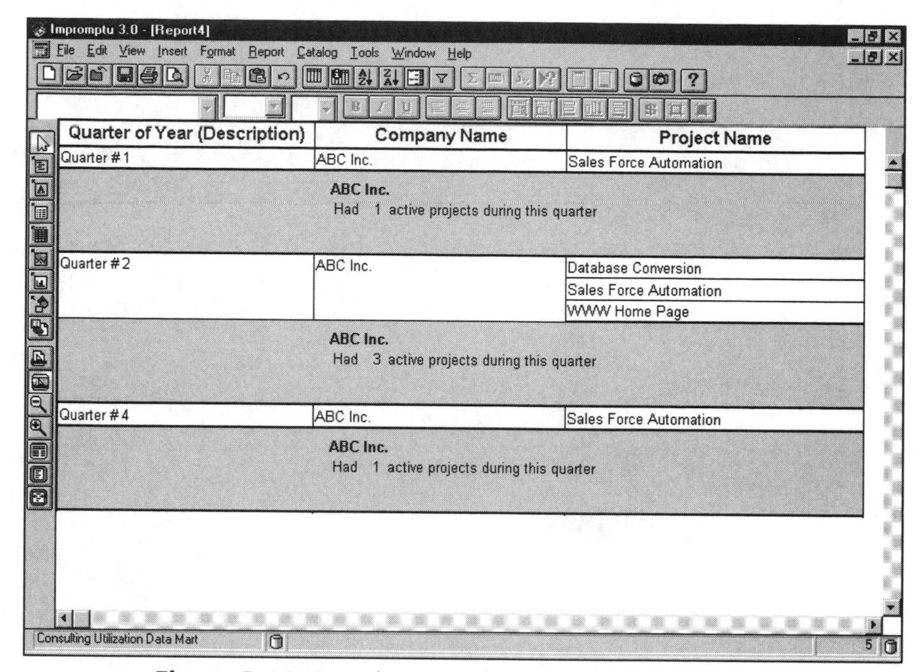

***Figure B.14:** Sample report from Cognos' Impromptu*

The Impromptu catalog allows placing data definitions in logical groupings, which offer better organization for the user to find the required data on which to report. This catalog can include traditional tables and columns as well as join strategies, report templates, standard reports, and predefined filters and calculations. Therefore, a lot of the work that would traditionally be accomplished through view management can now be done in an Impromptu catalog. This allows an administrator to better control how two objects are brought together, avoiding runaway queries.

To demonstrate these capabilities, we will walk through a detail listing of each consultant's billable days. Creating a new report in Impromptu is similar to creating a new document in Microsoft Word or a new spreadsheet in Microsoft Excel. The user simply presses the New button or selects the File|New menu item. Upon selecting this function, the user is presented with a query dialog, as illustrated in Figure B.15.

The Impromptu query dialog can be as powerful as the user wants it to be. Novices may never uncover some of the techniques here, while for advanced users this dialog presents virtually all of the subtle aspects of SQL in tab controls, including the *select* list, *order by* clause, and *group by* clause.

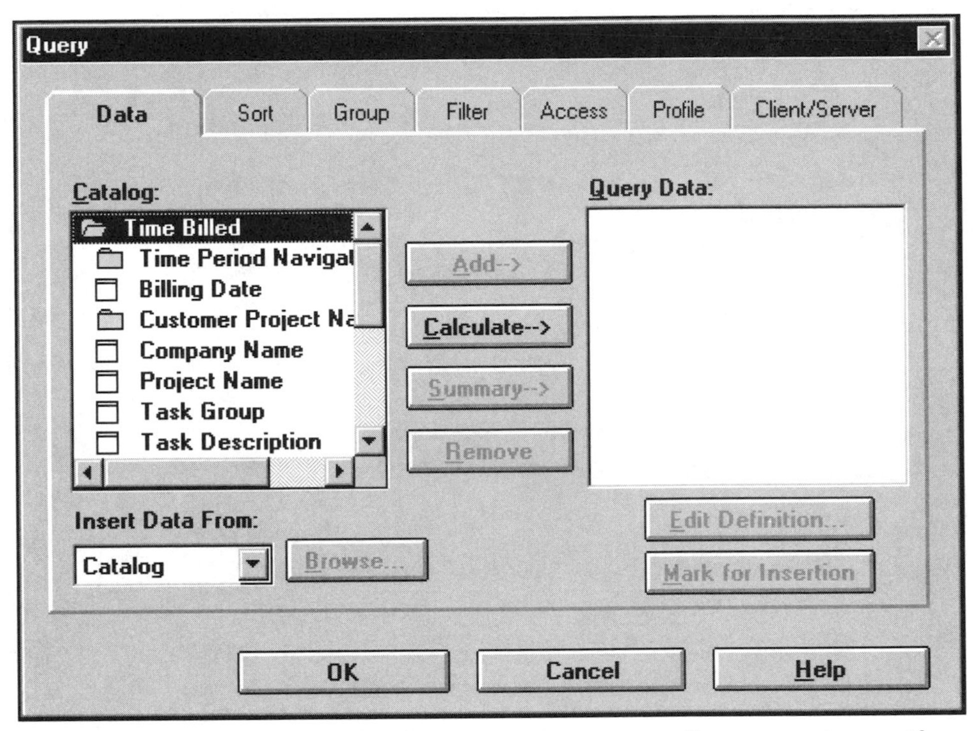

Figure B.15: *The query dialog for Cognos' Impromptu allows users to specify all required items for a relational query in a nonintrusive interface*

You will notice that we have taken great care to replicate the information package diagram structures in the Impromptu catalog as well as to present the user with business-oriented data columns. This information is mapped on top of the actual physical data structures that were shown earlier in Figure B.4. This dialog demonstrates two types of entities to the user, folders (the logical groupings of entities) and reportable columns. In Figure B.16, the Time Billed Information Package is open and has the data associated with the data model logically grouped into folders. Therefore, the navigational constructs of Time Periods and Customer Projects are displayed as folders. Opening these folders would further disclose the dimension and category definitions for those navigating components.

The user selects information from the groupings simply by highlighting the desired entity and selecting the Add button, though other advanced methods for performing these additions are available, such as drag and drop, and double clicking.

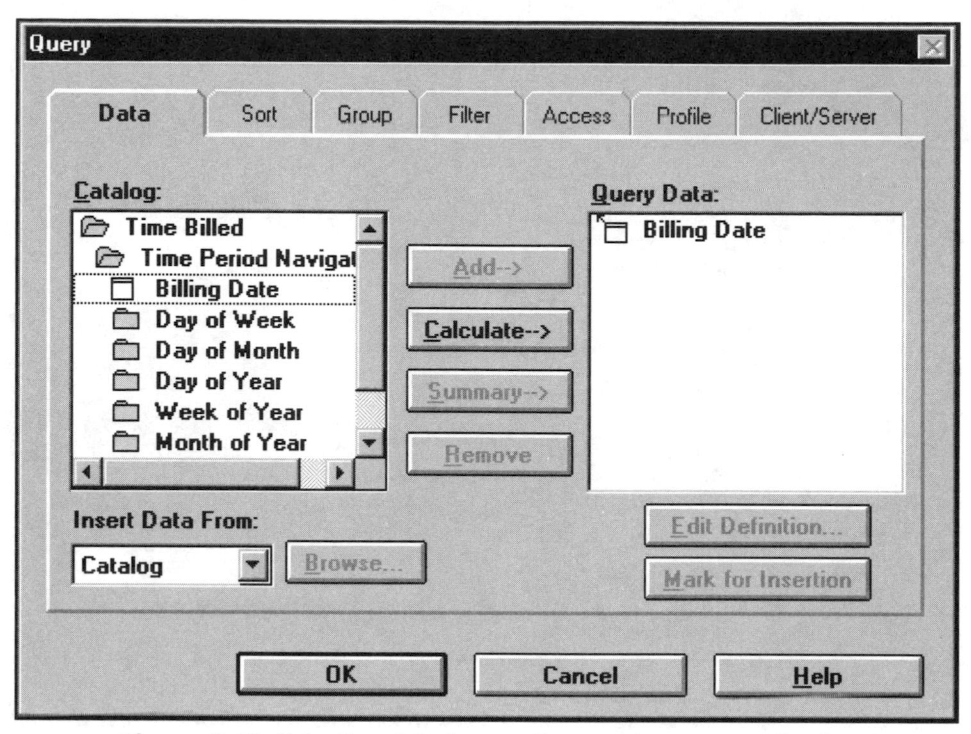

Figure B.16: *Selecting data from a Cognos' Impromptu Catalog from the Time Billed Information Package*

In Figure B.17, notice that we have traversed into the Customer Project Navigation folder and again opened the Customers logical grouping of report entities. From that folder, we selected Company Name, Project Name, Task Group, and Task Description for inclusion in the current report.

Calculations are also easy within the Impromptu environment. Calculations occur simply by pressing the Calculate button and filling in the proper definition. For purposes of this report, we simply want to see the revenue generated for any given billing. This calculation involves the hours billed and the billing rate, as shown in Figure B.18.

With this calculation, we now have all of the information required to present the data on consultant billings. The billing transaction data has been stored within the subject-oriented data warehouse. Therefore, this is a replica of the transaction system. For your data warehouse, this may not be desired, because in this example we have scaled down the data to present the concepts. The report will be produced by selecting the OK button on the query dialog. The results are presented as shown in Figure B.19.

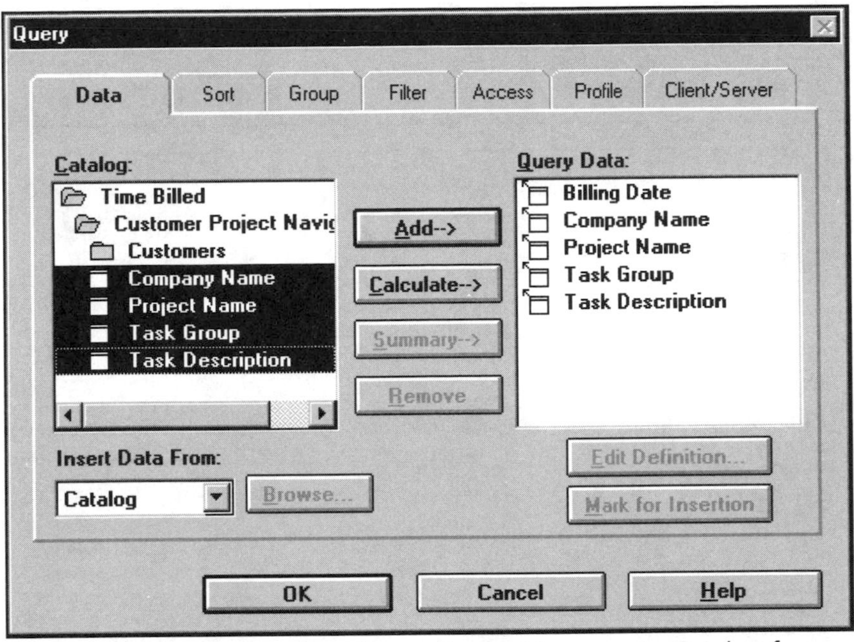

Figure B.17: *Selecting data from a Cognos' Impromptu Catalog from data in the Customer Project Dimension*

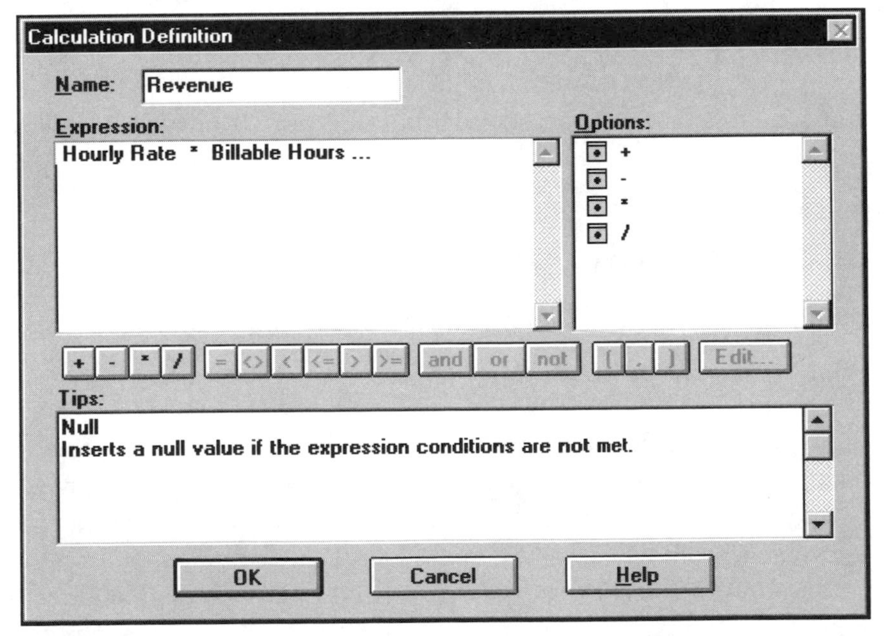

Figure B.18: *Performing calculations in Cognos' Impromptu reports*

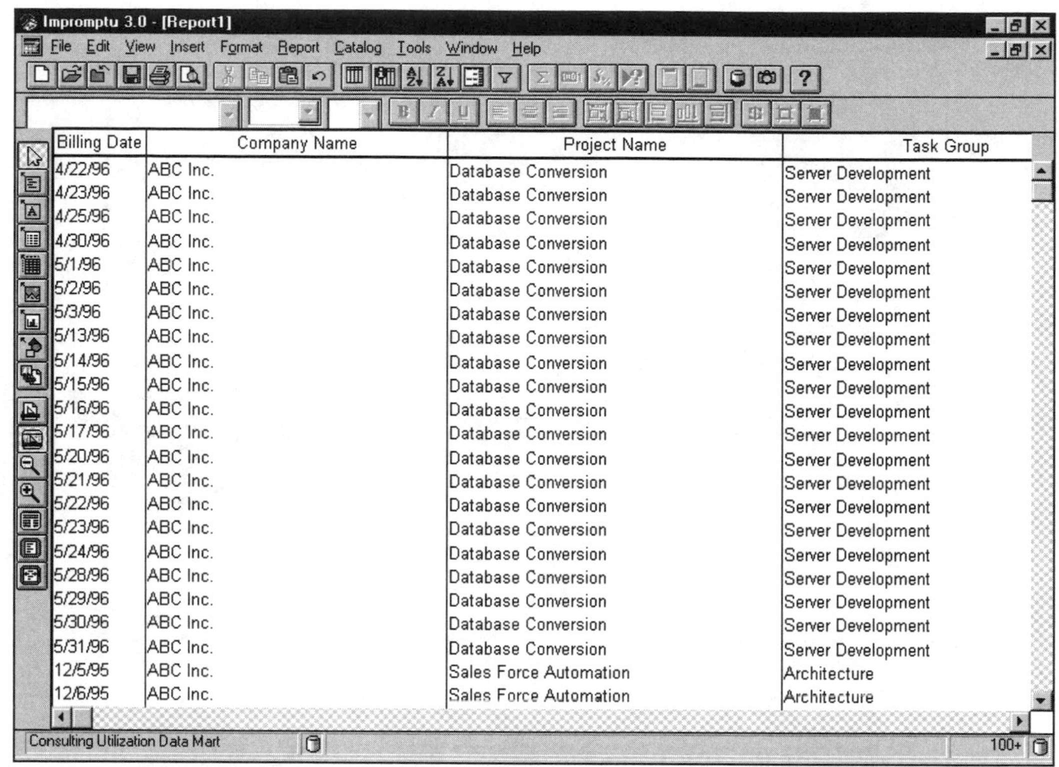

Billing Date	Company Name	Project Name	Task Group
4/22/96	ABC Inc.	Database Conversion	Server Development
4/23/96	ABC Inc.	Database Conversion	Server Development
4/25/96	ABC Inc.	Database Conversion	Server Development
4/30/96	ABC Inc.	Database Conversion	Server Development
5/1/96	ABC Inc.	Database Conversion	Server Development
5/2/96	ABC Inc.	Database Conversion	Server Development
5/3/96	ABC Inc.	Database Conversion	Server Development
5/13/96	ABC Inc.	Database Conversion	Server Development
5/14/96	ABC Inc.	Database Conversion	Server Development
5/15/96	ABC Inc.	Database Conversion	Server Development
5/16/96	ABC Inc.	Database Conversion	Server Development
5/17/96	ABC Inc.	Database Conversion	Server Development
5/20/96	ABC Inc.	Database Conversion	Server Development
5/21/96	ABC Inc.	Database Conversion	Server Development
5/22/96	ABC Inc.	Database Conversion	Server Development
5/23/96	ABC Inc.	Database Conversion	Server Development
5/24/96	ABC Inc.	Database Conversion	Server Development
5/28/96	ABC Inc.	Database Conversion	Server Development
5/29/96	ABC Inc.	Database Conversion	Server Development
5/30/96	ABC Inc.	Database Conversion	Server Development
5/31/96	ABC Inc.	Database Conversion	Server Development
12/5/95	ABC Inc.	Sales Force Automation	Architecture
12/6/95	ABC Inc.	Sales Force Automation	Architecture

Figure B.19: *Results of an ad hoc reporting session in Cognos' Impromptu*

Therefore, in its simplest form an Impromptu report is created by following these steps.

1. Opening a catalog
2. Selecting the New option
3. Selecting the desired report entities from an Impromptu catalog
4. Pressing OK on the query dialog

This simplicity is the power of such a tool, though for many tools this is also their greatest weakness. Impromptu has a lot of power behind this simplicity, which allows it to span not only a user base requirement from novice to expert, but also a report sophistication requirement from ad hoc query to production style reports.

The presentation of a report can then be modified through simple, direct manipulation techniques, like those shown within the PowerPlay examples. It is important to work with vendors to provide your users with a consistent interface among the spectrum of products that you offer in your warehouse tool suite.

In Impromptu, we can easily move columns by dragging their headings to the correct position on a report. This action changes the report so that it focuses on individual billings for given consultants. We can also organize the data along boundaries such as Consultant Name by selecting their heading and pressing the Group button. See Figure B.20.

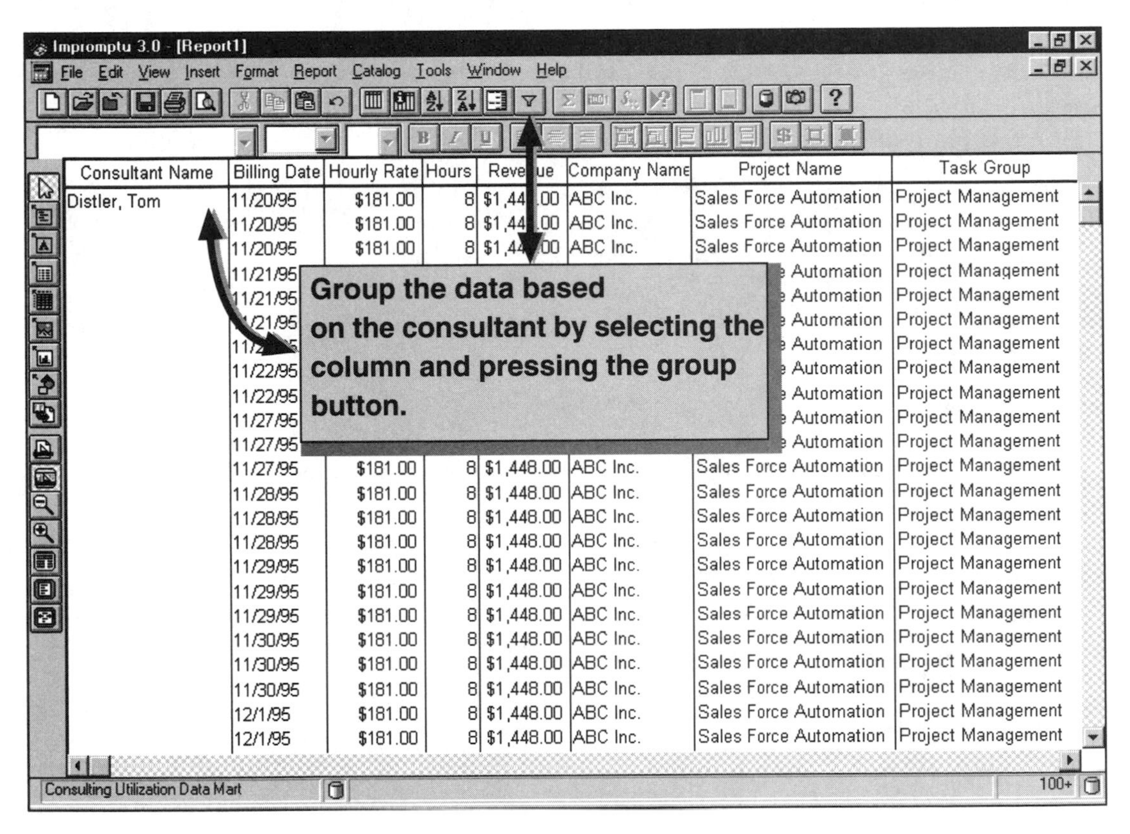

Figure B.20: *Using direct manipulation techniques in Cognos' Impromptu to modify cosmetics and grouping of data within a report*

This direct manipulation is typically utilized by novices; for more advanced users, this activity could have occurred within the query dialog. In fact, the query dialog is the preferred technique, because it reduces overhead associated with the query.

The Impromptu query engine is built to efficiently support your client/server, or distributed, data warehouse implementation. This means that when users request data, not all of the data is returned at once. Impromptu obtains enough data to present users with a meaningful representation of the report, allowing them to make modifications along the way and hoping they browse the data until they see what they need and avoid bringing down all the data. Of course, like most of the operations within Impromptu, this can be overridden so that if someone wants all of the data to be placed in a local cache, he or she can. This is another area of sophistication and capability that is incredibly important for mobile user communities, such as sales and marketing personnel, who need to disconnect from a data warehouse.

So in Figure B.20 you have a report that presents the following.

- The consultants
- The date on which the consultants billed their time
- How much time was billed
- At what rate
- Producing what revenue
- The details of the billing, including customer name, project, task group, and task

We could further enhance this report to present subtotals, percentages, maximums, minimums, averages, and so forth. By the way, how many joins do you think we did in the Impromptu report? How many tables were involved? Can you envision the SQL *select* statement that is required? Here it is.

```
select T1."NAME" as c1,
   T2."BILLINGDAT" as c2,
   T3."COMPANYNAM" as c3,
   T3."PROJECTNAM" as c4,
   T3."TASKGROUP" as c5,
   T3."TASKDESCRI" as c6,
   T2."HOURLYRATE" as c7,
   T2."BILLABLEHO" as c8,
   T2."BILLABLEHO" * T2."HOURLYRATE" as c9
from "BILL" T2,
   "NAVCUST" T3,
   "NAVCON" T1
where (T2."CUSTOMERID" = T3."CUSTOMERID"
   and T2."PROJECTID" = T3."PROJECTID"
   and T2."TASKID" = T3."TASKID")
   and (T2."EMPLOYEEID" = T1."EMPLOYEEID")
order by c1 asc,c2 asc
```

Summary

This appendix should allow you to see the ease of use that you can present to your user community when accessing a data warehouse. Tools—and complete tool suites like those presented in this appendix—assist your development team in avoiding writing a large number of standard reports, decision support applications, and executive information systems. This allows aggressive—and potentially unaggressive—users to take on more responsibility for deriving their own business intelligence.

Appendix C

Guide to Developing a Data Warehouse

The following appendix captures the key points of a quick reference guide to the information packaging methodology provided in this book. After reading this book, this appendix provides you with a project planning guide, highlighting the important tips of the overall work breakdown structure of your project plan. We also provide chapter references to guide you to the section in the book that covers the various content in detail.

Critical Success Factors

Prior to committing to a data warehouse project, it is critical that you address, scrutinize, and follow the following steps. Our experience is that the a of focus behind each of these items assists in the demise of a data warehouse project. Following these items will not guarantee success, but it will certainly place you on the path toward success.

- Obtain management commitment
- Begin with a manageable project
- Clearly communicate realistic expectations

- Assign a user-oriented manager
- Use proven methods
- Design based on queries rather than on transactions
- Load only data that is needed
- Define the proper system of record
- Clearly define unique subjects
- Force the use of, and reference to, a data warehouse

Note: *To refresh your memory about each of these items, please refer to Chapter 2, What Factors Drive a Successful Data Warehouse Project?*

Work Breakdown and Tips

A project plan defines the work and how it will be done. It provides a definition of each major task, an estimate of the time and resources required to complete the task, and a review process for management control. When properly documented, a project plan becomes an excellent learning vehicle—another data mart or knowledge base to assist future project managers. The benchmarking of actual execution of a plan will assist your organization in better managing and estimating tasks in the future, improving your overall accuracy. It is difficult to boilerplate a data warehouse project plan, but we include some of the major tasks that assist you in formulating your own plan. This should not be viewed as a complete project work breakdown structure, just as a framework to assist you in defining the specific tasks that you will require.

As with other projects, the work breakdown structure is only one element of an overall planning process. You need to define the initial requirements first. From these requirements, you can build the work breakdown structure, each item of which can then be estimated to allow you to project the required resources and formalize the schedule.

Step 0: The Architecture

To deliver all that is required by a data warehouse, you must establish a solid foundation of technology infrastructure—an architecture. The architecture is critical to the overall success of a data warehouse. Without a proper architecture, the connectivity among the required components and underlying technologies of a data warehouse will not occur.

After the architecture is completed, you can easily assess the benefit and impact of new data marts and expansions to a data warehouse.

Phase I: Plan the Architecture

Here are the consolidated steps to perform during this phase of the information packaging methodology.

1. Create a vision
2. Adopt a methodology
3. Assemble an architecture team
4. Define the architecture project scope
5. Define the business goals and objectives
6. Prepare the architecture plan and work breakdown structure
7. Obtain management commitment
8. Evaluate the current architecture
9. Model the existing enterprise
10. Phase review

Phase II: Build the Architecture Blueprint

Here are the consolidated steps to perform during this phase of the information packaging methodology.

1. Define the architecture requirements
2. Define the data architecture
3. Define the application architecture
4. Define the technology architecture
5. Establish the data warehouse tool suite
6. Document the data warehouse architecture in a standard document—a blueprint
7. Phase review

Here is a consolidation of the Architecture Tips that we have provided throughout the book, for your ready reference.

Architecture Tip 1: You should establish a replication technology that provides an unintrusive data warehouse agent—such as a Log Transfer Manager—to assist in the data warehouse loading and transformation processing. This type of technology minimizes the impact and interruptions that may occur on operational systems.

Architecture Tip 2: The architectural phase and architectural review are outside the development scope. However, they should not be forgotten, because they are the foundation of a proper enterprise data warehousing strategy. Would you build your house without a foundation or blueprint? Data warehouses should avoid the same philosophy.

Architecture Tip 3: Quality obviously is important; the guaranteed pursuit of quality should be too. Therefore, be sure to design an automated quality system in your architecture so that you can automate the testing process and more efficiently perform your integration testing.

Architecture Tip 4: Standards should be defined for each of the components of a data warehouse, including those that follow.

columns	constraints	databases	devices
datatypes	defaults	security groups	indexes
logins	rules	segments	servers
stored procedures	tables	triggers	information packages
views	standard reports	users	catalogs
domains	relationships		

Architecture Tip 5: Your data warehouse standards should be developed prior to tool selection. Try to find the tool that most matches your standards and continually monitor available tools to find the one that is best for your standards. *Do not build your standards based on tools. Over time, the tools will change and your standards will be left in the dark ages, or at least at the previous generation of tools.*

Architecture Tip 6: A data modeling tool should at a minimum support the following: logical data modeling; physical database modeling; automatic generation of the native, physical data definition language for your chosen database management system; domain management; reverse engineering of legacy data models; native database management system support; and complete reporting capabilities for impact analysis and documentation. Don't settle for less.

Architecture Tip 7: When choosing components of your architecture, choose products and tools that provide building blocks and expansion, or scalability options in the future. The components you select also should involve little to no disruption to your users when scaling or expanding. You should not be required to purchase all of your architectural components and tools in the beginning.

Architecture Tip 8: Look for impossible things in your vendor community, things you think can't be done—then have your vendor prove that they *can* be done. However, make sure to pay for the proof with something like a money-back guarantee. If you pay for a service, the vendor will realize you are serious and may assign more talented resources to your account than if you want a freebie proof.

Note: *Remember, an architecture consists of subarchitectures—namely data, application, and technology—and should also focus on the resources and organization required to support the target architecture. To refresh your memory about each of these items, please refer to Section II, Architecture—Building the Required Foundation.*

An Information Packaging Methodology Road Map

After the architectural work has been completed for overall enterprise, you begin to deliver subject-oriented data warehouses. To perform these tasks, you will want to follow the information packaging methodology covered in this book. This is a spiral methodology and should be utilized to build up to an enterprise data warehouse through implementation of several smaller subject-oriented data warehouses. This methodology is depicted in Figure C.1, and a step-by-step summary of its steps is provided in the sections that follow.

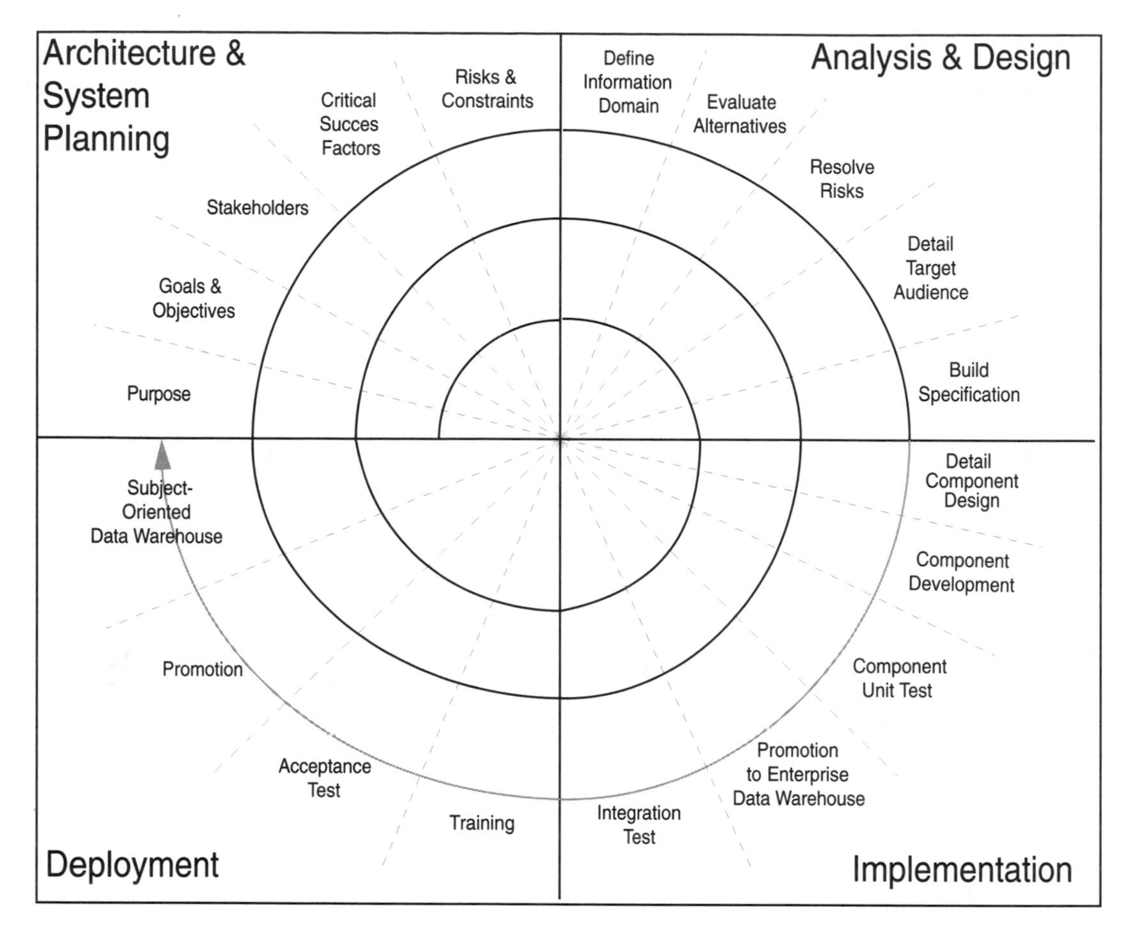

Figure C.1: *A project manager's road map to the information packaging methodology*

Step 1: Project Planning

Failing to plan is planning to fail. The planning phase of your project allows the proper scope to be set and assists your project team in clearly sizing the time and effort required to deliver a data warehouse solution. Here is a consolidation of the Planning Tips that were presented throughout the book.

Planning Tip 1: The planning process is one in which you must remember that the most important single factor in determining the final delivery date is the date on which a project begins.

Planning Tip 2: Remember that the initial plan is a starting point from which you will determine the size of a project. Managing this effectively means not over-committing resources by negotiating major time or cost cuts within tasks. Until you reach final agreement on time, resources, and cost, the project plan will not be solidified.

Here is a consolidation of the steps to perform during this phase of the information packaging methodology.

1. Define the project purpose
2. Define the project goals and objectives
3. Define the stakeholders who have an interest in the project's outcome
4. Define the project's management team
5. Define the project's critical success factors
6. Define the project's risks and constraints
7. Define the project team
8. Establish and enforce the project work flow
9. Phase review

Planning Tip 3: It is nearly impossible to build a "dream team" with any sort of staying power. Make sure to define a longer-term strategy that supports the needs of your initial team. Satisfying your goals and your people's goals will enhance your ability to succeed.

Planning Tip 4: Hourly rate should not be a decision criterion for selecting resources from the world of consulting. Experience and ability to stand behind a project far outweigh the hourly cost. Your consultants should be held accountable. Make sure their company can guarantee their work.

Note: *To refresh your memory about each of these items, please refer to Section III, Managing the Process.*

Step 2: Analysis and Design

The analysis and design phase assists your project team in defining what data is required by users as well as other relevant processing and background information required to successfully deliver a data warehouse. The analysis and design phase is greatly influenced by the knowledge of what is possible within a data warehouse. The final deliverables in this phase are specifications, in the form of dimension maps that define the subject areas and performance measures important to a business. Here is a consolidation of the steps to perform during this phase of the information packaging methodology.

1. Define the information domain
2. Evaluate alternate solutions
3. Resolve, or build plans to resolve, defined project risks
4. Develop detailed knowledge of the target audience
5. Assemble the specification
6. Map the requirements and specifications to the standard architecture
7. Map the information domain with information package diagramming techniques (user requirements)
8. Phase review

Here is a consolidation of the Analysis and Design Tips that were presented throughout the book.

Analysis and Design Tip 1: All project objectives and requirements for a data warehouse and associated data marts should be mapped to one or more components in the standard architecture. If the mapping cannot occur, the architecture or the requirements are incomplete.

Analysis and Design Tip 2: Preparation for user interviews is important. You will require input from the key personnel in the user community. You will do yourself and your team a large favor by being well prepared and optimizing your visits with users. Remember, their time is valuable to the enterprise. After all, they are making strategic and tactical decisions that are worth millions of dollars to the company.

Analysis and Design Tip 3: The data granularity required by users is typically one detail level lower than the decision point. For example, if a sales manager is only interested in quarterly variance of forecasted revenue to actual revenue because the selling cycle is 90 days and all decisions are based on the selling cycle, you want to deliver monthly variance figures in the data warehouse. By delivering this next layer of detail, you support the process of investigation that is required by the manager, his or her analysts, or the personnel within his or her organization who are typically asked for the reasons behind a change in trends. Though the ultimate business change might be made based on quarterly statistics, the monthly trends information provides insight when variances occur.

Analysis and Design Tip 4: Users will tag key information with common, *user-oriented keywords* such as *by* and *over*. These keywords give additional meaning to data requirements and allow you to easily package the information required by users into the proper structure. For example, a manager may desire to see product sales information by month, by geography, and by product during the last five years. The tags of *by* assist in defining the dimensions of month, geography, and product. The tag of *over* assists in defining the content of the time dimension, or how many months are required to fill the information request.

Analysis and Design Tip 5: Data warehouses contain data that is fundamentally dimension and measure oriented. Begin to listen and dissect your users' comments into dimensions (subjects) and measures (facts).

Analysis and Design Tip 6: When working with an information package diagram, try to minimize your access paths, or dimensions. This helps users by simplifying the manner in which the data is obtained. Keep the number of dimensions within a reasonable number, such as under 10. This is not a fixed limit, and many information models require a larger number of dimensions. However, usability is hampered when you exceed this number. Usability should be the number one focus of your warehouse project. The shaded areas on an information package diagram remind you of this usability tip.

Analysis and Design Tip 7: The relationship between category levels and a dimension should be under a 1:10 ratio. This assists users in navigating and understanding the data. This is not a fixed limit, and many information models require a larger ratio between dimensions and categories. However, usability is hampered when you exceed this number. Usability should be the top focus of your warehouse project. The shaded areas on an information package diagram remind you of this usability tip.

Analysis and Design Tip 8: If you get in a situation in which you exceed a reasonable ratio between category levels, you can place an artificial category in your information package that logically organizes the category level into a manageable ratio. A ratio between category levels that exceeds 1:150 should be further analyzed for applying this tip. This is not a fixed limit, and many information models require a larger ratio between category levels. However, usability is hampered when you exceed this number. Usability should be the number one focus of your warehouse project.

Analysis and Design Tip 9: Try to insert the numbers that represent the unique occurrences of a category value within your category cells. These numbers assist you in understanding the volume of potential data and the relationships on types of data that could greatly impact the size of your warehouse. This data assists you if you need to split an information package in the future.

Analysis and Design Tip 10: When analyzing information to design your data warehouse, use multiple information package diagrams. Don't try to cover all of the possible information requests with one information package diagram. Creating several information package diagrams, each tailored to suit a particular information request or information package, allows you to build a data warehouse that performs better and provides a higher degree of user satisfaction.

Note: *To refresh your memory about each of these items, please refer to Chapter 5, Project Life Cycle and Management, and Chapter 7, Data Gathering: Information Usage Analysis.*

Step 3: Implementation

Throughout the development process, the data warehouse team will gain a better understanding of the data warehousing process and user requirements. There are practical issues involved in the implementation of a data warehouse, such as how the user accesses the information, from which the development team gains a sense of judgment and experience, allowing it to begin delivering the ultimate data warehouse. A successful data warehouse implementation requires an interlocking of the development processes that guarantees that all elements work together in concert and harmony to provide users with the proper system. The implementation process focuses on the best way to physically implement the designs built in the analysis and design phase. Here is a consolidation of the steps to perform during this phase of the information packaging methodology.

1. Clearly define unique data warehouse entities
2. Build the logical data model by translating information package diagrams into star schemas
3. Build the physical data model by translating your star schema logical models
4. Develop the data import or loading components
5. Develop the data access components
6. Unit test all developed components
7. Perform integration testing of completed information packages, including data quality testing
8. Phase review

Here is a consolidation of the Implementation Tips that were presented throughout the book.

Implementation Tip 1: To give a more descriptive meaning to your star schema models, use graphics that communicate a clear meaning for each entity in the model. Recommended graphics are rectangles for measure entities, diamonds for dimension entities, and stop signs for category detail entities.

Implementation Tip 2: Measure entities are composed of the keys to the detail, or lowest level, categories in each dimension of an information package diagram. Each column must relate to all measures of the information package diagram. At this point, determine whether you will store calculated measurements. It is wise to estimate the overhead of users calculating the measurement data each time they access an information package versus the additional storage space and processing time required to precalculate the measurement data.

Implementation Tip 3: Dimension entities are placed on the points of a star schema and have a relationship that projects inward to the center of the star. The relationships among any dimension and measure entities is one to many; one dimension entity instance relates to many measure entity instances. Dimension entities are logical in nature and are the most denormalized of the three major data warehouse entities structures.

Implementation Tip 4: Category detail entity definitions contain information that enhances and adds qualitative data to the measurement, or quantitative, data. The category details transform your star schema diagram into a snowflake schema because of the branching effect that the category details deliver to the star schema. (Note: Some industry gurus have different meanings for snowflake schemas. The type we discuss is controlled and will not be a detriment to your implementation.)

Implementation Tip 5: It is important that you uniquely and clearly define all entities in your data warehouse: *What is a Customer? Product? Region?* You also need to realize that it is okay for different measure entities to require the same dimension entity to provide relationships at differing levels of category detail: *A Time Period relates to Measure Entity 1 at the month level, while Measure Entity 2 relates at a day level.* Remember, a relational database, which you typically utilize to implement your data warehouse, allows you to join tables with various entity columns. Therefore, you can take the Month column and join it from the Time Period Dimension Entity to the Month column within Measure Entity 1. You can also join the Date column from the Time Period Dimension Entity to the Date column within Measure Entity 2. Month and Date are both time periods and will be contained within the same entity even though theY provide different levels of detail.

Implementation Tip 6: Be sure to follow the complete refinement process when modeling your data; that is, from information package diagram through star schema to physical data model. This is a key part of the process that should be strictly followed to assist in the overall quality of a data warehouse and its components.

Implementation Tip 7: Data warehouse entities should be driven by the users' query behavior. To this end, dimension entities assist users in navigating and filtering measure entities, and proceed to allowing users to focus on data in category detail entities.

Implementation Tip 8: Become the leader in your company in driving an auditing standard for all operational systems, and data stores in general. This eases the process of extracting data from operational data stores and of loading the cleansed data into data warehouse data stores.

Implementation Tip 9: Just because SQL is a set-oriented language does not mean that everything can be easily and most efficiently done in one pass of data. Remember the policy of keeping things simple; simplicity often, but not always, equates to efficiency. Many cleansing and loading processes require more than one pass of the data. Design your load modules with your eye on the future and your mind in the past. That is, don't forget things such as checkpoint restart logic, which optimized batch jobs of old. These techniques can bridge to the future and optimize your loading process.

Implementation Tip 10: Replication technologies can be extremely useful for the data warehouse loading process. Search for the least intrusive method of trapping data modifications in operational systems. These systems can ill afford an increase in the transaction window, or code revisions. A good replication technology that monitors a data store's log file delivers this least intrusive solution.

Implementation Tip 11: Application packages should not be hard to integrate into your overall data warehouse strategy. However, often they are difficult to integrate due to your company's low technical knowledge in data management for the application. Guarantee that your development team receives adequate documentation and training on any in-house applications that will provide data to a data warehouse.

Note: *To refresh your memory about each of these items, please refer to Chapter 5, Project Life Cycle and Management; Chapter 8, Building a Data Model; Chapter 9, Database Design; Chapter 10, Data Extraction and Cleansing; Chapter 11, Publishing and Accessing Data; and Chapter 12, Avoiding Production Obstacles.*

Step 4: Deployment

After a data warehouse is built, you must guarantee success by formally defining a deployment strategy. This includes the concepts of training users, obtaining their acceptance and feedback, and in general promoting what is available in your data warehouse throughout the enterprise. Here is a consolidation of the steps to perform during this phase of the information packaging methodology.

1. Support staff training
2. User training
3. User acceptance—sign off
4. Promotion
5. Formal project review

Here is a consolidation of the Deployment Tips that were presented throughout the book.

Deployment Tip 1: A system is not complete until it is fully accepted by the user community. Only the users can say, "Done."

Deployment Tip 2: The users' interest is in the information contained in and managed by a data warehouse. Therefore, make sure to choose or build a deployment environment that is composed of tools and applications that support the business first—techie stuff way later, if at all.

Deployment Tip 3: In the area of tools, it is unfortunate but true that *you get what your pay for.* Don't be penny wise and pound foolish when deploying tools to your user community. The more sophisticated a tool is, the more productive users will be and the less burden will be placed on your development team.

Note: *To refresh your memory about each of these items, please refer to Chapter 5, Project Life Cycle and Management; Chapter 11, Publishing and Accessing Data; and Chapter 12, Avoiding Production Obstacles.*

Summary

This appendix has provided you with a synopsis of the information packaging methodology covered in this book. By following these steps and concentrating on the tips outlined in each phase, you and your data warehouse project team can quickly become information packaging experts, fully delivering a corporate knowledge base to your enterprise.

Appendix D

Sample Data Warehouse Forms

This appendix provides a collection of forms to assist in your quest to gather the requirements for a data warehouse, then to document those requirements. This appendix doesn't provide a form for every circumstance, but most of the key areas discussed in this book and in Appendix C are represented. Here are the forms that you will find on the following pages.

- **Project Planning Form** Use this form to clearly define the development cycle that you will be entering
- **Application/Data Source Description** Use this form to document existing systems that will feed a data warehouse
- **System/Business Function Matrix** Use this form to define the systems that support key business functions
- **System/Data Source Matrix** Use this form to define current database technologies utilized within an application or data source architecture
- **CRUD Matrix** Use this form to define how application systems interact with major data entities

- ***Data Source Volumetric Chart*** Use this form to log the growth and volatility of data sources
- ***User Category Map*** Use this form to log and document the different constituencies your data warehouse needs to support
- ***Specification Map*** Use this form to map data mart or data warehouse specifications to data warehouse architecture
- ***Information Package Diagram*** Use this form to build your conceptual data packages
- ***Multiple Access Path/Category Detail*** Use this form to define multiple access paths for any category of an information package diagram
- ***Information Package/Star Schema*** Use this form to build your logical data relationships and entity characteristics, transformed from information package diagrams
- ***Data Warehouse Entity Characteristics Chart*** Use this form to map summary information about all entities managed by a data warehouse
- ***Organization/Data Warehouse Entity Matrix*** Use this form to map security and access needs of a data warehouse
- ***Data Warehouse Entity Detail Characteristic Chart*** Use this form to define the details of each entity in a data warehouse
- ***Data Cleansing, Transformation & Loading Specification*** Use this form to define a single pass of data and all associated characteristics for the processing that will take place to transform the data into a suitable format for a data warehouse

Project Planning Form

Data Mart Name

Organization

Status

Business Function Supported

Purpose Definition

Goals

Objectives

Key Stakeholders

Name	Description of Involvement and Need

Project Planning Form - Page 2

Critical Success Factors

Risks and Constraints

Risk or Constraint	Description	Avoidance Action Plan

Potential Major Entities *(preliminary Measure, Dimension, Category Detail Entities)*

Application/Data Source Description

System Name

Organization

Status

Business Function Supported

Description

Processing Mode ☐ BATCH ☐ ONLINE Peak Hours of Operation:

Infrastructure *(Include hardware, software, communications, etc.)*

Input Systems

Output Systems

Information Domain

Table/File	Description	DBMS/FMS

Application/Data Source Description - Page 2

Key Contacts

Role	Name	Phone	EMail

Supplemental Material(s) ☐ Yes ☐ No

Description

Supplemental Item	Description	Filing Location

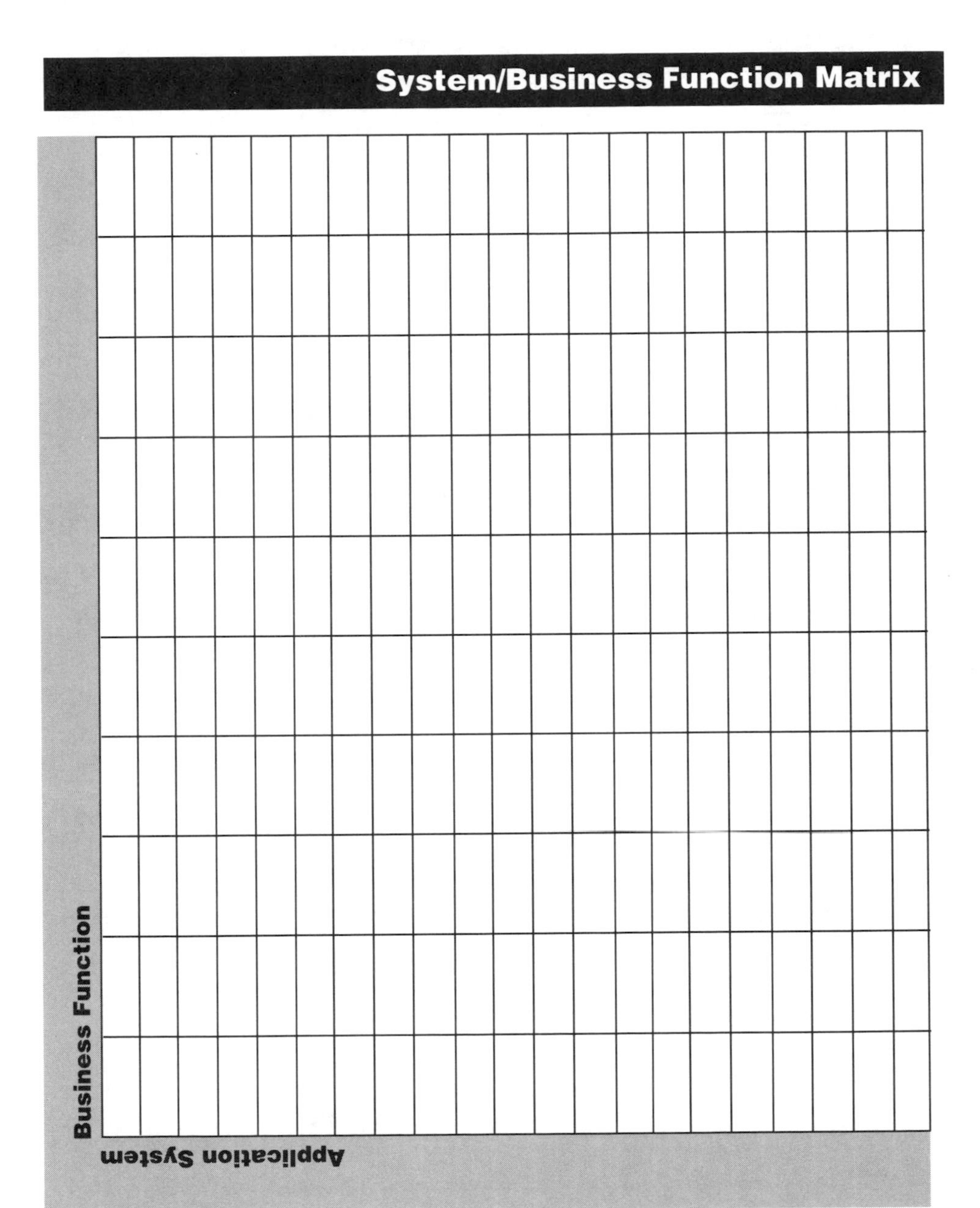
System/Business Function Matrix

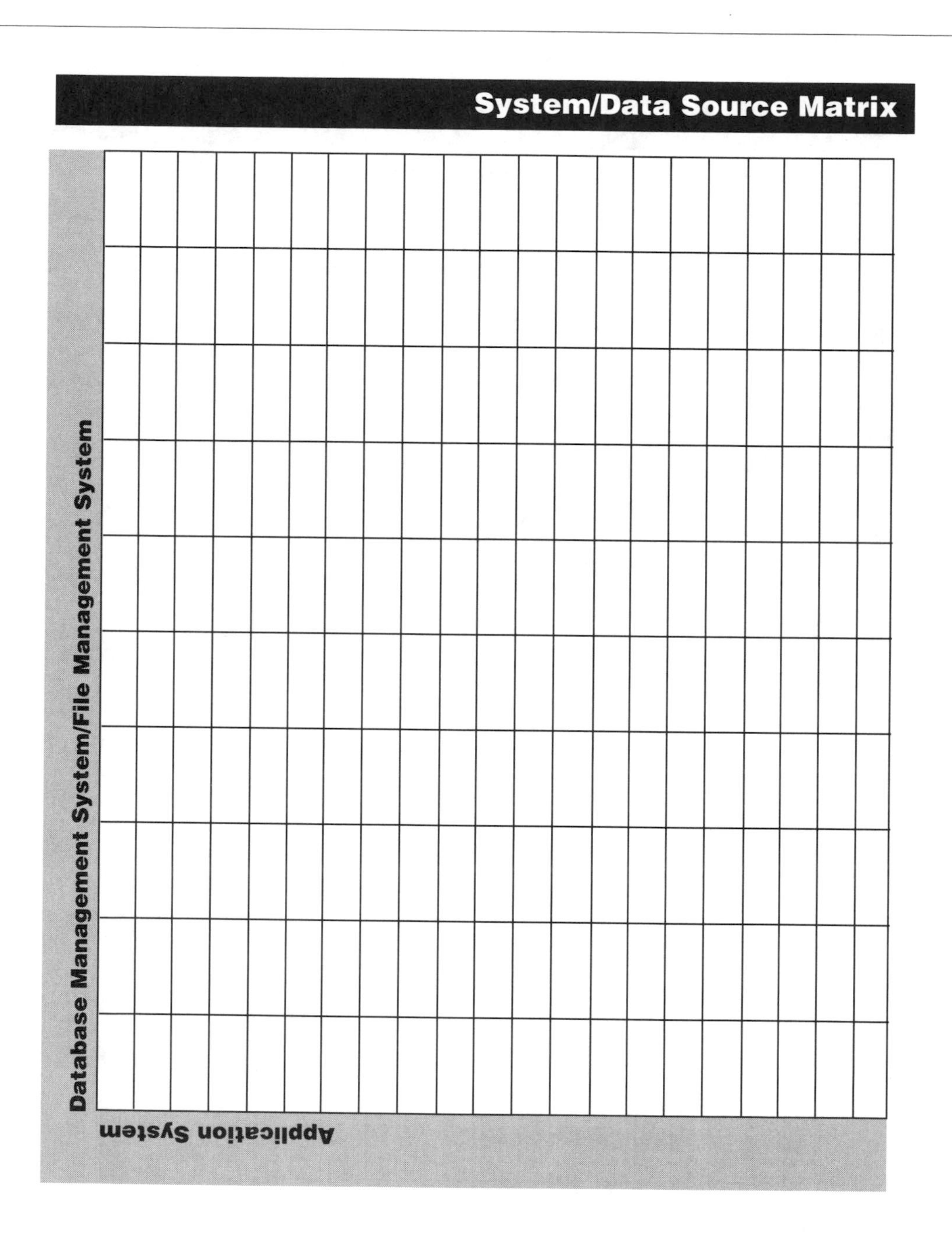
System/Data Source Matrix
Database Management System/File Management System
Application System

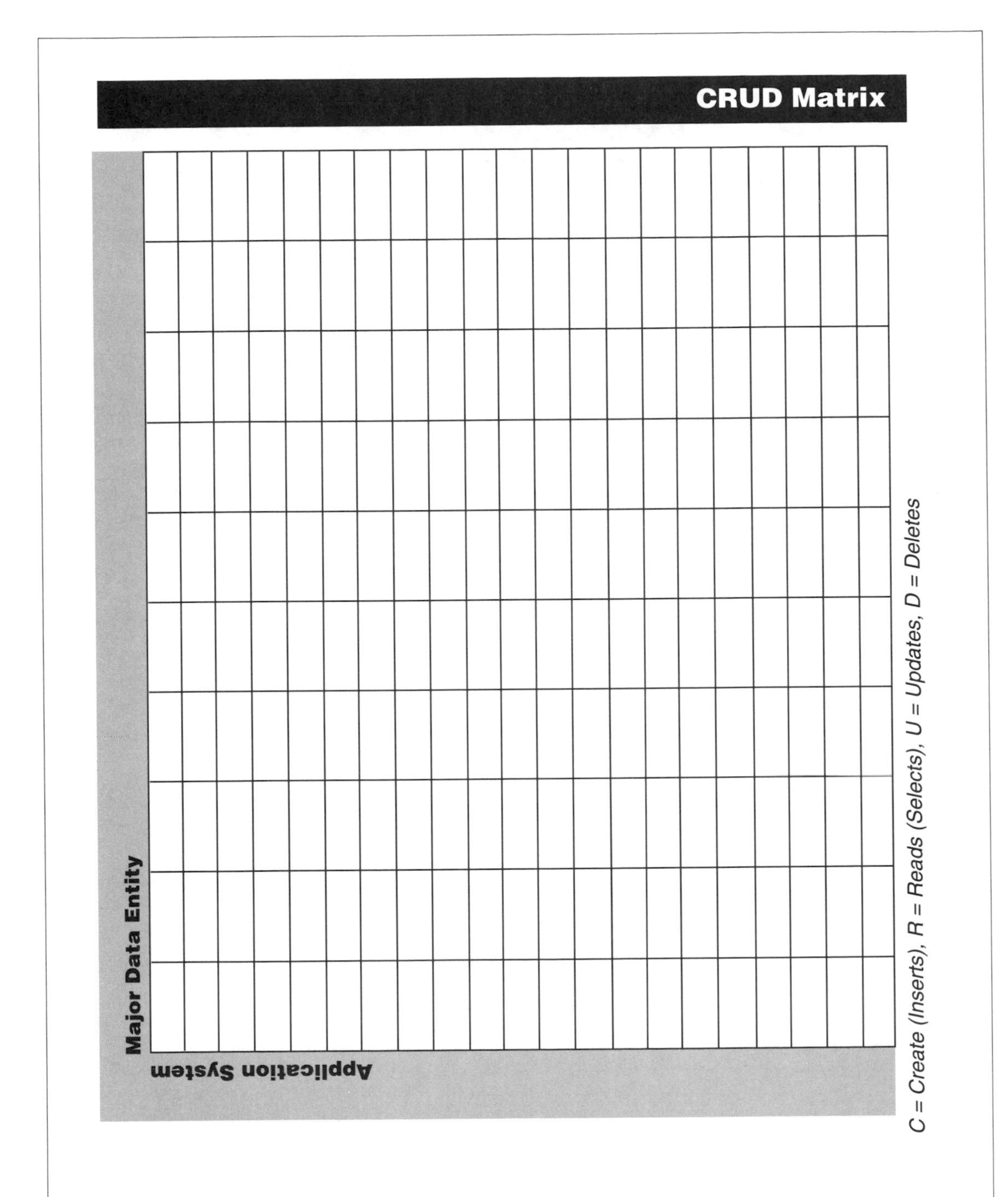
CRUD Matrix
Major Data Entity
Application System
C = Create (Inserts), R = Reads (Selects), U = Updates, D = Deletes

Data Source Volumetric Chart

Data Entry	Current Rows	Growth (Rows/Day)	Volatility (Trans/Day)	Projected Rows

User Category Map

User Category	Definition	Requirements

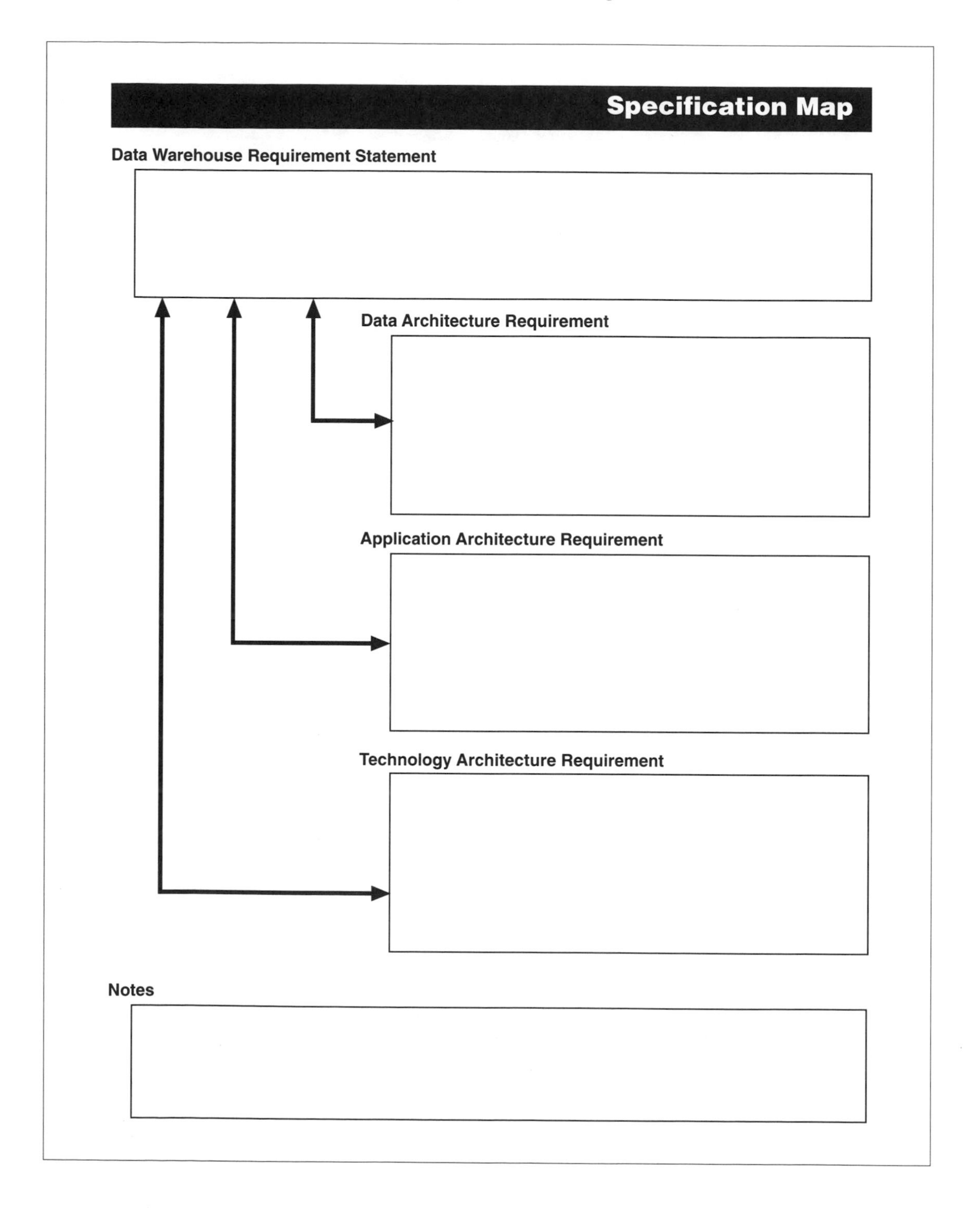
Specification Map
Data Warehouse Requirement Statement
Data Architecture Requirement
Application Architecture Requirement
Technology Architecture Requirement
Notes

Information Package Diagram

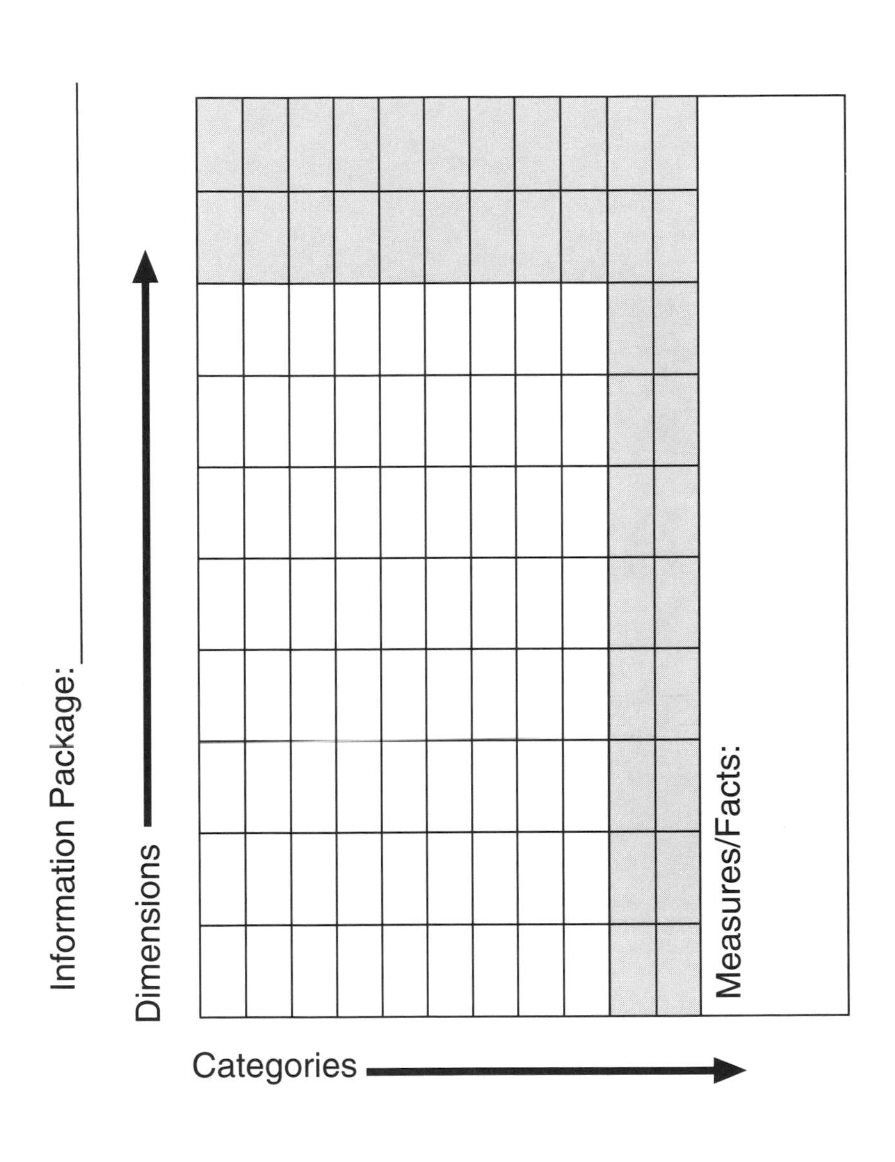

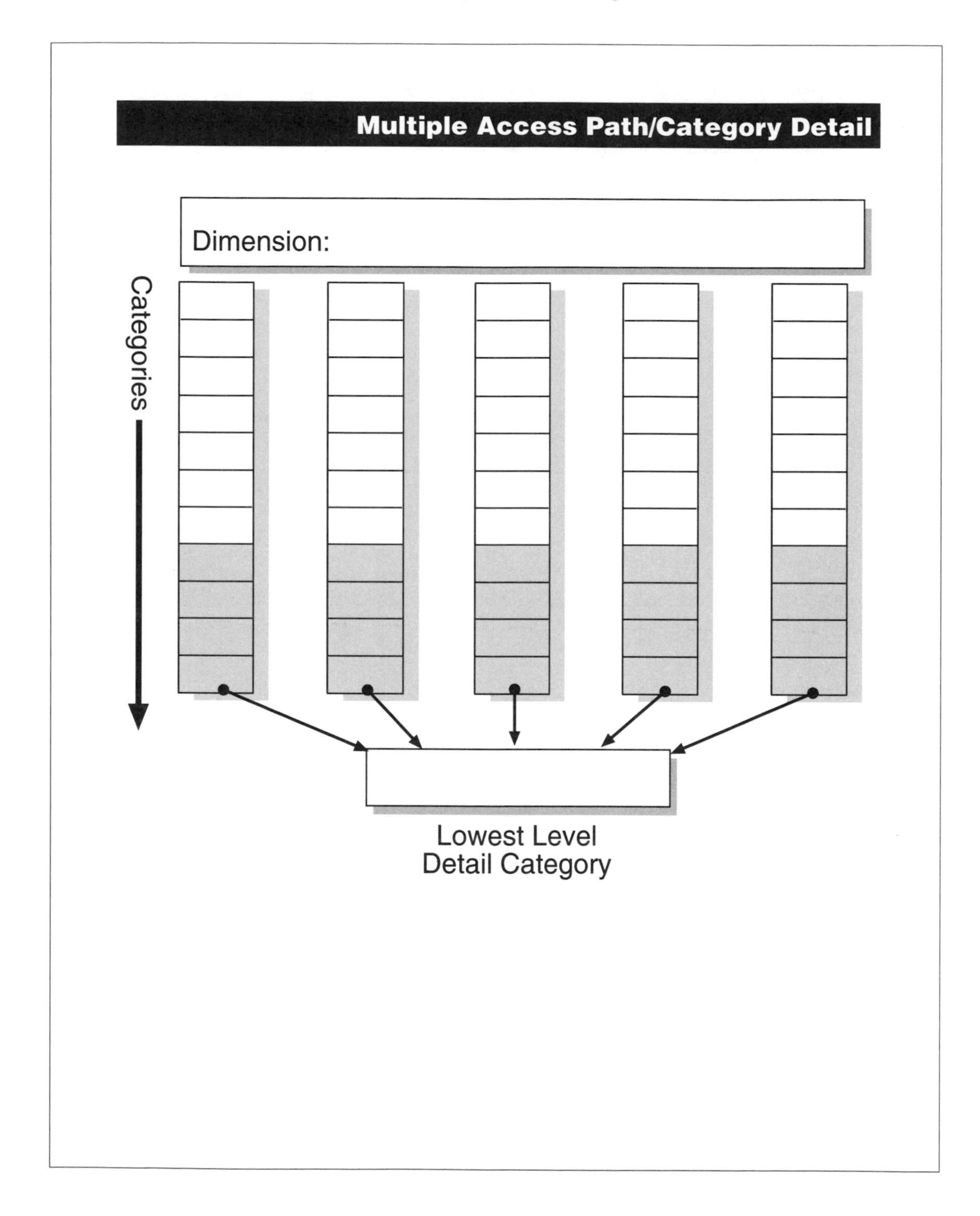
Multiple Access Path/Category Detail
Dimension:
Categories
Lowest Level
Detail Category

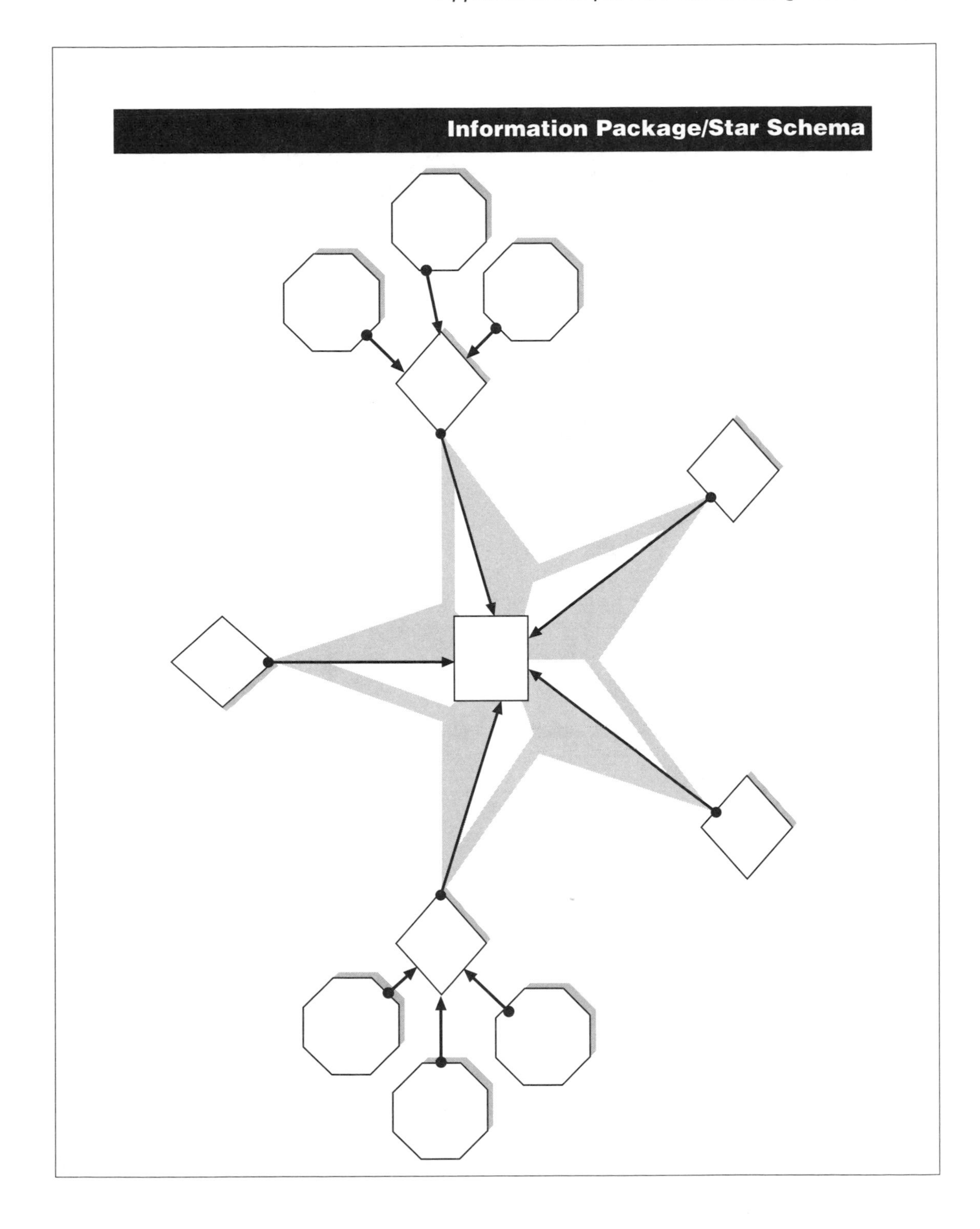
Information Package/Star Schema

Data Warehouse Entity Characteristic Chart

Data Warehouse Entity	Volumetric	Update Frequency

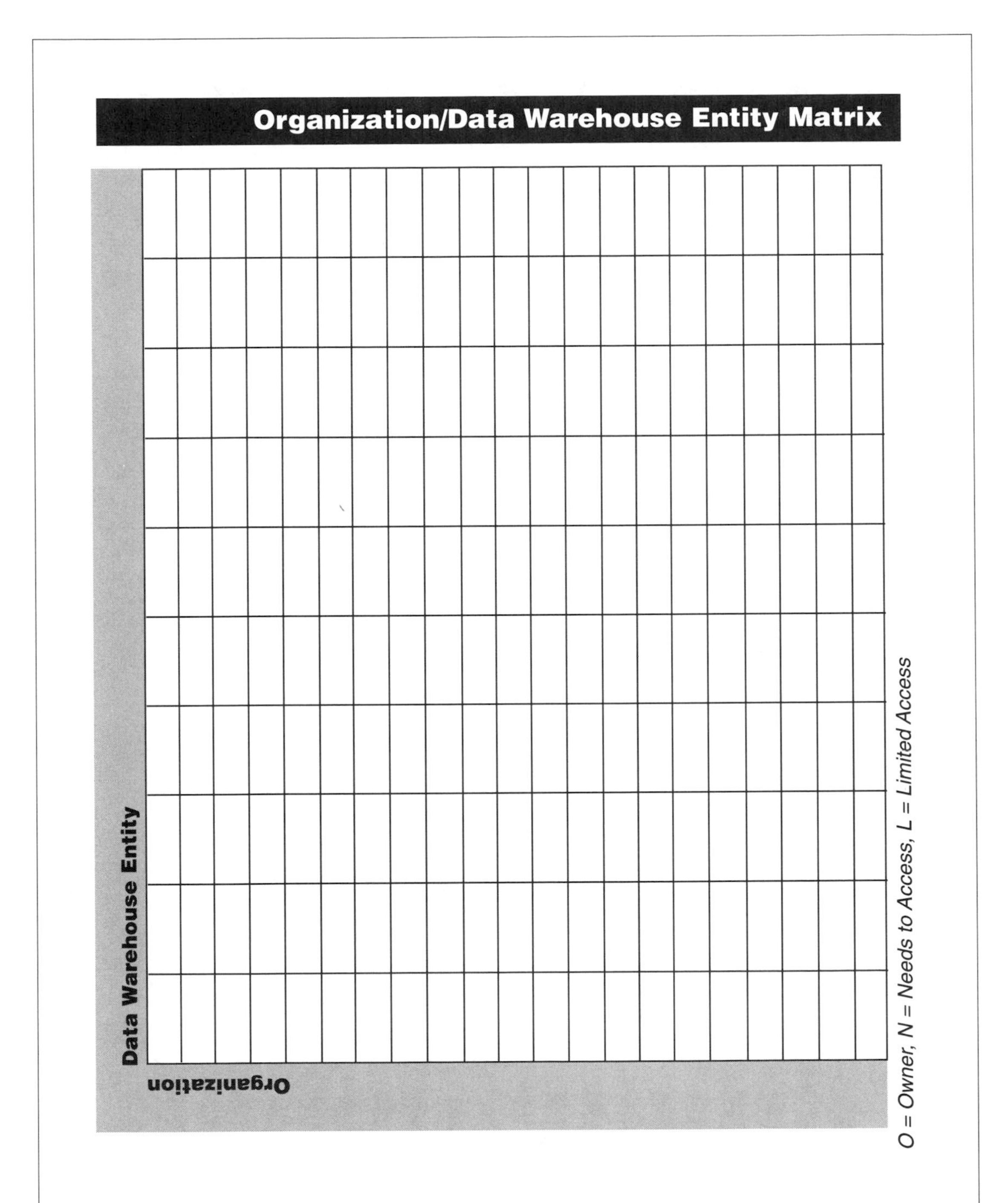
Organization/Data Warehouse Entity Matrix
Data Warehouse Entity
Organization
O = Owner, N = Needs to Access, L = Limited Access

Data Warehouse Entity Detail Characteristic Chart

Entity Name: ☐

Entity Type: ☐ Measurement ☐ Dimension ☐ Category Detail

Column	Key Attributes	Type and Size	Integrity Constraints	Valid Values Range

Data Cleansing, Transformation & Loading Specification

Specification Name ____________ **Process** ☐ **of** ☐

Description

Source Tables

Table	Database (System)	Platform

Filter and Join Criteria

And/Or Operation	Column	Operation	Value

Sorting and/or Aggregation Criteria

Column	Order	Group

Data Cleansing, Transformation & Loading Specification - Page 2

Target Column Definitions

Result Column	Source Column or Calculation	Description/Notes

Data Cleansing, Transformation & Loading Specification - Page 3

Processing Notes

Glossary

ad hoc An act such as a query against a data store that is not premeditated or that is without preparation, impromptu, and off the top of the head. This word often characterizes a set of query tools that support this behavior.

aggregate Generically, to gather into a mass, sum, or whole; to amount to; total. With regard to a data warehouse, aggregates or aggregation refers to the concept of rolling up data within its dimensional hierarchy. Each dimension contains many levels that, in turn, can present the user with a rolled-up version of data. Example: In a locations dimension, all districts add up to a region. Aggregates and aggregation provide a valuable type of computation within a decision support system or data warehouse. Most users want to see aggregations not only in one dimension, but across dimensional boundaries. Because dimensions are indexes into numerical business measures, this is possible. Example: A regional sales manager wants to see all sales figures, forecast and actual, for each district by product line. For this aggregation, sales figures must be summarized for each city within the district by product line and presented to the user. With regard to standard SQL statements, an aggregate refers to data returned in a result set with the average, summation, count, minimize, and maximize functions typically used with a *group by* clause.

alternate key An alternate key, or index, is a column or columns designated as a preferred or common means of accessing the instances of a given entity. Example: The primary key to a customer table might be CustomerNumber and the alternate key might be CustomerName. CustomerName does not guarantee uniqueness of the instance of a customer; therefore, a number that is typically generated by the operational system is used to uniquely represent the customer. However, users of the system are more likely to remember the name of the customer, so we provide them that way to access the data.

ANSI American National Standards Institute.

answer set *See result set.*

application architecture An application architecture defines and supports the software process for implementation of the required business functionality.

architecture A style and method of design and construction; an orderly arrangement of parts.

audit trail Data that links a sequence of events used to track transactions that have affected the contents of a record. This data allows tracing of the history on things such as accounts and product inventory.

back end process The area of a data warehouse system that utilizes the operational system's data stores to populate the staging area within a data warehouse. This process typically includes data collection and data gathering. The back end process prepares data into a transaction base that updates and feeds a data warehouse system.

batch A program, often referred to as a job, that performs a predefined series of actions with little or no interaction between the user and the system.

bitmap index An index in which a list of bits (either 1 or 0) represents the presence of a given value for a field. The bit represents *true* if 1 and *false* if 0. This technique is utilized in many modern data management tools that assist in optimizing data warehouse systems, such as Sybase-IQ.

b-tree index An indexing technique that has been utilized in traditional relational database management systems and indexed flat file systems to assist applications in rapidly locating data rows. This technique of indexing involves storing a representation of the index in a tree structure, typically balanced. The processing system works through the branches of the tree in an optimized fashion to find the actual physical page within a data store where data resides.

cardinality A term used in modeling data relationships; the definition of a relationship between two entities. Cardinality is normally stated in ratio terms such as one to many, or 1:M. Example: A customer has a one-to-many cardinality with orders. This example states that each customer places many orders—or 1 Customer:M orders.

Cartesian product A set of all pairs of elements (x, y) that can be constructed from given sets X and Y, such that x belongs to X and y to Y; every result from all tables contained within the join intersect.

category A specifically defined division in a dimension that provides a detailed classification system. This discrete member of a dimension is used to identify and isolate specific data within that dimension. Example: *Cincinnati* and *Central Region* are categories within a location dimension.

category detail entity An entity contained within a data warehouse to provide more detail information, often textual or qualitative, to the answer sets derived from measurement data. Examples of this data include legal contract information, warranty information, and contact information.

checkpoint A technique for monitoring the process of a long-running batch program. This technique records the status of execution points to speed recovery in the event of a failure. Upon recovering a failed program, the checkpoint logic allows skipping previously completed tasks and continuing with the items that were not successfully completed.

compound document A single document that contains components from multiple sources. Examples: dialogue from a word processor, graphics from a presentation package, and data from a spreadsheet.

conceptual design A preliminary design that captures the concepts behind a user's requirement; this design typically contains minimal information about data relationships and physical implementation. Within this book, a conceptual design is represented by a dimension map.

data architecture The organization of the sources and stores of business information throughout an enterprise.

data cleansing The process of taking operational data and applying quality, in essence removing dirty data through data transformation.

data collection A portion of back end processing in a data warehouse system. The data collection process involves intercepting and collecting data that has changed within operational data stores. This assists in the processing of data for a data warehouse's input feeds.

data control language The syntax provided within a data store's query language that allows control-oriented processing. Within Transact-SQL, this refers to syntax such as *begin...end, goto*, and *if...else.*

data cube A storage structure often utilized by products supporting a multidimensional data structure. Synonyms include *cube* and *hypercube.* A data cube typically comprises an information package defined by dimensions such as time, product, and geography; and their associated facts, such as revenue.

data definition language The syntax provided within a data store's query language that allows for the definition of the physical objects managed by a data store. Within SQL, this refers to syntax such as *create table* and *create database.*

data distribution The process of migrating data from a centralized location to remote locations that require copies of the data.

data extract The process of accessing a data store, retrieving a specified set of data, and populating another data store; typically a local file, such as a comma-delimited text file for importing into a user's spreadsheet application.

data gathering A portion of back end processing that occurs in a data warehouse system. Data gathering involves the pulling of operational data that is associated and related, then placing those transactions into a data warehouse or data warehouse's staging area.

data manipulation language The syntax provided within a data store's query language that allows data to be manipulated. Within SQL, this refers to the *select, insert, update,* and *delete* statements.

data mart A component of a data warehouse that is typically focused on a specific information package or business process. A data mart follows the same principles as an overall data warehouse; however, its content is not as comprehensive.

data placement The process of transferring data from either operational data stores or a data warehouse staging area into a data warehouse.

data scrubbing The process of massaging data to give it proper, uniform format and definition prior to placement in a data warehouse.

data store Where data is stored and managed by an application, such as a database.

data transformation The act of interpreting data and modifying its content to conform to a set of requirements and standards, typically involved in taking operational data and placing it into a data warehouse. Transformations include unifying transaction data along identifiers such as common customer numbers, or on populating additional information based on embedded data such as a vehicle identification number, which can identify the year, make, model, and other information about a vehicle.

data warehouse A place in which factual information, especially information organized for analysis or used to reason or make decisions, is stored; a corporate knowledge base.

database administrator A person responsible for a database system, including its design, development, operation, security, maintenance, and use.

database management system A software system that controls the creation, organization, access, and modification of data.

DBA *See database administrator.*

DBMS *See database management system.*

DCL *See data control language.*

DDL *See data definition language.*

decision support system A system that assists in providing users with relevant information that aids them in making informed decisions. The systems and tools used to build such systems are typically targeted toward knowledge workers and allow them to browse data stores in a free flowing, analytical style.

demographic Data that characterizes people and things, and that is typically the result of a study of their characteristics, such as size, growth, density, distribution, and vital statistics.

denormalize A data modeling technique that is typically utilized in decision support systems and data warehouse design. This technique allows for repetition of data within an entity and its key to data relationships, formulating a data column to key cardinality of one to many. Traditional transaction systems focus strongly on maintaining a normalized data structure in which the data within an individual entity maps in a one-to-one relationship to its key.

detail category A detail category is the lowest level of detail available within a dimension. Example: If a time dimension contains information about time periods that includes year, month, and day, day is a detail category, with the value 1996/11/19 considered an instance of the detail category.

dense data Density is often used with multidimensional databases to refer to the percentage of possible combinations for data compared to actual data. If a relatively high percentage of data combinations exists, the data is referred to as dense.

dimension A dimension is a physical property, such as time, location, or product, regarded as a fundamental way of accessing and presenting business information. A dimension typically acts as an index for identifying data. It is common to think of standard reports that present rows and columns as two dimensional. A manager who evaluates budgets may look at a two-dimensional spreadsheet containing accounts in the rows and cost centers in the columns. The intersecting point between the rows and columns, a cell, contains relevant numerical information about the specific cost center and account, such as product development's salary budget.

dimension entity A derived data structure managed by a data warehouse that assists users in navigating through measurement entities. These structures typically manage only the dimensional hierarchy data (keys and descriptions) and are optimized for user interface operations, filtering operations, and aggregation functions.

direct manipulation A user interface technique that allows an application object to be manipulated directly through items such as drill down, drill up, and drag and drop as distinguished from a more complicated technique such as a command line or syntax-oriented interface.

DML *See data manipulation language.*

domain The common attributes, including type, size, and possible values, that should be applied to a physical data item. A domain in essence provides a common and consistent data definition across data items that are related to the domain. Example: A money domain can define the presentation and storage attributes of payroll items, such as gross pay and deductions, providing commonality among these related items and avoiding conflict in areas such as calculations into which different storage types may require the data to be converted. In the strictest sense, domains define the columns that participate in a primary-to-foreign-key relationship, allowing data to be joined in a similar consis-tency as the calculation.

drill down *and* ***drill up*** Drilling down or drilling up is a navigational technique for users to further analyze detail information (down) or aggregate the data to another summary level (up) within a dimension. If you view the categories within a dimension, they formulate a hierarchy of valid data points. Example: When viewing information based on a location dimension, users may start by viewing the data organized by country. They could then drill down on a Western Region and further drill down to the state of California. Drilling up works in the opposite manner. Users viewing information organized by state could drill up to region and drill up again to a country view.

DSS *See decision support system.*

EIS *See executive information system.*

entity relationship diagram A data modeling technique typically used with relational database management systems that presents entities, or logical groupings of data columns, as tables and their relationships in terms of cardinality. The tables are typically presented using rectangular objects, which surround the columns of data. The relationships are typically presented utilizing lines and end connectors such as multiple arrows, or "chicken feet," to represent the relationship cardinality among the entities. These cardinalities are one to one, one to many, or many to many, and may involve either required or optional relationships.

ERD *See entity relationship diagram.*

executive information system A system that is highly focused on providing standard reports to executives that present specific information, often in line with an enterprise's overall goals. These systems comprise an easy-to-use front end application that presents a logical hierarchy of preplanned standard reports. These systems are characterized as easy to use yet expensive to maintain, because each executive typically requires a support staff to build a customized version.

fact *See measure.*

filter To remove data by passing through a condition, such as only reporting on people with the sex of *male*. *See* where *clause.*

foreign key Any column or group of columns within an entity whose values exist as primary key values in a parent entity. When verifying an entity instance's relationships at the key level, the value of the primary key must be present in the instance of the foreign key and vice versa. Example: In an order entry system, the order is typically represented by OrderHeader and OrderLine entities. OrderHeader is typically referred to as the parent entity and OrderLine as the child entity. OrderNumber is a primary key within OrderHeader because it defines a unique occurrence of an order. OrderNumber is considered a foreign key within the OrderLine entity because it defines the relationship between OrderLine and OrderHeader. Each OrderLine must contain an OrderNumber, because without an OrderHeader instance, an OrderLine instance will never exist.

from *clause* Specifies the tables or queries that contain the fields listed in a SQL *select* statement.

front end process The front end process of a data warehouse system involves granting proper access to users for the information contained within a data warehouse as well as repopulating any catalog or metadata information required by the user's tools.

GB Abbreviation for gigabyte.

gigabyte Unit of information equal to one billion (10^9) bytes.

graphical user interface A style of computer interface that presents users with pictorial representations of programs and associated application objects, and that allows users to interact with the system utilizing tools such as a mouse. The pictorial representation of application objects includes windows, icons, and menus. Examples: Microsoft Windows, MOTIF, X Windows, and Macintosh user interfaces.

group by clause Combines records with identical values in a specified *select* list into a single record. A summary value, or aggregate, is created for each record within the result set if you include an SQL aggregate function, such as sum or count, in a *select* statement.

GUI *See graphical user interface.*

incremental load The process of only loading data that has changed since the preceding loading process.

index A physical object managed by a data store that provides an optimized data access path. An index can be a single column, such as CompanyName, or multiple columns concatenated to create a single object, such as OrderNumber + OrderLine.

information Knowledge derived from the study of the data relating to a specific event or situation; a collection of facts or data; statistical information.

integrity The protection of data from inadvertent or malicious destruction or alteration.

iterative development A process of developing systems within shorter cycles that delivers portions of logically grouped and complete functions required by an overall system in more than one development cycle.

join A *where* clause operation that brings data from more than one table or query together in a query result set.

latency A term, often used in replication technology, that refers to the time period of a delay, such as a latency period of two seconds between transactions committing on two distributed data stores is acceptable.

legacy system A term in information management that refers to any application not developed using the applications development approach currently promoted as the standard. For data warehouses, a legacy application is a source of operational data.

location dimension A physical property, such as time or product, regarded as a fundamental way of accessing and presenting business information; typically the location dimension is composed of all cities in which a company has offices, the districts that contain the cities, the regions that contain the districts, and the countries that contain the regions.

logical design A data design that captures relevant data items derived from a conceptual design and from system and user requirements; this design typically defines data item groups or entities as well as relationships among these groups. Within this book, a conceptual design is represented by a star schema, which in turn is used to transform into traditional data modeling tools and their associated logical data models.

many to many A descriptive adjective to describe the cardinality or relationship between two entities. Example: A consultant participates in many projects and a project utilizes many consultants, sometimes expressed as M Projects:M Consultants. This relationship is typically viewed as a poor physical design, but it is quite common in logical designs. The resolution is to create a derived entity that manages the relationship between the tables in a one-to-many fashion. In this example, an entity such as Project_Participant would be created to resolve the many-to-many relationship, such that the project has many project participants and a consultant participates in many projects.

mass loading The process of totally refreshing the contents of a data warehouse. This process typically only occurs when new entities are added to the data warehouse or a component of the data warehouse is being recovered after a failure. However, depending on an operational data store's ability to monitor changes within its data, mass loads may be the only way to transform operational data to a data warehouse.

measure A measure—also referred to as a key performance measure, a fact, or a key business measure—is a device to measure business information along dimensions. Measures are typically quantities, capacities, or money that will be ascertained by comparison with a standard. These data points can then be used for the quantitative comparison of business performance.

measurement entity An entity that is managed by a data warehouse. This entity typically contains quantitative data, which is the primary focus of a data warehouse. The physical structure for a measurement entity is typically the lowest-level detail category key for each dimension mapped to the measurement, and the measurement data itself.

metadata Data about data. Metadata describes the structure, content, and source of the data within a data warehouse. Metadata must be as easily available through the data warehouse as the traditional data values maintained in an organization's databases.

metadata repository Refers to a dictionary providing details about data. This information includes an inventory of data sources and their associated standards. The data inventory describes the data that is available in both data capture and data access environments. The inventory information should also describe when the data was last updated and when future updates are planned—basically, the schedule of data maintenance. Data inventory also describes the physical attributes of the data; that is, how it is stored. This inventory is then utilized by data consumers to determine what data is available and where.

methodology A body of practices, procedures, and rules used by those who work in a discipline or engage in an inquiry; a set of working methods.

metric *See measure.*

mid-tier process The mid-tier process of a data warehouse system utilizes the staging area of the data warehouse to process and finalize the data that will be made available to users. This process typically incorporates data scrubbing, data placement, data distribution, and standard report compilation and indexing. The goal of a mid-tier process is to make the data more digestible by the user while minimizing the downtime of the data warehouse for any repopulation of data.

multidimensional Multidimensional refers to information that is defined or accessed by having several dimensions. In a geometric world, the easiest description of a multidimensional entity is a cube. The cube has three specified dimensions: width, height, and depth. Surprisingly, most business models are represented in a multidimensional view. The budgetary example described in the definition of *dimension* describes two dimensions—cost center and accounts. In reality, this is missing an important dimension, time. Most financial analysts evaluate their data with a minimum of three dimensions. A dimension map provides a technique for modeling a user's information in a multidimensional space. This design provides a visual representation of the business analyst's mental model of the information.

normalize A data modeling technique that is typically utilized in OLTP systems. The focus of this design technique is to maintain a data structure in which the data within an individual entity maps in a one-to-one relationship to its parent key.

null Refers to an entity's column that has no value.

OLAP *See online analytical processing.*

OLTP *See online transaction processing.*

one to many A descriptive adjective used to describe the cardinality or relationship between two entities. Example: An order has many line items describing what was ordered. This can be represented as 1 Order contains M Order Line Items, or 1:M.

one to one An adjective that describes the cardinality or relationship between two entities. Example: a US citizen has a social security number. This can be represented as 1 Citizen: 1 Social Security Number.

on-line Describes the user-to-program interaction that typically occurs through an interactive session with an input device such as a terminal and a program running on a computer.

online analytical processing A term used to describe the environment required to support business decision-making as opposed to on line transaction processing. An OLAP environment supports analytical queries against data representing an organization's state at a specific time.

online transaction processing A term used to describe the environment required to support business operations, as opposed to OLAP. An OLTP environment is transactional in nature, requiring access to current data.

operational data store The database associated with an operational system. These databases are typically required to support a large number of transactions on a daily basis with minimal latency for processing the transactions.

operational system An operational system is one that assists a company in its day-to-day business. These systems provide immediate focus on business functions and are typically run in an OLTP computing environment.

order by *clause* Sorts a query's result set on a specified field or fields in ascending or descending order.

parallel processing A query optimization technique in which a request is decomposed into a series of queries that is initiated simultaneously and distributed across multiple processors.

parent-child relationship In data modeling, this term refers to the relationship between two entities, one that is a controlling entity (parent) and the other that is the dependent entity (child).

physical design A data design that captures the relevant characteristics of data items (tables, columns, indexes, keys, and so forth) that are derived from a logical design; that is, from system and user requirements. This design is optimized to a physical database management system that will manage the data within the system being defined.

primary key Refers to a column or set of columns whose values can be used to uniquely identify instances of an entity. A means of access, control, or possession; a vital, crucial element. Example: The key to an order is typically an OrderNumber, which uniquely defines all associated data managed by that order.

prototype An early, typical example, form, or instance of a system that serves as a model on which later stages are based or judged. In iterative development, a prototype typically is produced as the first phase or development cycle to prove the concept and validate it with users.

query A request for information from a data store by a user or application. Example: A user issues a query requesting all year-to-date sales of widgets for the Northeast region.

query tool A component, a product, or an application that issues queries against information sources such as relational database management systems. These queries are often in the form of standard SQL *select* statements, which return result sets to the users. The tools automate the building of such statements as well as the execution of the process to retrieve and display the results produced from the statements.

RDBMS *See relational database management system.*

relational database management system A database management system that is organized and accessed according to relationships among items. The data is organized into normalized table structures that consist of rows and columns. The relationships among tables are defined among data values rather than pointers or location. Most relational database management systems adhere to such standards as SQL, which provide a common access syntax for users to retrieve and manipulate data managed within the systems.

replication The process of creating and maintaining associated replicas of original data at distributed sites. Within a replication architecture are typically a publisher of data and a subscriber of data. The publisher is the original, or controlling, source. If we utilize a CRUD diagram to represent the publisher, it would be characterized as the source that creates and deletes the data—or more easily stated, controls the capturing and purging of data from a corporation. A subscriber, on the other hand, is a system that needs access to the data, but only from a referential perspective; in other words it is a reader within the CRUD diagram of the specified entities.

result set The information returned from a database as a result of a query operation. With regard to an SQL *select* statement, this typically represents a set of records.

select list The names of the fields, columns, or calculations to retrieve data from within an SQL *select* statement. If you include more than one field, they are retrieved in the order listed.

select *statement* Instructs a database that utilizes the SQL standard to return information as a set of records.

snowflake schema Refers to an extended star schema. While a star schema typically creates a two-tier structure, one with dimensions and measures, a snowflake schema creates additional tiers. In the techniques discussed in this book, this is typically extended only to three tiers: dimensions (dimension entities), measures (measurement entities), and related, descriptive data (category detail entities). Snowflake schemas beyond a three-tier model should be avoided in data warehouse systems, because they begin to resemble normalized structures more prone to supporting OLTP applications versus the denormalized structures that are optimal for data warehouses and OLAP applications.

sparse data Often used with multidimensional databases to refer to the percentage of possible combinations for the data compared to the actual data. If a relatively low percentage of data combinations exist, the data is referred to as sparse.

SQL *See Structured Query Language.*

staging area A temporary storage location for organizing and cleansing data—where the data is assembled and processed prior to placing it into a production data warehouse.

standard report A report that is automatically created by a data warehouse. It typically has a fixed format and distribution, which makes it highly inflexible; however, it dictates how users should view the data. This is sometimes a desirable attribute.

star schema The optimal design model for data warehouse applications; named due to its physical appearance as a center entity, typically containing measurement data, and radiating data, typically dimensions assisting in navigating and aggregating the measurement data. The results of star schema modeling often are query-aware data structures that provide data structures optimized for rapidly responding to users' query requests. Star schemas frequently produce a two-tier model that contains dimensional data and measurement data.

Structured Query Language The standard language for accessing relational database management systems. SQL is defined and standardized through joint ANSI committees.

system of record The system from which data was obtained. Typically, this refers to a system that manages the creation and overall management of a data item. However, many operational systems have conflicting sources, each thinking it is the system of record. Example: An order entry system thinks it owns the customers and therefore uniquely provides customer numbers and other system-generated data items. Meanwhile, a sales management system also thinks it owns the customers and performs similar yet inconsistent data item maintenance.

TB Abbreviation for terabyte.

technology architecture A computing infrastructure that enables data and applications to successfully interact seamlessly throughout an enterprise.

terabyte A unit of information equal to one trillion(10^{12}) bytes.

time dimension A physical property, similar to location or product, that is regarded as a fundamental way to access and present business information. Often, a time dimension is composed of all days of the year, weeks of the year, months of the year, and possibly multiple years.

time stamping A data auditing technique that allows a user or application to determine when an activity occurred, such as when data was added or when it was last updated. A timestamp typically includes the date and time to the lowest possible level, such as hundredths of a second (11/19/1995 11:15:01.24).

tool suite A set of tools packaged together to assist in solving a spectrum of tasks. Example: Office automation tool suites typically include a word processor, spreadsheet, presentation package, and personal data manager. Within a data warehouse, a tool suite should be delivered that covers the user-requirement spectrum, including EIS, DSS, ad hoc reporting, standard reporting, and production reporting components, to name a few. Additional tool suites should also be defined for data warehouse administrators and for individual processes that comprise an entire data warehouse system, including front-end, mid-tier, and back-end processes.

transaction A logical unit of work that constitutes a business action.

trend analysis A method of proof in which a series of data samples are reviewed to determine sequences or series concerned with limits and convergence, or the general direction in which something tends to move.

where *clause* Specifies which records from the tables listed in a *from* clause are affected by a *select*, *update*, or *delete* statement in standard SQL.

Index

A

B

C

F

G

H

I

J

K

L

M

N

Q

R

S

T

U

V

W